Engineering the Computer Science and IT

Edited by

Safeeullah Soomro

Engineering the Computer Science and IT
Edited by Safeeullah Soomro

Republished by InTech
Janeza Trdine 9, 51000 Rijeka, Croatia

Technical Editor Zeljko Debeljuh

Additional hard copies can be obtained from orders@intechopen.com

Engineering the Computer Science and IT,
Edited by Safeeullah Soomro
p. cm.
ISBN 978-953-307-012-4

For EU product safety concerns:
IN TECH d.o.o., Prolaz Marije Krucifikse Kozulić 3, 51000 Rijeka, Croatia,
info@intechopen.com or visit our website at intechopen.com.

Meet the editor

Dr. Safeeullah Soomro received B.Sc (Hons) computer Science (1996) and M.Sc in Computer Science (1997) from University of Sindh, Jamshoro (www.usindh.edu.pk) Pakistan. He defended his PhD in 2007 from Graz University of Technology, Austria. He carried out research at Graz University of Technology (www.tugraz.at), Austria during 2003 - 2007. He has been involved in research and teaching since 1998. He has taught in different institutes of Pakistan. His research interest revolves around software debugging, formal verification and software testing. In particular, He is interested in applying model-based diagnosis and reasoning techniques to the field of automated software debugging of java programs. Furthermore, He is interested to carry out research in the formal methods. He is author of several national and international publications in conference proceedings, books and journals. He is a reviewer and committee member of different international and national conferences. He has more than 12 years of experience in teaching and research. He is an approved supervisor of Higher Education Commission (HEC) Pakistan and can supervise PhD Students. He is a member of IEEE, IEEE Computer Society, ISOC and SUCSA. Previously He supervised MS students from top ranking university in Pakistan. He is editor of three books and these are recognized internationally.

Preface

It has been many decades, since Computer Science has been able to achieve tremendous recognition and has been applied in various fields, mainly computer programming and software engineering. Many efforts have been taken to improve knowledge of researchers, educationists and others in the field of computer science and engineering. This book provides a further insight in this direction. It provides innovative ideas in the field of computer science and engineering with a view to face new challenges of the current and future centuries.

This book comprises of 25 chapters focusing on the basic and applied research in the field of computer science and information technology. Authors have made efforts to provide theoretical as well as practical approaches to solve open problems through their excellent research work. This book increases knowledge in the topics such as web programming, logic programming, software debugging, real-time systems, statistical modeling, networking, program analysis, mathematical models and natural language processing.

Basically this book opens a platform for creative discussion for current and future technologies in the field of computer science and engineering, these are essential for students, researchers, academicians and industry related people to enhance their capabilities to capture new ideas. Also they provide valuable solutions regarding information technology to an international community.

The editor and authors hope that this book will provide valuable platform for the new researchers and students who are interested to carry out research in the fields of computer science and information technology. Finally, we are thankful to I-Tech Education and publishing organization which provides the best platform to integrate researchers of the whole world though this book.

Editor

Dr. Safeeullah Soomro
Yanbu University College
Kingdom of Saudi Arabia

Contents

Preface VII

1. Extensions of Deductive Concept in Logic Programming and Some Applications 001
Ivana Berkovic, Biljana Radulovic and Petar Hotomski

2. Regular Language Induction with Grammar-based Classifier System 013
Olgierd Unold

3. Fault Localization Models Using Dependences 023
Safeeullah Soomro, Abdul Hameed Memon, Asif Ali Shah and Wajiha Shah

4. Assisted form filling 041
Łukasz Bownik, Wojciech Górka and Adam Piasecki

5. Transatlantic Engineering Programs: An Experience in International Cooperation 065
Andrew J. Kornecki, Wojciech Grega, Thomas B. Hilburn, Jean-Marc Thririet, Miroslav Sveda, Ondrei Rysavy and Adam Pilat

6. Methodology To Develop Alternative Makespan Algorithm For Re-entrant Flow Shop Using Bottleneck Approach 085
Salleh Ahmad Bareduan and Sulaiman Hj Hasan

7. Flexible Design by Contract 103
Koen Vanderkimpen and Eric Steegmans

8. Application of semantic networks in natural language issues 127
Wojciech Górka, Adam Piasecki and Łukasz Bownik

9. Towards the Methodological Harmonization of Passive Testing Across ICT Communities 143
Krzysztof M. Brzeziński

10. Application of Automata Based Approach for Specification of Model Transformation Strategies 169
Anna Derezińska and Jacek Zawłocki

11. Dissociation of Colloidal Silver into Ionic Form through Membrane under Electric Field 193
Kuo-Hsiung Tseng, Chih-Yu Liao, Der-Chi Tien and Tsing-Tshih Tsung

12. SOA and supporting software processes integrated with self-organizing business networks 213
Francesco Rago

13. Algebraic Algorithms for Image Tomographic Reconstruction from Incomplete Projection Data 231
Nadiya Gubareni

14. Templates for Communicating Information about Software Requirements and Software Problems 261
Mira Kajko-Mattsson

15. Ontological description of gene groups by the multi-attribute statistically significant logical rules 277
Aleksandra Gruca and Marek Sikora

16. Mathematical modeling of the Internet survey 303
Getka-Wilczyńska Elżbieta

17. Toward Personalized RSS Retrieval Service: The Effect of Using User's Context 329
Haesung Lee and Joonhee Kwon

18. Client-based Relay Infrastructure for WiMAX MAN Networks 347
Gierłowski, Woźniak and Nowicki

19. The Decoding Algorithms as Techniques for Creation the Anomaly Based Intrusion Detection Systems 369
Evgeniya Nikolova and Veselina Jecheva

20. Transition Parameters For Successful Reuse Business 391
Jasmine K.S.

21. Interactivity of 3D social Internet as a marketing tool 427
Urszula Świerczyńska-Kaczor

22. Performance evaluation of protocols of multiagent information retrieval systems 445
Zofia Kruczkiewicz

23. Measurement of Production Efficiency in Semiconductor Assembly House: Approach of Data Envelopment Analysis 465
Chien-wen Shen, Ming-Jen Cheng

24. Portable ID Management Framework for Security Enhancement of Virtual Machine Monitors 477
Manabu Hirano, Takeshi Okuda, Eiji Kawai, Takahiro Shinagawa, Hideki Eiraku, Kouichi Tanimoto, Shoichi Hasegawa, Takashi Horie, Seiji Mune, Kazumasa Omote, Kenichi Kourai, Yoshihiro Oyama, Kenji Kono, Shigeru Chiba, Yasushi Shinjo, Kazuhiko Kato and Suguru Yamaguchi

25. Task Jitter Measurement in Multi-purpose Real-time Systems 489
Pavel Moryc and Jindrich Cernohorsky

1

Extensions of Deductive Concept in Logic Programming and Some Applications

Ivana Berkovic, Biljana Radulovic and Petar Hotomski
University of Novi Sad, Technical faculty "Mihajlo Pupin" Zrenjanin
Serbia

1. Introduction

Automated reasoning systems are computer programs which have certain "intelligent" components and can be used as: shells of expert systems, dialog systems, human language translators, educational software etc. Inferring the conclusion in such systems is often based on resolution refutation method from a certain set of rules and facts. In order to infer a conclusion, these systems, apart from negating set query, use rules for deducting facts in axiom form and working fact base. Automated reasoning systems give answers to a set query which depend upon the knowledge base and fact base (Hotomski, 2004). In this sense, "automated reasoning is concerned with the discovery, formulation, and implementation of concepts and procedures that permit the computer to be used as a reasoning assistant" (Wos, 1985).

The developing of automated reasoning results into the developing of logic programming languages, especially PROLOG. In this paper the advantages and applications of changing one system for automated reasoning by the other are described. The determinate resolution system for automated theorem proving ATP (OL-resolution with marked literals) is especially put into the base of prolog-like language, as the surrogate for the concept of the negation as definite failure (SLDNF resolution) in PROLOG.

2. Ordered Linear Resolution as the Foundation of Automatic Theorem Proving

The most popular method for automatic theorem proving is the resolution method, which was discovered by J. A. Robinson in 1965 (Barr et al., 1982, Gevarter, 1985, Wos et al., 1992). Since 1965, many resolution forms and techniques have been developed because the pure resolution rule was unable to handle complex problems (Hotomski, 2004).

Here is used the general automatic method for determining if a theorem (conclusion) **A** follows from a given set of premises (axioms) **F**:

$$\mathbf{F} \vdash \mathbf{A}.$$

Each formula will be transformed to the *clauses form*. The *clauses* have the form:

$$L_1 \vee L_2 \vee \ldots \vee L_m$$

where L_i are literals. The symbol for disjunction is: $\vee$.

The *literals* L_i have the form: $\mathbf{P(t_1, t_2, \ldots, t_n)}$ or $\neg P(\mathbf{t_1, t_2, \ldots, t_n})$, where **P** is predicate symbol, ti is term, $\neg$ is negation. The literal $\mathbf{P(t_1, t_2, \ldots, t_n)}$ is called *positive* literal, the literal $\neg\mathbf{P(t_1, t_2, \ldots, t_n)}$ is called *negative* literal.

Resolution method is a syntactic method of deduction. *Reduction ad absurdum* is in the basis of resolution method:

$$\mathbf{F} \;|\!\!-\; \mathbf{A} \quad \textbf{iff} \quad \mathbf{F} \cup \{\neg\mathbf{A}\} \;|\!\!-\; \textbf{contradiction}.$$

Resolution rule will be applied on the set of clauses - axioms which was expanded by negating the desired conclusion in clause form.

Ordered Linear (OL) resolution rule with marked literals (Hotomski & Pevac, 1991, Hotomski, 2004, Kowalski & Kuchner, 1971) increases efficiency and doesn't disturb completeness of pure resolution rule.

The generating process of OL-resolvent from central clause (**d1**) and auxiliary clause (**d2**):

1. Redesignate variables (without common variables in the clauses).
2. Determine universal unificator **Θ** for last literal of **d1** and **k**-literal (**k=1,2,...**) of **d2** (if it exists for some k, else it is impossible to generate OL-resolvent for specification clauses).
3. Create resolvent with marked last literal in **d1Θ** and add the rest of clause **d2Θ** without **k**-literal (**d1Θ** and **d2Θ** are clauses, which were formed by universal unificator **Θ** applied on **d1** and **d2**, respectively).
4. Eliminate identical non-marked literals and tautology examination (tautologies are not memorized).
5. The Shortening Operation (delete all ending marked literals)
6. The Compressing Operation (delete the last non-marked literal, which is complemented in relation to negation, with some marked literal for unificator λ).
7. Repeat steps: 5 and 6 until the empty clause is got, or the Compressing Operation is not applied on the last non-marked literal.

The rule of OL-resolution with marked literals is separated in two parts: ***in-resolution*** and ***pre-resolution***. The steps: 1 - 5 are represented in-resolution. The steps: 6 - 7 are represented pre-resolution. Mid-resolvents are the products of in-resolution and without their memorizing, the completeness of the method can be lost. This modification of Ordered Linear resolution rule is served as the base for development of the system for automatic theorem proving ATP.

3. ATP System for Automatic Theorem Proving

ATP is a system for automatic theorem proving (Berkovic, 1994), which is implemented on personal computer by Pascal language. The rule of Ordered Linear Resolution with marked literals presents the system base. The system is developed at Technical Faculty “Mihajlo Pupin” in Zrenjanin. ATP is projected for scientific - researching, teaching and practical purpose. ATP system disposes three search strategies: breadth-first, depth-first and their combination. Numerously experiments with ATP system show that depth-first strategy is the most efficient. In depth-first search, a new node is generated at the next level, from the one current, and the search is continuing deeper and deeper in this way until it is forced to backtracking.

The main characteristics of ATP system:

- This system presents a complete logical deductive base: *the clauses-set is unsatisfied (contradictory) iff the empty clause is generated by finite use of the resolution rule*. So, the proof of conclusion **A** is completed (**F** $|$— **A**) when the empty clause is generated by the resolution from clauses-set $\mathbf{F} \cup \{\neg \mathbf{A}\}$.
- Besides the theoretical completeness of the system, it has the satisfying practical efficiency limited by the space-time computer resources.
- The first-order logic is the form of representation in ATP system (each formula is transformed into the clause form). This deductive base has no restriction in Horn clause (expansions concerning Horn clauses) and it allows the logical treatment of negation (escaping negation treatment as a definite failure).

Therefore, the system of automated reasoning ATP is put into the base for development of the descriptive language for logic programming LOGPRO. This logical complete deductive base is used for building a new descriptive logical programming language (Berkovic, 1997, Berkovic & Hotomski , 1997, Berkovic et al., 2003).

4. The Concept of LOGPRO – LOGic PROgramming Language Based on ATP System

Many logic programming languages have been implemented, but PROLOG is the most popular language and it is useful for solving many problems. PROLOG as a logic-oriented language (Bratko, 1986, Malpas, 1987, Pereira & Shieber, 1987) contains a resolution-based theorem-prover (PROLOG-system). The theorem-prover in PROLOG appears with the depth-first search approach. It uses the special resolution rule: ***SLDNF*** (Linear resolution with Selection function for Definite clauses and Negation as Failure).

4.1 Formalization on PROLOG

The first-order predicate logic is the form of representation in PROLOG. PROLOG-program is a set of sentences. Every sentence is finished by full stop. Program in PROLOG consists of axioms (rules, facts) and a theorem to be proved (goal). The axioms are restricted in ***Horn clauses*** form. ***Horn clauses*** (Hotomski & Pevac, 1991), are clauses with at most one positive literal.

The ***rules*** have the form: $\mathbf{G :- T_1, T_2, \dots , T_n .}$

where **G** is positive literal and $\mathbf{T_j}$ ($\mathbf{j=1,2,\dots,n}$) are literals (positive or negative). The symbol for conjunction is: **,** . The element **G** is presented head of the rule. The elements $\mathbf{T_j}$ ($\mathbf{j=1,2,\dots,n}$) are presented body of the rule. The separator **:-** corresponds to implication ($\Leftarrow$). The symbol for negation is: **not**.

The ***facts*** have the form: **G.**

where **G** is positive literal.

The ***goals*** (questions) have the form: $\mathbf{?- T_1, T_2, \dots , T_n .}$

where $\mathbf{T_i}$ ($\mathbf{i=1,2,\dots,n}$) are literals.

Practically, programming in PROLOG is restrictive in a subset of first-order logic. Horn clauses are represented the first defect of PROLOG. The concept of negation as definite failure is represented the second defect of PROLOG.

4.1 Formalization on LOGPRO

An other approach to logic programming is implementation of a different deductive concept. The determinate system ATP for automated theorem proving is especially put into the base of prolog-like language LOGPRO, as the surrogate for the concept of negation as definite failure. This logical complete deductive base is used for building a new descriptive logic programming language.
The first-order logic is the form of representation in ATP system, too. But, this system has not restriction in Horn clauses. The program on logic language LOGPRO based on the ATP system is a set of sentences (clauses). There are three kinds of sentences: rules, facts and goals. Every sentence is finished by full stop.
The ***rules*** have the form: $\mathbf{G_1, G_2, \dots, G_m :- T_1, T_2, \dots, T_n}$ **.**
where $\mathbf{G_i}$ **(i=1,2,...,m)** and $\mathbf{T_j}$ **(j=1,2,...,n)** are literals (positive or negative). The symbol for conjunction is: **,** . The elements $\mathbf{G_i}$ **(i=1,2,...,m)** present head of the rule. The elements $\mathbf{T_j}$ **(j=1,2,...,n)** present body of the rule. The separator **:-** corresponds to implication ($\Leftarrow$). The symbol for negation is: ~ .
The ***facts*** have the form: **G.**
where **G** is literal (positive or negative).
The ***goals*** (questions) have the form: **?-** $\mathbf{T_1, T_2, \dots, T_n}$ **.**
where $\mathbf{T_i}$ **(i=1,2,...,n)** are literals (positive or negative).
The rules and facts (axioms) are presented by auxiliary clauses. The goal (central clause) is negating the theorem to be proved. Symbol **?-** in goal is the substitution for negation. The execution procedure is ATP system based on OL-resolution with marked literals. This formulation enables eliminating the defects of PROLOG-system.
The logic programming languages PROLOG and LOGPRO are compared. PROLOG rules and facts do not allow the explicit statement of negative information. But, the declarative syntax of the logic programming language LOGPRO allows the expression of negative information in rules and facts. Also, it is possible to construct the rule with more than one element in the rule's head.

Example 1.
The problem of trying to formulate sentence:
"Alice likes whatever Queen dislikes, and dislikes whatever Queen likes." into PROLOG form (Subrahmanyam, 1985).
The representations:

```
likes(alice,X1) :- not likes(queen,X1).
not likes(alice,X1) :- likes(queen,X1).
```

are illegal in PROLOG because the second rule has a negation in head (it isn't Horn clause). It is possible to solve the problem by trick - using a modified predicate likes, and expressing the statement as:

```
likes(alice,X1,true) :- likes(queen,X1,false).
likes(alice,X1,false) :- likes(queen,X1,true).
```

The expansion concerning Horn clauses on the logic programming language based on ATP system has the possibilities to express the statement as:

```
likes(alice,X1) :-  ~ likes(queen,X1).
~ likes(alice,X1) :-  likes(queen,X1).
```

PROLOG-system has the negation defect (Brtka, 2001). This defect is corrected in ATP system. It can be illustrated by the following example.

Example 2.

Program in PROLOG:

```
vegetarian(tom).
vegetarian(ivan).
smoker(tom).
likes(ana,X1) :- not (smoker(X1)), vegetarian(X1).
```

PROLOG-system gives unconnected answers on the following questions:

```
?- likes(ana,X1).
no
?- likes(ana,ivan).
yes
```

If the last clause is now:

```
likes(ana,X1) :-  vegetarian(X1), not (smoker(X1)).
```

PROLOG-system gives wrong answers on the following questions:

```
?- likes(ana,X1).
X1=ivan
?- likes(ana,ivan).
yes
```

These answers are incorrect because we have not data about Ivan and smoking. We don't know if Ivan is a smoker or not. The correct answer will be: "I don't know".

The program in LOGPRO:

```
vegetarian(tom).
vegetarian(ivan).
smoker(tom).
likes(ana,X1) :- ~ smoker(X1), vegetarian(X1).
```

ATP-system gives answers on the following questions:

```
?- likes(ana,X1).
Success=0
```

The proof isn't completed

```
?- likes(ana,ivan).
Success=0
```

The proof isn't completed

When the last clause is:

```
likes(ana,X1) :- vegetarian(X1), ~smoker(X1).
```

ATP system also gives the correct answers: **"Success=0, the proof isn't completed"**.

In fact, the system generates resolvents, but can not complete the proof with depth-first strategy. The treatment of negation as definite failure in this system is escaped. The concept of LOGPRO allows eliminating of endless branches, recursion using and works with structures and lists, as well as PROLOG. It is presented in some concrete examples (Berkovic, 1997).

5. Applications of ATP System and LOGPRO

5.1. Time-Table and Scheduling System DEDUC

This system ATP is incorporated in the system for automatic creating of the combinatorial disposition DEDUC, where it has presented the satisfying practical efficiency.

DEDUC is a software package that integrates scientific results of Constraint Logic Programming and practical needs in generating combinatorial schedules. The work on the system started in 1991. After ten years the powerful system was developed.

System is based on synchronized work of two processes: data storing and optimization of gaps in the timetable. Theorem prover controls both processes to secure that initial requirements are not violated

System facilities and performances:

- Automatic and interactive generating of schedules for the initial data and conditions;
- Setting up and maintenance of the initial data and requirements by using the user friendly interface;
- Setting up various initial requirements like splitting classes into groups, connecting groups and classes, enabling multiple lessons; setting restrictions in using laboratories and rooms; setting teachers' requirements and the other pedagogic obligations and desirable demands;
- Generating schedules respecting school shifts;
- Screen browsing and printing the general, per-class and per-teacher schedules;
- Generating and archiving different versions of the schedules generated for the same initial data and conditions;
- Maintenance of the archived versions, data and conditions.

The practical efficiency and system limits can be observed for complicated examples as well as for the simple ones. Essentially, getting the acceptable version of the schedule depends on structure of the initial requirements and their connections with data, although the number of requirements has no influence.

Practical experiences in the real world assure that DEDUC system generates timetables with quality level higher than quality level of hand-made timetables. The time needed for generating a timetable varies from few minutes to several hours, and depends on amount of data, structure of conditions as well as on computer performances. More informations at http://deduce.tripod.com

5.2. A Technique for the Implicational Problem Resolving for Generalized Data Dependencies

A mechanism for generalized representation of various data dependency types, such as functional (*fd*), multivalued (*mvd*), join (*jd*), implied (*imd*) and inclusion (*id*) dependencies, has been developed in the relational data model theory. The initial supposition was that all the data dependencies (i.e. "rules" which hold among data) can be represented, in unified manner, by one, or more symbolic data templates, satisfying certain criteria, according to defined interpretation rules for such symbolic templates. On the basis of that supposition, the term of generalized data dependency has been introduced, so as to represent the other dependency types in the same way. One of the important questions, arising when new data dependency type is introduced, is how it can be stated if a data dependency is a logical consequence of a given set of data dependencies. This problem in relational databases is known as the *implicational problem.*

At the beginning, the terms of: tableau, as a symbolic data template, generalized dependency (*gd*) and its interpretation are defined without explanations, because they are considered as already known. In (Lukovic et al., 1996, Lukovic et al., 1997) is presented a possible approach to resolving the implicational problem for *gds,* it is established at the same time a way of testing the implicational problem for all the specific data dependency types which can be formalized by means of *gds*. The proposed approach considers a usage of the ATP System.

To resolve the implicational problem for a given sets of *gds* Γ and arbitrary *gd* γ means to establish if $\Gamma \mid= \gamma$ holds. It is not practically possible to test he implicational problem $\Gamma \mid= \gamma$ by exact applying of definition of generalized dependencies by systematic generating of all the relations form *SAT (R)* and checking the implication $r \mid= \Gamma \;\Rightarrow\; r \mid= \gamma$, because *SAT(R)* is, in most cases, the set of high cardinality and it can be even infinite. Therefore, the other methods have to be applied so as to resolve the problem. According to the nature of *gds,* it is concluded that for the automations of the test $\Gamma \mid= \gamma$, the resolution procedure can be applied. Therefore, the set of Γ and the dependency γ will be represented by appropriate predicate formulas. According to the resolution theorem and theorem of generalized dependencies, the test of the condition $\Gamma \mid= \gamma$, where $\Gamma = \{\gamma_1,\ldots, \gamma_n\}$, is performed by disproving procedure, on the basis of the set of initial assumptions $\mathbf{F}(\Gamma)$ and the negation of the conclusion $\neg F$. In that case, the theorem that should be proved by ATP System is of the form: $\mathbf{F}(\Gamma) \rightarrow F$.

To prove the theorem, the clauses should be built from the set of assumptions $\mathbf{F}(\Gamma)$ and negation $\neg F$. They represent the input for ATP. Beside that, two additional input parameters are: (i) maximal searching deep and (ii) maximal clause length. With respect to the resolution theorem, there are three possible outcomes from ATP. (a) *"positive"*; an empty clause has been reached, which means that the assertion *F* holds. According to theorem of generalized dependencies, $\Gamma \mid= \gamma$ holds, too; (b) *"negative"*: the empty clause has not been reached and there are no more possibilities for new clause generating. It means that the conclusion *F* cannot be derived from $\mathbf{F}(\Gamma)$. According to theorem of generalized dependencies, we conclude $\Gamma \mid= \gamma$ does not hold; (c) *"uncertain"*: the empty clause has not been obtained, whereas maximal searching deep and maximal clause length have been reached, or memory resources have been exhausted.

5.3. Intelligent Tutoring System Based on ATP System

The concept of LOGPRO can be an excellent base for an intelligent tutoring system iTUTOR (Brtka, 2001, Berkovic et al., 2003). Such deductive logic programming language can perform tasks that standard PROLOG system could not (Hotomski, 2004).

It is now possible to define predicate:

know(student_name, concept, degree).

where studentname is name of a student, concept is name of a concept that student should know and degree indicates grade of concept cognition.

Negation in the head of the rule can be implemented as:

~know(student_name, concept, degree):-

know(student_name, concept$_1$, degree$_1$),
know(student_name, concept$_2$, degree$_2$),
...
know(student_name, concept$_n$, degree$_n$),
degree$_1$<c$_1$,
degree$_2$<c$_2$,
...
degree$_n$<c$_n$.

which means that student does not know concept in certain degree if he does not know minor concepts concept$_1$, concept$_2$, ..., concept$_n$ in degree greater than or equal with c_1, c_2, ..., c_n where c_1, c_2, ..., c_n are predefined constants. Furthermore, one can calculate degree of concept cognition by adding a line at the end of previous rule:

degree is (degree$_1$+ degree$_2$+...+ degree$_n$)/n.

Rule:

~nextlesson(student_name, lesson_name):-

know(student_name, concept$_1$, degree$_1$),
know(student_name, concept$_2$, degree$_2$),
...
know(student_name, concept$_n$, degree$_n$),
degree$_1$>c$_1$,
degree$_2$>c$_2$,
...
degree$_n$>c$_n$.

indicates lessons that particular student should not learn because he knows all belonging concepts in degree greater than predefined constant.

Similar rule:

~nextlesson(student_name, lesson_name):-

~know(student_name, concept$_1$, degree$_1$),
know(student_name, concept$_2$, degree$_2$),
...
know(student_name, concept$_n$, degree$_n$),
degree$_1$>c$_1$,
degree$_2$>c$_2$,
...
degree$_n$>c$_n$.

where some predicates in the body of the rule are negated, indicates lessons that student should not learn because he does not know all belonging concepts in degree greater than predefined constant. Application of such logic programming language LOGPRO can overcome some problems during the process of student modelling in an intelligent tutoring system.

5.4. Baselog System as Deductive Databases

Baselog system concept and its program implementation enabled the integration of good properties of Datalog, Prolog and ATP system, and so is realized a more flexible system in reference to the work in the closed, respectively opened world. Specifically needs in the development for the work with databases ask just development and application of a such system, and it makes it more superior in reference to Datalog, Prolog and ATP system, considered separately (Radulovic, 1998, Radulovic & Hotomski, 2000).

Some automated reasoning systems can give incorrect answers if they work in closed world concept, or correct answers if they work in open world concept where the answer depends on fact base completeness. If fact, the base is incomplete, some of automated deduction systems can consult facts from various extension files. In order to enable work with greater data amount there arose a need to access certain databases which can even be distant and then take the piece of data which could be used for deducting a conclusion (Hotomski, 2004).

5.4.1. Close/Open World Assumption in Baselog

In (Ceri, 1989, Stonebraker et al., 1990, Ullman, 1994) is described Datalog, the logic programming language in the field of the database that is implemented in the post-relation software for database management system PROGRESS. Datalog works on the CWA-principle, respectively (by) adopting the Closed World Assumption. The CWA-principle declares (Radulovic, 1998, Radulovic & Hotomski, 2000) :

Definition 1. (The CWA - principle) If a fact does not logically follow from a set of Datalog clauses, then we conclude that the negation of this fact is true.

For knowledge databases is also characteristic the open world assumption. In the open world regime work classic systems for the automatic theorem proving, especially, ATP system (Berkovic, 1994, Berkovic, 1997). The knowledge bases contain limited knowledge segments from a certain field. They can be incomplete, i.e. they do not present total relevant knowledge. The applying of the closed world concept on such databases, can bring wrong answers to the asked questions. Because of that the pure concept of the closed world can not be applied for the databases used in the education computing software.

Universal resolution systems from theoretic aspect totally support the work with databases as well, but they show a practical deficiency. It can be seen in the fact that because of the endeavoring to get a semantically expected answer, it is necessary to give a complete space description where the solution is claimed.

In the database area it is, for example, exposed through the necessity of proposing following axiom:

$$t \neq t_1 \wedge t \neq t_2 \wedge \ldots \wedge t \neq t_n \Rightarrow \sim P(t)$$

where $t_1,\ldots,t_n$ are the relation database tuples, and P(t) means the tuple t belonging to the database relation (~ is negation).

As it can be seen, already for little number of tuples in database, this axiom has big length, so this theoretic possibility is left in practical applications. Both in Datalog and in Prolog it is made the attempt for solving this deficiency in specific ways. In Prolog it is the strategy of definite failure (Bratko, 1986, Berkovic, 1997) and in Datalog the CWA-principle

(Stonebraker et al., 1990). Meanwhile, no one of these solutions can satisfy education needs in fullness, for the following reasons.
In reference to possible user's questions, there are following options:

a) the answer to the question is deducible from the base,
b) the answer to the question is not deducible from the base,

where in b) we differ:

b1) the answer needs to be affirmative,
b2) the answer needs to be negative.

In a) when the answer is deducible from the base, it will be found and presented to a user either Prolog, Datalog or Logpro based on ATP-system.
Specificities are being reflected in b). According to the adopted the CWA-assumption in Datalog, respectively the definite failure concept in Prolog, there are possible incorrect or indefinite answers. So in b1) Datalog can generate the incorrect answer NO, while Prolog's answer "NO" can be interpreted as "*uncertain*". In b2) Datalog answer "NO" is correct, and Prolog answer "NO" can be interpreted as "NO". In both cases b1) and b2) Logpro based on ATP gives answer "*uncertain*".

We observe that in educative meaning Datalog according to the b1) does not satisfy, while Prolog and Logpro based on ATP give acceptable, but uncertain answers. In b2) Datalog gives correct and precise answer, while Prolog and Logpro based on ATP gives inadequately precise answers. From the educative aspect it is desirable to lessen the indefiniteness of the system answer and it is necessary to eliminate the non-allowed answers. Otherwise, there is need to keep the definiteness present in Datalog for b2) and eliminate non-allowed answer from b1). Implementing Baselog - system projected on the list of the CWA-predicate and the CWA-rule, a flexible concept has been realized. Such system all predicates which are in the CWA-list treats as Datalog, in closed-world, while all the other predicates treat in open world, i.e. works as ATP. With it, it is free of Prolog defects in reference to the negation treatment and the definite failure concept.

The basis for Baselog - system make following components (Radulovic & Hotomski, 2000, Radulovic, 1998):

- The CWA-predicate list, which is a part of the program,
- The CWA-rule,
- The CWA-controller by which is enlarged ATP resolution system.

The whole Baselog - system is the extension of the resolution method by the concepts of the opened and closed world. By the CWA-controller one provides dozing a degree of the world openness/closeness for the program predicates.
Every literal of the form $R(w_1,...,w_m)$ where R is predicate name mentioned in the CWA-predicate list, and $w_1,...,w_m$ are arguments, Baselog - system will treat in the closed system regime, while all the other predicates that are not in the CWA-predicate list, by the system will be treated in the open world regime. Here, the CWA-controller of Baselog -system uses the CWA-rule, formulated in the following way.

The CWA - RULE:

Let D is the clause of the forms $L_1 \vee L_2 \vee ... \vee L_p$ *and let* L_i, $1 \leq i \leq p$ *is literal of the form* $R(w_1,...,w_m)$, *where the predicate R is declared as the CWA–predicate. If* $R(w_1,...,w_m)$ *can not be unified with no one base element, then* $R(w_1,...,w_m)$ *will be deleted from clause D.*

If exists unificator for L_i *and some element from base, then clause D is not changed, there is no deleting.*

The proof of the CWA–rule correctness is described in (Radulovic, 1998).

6. Conclusion

Completeness and universality of the resolution method, as the base of ATP system, enables it to be applied as the deductive base of prolog-like language. The relationship between programming language based on ATP system and programming language PROLOG are emphasized. The logic programming language based on ATP system enables eliminating the defects of PROLOG-system (the expansion concerning Horn clauses, escaping negation treatment as definite failure, eliminating of endless branches), keeping the main properties of prolog-language. In this paper are also described some applications of ATP system and LOGPRO such as: time-table and scheduling (DEDUC), a technique for the implicational problem resolving for generalized data dependencies, deductive databases (Baselog System) and intelligent tutoring system based on ATP system (iTUTOR). Also, ATP system is used for the development inference system and data mining (Brtka, 2008).

7. References

Barr, A.; Cohen, P.R. & Feigenbaum, E.A. (1982). *The Handbook of Artificial Intelligence*, Vol.I,II,III, Heuris Tech Press, W. Kaufmann, Inc., California

Berković, I. (1994). Variable Searching Strategies in the Educationally Oriented System for Automatic Theorem Proving, M.Sc. Thesis, Technical Faculty "Mihajlo Pupin", Zrenjanin, (in Serbian)

Berković, I. (1997). The Deductive Bases for the Development of the Descriptive Languages for the Logical Programming, Ph.D. Thesis, Technical Faculty "Mihajlo Pupin", Zrenjanin, (in Serbian)

Berković, I. & Hotomski, P. (1997). The concept of logic programming language based on resolution theorem prover, *Proceedings of VIII Conference on Logic and Computer Science LIRA*, pp. 111-120, Sept 1-4 1997, Novi Sad, Serbia

Berković, I.; Hotomski P. & Brtka V. (2003). The Concept of Logic Programming Language Based on the Resolution Theorem Prover and its Appliance to Intelligent Tutoring Systems; *IEEE Proceedings of 7th International Conference on Intelligent Engineering Systems*, pp 169 - 172; ISSN: 977.246.048.3/1562, Assiut – Luxor, Egypt, March 4 - 6. 2003.

Bratko, I. (1986). *PROLOG Programming for Artificial Intelligence*, Addison-Wesley Publ. Comp.

Brtka, V. (2001). Tutoring educational software, M.Sc. Thesis, Technical Faculty "Mihajlo Pupin", Zrenjanin, (in Serbian).

Brtka, V. (2008). Automated Synthesis of Rule Base in Inference Systems, Ph.D. Thesis, Technical Faculty "Mihajlo Pupin", Zrenjanin, (in Serbian)

Ceri, S.; Gottlob, G. & Tanza, L. (1989). What You Always Wanted to Know About Datalog (And Never Dared to Ask), *IEEE Transactions on Knowledge and Data Engineering*, Vol. 1, No. 1 March 1989, pp. 146-167

Gevarter, W.B. (1985). *Intelligent Machines*, Prentice-Hall, Inc., Englewood Cliffs, New Jersey

Hotomski, P. & Pevac, I. (1991). *Mathematical and Programming Problems of Artificial Intelligence in the Field of Automatic Theorem Proving*, Naučna knjiga, Belgrade, (in Serbian)

Hotomski, P. (2004). *Systems of Artificial Intelligence*, University of Novi Sad, Technical Faculty "Mihajlo Pupin" Zrenjanin, (in Serbian)

Kowalski, P. & Kuchner, D. (1971). Linear Resolution with Selection Function, *Artificial Intelligence*, Vol. 2, pp. 227-260

Luković, I.; Hotomski, P.; Radulović, B. & Berković, I. (1996). A Proof of Generalized Data Dependency Satisfaction by The Automatic Reasoning Method, *Proceedings of the Second Symposium on Comp, Sc. and Informatics YU INFO*, Brezovica, 02-05.-4.1996. (in Serbian)

Luković, I.; Hotomski, P.; Radulović, B. & Berković, I. (1997). A Technique for the Implicational Problem Resolving for Generalized Data Dependencies, *Proceedings of VIII Conf. on Logic and Computer Science LIRA '97*, pp. 111-119, Novi Sad, 01-04.09.1997,

Malpas. J. (1987). *PROLOG: A Relational Language and Its Applications*, Prentice-Hall International Inc.

Pereira, F.C.N. & Shieber, S.M. (1987). *PROLOG and Natural - Language Analysis*, CLSI, Leland Stanford Junior University

Radulović, B. & Hotomski, P. (2000). Projecting of Deductive Databases with CWA Management in Baselog System, *Novi Sad Journal of Mathematics*, pp 133-140. Vol 30, N2, 2000, Novi Sad, Serbia

Radulović, B. (1998). Database Projecting in the Field of Education Computer Software, Ph.D. Thesis, Technical Faculty "Mihajlo Pupin", Zrenjanin, (in serbian)

Radulović, B. & Hotomski, P. (1997). Database projecting in the Baselog-system, *Proceedings of VII Conf. "Informatics in eduation and new information technologies"*, pp. 71-77, Novi Sad, 1997, (in serbian)

Radulović, B.; Berković, I.; Hotomski, P. & Kazi, Z. (2008). The Development of Baselog System and Some Applications, *International Review on Computers and Software (I.RE.CO.S.)*, pp 390-395, Vol. 3 N. 4, July 2008, Print ISSN: 1828-6003

Stonebraker, M.; Rowe, L. A. & Hirohama, M. (1990). The Implementation of POSTGRES, *IEEE Transactions on Knowledge and Data Engineering*, pp. 125-142, Vol. 2, No. 1, March 1990

Subrahmanyam, P.A. (1985). The "Software Engineering" of Expert Systems: Is Prolog Appropriate?, *IEEE Transactions on Software Engineering*, pp. 1391-1400, Vol. SE-11, No. 11, november 1985.

Ullman, J. (1994). Assigning an Appropriate Meaning to Database Logic With Negation, www-db.stanford.edu/pub/papers/negation.ps

Wos, L. (1985). Automated Reasoning, *The American Mathematical Monthly*, pp. 85-93 Vol. 92, No. 2, february 1985.

Wos, L.; Overbeek, R.; Lusk, E. & Boyle J. (1992). *Automated Reasoning: Introduction and Applications*, Prentice-Hall

2

Regular Language Induction with Grammar-based Classifier System

Olgierd Unold
Wroclaw University of Technology
Poland

1. Introduction

In this chapter, we are interested in inducing a grammar that accepts a regular language (Hopcroft & Ullman, 1969) given a finite number of positive and negative examples drawn from that language. Learning regular languages is equivalent to the problem of learning Deterministic Finite Automata (DFA). Both problems have been extensively studied in the literature and it has been proved that learning DFA or regular languages is a hard task by a number of criteria (Pitt & Warmuth, 1993). Note, that induced DFA should not only be consistent with the training set, but also DFA should proper estimate membership function for unseen examples.

The approaches to learning DFA or equivalent regular languages (RL) base mainly on evolutionary algorithms (Dupont, 1996), (Luke et al., 1999), (Lucas & Reynolds, 2005), recurrent neural network (Giles et al., 1990), (Waltrous & Kuhn, 1992) or combination of these two methods (Angeline et al., 1994). While speaking about DFA/regular grammar induction, one cannot help mentioning one of the best known algorithm for learning DFA – EDSM (Cicchello & Kremer, 2002), which relies on heuristic compressing an initially large DFA down to a smaller one, while preserving perfect classification before and after each compression.

In this chapter we examine RL induction using Grammar-based Classifier System (GCS) – a new model of Learning Classifier System (LCS). GCS (Unold, 2005a), (Unold & Cielecki, 2005) represents the knowledge about solved problem in Chomsky Normal Form (CNF) productions. GCS was applied with success to natural language processing (Unold, 2007a), biological promoter regions (Unold, 2007b), and toy grammar (Unold, 2005b). In spite of intensive research into classifier systems in recent years (Lucas & Reynolds, 2005) there is still a slight number of attempts at inferring grammars using LCS. Although there are some approaches to handle with context-free grammar (Bianchi, 1996), (Cyre, 2002), (Unold, 2005a), there is no one work on inducing regular languages with LCS. This article describes GCS approach to the problem of inferring regular languages.

The generic architecture of learning classifier system is presented in the second paragraph. The third section contains description of GCS preceded by short introduction to context-free grammars. The fourth paragraph shows some selected experimental results in RL grammar induction. The chapter is concluded with a summary.

2. Learning Classifier System

A Learning Classifier System, introduced by Holland (1976), learns by interacting with an environment from which it receives feedback in the form of numerical reward. Learning is achieved by trying to maximize the amount of the reward received. There are many models of LCS and many ways of defining what a Learning Classifier System is. All LCS models, more or less, comprise four main components (see Fig. 1): (i) a finite population of condition-action rules (classifiers), that represent the current knowledge of a system; (ii) the performance component, which governs the interaction with the environment; (iii) the reinforcement component, called credit assignment component), which distributes the reward received from the environment to the classifiers accountable for the rewards obtained; (iv) the discovery component responsible for discovering better rules and improving existing ones through a genetic algorithm (GA).

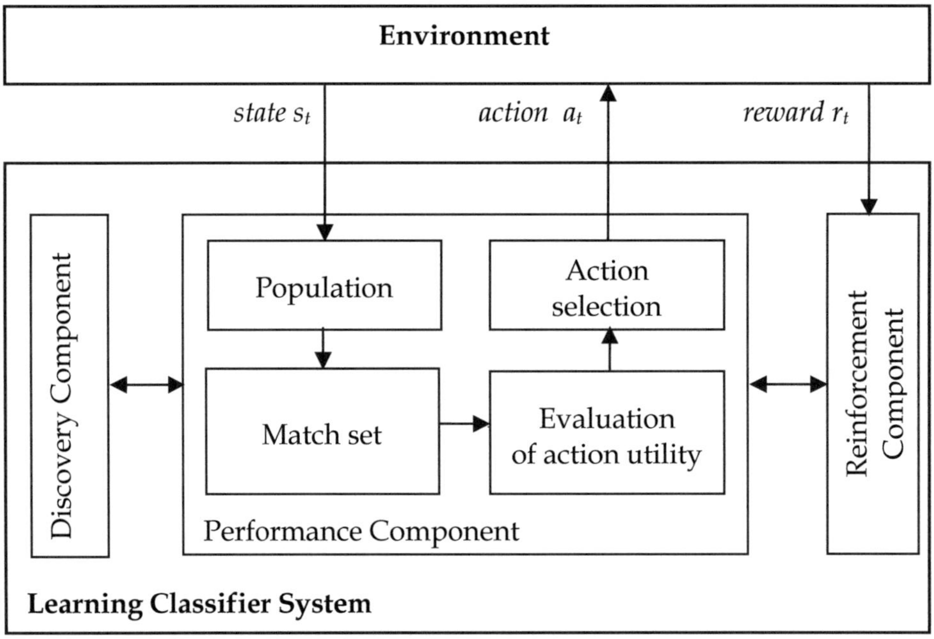

Fig. 1. The generic architecture of Learning Classifier System (Holmes et al., 2002)

Classifiers have two associated measures: the prediction and the fitness. Prediction estimates the classifier utility in terms of the amount of reward that the system will receive if the classifier is used. Fitness estimates the quality of the information about the problem that the classifier conveys, and it is exploited by the discovery component to guided evolution. A high fitness means that the classifier conveys good information about the problem and therefore it should be reproduced more trough the genetic algorithm. A low fitness means that the classifier conveys little or no good information about the problem and therefore should reproduce less.

On each discrete time step t, the LCS receives as input the current state of the environment s_t and builds a match set containing the classifiers in the population, whose condition matches the current state. Then, the system evaluates the utility of the actions appearing in the match

set; an action at is selected from those in the match set according to a certain criterion, and sent to the environment to be performed. Depending on the current state s_t and on the consequences of action at, the system eventually receives a reward r_t. The reinforcement component distributes a reward r_t among the classifiers accountable of the incoming rewards. This can be either implemented with an algorithm specifically designed for the Learning Classifier Systems (e.g. bucket brigade algorithm (Holland, 1986)) or with an algorithm inspired by traditional reinforcement learning methods (e.g., the modification of Q-learning (Wilson, 1995)). On a regular basis, the discovery component (genetic algorithm) randomly selects, with the probability proportional to their fitness, two classifiers from the population. It applies crossover and mutation generating two new classifiers.
The environment defines the target task. For instance, in autonomous robotics the environment corresponds roughly to the robot's physical surroundings and the goal of learning is to learn a certain behaviour (Katagami & Yamada, 2000). In classification problems, the environment trains a set of pre-classified examples; each example is described by a vector of attributes and a class label; the goal of learning is to evolve rules that can be used to classify previously unseen examples with high accuracy (Holmes et al., 2002) (Unold & Dabrowski, 2003). In computational economics, the environment represents a market and the goal of learning is to make profits (Judd & Tesfatsion, 2005).
For many years, the research on LCS was done on Holland's classifier system. All implementations shared more or less the same features which can be summarized as follows: (i) some form of a bucket brigade algorithm was used to distribute the rewards, (ii) evolution was triggered by the strength parameters of classifiers, (iii) the internal message list was used to keep track of past input (Lanzi & Riolo, 2000).
During the last years new models of Holland's system have been developed. Among others, two models seem particularly worth mentioning. The XCS classifier system (Wilson, 1995) uses Q-learning to distribute the reward to classifiers, instead of bucket brigade algorithm; the genetic algorithm acts in environmental niches instead of on the whole population; and most importantly, the fitness of classifiers is based in the accuracy of classifier predictions, instead of the prediction itself. Stolzmann's ACS (Stolzmann, 2000) differs greatly from other LCS models in that ACS learns not only how to perform a certain task, but also an internal model of the dynamics of the task. In ACS classifiers are not simple condition-action rules but they are extended by an effect part, which is used to anticipate the environmental state.

3. Grammar-based Classifier System

GCS (Unold, 2005a) (Unold & Cielecki, 2005) operates similarly to the classic LCS but differs from them in (i) representation of classifiers population, (ii) scheme of classifiers' matching to the environmental state, (iii) methods of exploring new classifiers (see Fig. 2).
The population of classifiers has a form of a context-free grammar rule set in a Chomsky Normal Form (population P in Fig. 2). Actually, this is not a limitation, because every CFG can be transformed into equivalent CNF. Chomsky Normal Form allows only for production rules, in the form of $A \rightarrow a$ or $A \rightarrow BC$, where A, B, C are the non-terminal symbols and a is a terminal symbol. The first rule is an instance of *terminal rewriting rule*. Terminal rules are not affected by the GA, and are generated automatically as the system meets an unknown (new) terminal symbol. The left hand side of the rule plays a role of the classifier's

action while the right hand side - a classifier's condition. The system evolves only one grammar according to the so-called Michigan approach. In this approach, each individual classifier – or grammar rule in GCS – is subject of the genetic algorithm's operations. All classifiers (rules) form a population of evolving individuals. In each cycle a fitness calculating algorithm evaluates a value (an adaptation) of each classifier and a discovery component operates only on single classifiers.
The automatic learning CFG is realized with grammar induction from the set of sentences. According to this technique, the system learns using a training set that in this case consists of sentences both syntactically correct and incorrect. Grammar which accepts correct sentences and rejects incorrect ones is able to classify sentences unseen so far from a test set. Cocke-Younger-Kasami (CYK) parser, which operates in Θ(n3) time (Younger, 1967), is used to parse sentences from the corpus.

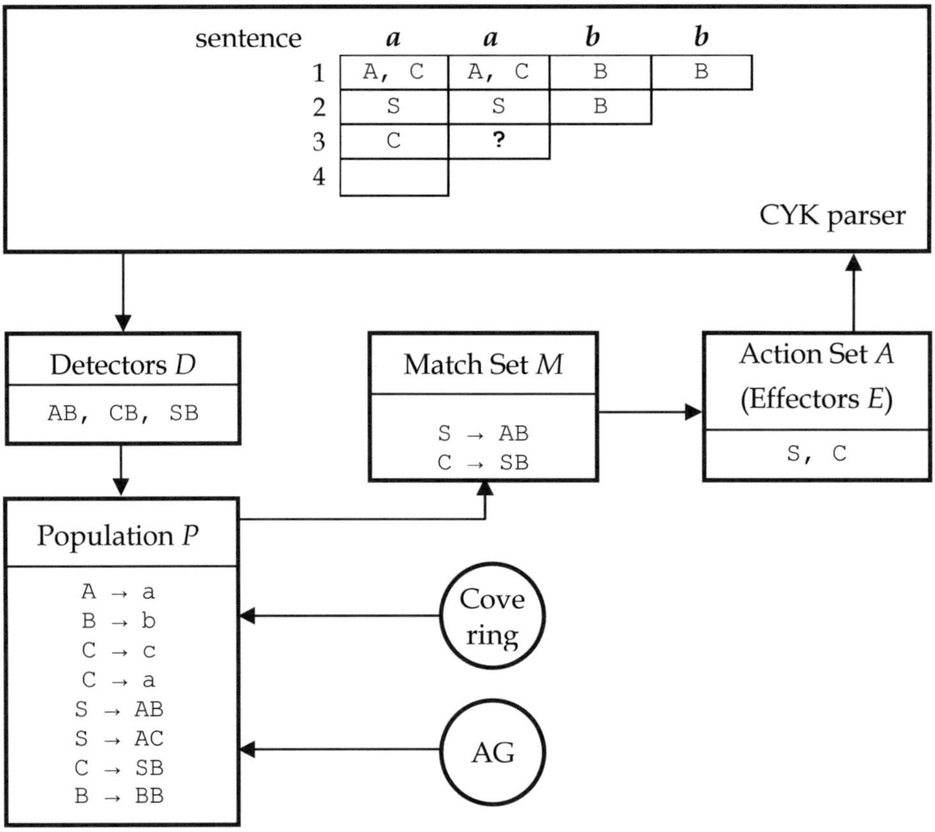

Fig. 2. The environment of Grammar-based Classifier System

The environment of a classifier system is substituted by an array of CYK parser (CYK parser module in Fig. 2). The classifier system matches the rules according to the current environmental state (state of parsing, Matching Set M in Fig. 2) and generates an action (or set of actions in GCS, effectors E in Fig. 2), pushing the parsing process toward the complete derivation of the analyzed sentence.

The discovery component in GCS is extended in comparison with a standard LCS. In some cases, a "covering" procedure may occur, adding some useful rules to the system. It adds productions that allow continuing of parsing in the current state of the system. This feature utilizes for instance the fact that accepting 2-length sentences requires separate, designated rule in grammar in CNF.

Apart from a "covering", a genetic algorithm also explores the space, searching for new, better rules. The first GCS implementation used a simple rule fitness calculation algorithm which appreciated the ones commonly used in correct recognitions. Later implementations introduced the "fertility" technique, which made the rule fitness dependant on the amount of the descendant rules (in the sentence derivation tree) (Unold, 2005b). In both techniques classifiers used in parsing positive examples gain highest fitness values, unused classifiers are placed in the middle, while the classifiers that parse negative examples gain lowest possible fitness values.

GCS uses a mutation of GA that chooses two parents in each cycle to produce two offspring. The selection step uses the roulette wheel selection. After selection a classical crossover or mutation can occur. The offspring that are created replace existing classifiers based on their similarity using crowding technique, which preserves diversity in the population and extends preservation of the dependencies between rules by replacing classifiers by the similar ones.

4. Regular Language Induction

4.1 Experimental testbed

The datasets most commonly used in DFA learning is Tomita sets (Tomita, 1982). The definition of Tomita languages is as follows:

L1: *a*,*

L2: *(ab)*,*

L3: *(b | aa)*(a* | (abb(bb | a)*))*
any sentence without an odd number of consecutive *a*'s after an odd number of consecutive *b*'s,

L4: *a*((b | bb)aa*)*(b | bb | a*)*
any sentence over the alphabet *a,b* without more than two consecutive *a*'s,

L5: *((aa | bb)*((ba | ab)(bb | aa)*(ba | ab)(bb | aa)*)*(aa | bb)**
any sentence with an even number of *a*'s and an even number of *b*'s,

L6: *((b(ba)*(a | bb)) | (a(ab)*(b | aa)))**
any sentence such that the number of *a*'s differs from the number of *b*'s by 0 modulo 3,

L7: *b*a *b*a*.*

By the way, it is worth mentioning that the L3 language given in (Luke et al., 1999) comprises improper, i.e. not according to the definition, two sentences *baaabbaaba* oraz *aabaaabbaab*. The same work gives incorrect definition of L5 language, permitting sentences which contain odd number of symbols a and b.

Grammatical (grammar) inference methods that employ DFAs as models can be divided into two broad classes: passive and active learning methods (Bongard & Lipson, 2005). In passive methods, a set of training data is known before learning. In active learning

approaches, the algorithm has some influence over which training data is labeled by the target DFA for model construction.
Passive methods, and to this class belongs GCS, usually make some assumption about the training data. In (Pitt, 1989), (Porat & Feldman, 1991), (Dupont, 1996), (Lang et al., 1998) a learning data was selected at random from sample data, in (Pao & Carr, 1978), (Parekh & Honavar, 1996) a learning data consisted of a structurally complete set, (Oncina & Garcià, 1992) assume a characteristic sample; and (Angluin, 1981) assumes a live complete set. Luke et al. (1999) and Lucas & Reynolds (2005) used equal amounts of positive and negative training examples when inferring the Tomita languages, so a learning set was balanced as in (Tomita, 1982), (Angeline, 1997), (Waltrous & Kuhn, 1992). In passive methods once the sample data has been generated and labeled, learning is then conducted.
In this chapter Grammar-based Classifier System, a method which employs evolutionary computation for search, will be compared against the evolutionary method proposed by Lucas & Reynolds (2005), and Luke et al. (1999). (Lucas & Reynolds, 2005), as well as (Luke et al., 1999) present one of the best-known results in the area of DFA/regular language induction. All of compared evolutionary methods will assume the same training and test sets. Some comparisons will be made also to EDSM method (Cicchello & Kremer, 2002), the current most powerful passive approach to DFAs inference.
Table 1 shows the details of applied data sets: number of all learning examples |U|, number of positive learning examples |U+|, number of negative learning examples |U–|, number of all test examples |T|, number of positive test examples |T+|, and number of negative test examples |T–|. Note, that test sets are not balanced, and contain much more negative sentences than positive once.

Lang.	$\|U\|$	$\|U^+\|$	$\|U^-\|$	$\|T\|$	$\|T^+\|$	$\|T^-\|$
L1	16	8	8	65 534	15	65 519
L2	15	5	10	65 534	7	65 527
L3	24	12	12	65 534	9447	56 087
L4	19	10	9	65 534	23 247	42 287
L5	21	9	12	65 534	10 922	54 612
L6	21	9	12	65 534	21 844	43 690
L7	20	12	8	65 534	2515	63 019

Table 1. Learning and test data sets.

4.2 Experiments

A comparison set of experiments with GCS was performed on the above Tomita corpora. Fifty independent experiments were performed, evolution on each training corpus ran for 5,000 generations, with the following genetic parameters: number of non-terminal symbols 19, number of terminal symbols 7, crossover probability 0.2, mutation probability 0.8, population consisted of maximal 40 classifiers where 30 of them were created randomly in the first generation, crowding factor 18, crowding size 3.
In the first attempt GCS was compared to the approach presented in (Luke et al., 1999) (denoted by GP). GP applies gene regulation to evolve deterministic finite-state automata. In this approach genes are states in the automaton, and a gene-regulation-like mechanism determines state transitions. Each gene has Boolean value indicating whether or not it was an accepting state. The main results are summarized in Table 1. For each learning corpus,

the table shows the target language, and three sets of results. The first indicator nSuccess is the number of runs with success gained by GCS within 50 experiments and compared approach presented in (Luke et al., 1999). The second one nEvals indicates the average number of generations needed to reach the 100% fitness, and the last one nGen is the percentage of all unseen strings correctly classified.

Lang.	*nSuccess*		*nEvals*		*nGen*	
	GP	**GCS**	**GP**	**GCS**	**GP**	**GCS**
L1	31/50	**50/50**	30	**2**	88.4	**100**
L2	7/50	**50/50**	1010	**2**	84.0	**100**
L3	1/50	1/50	12 450	**666**	66.3	**100**
L4	3/50	**24/50**	7870	**2455**	65.3	**100**
L5	0/50	**50/50**	13 670	**201**	68.7	**92.4**
L6	47/50	**49/50**	2580	**1471**	95.9	**96.9**
L7	1/50	**11/50**	11 320	**2902**	67.7	**92.0**

Table 2. Comparison of GCS with GP approach (Luke et al., 1999).

For compared methods induction of L3 language appeared to be hard task. Both in GP and in GCS only the one run over 50 successfully finished. But GP found the solution in 12450 iterations, whereas GCS in only 666 steps. For the same language GCS correctly classified all of the unseen examples, while GP achieved 66%. As to an indicator nGen, GP was not able correctly classified unseen strings for any language from the tested corpora, while GCS induced a grammar fully general to the language in 4 cases. It is interesting to compare the results of induction for L5 language. GP approach could not find the proper grammar (DFA) for any run, while GCS found the solution in all runs, on average in 201 steps. While learning L1 and L2 languages, GP found the proper grammars not in all runs, whereas for GCS this task appeared to be trivial (100% nGen, 50/50 nSuccess, and nEvals 2 steps).
Table 3 shows the cost of induction (an indicator nEvlas) for the methods Plain, Smart, and nSmart taken from (Lucas & Reynolds, 2005), GP approach, and GCS.

Lang.	**Plain**	**Smart**	**nSmart**	**GP**	**GCS**
L1	107	25	15	30	**2**
L2	186	37	40	1010	**2**
L3	1809	237	833	12 450	666
L4	1453	177	654	7870	2455
L5	1059	195	734	13 670	201
L6	734	93	82	2580	1471
L7	1243	188	1377	11 320	2902

Table 3. Cost of induction (nEvals) for different evolutionary methods.

Lucas and Reynolds (Lucas & Reynolds, 2005) used different method to evolving DFA. In contrary to (Luke et al., 1999), only transition matrix was evolved, supported by a simple deterministic procedure to optimally assign state labels. This approach is based on evolutionary strategy (1+1). Three versions of induction algorithm were prepared: an approach in which both the transition matrix and the state label vector evolve (Plain), so-called Smart method evolving only the transition matrix and the number of the states was fixed and equal to 10, and finally nSmart method in which the number of the DFA states is

equal to the size of minimal automata. Recall that both GP and GCS belong to the so-called variable size methods, whereas Plain, Smart, and nSmart approaches represent the fixed-size structure methods. In general, the second group of methods gains better results.
GCS obtained the best results for the L1 and L2 languages among comparable methods. The result 201 steps for L5 is comparable with the best result of 195 reached by nSmart. Although GCS reached similar result for language L3 as the best method (666 for GCS, and 237 for Smart), it is hard to compare for this language these methods, because of low value of nSuccess for GCS - only one run over 50 finished with success (see table 2). For the languages L4, L6, and L7 fixed-size structured methods achieved better results than variable-size methods.

Lang.	Smart	nSmart	EDSM	GP	GCS
L1	81.8	100	52.4	88.4	100
L2	88.8	95.5	91.8	84	**100**
L3	71.8	90.8	86.1	66.3	**100**
L4	61.1	100	100	65.3	100
L5	65.9	100	100	68.7	92.4
L6	61.9	100	100	95.9	96.9
L7	62.6	82.9	71.9	67.7	**92**

Table 4. Percentage of all unseen strings correctly classified (nGen) for different methods.

Table 4 shows the percentage of all unseen strings correctly classified (an indicator nGen) for the methods Smart, nSmart, EDSM, GP, and GCS. Recall that the EDSM, as a heuristic and non-evolutionary method, was single-time executed during learning phase. Model GCS achieved the best results from all tested approaches for L1, L2, L3, and L7 languages. For the language L4 the same 100% accuracy was obtained by proposed method, nSmart, and EDSM. For the L5 and L6 languages GCS obtained the second result, higher than 90%.

5. Summary

Our experiments attempted to apply a Grammar-based Classifier System to evolutionary computation in evolving an inductive mechanism for the regular language set. Near-optimal and/or better than reported in the literature solutions were obtained. Moreover, performance of GCS was compared to the Evidence Driven State Merging algorithm, one of the most powerful known DFA learning algorithms. GCS with its ability of generalizations outperforms EDSM, as well as other significant evolutionary method.

6. References

Angeline, P. (1994). *Evolutionary Algorithms and Emergent Intelligence*. PhD Thesis. Computer Science Department, Ohio State University

Angeline, P. (1997). An alternative to indexed memory for evolving programs with explicit state representations, In: Koza, J.R. et al (eds.) *Proc. 2nd Conf. Genetic Programming (GP97)*, pp. 423–430, Morgan Kaufmann, San Francisco, CA

Angeline, P.; Saunders, G.M. & Pollack, J.P. (1994). An Evolutionary Algorithm that Constructs Recurrent Neural Networks, *IEEE Trans. Neural Networks*, vol. 5, no. 1, 54–65

Angluin, D. (1981). A note on the number of queries needed to identify regular languages, *Information and Control*, 51, 76–87

Bianchi, D. (1996). Learning Grammatical Rules from Examples Using a Credit Assignement Algorithm, In: *Proc. of The First Online Workshop on Soft Computing (WSC1)*, pp. 113–118, Nagoya

Bongard, J. & Lipson, H. (2005). Active Coevolutionary Learning of Deterministic Finite Automata, *J. of Machine Learning Research*, 6, 1651–1678

Cicchello, O. & Kremer, S.C. (2002). Beyond EDSM, In: *Proc. Int'l Colloquium Grammatical Inference*, vol. 2484, pp. 37–48

Cyre, W.R. (2002). Learning Grammars with a Modified Classifier System, In: *Proc. 2002 World Congress on Computational Intelligence*, pp. 1366–1371. Honolulu, Hawaii

Dupont, P. (1996). Incremental regular inference. In: Miclet, L. & de la Higuera, C. (eds.) *Proc. 3rd ICGI-96*, pp. 222–237, LNAI, vol. 1147

Dupont, P.; Miclet L. & Vidal, E. (1994). What Is the Search Space of the Regular Inference? In: Carrasco, R.C. & Oncina, J. (eds.) *Proc. Grammatical Inference and Applications: Second Int'l Colloquium (ICGI-94)*, pp. 25–37

Giles, C.; Sun, G.; Chen, H.; Lee Y. & Chen, D. (1990). Higher order Recurrent Neural Networks and Grammatical Inference, In: Touretzky, D. (ed.) *Advances in Neural Information Processing Systems 2*, pp. 380–387. San Mateo, Calif.: Morgan Kaufman

Holland, J. (1976). Adaptation. In: Rosen, R. & Snell, F.M. (eds.) *Progress in theoretical biology*, Plenum, New York

Holland, J. (1986). Escaping Brittleness: The possibilities of General-Purpose Learning Algorithms Applied to Parallel Rule-Based Systems. In: Michalski, R.S. et al. (eds.) *Machine Learning, an Artificial Intelligence Approach*, vol. II, 593–623. Morgan Kaufmann

Holmes, J.H.; Lanzi, P.L.; Stolzmann, W. & Wilson, S.W. (2002). Learning classifier systems: new models, successful applications, *Information Processing Letters* 82(1), 23–30

Hopcroft, J.E. & Ullman, J.D. (1969). *Formal Languages And Their Relation to Automata*, Reading, Mass.: Addison-Wesley

Judd, K.L. & Tesfatsion, L. (2005). Agent-Based Computational Economics, *Handbook of Computational Economics*, vol. 2, Elsevier, North-Holland

Katagami, D. & Yamada, S. (2000). Interactive Classifier System for Real Robot Learning. In: *IEEE International Workshop on Robot-Human Interaction ROMAN-2000*, pp. 258–263, Osaka, Japan

Lang, K.; Pearlmutter, B. & Price R. (1998). Results of the Abbadingo One DFA Learning Competition and a New Evidence Driven State Merging Algorithm. In: *Proc. Int. Colloquium on Grammatical Inference ICGA-98*, pp. 1–12, LNAI, vol. 1433, Springer, Berlin, Heidelberg

Lanzi, P.L. & Riolo, R.L. (2000). A Roadmap to the Last Decade of Learning Classifier System Research, In: *LNAI*, vol. 1813, pp. 33–62. Springer Verlag

Lucas, S. & Reynolds, T.J. (2005). Learning Deterministic Finite Automata with a Smart State labeling Evolutionary Algorithm, *IEEE Trans. on Pattern Analysis and Machine Intelligence*, 27 (7), 1–12

Luke, S.; Hamahashi, S. & Kitano, H. (1999). 'Genetic' Programming". In: Banzhaf, W. et al. (eds.) *Proc. Genetic and Evolutionary Computation Conf.*, pp. 1098–1105

Oncina, J. & Garcià, P. (1992). Inferring regular languages in polynomial update time, In: Perez, N. et al. (eds.) *Pattern recognition and image analysis*, pp. 49–61, Singapore, World Scientific

Pao, T. & Carr, J. (1978). A solution of the syntactic induction-inference problem for regular languages, *Computer Languages*, 3, 53–64

Parekh, R.G. & Honavar, V.G. (1996). An incremental interactive approach for regular grammar inference. In: *Proc. 3rd ICGI-96*, pp. 238–250, LNAI, vol. 1147, Springer, Berlin, Heidelberg

Pitt, L. (1989). Inductive inference, DFAs and computational complexity. In: *Proc. Int. Workshop on Analogical and Inductive Inference*, pp. 18–44, LNAI, vol. 397, Springer, London, UK

Pitt, L. & Warmuth, M. (1993). The Minimum Consistent DFA Problem Cannot Be Approximated within Any Polynomial, *J. ACM*, vol. 40, no. 1, 95–142

Porat, F. & Feldman, J. (1991). Learning automata from ordered examples, *Machine Learning*, 7, 109–138

Stolzmann, W. (2000). An Introduction to Anticipatory Classifier Systems, In: *LNAI*, vol. 1813, pp. 175–194, Springer-Verlag

Tomita, M. (1982). Dynamic construction of finite automata from examples using hill climbing, In: *Proc. 4th Annual Cognitive Science Conf.*, pp. 105–108, USA

Unold, O. (2005a). Context-free grammar induction with grammar-based classifier system, *Archives of Control Science*, vol. 15 (LI) 4, 681–690

Unold, O. (2005b). Playing a toy-grammar with GCS, In: Mira, J & Álvarez, J.R. (eds.) *IWINAC 2005*, pp. 300–309, LNCS, vol. 3562,. Springer Verlag

Unold, O. (2007a). Learning classifier system approach to natural language grammar induction, In: Shi, Y. et al. (eds.) *ICCS 2007*, pp. 1210–1213 Part II, LNCS, vol. 4488

Unold, O. (2007b). Grammar-based classifier system for recognition of promoter regions, In: Beliczynski B. et al. (eds.) *ICANNGA07*, pp. 798–805, Part I, LNCS, vol. 4431

Unold, O. & Cielecki, L. (2005). Grammar-based Classifier System, In: Hryniewicz, O. et al. (eds.) *Issues in Intelligent Systems: Paradigms*, EXIT Publishing House, Warsaw, 273–286

Unold, O. & Dabrowski, G. (2003) Use of learning classifier system for inferring natural language grammar. In: Abraham, A et al. (eds.) *Design and application of hybrid intelligent*, Amsterdam, IOS Press, 272–278

Waltrous, R. & Kuhn, G. (1992). Induction of finite state automata using second-order recurrent networks. In: Moody, J. et al. (eds.) *Advances in Neural Information Processing 4* , pp. 309–316, Morgan Kaufmann, San Francisco, CA

Wilson, S.W. (1995). Classifier Fitness Based on Accuracy, *Evolutionary Computation* 3 (2), 147–175

Younger, D. (1967). *Recognition and parsing of context-free languages in time n3,* University of Hawaii Technical Report, Department of Computer Science (1967)

Fault Localization Models Using Dependences

Safeeullah Soomro[1], Abdul Hameed Memon[2],
Asif Ali Shah[3, 4] and Wajiha Shah[3, 4]
Emails: safee@ieee.org, memon@yic.edu.sa &
{asif.shah,wajiha.shah}@tuwien.ac.at
[1]*Yanbu University College, KSA*
[2]*Yanbu Industrial College, KSA*
[3]*Vienna University of Technology, Austria*
[4]*Mehran University of Engineering & Technology Jamshoro, Pakistan*

Abstract

In recent years Mode-Based Diagnosis has an acheived a tremendous recognition and has been applied to variety of disgnosis problems, mainly software debugging. Many efforts have been taken to improve software development and prevent faults. Still software faults pose challenging problems to software designers. Fault localization is next step after detecting faults in programs. This chapter makes use of dependences between program variables to detecting and localization faults from strucural programs. Further more we discuss the relationship between the FDM (functional-dependences model) and VBM (verification-based model) under presence of partial specifications artifacts like assertions are pre and post conditions by exemplifying specific scenarios in software debugging. Moreover, we discuss the relationship between VBM model and the well-known functional-dependence model particularly under presence of partial specification artifacts like assertions or pre- and post conditions. In the last we present the summary regarding dependences models that helps us to choose which model is detecting and locating errors from different type of data structures. Finally we discuss the case studies between FDM and VBM with some test programs.

Keywords: *Model Based Software Debugging, Software Debugging, Model-Based Diagnosis, Fault Detection and Localization.*

1. Introduction

Within the last decades several techniques for debugging, i.e., detecting, locating, and repairing faults in programs, have been proposed. Some of the techniques make use of models of the program's structure and behavior like algorithmic debugging or model-based debugging. Other techniques try to find bugs by examining code for suspects, i.e., code fragments that do not obey given rules, by finding differences between different program runs, or by finding (structural) differences between a program and another implementation.

The latter technique is used mainly for tutoring systems where the desired implementation is known in advance.

We introduce the basic idea of automated fault localization in software by means of a small Java program example. The program given in Figure 1. multiplies two integer variables x and y and returns the product and the product's sign. In line 11 we assign 0-y to the loop counter i, thus our program is buggy. For the test case x=-2 and y=+4 we obtain that result is 0, which contradicts our expectation result = -8.

In localizing the misbehavior's cause we start with static code analysis techniques. For example, we compute a static slice in line 18 with respect to the variable result. This rules out irrelevant statements by considering solely statements influencing the variable result. Our static slice contains the statements [2,6,7,8,9,11,12,14,15,16] - that is, we can exclude the statements 5 and 10 from causing the result's wrong value.

In addition we know that our loop counter *i* is always bigger or equal to 0 thus we might add the assertion in line 13. When executing the program with the test case x=-2 and y=+4 the variable i becomes -4 which causes the assertion to fail. At this point we again compute the static slice obtaining the lines [2,7,9,11]. Thus at this point we definitely know that one of the statements given in this slice causes the misbehavior with regard to variable i. Moreover, the second slice is a subset of the first one, thus we suspect the same error being responsible for both assertion violations, line 13 and 17.

In the next step we incorporate the specific test case's outcome. Notably, dynamic slices cannot localize the fault's real cause, thus the authors (Gyimothy et al, 1999 ; Agrawal et al, 1993) extend this notion to a so called relevant slice. A relevant slice is a dynamic slice augmented with potentially affecting conditions and their data dependences. We employ this notion of a slice for the given test case and the slicing criterion *(13,{result =0})*. When taking into account this kind of slice we can further rule out line 7. Since, for the given test case, the condition in line 8 is true, line 11 rather than 7 determines the value of i in line 13.

In our example, slicing techniques alleviate localizing the misbehavior's cause. In general, fault localization is a difficult task and requires the incorporation of various models (the spectrum ranges from abstract models relying on dependences (Jackson, 1995) to concrete value-level models) and techniques (e.g. algorithmic debugging (Shapiro, 1983), model-based debugging (Wotawa, 2000 ; Kleer & Williams, 1987) into a debugging environment.

```
// pre true
public int mult (int x,y) {
int add,i,result;

sign = 1;
add = y;
i = x;
result = 0;
if (x < 0) {
        sign = -1;
        i = 0 - y; // should be 0 - x
        add = 0 - y; }
ASSERT (i >= 0)
while ( 0 < i ) {
        i = i - 1;
        result = result + add;}
ASSERT (result = xy);
output result, sign;
}
// post result = xy
// post sign = sign xy
```

Fig. 1. Multiplication of two integer values.

The chapter is organized as follows. In Section 2 we present our Verification Based Model (VBM). The comparison between VBM and (Functional Dependence Model) FDM is given in Section 3. In Section 4 we present case studies regarding debugging model. In section five we present the related research work of dependences based models. Finally we summarize the chapter including furure research.

2. Verification Based Model

Our novel debugging model allows one for reasoning about functions over dependence relations under given assumptions. Therefore the notion of a dependence relation is fundamental to our approach:

Definition 1 ***(Dependence Relation)*** *Given a program with variables V, and a set of model variables* $M=\{\xi_1 \ldots\}$. *A dependence relation is a subset of the set* $D = 2^V X ((M \upsilon V)$.
The key idea is to abstract over the actual state transitions of the program and instead view its behavior as a dependence relation between inputs and outputs. Any pair $(x,y) \in D$ says that the value of x after depends on the value of y before statement execution.

We obtain the dependence relation of compound statement by putting together the dependence relation of its constituent parts. Given two statement S_1 and S_2, the dependence relation of the compound statement $S_1 ; S_2$ is given by $D(S_1 ; S_2)=D(S_1) \bullet D(S_2)$. To reflect this we define two composition operators:

Definition 2 ***(Composition1)*** *Given two dependence relations R_1, R_2 Є Don V and M. The composition of R_1 and R_2 is defined as follows:*

$$R_1 \bullet R_2 = \begin{array}{l} \{ (x,y) \mid \exists \text{ exists } (z,y) \text{ in } R_1 \;\&\; \exists\, (x,z) \in R_2 \} \cup \\ \{ (x,y) \mid \exists \text{ exists } (z,y) \text{ in } R_1 \;\&\; \nexists\, (x,z) \in R_2 \} \cup \\ \{ (x,y) \mid \nexists \text{ exists } (z,y) \text{ in } R_1 \;\&\; \exists\, (x,z) \in R_2 \} \end{array}$$

This definition ensures that no information is lost during computing the overall dependence relation for a procedure or method. Hence, the first line of the definition of composition handles the case where there is a transitive dependence. The second line states that all dependences that are not re-defined in R_2 are still valid. In the third line all dependences that are defined in R_2 are in the new dependence set provided that there is no transitivity relation.

Note that functional composition is not a commutative operation and that { } is the identity element of composition. For example, the combined dependences of our below examples are:

$$r^1 \bullet r^2 = \{(c,r),(d,r)\} = r' \text{ and } r' \bullet r_3 = \{(a,r), (a, pi), (c,r),(d,r)\} = r''$$

In the following we explain the basic ideas using the following small program which implements the computation of the circumference and area of a circle. The program contains one fault in line 2 where a multiplication by **Π (pi)** is missing.

```
0. // pre true
1.        d = r * 2;
2.        c = d; // BUG! a = d * pi;
3.        c = r * r * pi;
4. // post c = r2 ·Π ^ a = 2 ·r ·Π
```

These dependences solely are given by a statement whenever we assume that the statement is correct (w.r.t. the dependences). If a statement is assumed to be incorrect, the dependences are not known. We express the latter fact by introducing a new type of variable, the so called model variables. Model variables are variables that work as place-holder for program variables. For example, if we assume statement 2 to be incorrect, we introduce a model that says that program variable a depends on model variable ε_2 (where ε_2 is unique).

To point out intricacies with the previous definition we further need to define relation composition as follows:

Definition 3 ***(Relational Composition)*** *Given two dependence relations R_1, R_2 Є D on V and M. Given two statement S_1 and S_2, the dependences of the compound statement $S_1; S_2$ in terms of* *relational composition is given by D(S1; S2) = D(S2) o D(S1). The relational composition of R_1 and R_2 is defined as follows:*

$$R_1 \circ R_2 = \{ (x,y) \mid (x,y) \in R_1 \,\&\, (z,y) \in R_2 \}$$

Note, that as long as we rely on the simple dependence definition given previously, this operator suffers from information loss since it solely preserves transitive relationships. For our running example we obtain $r_1 \circ r_2 = \{(c,r)\} = r'$ and $r_3 \circ r' = \{\ \} = r''$.

In order to allow the direct comparison of specified dependences with the computed ones we introduce a projection operator which deletes all dependences for variables that are not of interest like the internal variable d.

Definition 4 *(Projection)* *Given a dependence relations R ∈ D and a set of ariables A ⊆ M υ V. The projection of R on A written as ∏ A(R) is defined as follows:*

$$\prod_{A}(R) = \{ (x,y) \mid (x,y) \in R \,\&\, x \in A \}$$

For example, $\prod_{\{r,c,a,pi\}} (r'')$ *is {a,r), (c, r),(c, pi)}* which is equivalent to the specification.

From here on we assume that the computed dependence relation is always projected onto the variables used within the specification before comparing it with the specification - that is, *A= {x | (x,y) ∈ SPEC* denotes the specified dependences.

Definition 5 *(Grounded dependence relation*) *A dependence relation is said to be grounded (or variable-free) if it contains no model variables.*

We assume that all specification are grounded dependencerelations. Thus, we have to compare dependence relations containing model variables with grounded dependence relations. Wepropose a similar solution to that employed in the resolution calculus of first-order logic, namely substitution and finding the most general unifier. However, in contrast to variable substitution in first-order logic, we do not only replace one variable by one term but one model variable by a set of program variables.

Definition 6 *(Substitution)* A substitution σ is a function which maps model variables to a set of program variables, i.e., $\sigma: M \rightarrow 2^v$. The result of the application of the substitution σ on a dependence relation R is a dependence relation where all model-variables x from R have been replaced by σ (x).

For the purpose of finding an efficient algorithm for computing asubstitution that makes a dependence set equivalent to its specification we first map the problem to an equivalent constraint satisfaction problem (CSP). A CSP (Dechter, 1992 & Dechter 2003) comprises variables Vars, their domains *Dom,* and a set of constraints *Cons* that have to be fulfilled when assigning values to the variables. A value assignment that fulfills all constraints is said to be a σ solution of the CSP. Every solution to the corresponding CSP is a valid substitution. For more details about how make use of standard CSP algorithms for computing substitutions. we refer the reader to (Jackson, 1995).

Finally, we are now able to define the equivalence of a dependence set and its grounded specification.

1. Assignmnts:
   $\neg Ab(x = e) \rightarrow D(x = e) = \{(x,v) \mid v \in vars(e)$ where vars is assumed to return all variables which are used in exression *e*.
   $M(x = e)= \{x\}$
   $Ab(x = e) \rightarrow D(x =e) =\{(x,\xi_i)\}$
2. Conditionals:
   $\neg Ab(if\ e\ then\ S_1\ else\ S_2) \rightarrow D(if\ e\ then\ S_1\ else\ S_2) = D(S_1)\ \upsilon\ D(S_2)\ \upsilon\ \{(x,x) \mid x \in (M(S_1)\ \upsilon\ M(S_2))\}\ \upsilon\ ((M(S_1)\ \upsilon\ M(S_2))\ x\ vars(e))$
   $M(if\ e\ then\ S_1\ else\ S_2) = M(S_1)\ \upsilon\ M(S_2)$
   $Ab(if\ e\ then\ S_1\ else\ S_2)\ \ D(if\ e\ then\ S_1\ else\ S_2)= D(S_1)\ \upsilon\ D(S_2)\ \upsilon\ \{(x,x) \mid x \in (M(S_1)\ \upsilon\ M(S_2))\}\ \upsilon\ ((M(S_1)\ \upsilon\ M(S_2))\ x\ \{\ \xi_i\ \})$
3. Loops:
   $\neg Ab(while\ e\ \{S\}) \rightarrow D(while\ e\ \{\ S\ \}) = D(S)^+\ \upsilon\ (M(S)\ x\ vars(e)))\ \bullet\ D(S)^+$
   $M\ (while\ e\ \{S\}) = M(S)$
   $Ab(while\ e\ \{\ S\ \}) \rightarrow D(while\ e\ \{\ S\ \}) = D\ (S)^+\ \upsilon\ \ (M(S)\ X\ \{\ \xi_i\ \})\ \bullet\ D(S)^+$
   In the above rules $D(S)^+$ *is the transiive closure of* $D(S)$.
4. No-operation (NOP):
   $D((nop)= I\ where\ I =\{(x,x) \mid x \in V\}$
   $M(nop) = \{\ \}$
5. Sequence of statements:
   $D(S_1; S_2) = D(S_1)\ \bullet\ D(S_2)$
   $M(S_1 ;S_2) = M(S_1)\ \upsilon\ M(S_2)$

Fig. 2. The Verification-Based Model.

Definition 7 ***(Equivalence)*** *A dependence set R is equivalent to its grounded specification S iff there exists a* $\sigma = findSubstitution\ (R,S) \neq \perp$ *and* $\sigma\ (R) = S$.

Formally, it remains to introduce how to extract dependence information from the source code. Figure 2 shows the appropriate rules. In the figure function *D* returns the dependences for a given statement and function M returns the variables employed within a given statement. Moreover, function var returns a given expression's variables. For more details about how to extract dependences we refer the reader to (Jackson, 1995). In Figure 2 we presented rules of of extracting dependences from multiples statements and more details about how to extract dependences from procedures we refer to reader (Soomro., S. 2007).

3. Comparison Between VBM and FDM

In order to compare different models of programs for fault detection and localization, we first introduce the debugging problem formally. Similar to Reiter's definition of a diagnosis problem (Wotawa, 2002) a debugging problem is characterized by the given program and its expected behavior. In contrast to Reiter we assume the existence of a specification that captures the whole expected behavior and not only behavioral instances like given by the set of observations *OBS* in Reiter's original definition.

Definition 8 ***(Debugging Problem)*** *A debugging problem is characterized by a tuple ($\prod$, SPEC) where $\prod$ is a program written in a certain programming language and SPEC is a (formal) specification of the program's intended behavior. The debugging problem now can be separated into three parts:*

1. **Fault Detection**: *Answer the question: Does $\prod$ fulfill SPEC?. In case a program fulfills (does not fulfill) its specifications we write $\prod \upsilon$ SPEC $\not\models \perp$ ($\prod \upsilon$ SPEC $\models \perp$ respectively).*
2. **Fault Localozation** : *Find the root cause in $\prod$ which explains a behavior not given in SPEC.*
3. **Fault Correction** : *Change the program such that $\prod$ fulfills SPEC.*

Note that SPEC is not required to be a formal specification. It might represent an oracle, i.e., a uman, which is able to give an answer to all questions regarding program $\prod$. In this section we focus on the first two tasks of the debugging problem. Because fault localization and correction can only be performed when identifying a faulty behavior, from here on we assume only situations where ($\prod$, *SPEC*) $\models \perp$. The question now is how such situations can be detected in practice.

The availability of a specification that is able to answer all questions is an assumption which is hardly (and not to say impossible) to fulfill. What we have in practice is a partial specification. Therefore, we are only able to detect a faulty behavior and not to prove correctness. Obviously different kind of specifications may lead to different results to the first task of the debugging problem, i.e., identifying a faulty behavior. In the context of this chapter the question about the satisfiability of $\prod$ υ *SPEC* $\models$ is reduced to checking the satisfiability of two entences, i.e., $FDM(\prod)\ \upsilon\ SPEC_{FDM} \models \perp$ and $VBM(\prod) \upsilon\ SPEC_{VBM} \models \perp$ where $SPEC_{VBM}$ and $SPEC_{FDM}$ are the partial specification which belong to the FDM and VBM respectively.

1. *proc (a,b) {.....*
2. *x= a+b;*
3. *y = a / b; //instead of y= a * b*
4. *assert (y = = a * b)*
5. *}...*

$\neg AB(2) \wedge ok(a) \wedge ok(b) \rightarrow ok(x)$	$SPEC(proc) = \{(y,a), (y,b)\}$
$\neg AB(3) \wedge ok(a) \wedge ok(b) \rightarrow ok(y)$	$dep(proc) = \{(y,a), (y,b)$
	$dep(proc) \supseteq SPEC(proc)$
$\rightarrow ok(a), \rightarrow ok(b), \rightarrow \neg ok(y)$	$DIAG = \{\ \}$
$DIAG = \{\{AB(3)\}\}$	

Fig. 3. Code Snippet, FD model, Specified and Computed Dependences.

The model comparison we present in the following relies on a couple of (reasonable) assumptions. First, for the FDM we need to have a test case judging the correctness of specific variables. In general, finding an appropriate test case revealing a misbehavior w.r.t. specific variables is a difficult task, however, the presence of such a single test case is a requirement for the applicability of the FDM. For the VBM, we assume an underlying assertion language, and a mechanism for deducing dependence specifications from this language. Dependences are further oriented according to last-assigned variables and specified in terms of inputs or input parameters rather than intermediate variables. For simplicity, we further assume that there are no disjunctive post conditions.

In the following we illustrate the introduced models' strength and weaknesses in terms of simple scenarios. In the figures the left hand side is a summary of the FDM model including the observations obtained from running the test case and the left hand side outlines the VBM. For both columns we summarize the obtained diagnosis candidates in terms of the set *DIAG*. Note that we only focus on single-fault diagnosis throughout the following discussion.

Figure 3 outlines a code snippet together with the assertion checking a certain property, the FDM, and the specified computed dependences. Obviously, the VBM is unable to detect and thus localize this specific (functional) fault. In contrast to this, the FDM is able to localize this specific fault. Due to the failed assertion we can conclude that there is something wrong with variable y, thus ¬ ok(y) holds. We also can assume that inputs *a* and *b* are correct, thus the assumptions *ok(a)* and *ok(b)* directly deliver line 3 (AB(3)) as the sole single-fault diagnosis.

```
1.  proc (a,b,x,y) {.....
2.  x= a+b;
3.  x = +2; //instead of y= x+2
4.  assert (y = = x +2, x = = a+b)
5.  }...
```

$\neg AB(2) \wedge ok(a) \wedge ok(b) \rightarrow ok(x')$	$SPEC = \{(y,a), (y,b)(x,a)(x,b)\}$
$\neg AB(3) \wedge ok(a) \wedge ok(b) \rightarrow ok(y)$	$dep(proc) = \{(x,a), (x,b)$
$\rightarrow ok(x), \rightarrow ok(a); \rightarrow ok(b)$	$dep(proc) \subseteq SPEC(proc)$
	$\sigma(\xi_2) = \{\}; \sigma(\xi_3) = \{\}$
$\rightarrow \neg ok(x''); \rightarrow ok(a), \rightarrow ok(b)$	
$DIAG = \{\{AB(3)\}, \{AB(3)\}\}$	$DIAG = \{\}$

Fig. 4. The misplaced Left-hand Side Variable.

Moreover, as Figure 4 illustrates, although the FDM allows for detecting misplaced left-hand side variables, the VBM cannot localize these kind of faults. Assume that $a=1,b=1,x=2$ thus $y=4$. Our assertion suggests to assume the dependences $\{(y,a),(y,b),(x,a),(x,b)\}$. Both models allow for detecting the fault. When employing the FDM, from the raised assertion we know that $\neg\, ok(x)$ holds. In order to conclude that the outcome of statement 3 is correct, we need to know that x is correct prior to this statement's execution. Thus, to obtain the contradiction we have to assume that both statements are correct.

By reverting the correctness assumption about statement 2 we obviously can remove the

contradiction. Moreover, reverting the assumption about statement 3 also resolves the contradiction. Thus, we obtain two single-fault diagnosis *AB(2)* and *AB(3)*. In contrast to this, since y never appears as target variable, we cannot obtain dependences for variable y and thus the VBM cannot localize these kind of (structural) faults.

1. *proc (a,b,x,y) {.....*
2. *x= a+b;*
3. *y = x+c+d; //instead of y= x+c*
4. *assert (y = = x +c)*
5. *}...*

$\neg AB(2) \wedge ok(a)\ C) \rightarrow ok(x)$
$\neg AB(3) \wedge ok(x) \rightarrow ok(c) \wedge ok(d) \rightarrow ok(y)$
$\rightarrow \neg ok(y), \rightarrow ok(a), \rightarrow ok(b)$
$DIAG = \{\{AB(2)\}, \{AB(3)\}\}$

$SPEC(proc) = \{Y,a),(y,b)(y,c)\}$
$Dep(proc) = \{(y, a), (y, b), (y, c), (x, a), (x, b)\}$
$Dep(proc) \supseteq SPEC(proc)$
$DIAG = \{\ \}$

Fig. 5. A Typical (Structure) Fault Inducing Additional Dependences.

The next example points out that the VBM fails in case the fault introduces additional dependences. In Figure 5 we assign $x + c + d$ instead of $x + c$ to the variable y. Our assertion indicates that y depends upon x and c, thus $SPEC(proc) = \{(y,a),(y,b),(y,c)\}$. Computing the program's actual dependences dep(proc), however, yields to {(y,a),(y,b),(y,c),(y,d)} □ $\{(y,a),(y,b),(y,c)\}$ and thus VBM cannot detect this specific malfunctioning nor locate the misbehavior's cause. By employing the FDM under the assumption $\neg ok(y)$ we obtain two single-fault diagnosis *AB(2)* and *AB(3)*.

Figure 6 illustrates an example where the fault manifests itself in inducing less dependences than specified. Our specification is $SPEC(proc) = \{(y,a),(y,b),(y,c)\}$. Obviously, the computed dependences $\{(y,a),(y,b)\} \not\supseteq SPEC(proc)$. As the figure outlines, we obtain two single-fault diagnosis candidates, *AB(2)* and *AB(3)*. In this case, the FDM is also capable of delivering the misbehavior's real cause, it returns two single-fault diagnosis candidates: *AB(2)* and *AB(3)*.

The Author (Stumptner, 2001) shows that localizing structural faults requires exploiting design information like assertions, and pre- and post conditions. Again, we outline this in terms of a few small examples. Although the previous examples show that the VBM cannot detect neither locate certain types of faults, it may provide reasonable results in capturing structural faults.

Our final example in Figure 7 illustrates that both approaches might deliver reasonable but different results. We assume $a=1,b=1,e=0$, thus we expect $z=2$ and $d=0$. However, due to the introduced fault, we obtain $z=1$ *and* $d=0$. Since the value of z is incorrect, but $d=0$, we conclude that $\neg\, ok(z)$ and $ok(d)$ holds. Thus, we btain $AB(2)$ and $AB(4)$ as diagnosis candidates. Note that this result primarily roots in the coincidental correctness of variable d.

```
1. proc (a,b,c) {.....
2. x= a+b;
3. y = x; //instead of y= x+c
4. assert (y = = a+b +c)
5. }...
6.
```

$\neg AB(2) \wedge ok(a) \wedge ok(b) \rightarrow ok(x)$	$SPEC = \{(y,a), (y,b)(y,c)\}$
$\neg AB(3) \wedge ok(a) \rightarrow ok(y)$	$dep(proc) = \{(y,a), (y,b)\}$
$\rightarrow \neg ok(y), \rightarrow ok(a), \rightarrow ok(b)$	$dep(proc) \not\supseteq SPEC(proc)$
	$\sigma(\xi_2) = \{a,b,c\}, \sigma(\xi_3) = \{a,b,c\}$
$DIAG = \{\{AB(2)\}, \{AB(3)\}\}$	$DIAG = \{\{AB(2)\}, \{AB(3)\}\}$

Fig. 6. A Typical (Structural) Fault Inducing Fewer Dependences than Specified

Given the assertion in Figure 7 we are aware of the dependences $\{(d,a),(d,b),(d,e),(z,a),(z,b),(z,e)\}$. As the figure outlines, we obtain two single-fault diagnosis $AB(2)$ and $AB(3)$. As is also indicated in the figure, when solely employing a single assertion requiring $z == c + d$, we obtain $SPEC'(proc)=\{ (z,a),(z,b),(z,e)\}$ and $dep'(proc) \supseteq SPEC'(proc)$. Consequently, we obtain 3 diagnoses ($AB(2)$, $AB(3)$ and $AB(4)$) in this case. However, even when employing the FDM we cannot exclude a single statement, thus, in this specific case, both models deliver the same accuracy.

The examples outlined above should have made clear that a comparison of both models in terms of their diagnostic capabilities inherently depends on how we deduce observations from violated properties. Note that the FDM itself cannot detect any faults, rather faults are detected by evaluation of the assertions on the values obtained from a concrete test run.

The VBM can reliably detect and localize faults that manifest in missing dependences on the right-hand side of an assignment statement. Due to the over-approximation of dependences we cannot locate faults manifesting in additional dependences as it is impossible to distinguish if (1) the specification is incomplete, (2) the model computes spurious dependences, or (3) an unwanted dependence is present due to a fault.

Table 1 summarizes the illustrated examples by listing the individual models' fault detection and localization capabilities. For those examples, where both models deliver diagnosis candidates, we checked whether the diagnoses provided by the VBM are a subset of those provided by the *FDM*.

In comparing both models, we start by contrasting the well-known artifacts in the area of MBSD. Table 2 summarizes the most notable differences in employing the VBM and FDM for fault localization. In both models we employ a partial specification (e.g. test case, assertion, invariant) for deducing a number of observations. Whereas the VBM encodes observations in terms of dependence relations, the FDM relies on a program's execution and subsequent classification of the observed variables. Variables are merely classified as being correct or incorrect with respect to a given (partial) specification.

```
1. proc (a,b,c) {.....
2. c= a;// should be c=a+b
3. d=c * e;
4. z =c+d;
5. assert (z = =c+d, [d = = c * e])
6. }...
```

$\neg AB(2) \wedge ok(a) \rightarrow ok(c)$

$\neg AB(3) \wedge ok(c) \wedge ok(e) \rightarrow \neg ok(d)$

$[\rightarrow \neg ok(d)], \rightarrow \neg ok(z)$

$DIAG = \{\{AB(2)\}, \{AB(4)\}\}$

$DIAG' = \{\{AB(2)\}, \{AB(3)\}, \{AB(4)\}\}$

$SPEC(proc) = \{(z,a), (z,b), (z,e), (d,a), (d,b), (d,e)\}$

$dep(proc) = \{(z,a), (z,e), (d,a), (d,e)\}$

$dep(proc) \not\supseteq SPEC(proc)$

$\sigma(\xi_2) = \{a,b\}, \sigma(\xi_3) = \{a,b,e\}, \sigma(\xi_4) = \{\}$

$DIAG = \{\{AB(2)\}, \{AB(3)\}\}$

$SPEC'(proc) = \{(z,a), (z,b), (z,e)\}$

$dep'(proc)=\{(z,a),(z,e)\}$

$dep'(proc) \not\supseteq SPEC'(proc)$

$\sigma(\xi'_2) = \{a,b\}, \sigma(\xi'_3) = \{a,b,e\}, \sigma\, \sigma(\xi_4) = \{a,b,e\}$

Fig. 7. A Degenerated Example (Error Masking), Diags (FDM) (symbol) diags(VBM)

Example	FDM loc	VMB		Diags (FDM) ⊇ diags (VBM)
		det.	loc	
Fig. 3	✓	X	X	-
Fig. 4	✓	X	X	-
Fig. 5	x	✓	✓	-
Fig. 6	✓	✓	✓	✓
Fig. 7	✓	✓	✓	x

Table 1. Summary on the Outline Scenarios

Furthermore, the VBM models the program in terms of functions over ependence relations, the FDM captures the programs behavior by a number of logical sentences, in particular we employ a Horn clause theory. The VBM detects a fault by checking whether the system description fulfills the given specification. In case this relationship does not hold, a fault has been detected. In contrast, we detect a fault with the FDM if the system description together with the specification yields to logical contradiction.

artifact	VBM	FDM
observatuibs	dependence relations	Ok, $\neg$ (ok)
systemn descr	function over dependences relation VBM (Π)	Horn clauses FDM(Π)
fault detect.	VBM (Π) $\not\supseteq$ SPEC	-
fault localiz.	VBM (Π) $\supseteq$ SPEC	FDM(Π) $\cup$ Spec $\neq \perp$
assumptions	Varible substitution $\xi = \ldots$	$\neg$ AB
theorem prover	CSP solver	Horn clauses theorem prover
structureal faults	detect., localiz,	detect, localiz.
functional faults	no detect., no localiz	detect., localiz.

Table 2. Comparing the Most Common Artifacts

The VBM locates possible causes for detected misbehavior by assuming that specific statements depend on model variables, and checking whether there is a valid substitution. As authros outlined in (Peischl et al, 2006), this process is an efficiently done by solving a CSP. Instead, the FDM employs a Horn clause theorem prover under the assumption of statement abnormality in computing diagnosis candidates. Note, that whereas the FDM does not assume any faulty behavior for specific statements, the VBM assumes specific dependences guided by the specification.

As indicated by the example above, the VBM is tailored towards detection and localization of structural faults, whereas the FDM may capture structural but particularly functional faults. Similar to static slicing capturing control as well as data flow dependences, the FDM must comprise all statements responsible for the computation of an erroneous variable. Thus, the FDM always provides diagnosis candidates under presence of an erroneous variable. The author (Wotawa, 2002) points out that the FDM delivers at least the same results as static slicing. Moreover, we know that the misbehavior's real cause is always among the delivered diagnosis candidates when employing the FDM. This perspective is supported by theoretical foundation (Friedrich et al, 1999) as well as practical evidence in numerous case studies.

Particularly, a comparison w.r.t. the accuracy and completeness of the obtained diagnosis is of interest. Figure 8 summarizes the relationship of the FDM and the VBM regarding their abilities of checking satisfiability. The lines between the nodes building up the lattice denote a subset relationship. As illustrated by the examples, there are debugging problems where the VBM allows for finding a discrepancy but the FDM does not and vice versa.

4. Case Studies

Authors (Peischl et al, 2006) present first experimental results indicating the approaches' applicability. The results presented there solely stem from small programs. In evaluating the model's fault localization capabilities under presence of procedural abstraction, we decompose a program into several procedures in a step by step fashion. This procedure allows for a first evaluation of both, the model for (1) parameter passing and (2) handling of return values.

Table 3 summarizes our most recent results. Specifically, the program *eval* evaluates the arithmetic expression $z \leftarrow (r \times h)+(c/d) - (d+h) \times (e+f)$. The specification says that the left-hand side z depends on the variables r,h,c,d,e, and f. We introduced a single structural fault and decomposed this program by adding procedures computing specific subexpressions in a step by step fashion. A specific subexpression is thus evaluated by a single procedure and replaced by the variable capturing this procedure's evaluation. We refer to the decomposed programs comprising i ethods by *eval(i)*. In the remaining programs, which perform simple computations like taxes or evaluate simple arithmetic expressions, we also introduced a single structural fault.

Removing certain dependences from the specification allows for evaluating our odel's capabilities in localizing structural faults under presence of partial knowledge of the dependences of the output variables. Thus, we observed a subset of the output dependences involving up to 5 variables and recorded the minimum and maximum number of diagnosis candidates.

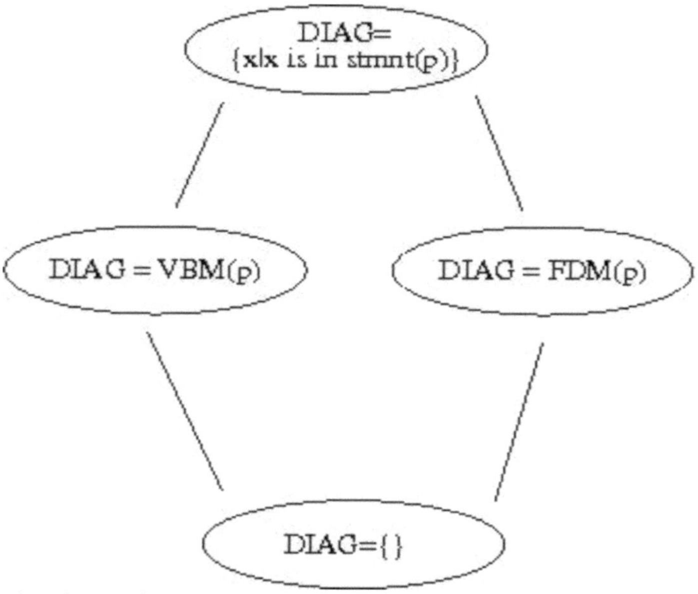

Fig. 8. The (Open) Relationship Between VBM and FDM

Method no	LOC	Total dep.no	Min-Max no. Diagnosis Candidates				
			5	4	3	2	1
eval (1)	10	9	-	-	-	-	4
eval (2)	14	10	-	-	-	4	4-11
eval (3)	18	11	-	-	4	4-13	4-18
eval (4)	22	12	-	4	4-15	4-22	4-22
eval (5)	26	13	4	4-17	4-26	4-26	4-26
sum	22	11	-	-	4	4-13	4-18
arithmetic	26	12	-	4	4-15	4-15	4-22
tax comp.	30	13	4	4-17	4-26	4-26	4-26
calculator	40	12	1-31	1-31	1-33	1-34	1-34

Table 3. Number of single-Faults Diagnosis with Decreasing Number of Specified Output Variables.

For example, regarding the program eval(3) we obtained 4 diagnosis candidates when observing all outputs. Afterwards we selected 2 output variables out of the 3 output variables, and for all possible combinations of selecting 2 out of 3 outputs, we recorded the number of diagnoses. The table specifies the minimal and maximal number of diagnosis candidates obtained in this way (in this specific case of considering 2 output variableswe obtain at least 4 and at most 13 diagnosis andidates). We checked whether or not the introduced faults appear among the delivered diagnosis candidates. Regarding all our experiments, we have been able to locate the misbehavior's real cause.

Furthermore, the table lists the number of total dependences (column 3) and the program's size in terms of the lines of code (column 2). Our experiments indicate an increase in the number of candidates with a decreasing number of outputs being considered. In the table, we did not take into account cases where the reduced output dependences are not capable of detecting the fault. In this case our approach obviously returns *{ }*. In summary, the obtained results, confirm the findings in (Hamscher & Davis 1984): As our problem becomes under-constrained by removing certain output dependences, the number of diagnosis candidates may increase drastically. As our experiments indicate, this also appears to hold for the novel model introduced herein.

5. Related Research

We present related work which provides an overview of related research of our chapter.

5.1 Model-Based Software Debugging

Model-based diagnosis(MBD) is a well-known Artificial Intelligence(AI) Technique for the localization and malfunctioning parts in (mostly physical) systems. The definitions of MBD as given in (Reiter, 1987; Kleer & Williams 1987) and show how this approach can be used to locate faulty components in a given system. First-order logic produced formal model for MBD and covers sound framework. Test cases are uses to examine the specifications and diagnostic engine locates single or multiple faults from derived system. Several authors (Hamscher, W.C 1991, Greiner, R et. al. 1989) provides the well-founded theory underlying

Model-Based Diagnosis (MBD). Traditionally MBD focuses on diagnosing physical systems (Console, L. et. al. 1993, Cascio., F. et. al. 1999, Williams., B.C. 1996 & Malik., A. 1996), however several authors (Console, L. et. al. 1993, Bond., G. W. 1994, Stumptner., M & Wotawa., F. 1999a, Stumptner., M & Wotawa., F. 1999b, Stumptner., M & Wotawa., F.1999c & Stumptner., M & Wotawa., F. 1999d) employing model-based diagnosis techniques in software debugging.

Authors (Stumptner., M & Wotawa., F. 1999a & Stumptner., M & Wotawa., F. 1999b) covers model-based software debugging of functional programs and the other authors of these publications (Mayer., W. & Stumptner., M. 2003, Mayer., W. et. al 2002a & Wieland., D. 2001) focus on software debugging of Java programs, particularly objected-oriented programming features. These authors work together ***JADE*** project to develop functional dependency model and value based model for software debugging. The comparison between two models are presented in (Mayer., W. et. al 2002a, Mayer., W. et. al 2002b, Stumptner., M. et. al. 2001a & Stumptner., M. et. al. 2001b) where they discussed capabilities of both models in respect with advantages and weaknesses.

The work described in this chapter is solely based on diagnosis from first principle (Reiter, 1987). According to Reiter's (Reiter, 1987) a precise theoretical foundation of diagnostic reasoning from first principle will be a essential ingredient in any common theory of diagnostic reasoning.Applying theory of model-based diagnosis to software debugging first requires an adaption of the diagnosis theory. We wrote some articles (Wotawa., F. & Soomro., S. 2005, Peischl., B., et. al. 2005, Soomro., S. 2007., Soomro., S. 2008, ., Soomro., S. et. al. 2008; Soomro., S. & Wotawa., F. 2009) for software debugging to localize faults using model-based diagnosis technique.

5.2 Aspect System: Abstract Dependencies

Aspect is a static analysis technique for detecting bugs in imperative programs, consisting of an annotation language and a checking tool. This system introduced by (Jackson, 1995) which is based on the abstract dependencies that are used by the Aspect system (Jackson, 1995) for detecting faults.The Aspect system analysis the dependences between variables of a given program and compares them with the specified dependences.The computed dependencies are compared to expected ones specified by software engineer. After comparing these dependencies with derived ones this system pinpoint the missing dependencies. This work employs abstract dependences for detecting rather than for localizing a fault.Aspect system (Jackson, 1995) which has been used for dependency based verification of C programs. Aspect system provides a very simple way to specify and verify properties of software system, even though the results of this approach is limited,as the correctness of program is hardly expressable due to terms of variable dependences.

The work described in this thesis is based on the abstract dependencies that are used by the Aspect system (Jackson, 1995) for detecting faults.The verification-based model for debugging is an extension of the dependence model from Jackson's Aspect system (Jackson, 1995) which has been used for dependency based verification of C programs. The Aspect system analysis the dependences between variables of a given program and compares them with the specified dependences. In case of a mismatch the program is said to violate the specification. Otherwise, the program fulfills the specification. Unfortunately, the Aspect system does not allow to locate the source of a mismatch. In the following we extend Jackson's idea towards not only detecting misbehavior but also localizing the malfunctioning's real cause.

5.3 Program Slicing

The author (Weiser, 1982 & 1984) introduces program slicing towards debugging systems. Program slicing is an approach for reduce to complexity of programs by focusing on selected aspects of semantics. The process of slicing deletes those parts of the program which can be determined to have no effect upon the semantics of interest. Slicing has applications in testing and debugging, re-engineering, program comprehension and software measurement. The author (Tip, 1995) scrutinize various approaches of slicing with respect with static and dynamic slicing.

Program slicing is a general, widely-used, and accepted technique applicable to different software engineering tasks including debugging, whereas model-based diagnosis is an AI (Artificial Intelligence) technique originally developed for finding faults in physical systems. During the last years it has been shown that model-based diagnosis can be used for software debugging (Console, L. et. al. 1993, Bond., G. W. 1994, Stumptner., M & Wotawa., F. 1999a, Stumptner., M & Wotawa., F. 1999b, Stumptner., M & Wotawa., F.1999c & Stumptner., M.) The author (Wotawa, 2002) clarifies that model-based diagnosis is related to program slicing. In case of diagnosis it proves that slices of a program in a fault situation are equivalent to conflicts in model-based debugging. This result helps debugging community to compute diagnosis faster and gives more information about possible bugs in certain situations.

6. Conclusion and Future Research

In this chapter we focused on verification-based model (VBM) specifically tailored towards detecting and localizing structural faults. We discussed the relationship between this model and the well-known functional dependence model (FDM) by exemplifying the weaknesses and strengths of both models. Our examples show, that there are debugging problems where the verification-based model (VBM) delivers different diagnoses than the functional-dependence model (FDM) and vice versa. Furthermore, we present case studies conducted recently. Notably, whenever our novel model detects a structural fault, it also appears to be capable of localizing the misbehavior's real cause.

A future research challenge is the empirical evaluation of the modeling approaches discussed herein. Also include another extensions of the Verifcation Based Model, e.g, to handle object oriented features and to provide an emprical anaylsis. Another open issued which is the connection with program slicing that is also based on abstract dependences.

7. References

Bond., G. W. (1994). Logic Programs for Consistency Based Diagnosis. *Phd. Thesis Dissertation,* Carleton University, Faculty of Engineering, Ottawa, Canada.

Cascio., F., Console., L, Guagliumi., M, Osella., M., Panato., A., Cauvin., S., Cordier. M., Theseider, D & Sottano. S. (1999) . Generating on-board diagnostics of dynamic automotive systems based on qualitative models. *Artificial Intelliegence Communication,* Vol., No. 12, 1999.

Cauvin., S., Cordier. M. & Dousson.C (1998). Monitoring and Alarm Interpretation in Industrial Environments. *Artificial Intelliegence Communication,* Vol., No. 11, 1998.

Console, L., Friedrich, G. & Theseider, D. (1993). Model-Based Diagnosis Meets Error Diagnosis in Logic Programs, *Proceedings of Joint International Conference on Artifical Intelligence,* pp. 1494-1499, Chambery, August and 1993.

Greiner, R., Smith, B & Ralph, W. (1989). A Correction to the Algorithm in Reiter's Theory of Diagnosis. *Artificial Intelliegence,* Vol., No., 41, pp. 79-88.

Hamscher, W.C (1991). Modeling Digital Circuits for Troubleshooting. *Artificial Intelliegence,* Vol., No., 51 (October & 1995) pp. 223-271.

Hamscher, W.C; Console, L. & Kleer, J. (1992). Readings in Model-Based Diagnosis. *Morgan Pulisher,* (October & 1992).

Jackson, D. (1995). Aspect Detecting Bugs with Abstract Dependences. *Transaction on Software Engineering and Mrthodology,* Vol., No., 3, (April & 1995) pp. 109-145.

Kleer, J. & Williams, B C (1987). Diagnosing multiple faults. *Artificial Intelligence,* pp. 97–130.

Malik., A., Struss., P. & Sachenbacher., M. (1996). Case Studies in Model-based Diagnosis and Fault Analysis of Car-Subsystems. *Proceedings of European Conference ofArtifical Intelligence.* Pp. 1322-1334. 1996.

Mayer., W. & Stumptner., M. (2003). Extending Diagnosis to Debug Programs with Exceptions. *Proceedings of 18th International IEEE Conference on Automated Software Engineering,* pp. 240-244, Montreal, Canada, October 2003.

Mayer., W., Stumptner., M., Wieland., D. & Wotawa., F (2002a). Can AI help to improve debugging substantially? Debugging experiences with value-based models. *Proceedings of European Conference ofArtifical Intelligence.* Pp. 417-421. IOS Press, Lyon, France 2002.

Mayer., W., Stumptner., M., Wieland., D. & Wotawa., F (2002b). Towards an Integrated Debugging Environment *Proceedings of European Conference ofArtifical Intelligence.* Pp. 422-426. IOS Press, Lyon, France 2002.

Peischl., B., Soomro., S. & Wotawa., F. (2006). Towards Lightweight Fault Localization in Procedural Programs. *Proceedings of the 19th Conference on International Conference on Industrial, Engineering and Applications of Applied Intelligent Systems (IEA/AIE).* Lecture Notes in Compter Science, Springer 2006.

Reiter, R. (1987). A theory of diagnosis from first principles. *Artificial Intelligence,* pp. 57–95.

Stumptner., M & Wotawa., F. (1999a). Debugging Functional Programs. *Proceedings of Joint International Conference on Artifical Intelligence,* pp. 1074-1097, August, Stockholm, Sweden, 1999.

Stumptner., M & Wotawa., F. (1999b). Reconfiguration Using Model-Based Diagnosis. *Proceedings of Diagnosis Worksshop Series* , Loch Awe, Scotland.

Stumptner., M & Wotawa., F. (1999c). Detecting and Locating Faults in Hardware Designs. *Proceeding AAAI 99 Workshop on Intelligent Software Engineering,* Orlando, Florida.

Stumptner., M & Wotawa., F. (1999d). Jade -- Java Diagnosis Experiments -- Status and Outlook. *IJCAI '99 Workshop on Qualitative and Model Based Reasoning for Complex Systems and their Control* August, Stockholm,Sweden, 1999.

Stumptner., M., Wieland., D. & Wotawa., F. (2001a). Analysis Models of Software Debugging.*Proceedings of Diagnosis Worksshop Series* , Sansicario, Italy.

Stumptner., M., Wieland., D. & Wotawa., F. (2001b). Comparing Two Models for Software Debugging. *Proceedings of the Joint German/Austrian Conference on Artificial Intelligence (KI),* Vienna, Austria.

Soomro., S. (2007). Using Abstract Dependences to localize faults from procedural Programs *Proceeding of Artificial Intelligence and Applications.* pp. 180-185, Inssbruck, Austria

Soomro., S., Shah. A.A & Shah., Wajiha (2008). Localize Faults from ALias-free Programs using Verification Based Model. *Proceeding of Artificial Intelligence and Soft Computing ASC 2008.* pp. 190-196, Palma-DelMalorca, Spain. 2008.

Soomro., S. (2008). Verification Based Model Localizes Faults from Procedural Programs. *Frontiers in Robotics and Automation Control* International Book of Advanced Robotic System. ISBN 978-953-7619-17-6, October 2008.

Soomro. S. & Wotawa. F. (2009). Detect and Localize Faults in Alias-free Programs using Specification Knowledge. *Proceedings of the 19th Conference on International Conference on Industrial, Engineering and Applications of Applied Intelligent Systems (IEA/AIE).* Lecture Notes in Compter Science, Springer, Taina,, Taiwan 2009.

Tip, F. (1995). A Survey of Program Slicing Techniques. *Journal of Programming Languages,* Vol., No., 3, (September & 1995) pp. 121-189.

Wieland., D. (2001). Model Based Debugging of Java Programs Using Dependencies. *Phd. Thesis Dissertation,* Vienna University of Technology, Computer Science Department, Institute of Information Systems (184), Database and Artificial Intelligence Group (184/2) Austria , November 2001.

Williams., B.C. & Nayak., P.P. (1996). Immobile Robots -- AI in the New Millennium. *Artificial Intelligence Magzine,* AAAI Press, pp. 16-35.

Weiser. M. (1982). Programmers Use Slices when Debugging. *Communication of The ACM,* Vol. No. (7), pp. 446-452. July 1982.

Weiser. M. (1984). Programmers Use Slices when Debugging. *IEEE Transaction of Software Engineering,* Vol. No. (4) , pp. 352-357. July 1984.

Wotawa., F. & Soomro., S. (2005). Using abstract dependencies in debugging. *Proceedings of 19th International Workshop on Qualitative Reasoning QR-05* pp. 23-28., Graz-Austria.

4

Assisted form filling

Łukasz Bowník, Wojciech Górka and Adam Piasecki
Centre EMAG
Poland

1. Introduction

Semantic technologies that form the basis of the idea of the Semantic Web (Berners-Lee et al. 2001) are currently one of the most popular points of interest in the field of computer science. The main emphasis here is on issues related to the logical layer of semantic applications, that is exploring the methods of machine reasoning within an ever wider range of logic, and the issues of data exploration and integration. This article features a practical application of semantic technologies for solving problems more closely affecting an average computer user. We present a solution to the issue of accelerating the filling of electronic forms based on previous achievements in this field, which combines the capabilities of inference engines with the expressiveness of ontologies stored in OWL (Web Ontology Language) (OWL Guide 2004) and flexibility of data stored in RDF (Resource Description Language) (RDF Primer 2004). The article assumes that the reader has a basic knowledge on the construction and use of the RDF and OWL languages.

1.1. Objective of the article

The objective of this article is to describe ways to facilitate electronic form filling. At the beginning we described the issue and the requirements placed on the solution. Then we described the solution. We characterized the reasons for the selection of specific techniques and architecture of the proposed solution, as well as two alternative approaches to the interaction with the user. Finally, we presented the investigated results of the acceleration of assisted form filling, which was compared with other existing solutions of the stated issue.

1.2. The Issue

The basic issue associated with the concept of public services is the need to fill the forms containing repeated data. Most forms require entering the same data, similar data sets or data dependent on other data contained in another part of the form. This causes psychological discomfort associated with repeated, from the user's perspective, contents. Such an approach is not only unproductive but also increases the risk of errors. Errors in the completed forms, if not detected during the interaction with the system, may have serious and far-reaching consequences, including legal ones. A mechanism capable of assisting in the process of electronic form filling would not only result in a positive acceleration of the process but could also potentially reduce the risk of errors.

1.3. Requirements

The proposed solution of the stated issue is to assist the user in the process of filling in any electronic form through the automatic and pseudo-intelligent filling of the form fields with information available to the system. The basic assumptions that guided the search for solutions were:

- modularity of the developed software that will allow integration with a broad class of information systems;
- independence from the domain of the form which will minimize the number of assumptions about the meaning and format of processed data;
- minimization of interactions with the user that is both a target and measure of the quality of the resulting solution.

The result of research is a portable Java library that implements assisted electronic form filling processes. Later in the article we will present the results of the work and a description of the architecture and operation of the developed software, hereinafter referred to as "the forms module".

1.4. Other solutions

Similar solutions have been proposed, *inter alia* in the projects "RoboForm"[1] and "Mojo Navigator"[2] however they focus primarily on the functionality of a portfolio of passwords integrated with a web browser with an additional history of the field values associated with the forms available on the Internet. They also lack the dynamics associated with the automatic acquisition of data, which is presented by the described solution. On the market there are a lot of other solutions based on a dialogue form of form filling but most of them are firmly based on the dialogue recorded on a particular form (the wizards). Finally, it should be noted that a simple form of field values suggestion is available directly in browsers. However, it is characterized by a very small degree of ergonomics both with regard to the interaction with the user, who must enter the desired values prefixes, and the lack of contextuality, which makes it impossible to fill the whole form at once.

---

[1] http://www.roboform.com, 2009-01

[2] http://www.mozilla.org/projects/ui/communicator/browser/formfill, 2009-01

2. Design

The following section describes the design of the forms module along with the reasons for selecting particular data representation and architecture.

2.1. Data representation

The main idea of assisted form filling is pseudo-intelligent matching of existing data to form fields. For this purpose, it is necessary to identify the meaning of the fields and sections of the form and find an adequate available data set. The data for assisted filling may come from the user's ontoprofile, whose task is to accumulate the data from the completed forms, or from an external system. In the case when the data are not available (as it will be the case with every new user), assisted filling will not be available either.

Identification of the meaning of data requires their explicit tagging with metadata. For this reason, we need data representation that supports their binding to the metadata. The binary representation and simple text representation, for example in the csv format, do not allow to record the metadata and therefore are not useful. For this purpose, the most suitable are the relational data model (in whose case the metadata consist of names of relations and fields) and languages like XML (eXtensible Markup Language) (XML 2006) and RDF.

The objective of this work was to develop software with a minimum number of assumptions about the meaning and format of the processed data. In the relational data model the meaning and format of data is contained in the database schema that can be subjected to a variety of analyses performed by the software. The relational database schemas have, however, two significant drawbacks. First, the producers of databases quite freely implement the DDL language standard and extend it with many product-specific features. Such diversity results in considerable difficulty in automatic analyzing of database structures. Second, solving the issue of assisted form filling requires maximum flexibility of data representation. The relational database model does not satisfy this condition as it assumes constant or slowly changing structure of the database. Application of the representation of data based on this model would be a very hard assumption regarding the meaning and format of data in a particular installation (e.g. installing a module with respect to a database which describes the forms of medical service appointments would allow to fill only this type of forms). For this reason, the relational data model has been rejected as a representation of the processed data.

Rejection of the relational model narrowed the choice of data representations to those based on XML and RDF. Data stored in these languages are very dynamic in their structure defined by XML schemas and ontologies that can be dynamically loaded and analyzed by an application. XML requires that all data have a tree structure. This structure does not fully correspond with the "natural" structure of data which more often resembles graphs. For this and other less significant reasons, the RDF language was chosen because it allows very natural data recording in the form of graphs and a flexible description of their structure by means of ontologies stored in OWL. An additional advantage is the possibility of using machine-based inference with ontologies and rules which allowed the development of pseudo-intelligent software by means of very expressive logic programs.

2.2. Structure

Data structures on which the module operates are defined by means of ontologies written in OWL. In order to understand the operations of the dialogue module, it is necessary to grasp the data ontology and the form ontology (a kind of data ontology) ideas which lie at the basis of the process.

2.2.1. Data ontologies

Data ontologies define the vocabulary (concepts) used in the course of data exchange between systems. A data ontology is not meant to organize knowledge (which is the case of expert systems) but to determine concepts describing the data which can be understood by many systems. In terms of their concept, data ontologies correspond with XML diagrams and are their functional equivalents.

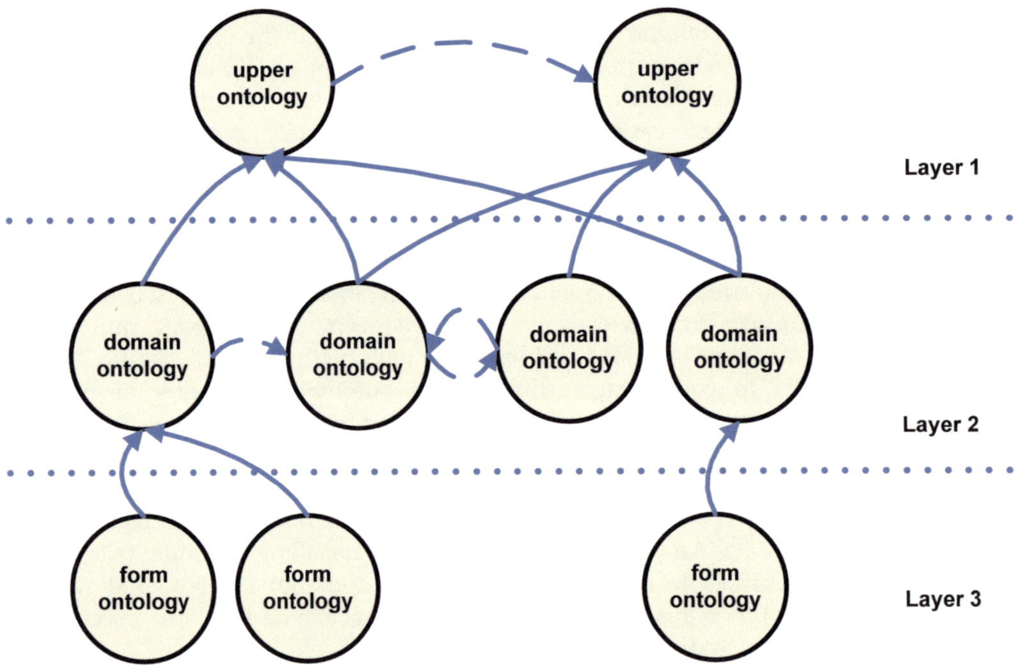

Fig. 1. Layered-tree ontology structure [own].

Data ontologies are naturally arranged in a tree-layer structure shown in Figure 1.
The first and highest level contains definitions of the most general vocabulary (concepts) commonly used by many IT systems (e.g. *person, age, name, family name*). The concepts defined at this level are the basis for the definitions of more specialized concepts placed at lower levels of abstraction. **General ontologies should not (must not, to be precise) impose any restrictions** (e.g. in the form of limits as to the format of field value or number of fields in the form) on the defined concepts because each restriction placed at this level of generalization will diminish the universal force of the defined vocabulary and will raise the probability of conflicts with restrictions defined at lower levels (redundant or contrary restrictions). General ontologies must have total horizontal coherence, i.e. mutual coherence within the entire level of abstraction.

The second, middle level contains definitions of concepts shared by IT systems which operate within a given domain (e.g. medicine). These ontologies should use, to the highest possible extent, the concepts defined at a higher level of abstraction (i.e. they should not define their own concepts indicating, for example, *family name*) as well as add the concepts from this very domain (e.g. *clinic, doctor, vaccine*). At this level of abstraction **only most obvious restrictions** should be defined, i.e. the restrictions which will be forced by all existing and future IT systems operating within a given domain. If it is not possible to explicitly define such restrictions, one should not define them at all because, as it is the case with general ontologies, they may provoke conflicts between ontologies. Domain ontologies must have horizontal coherence within a certain domain, i.e. mutual coherence within each domain at this level of abstraction as well as coherence with general ontologies.

The third and lowest level contains definitions of forms, i.e. specific data packages exchanged between IT systems. A form is a structure of data exchanged between two IT systems. The structure may, but does not have to, be related to the form filled by the system user. Each form there should have a form ontology describing its structure. The ontologies of the form should use, to the highest possible extent, the concepts defined at higher levels of abstraction and **define only such new concepts which are specific to a given form** and cannot be shared with other forms. The form ontology should define all necessary restrictions which will ensure logical coherence and correctness of the form required by the specifications of the IT system. Since for each form there are different rules (restrictions) which determine its coherence and correctness (e.g. one form requires an ID number, the other does not), it is not advisable to define restrictions at higher levels of abstraction. The form ontologies do not have to demonstrate any horizontal coherence (it is practically impossible to provide it). A logical error resulting from horizontal incoherence will never occur because there is separate processing of each ontology in each processing path in the IT system, which was depicted in Figure 2. The form ontologies must be coherent with the applied domain ontologies and general ontologies.

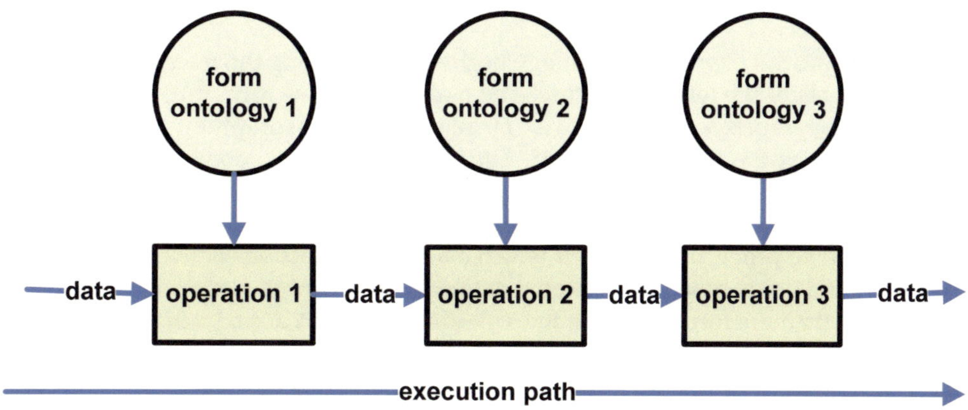

Fig. 2. Physical separation of processing of form ontologies within a single processing path [own].

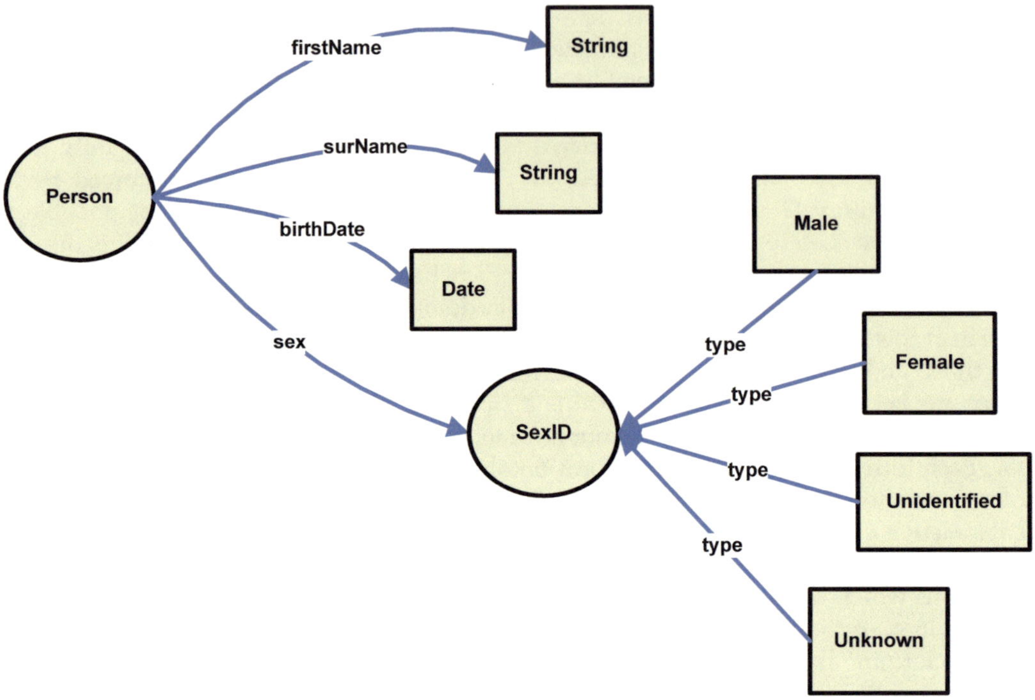

Fig. 3. Example of data ontology [own].

Figure 3 shows a sample ontology describing personal data.

2.2.2. Form ontologies

Form ontologies define the structure as well as coherence and correctness rules of data contained in the described form. A form ontology describes a specific set of data exchanged between IT systems.

The process of constructing a form ontology begins from building the main form class which will lie at the roots of the whole structure. The main class of the form must be marked with the appropriate property `isFormRoot`. Thanks to this assumption, it is possible to automatically detect the root of the form. The definition of the successive sections of the form is carried out by defining separate classes (e.g. *Person* class or *Address* class) linked with object properties to form a tree structure. The definitions of data fields are carried out with the use of data-type properties of classes which make up the sections of the form.

As the form ontology is based on concepts defined in data ontologies which may be much more extensive than the form requires, the `isRequired` and `isOptional` properties were defined. They connect the desired properties with the classes being the sections of the form (see Fig. 4). In order to force the order of processing sections and fields of the form, it is necessary to define the processing order for each pair of properties, representing these sections, by means of the *askBefore* property (see Fig. 4).

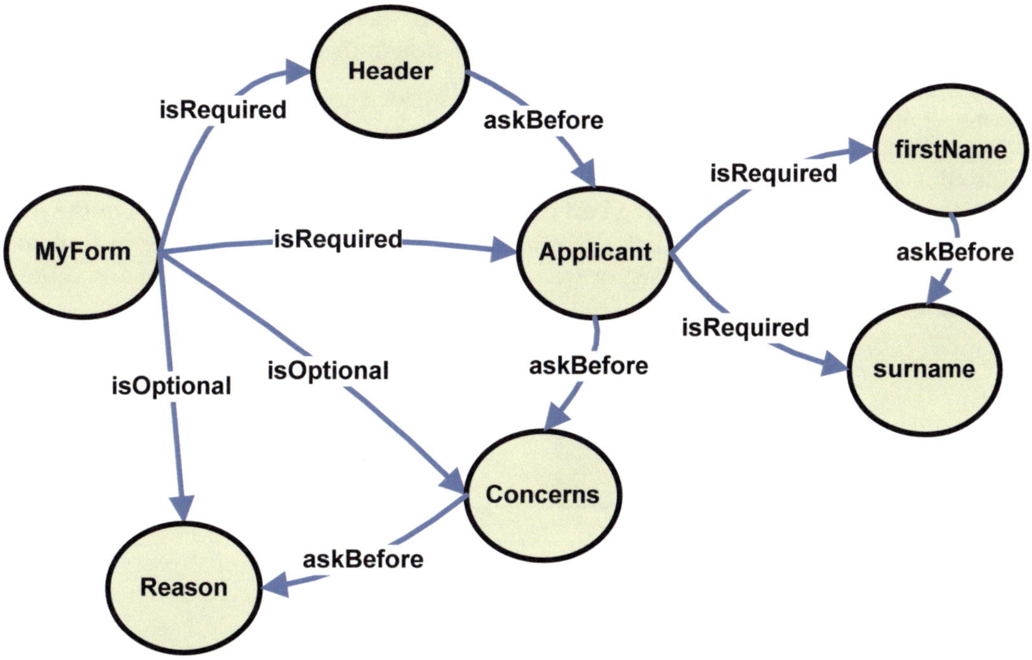

Fig. 4. An example of form ontology[own].

In order to define the desired restrictions, it is necessary to determine new concepts due to the fact that the built-in cardinality concepts have their own defined semantics which does not suit the issue to be solved (OWL Guide 2004).

Form ontologies can contain rules (Horn clauses ((Horn 1951) that extend the functionality of the OWL language. In order to secure logical non-contradiction, the rules must belong to the "DL-safe" set (Grosof et al. 2003). The most frequent application of the rules is the structure of section labels (enabling, for example, creation of a section label for personal data on the basis of the entered name and surname) and automatic assigning of values to certain fields based on the values of other fields.

2.3. The operating principle

The operating principle of the module is based on the fact that a form makes up a tree structure in which successive embedded sections make branches, while fields - leaves of the tree. Thus it is possible to process a form with the use of tree-searching algorithms. To fulfill this task the depth-first search algorithm was selected. This algorithm is the most compliant with the way people fill real forms. The functioning principle of the dialogue module is presented below in a simplified way. While analyzing successive steps one should remember about the iteration-recurrent nature of the algorithm.

1. At the beginning of each dialogue, the forms module detects a proper form class in the form ontology and creates its instance.
2. The newly created instance becomes a currently processed node and, at the same time, the top of the tree.

3. For the currently processed node, all required and optional properties are found and sorted according to the arrangement determined in the ontology. Then the successively found properties are processed.
4. If the currently processed property points at a section of the form, the section is then processed recursively.

In the course of processing the successive properties of the node, the dialogue module tries to detect, in the set of input data, the best adjustments both for the single fields of the form and for the whole sections. The dialogue module asks the user questions only in situations when the desired values do not exist or when it is possible to adjust more than one value to one field or section.

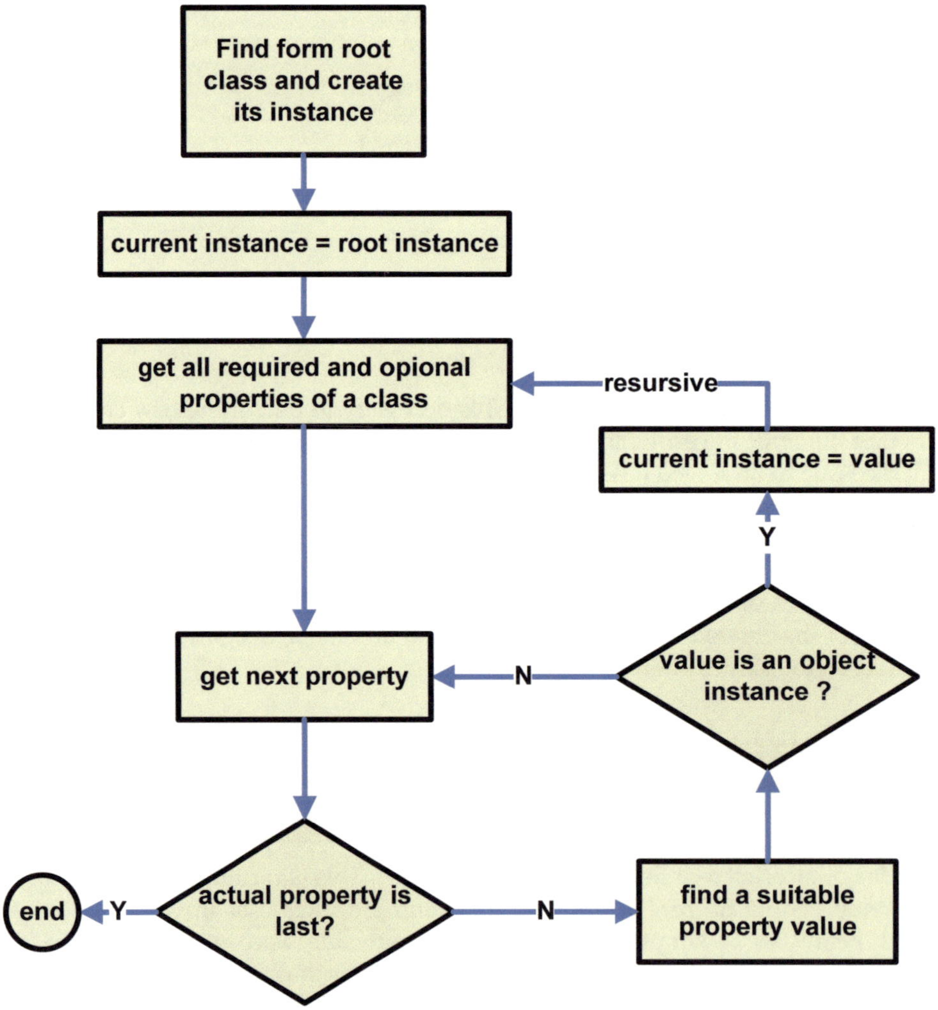

Fig. 5. A simplified version of the algorithm. [own].

During the subsequent processing of the properties of the node the software tries to find in the collection of input data the best match of both the individual form fields as well as the entire section of the form. The forms module communicates with the user only in situations where the desired values do not exist or if it is possible to fit more than one value into onefield or section. A simplified version of the algorithm is presented in Figure 5.

2.4. The reasoning

The proposed machine reasoning is mainly based on the OWL language but is limited in its expressiveness to a subset called DLP (Description Logic Programs) (Grosof et al. 2003). DLP is a logic system that is a subset of a description logic, on which the OWL language is based, that can be expressed by means of Horn clauses (Horn 1951). DLP provides the key inference capabilities found in OWL necessary for the implementation of assisted form filling, that is the reasoning with class hierarchies and properties. In addition, it allows flexible extension of specific rules for the process itself or even for a specific form.
Applying an inference engine brought a significant simplification of the code responsible for retrieving the data with required meaning through moving a significant computing burden into a logic program which contains the rules of logical inference. This way, the matching algorithm is limited to the search of resources belonging to the respective classes or values of the respective properties.

2.5. Architecture

The architecture of the proposed solution is briefly described below. The basic elements of the forms module are responsible for performing assisted filling process logic, and storing the data gathered during filling forms. The user interface and data access layers have been omitted.

2.5.1. The form processor

The forms module is composed of four basic parts:

- RDF storage providing access to RDF data and ontologies[3] ;
- a forward inference engine based on the RETE algorithm (Forgy 1979);
- a module that controls the process of form filling developed as a result of the work (implemented in Java), which, together with two previous elements, makes up a forms processor;
- an ontoprofile allowing the storage of the data collected during form filling processes

Figure 6 presents a layered structure of the forms module.

---

[3] Jena – A Semantic Web Framework for Java. http://jena.sourceforge.net, 2009-01

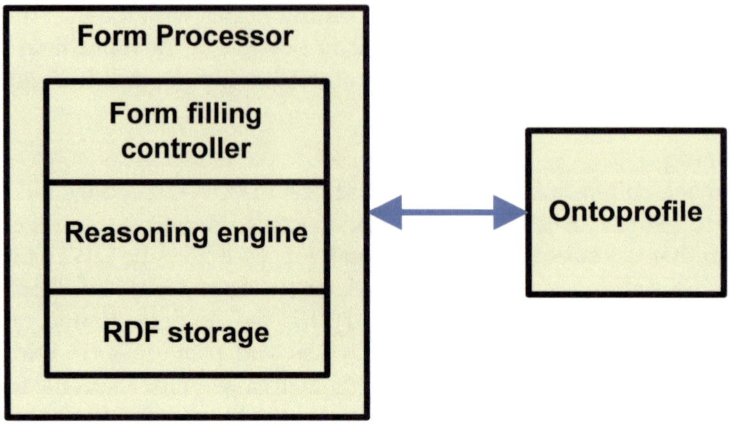

Fig. 6. The forms module structure [own].

Effectiveness of the module depends on the input data stored in the user profile.

2.5.2. The ontoprofile

The ontoprofile is used to store data collected during the assisted form filling processes which are used to support the filling of successive forms. Its main task is to integrate data coming from completed forms with the data collected so far and to make these data accessible to the successive forms. Proper integration is driven by the integration policy which determines what should be integrated and how. The data contained in the ontoprofile are stored in the form of RDF graphs. A physical way in which they are stored is not important but for the prototype installation a relational database has been used.

3. Prototypes

The following describes the two prototypes built during the experimental work. We described the way of interaction with each of the prototypes and the reason for the rejection of one of them.

3.1. The dialogue version

The first prototype of the forms module assumes a dialogue based interaction between the user and the computer in the form of a sequence of questions and answers, which recalls the manner of interaction with the wizard. The questions are asked by the software, and the answers are provided by the user. The forms module operates as a filter of information. With a set of input data (may be empty) and ontologies, the forms module "tries to" fill in the form with input data and data supplied by the user. Filling the form takes on a dialogue with the user while maintaining the principle of minimal interaction which assumes that the user is queried only in such cases where the data are unavailable or inconclusive. The usefulness of the forms module, as measured by the number of interactions with the user (the fewer the better), increases with the amount of input data available in the system.

In order to illustrate the functioning of the dialogue module let us check how the module works with a simple form. We assume that it is necessary to fill the form as follows:

Form:
- Personal data of the user:
  - Name;
  - Surname;
  - Address:
    - City;
    - Street;
    - House No;
- Purpose of submitting the form;

When the process of filling the form is invoked for the first time, the dialogue with the user will look as follows:

System: Enter "Name".
User: John
S: Enter "Surname".
U: Brown
S: Enter "City".
U: London
S: Enter "Street".
U: Portland Place
S: Enter "House No".
U: 47
S: Enter "Purpose of submitting the form".
U: Application for the permission to use a company car

After filling and accepting the form, the data from the form are stored in the user's ontoprofile. At the next interaction between the user and the module, the dialogue will look as follows:

S: I have found personal data for "John Brown, Portland Place 47, London". Shall I apply them (Y/N)?
U: Y
S: Enter "Purpose of submitting the form".
U: Application to access financial data.

As one can see in the above successive filling of the form, the number of necessary interactions with the user is 6 times smaller. The reduction was possible due to the fact that the forms module was able to automatically fill the fields with available personal data. Asking the question about the field "Purpose of submitting the form" results from the updating policy of the user's profile – this issue, however, is beyond the scope of the paper. Please note that the functioning of the module is based on the real meaning of data defined in an ontology which allows to move data between different forms using common concepts defined in the shared data ontologies.

3.2. The form view based version

The dialogue based version of the forms module described in the previous chapter is an initial prototype that enabled to verify the validity of the approach and demonstrated the ability to achieve the stated goals. From the point of view of ergonomics, however, the use of the prototype proved to be inadequate. The assisted form filling based on a dialogue which involves asking the user about the values of consecutive fields turned out to be uncomfortable. The user was constantly losing context in which the currently filled field existed. He/she was also unable to determine at what stage of the process he/she currently is and when the process will be completed. In addition, the inability to go back in the process of form filling made the solution unacceptable.
These problems resulted in a departure from the dialogue based approach to a more natural way, based on the form view, in which the user can freely choose the order in which he/she completes the form, and freely modify the contents of already completed parts. In this prototype the software tries to pre-fill the largest possible part of the form, at the same time giving the user the right to accept or change the suggested values. This approach has significantly increased the comfort of working with the software, which no longer imposes the schema of work with the form and brings its action to the role of an assistant. It should be noted that the change in the interaction has not changed the idea of the forms module and its architecture.
The operation rules of the assisted filling based on the form view will be described by examples. The following is a series of screenshots of a working forms module.

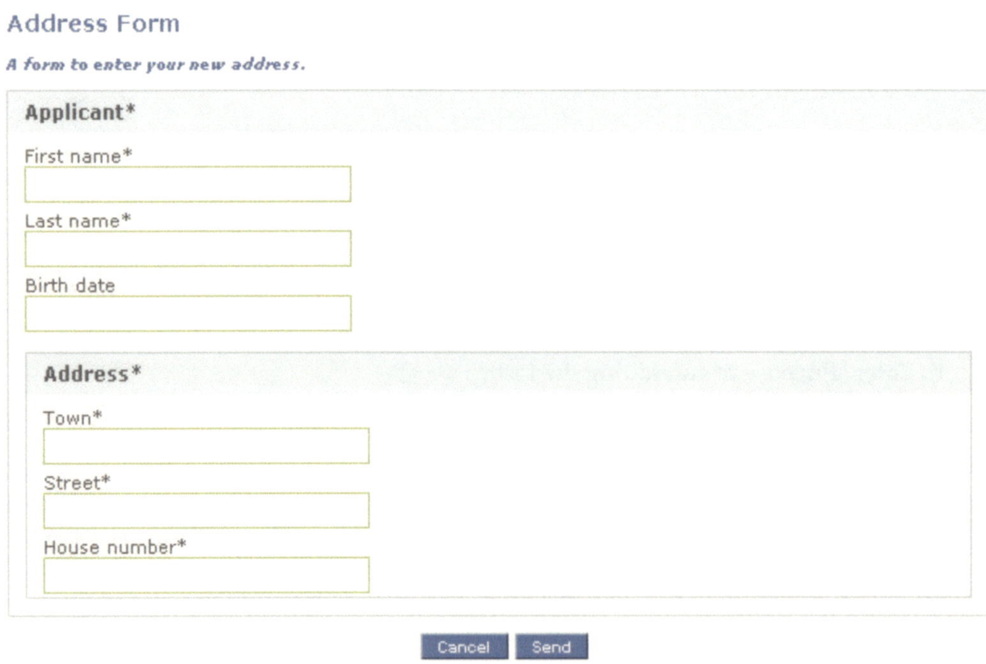

Fig. 7. An empty form.

Figure 7 presents a blank form at the first run. The form is used to update the address of a system user. A user profile does not contain any data yet because no form has been completed so far, so all fields are empty.
Figure 8 shows the same form after the introduction of sample data. After submitting the form to the system, the data will be saved in the user's ontoprofile. Their meaning will be stored as metadata that will come from the form fields from which they originate.
Figure 9 shows a re-run of the forms module. In this case, the software was able to retrieve data from ontoprofile and attribute it to the form according to their meaning. As you can see, it is so accurate that the form no longer requires any interaction with the user. In addition, the software was able to create objects representing labels of the identity and address data and place them in dropdown boxes located below the sections headers. This enables the user to select alternative proposals. The lists also allow to select an empty position which deletes the contents of each field in the section.
Figure 10 represents a situation in which the user has deleted the contents of the form fields and introduced the new values of personal data. In an attempt to minimize the number of necessary interactions, the software suggests him/her an existing address value stored from a previous interaction. The user can choose the proposed address or enter new values.

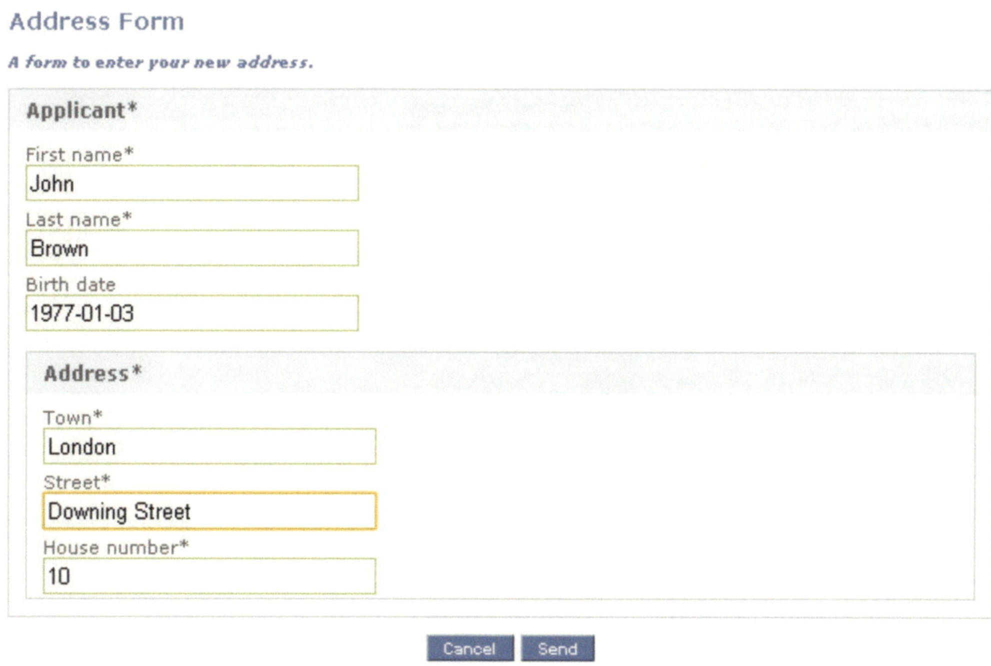

Fig. 8.A fully filled form.

Fig. 9. Second run of the forms module.

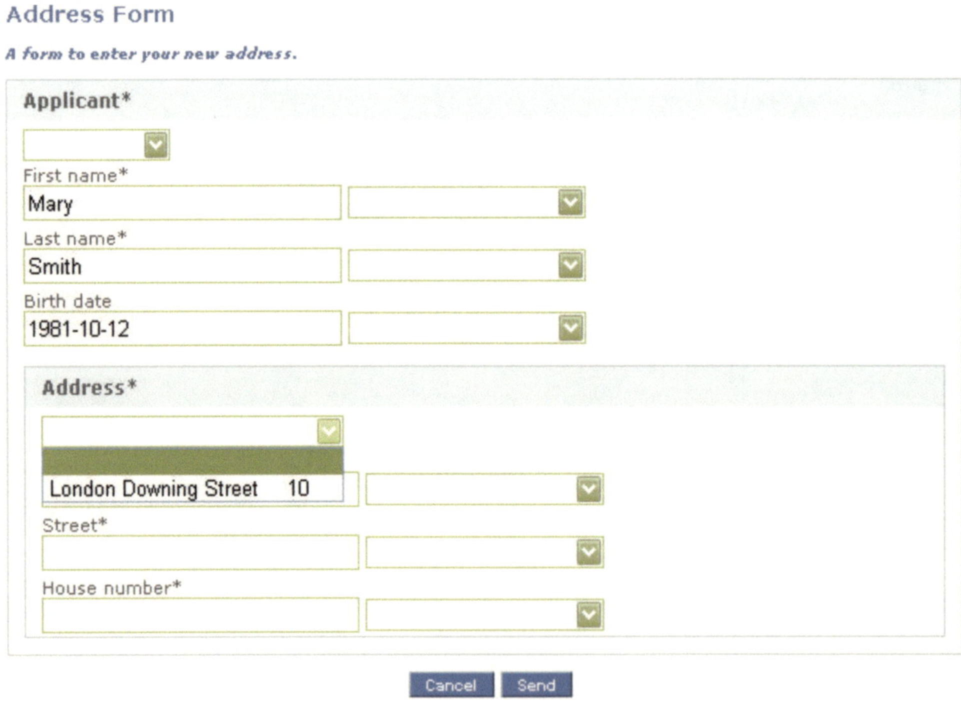

Fig. 10. Changing the data during a second run of the forms module.

Fig. 11. The third launch of the form module.

Figure 11 demonstrates the third launch of the form module. In this case, the software found two objects with the meaning matching to the "Applicant", and therefore allowed the user to select from two proposals.

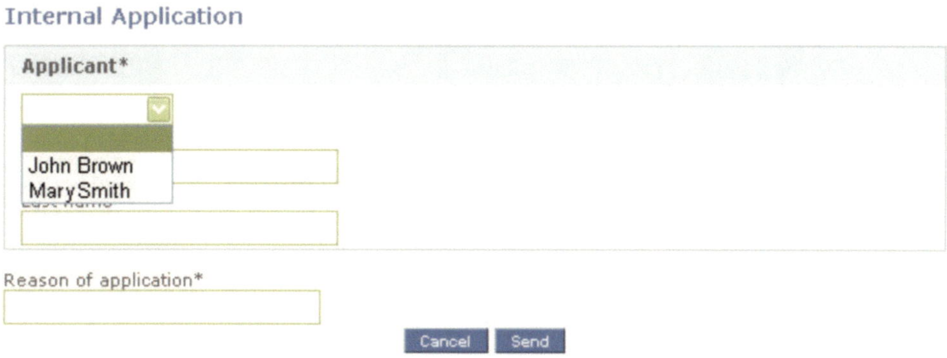

Fig. 12. Matching data to a different form.

In Figure 12 there is a different form launched for the first time. The user's ontoprofile already includes data gathered during the processing of earlier forms, which can be used in assisted filling. It should be noted that although the form shown in Figure 12 is different from the one you saw in the previous figures, the semantic description of the data and forms made it possible to match the correct data to the corresponding fields and sections of the form. Such a solution makes it possible to transfer data between forms if only they are assigned the same meaning.

4. The acceleration measurements of assisted form filling processes

The measurements of acceleration of assisted form filling processes were made on the two forms shown earlier and on a more complex form shown in Figure 13. The measurements allowed to estimate the degree of acceleration of the process of assisted form filling in relation to the time required to fill out the forms without support.

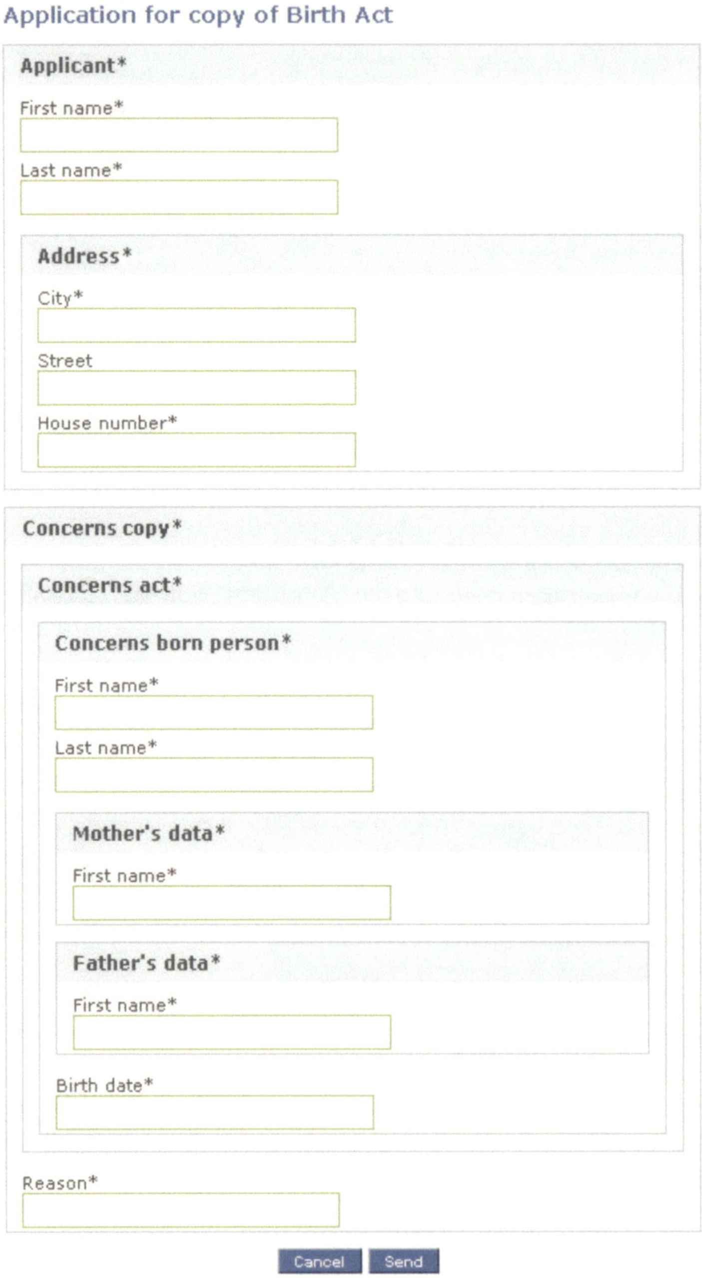

Fig. 13. A complex form [own].

4.1. The estimation of maximal acceleration

To estimate the maximum acceleration it was required to construct test scenarios involving the best (fastest) and worst (the most interaction intensive) processes of filling in the forms. For this purpose, we constructed the following test cases:

- T1 – the user manually completes all fields (the ontoprofile is empty) - requires a large amount of interactions (key presses) because, due to the lack of data, the assisted filling functionality is not available;
- T2 - the user accepts all proposed values of the fields making up only those which are missing - this case is optimal;
- T3 - the user deletes all proposed fields and brings his/her own values - the worst case because, apart from entering the data, it is necessary to delete already suggested values;
- T4 - for each section the user selects a proposed value from the list - it is an almost optimal case but most often it appears while using a module.

Before we began to measure real acceleration of assisted form filling processes we had estimated the maximum possible accelerations. The estimates were made by counting the number of interactions (clicks and key presses) required to fill each form. This quantity was obtained by counting all actions (filling in the fields, selecting a value from the list, etc.) necessary to complete the case at the optimal test conditions, and then by multiplying them by the appropriate weight of each action. We defined the following actions:

- approval of the form = 1 interaction (a mouse-click on the button);
- selecting a proposed field or section value from the list = 2 interactions (a click on a dropdown list unroll button and a click on the selected item);
- filling in a field = 7 interactions (6 key presses corresponding to the average length of words in the Polish language and a tab key press to make a transition to the next field).

Test case	Number of interactions		
	Internal Application	Address Form	Application for copy of Birth Act
T1	22	43	78
T2	8	1	1
T3	24	45	82
T4	10	3	12
Average acceleration	2,59	29,33	43,33

Table 1. Estimated maximum acceleration of the process of filling in the forms using the forms module [own].

Table 1 presents the estimated peak acceleration of the form filling processes. As you can see, these estimates are very high and the most complex form called *Application for copy of Birth Act* can be traced up to even 40-times here. In addition, it can be seen that the acceleration increases with the complexity of the form (Figure 14). This is due to the fact that with an increase in the nesting of sections of a form the efficiency of the process increases too, because it is possible to suggest values of the whole form tree branches.

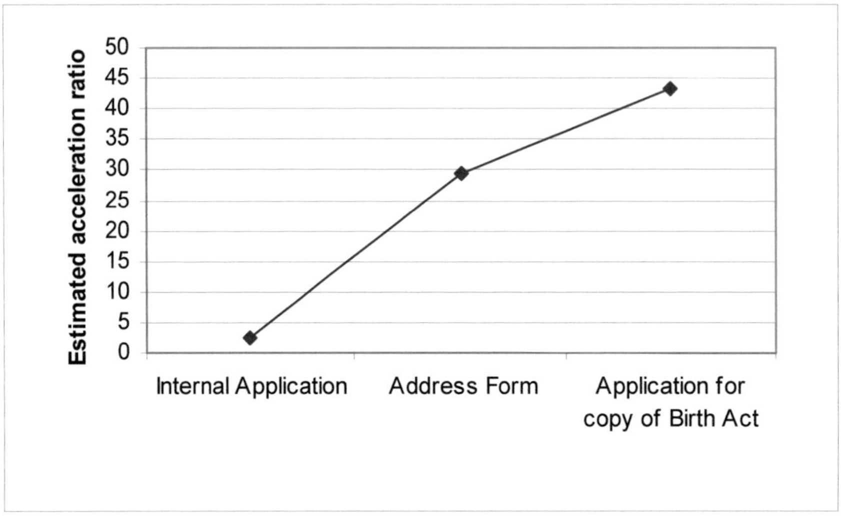

Fig. 14. Estimated acceleration of the process of filling in the form in relation to the degree of complexity, with the use of the module forms [own].

To highlight the difference of the solution, we estimated the acceleration of the processes of filling the same forms with the use of the functionality available in the Firefox 3 browser. In this case, the following events were recognized as actions:

- approval of the form = 1 interaction (a mouse-click on the button);
- selecting the proposed value for a field = 3 interactions (typing the first letter which activates the auto complete option, a click of the mouse selecting a proposed value, transition to the next field with a tab key press);
- filling in a field = 7 interactions (6 presses of the keys corresponding to the average length of words in the Polish language and a tab key press to make the transition to the next field).

Table 2 presents the results of the calculation of the estimated acceleration for specific test cases. The acceleration growth as a function of the complexity of a form is indicated in figure 15.

Test case	Number of interactions		
	Internal Application	Address Form	Application for copy of Birth Act
T1	22	43	78
T2	10	19	34
T3	22	45	82
T4	10	19	34
Average acceleration	2,20	2,32	2,35

Table 2. Estimated maximum acceleration of the process of filling in the forms using the mechanism available in the Firefox 3 browser [own].

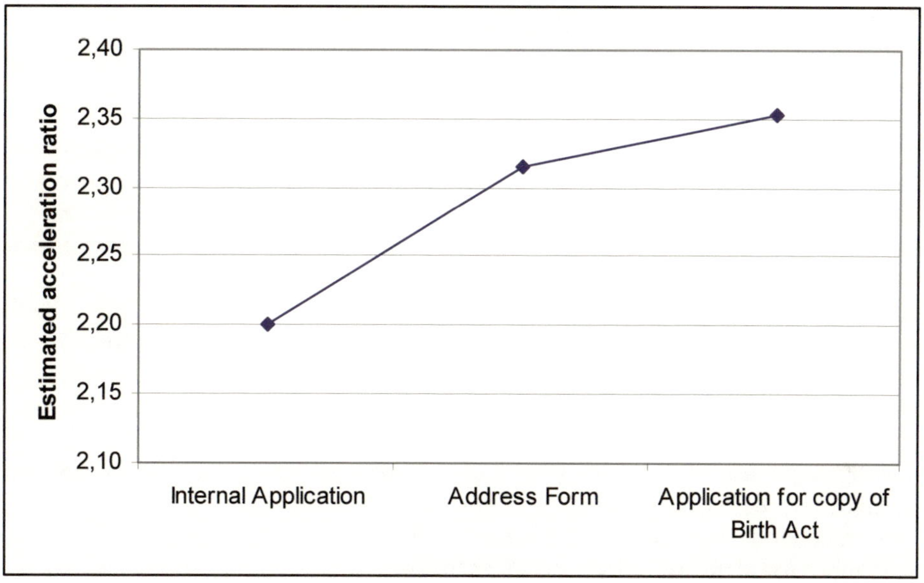

Fig. 15. Estimated acceleration of the process of filling in the form in relation to the degree of complexity, using the mechanism available in the Firefox 3 browser [own].

As you can see, the difference between the estimated acceleration offered by the forms module as compared to the one offered by Firefox is dramatic as the former exceeds the latter 20-times. In addition, it should be noted that the solution offered in the browser does not show a significant growth of acceleration with the increasing degree of complexity of the form (only about 5%).

In the following section we present the results of tests performed on the acceleration of assisted form filling with the users' participation. The results will verify the above estimates.

4.2. Acceleration measurements with the users' participation

After having estimated the maximum acceleration of the forms completion, actual measurements were made with test users. The group consisted of four people. The first three had no previous contact with the tested software, while the fourth was one of its developers, thus an advanced user. The scenario was to perform four test cases described earlier for each of the three sample forms. To reduce the size of the table we changed the names of the forms to:

- F1 - Internal Application
- F2 - Address Form
- F3 - Application for Copy of Birth Act.

We measured the time the users took to fill out the forms in the specific test cases. The acceleration of the form filling processes has been defined as the average ratio of the best to the worst cases. The acceleration was calculated using the formula below, where a is the acceleration of the process of filling a specific form, and t_n is the time of completion of the n-th test case.

$$a = \left(\frac{t_{T1}}{t_{T2}} + \frac{t_{T1}}{t_{T4}} + \frac{t_{T3}}{t_{T2}} + \frac{t_{T3}}{t_{T4}}\right) / 4$$

Then we calculated the average acceleration for each user (Table 3). At this point, you may notice a significant difference between the acceleration achieved by the new users and the value of acceleration achieved by the advanced user (User 4) which was two times higher. For this reason, the fourth user's samples were considered abnormal and excluded from further calculations.

Finally, the arithmetic means of accelerations were calculated for each form (on the basis of the results of users 1, 2 and 3) as well as the arithmetic mean of acceleration for all forms which is 3.36 times.

Then we measured the accelerations of form filling processes using mechanisms available in Firefox 3. Because of a different mechanism, the test cases T3 and T4 have become synonymous with cases T1 and T2 (the same scenario of interaction) and therefore have been omitted. The results of the measurements can be found in Table 4.

Then we calculated the arithmetic means of the acceleration for each form, and the arithmetic mean for all forms, which was 1.13 times.

Scenario	Time needed to fill in a form(in seconds)												Average acceleration for users 1,2,3	
	User 1			User 2			User 3			User 4				
	Time	Acceleration		Time	Acceleration		Time	Acceleration		Time	Acceleration			
			Average			Average			Average			Average		Average
F1-T1	12			46			25			10				
F1-T2	10			24			14			6				
F1-T3	17			23			55			14				
F1-T4	7	1,76		23	1,47		14	2,86		8	1,75		2,03	
F2-T1	22			51			35			18				
F2-T2	4			16			11			1				
F2-T3	31			46			62			23				
F2-T4	5	5,96		10	3,94		15	3,82		15	10,93		4,57	
F3-T1	54			110			68			49				
F3-T2	16			38			24			5				
F3-T3	65			131			78			52				
F3-T4	17	3,61	3,78	28	3,74	3,05	23	3,11	3,26	11	7,35	6,68	3,48	3,36

Table 3. The results of the measurements of acceleration of the assisted form filling using the forms module [own].

Scenario	Time needed to fill in a form(in seconds)												Average acceleration
	User 1			User 2			User 3			User 4			
	Time	Acc.	Avg.	Time	Acc.	Avg..	Time	Acc.	Avg.	Time	Acc.	Avg.	
F1-T1	12			46			25			10			
F1-T2	10	1,20		51	0,90		22	1,14		7	1,43		
F2-T1	22			51			35			18			
F2-T2	18	1,22		46	1,11		33	1,06		17	1,06		
F3-T1	54			110			68			49			
F3-T2	49	1,10	1,17	99	1,11	1,04	61	1,11	1,10	43	1,14	1,21	1,13

Table 4. The measurements of acceleration using a form-filling mechanism for Firefox 3[own].

4.3. Analysis of results

The analysis of estimates let us assume that the acceleration processes of assisted form filling will grow more or less linearly with the increase of the forms complexity. This fact has not been confirmed by the results of tests presented in Figure 16.

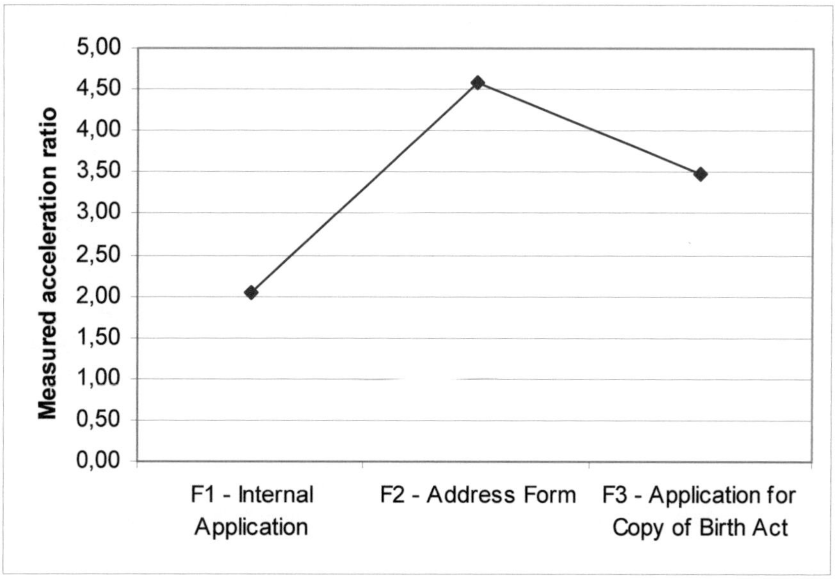

Fig. 16. The measured average acceleration of the process of assisted form filling in relation to the degree of complexity of forms [own].

The dramatic difference between the estimated and the measured acceleration comes from the time the users spent on analyzing the structure and meaning of forms being filled, which was not included in the estimates. The time needed to analyze the meaning and structure of forms is also responsible for the noticeable decline of acceleration of processes with the increase in the form complexity, which was depicted in the figure 16. It is reasonable to assume that the two trends are going to cancel each other out resulting in roughly constant acceleration. However, it is necessary to perform tests with more users and more diverse forms to determine which trend has a dominating influence on the final value of the acceleration.

Despite the need for further research we can already predict some consequences. In case of users with well-developed motor skills the dominant factor will be the time they spend on the analyzing the meaning of the form. In such cases, the benefit associated with accelerating the process of form filling will be small, and the usefulness of this solution will be considered only in terms of easy use.

Another extremely different group will consist of people with low motor skills, for whom the main concern will be to type in the field values using the keyboard. They can be both disabled people and novice computer users who have not yet dealt with rapid typing. For such people the dominant factor will be the time taken to fill in individual fields. In such cases, the mechanism of assisted form filling will provide a significant time benefit and a significant increase in the convenience of the software use.

However, the largest group of users will probably be represented by those with the average motor skills for whom the acceleration of the form filling processes in the order of three to four times is sufficiently good.
In addition, it should be noted that, despite the difference between the estimated and the measured acceleration of assisted form filling processes, the solution presented by the forms module obtains significantly better results (by order of magnitude) than the mechanism available in web browsers, which at the efficiency of 10-20% puts the solution into question.

5. Conclusions

The application of semantic technologies allowed to implement working software that assists the user in filling any electronic forms. As both research and implementation are still in progress, the usefulness of this solution was based only on approximate estimates and on several studies involving the users, which does not allow a thorough evaluation. The outcome of the work, however, allows us to believe that the chosen direction has good chances of success.

6. References

Berners-Lee T., Hendler J., Lassila O., The semantic web. Scientific American Magazine, May, 2001.

Forgy C., On the efficient implementation of production systems. Carneggie-Mellon University, 1979.

Grosof B., Horrocks I., Volz R., Decker S., *Description Logic Programs: Combining Logic Programs with Description Logic .2003,* http://www.cs.man.ac.uk/~horrocks/Publications/download/2003/p117-grosof.pdf, 2009-01.

Horn A., On sentences which are true of direct unions of algebras. Journal of Symbolic Logic, 16, 14-21, 1951.

OWL Web Ontology Language Guide. W3C, 2004, http://www.w3.org/TR/owl-guide, 2009-01.

OWL Web Ontology Language Overview. W3C, 2004, http://www.w3.org/TR/owl-features, 2009-01.

OWL Web Ontology Language Reference. W3C, 2004, http://www.w3.org/TR/owl-ref, 2009-01.

OWL-S: Semantic Markup for Web Services, W3C, 2004, http://www.w3.org/Submission/OWL-S, 2009-01.

OWL Web Ontology Language Semantics and Abstract Syntax. W3C, 2004, http://www.w3.org/TR/owl-semantics, 2009-01.

Resource Description Framework (RDF); Concepts and Abstract Syntax. W3C, 2004, http://www.w3.org/TR/rdf-concepts, 2009-01.

RDF Primer. W3C, 2004, http://www.w3.org/TR/rdf-primer, 2009-01.

RDF Vocabulary Description Language 1.0: RDF Schema. W3C, 2004, http://www.w3.org/TR/rdf-schema, 2009-10.

RDF Semantics. W3C, 2004, http://www.w3.org/TR/rdf-mt, 2009-01.

Extensible Markup Language (XML) 1.0 (Fourth Edition). W3C, 2006, http://www.w3.org/XML, 2009-01.

Transatlantic Engineering Programs: An Experience in International Cooperation

Andrew J. Kornecki[1], Wojciech Grega[2], Thomas B. Hilburn[1], Jean-Marc Thririet[3], Miroslav Sveda[4], Ondrei Rysavy[4] and Adam Pilat[2]
[1] *Embry Riddle Aeronautical University*
USA
[2] *University of Mining and Metallurgy*
Poland
[3] *Universite Joseph Fourier*
France
[4] *Brno University of Technology*
Czech Republic

1. Introduction

Computing curricula are designed to promote the education of engineers and scientists using a sound theoretical basis and practices useful in the job market. The major objective of a well established curriculum is to provide a rigorous educational background, while giving students tools for future life-long learning. Typically, the faculty experience allows them to design curricula considering the fundamental concepts and basic principles of their discipline. However, feedback from future employers of graduates is critical to the design of modern curriculum fully matching the continuously changing job market demands.

Real-Time Software-Intensive Control systems (RSIC) are often safety-critical, and their reliability is paramount. There is an increasing importance and demand for efficient development of high quality RSIC systems. No other technology domain has experienced progress with more impact on engineering education. To keep up with this progress, engineering curricula require continuous modifications to prepare students for the technological challenges of the modern workplace. Rapid progress of computing technologies is the major reason programs like electronics, computer and software engineering, robotics, and control engineering need continuous updates.

An additional issue is the internationalization and globalization of complex systems development. Several large companies, specifically in the aerospace industry, engage international teams working in geographically diverse locations often using diverse standards, guidelines, and processes. It is advantageous for future engineers to understand the implications of international collaboration and to appreciate cultural differences.

The findings presented in this paper are results of a two-year long project called ILERT (International Learning Environment for Real-Time Software Intensive Control Systems), supported by the American Fund for Improvement of Postsecondary Education (FIPSE) and the European Commission, and executed by a consortium of one American and three European universities: Embry Riddle Aeronautical University (ERAU - Daytona Beach, FL, USA), AGH University of Science and Technology (AGH - Krakow, Poland), University of Technology (BUT - Brno, Czech Republic), and Université Joseph Fourier (UJF - Grenoble, France). The key documents resulting from the project are located at the project website (ILERT, 2009). This paper describes a methodology for the creation of a multinational engineering program, designed to produce graduates capable of working efficiently in multidisciplinary teams engaged in international collaboration on industrial RSIC projects -- projects that additionally may require conformance to specific standards mandated by regulatory authorities. Related issues explored in the ILERT project were identification of learning objectives and outcomes, analysis of credit transfer and program assessment, and development of a RSIC curriculum framework that could be easily adapted in diverse engineering curricula with different program emphases like software, control, communication, and digital systems.

The paper is structured as follows. We first describe the methodology leading to creation of an international engineering program based on the ILERT project experiences. The subsequent sections describe the components of the methodology: the identification of the curriculum learning objectives and outcomes, program assessment, student mobility and credit transfer, and the proposed curriculum framework.

2. Methodology

The development and implementation of international transatlantic engineering curricula was conducted in several phases (Kornecki 2009). The Atlantis-ILERT project defined three phases: Preparatory Phase, Research Phase, and Pilot Implementation Phase (see Fig. 1). The fourth phase (Long Term Application) started later as a separate project: Atlantis–DeSIRE^2.

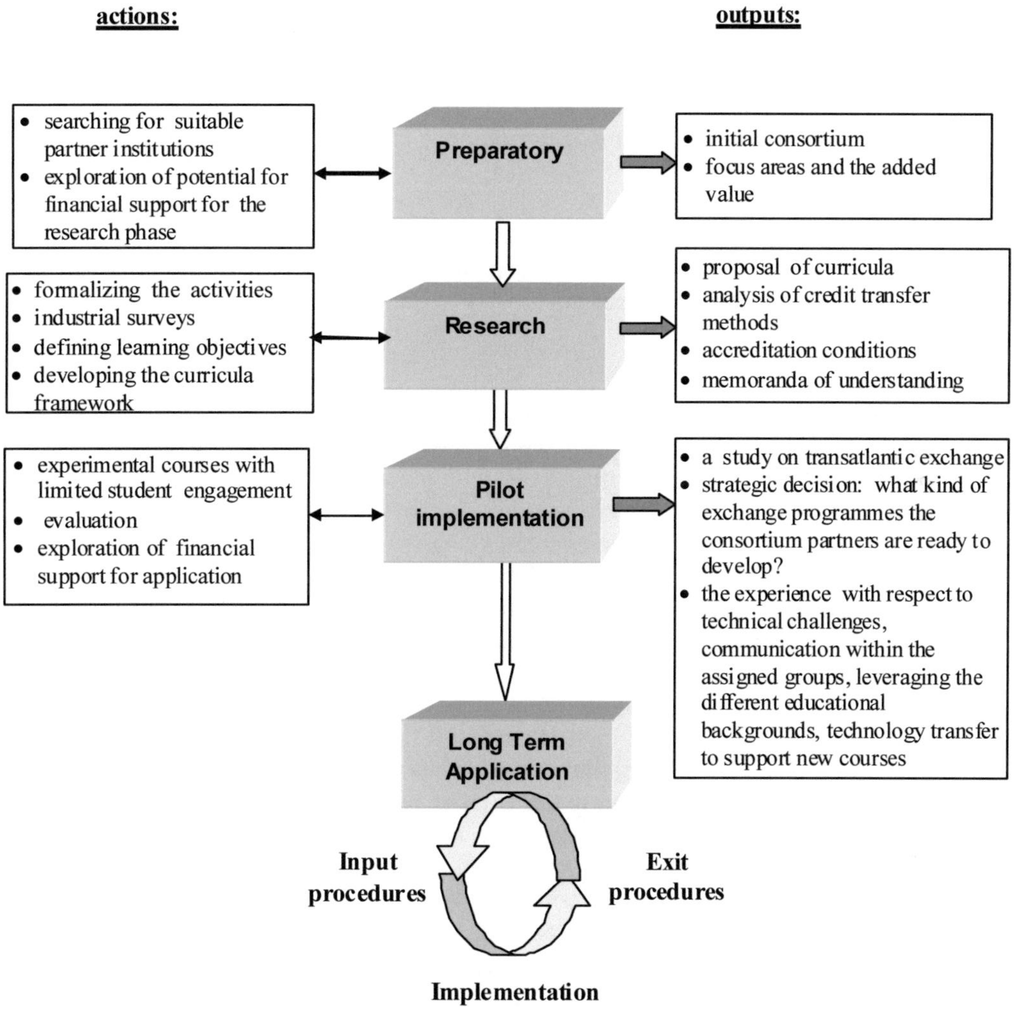

Fig. 1. Atlantis-ILERT Project Methodology

2.1 Preparatory Phase

The Preparatory Phase started with informal discussion between faculty of academic institutions of both sides of Atlantic about advantages of international relationships. The following identify the activities of this phase:

- Inventory of international informal personal contacts already existing in institutions.
- Brainstorming on the type of activities to be engaged and potential partners, defining goals and priorities (like curriculum-related cooperation and international exchanges of the faculty expertise).
- Proposing an initial consortium of universities offering expertise in the similar lines of engineering education. A common thread within the programs at all the partner institutions must be identified.

- Identifying the focus areas in the existing programs of the consortium partners. It was assumed that the selected courses from the focus areas must constitute a coherent value added, if selected by exchange students.
- Exploration of potential for financial support for research (including industry funding, international cooperation programs, international projects, international and national systems of grants).

The preparatory phase was concluded by formalities leading to establishing of the consortium of university partners and writing a successful proposal for funding the described here educational research project.

2.2 Research Phase

The research phase started with the analysis of industry requirements related to graduates in the proposed domain. The collected data were analyzed and the results were used to help identify academic program learning objectives and outcomes, thus preparing a base for creation of a new curriculum framework.

The following steps can be identified in this phase:

- **Defining learning objectives** and outcomes, developing the curriculum framework, exploring the partners' programs commonalities and laboratory infrastructure, comparing the curriculum content, and analyzing of the educational process assessment. The existing curricula were reviewed as a way of prioritizing and integrating the various elements, in order to fulfill the requirements of interdisciplinary specialization. It should be noted, that the existence of common characteristics does not imply automatic commonality among the ways in which individual institutions pursue common educational objectives. Universities often create their own procedures and methods. By reviewing existing programs and comparing them with industry needs, this research phase has identified missing topics and topics that could be strengthened. As the final outcome of this phase, a comprehensive list of courses related to the RSIC domain offered at all of the partner institutions was compiled.
- **Curriculum development** started with classifying courses into one of four categories: General Education (languages, humanities, social science), Math and Science (mathematics, physics), Basic (required towards the completion of the degree in the given line of study), and Advanced, which focuses on a selected engineering specialization. It was critical to identify and agree on the minimal number of contact hours required to complete the entire engineering program and the percentage of effort assigned to the four curriculum categories given above. This was followed by a practical case study adapting selected curricula of partner institutions by including components of interdisciplinary specialization, thus creating an engineering program acceptable to all partner organizations.
- **Credit transfer and accreditation issues.** The development of new curriculum framework in engineering may in turn require new approaches to their validation and accreditation. The transfer of credits and grades is a challenging undertaking for university systems, which are significantly different in Europe and the U.S. Existing and emerging structures for accreditation, quality control, and credit transfer (such as the European Credit Transfer and Accumulation Scheme) have been analyzed. It should

be noted that the proposed curriculum units must be reviewed according to ABET standards (and the applicable standards of Ministry of Higher Education in the European countries), focusing on the objectives and outcomes of the educational activity.

- **Students' mobility plan.** Based on the developed curricula, a general schedule of students' mobility between partners' institutions was proposed, opening the possibility of collaborating and enrolling in the courses offered in four partner sites.
- **Formalizing the activities** included signing formal agreements or memoranda of understanding, defining responsibilities and structure of communication.

2.3 Pilot Implementation Phase

Agreements between partner institutions, or "memoranda of understanding," in delivery and mutual recognition of courses were prepared at the beginning of this phase. During the pilot implementation phase, the experimental courses were created, instructional material was developed, and experimental concurrent delivery with limited student engagement was initialized. The participating students were supervised by coordinators from the partners' institutions. During this phase, a lot of experience was gained on the technical challenges, international cooperation, communication within the assigned groups, leveraging the different educational backgrounds in the interdisciplinary context, technology transfer, and interactions between international students and staff. The Final Report, including guidelines for extension of the approach for long-term application, is the most valuable output of this phase.

An important part of the pilot implementation phase is the analysis of the sources and mechanisms of financial support for future transatlantic educational collaboration. Generally, tangible and intangible resources, essential to the success of the project's future, must be considered. Tangible resources include finances, facilities, and time. Intangible resources include will, commitment, and the ability to sustain the effort to conclusion.

This phase can be concluded with important strategic analysis and decision-making: What kind of exchange programs would the consortium partners be able to develop? Would a partner institution initiate a dual degree program or develop one or more aspects of a current program with other international partners? The general goals, including number of mobility years and the number of mobility students must be decided at this stage.
The selection between single or dual degree programs or other forms of partner institution engagement should also be made (see Table 1).

2.4 Long Term Application Phase

In the long term application and evaluation phase, internal and external procedures are developed. The final agreement between partners on credit transfer, accreditation, tuition, and student selection must be accepted by all partner institutions. The agreement must also define: responsibility of institution and students, admission requirements, registration procedures, specific learning agreement form (e.g. one semester course, receives recognition upon return), tuition waiver, language/culture engagement of the students and logistic/administration details.

Student spends abroad	Expected results	Formal effects	Comments
One semester in a partner university	• single diploma in home institution • mobility students focus on an area of concentration not available at home institution • experiences related to cultural immersion	• US student receive special certificate of completion of a specific focus area • EU student receive appropriate entry in their Diploma and the Supplement identifying the focus area.	• bilateral agreements are necessary
Two-three semesters in the partner university	• two diplomas are received • students may receive a new specialization, not offered at single university • experiences related to cultural immersion	Dual degree	• more detailed bilateral agreements are necessary • requires full validation and accreditation of learning programs. • ethical issue: is it fair that student receives two diplomas without any increase of his work?

Table 1. Examples Of Final Partner Institution Engagement

The long-term mobility of students includes two cyclic steps: input and implementation procedures.

2.4.1 Input Procedures

a) Internal Procedures:

- Setting deadlines for the partners' institutions
- Distributing information on international mobility - to recruit students
- Performing internal selection procedures for applicants from the home university (eligibility, mandatory orientation, interviews, language skills)
- Performing placement procedures for incoming exchange students:
- Assigning the mentors to incoming students
- Internal selection of the teachers interested to participate in the mobility exchange.

b) External Procedures:

- Exchange information with the partner university on the selection results.
- Identify the courses available for overseas students during the mobility period
- Signing joint learning agreement forms.
- Procedures for practical issues such as housing, insurance, etc.

2.4.2 Implementation Procedures

a) Assistance to the Internal Applicants

- Explaining the program options and site/course selection
- Helping students with the application procedure.

b) Assistance to the External Applicants

- Helping with questions from students/teachers interested in mobility exchange (terms of exchange, reporting, application process).
- Facilitating mentoring process for incoming students
- Monitoring and reporting the students' progress

It should be noted that the long-term phase, in addition to continuous evaluation of the program, must include the exit and evaluation component, where the entire program is given to critique and scrutiny with the goal to learn the lessons and improve the process. The components of such evaluation will include the assessment and evaluation of the individual students at the end of the mobility period and the overall assessment and evaluation of the mobility exchange.

3. Identification of Learning Objectives and Outcomes

There is a general agreed upon set of non-technical skills and behaviors expected from engineering school graduates, such as oral and written communications, professional ethics, team skills, etc. The starting point for designing a specific program curriculum is to identify the technical knowledge areas and skills required from the graduating students. The program educational objectives can be defined in terms of the expected graduates' proficiency, specifying the profile of graduates and their competencies. An often used phrase when defining the objectives is that the graduates of the program "are able to" perform certain specific tasks. Examples may be: analyze the problem, elicit requirements, design a circuit, apply a method, use a tool, etc.

There are two common ways to define an objective. One is a "know how" objective: describing a task one performs. Another is a "knowledge" objective: describing a topic that one understands and is able to convey knowledge about. Examples of such would be:

- "Know How" to manage database: e.g. to install the database software, to manage users, to create/update/delete database record, etc.
- "Knowledge" of a database concept and model: e.g. to describe the attributes of a database logical model, to give examples of such models, to identify security vulnerabilities, to describe SQL syntax, etc.

The Accreditation Board of Engineering Technology, ABET, (ABET, 2007) defines Program Educational Objectives (PEO) and Program Outcomes (PO). Program Educational Objectives are broad statements that describe the career and professional accomplishments that the program is preparing graduates to achieve. An example of PEO would be: "graduates will pursue successful careers as professional software engineers". Program Outcomes are narrower statements that describe what students are expected to know and be able to do by the time of graduation. The PO relate to the skills, knowledge, and behaviors that students acquire in their matriculation through a program. An example would be: "graduates will be able to work effectively as part of a software development team." The PO can be assessed during the course of studies and immediately after students' graduation. The RSIC PEO and PO presented in this document were developed using the ABET interpretation.

A survey (Pilat, 2008), solicited from a representative sample of industry engaged in real-time software-intensive control systems, was designed to get feedback on what the employers expect graduates to possess in terms of skills and attitudes, as well as the knowledge of technical topics. The data collected from 43 companies in four countries (USA, France, Poland, and Czech Republic) were analyzed and the results were used to help identify academic program educational objectives and outcomes, thus preparing a base for creation of a new curriculum framework. The resulting objectives and outcomes, listed in (Kornecki, 2008), guided subsequent ILERT activities and the development of the RSIC Curriculum Framework.

4. Program Assessment

To help ensure achievement of program objectives and outcomes, an assessment and evaluation process, based on student performance and other indicators, must be in place. Considering long term impact, the assessment process for program educational objectives may involve instruments, such as the following:

- Surveys of alumni and their employers
- Feedback from an industry advisory board
- Alumni focus group meetings
- Examination of a successful industrial project, involving program alumni

A short-term focused assessment process for program outcomes might involve instruments, such as the following:

- Annual review of student performance in selected indicator courses by the program faculty
- Feedback from graduating seniors and recent graduates
- Feedback from an industry advisory board
- Discussion of the department curriculum committee
- Analysis of data reflecting student cooperative education activities, involvement in professional societies, choice of minor programs, etc.
- Student Portfolios

Table 2 describes a process for the assessment and evaluation of achievement of program educational objectives and program outcomes. This table provides a high-level description of the steps and activities that are part of the assessment process. This process is meant to provide a framework for carrying out assessment and evaluation; the actual process might vary from one RSIC program to another. The indicator courses, defined by the faculty, are critical in assessing program outcomes. Each program outcome should have one or more courses that contribute to its achievement. Performance in indicator courses also provides information to the faculty regarding performance in prerequisite courses.

A survey of graduating seniors and an exit interview can be a good source of information regarding the curriculum. While senior information is valuable, graduating seniors may lack sufficient context to correctly identify the degree to which the program achieves program outcomes; thus, information from the senior survey is considered only moderately reliable. In contrast, feedback from the program alumni employed for two or more years, as well as the feedback from industry employing graduates, provides stronger evidence of the degree to which the program has achieved the desired outcomes.

Step	Description	Schedule
Determine Constituencies	A discussion at the faculty meeting identifies the constituencies for the RSIC program. (e.g., students, employers, faculty)	Initially
Determine Objectives and Outcomes	Based on the needs of the constituencies, the faculty, determine RSIC Program Educational Objectives and Program Outcomes	Initially
Determine Assessment Items and Process	The program faculty identify what will be assessed and how and when achievement of objectives and outcomes will be evaluated (with the use of elements such as indicator courses, surveys, interviews, data collection methods)	Start of Assessment
Collect Data and Opinion	Information and opinion about achievement of Program Outcomes is collected.	Annually
Assess Program Outcomes	The data collected is used to assess whether the Program Outcomes are being achieved.	Annually
Evaluate Program Educational Objectives	The data collected is used to evaluate whether the PEOs of the RSIC program are achieved. There is a determination of whether the objectives need to be modified.	Every Three Years
Modify Program	Based on outcomes assessment and on the results of program educational objectives evaluation and review, the faculty make changes in the program, its educational objectives, and/or the program outcomes.	Every Three Years
Evaluate Assessment Process	The faculty evaluate the effectiveness of the assessment process and make changes as appropriate.	Every Three Years

Table 2. Assessment Process

5. Student Mobility and Credit Transfer

The credit systems are used not only to evaluate the students but also for mobility, i.e. the situation when a student leaves an institution to continue studies in another one. Such a situation is called permanent mobility (in Europe) or transfer student (in USA). With the impact of the Erasmus Program, a new type of transient mobility exists, when a student spends a semester, or a year, in a partner university. In such situation, the student gets the diploma from his home university, except in the case of double-degree curricula. The same situation exists in the USA also, allowing a student to spend part of his program in another institution as a visiting student. The procedures require an agreement between the exchange institutions that considers the content and learning outcomes of the partner curriculum.

When credits are used for mobility, the courses must be "equivalent". The rules of equivalence could vary between the institutions and academic programs but, generally, the student will keep academic record in the home university and adhere to the admission procedure in the host university. This admission procedure will be based on the actual contents and learning outcomes of the courses followed by the student in the sending institution.

When credits are used for students' evaluation, the situation is the same in the USA and in the Europe. Note that the European countries generally use their own national or local grading systems (Hilburn, 2008). The credits are given after a semester (or a term) to continue the academic program, or after the completion of the entire curriculum to be recorded in the final diploma.

5.1. In Europe

The European Credit Transfer System (ECTS) (Bologna Working Group, 2005) has been designed to facilitate the mobility of students among the member countries. The initial purpose was not to use ECTS as an accumulation system for life-long learning, nor to use them to characterize the level of the course. As a result of the Bologna declaration in June 1999, it was decided to use ECTS as an accumulation system.

The ECTS is designed to measure the actual workload of students for a given course. The workload reflects the quantity of work and includes all the pedagogical components such as lectures, seminars, independent and private study, preparation of projects and examinations, placements, dissertation work, etc. The workload measure is based on a student-centered approach. A complete year is equivalent to 60 ECTS credits. The credits are allocated on a relative basis, since the complete year is fixed. The student workload of a full-time study program in Europe amounts, in most cases, to 1500-1800 hours per year, so one ECTS credit reflects about 30 hours of workload for an average student.

Credits in ECTS can only be obtained after successful completion of the work required, and appropriate assessment of the learning outcomes achieved. Learning outcomes are sets of competencies, expressing what the student will know, understand or be able to do after completion of a process of learning.

The performance of a student is documented by a local/national grade. It is good practice to also add an ECTS grade, in particular in case of credit transfer. The ECTS grading scale ranks the students on a statistical basis. Therefore, statistical data on student performance is a prerequisite for applying the ECTS grading system. Grades are assigned among students with passing grades as follows: A best 10%, B next 25%, C next 30%, D next 25%, and F last 10%. A distinction is made between the grades FX and F that are used for unsuccessful students. FX means: "fail- some more work required to pass" and F means: "fail - considerable further work required". The inclusion of failure rates in the Transcript of Records is optional.

Since the ECTS does not measure the quality of performance, content, or level, certain additional rules must apply when ECTS is used as an accumulation system. In addition to the number of credits required, the type of the course and the level at which those credits must be obtained must be added. The levels are defined as:

- Basic Level Course - Introduction to a subject

- Intermediate Level Course - Expand basic knowledge
- Advanced Level Course - Further strengthen of expertise
- Specialized Level Course - To build up knowledge and experiences in a special field or discipline

The following types of courses are defined:

- Core course (part of the core of a major program of studies)
- Related course (supporting course for the core)
- Minor course (optional course or supplementary course)

These accumulation system features were preliminary work for the introduction of the European Qualification Framework (EQF).

To support the administration and management of student progress, the European Commission proposed accompanying documents:

- Application Form: the agreement to be signed by the partners.
- Learning Agreement: contains the list of courses to be taken, with the ECTS credits which will be awarded for each course.
- Transcript of Records: documents the performance of a student by showing the list of courses taken, the ECTS credits gained, local or national credits, if any, local/ECTS grades awarded; the transcript of records comprises information about the type of courses followed abroad, the duration of the course (one year (Y), one semester (1S) or one term (1T)), the local grades (in the national grading system), the ECTS grades and the ECTS credits.

Table 3 gives an example of a Transcript of Records, which means that the student followed the course "RT-M7 Security of information systems", the duration of the course was one semester, the local grade was 14/20, which stands for an ECTS grade of B (statistical, depending on the actual results of the whole class), and the amount of ECTS credits for this course is 4. The institutional or local grading system should be explained. For instance, in France, the grading system is equivalent to a percentage, but it is given in a scale on which the higher mark is 20 (14/20 for example means 70 %).

Course unit code	Title of the course unit	Duration of the course unit	Local grade	ECTS grade	ECTS credit
RT-M7	Security of information systems	1S	14/20	B	4

Table 3. Example of Transcript of Records

The Diploma Supplement is a document attached to a higher education diploma, providing a standardised description of the nature, level, context, content, and status of the studies successfully completed by the graduate. The purpose of the Diploma Supplement is to provide a description of the competences acquired by the students as a function of the various pedagogical sequences which were validated but also as a function of specific activities (special project, elective course, associations or student organizations engagement, social activities if there are recognized and validated by the instructor).

The Dublin descriptors are descriptors for qualifications awarded to students that signify completions of:

- higher education short cycle (within first cycle)
- Bachelor - first cycle
- Master - second cycle
- Doctorate - third cycle

Descriptors are associated with national frameworks of qualification. Table 4 describes competencies for each of the cycles. The implementation of the competences would vary across institutions.

These features were the preliminary work from the introduction of the European Qualifications Framework (EQF) for lifelong learning (European Commission, 2008). This framework defines three criteria:

- Knowledge: described as theoretical and/or factual,
- Skills: cognitive (use of logical, intuitive and creative thinking) and practical (involving manual dexterity and the use of methods, materials, tools and instruments)
- Competencies: responsibility and autonomy.

For each of the criteria, eight levels have been defined, from the basic to the most advanced. The EQF proposes the following equivalence between the level of a course and the cycles of study:

- The descriptor for the higher education short cycle (within or linked to the first cycle), corresponds to the learning outcomes for EQF level 5.
- The descriptor for the first cycle in the Framework for Qualifications of the European Higher Education Area in the framework of the Bologna process corresponds to the learning outcomes for EQF level 6.
- The descriptor for the second cycle in the Framework for Qualifications of the European Higher Education Area in the framework of the Bologna process corresponds to the learning outcomes for EQF level 7.
- The descriptor for the third cycle in the Framework for Qualifications of the European Higher Education Area in the framework of the Bologna process corresponds to the learning outcomes for EQF level 8.

Descriptors draw upon other sources some of which are associated with national frameworks of qualification. The descriptors describe variable knowledge, skills, and competencies for each of the levels, and the implementation of the competences is different as a function of the level of the degree.

Competences	1 (Bachelor)	2 (Master)	3 (Doctorate)
Knowledge and understanding	supported by advanced text books with some aspects learned including knowledge at the forefront of their field of study	provides a basis or opportunity for originality in developing or applying ideas often in a research context ..	[includes] a systematic understanding of their field of study and mastery of the methods of research associated with that field..
Applying knowledge and understanding	[through] devising and sustaining arguments	[through] problem solving abilities [applied] in new or unfamiliar environments within broader (or multidisciplinary) context	[is demonstrated by the] ability to conceive, design, implement and adapt a substantial process of research with scholarly integrity .. [is in the context of] a contribution that extends the frontier of knowledge by developing a substantial body of work some of which merits national or international refereed publication ..
Making judgments	[involves] gathering and interpreting relevant data ..	[demonstrates] the ability to integrate knowledge and handle complexity, and formulate judgments with incomplete data ..	[requires being] capable of critical analysis, evaluation and synthesis of new and complex ideas..
Communication	[of] information, ideas, problems and solutions ..	[of] their conclusions and the underpinning knowledge and rationale (restricted scope) to specialist and non-specialist audiences (monologue) ..	with their peers, the larger scholarly community and with society in general (dialogue) about their areas of expertise (broad scope)..
Learning skills	have developed those skills needed to study further with a high level of autonomy ..	study in a manner that may be largely self-directed or autonomous..	expected to be able to promote, within academic and professional contexts, technological, social or cultural advancement ..

Table 4. Dublin Descriptor Competencies

5.2. In the USA

In the United States, there is no national policy or procedure for transfer and acceptance of credit between academic institutions; that is, there is no system similar to the ECTS for governing or administering the transfer of academic credit. Transfer policies and procedures vary from state to state, and from institution to institution. Hence, transfer of credit on a nation-wide basis is complex, and sometimes confusing and inconsistent. The list below describes a variety of transfer categories. These categories presume all colleges and universities are regionally accredited and are either public or independent (not-for-profit).

- Two-year (A.S "Associate of Science" degree and A.A "Associate of Arts" degree) to four-year colleges and universities – these transfer arrangements are often formalized by states or state systems. Students completing an associate of arts or associate of science degree from a community college often can receive full credit and junior standing at another state institution through articulation agreements. Transfer from two-year to four-year may also be by design, in what is called a "two plus two" arrangement. For this arrangement, the student completing the associate's degree moves directly into a coordinated upper level program to complete the bachelor's degree.
- Four-year to four-year colleges and universities – typically not covered by formal arrangements, these may be situations where students enrolled as a regular or "non-degree" students, accumulate credits and wish to transfer them to their "home" institution. The credits often will transfer (assuming a student has earned an acceptable grade), but may not meet specific requirements or may be accepted as elective credit or as "additive" credit (meeting no requirements but listed as transfer credits on your transcript).
- Four-year to two-year institutions – some students take a reverse path, possibly having completed some coursework at a four-year institution and now are seeking a degree at a two-year institution. There are also some "reverse two plus two" programs where a student completes coursework at a four-year institution and returns to a two-year institution to complete a program of study.
- Multiple credits from multiple institutions to a "home" institution – a student may take courses from a variety of institutions, hoping to "bank" them eventually at an institution and earn a degree. This can work, but credits earned in this fashion are subject to greater scrutiny – particularly if the student was not a regularly admitted student at the college or university where credit was earned.
- Proprietary (even when regionally accredited) to public and independent institutions – whether appropriate or not, students attempting to transfer credit from a proprietary institution to a public or independent college or university often face a loss of credit in the transfer process.
- Credits earned through assessment, prior learning, credit equivalency, and other non-traditional means to a "home" institution – there are significant differences in institutional policy regarding the acceptance of credits earned through alternative methods, both in terms of the number that might be acceptable and use of the credits.

Institutions and academic degree programs are accredited by various organization and agencies. Accreditation organizations (state, regional or professional) typically specify high-level requirements for acceptance of transfer credit. Here are two examples:

- The Southern Association of Colleges and Schools (SACS, 2007) is the recognized regional accrediting body in the eleven U.S. Southern states (Alabama, Florida, Georgia, Kentucky, Louisiana, Mississippi, North Carolina, South Carolina, Tennessee, Texas and Virginia) for those institutions of higher education that award associate, baccalaureate, master's or doctoral degrees. SACS specifies the following standard regarding transfer credit:

  The institution has a defined and published policy for evaluating, awarding, and accepting credit for transfer, experiential learning, advanced placement, and professional certificates that is consistent with its mission and ensures that course work and learning outcomes are at the collegiate level and comparable to the institution's own degree programs. The institution assumes responsibility for the academic quality of any course work or credit recorded on the institution's transcript.

- The Engineering Accreditation Commission (EAC) of the Accreditation Board for Engineering and Technology (ABET) is responsible for accrediting U.S. engineering programs. EAC specifies the following criterion regarding transfer credit (EAC, 2008):

  The institution must have and enforce policies for the acceptance of transfer students and for the validation of courses taken for credit elsewhere.

6. Curriculum Framework

The section describes the organization and content of the RSIC curriculum framework. The framework is a high-level curriculum specification describing the architecture and content of the RSIC curriculum, which is detailed enough to guide the development of a RSIC program and to support the RSIC objectives and outcomes (Kornecki, 2008); however, it is flexible enough to account for specializations, constraints, and requirements of various programs, institutions, and regions.

6.1 Curriculum Components

The basic organizational unit for the framework is a RSIC "component". A RSIC component is a curriculum unit which covers theory, knowledge, and practice that supports the RSIC curriculum objective and outcomes. Table 5 describes the RSIC components in six identified RSIC areas: Software Engineering, Digital Systems, Computer Control, Real-Time Systems, Networking, and Systems Engineering.

The proposed RSIC Curriculum Framework does not specify the way in which component topics might be formed into modules or courses. Component topics might be focused in one or two courses, or spread among several courses, along with other non-RSIC topics. The "Final Result" link at (ILERT, 2009) contains the full report on RSIC Curriculum Framework, which provides more detailed specifications for each component: prerequisite knowledge, component learning objectives, information about required facilities and equipment, and guidelines and suggestions for course design and delivery.

In addition to the RSIC components, a curriculum must support requirements for prerequisite knowledge and other material that is required for a graduate of the program to achieve the education objectives and graduation outcomes. It is recommended that the following non-RSIC courses or units be part of a RSIC curriculum, as part of entrance requirements or as courses to provide prerequisite knowledge or to supplement the components as part of a full degree program. The prerequisite knowledge includes such areas as Mathematics (Differential and Integral Calculus, Differential Equations, Discrete Mathematics, Statistics, Linear Algebra...), Physics (Mechanics, Electromagnetism, Thermodynamics, Fluids...), Electrical Engineering (Circuit Analysis, Basic Electronics...), Engineering Economics, and Introduction to Computer Science with Programming.

Software Engineering - **SoftEng**
software engineering concepts and practices, software lifecycle models, project management, software processes, software modeling and formal representation; software requirements; software architectural and module design; software construction methods and practices, testing and quality assurance; software maintenance; and notations and tools
Digital Systems - **DigSys**
concepts, methods, techniques, and tools used to support the design of combinational and sequential digital circuits and the design of fault tolerant and advanced networked hardware components.
Computer Control - **CompCtrl**
concepts of feedback control, time and frequency domains, continuous and discrete models of dynamical systems, state analysis, stability, controllability and observability, controller design, implementing control algorithms in real-time, integrated control design and implementation, use of analysis and design tools
Real-Time Systems - **RTSys**
timing and dependability properties of software intensive systems, RTOS concepts and applications, concurrency, synchronization and communication, scheduling, reliability and safety
Networking - **Network**
data communication, network topology, analysis and design, information security, algorithms, encryption, bus architectures, wireless, distributed control and monitoring, etc.
System Engineering - **SysEng**
system engineering concepts, principles, and practices; system engineering processes (technical and management); system requirements, system design, system integration, and system testing; special emphasis on the development of a RSIC system and the integration of RSIC system elements

Table 5. RSIC Components

In addition to the above areas, there may be institutional, regional, or national requirements in areas of "general education"; for example, there may be requirements for oral and written communication, for arts and humanities, or for the social sciences. These areas also support the RSIC curriculum objectives and outcomes concerned with ethical and professional responsibility, effective communications skills, ability to work as part of a team, and life-long learning.

6.2 Curriculum Structure

The project consortium discussed the potential curricula to include the RSIC curricular areas. The consortium partners not only represents computing programs at four schools from different countries; it represents four programs that provide focus and depth in diverse areas of computing: ERAU - software engineering, AGH - controls and automatics, UJF - networking and telecommunication, and BUT - digital systems.

To verify the practicality and efficacy of the RSIC Curriculum Framework, each ILERT partner analyzed how the Framework could be applied to their program. The challenge was to maintain the program integrity and at the same time include all necessary elements of the

RSIC Framework. Obviously, different programs will treat the RSIC areas differently. For example, the ERAU program may include more courses/units dedicated to software engineering, while AGH will have more content dedicated to controls. Tables 6, 7, 8, and 9 show examples of curricula (semester by semester) in the four partner organizations that meet the above criteria including one or more RSIC components. We abstract from the concrete course names and classify them into eleven categories. Six of them correspond with RSIC components: **SoftEng, DigSys, CompCtrl, RTSys, Network,** and **SysEng**. The other categories include courses that are fundamental to engineering education and are usually considered as prerequisites for RSIC components:

- **Math** - calculus for engineers, differential equations, mathematical logic, discrete mathematics, and probability and statistics.
- **Physics** - general physics, and more specific topics from, e.g. chemistry, mechanics, and fluid theory (includes also preliminary courses in electrical engineering)
- **CompSc** - programming, computer algorithms and data structures, programming languages, operating systems, computer organization.
- **Elective** - technical courses that are outside the RSIC areas, such as advanced databases, compiling techniques, computer graphics, etc. and non-technical elective courses.
- **GenEd** - ethics, philosophy, history, economics, technical writing, communication skills, presentation skills.

Year 1		**Year 2**		**Year 3**		**Year 4**	
Sem 1A	**Sem 1B**	**Sem 2A**	**Sem 2B**	**Sem 3A**	**Sem 3B**	**Sem 4A**	**Sem 4B**
CompSc	CompSc	**SoftEng**	SoftEng	SoftEng	SoftEng	**SysEng**	SysEng
Math	Math	CompSc	**DigSys**	SoftEng	SoftEng	SoftEng	TechElect
Math	Math	Physics	Physics	DigSys	**RTSys**	Practice	TechElect
GenEd	GenEd	GenEd	Math	**CompCtrl**	**Network**	GenEd	OpenElect
GenEd	GenEd	Math	Physics	Network	Math	GenEd	GenEd

Table 6. RSIC Software Engineering Oriented Curriculum (ERAU)

Year 1		**Year 2**		**Year 3**		**Year 4**	
Sem 1A	**Sem 1B (2)**	**Sem 2A (3)**	**Sem 2B (4)**	**Sem 3A (5)**	**Sem 3B (6)**	**Sem 4A (7)**	
Math	Math	**DigSys**	DigSys	DigSys	CompCtrl	CompCtrl	
Math	Math	**CompCtrl**	CompCtrl	CompCtrl	CompCtrl	CompCtrl	
Physics	Physics	Physics	Physics	CompCtrl	CompCtrl	SoftEng	
GenEd	Math	**RTSys**	**SysEng**	SysEng	CompCtrl	RTSys	
GenEd	GenEd	Math	CompCtrl	SysEng	SysEng	SysEng	
CompSc	CompSc	SoftEng	Physics	CompCtrl	CompCtrl	Project	
CompCtrl	**SoftEng**	Math	Physics		**Network**		

Table 7. RSIC Control Oriented Curriculum (AGH)

Year 1		Year 2		Year 3		Year 4
Sem 1A	**Sem 1B**	**Sem 2A**	**Sem 2B**	**Sem 3A**	**Sem 3B**	**Sem 4A**
Math	Math	CompSc	SoftEng	SoftEng	Network	B.S. Thesis
Physics	Physics	CompSc	Network	DigSys	DigSys	
DigSys	**DigSys**	DigSys	CompSc	**SysEng**	CompCtrl	
SoftEng	**SoftEng**	DigSys	**CompCtrl**	**RTSys**	Term Project	
SoftEng	DigSys	**Network**	CompCtrl	Network		
GenEd	GenEd	GenEd	GenEd	GenEd	GenEd	

Table 8. RSIC Digital System Oriented Curriculum (BUT)

Year 1		Year 2		Year 3		Year 4	
Sem 1A	**Sem 1B**	**Sem 2A**	**Sem 2B**	**Sem 3A**	**Sem 3B**	**Sem 4A**	**Sem 4B**
Math	Math	Math	Physics	SoftEng	TechElect	**DigSys**	SoftEng
GenEd	GenEd	GenEd	Network	GenEd	GenEd	GenEd	EMC
Physics	Physics	Physics	**SysEng**	Network	Project	DigSys	**CompCtrl**
CompSc	**SoftEng**	Network	Project	Network		Physics	DigSys
Network	**Network**	Network		Network		**RTSys**	Project
1. The program represents three year of a bachelor program and the 1st year of a 2-year master program. *2. The project is sometimes completed in industry (in particular in the last year of the bachelor or masters' programs).*							

Table 9. A RSIC Network Oriented Curriculum (UJF)

A capstone design project is a key feature of most (if not all) undergraduate engineering curricula. Because of the complexity and criticality of the RSIC curriculum and its international nature, a team project is essential and challenging. Such course shall have the following features:

- Distributed student teams, with members from four partner institutions, design, develop and test a multi-robot system involving search and communication.
- The project made use of the material from all six of the RSIC components areas.
- Teams followed a defined process, use proven engineering practices, and document all work.

7. Conclusions

We believe the Atlantis-ILERT project has strengthened international cooperation and the global links in engineering education. The Project Methodology discussed in this paper summarizes and formalizes the lessons learned by the project partners, and presents principles and practices that can be used by other international collaborative groups seeking to develop curricula that serve the global community.

The RSIC curriculum framework not only provides a model for development of curricula that are critical to so much of human endeavor, but also serves as a meta-model for general curriculum development. The framework elements (industrial survey, objectives and outcomes, assessment process, architecture, and curriculum content) characterize the structure, scope, and content that we believe should be part of any curriculum development project.

Finally, a significant side effect of the ILERT project has been the increased understanding and appreciation by the project partners of the importance of working across borders and oceans to educate the world's future engineers. We are hopeful that the ILERT project will influence not only the technical capability of these engineers, but will better prepare them for work in a global community.

8. Acknowledgements

This work was supported by the following grants: European Commission ATLANTIS EU/EC: 2006-4563/006-001, Department of Education FIPSE ATLANTIS US: P116J060005, AGH University of Science and Technology 2009 Grant.

9. References

ABET (2007). Accreditation Policy and Procedure Manual, 2008-2009 Accreditation Cycle, ABET Inc., November 3, 2007, Baltimore, MD. (April 20, 2009, from the Website http://www.abet.org/forms.shtml)

ACM/IEEE-CS (2004). ACM/IEEE-CS Joint Task Force on Computing Curricula, *Software Engineering 2004,Curriculum Guidelines for Undergraduate Degree Programs in Software Engineering*, Aug. 2004 (April 20, 2009, from the Website http://www.acm.org/education/curricula.html)

Bologna Working Group (2005). *A Framework for Qualifications of the European Higher Education Area*, Ministry of Science, Technology and Innovation, February 2005 (April 20, 2009, from the Website http://www.bologna-bergen2005.no/Docs/00-Main_doc/050218_QF_EHEA.pdf)

EAC (2008). *Criteria For Accrediting Engineering Programs, 2007-2008 Accreditation Cycle*, Engineering Accreditation Commission, ABET Inc., March 18, 2007 (April 20, 2009, from the Website http://www.abet.org/forms.shtml)

European Commission (2008). *The European Qualifications Framework For Lifelong Learning*, Office for Official Publications of the European Communities, April 2008 (April 20, 2009, from the Website http://ec.europa.eu/dgs/education_culture/publ/pdf/eqf/broch_en.pdf)

ILERT (2009) Home page for International Learning Environment for Real-Time Software Intensive Control Systems (April 20, 2009, from the Website: http://www.ilert.agh.edu.pl/)

Thiriet, J.-M., Hilburn, T.B., Kornecki, A.J., Grega, W., Sveda, M.: "Implementation for a US-European Trans-national Degree in Real-Time Software Engineering." *Proceedings of the 19th EAEEIE Annual Conference*, Tallin, Estonia, June 29 - July 2, 2008, pp. 134-137, ISBN: 978-1-4244-2009

Hilburn, T.B., Thiriet, J.-M., Kornecki, A.J., Grega W., Sveda, M. (2008) "Credits and Accreditation in the U.S.A. and Europe: Towards a Framework for Transnational Engineering Degrees.", Chapter 4 in *INNOVATIONS 2008 - World Innovations in Engineering Education and Research*, Edited by Win Aung at all, iNEER Innovations Series, Begell House Publishing, ISBN 978-0-9741252-8-2, pp. 29-42

Kornecki, A., Hilburn, T., Grega, W., Thiriet, J-M., Sveda, M., (2008) "A Common US-Europe Curriculum: an Approach for Real-Time Software Intensive Systems", *Proceedings of the 2008 ASEE Annual Conference & Exposition*, Pittsburgh, PA, Jun 22-25, 2008, pp. 1359-1371

Pilat, A., Kornecki, A., Thiriet, J-M., Grega, W., Sveda, M., (2008) "Industry Feedback on Skills and Knowledge in Real-Time Software Engineering" *19th EAEEIE Annual Conference*, Tallinn, Estonia, June 29 - July 2, 2008, pp. 129-133, ISBN: 978-1-4244-2009-4

Hilburn, T.B., Kornecki, A.J., Thiriet, J.-M., Grega W., Sveda, M. (2008) "An RSIC-SE2004 Curriculum Framework." *Proceedings International Multiconference on Computer Science and Information Technology - Real-Time Software, IMCSIT*, Wisla, Poland, 2008, pp. 633-638

Kornecki, A., Hilburn, T., Grega, W., Thiriet, J-M., Sveda, M. (2009), "ILERT - International Learning Environment for Real-Time Software-Intensive Control Systems", *JAMRIS - Journal of Automation, Mobile Robotics and Intelligent Systems*, ISSN 1897-8649, Vol. 3, No. 3, 2009, pp. 66-71

SACS (2007). *The Principles of Accreditation: Foundations for Quality Enhancement*, Commission on Colleges, Southern Association of Colleges and Schools, December 2007. (April 20, 2009, from the Website http://www.sacscoc.org/pdf/2008PrinciplesofAccreditation.pdf)

Methodology To Develop Alternative Makespan Algorithm For Re-entrant Flow Shop Using Bottleneck Approach

Salleh Ahmad Bareduan and Sulaiman Hj Hasan
Universiti Tun Hussein Onn Malaysia, Malaysia

1. Introduction

The Flow shop manufacturing is a very common production system found in many manufacturing facilities, assembly lines and industrial processes. It is known that finding an optimal solution for a flow shop scheduling problem is a difficult task (Lian *et al.*, 2008) and even a basic problem of $F3 \mid\mid C_{max}$ is already strongly NP-hard (Pinedo, 2002). Therefore, many researchers have concentrated their efforts on finding near optimal solution within acceptable computation time using heuristics.

One of the important subclass of flow shop which is quite prominent in industries is re-entrant flow shop. The special feature of a re-entrant flow shop compared to ordinary flow shop is that the job routing may return one or more times to any facility. Among the researchers on re-entrant flow shop, Graves et al. (1983) has developed a cyclic scheduling method that takes advantage of the flow character of the re-entrant process. This work illustrated a re-entrant flow shop model of a semiconductor wafer manufacturing process and developed a heuristic algorithm to minimize average throughput time using cyclic scheduling method at specified production rate. The decomposition technique in solving maximum lateness problem for re-entrant flow shop with sequence dependent setup times was suggested by Dermirkol & Uzsoy (2000). Mixed integer heuristic algorithms was later elaborated by Pan & Chen (2003) in minimizing makespan of a permutation flow shop scheduling problem. Significant works on re-entrant hybrid flow shop can be found in Yura (1999), Pearn et al. (2004) and Choi et al. (2005) while hybrid techniques which combine lower bound-based algorithm and idle time-based algorithm was reported by Choi & Kim (2008).

In scheduling literature, heuristic that utilize the bottleneck approach is known to be among the most successful methods in solving shop scheduling problem. This includes shifting bottleneck heuristic (Adams et al., 1988),(Mukherjee & Chatterjee, 2006) and bottleneck minimal idleness heuristic (Kalir & Sarin, 2001)(Wang et al., 2006). However, not much progress is reported on bottleneck approach in solving re-entrant flow shop problem.

Among the few researches are Dermirkol & Uzsoy (2000) who developed a specific version of shifting bottleneck heuristic to solve the re-entrant flow shop sequence problem.

This chapter explores and investigates an Internet based collaborative design and manufacturing process scheduling which resembles a four machine permutation re-entrant flow shop. It presents the methodology to develop an effective makespan computation algorithm using bottleneck analysis. This computation is specifically intended for the cyber manufacturing centre at Universiti Tun Hussein Onn Malaysia (UTHM).

2. Cyber Manufacturing Centre

UTHM has developed a web-based system that allows the university to share the sophisticated and advanced machinery and software available at the university with the small and medium enterprises using Internet technology (Bareduan et al., 2006). The heart of the system is the cyber manufacturing centre (CMC) which consists of an advanced computer numerical control (CNC) machining centre fully equipped with cyber manufacturing system software that includes computer aided design and computer aided manufacturing (CAD/CAM) system, scheduling system, tool management system and machine monitoring system.

The Petri net (PN) model that describes a typical design and manufacturing activities at the CMC is shown in Fig. 1. The places denoted by P22, P23, P24 and P25 in Fig. 1 are the resources utilized at the CMC. These resources are the CAD system, CAM system, CNC postprocessor and CNC machine centre respectively. At the CMC, all jobs must go through all processes following the sequence represented in the PN model. This flow pattern is very much similar with flow shop manufacturing (Onwubolu, 1996 and Pinedo, 2002). However, it can be noticed from the PN model that there a few processes that share common resources. The process of generating CNC program for prototyping (T3) and the process of generating CNC program for customer (T5) are executed on the same CNC postprocessor (P24). Similarly, the processes of prototype machining (T4) and parts machining (T6) are executed on the same CNC machine centre. These indicate that there are re-entries at both CNC postprocessor (P24) and CNC machine centre (P25) for each job going through the CMC process activities. Thus, this process flow is considered as a re-entrant flow shop as described by Graves et al. (1983). It can also be noticed that both shared resources (P24 and P25) must completely finish the processing of a particular job at T5 and T6 before starting to process any new job at T3 and T4. This means that the CMC scheduling will always follow the permutation rule in executing its functions. In other words, considering all characteristics of the CMC, this problem can be identified as four machine permutation re-entrant flow shop with the processing route of M1,M2,M3,M4,M3,M4 as similarly described by Yang et al. (2008).

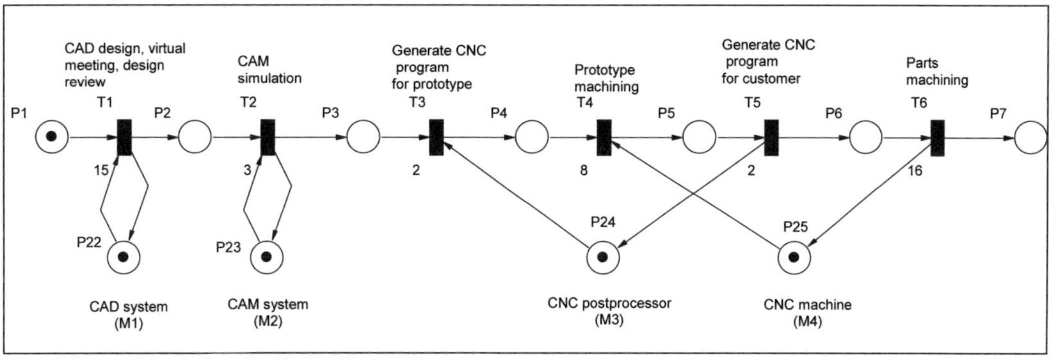

Fig. 1. Petri Net Model of CMC activities

3. Absolute Bottleneck Analysis

Let say, the CMC is currently having four jobs that need to be processed. Typical processing time ranges for all processes are shown in Table 1. From this table, it is obvious that most probably $P(1,j)$ is the bottleneck for the overall process because it is having the longest processing time range. By using the time ranges in Table 1, sets of random data was generated for four jobs that need to be processed. These data is shown in Table 2. Assuming that the data in Table 2 is arranged in the order of First-come-first-served (FCFS), then a Gantt chart representing a FCFS schedule is built as illustrated in Fig. 2. The Gantt chart is built by strictly referring to the PN model in Fig. 1 together with strict permutation rule.

	$P(1,j)$	$P(2,j)$	$P(3,j)$	$P(4,j)$	$P(5,j)$	$P(6,j)$
Minimum time	70	2	2	8	2	8
Maximum time	100	8	8	40	8	40

Table 1. Processing Time Range (hr)

	$P(1,j)$	$P(2,j)$	$P(3,j)$	$P(4,j)$	$P(5,j)$	$P(6,j)$
Job A	73	8	3	8	5	30
Job B	90	2	5	32	5	32
Job C	98	2	3	8	8	17
Job D	75	6	3	36	4	35

Table 2. Processing Time Data (hr)

Referring to Table 2, Figure 1 and Figure 2, the scheduling algorithm for the CMC can be written as the followings and is identified as Algorithm 1 (Bareduan & Hasan, 2008):

Algorithm 1

Let i = Process number or work centre number (i=1,2,3,....)
j = Job number (j=1,2,3,...)

Start (i,j) = start time of the jth job at i^{th} work centre.
Stop (i,j) = stop time of the jth job at i^{th} work centre.
P(i,j) = processing time of the jth job at i^{th} work centre.

For i=1,2,5,6 and j=1,2,3,…n
Start (i,j) = Max [Stop $(i,j-1)$, Stop $(i-1,j)$] except Start (1,1) = initial starting time
Stop (i,j) = Start (i,j) + P (i,j)

For i =3,4 and j=1,2,3,…n
Start (i,j) = Max [Stop $(i,j-1)$, Stop $(i-1,j)$, Stop $(i+2,j-1)$]
Stop (i,j) = Start (i,j) + P(i,j)

Work centre (resource)	Job	Time (hours)																		
		0	24	48	72	96	120	144	168	192	216	240	264	288	312	336	360	384	408	432
1 (M1)	JA	24	24	24	1															
	JB				23	24	24	19												
	JC							5	24	24	24	21								
	JD											3	24	24	24					
2 (M2)	JA				8															
	JB							2												
	JC											2								
	JD															6				
3 (M3)	JA				3															
	JB							3	2											
	JC											1	2							
	JD															3				
4 (M4)	JA				8															
	JB								22	10										
	JC												8							
	JD															15	21			
5 (M3)	JA				4	1														
	JB									5										
	JC												8							
	JD																3	1		
6 (M4)	JA					23	7													
	JB									9	23									
	JC												6	11						
	JD																	23	12	

Fig. 2. Gantt Chart for ABCD Job Sequence

Upon thorough study on the schedule Gantt chart at Fig. 2 inwhich $P(1,j)$ appears to be the clear bottleneck, a general makespan computation algorithm for the example problems can be described as below:

$$C_{max} = \sum_{j=1}^{n} P(1,j) \quad + \quad \sum_{i=2}^{6} P(i,n) \tag{1}$$

The bottleneck of $P(1, j)$ in Fig. 2 is represented by the value of $\sum_{j=1}^{n} P(1,j)$ in Equation (1).

Since $\sum_{j=1}^{n} P(1,j)$ will always result to the same value at any job sequence, then the makespan is directly influenced by $\{P(2,n) + P(3,n) + P(4,n) + P(5,n) + P(6,n)\}$ which is the sum of the second, third, fourth, fifth and sixth task processing time for the last job.

Equation (1) is similar with completion time algorithm described by Ho & Gupta (1995) and Cepek *et al.* (2002) for the problem $Fm \mid ddm \mid \gamma$. They illustrated the scheduling sequence of decreasing dominant machine (*ddm*) which follows the criteria of Min{j=1,2…n}[$P(k, j)$] ≥ Max{j=1,2…n}[$P(r, j)$]. While these two researches concentrated on strict *ddm* flow shop case study, this chapter focuses on the problem of a special type of flow shop which is known as re-entrant flow shop that exhibits dominant or bottleneck machine characteristics.

To illustrate the usage of Equation (1), the data in Table 2 is used to compute the makespan for the scheduling sequence of DCBA.

$$\begin{aligned} C_{max}\,(\text{DCBA}) &= \{P(1,1) + P(1,2) + P(1,3) + P(1,4)\} \\ &\quad + \{P(2,4) + P(3,4) + P(4,4) + P(5,4) + P(6,4)\} \\ &= \{75 + 98 + 90 + 73\} + \{8 + 3 + 8 + 5 + 30\} \\ &= 390 \text{ hours} \end{aligned}$$

Equation (1) can also be used to obtain the optimum job sequence. This is achieved by assigning the last job sequence to the job that has the smallest value of $\{P(2,j) + P(3,j) + P(4,j) + P(5,j) + P(6,j)\}$ (Bareduan et al., 2008). From Table 2, it can be noticed that Job C has the smallest value of $\{P(2,j) + P(3,j) + P(4,j) + P(5,j) + P(6,j)\}$. Therefore, by assigning Job C as the last sequence, an optimal schedule can be expected. The job sequences that end up with Job C as the last sequence are ABDC, ADBC, BADC, BDAC, DABC and DBAC. The makespan computation for ABDC sequence using Equation (1) is as the followings:

$$\begin{aligned} C_{max}\,(\text{ABDC}) &= \{P(1,1) + P(1,2) + P(1,3) + P(1,4)\} \\ &\quad + \{P(2,4) + P(3,4) + P(4,4) + P(5,4) + P(6,4)\} \\ &= \{73 + 90 + 75 + 98\} + \{2 + 3 + 8 + 8 + 17\} \\ &= 374 \text{ hours} \end{aligned}$$

Job Sequence	Makespan (hr)	Job Sequence	Makespan (hr)	Job Sequence	Makespan (hr)	Job Sequence	Makespan (hr)
ABCD	420	ABDC	374	ACDB	412	BCDA	390
ACBD	420	ADBC	374	ADCB	412	BDCA	390
BACD	420	BADC	374	CADB	412	CBDA	390
BCAD	420	BDAC	374	CDAB	412	CDBA	390
CABD	420	DABC	374	DACB	412	DBCA	390
CBAD	420	DBAC	374	DCAB	412	DCBA	390

Table 3. Makespan for different job sequences using Algorithm 1

In searching for the optimum solution for the 4 job problems in Table 2, a complete enumeration consisting of 24 schedule sequences representing ABCD, ABDC, BADC, etc arrangements were investigated. Algorithm 1 was used to obtain the makespan for all possible sequences and the results are shown in Table 3. From this table, it is noticed that 374 hours is the minimum makespan value and this value belongs to all sequences that end up with Job C as the last sequence. This indicates that minimum makespan solution provided by Equation (1) in the specific example problem of Table 2 is correct. A further detail observation of Equation (1) suggests that this equation works well for CMC makespan computation under a strict bottleneck conditions. The conditions are imposed to ensure that all first tasks of the CMC activities ($P(1, j)$) are always the bottleneck. These conditions are identified as absolute bottleneck in which regardless of any job sequence arrangement, $P(1,j)$ without fails are always the schedule bottleneck. The absolute bottleneck conditions of Equation (1) are written as the followings:

$$\text{Max}\{j=1\ldots n\}[\,P(2,j)\,] \leq \text{Min}\{j=1\ldots n\}[\,P(1,j)\,] \tag{2}$$

$$\text{Max}\{j=1\ldots n\}[P(2,j)+P(3,j)+P(4,j)+P(5,j)] \leq \text{Min}\{j=1\ldots n\}[P(1,j)+P(2,j)] \tag{3}$$

$$\text{Max}\{j=1\ldots n\}[P(2,j)+P(3,j)+P(4,j)+P(5,j)+P(6,j)] \leq \text{Min}\{j=1\ldots n\}[P(1,j)+P(2,j)+P(3,j)] \tag{4}$$

Condition (2) implies that every job takes less time going through task 2 compares to any job going through task 1. It functions to make sure that no matter how the jobs are arranged, $P(2,j)$ will never imposed a bottleneck to the system. $P(2,j)$ will always complete earlier than $P(1,j+1)$ and this guarantees that task 2 of any job can immediately begins after the completion of its task 1 process. This environment is illustrated in Fig. 3 in which X2 completes earlier than Y1. As a result, Y2 can begin immediately after the completion of Y1.

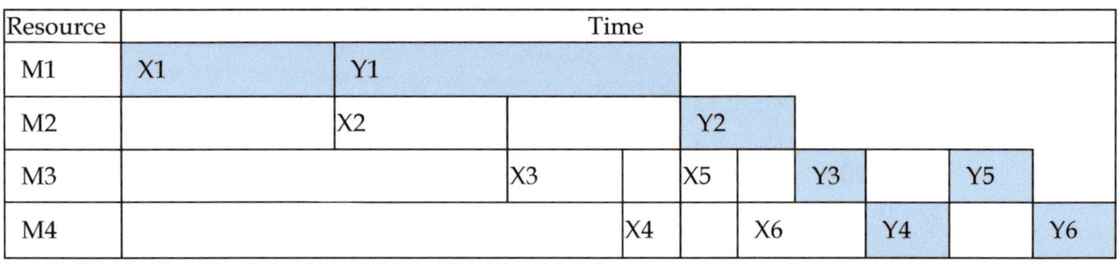

Fig. 3. Example schedule that fulfils (2), (3) and (4)

Condition (3) states that every job takes less time going through task 2, 3, 4 and 5 than any job going through task 1 and 2. This means that for a job X starting on task 2, and job Y starting at task 1 at the same time, this condition guarantees that job X would have released the CNC postprocessor M3 (refer Fig. 1) after its task 5 no later than when job Y needs the postprocessor for its task 3. This is due to the fact that tasks 3 and 5 are sharing the same M3 CNC postprocessor. However, this achievement is only guaranteed if (2) is also satisfied. Fig. 3 also illustrates the example of a schedule that fulfils (3). In this figure, Y3 can begin immediately after completion of Y2 because Y1+Y2 is longer than or equal to X2+X3+X4+X5.

Similarly, condition (4) implies that every job takes less time going through task 2, 3, 4, 5 and 6 than any job going through task 1, 2 and 3. This means that for a job X starting on task 2, and job Y starting at task 1 at the same time, this condition guarantees that job X would have released CNC machine M4 (refer Fig. 1) after its task 6 no later than when job Y needs the CNC machine for its task 4. However, this achievement is only guaranteed if both Condition (2) and (3) are also satisfied. This is also shown in Fig. 3 in which

X2+X3+X4+X5+X6 is less or equal to Y1+Y2+Y3. As a result, it is guaranteed that Y4 can begin immediately after the completion of Y3.

Condition (2), (3) and (4) were then tested on the data from Table 2. The result of this test is shown in Table 4. It can be seen clearly that Condition (2) is satisfied by the values of all $P(2, j)$ which are always smaller than the minimum value of $P(1, j)$. At the same time Condition (3) is also satisfied by the value of $\sum_{i=2}^{5} P(i,j)$ for each job "j" which is never greater than the minimum value of $\sum_{i=1}^{2} P(i,j)$ over all jobs. Similarly, Condition (4) is not violated by looking at the fact that the value of $\sum_{i=2}^{6} P(i,j)$ for each job "j" is always smaller or equal to the minimum value of $\sum_{i=1}^{3} P(i,j)$.

	Condition (2)						Condition (3)		Condition (4)	
Job	$P(1,j)$	$P(2,j)$	$P(3,j)$	$P(4,j)$	$P(5,j)$	$P(6,j)$	$\sum_{i=1}^{2} P(i,j)$	$\sum_{i=2}^{5} P(i,j)$	$\sum_{i=1}^{3} P(i,j)$	$\sum_{i=2}^{6} P(i,j)$
Job A	73	8	3	8	5	30	81	24	84	54
Job B	90	2	5	32	5	32	92	44	97	76
Job C	98	2	3	8	8	17	100	21	103	38
Job D	75	6	3	36	4	35	81	49	84	84

Table 4. Condition (2), Condition (3) and Condition (4) observations

If a set of scheduling data fulfils Condition (2), (3) and (4), then Equation (1) can be used to calculate the schedule makespan as well as to find the job sequences that provide the optimum makespan. Strictly depending on the job sequence, the completion time for each job (C_j) then can be computed as the followings:

$$C_j = \sum_{k=1}^{j} P(1,k) \quad + \quad \sum_{i=2}^{6} P(i,j) \tag{5}$$

Using the data at Table 2, the completion time of Job B under DCBA job sequence can be computed using Equation (5) as the followings:

$$\begin{aligned} C_B &= \{P(1,1) + P(1,2) + P(1,3)\} \\ &\quad + \{P(2,3) + P(3,3) + P(4,3) + P(5,3) + P(6,3)\} \\ &= \{75 + 98 + 90\} + \{2 + 5 + 32 + 5 + 32\} \\ &= 339 \text{ hours} \end{aligned}$$

The explanations on the absolute bottleneck conditions indicate that Equation (1) produces accurate makespan computation result if Condition (2), Condition (3) and Condition (4) were met. In order to test this statement, a total of 10000 simulations for four job sequence were conducted using random data between 1 to 20 hours for each of $P(2,j)$, $P(3,j)$, $P(4,j)$, $P(5,j)$ and $P(6,j)$. The value of $P(1,j)$ were set to be between 1 to 100 in order to have a more evenly distributed matching of either Condition (2), Condition (3) and Condition (4) or any of their combinations. These simulations were conducted in Microsoft® Excel using Microsoft® Visual Basic for Application programming.

Each set of random data obtained was tested with a total of 24 different sequences that resembles the sequence arrangements of ABCD, ABDC, ACBD etc. This means that with 10000 simulations, a total of 240,000 job sequence arrangements were tested. The makespan results from Algorithm 1 were compared with the makespan value obtained from Equation (1). In analyzing the test result, a set of data is said to produce perfect result if all the 24 different job sequences makespan from Equation (1) are the same with Algorithm 1. The test analysis result is shown in Table 5. The results from the simulations showed that all makespan value from both Equation (1) and Algorithm 1 are equal for random data sets that fulfill all the three conditions. This indicates that Equation (1) produces accurate makespan computation if Condition (2), Condition (3) and Condition (4) were met. With all these three conditions met, we can conclude that $P(1, j)$ is the absolute bottleneck of the scheduling system. Then, Equation (1) can also be used to determine the optimum job sequences and Equation (5) can be used to calculate the completion time for each job.

Conditions Met	Sets of Data Fulfill The Conditions	Percentage of Perfect Result
4.7+4.8+4.9	900	100%
4.7+4.8	286	8.74%
4.7+4.9	185	19.46%
4.7	3729	1.13%
-	4898	0%

Table 5. Accuracy of Equation (1) at various conditions

4. Bottleneck Correction Factor

During the simulation process to investigate the accuracy of makespan computation using Equation (1) in relation with Condition (2), (3) and (4), it was observed that within a data set that violates these conditions, Equation (1) still produces accurate makespan result at some sequence arrangements but not on all of them. It is worth to investigate further whether there are rules or conditions that might be used to describe this phenomenon. This can only be done by comparing the makespan computation for all possible job sequences within the specific data set using both Algorithm 1 and Equation (1). A sample of data set that exhibits this phenomenon is illustrated in Table 6 in which, Condition (4) is violated. Table 7 shows the makespan computation of data from Table 6 using Algorithm 1 while Table 8 is the makespan computation using Equation (1).

	Condition (2)						Condition (3)		Condition (4)	
Job	$P(1,j)$	$P(2,j)$	$P(3,j)$	$P(4,j)$	$P(5,j)$	$P(6,j)$	$\sum_{i=1}^{2} P(i,j)$	$\sum_{i=2}^{5} P(i,j)$	$\sum_{i=1}^{3} P(i,j)$	$\sum_{i=2}^{6} P(i,j)$
Job A	73	8	3	8	5	30	81	24	84	54
Job B	90	2	5	32	5	32	92	44	97	76
Job C	98	2	3	35	8	39	100	48	103	87
Job D	75	6	3	36	4	35	81	49	84	84

Table 6. Condition (4) violations

Job Sequence	Makespan (hr)	Job Sequence	Makespan (hr)	Job Sequence	Makespan (hr)	Job Sequence	Makespan (hr)
ABCD	423	ABDC	423	ACDB	412	BCDA	393
ACBD	420	ADBC	423	ADCB	412	BDCA	393
BACD	423	BADC	423	CADB	412	CBDA	390
BCAD	420	BDAC	423	CDAB	412	CDBA	390
CABD	420	DABC	423	DACB	412	DBCA	393
CBAD	420	DBAC	423	DCAB	412	DCBA	390

Table 7. Makespan computation using Algorithm 1

Job Sequence	Makespan (hr)	Job Sequence	Makespan (hr)	Job Sequence	Makespan (hr)	Job Sequence	Makespan (hr)
ABCD	420	ABDC	423	ACDB	412	BCDA	390
ACBD	420	ADBC	423	ADCB	412	BDCA	390
BACD	420	BADC	423	CADB	412	CBDA	390
BCAD	420	BDAC	423	CDAB	412	CDBA	390
CABD	420	DABC	423	DACB	412	DBCA	390
CBAD	420	DBAC	423	DCAB	412	DCBA	390

Table 8. Makespan computation using Equation (1)

Comparing Table 7 and Table 8, it can be noticed that majority of the makespan value using Equation (1) are equal with the makespan value from Algorithm 1. This means that Equation (1) works very well with majority of the job sequences except ABCD, BACD, BCDA, BDCA and DBCA. In other words, even though Condition (4) is violated, Equation (1) still produces accurate makespan value for majority of the job sequences. To further investigate the failure characteristics of Equation (1) in computing the makespan of some job sequences, a detail analysis of the Gantt charts representing the job arrangements that were wrongly computed by the equation was conducted. During the analysis, it was observed that Equation (1) is still valid for makespan computation if some localized sequence dependent conditions were met. These localized sequence dependent conditions for the 4-job example case in Table 6 are (Bareduan & Hasan, 2008):

$$P(1,2) + P(1,3) + P(1,4) \geq VP(2,1) + VP(2,2) + VP(2,3) \quad (6)$$

$$P(1,2) + P(1,3) + P(1,4) + P(2,4) \geq P(2,1) + VP(3,1) + VP(3,2) + VP(3,3) \quad (7)$$

$$P(1,2)+P(1,3)+P(1,4)+P(2,4)+P(3,4) \\ \geq P(2,1)+P(3,1)+VP(4,1)+VP(4,2)+VP(4,3) \quad (8)$$

where VP = Virtual Processing Time.

Condition (6) is meant to make sure that for the last job sequence, task 2 can immediately be started as soon as task 1 completed its process. For example, if Condition (6) is violated, $P(2,n\text{-}1)$ completion time is later than the completion time of $P(1,n)$, this means that $P(2,n)$ cannot start immediately after the completion of $P(1,n)$. It can only begin after the completion of $P(2,n\text{-}1)$ which is also indicated by the completion time of $VP(2,n\text{-}1)$. This introduces a delay between $P(1,n)$ and $P(2,n)$ thus affecting the accuracy of Equation (1). Fig. 4 shows an example schedule that violates Condition (6). The completion time of *P23* which is later than the completion time of *P14* prevents *P24* from starting immediately after the completion of *P14*.

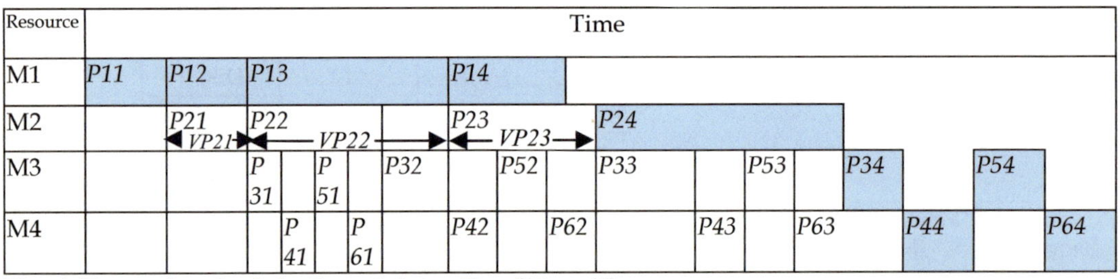

Fig. 4. Example schedule that violates Condition (6)

The virtual processing times for task 2 in Condition (6) are assigned as the followings:

$$\text{For } j = 1,\ VP(2,1) = \text{Max}\,[\,P(2,1), P(1,2)\,]$$

$$\text{For } j = 2,3\ldots n\text{-}1,\ VP(2,j) = \\ Max\left[\left[\sum_{k=1}^{j-1} VP(2,k)\right]+P(2,j), \left[\sum_{k=2}^{j+1} P(1,k)\right]\right]-\sum_{k=1}^{j-1} VP(2,k) \quad (9)$$

Condition (7) functions to ensure that for the last job sequence, task 3 can immediately be started as soon as task 2 completed its process. For example, if Condition (7) is violated, this means that the right side value of this condition is larger than its left side value. Since *P*3 and *P*5 are sharing the same M3 processor (refer Fig. 1), the violation of Condition (7) will result to a later completion time of $P(5,n\text{-}1)$ compares to the completion time of $P(2,n)$. Consequently, $P(3,n)$ cannot start immediately after the completion of $P(2,n)$. It can only begin after the completion of $P(5,n\text{-}1)$ which is the completion time of $VP(3,n\text{-}1)$. This introduces a delay between $P(2,n)$ and $P(3,n)$ thus affecting the accuracy of Equation (1). Fig. 5 shows an example schedule that violates Condition (7). The completion time of *P53* which is later than the completion time of *P24* prevents *P34* from starting immediately after the completion of *P24*.

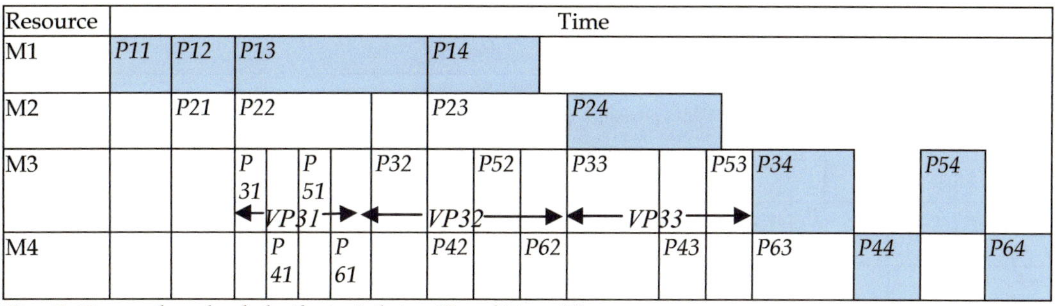

Fig. 5. Example schedule that violates Condition (7)

The virtual processing times for task 3 are assigned as the followings:

$$\text{For } j = 1,\ VP(3,1) = \text{Max}\,[\{VP(2,1) + P(2,2)\},\{P(2,1) + P(3,1) + P(4,1) + P(5,1)\}] - P(2,1)$$

$$\text{For } j = 2,3\ldots n\text{-}1,\quad VP(3,j) =$$

$$Max\left[\begin{array}{l}\left[\sum_{k=1}^{j} VP(2,k)\right] + P(2,j+1), \left[P(2,1) + \sum_{k=1}^{j-1} VP(3,k) + \sum_{i=3}^{5} P(i,j)\right], \\ P(2,1) + P(3,1) + \sum_{k=1}^{j-1} VP(4,k) + \sum_{i=4}^{5} P(i,j)\end{array}\right] - \tag{10}$$

$$\left[P(2,1) + \sum_{k=1}^{j-1} VP(3,k)\right]$$

Condition (8) functions to guarantee that for the last job sequence, task 4 can immediately be started as soon as task 3 completed its process. For example, if Condition (8) is violated, this means that the right side value of this condition is larger than its left side value. Since *P4* and *P6* are sharing the same M4 CNC machine (refer Fig. 1), the violation of Condition (8) will result to a later completion time of $P(6,n\text{-}1)$ compares to the completion time of $P(3,n)$. Consequently, $P(4,n)$ cannot start immediately after the completion of $P(3,n)$. It can only begin after the completion of $P(6,n\text{-}1)$ which is indicated by the completion time of $VP(4,n\text{-}1)$. This introduces a delay between $P(3,n)$ and $P(4,n)$ thus affecting the accuracy of Equation (1). Fig. 6 shows an example schedule that violates Condition (8). The completion time of *P63* which is later than the completion time of *P34* prevents *P44* from starting immediately after the completion of *P34*.

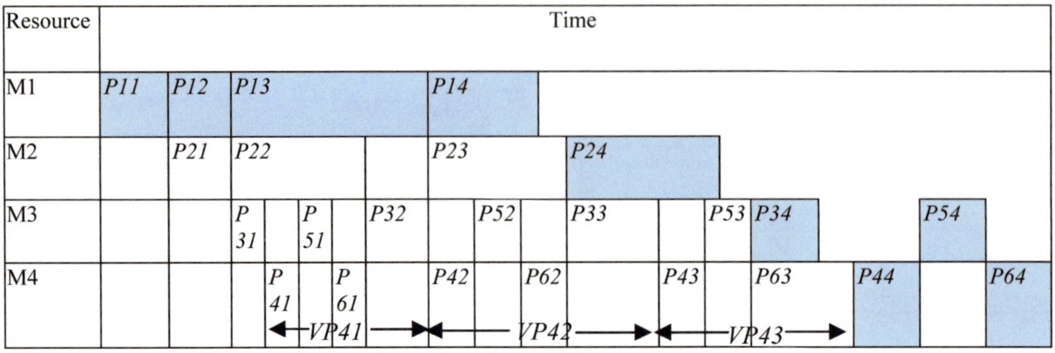

Fig. 6. Example schedule that violates Condition (8)

The virtual processing time for task 4 are assigned as the followings:

$$\text{For } j = 1,\ VP(4,1) =$$

$$\text{Max } [\{VP(3,1) + P(3,2)\},\{P(3,1) + P(4,1) + P(5,1) + P(6,1)\}] - P(3,1)$$

$$\text{For } j = 2,3\ldots n\text{-}1,\ VP(4,j) =$$

$$Max\left[\left[\sum_{k=1}^{j} VP(3,k)\right] + P(3,j+1), \left[P(3,1) + \sum_{k=1}^{j-1} VP(4,k) + \sum_{i=4}^{6} P(i,j)\right]\right] - \left[P(3,1) + \sum_{k=1}^{j-1} VP(4,k)\right] \quad (11)$$

If any of the Condition (6), (7) and (8) is violated, Equation (1) is no longer valid for the makespan computation. This equation has to be modified and improved by introducing a dedicated correction factor in order to absorb the violated conditions if it is still to be used for makespan computation beyond the above stipulated conditions.

Detail observations of Condition (6), (7) and (8) reveal that the inaccuracy of Equation (1) due to the violation of Condition (6) is inclusive in Condition (7). Similarly, the error of Equation (1) resulted from the violation of Condition (7) is also inclusive in Condition (8). These are due to the fact that the computations of $VP(4,j)$ in Condition (8) are inclusive of all errors resulting from violations of both Condition (6) and (7). As such, by evaluating and monitoring only Condition (8), all the errors of Equation (1) resulted from the violations of either Conditions (6), (7) and (8) or their combinations are actually covered.

Job	j	$P(1,j)$	$P(2,j)$	$P(3,j)$	$P(4,j)$	$P(5,j)$	$P(6,j)$
Job A	1	73	8	3	8	5	30
Job B	2	90	2	5	32	5	32
Job C	3	98	2	3	35	8	39
Job D	4	75	6	3	36	4	35

	A	B	C	D	E	F	G	H	K
j	Sum $P(1,k)$ $k=2, j+1$ For $j=1,2..n-1$	$VP(2,j)$ For $j=1,2..n-1$	Sum $VP(2,k)$ $k=1, j-1$ For $j=2,3..n-1$	Sum $VP(2,k)$ $k=1, j$ For $j=1,2..n-1$	$VP(3,j)$ For $j=1,2..n-1$	Sum $VP(3,k)$ $k=1, j-1$ For $j=2,3..n-1$	Sum $VP(3,k)$ $k=1, j$ For $j=1,2..n-1$	$VP(4,j)$ For $j=1,2..n-1$	Sum $VP(4,k)$ $k=1, j-1$ For $j=2,3..n-1$
1	90	90		90	84		84	86	
2	188	98	90	188	98	84	182	96	86
3	263	75	188	263	79	182	261	82	182

Table 9. Table for makespan computation

Table 9 is developed in order to determine the values of $VP(2,j)$, $VP(3,j)$ and $VP(4,j)$ from the data in Table 6. These values will be used to monitor Condition (8). Referring to Table 9, Cell B1 represents $VP(2,1)$. This is computed using Equation (9) as the followings:

For $j = 1$, $VP(2,1) = \text{Max}\,[P(2,1), P(1,2)]$
$= \text{Max}\,[8,90]$
$= 90$

Cell B2 represents $VP(2,2)$. This is also computed using Equation (9) as the followings:

For $j = 2,3\ldots n-1$,

$$VP(2,j) = Max\left[\left[\sum_{k=1}^{j-1} VP(2,k)\right] + P(2,j), \left[\sum_{k=2}^{j+1} P(1,k)\right]\right] - \sum_{k=1}^{j-1} VP(2,k)$$

Therefore,

$$VP(2,2) = Max\left[\left[\sum_{k=1}^{2-1} VP(2,k)\right] + P(2,2), \left[\sum_{k=2}^{2+1} P(1,k)\right]\right] - \sum_{k=1}^{2-1} VP(2,k)$$

$= \text{Max}\,[\text{C2} + P(2,2), \text{A2}] - \text{D1}$
$= \text{Max}\,[90 + 2, 188] - 90$
$= 188 - 90$
$= 98$

Using the same equation, Cell B3 is computed as follows:

$VP(2,3) = \text{Max}\,[\text{C3} + P(2,3), \text{A3}] - \text{D2}$
$= \text{Max}\,[188 + 2, 263] - 188$
$= 263 - 188$
$= 75$

The value for $VP(3,1)$ which belongs to Cell E1 is computed using Equation (10) as the followings:

For $j = 1$, $VP(3,1)$ = Max [{$VP(2,1) + P(2,2)$}, {$P(2,1) + P(3,1) + P(4,1) + P(5,1)$}] - $P(2,1)$
= Max [{90 + 2}, {8+3+8+5}] - 8
= Max [92, 24] - 8
= 92 - 8
= 84

Cell E2 represents $VP(3,2)$. This is also computed using Equation (10) as the followings:
For $j = 2,3\ldots n\text{-}1$, $VP(3,j)$ =

$$Max\begin{bmatrix}\left[\sum_{k=1}^{j} VP(2,k)\right] + P(2,j+1), \left[P(2,1) + \sum_{k=1}^{j-1} VP(3,k) + \sum_{i=3}^{5} P(i,j)\right], \\ P(2,1) + P(3,1) + \sum_{k=1}^{j-1} VP(4,k) + \sum_{i=4}^{5} P(i,j)\end{bmatrix} - \left[P(2,1) + \sum_{k=1}^{j-1} VP(3,k)\right]$$

Therefore,

$VP(3,2)$ =

$$Max\begin{bmatrix}\left[\sum_{k=1}^{2} VP(2,k)\right] + P(2,2+1), \left[P(2,1) + \sum_{k=1}^{2-1} VP(3,k) + \sum_{i=3}^{5} P(i,2)\right], \\ P(2,1) + P(3,1) + \sum_{k=1}^{2-1} VP(4,k) + \sum_{i=4}^{5} P(i,2)\end{bmatrix} - \left[P(2,1) + \sum_{k=1}^{2-1} VP(3,k)\right]$$

= Max [{D2 + $P(2,3)$}, {$P(2,1)$ + F2 + $P(3,2) + P(4,2) + P(5,2)$},
{$P(2,1) + P(3,1)$ + K2 + $P(4,2) + P(5,2)$}] - {$P(2,1)$ + F2}
= Max [{188 + 2}, {8 + 84 + 5 + 32 + 5}, {8 + 3 + 86 + 32 + 5}] - {8 + 84}
= Max [190, 134, 134] - 92
= 190 - 92
= 98

$VP(3,3)$
= Max [{D3 + $P(2,4)$}, {$P(2,1)$ + F3 + $P(3,3) + P(4,3) + P(5,3)$},
{$P(2,1) + P(3,1)$ + K3 + $P(4,3) + P(5,3)$}] - {$P(2,1)$ + F3}
= Max [{263 + 6}, {8 + 182 + 3 + 35 + 8}, {8 + 3 + 182 + 35 + 8}] - {8 + 182}
= Max [269, 236, 236] - 190
= 269 - 190
= 79

Referring again to Table 9, Cell H1 represents $VP(4,1)$. This is computed using Equation (11) as the followings:

For $j = 1$, $VP(4,1)$ = Max [{$VP(3,1) + P(3,2)$}, {$P(3,1) + P(4,1) + P(5,1) + P(6,1)$}] - $P(3,1)$
= Max [{84 + 5}, {3 + 8 + 5 + 30}] - 3
= Max [89, 46] - 3
= 89 - 3
= 86

Cell H2 represents $VP(4,2)$. This is also computed using Equation (11) as the followings:

For $j = 2,3\ldots n\text{-}1$, $VP(4,j) =$

$$Max\left[\left[\sum_{k=1}^{j} VP(3,k)\right] + P(3,j+1), \left[P(3,1) + \sum_{k=1}^{j-1} VP(4,k) + \sum_{i=4}^{6} P(i,j)\right]\right] - \left[P(3,1) + \sum_{k=1}^{j-1} VP(4,k)\right]$$

Therefore, $VP(4,2) =$

$$Max\left[\left[\sum_{k=1}^{2} VP(3,k)\right] + P(3,2+1), \left[P(3,1) + \sum_{k=1}^{2-1} VP(4,k) + \sum_{i=4}^{6} P(i,2)\right]\right] - \left[P(3,1) + \sum_{k=1}^{2-1} VP(4,k)\right]$$

= Max [{G2 + $P(3,3)$}, {$P(3,1)$ + K2 + $P(4,2)$ + $P(5,2)$ + $P(6,2)$}] - {$P(3,1)$ + K2}
= Max [{182 + 3}, {3 + 86 + 32 + 5 + 32}] - {3 + 86}
= Max [185, 158] - 89
= 185 - 89
= 96

$VP(4,3)$
= Max [{G3 + $P(3,4)$}, {$P(3,1)$ + K3 + $P(4,3)$ + $P(5,3)$ + $P(6,3)$}] - { $P(3,1)$ + K3}
= Max [{261 +3}, {3 + 182 + 35 + 8 + 39}] - {3 + 182}
= Max [264, 267] - 185
= 267 - 185
= 82

The values of $VP(2, j)$, $VP(3, j)$ and $VP(4, j)$ from Table 9 are used to detect the occurrences of bottleneck at processes other than $P(1, j)$. In other words, this table will be used to suggest the correction factor need to be added to Equation (1) if the previously described Condition (8) is violated. This correction factor is computed as the followings:

From Condition (8):

$$P(1,2) + P(1,3) + P(1,4) + P(2,4) + P(3,4) \geq P(2,1) + P(3,1) + VP(4,1) + VP(4,2) + VP(4,3)$$

If Condition (8) is violated, it means:

$$P(1,2) + P(1,3) + P(1,4) + P(2,4) + P(3,4) < P(2,1) + P(3,1) + VP(4,1) + VP(4,2) + VP(4,3)$$

Therefore, the correction factor ($P1BCF$) is:

$$P1BCF = \{P(2,1) + P(3,1) + VP(4,1) + VP(4,2) + VP(4,3)\} - \{P(1,2) + P(1,3) + P(1,4) + P(2,4) + P(3,4)\}$$

If $\{P(2,1) + P(3,1) + VP(4,1) + VP(4,2) + VP(4,3)\} - \{P(1,2) + P(1,3) + P(1,4) + P(2,4) + P(3,4)\} < 0$ then, $P1BCF = 0$

The general formulation of the correction factor is written as the following:

$$P1BCF = \text{Max}\left[0, \sum_{i=2}^{3} P(i,1) \quad + \quad \sum_{j=1}^{n-1} VP(4,j) \quad - \quad \sum_{j=2}^{n} P(1,j) \quad - \quad \sum_{i=2}^{3} P(i,n)\right] \tag{12}$$

where, *P1BCF* = Process 1 Bottleneck Correction Factor

With the introduction of *P1BCF*, then the generalized makespan computation algorithm for the CMC is:

$$C_{max} = \sum_{j=1}^{n} P(1,j) \quad + \quad \sum_{i=2}^{6} P(i,n) \quad + P1BCF \tag{13}$$

By using Equation 4.11 and 4.12, the makespan computation for the ABCD job sequence in Table 9 is as the followings:

$$\begin{aligned} P1BCF &= \text{Max}\ [0, \{P(2,1) + P(3,1)\} + \{VP(4,1) + VP(4,2) + VP(4,3)\} \\ &\qquad - \{P(1,2) + P(1,3) + P(1,4)\} - \{P(2,4) + P(3,4)\}] \\ &= \text{Max}\ [0, \{8 + 3\} + \{86 + 96 + 82\} - \{90 + 98 + 75\} - \{6 + 3\}] \\ &= \text{Max}\ [0, 3] \\ &= 3 \text{ hours} \end{aligned}$$

Therefore, the makespan is equal to:

$$\begin{aligned} C_{max}\,(\text{ABCD}) &= \{P(1,1) + P(1,2) + P(1,3) + P(1,4)\} \\ &\quad + \{P(2,4) + P(3,4) + P(4,4) + P(5,4) + P(6,4)\} + P1BCF \\ &= \{73 + 90 + 98 + 75\} + \{6 + 3 + 36 + 4 + 35\} + 3 \\ &= 336 + 84 + 3 = 423 \text{ hours} \end{aligned}$$

The makespan of 423 hours is equal to the results using Algorithm 1 as in Table 7 for ABCD job sequence. This shows that Equation (13) is capable to perform accurate makespan computation even if the absolute bottleneck condition is violated. To verify the accuracy of Equation (13) in performing the makespan computations, a total of 10,000 simulations were conducted using random data of between 1 to 80 hours for each of $P(1,j)$, $P(2,j)$, $P(3,j)$, $P(4,j)$, $P(5,j)$ and $P(6,j)$ with four job sequence for each simulation. These simulations were conducted in Microsoft® Excel using Microsoft® Visual Basic for Application programming. Each set of random data obtained was also tested with a total of 24 different sequences that resembles the sequence arrangement of ABCD, ABDC, ACBD etc. This means that with 10000 sets of random data, a total of 240,000 job sequence arrangements were tested. The makespan results from using Equation (13) were compared with the makespan value obtained from Algorithm 1. The results from the comparisons showed that all makespan value from both Equation (13) and Algorithm 1 are equal. This indicates that Equation (13) produces accurate makespan results for 4-job CMC scheduling problem. Equation (13) was also tested for computing the makespan for 6-job, 10-job and 20-job CMC scheduling. Each test was conducted with 10,000 sets of random data between 1 to 80 hours for each of $P(1,j)$, $P(2,j)$, $P(3,j)$, $P(4,j)$, $P(5,j)$ and $P(6,j)$. Each set of random data obtained was also tested with different sequences that resemble the sequence arrangement of ABCDEF, ABCDFE, ABCEDF etc. All results indicate that Equation (13) produces makespan value equal the results of Algorithm 1. This shows the accuracy of Equation (13) in computing the makespan of the CMC scheduling arrangements.

5. Conclusion

This chapter presented the methodology to develop an effective makespan computation algorithm using bottleneck analysis for M1,M2,M3,M4,M3,M4 permutation re-entrant flow shop in which M1 has high tendency of exhibiting bottleneck characteristics. It was shown that under the absolute bottleneck characteristics, both the makespan and optimum job sequence can be accurately determined by the makespan algorithms developed using bottleneck analysis. In cases where the absolute bottleneck condition is violated, the makespan can still be accurately determined by the introduction of bottleneck correction factors. The bottleneck-based methodology or approach presented in this chapter is not only valid for the specific case study alone, but can also be utilised to develop alternative makespan algorithms for other flow shop operation systems that shows significant bottleneck characteristics. With the successful development of makespan computation method using bottleneck analysis, future work can be concentrated to further utilize the bottleneck approach in developing heuristic for optimizing the CMC re-entrant scheduling problems.

6. Acknowledgement

This work was partially supported by the Fundamental Research Grant Scheme (Ministry of Higher Education), Malaysia (Vot 0368, 2007).

7. References

Adams J, Balas E & Zawack D. (1988). The shifting bottleneck procedure for job shop scheduling, *Management Science,* 34, 391-401

Bareduan SA, Hasan SH, Rafai NH & Shaari MF. (2006). Cyber manufacturing system for small and medium enterprises: a conceptual framework, *Transactions of North American Manufacturing Research Institution for Society of Manufacturing Engineers,* 34, 365-372

Bareduan SA & Hasan SH. (2008). Makespan Computation for Cyber Manufacturing Centre Using Bottleneck Analysis: A Re-entrat Flow Shop Problem, Proceedings of International Multiconference of Engineers & Computer Scientists (IMECS 2008) Hong Kong, 19-21/3/2008, pp. 1644-1648

Bareduan SA, Hasan SH & Ariffin S. (2008). Finite scheduling of collaborative design and manufacturing activity: a Petri net approach, *Journal of Manufacturing Technology Management,* 19(2), 274-288

Cepek O, Okada M & Vlach M. (2002). Nonpreemptive Flowshop Scheduling With Machine Dominance, *European Journal of Operational Research.* 139, 245-261

Choi SW & Kim YD. (2008). Minimizing makespan on an *m*-machine re-entrant flowshop, *Computers & Operations Research,* 35(5), 1684-1696

Choi SW, Kim YD & Lee GC. (2005). Minimizing total tardiness of orders with reentrant lots in a hybrid flowshop, *International Journal of Production Research,* 43(11), 2149-2167

Demirkol E & Uzsoy R. (2000). Decomposition methods for reentrant flow shops with sequence dependent setup times, *Journal of Scheduling*, 3, 115-177

Graves SC, Meal HC, Stefek D & Zeghmi AH. (1983) Scheduling of re-entrant flow shops, *Journal of Operations Management*, 3(4), 197-207

Ho JC & Gupta JND. (1995). Flowshop Scheduling With Dominant Machines, *Computers and Operations Research*, 22(2), 237-246

Kalir AA & Sarin SC. (2001). A near optimal heuristic for the sequencing problem in multiple-batch flow-shops with small equal sublots. *Omega*, 29, 577-584

Lian Z, Gu X & Jiao B. (2008). A novel particle swarm optimization algorithm for permutation flow-shop scheduling to minimize makespan, *Chaos, Solitons and Fractals*, 35(5), 851-861

Mukherjee S & Chatterjee AK. (2006). Applying machine based decomposition in 2-machine flow shops, *European Journal of Operational Research*, 169, 723-741

Onwubolu GC. (1996). A flow-shop manufacturing scheduling system with interactive computer graphics, *International Journal of Operations & Production Management*, 16(9), 74-84

Pan JC & Chen JS. (2003). Minimizing makespan in re-entrant permutation flow-shops, *Journal of Operation Research Society*, 54(6), 642-653

Pearn WL, Chung SH, Chen AY & Yang MH. (2004). A case study on the multistage IC final testing scheduling problem with reentry, *International Journal of Production Economics*, 88(3), 257-267

Pinedo M. (2002). *Scheduling: Theory, algorithms, and systems*, 2nd ed., Upper Saddle River, N.J., Prentice-Hall

Wang JB, Shan F, Jiang B & Wang LY. (2006). Permutation flow shop scheduling with dominant machines to minimize discounted total weighted completion time, *Applied Mathematics and Computation*, 182(1), 947-954

Yang DL, Kuo WH & Chern MS. (2008). Multi-family scheduling in a two-machine re-entrant flow shop with setups, *European Journal of Operational Research*, 187(3), 1160-1170

Yura K. (1999). Cyclic scheduling for re-entrant manufacturing systems, *International Journal of Production Economics*, 60, 523-528

7

Flexible Design by Contract

Koen Vanderkimpen and Eric Steegmans
K.U.Leuven
Belgium

1. Introduction

Advances in computer science are made at many different levels and in many areas. One important area of research is reusability, a goal achievable in many ways, from the improvement of programming languages to the development and use of components off the shelve. In this chapter, we focus on methodology to improve reusability.

More precisely, we improve the practice of design by contract, a system of rules for specification of code that aims at improving reliability and clarity of code, two factors that contribute to reuse. The practice, however, conflicts with another practice, that of maximizing the adaptability of code, which is also an important factor to improve reuse. More on this conflict and on the limits of design by contract is explained in section 2.

Our first improvement to design by contract, the flexibility principle, aims to reconcile the methodology with adaptability. The second contribution, the distinction between restrictions and permissions, aims to improve the expressiveness of contracts.

The flexibility principle divides contract clauses between flexible and rigid clauses. The latter are inherited, the former are only valid in the containing class, which allows for more adaptations in subclasses. The second distinction, between restrictive and permissive clauses, allows splitting the domain of possible states for an object in three: a part that's valid, a part that's invalid, and a third left undefined, which can still be adapted in the future. Traditional contracts define only valid and invalid states, leaving little room for future change. We elaborate on our principle in section 3, defining the four important kinds of contract clauses (two times two) and their behaviour under inheritance.

Of course, a programming practice can reap great benefits of language support to make it more useful. That's why, in section 4, we introduce properties, part of our previous research, as the basis to which we will apply flexible design by contract. To do this, we demonstrate the readonly modifier for properties, and we show how this modifier is an application of our principle.

In section 5, we demonstrate the principle in full, applying it to the contract clauses of invariants, preconditions and postconditions. We demonstrate how our work improves the coherence of design by contract by creating symmetry between permissions and restrictions and the way they are strengthened or weakened in subclasses.

In section 6, we provide an evaluation of our work. Section 7 elaborates on a possible implementation. In section 8, we discuss related work, and we end with a conclusion and discussion of future work in section 9.

2. Problem Statement

The goal of design by contract, as explained in (Meyer, 1992), is to improve the reliability of software systems. The methodological guidelines enforce a relationship between the client and the supplier, here called the client and the developer. This reliability, however, comes at a price: the contract of a class can only be changed in certain specific ways that hamper the flexibility with which future changes can be made. Furthermore, a contract does not completely specify exactly what is correct, what is incorrect, and what is left undetermined.
This section first elaborates on the benefits of programming by contract and the detrimental effect of unbridled adaptability in the absence of contracts, and then explores both of the principle's problems of flexibility and expressivity.

2.1 Adaptability versus Contracts

To improve adaptability is often considered to be the best way to improving reusability. We can, for example, make systems as customizable as possible, so that they can be reused in many different ways by changing parameters and making adaptations to the code. This kind of adaptability is often found in large software systems that need to be customized for each client individually. It is often accomplished by putting hooks in the code, by which the normal control flow is interrupted and custom code injected. It can also be done by injecting code using aspect oriented software development. Inheritance, with its ability to override the current behaviour, is also a powerful tool to accomplish this.
Contracts pose a serious obstacle when implementing adaptability in such a way, because the behaviour of subroutines that leave hooks and other insertion points for foreign code, is difficult to predict and even more difficult to correctly specify. A contract would limit the options for inserted code, while the ability to insert code often limits what can be described in the contract, or even makes it impossible to create any contract.
Another way to improve reuse is to divide the system in reusable building blocks, called components, which perform certain tasks with high reliability and usually offer some form of abstraction. This abstraction allows the component to be reused in different ways, and in different systems. The reliability of the component, combined with good documentation, makes sure developers will want to reuse the component, because they know what it will do and they know that it will work. A good approach to achieving reliability in such components is the use of contracts. This principle not only improves robustness and correctness, two key components of reliability, by formalizing the component's behaviour, but also automatically provides developers with good documentation, which increases the potential for reuse by lowering the learning curve required to reuse the code. Software written with a clear contract will tell developers what it can and cannot do, so any potential reuse is more easily identified.
To conclude, adaptability and the use of contracts cannot easily be combined. The problem lies in the difficulty of writing a good contract to specify a component that is designed for high adaptability. This reason for this is that class contracts are usually about what is constant: what will always be true about a system; and the more adaptable we make a system, the fewer constant features it will have. We believe, however, in improving the reliability of software systems by the rigorous use of class contracts, and strongly discourage making a system adaptable to the point where class contracts lose any meaning. The detrimental effect of class contracts on the potential adaptability of a system, should,

however, be minimized. In that manner, both reliability and adaptability may lead to increased reusability.

2.2 Flexibility

The first problem of design by contract we consider, is its lack of flexibility. Once we introduce a contract clause in a class, it is automatically inherited by all subclasses, and it can only be changed in certain ways, depending on what kind of clause it is.

```
public class Stack {

  /**
   * push object o on the stack
   *
   * Precondition for this method: none
   * Which means precondition: true
   * The method can always be executed
   */
  public void push (Object o) { … }
}

public class BoundedStack extends Stack {

  /**
   * New Precondition: getNbItems() < getCapacity()
   * The stack must not be full!
   */
  @Overridden public void push (Object o) { … }
}
```

Fig. 1. The Classes of Stacks and BoundedStacks

Consider the example in Figure 1; it is a Java-version of a class of stacks and a subclass of BoundedStacks, based on an example in (Meyer, 1997). The example clearly does something illegal: it introduces a precondition for a method in a subclass, which overrides a method in the superclass without precondition. This is against the Liskov principles of substitution (Liskov, 1994), which state that a precondition may only be weakened in subclasses, not strengthened. The lack of any precondition is identical to a precondition of 'true', which is the weakest possible precondition, so introducing any precondition in the subclass breaks the contract.

Yet exactly this illegal introduction of a precondition is often what we need when creating new subclasses based on classes built by a third party that did not know what our exact requirements would be. It is a good example of the lack of flexibility in specification of contracts. The developer of the class of stacks never considered the possibility of the introduction of a precondition, so he did not provide one, making it impossible for any client to do so either. Meyer (Meyer, 1997) solves this issue by introducing an abstract precondition in the class of Stacks, that can be made concrete by the clients; indirectly, this is a strengthening of the precondition, but by using an undetermined postcondition (read: the absence of a postcondition, which actually defaults to a true postcondition), he stays within the rules and avoids being accused of 'cheating'.

There are two problems with Meyer's approach: the first is the lack of coherence between the different kinds of assertions available: the lack of any assertion, whether it is a pre- or postcondition, means the assertion is true, but this still defines a big difference between the two kinds of assertions, because they are inherited differently. Preconditions in subclasses are OR'ed with those in superclasses, whereas postconditions are AND'ed. This results in preconditions that can only be made weaker (once you have true, the or-operation will make the result always true) and postconditions that can only be made stronger (once you have false, the and-operation will make the result always false).

The second problem lies in the fact that the developer of Stack needs to know he has to make an abstract precondition. If the developers of the two classes are different, however, they usually do not know such things. The superclass provider may guess that a precondition will be necessary in a subclass, but how is he to know which one and how it will be introduced?

So what we need is the option to leave certain things undetermined in a superclass, so subclass developers can still choose for themselves. Having a postcondition of 'true' comes close to non-determination, but for the precondition, there's no easy way to introduce it (a precondition of 'false' would make the execution of the method in the superclass impossible, regardless of the fact we can still weaken it in subclasses). Furthermore, we also need a more symmetrical approach to assertions, which will make it easier to reason about them.

2.3 Expressivity

When discussing flexibility, we already mentioned the problem of inconsistency: preconditions and postconditions being handled differently. The problem is actually much wider than simply the default precondition being false and the default postcondition being true: it is generally difficult to express that which is left undetermined. Lack of any assertion, whether it be pre- or postcondition, should mean that the assertion is left unspecified. We should generally be able to express what is certainly a precondition, what is certainly not a precondition, and what is left in the middle. The same is true for postconditions and invariants.

Consider the example in Figure 2: again, we've made an illegal strengthening of the precondition. Nevertheless, what we want to express here, is that a general Person can have an age from 0 to 200, but a Customer – clearly a subclass of Person, because not everyone is our customer – needs to be older than 18.

For this to work, we would need to be able to introduce a distinction between necessary preconditions and sufficient preconditions. For a Person, it is necessary and sufficient to have an age between 0 and 200. For a customer, however, this is also necessary but not sufficient.

What we would like to express is that values outside of the range between 0 and 200 are always illegal values, but the legality of the values inside that range is left undetermined for now. This is only possible by using tricks such as using a boolean method in the precondition, of which the postcondition can be strengthened. The method would state 'if (age<0 || age >200) then result==false', leaving unspecified when it returns true.

To conclude this section, we list what we need to be able to specify: first, we want to be able to specify that which is not to change in subclasses, whether it is an assertion that restricts certain things or one that permits certain things. Second, we also want to be able to specify what is not to change in future versions of some class (also called: a change in time). Being able to express what will not change will provide guarantees to clients. Third, we want the option of being able to change what is still allowed to change in flexible ways, giving us full control over all which is not yet specified. Being able to specify anything left unspecified however we wish, will give us, and our clients, the possibility to make more adaptable software.

```
public class Person {

  /**
   * Precondition: argument should be a reasonable number
   * arg >= 0 && arg <= 200
   */
  public void setAge(int arg) {…}
}

public class Customer extends Person {

  /**
   * Precondition: our customers must be adults
   * arg >= 18
  public void setAge(int arg) {…}
}
```

Fig. 2. The Classes of Person and Customer

3. Flexible Design by Contract

This section explains the two pillars of our solution to improve the flexibility and expressiveness of design by contract. First we explore flexibility, which is accomplished by the distinction between flexible and rigid contract clauses. Second, we look into restrictions versus permissions, a classification of contract clauses which allows a more powerful specification than the traditional restrictive clauses.

3.1 The Flexibility Principle

The first constituent of our principle is the flexibility principle. In programming by contract, the definitions of all possible clauses in a contract state that the clause is valid for a class and all its subclasses. The flexibility principle changes the way in which this validity is determined: a contract clause will no longer automatically be always valid, nor valid for all subclasses. Instead, this will be optional and configurable. The definitions of the principle state as follows:

> The Flexible Restriction Principle classifies contract clauses in two kinds: flexible clauses and rigid clauses. Flexible clauses are not inherited through subclassing, and are therefore not subject to any principles of substitutability. Rigid clauses are the traditional kind.

Actually, three different levels of guarantee are defined by this principle. The least level, not included in the definition, guarantees nothing: anything not specified by a flexible or rigid restriction is left undetermined and thus unguaranteed. The flexible level is therefore an intermediate level: anything guaranteed by a flexible clause, is guaranteed for the current class, whatever versions of the class are still to come. It is thus a guarantee in time. The highest level of guarantee is given by a rigid clause: the specification given by such clauses remains guaranteed not only through time, but also through inheritance. Hence, this can be called a guarantee in all dimensions.

It would not make sense to establish a form of guarantee that would be fixed for inheritance, and thus inherited by subclasses, but not in time, which means it could be changed in future versions. This would cause a fragile base class problem (Szyperski, 1998), as such an assertion could be dropped in a future version of a superclass, possibly invalidating a subclass depending on it.

The two kinds of clauses, and the absence of clauses, can now be defined:

A flexible contract clause is a contract clause asserting a fact about objects of the current class. It may or may not be inherited in subclasses, where it can also, as a convenience, be converted into a rigid clause. It can be changed in time, but only according to well-defined principles of substitutability

A rigid clause is a contract clause asserting a fact about objects of the current class and all of its subclasses. It is automatically inherited and can only be changed in subclasses according to well-defined principles of substitutability

Anything that cannot be asserted by a contract clause, whether because of the lack of any clauses or because the existent clauses do not cover every possible ascertainable fact, is left undetermined, it can be changed at will

A simpler way of understanding these three definitions is as follows: as long as we have no contract at all, we can still add contract clauses. Once we introduce certain contract clauses, we can only add new clauses as long as these do not somehow conflict with the already existing clauses. We could also change these existing clauses, but only in ways that do not conflict with their previous version. In subclasses, we only have to take the rigid classes of the superclass into account, not the flexible ones. For example, suppose we have a method returning an integer. In its initial version, the method has no postcondition and can thus return any number in the integer range determined by the language. We then add a traditional, restrictive postcondition, stating the result has to be greater than or equal to 10. We call this a restrictive postcondition because it restricts any values smaller than 10, but does not specify anything about values greater than 10 (see the next subsection). If this is a flexible clause, the subclasses are still able to add any postcondition, even that the result would have to be smaller than 10. In the class itself, or also in subclasses if our postcondition were rigid, we can only add a postcondition that does not conflict. For example, we could state that the method only returns numbers smaller than 30. The new postcondition would be combined with the existing one using boolean conjunction. We could also introduce a postcondition stating the result has to be greater than 15, which can be combined with the existing clauses, but can also replace the greater-than-10 clause without conflict.

The flexibility principle allows developers to specify contracts for a certain class without compromising the possibility to specify adapted contracts in its subclasses. Any contract clause is enforced for objects of that specific class, but not automatically for instances of subclasses. The developer can, however, also provide rigid clauses to deal with important restrictions that also apply to subclasses, and supplement these rigid clauses with flexible ones, that function more as guidelines, which can speed up the decision making process of subclass developers by providing easily accessible examples of further assertion statements. Furthermore, if a programming or specification language provides syntactic sugar to easily transform a flexible clause into a rigid one, the flexible clauses can also function as 'pick and choose' kind of clauses, speeding up the actual specification work of subclass developers by providing reusable assertions.

3.2 Restrictive versus Permissive

Sometimes it becomes necessary in a specification to express not only what is certainly incorrect, but also what will always be correct. Traditionally, this is only possible in a contrived way. For example, suppose we want to express, as an invariant, that the value of a certain integer field must always be positive, and is always allowed to be bigger than 18, leaving the interval between 0 and 18 unspecified. This would allow subclass developers to decide about that interval, and only that interval. Using only restrictions, the most we can do in a straightforward manner, is force subclass developers to accept that negative values are unacceptable; we cannot force them to leave the 18+ interval alone, since they are usually only allowed to make restrictions stronger.

To express these kinds of permissive domains, we introduce permissions. They are the opposite of restrictions, which are the traditional contract clauses. When permissions converge with restrictions, they become immutabilities. In the next section, we will see what the permissive qualification alters about the three simplest contract clause types: invariants, preconditions and postconditions. In this section, we provide the general definition:

A permission is a contract clause that expresses a fact that, although it will sometimes be false, is always allowed to be true. No other contract clause may be introduced that contradicts this fact. A rigid permission can be made more permissive, or less restrictive, in subclasses, as long as it does not contradict other contract clauses.

A restriction is a contract clause that expresses a fact that must always be true. It is never allowed to be false. No other contract clause may be introduced that contradicts this fact. A rigid restriction can be made more restrictive, or less permissive, in subclasses, as long as it does not contradict other contract clauses.

An immutability is a permission and a restriction at the same time. It is a fact that must always be true. No other contract clause may be introduced that contradicts this fact. A rigid immutability cannot be changed in subclasses.

The difference between these definitions is apparently small: a permission is always allowed to be true, whereas a restriction is simply always true. Yet they are two opposites that perfectly complement each other, allowing the expression of complex specifications. They relate to each other in the following way: a permission may be made less restrictive in subclasses, but not less restrictive than any restrictions about the same fact that could be present. The reciprocal is true for the restriction: it can be made more restrictive in sub-

classes, but not more so than any present permission about the same fact. When both a restriction and permission are maximally made more or less restrictive, they can no longer be changed in subclasses. This we call an immutable contract clause. The different possibilities for contract clauses are put together in Figure 3.
Different contract clauses in a class will be combined as follows: restrictions of the same kind (invariants, preconditions…) will be logically conjoined to make the complete restriction. Permissions of the same kind will also be logically conjoined, and also conjoined with the complete restriction. This is because we cannot permit anything that is already restricted, so any permission always implies the active restrictions.

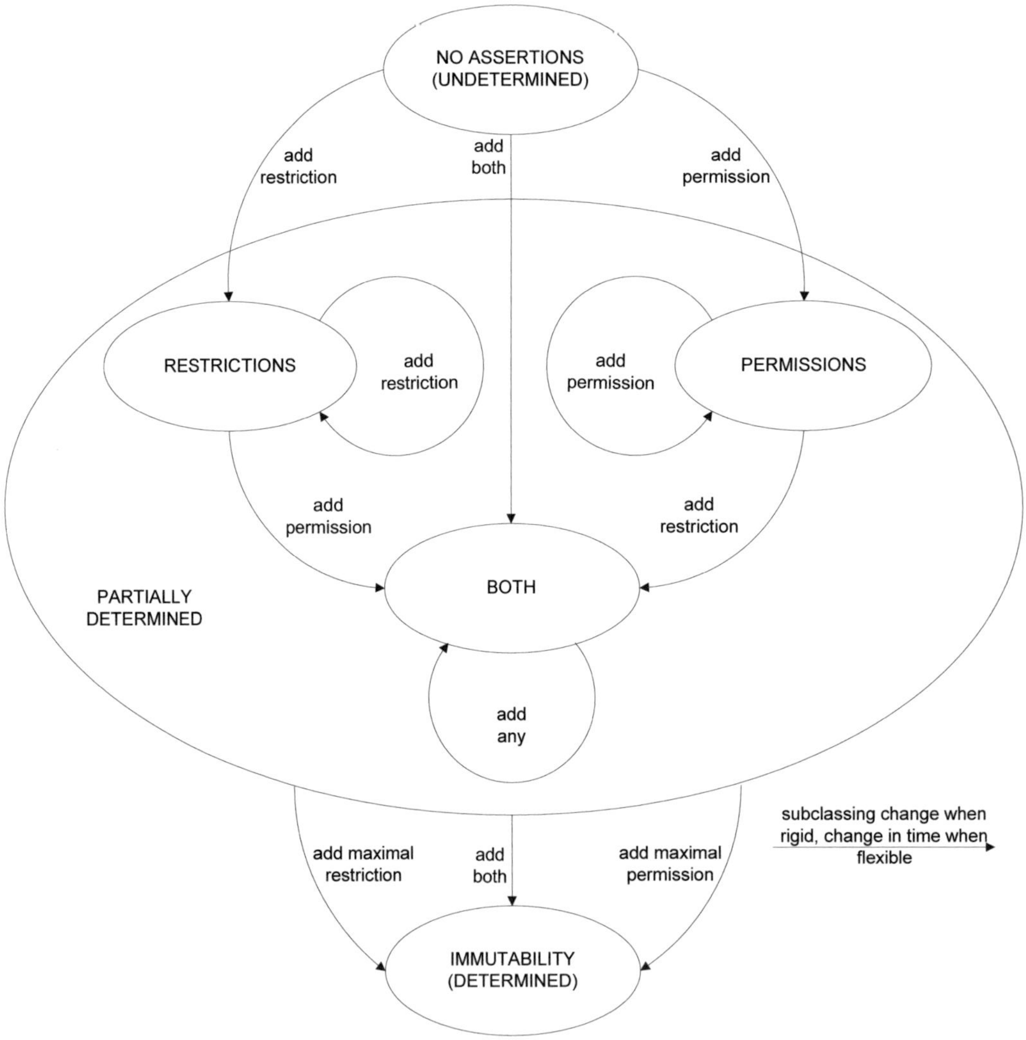

Fig. 3. State Diagram of Restrictions and Permissions

When inheriting rigid contract clauses, they will always be logically conjoined with the clauses of the same kind that are added in the subclass: restrictions with new restrictions of

the same kind (invariants, preconditions,...) and permissions with permissions of the same kind. This coherence is different from traditional design by contract, where inherited preconditions were combined using the disjunctive boolean operator instead of conjoined like postconditions.
When using flexible contract clauses, they are similarly conjoined with the rigid clauses of the same kind, whether inherited or local, to form the complete assertion for the current class.

4. Application to Properties

In this section we will digress from flexible design by contract and introduce properties; part of our previous research. In the following section, our principles will be applied to properties to demonstrate them in detail. Properties were first introduced in (Vanderkimpen et al., 2007a) and further elaborated on in (Vanderkimpen et al., 2007b). They are a language feature introduced in statically typed object oriented programming languages to replace the concept of fields with a more versatile concept. In section 4.2, we will demonstrate that the readonly modifier for properties is already an early example of flexible design by contract.

4.1 Basic Properties

The main contribution of properties is the greatly increased flexibility when they are used under inheritance. Many things about a property, such as its being a stored or a derived property, can be overridden in subclasses. The traditional fields in languages like JAVA (Gosling et al., 2005) do not leave room for redefinitions at all, which is why good practices such as using beans have been established. With properties, there's no more need for beans; all their benefits are now part of the language.
Properties are best demonstrated using an example. Consider Figure 4, it demonstrates two classes: the class of Persons, and its subclass of BornPersons. The first class has a simple property age, denoting, in a number of years, the age of a Person. The keyword property denotes that the age is a property, which means it is actually the combination of a field, an accessor or getter, and a mutator or setter. Since this property has a primitive type, we call it a primitive property. Unlike the properties in the subclass, the age property in Person does not have a property block, which means it will be a default stored property. Default stored properties have a private value, stored in a field with the same type as the property, a default getter, which simply returns the stored field, and a default setter, which stores its argument in the field. The purpose of properties is to allow access to a field through the methods that encapsulate it, but with the same syntax as if it were a public field. An example of the use of a property is seen in the first and last lines of the setter for the age property in the subclass, where the birthDate property is first accessed, and later assigned to. This access actually uses the getter and setter defined in the birthDate property.
So far, we see no difference with C# properties, which are syntactic sugar for a field with a getter and a setter. The main benefit of our properties lies in its use with inheritance. Suppose we were not allowed to change the class of Persons, but we still wanted to make a better implementation, using a birth date to represent a Person's age instead of an integer denoting the age in years. For this purpose, we introduce a BornPerson class, subclassing Person and introducing a birthDate property. The age of a person must now be derived from that person's birthDate, which means we have to override the age property to make

sure the birthDate property is used behind the scenes. The age property is now completely derived, which can be inferred by the compiler: the value keyword representing the private field to store the property in is absent from the implementation. The only other special keyword is argument, which denotes the argument given to the setter. Since our properties are more than just syntactic sugar and since the private values of stored properties are kept completely encapsulated inside the properties at all times, we can drop the private field from the storage space needed to store an object of type BornPerson.
A second benefit of properties can be seen in the implementation of the getter and setter for the birthDate property: by default, we do not have to declare the private value, since it will have the same type as the property. For the birthDate property, however, we were able to declare a private value of a completely different type: the primitive type long. This is an acceptable choice, as long as we also make sure that the getter and setter of the property take this difference in types into account (otherwise, this would create an error at compile-time). This mechanism is so versatile, we can even change the type when overriding the property.

```
public class Person {
    public property int age;
}

public class BornPerson extends Person {
    public property Date birthDate {
        long value = 0;
        get {
            if (value==0) return null;
            return new Date(value);
        }
        set {
            if (argument==null) value = 0;
            value = argument.getTime();
        }
    }
    public property int age {
        get {
            return (new Date()).getYear()-birthDate.getYear();
        }
        set {
            Date date = birthDate;
            date.setYear((new Date()).getYear()-argument);
            birthDate = date;
        }
    }
}
```
Fig. 4. The Classes of Persons and BornPersons

4.2 Readonly Properties
As the name implies, a readonly property is a property that can only be read. This means the property cannot be assigned to by clients. As demonstrated in figure 5, it can be introduced

by adding the readonly modifier to the declaration. For default properties, the result will be the absence of a setter, and hence a compile-time error will occur when an attempt to assign to the property is made. For a readonly property with customizations, it would be a compile-time error to introduce a setter inside the property block. Readonly properties should not be confused with constant properties: they can still change, only not through assignment.

In (Vanderkimpen et al., 2007b), we introduced one more modifier: the immutable modifier. The reason for this is that a readonly property can still be overridden to become writable. According to the substitution principles, this is acceptable: only when accessed through its subtype, the redeclared property can be written to. Clients relying on the supertype declaration experience no problems, because a readonly property is not the same as a constant property: it can still change, only not through assignment. An immutable property, contrary to a readonly property, can no longer be made writable in subclasses, making it a stronger constraint.

```
public class Person {
    public readonly property String firstName;
    public readonly property String lastName;
}

public class BornPerson extends Person {
    public property String firstName;
    public immutable property String lastName;
}
```

Fig. 5. Readonly Modifiers

In the example in Figure 5, we introduce names in the class of Persons: a first name and a last name, both readonly. In the class of BornPersons, the first name is made writable: from now on, it can be changed and this option can no longer be taken away in further subclasses. The lastname property, on the other hand, is made immutable, which means the option of making it writable is unavailable for any further subclasses.

Making a property readonly is a restriction: the ability to change it is completely taken away, and thus maximally restricted (so actually it is an immutability). Furthermore, this restriction can be seen as flexible, as it is only applied to the current class (although by default repeated in subclasses, but this is only a matter of choice and a syntactic convenience). Finally, it could also be seen as a 'false' precondition for the setter of the property, because having a precondition of false means it cannot be used.

Making a property writable, on the other hand, is the absence of a restriction or permission. It could actually be seen as a maximal permission, but this would hamper future change, because it would also be rigid. This is because the writable status is automatically inherited. In the absence of any other restrictions or permissions, the ability to write the property is thus left undetermined, with the syntactical effect of being able to assign to it.

Finally, the immutable modifier for properties, like the readonly modifier, is a maximal restriction, but unlike the readonly modifier, it is rigid, as it is automatically inherited in subclasses.

So, what we have demonstrated here, is that the readonly modifier for properties is actually already a special case of the application of flexible design by contract to the precondition of a property's setter. Readonly is a flexible immutability, immutable is a rigid immutability and writable is the absence of any assertion. In figure 5, we show a state diagram demonstrating the possibilities of the readonly modifier for properties. The full application of our principle to preconditions in general, and also to other kinds of contract clauses, will be elaborated in the next section.

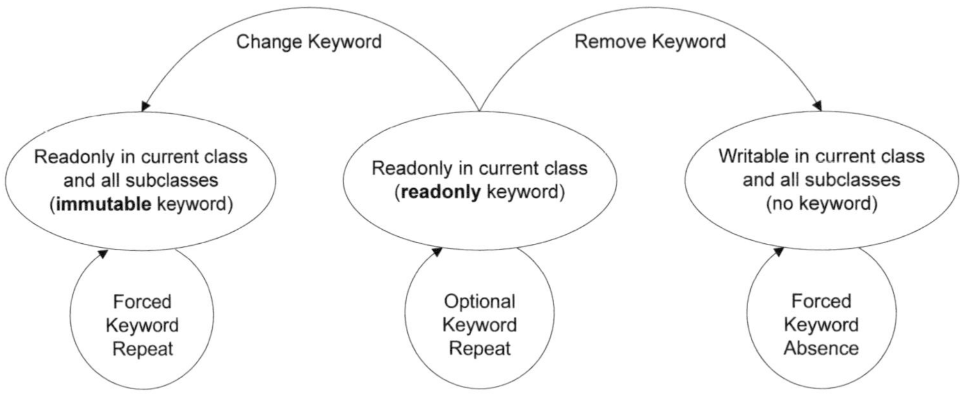

Fig. 6. Readonly State Diagram

5. The Principle in General

In section 3, we explained the new principle's general semantics, introducing the concepts of flexibility versus rigidity and restrictive versus permissive contract clauses. In this section, we apply these formalisms to invariants, preconditions and postconditions, introducing syntax to apply these contract clauses to the property concept from section 4. We present a set of short keywords to indicate these constructs as flexible or rigid and as restrictions or permissions. Furthermore, some single-word modifiers, which map to invariants, can be easily adapted to be used with our principle, similar to the readonly concept in the previous section. These modifiers are not supported in Java by default, so we will also provide a short explanation on them.

5.1 Invariants

In design by contract (Meyer, 1992), an invariant is a clause in the contract denoting a fact that will always be true. For a class contract, this fact will be true for all objects of that class throughout the object life cycle, starting immediately after construction and ending immediately before destruction. Usually, with 'objects of that class', objects of that class and all its subclasses are meant. Using the flexible restriction principle, however, we will make a clear distinction between invariants valid for a single class and invariants valid for the whole hierarchy. Additionally, we will make a distinction between the traditional restrictive invariants and the newly introduced permissive invariants.
For the scope of this work, we limit the invariants in our contracts to invariants that revolve around specific properties. Consequentially, the invariants will be added to the property block. We call these invariants 'property invariants', as opposed to the regular class invariants. They do, however, have the same semantics.

We explain all these different invariants by means of an example. In these examples, Java code will sometimes be complemented with pseudo code (in italics) to increase readability and conciseness.

In Figure 7, we see the class of Files, having several invariant clauses for its property name. A first distinction is made between flexible and rigid invariants: all contract clauses will by default be flexible, unless the keyword rigid is added, that's why the invariants without the rigid keyword are flexible. A second distinction is the presence or absence of the permit keyword, which indicates a clause as being a permission, rather than a restriction, which is, again, the default. Finally, all invariants are indicated as such by the keyword invar, which is followed by an optional name and an obligatory boolean statement enclosed in braces, indicating the actual invariant.

The class of Files has four invariant clauses. The first two are rigid restrictions; they tell us, that for all files, including subclasses of File, the name must never contain a slash or a delete character and the name must be between 0 and 256 characters. This is the traditional invariant clause: any object of type File for which the boolean statement is not true, is violating the class invariant. The invariant clause is inherited in all subclasses and can never be made less restrictive, according to the Liskov substitution principles (Liskov 1994).

```
public class File {
  public property String name {
    rigid invar(!name.contains(/,DEL) && name.length()<256);
    rigid invar(name.length()>=1);
    rigid permit invar(name.length()<=12);
    rigid permit invar(name.matches(alphanumerics));
    permit invar wildcards(!name.contains(?,*));
    permit invar (name.length()<=16);
    invar (name.length()<=32);
    invar notnull(name!=null);
  }
}
```

Fig. 7. The Class of Files

The third and fourth clauses indicate rigid permissions. They tell us, that for all files, including subclasses of File, if the name has at most 12 alphanumeric characters, it will be a valid name. This is the opposite of the traditional invariant: any object of type File for which the boolean statements are all true, is obeying the class invariant. The invariant clause is inherited in all subclasses and cannot be made more restrictive, which means it also defines a limit to how strong the class invariant can become.

In the absence of flexible invariant clauses, the combination of the rigid restrictions and permissions determines how the full domain of possible objects is divided into objects that respect the class invariant, objects that violate it, and objects for which this is undetermined. The third group are the objects for which the restriction conditions all evaluate to true, but not all of the permissions evaluate to true. For example, a filename that does not contain slashes or delete signs, but does contain non-alphanumerical characters, is not a restricted filename, but we cannot be certain it will always be a permitted one.

The situation is slightly different when flexible invariants are present. In such a case, the flexible invariant clauses further shrink the domain of undetermined values for an object's properties, if that object is a direct instance of the current class. Flexible contract clauses are logically conjoined with their rigid counterparts.

Consider the fifth and sixth clause in Figure 7. They are flexible permissive invariant clauses, which tell us that, for instances of File, names shorter than 16 characters and not containing wildcards, will always be valid names, when they also respect the restrictive invariant clauses. Note that the fifth clause is named as the wildcards clause; this will prove convenient when the clause becomes important for a subclass, as it is easily referred to. Furthermore, an error-reporting tool able to detect the violation of invariants can create more meaningful error messages by using the name of the invariant clauses involved.

The last two clauses are flexible restrictions, further restricting the rigid restrictions for instances of File to the point where names of files cannot be null and can at most count 32 characters.

Please note a hypothetical conflict between the wildcards flexible permission and the first rigid restriction: it seems as if names not containing wildcards would always be valid names, even if they contain deletion sign or slashes, because the permission does not repeat those characters in the list of prohibited characters. This is of course not a real conflict: the rules we introduce to combine restrictions and permissions state that permissions always automatically imply any active restrictions, which means that only objects that respect the restrictions as well as the permissions are valid objects (objects respecting only the restrictions but not the permissions have an undefined validity; objects that don't comply with the restrictions are, of course, invalid). This is also the case for inherited rigid restrictions and permissions, which are AND'ed with the restrictions and permissions of the subclass.

An illustration of the invariant clauses determining filename length can be seen in figure 8. There is still a range of values not covered by any of the invariants: it is the range between 16 and 32. This is left undetermined by the developer: no guarantees are given that these values will be legal, and likewise, no guarantee is given that they will be illegal. This allows the developer of the class to further restrict or slacken the invariant in future versions of the class of Files. Clients are guaranteed the current restrictions and permissions; use of the undetermined range of values is at their own risk.

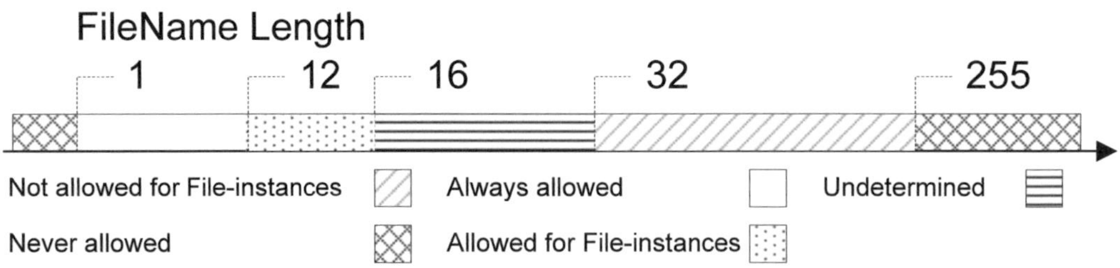

Fig. 8. Filename Length

In the subclass of files for ms-dos operating systems, shown in Figure 9, the invariants for the filename are altered. The first rigid clause further restricts the list of available characters for filenames; obviously, the new illegal symbols cannot be alphanumerical characters, since they are already explicitly permitted in the superclass. The second line in the contract states that the name will only contain majuscules.

The third contract clause in DosFile is an immutable invariant clause: it restricts the length of filenames to 12 characters or less. Since there is already a rigid permission, defined in the superclass File, that allows filenames to have up to 12 characters, we cannot restrict the length to shorter than this, and we must therefore make this clause an immutability. This means it cannot be further restricted or slackened; it is a rigid permission as well as a rigid restriction.

```
public class DosFile extends File {
  public property String name {
    rigid invar(!name.contains(0x00-0x1F, ,",:,<,>,\,|));
    rigid invar(name.equals(name.toUpperCase());
    immutable invar(name.length()<=12);
    rigid invar wildcards,notnull;
  }
}
```
Fig. 9. The Class of DosFiles

The fourth invariant clause is a syntactic convenience: the flexible invariant clauses from the superclass are normally not inherited, but we wish to repeat them nevertheless, and even make them rigid. Since they have names, we can easily do this by modifying them with the right keywords, which of course is only syntactic sugar for repeating the code.

When discussing inheritance of class contracts, we cannot fail to mention the Liskov principles of substitution (Liskov, 1994). According to these, traditional class invariants can only be made more restrictive than the invariants in the superclass, as objects of the subclass must comply with the same rules as objects of the superclass, and optionally some extra rules. The situation is different using the flexible restriction principle. First and foremost, flexible invariants are not inherited at all, so we can ignore them for the remainder of this discussion. The system of restrictions and permissions, however, has a notable effect. Ordinarily, anything not explicitly forbidden by a class invariant is allowed; this is no longer the case: only that which is explicitly permitted is by default allowed, and vice versa, only that which is explicitly restricted is by default forbidden. The most important consequence of this is that a part of the domain of legal objects can remain undetermined, which allows us to later enlarge the part that is legal. Using only restrictions, we were only allowed to increase the part of the domain that was illegal.

The new principles of substitution are thus as follows: a rigid restrictive invariant can be made more restrictive, as long as it does not conflict with a rigid permissive invariant, and a rigid permissive invariant can be made less restrictive, as long as it does not conflict with a rigid restrictive invariant. When both are impossible because of conflicts, we have created an immutable invariant clause, which means the domain of legal values for what concerns that specific invariant clause, is completely determined.

5.2 Preconditions

A precondition, in programming by contract, is a fact that has to be made true by the caller of a method before that method may be called. Failure to do so would result in undefined behaviour. Preconditions, when applied to properties, will be facts that have to be true before calling the setter of the property, and thus before assigning a value to the property.

Consider Figure 10: the argument keyword represents the argument that will be passed to the setter, as explained in section 4. The first precondition of the name property in the figure, states that the property must not be assigned values containing slashes or delete characters.

It is a rigid precondition, which means it can be made more restrictive. The rest of the preconditions in the example are strongly akin to the invariants from section 5.1. This is typical: in order to guarantee the class invariant, the developer introduces preconditions that make it illegal for the client to invalidate the object by assigning a value to it that would be against the invariant. It is, however, not mandatory; for example, we omitted a precondition reflecting the permissive invariant that makes alphanumerical file names legal.
This classical similarity between invariants and preconditions pleads for a way to declare in short that the preconditions are meant to enforce the invariants. This would be a beautiful addition to our concepts, but is, for now, out of scope. We will re-examine it in section 9, together with other future work.

```
public class File {
  public property String name {
    rigid pre(!argument.contains(/,DEL));
    rigid pre(1<=argument.length()<256);
    rigid permit pre(argument.length()<=12);
    permit pre wildcardsarg(!argument.contains(?,*));
    permit pre (argument.length()<=16);
    pre (argument.length()<=32);
    pre notnullarg(argument!=null);
  }

  someMethod() {
    File someFile = getSomeFile();
    someFile.name ?= "myFileNamedTooLong"; //returns true
    someFile.name ??= "myFileNamedTooLong";//returns false
  }
}
```

Fig. 10. The Class of Files, Preconditions

In the method someMethod in Figure 10, the single question mark-equation mark operator checks if a given value satisfies the restrictive preconditions of a property setter. The operator takes an object or primitive value of the same type on its left-hand and right-hand side. Its result will always be boolean. It differs from the regular assignment operator because it does not actually assign anything, it only checks the preconditions. When it returns true, we know our argument is not invalid, but we are not sure it is valid, as it could still be in the undetermined domain of values.
The double question mark-equation mark operator, on the other hand, checks the permissive preconditions and returns true only if these are met. The restrictive preconditions are of course automatically met in this case, since they are implied by the permissive ones. This check can thus give a stronger guarantee if it returns true, because we know the argument is valid for certain. In the example, the second check returns false because the permissive precondition '<=16' is not met.
Both operators are an easy way for clients that wish to make an assignment to a property depending on its preconditions. It would be an easy exercise to introduce assignment operators that would check the preconditions and then make the assignment if they are met, which is simply syntactic sugar for an if-statement; we leave this to future work.
An example of rigid preconditions being inherited can be seen in Figure 11.

```
public class DosFile {

  public property String name {
    rigid pre(!argument.contains(0x00-0x1F, ,",:,<,>,\,|));
    immutable pre(argument.length()<=12);
    rigid pre wildcardsarg,notnullarg;
  }
}
```
Fig. 11. Precondition in the class of DosFiles

In the class of DosFiles, the first rigid restrictive precondition strengthens the precondition by disallowing more characters. The second line makes the permission to have a name shorter than 12 characters immutable, meaning this is now also a restriction. The third line turns the flexible permissions wildcardsarg and notnullarg of the superclass into an immutable precondition: the argument is now required not to contain wildcards and must also be non-null. Note that a restriction for the argument to consist only of capitals, is not given. This means the implementation of the setter will somehow have to make sure that the name is capitalized in order not to break the class invariant for DosFile. We will see to this when discussing postconditions.
From the example, we see that the substitution principles for preconditions are analogous to those for invariants. One important fact must be mentioned: the traditional precondition, when inherited, can only be made weaker, as opposed to the traditional invariants, which can only be made stronger. This is because the client is key in design by contract, and the actions of the client cannot be further restricted. Using the flexible restriction principle, this inconsistency is absent: restrictive preconditions can be made more restrictive, just like restrictive invariants. This correspondence is granted by the fact that our principles allow part of the domain of legal values to remain unspecified. From client-centric, we have evolved to a system where the provider still has some freedom in adapting the specification.

5.3 Postconditions

A postcondition, in programming by contract, is a fact that has to be made true by a method by the end of that method. Postconditions, when applied to properties, pertain only the result of the setter, which usually means they will be little used with simple single-valued properties. The default postcondition for non-primitive properties is shown in Figure 12. For primitive properties, it would make use of identity (==). This default does not need to be provided and is overridden by the user when a postcondition is introduced in the property block. A more useful set of postconditions is shown for the copy method in Figure 12.
Postconditions differ from invariants in that they need not always be true. They only have to be true immediately after the execution of a method. The flexible restriction principle, applied to postconditions, alters the definition of the standard postcondition in the following way: The postcondition must be true after execution of an assignment to a property, if the assignment was dynamically bound to the property's setter as defined in the class declaring the postcondition. Adding the rigid keyword to the postcondition ensures that the postcondition must always be made true after executing the method call, regardless of which class the object containing the property belongs to. Just as was the case with invariants, this does not break the substitution principles, because the definition of the flexible postcondition is different from the definition of a rigid one.

To illustrate the difference between restrictive and permissive postconditions, we consider the File example again, in Figure 12. The rigid restriction of the copy method tells us that we can expect the method to always create a file with a name that is at least equal to the copied file's name, ignoring case and dropping any part beyond the first 12 characters. The flexible restriction strengthens this further by stating the names need to be exactly equal, but only for direct instances of File.
The rigid permission of the copy method tells us that if the new name equals the existing name, the postcondition will always be fulfilled. This means a permission is the maximum postcondition that well ever need to be achieved by the method's developer, and the restrictive postcondition is the minimum required. Another way of explaining this, is that a restrictive postcondition is the necessary condition a method needs to fulfil, and the permissive postcondition a sufficient condition. Clients can rely on the necessary condition to be met, but not on the sufficient one. The (rigid) permission can be made less restrictive in subclasses, while the restrictive postcondition, like traditional postconditions, can only be made stronger.

```
public class File {
  public property String name {
    post(this.name.equals(argument)) //default postcondition
  }

  public File copy(Directory target) {
    rigid pre(target!=this.getDirectory())
    rigid post
        (result.name.substring(0,11).equalsIgnoreCase(
        name.substring(0,11))
    rigid permit post(result.name.equals(name))
    post(result.name.equals(name))
  }
}

public class DosFile {
  public property String name {
    post(this.name.equals(argument.toUpperCase()))
  }

  public File copy(Directory target) {
    immutable post(result.name.equals(name))
  }
}
```
Fig. 12. Postconditions in the Class of Files

In the subclass of DosFiles, also in Figure 12, the postcondition of the setter needs to be changed from the default, because the invariant for DosFile (in Figure 9) names state they need to be capitalized, so this is exactly what the setter will do. The rigid postcondition of the copy method becomes immutable: it needs to be rigid, because the name of the result being equal to the current name is a necessity, and it is also equally restrictive as the rigid permission in the superclass, which means it cannot be further restricted or weakened anymore.

5.4 More Modifiers

In specification languages like JML (Leavens, 1999), many single-word assertions are introduced on fields or methods. These can sometimes be brought back to some invariant or pre- or postcondition.

An example is the nullable keyword. In JML, all declarations are by default declared non-null, which means the declaration in question cannot evaluate to null. The nullable keyword is introduced to declare that something is allowed to be null.

Applying our principle, we could state that any property declaration has, by default, a flexible immutable invariant stating that the property is not allowed to be null. If we want the property to be able to become null, we can use the same keyword, nullable, to declare a flexible permission invariant stating that the property is valid when null. This, as usual, replaces the default, so it is not conflicting.

Another option is to enforce non-null even further, by making it a rigid immutable invariant. We introduce the keyword 'nevernull' for this purpose. At the other extreme, we could make the nullable permission rigid, by modifying the property with an 'alwaysnullable' keyword.

As we can see, our principles are applicable to many forms of assertions, even single-word modifiers, like nullable.

6. Evaluation

The flexible restriction principle adds qualifiers to clauses of a class contract denoting their precise meaning. At first sight, this adds complexity to programming by contract. It replaces three standard kinds of contract clauses - the precondition, postcondition and invariant - by the same number of clauses, multiplied by two times two distinctions: either a flexible or a rigid clause, and either a restrictive or a permissive clause. This distinction, however, also simplifies the paradigm. The division in four kinds of clauses can be seen as a modification of the clauses by additional meta-information that makes the clause easier to use. Once you know what kind of clause you're dealing with, you know how it impacts the contract, how far its influence goes, and by how much it limits future change. Furthermore, the three revised standard contract clauses are now completely consistent in the way they can be used and transformed.

Another benefit is the increased flexibility with which contracts can be written, thanks to the flexibility principle. The distinction between no clause, a flexible clause and a rigid clause allows developers to exactly determine which parts of the contract are fixed, and which are still flexible, and thus open to future adaptation. Lack of adaptability is an oft-used reason not to use programming by contract, a paradigm which, even in its traditional form, has a great impact on software quality. The increased flexibility established by our ameliorations makes this reason obsolete.

This increased flexibility nevertheless comes at a cost: we are now forced to think about assertions when we write code. How de we know which facts are true or false for all subclasses? How do we know what is sure not to change in future versions of the current class? How much flexibility do clients need? How many guarantees? Of course, this need to think, just as the lack of adaptability, is likewise a popular reason not to use traditional programming by contract. Our enhanced principles are designed to make it easier to reason about these issues in a controlled way. For each assertion conceivable, developers can now take two recurring steps to decide how to put them in the contract: first, decide if you want to restrict the options, or to delimit a domain of permitted options. Second, decide if you want this assertion in subclasses or not. In traditional programming by contract, these decisions had to be taken implicitly and they impacted how the actual assertions needed to be written instead of simply being expressed by a number of contract clause modifiers. Making developers think about these questions in a controlled way will have a positive effect on the quality of the code they write.

Besides ease of use and flexibility, there is also an increase in expressiveness, thanks to the permission principle. This makes the writing of contracts easier, since certain assertions can now be expressed within a single clause, whereas they traditionally required the use of contrived mechanisms using auxiliary methods.

The possibility to add meta-information to contract clauses allows developers of the class to decide exactly which parts of the implementation are under a strict contract, fostering better robustness, and which parts are more suitable to change by subclasses. A criticism that can be made, is that the flexible assertions used to indicate the latter parts, do not provide any real guarantees: because of polymorphism, clients may not know if they are using instances of a class, or of its subclasses. For the developers of a class, this is not really a problem, since they have full control. For clients, a small amount of discipline when using the class is enough to ensure the flexible guarantees. For example, clients could create a subclass in which all flexible guarantees are made rigid, neutralizing the need for instances to be of a certain type as long as they use this subclass's static type. At the same time, the clients could introduce changes to any parts of the class contract that are still flexible. These changes can either be a fortification of the restrictions of the contract, improving robustness, or a fortification of its permissions, where more customization is required.

Another way of making sure objects of a certain type are used, is to create them in factories, and have those factories state in their postconditions that the created objects will be of a certain type, which guarantees the flexible assertions of that type will be applicable to the created objects. In Java (Gosling et al., 2005) for example, this can be done with the 'getClass' method and the '.class' expression, both resulting in types that can be compared with the '==' operator (using the instanceof would prove of no use, since it returns true even for subtypes).

7. Implementation

Implementing the proposed principle in Java would require language support for properties and class contracts. Several languages, Eiffel (Meyer, 1997), for example, exist already that integrate contracts in the language, as opposed to creating a separate specification language to be used on top of the programming language, like the Java Modelling Language (Leavens, 1998) for Java. Both of these approaches have the benefit of seamlessness: the fact that documentation and code should be one, which means: in the same document. This seamlessness is the best way to ensure that the code and its specification remain consistent, which is indispensable for reliable reuse.

A benefit that direct language support has over third party languages is easier acceptance: if the assertions are part of the language, nothing else is needed to start using them, so developers will more easily be inclined to do so.

In any case, language support, whether in a separate documentation language or in the core programming language, requires a compiler, and optionally modifications to the virtual machine (for runtime support). We are currently working on adapting the Java compiler to support our properties, and support for design by contract is future work.
Language support for flexible design by contract would allow for a myriad of useful tools. IDEs could do syntax checking on our assertions, and simple analysis tools could check them for inconsistencies, such as restrictions that restrict further than an already present permission. More advanced tools could check if the program code adheres to the provided assertions, and hence check if it is correct. How far this can go depends on the state of the art of tools for static verification. As it is now, a lot can be accomplished with certain tools (Chalin, 2006; Barnett et al., 2006), but complete verification of the correctness of general program code is not entirely possible. The development of such tools for our concepts, while extremely beneficial, is out of scope.

8. Related Work

The two main ingredients of this work are inheritance and class contracts. We are not the first to focus on these concepts to improve reuse of software.
Concentrating on inheritance, the notion of weak subtyping (Lowe et al., 1998) alleviates the principles of substitutability (Liskov & Wing, 1994) by looking at conformance not in general, but for a concrete application. This is called weak conformance. The difference with our approach is that we do not slacken the principles of substitution, but introduce new concepts which allow the easy identification of parts in the code or contract that are not subject to them.
Weak subtyping is not to be confused with the notion of weak behavioural subtyping (Dhara & Leavens, 1995). The latter defines a different weakening of the subtyping rules, which, as its most important contribution, allows mutable types to be subtypes of immutable types. The possible unexpected side effects resulting from this are prevented by prohibiting direct aliasing between objects of different types.
Weak behavioural subtyping is a weak version of Liskov's strong behavioural subtyping, simply called behavioural subtyping in (Liskov & Wing, 1994), which explicitly forbids mutations of immutable supertype state by mutable subtypes. Using strong behavioural subtyping, inheritance between such types can usually be accomplished by providing an abstract supertype to both the mutable and immutable versions of the type in question. Such a supertype leaves mutability undetermined. This is similar to our notions: our version of programming by contract explicitly states that anything left unspecified is also undetermined. The difference with our approach is the scope: certain assumptions about unspecified constraints still appear in Liskov's notions of subtyping that do not occur in ours. For example, we do not automatically presume that the only state-changes that occur are the explicitly specified ones.
The same example can be found in the Java Modelling Language (Leavens et al., 1999), a language to write contracts for Java-code (Gosling et al., 2005), JML introduces an assignable clause, specifying the allowed state-changes done by methods; the default for this clause is '\everything', which means there is no constraint on what state-changes are affected by the method. In general, the assignable clauses in JML are called frame axioms (McCarthy & Hayes, 1987). One could argue the default frame axiom be that anything not mentioned is

not allowed to change. Unfortunately, this is often too restrictive for systems that need to be highly adaptable, and therefore, our principles make this optional, stating that anything left undetermined is not under any contract. However, the use of properties (Vanderkimpen et al., 2007a) as a means of implementing our principles, fosters encapsulation (Snyder, 1986) and high cohesion, which lower the chance for unexpected (or undocumented) side effects and thus reduces the frame problem (Borgida et al., 1995). The JML is widely adopted and several tools exist for both static analysis (Chalin et al., 2006) as runtime checking of the contracts. Beyond the new principles introduced by this chapter, using JML differs from our approach because we make the specification part of the programming language, making it more natural in use.

Other languages exist that incorporate class contracts in the code. An important example is Eiffel (Meyer, 1997), which was invented by Bertrand Meyer, who also was the first to introduce the notion of design by contract (Meyer, 1992). Our approach is based on this notion, and expanded with the new concepts of flexibility and permissions.

Inheritance and contracts have also been combined before in a different way. Reuse contracts (Steyaert et al., 1996) allow developers and users of reusable code to specify a protocol for reuse. The contract's main contribution is the identification of method dependencies, which, in the absence of contracts, can cause problems like the fragile base class problem (Mikhajlov & Sekerinski, 1998). Subclassing Contracts (Ruby & Leavens, 2000) are a similar construct, but add this dependency identification to the more general class contracts of JML. Whatever their name, such contracts are indeed an interesting addition to general contracts and can thus also be combined with this work.

The distinction between inherited and uninherited parts of a contract, reflected in our approach by the flexibility principle, is also not entirely new. In Verified Design by Contract (Crocker, 2004) a distinction is made between postconditions and postassertions. Postassertions are actually the traditional, inherited postconditions, stating the facts that need to be true after execution of a method. They must be provable consequences of the postconditions, which are not inherited and thus have to be supplied anew in the subclass in order to still be able to prove the inherited postassertion. These postconditions, however, are more expressive than the traditional ones; they are in fact complete, which means they specify precisely what state is changed and how it is changed, which brings us back to frame axioms. The biggest difference between VDBC and our approach is precisely this completeness: in our approach, we are deliberately incomplete in specifications, to allow maximum flexibility of the design.

9. Conclusion & Future Work

In this chapter, we have shown how design by contract can impede the development of adaptable software because of its lack of flexibility. We have also shown how the expressivity of many contracts is often too limited. Focusing on the importance of both adaptable and reliable software, we have introduced flexible design by contract, a methodology aimed at reconciling the reliability of design by contract with a programming style that fosters adaptability.

Flexible design by contract introduces the distinction between flexible and rigid assertions, the latter of which concern whole type hierarchies, as in traditional design by contract, while the former focus only on a single type, not its subtypes. Furthermore, flexible design by contract clarifies the third option, not to provide an assertion, as undetermined, maximizing the opportunities for future change.

A second distinction principle introduced by flexible design by contract is the distinction between restrictions and permissions, which allow for the division of a domain of possible values for a certain feature in three parts: valid, invalid and undetermined. This goes against the tradition of making anything left unspecified automatically valid or invalid, depending on which of the two has been specified.

We have demonstrated how both these changes to design by contract not only increase flexibility and expressiveness, but also the coherence of the paradigm, by eliminating certain ambiguities such as allowing preconditions only to weaken under inheritance, but postconditions only to strengthen.

We have shown how flexible design by contract can be applied to properties, part of our previous research, by adding invariants, preconditions and postconditions to property declarations. We have also discussed how an implementation in the form of language support can help developers use our methodology and how tools can be used to better test software written this way.

Finally, we have considered the benefits and drawbacks of our principles, and contrasted them with existing work.

Future work could include the addition of more kinds of contract clauses, such as the exception clause, which will be similar to the precondition clause, and clauses that can express the frame axioms of the code. Another branch of future work involves implementation in the form of adaptations to the Java compiler, and tool support. Finally, we note that there are often important similarities between invariant clauses and precondition clauses. Devising a short-hand notation to make preconditions implement the invariants can thus be future work that would strongly alleviate the burden of writing semi-duplicate specifications.

10. References

Barnett, M.; Chang, B.; DeLine, R.; Jacobs, B. & Leino, K. (2006). Boogie: A Modular Reusable Verifier for Object-Oriented Programs, In: *Formal Methods for Components and Objects*, de Boer, F.; Bonsangue, M.; Graf, S. & de Roever, W.-P., (Ed.), 364-387, Springer, 978-3-540-36749-9, Heidelberg, Germany

Borgida, A.; Mylopoulos, J. & Reiter, R. (1995). On the Frame Problem in Procedure Specifications. *IEEE Trans. Softw. Eng.*, 21, 10, (October 1995) 785-798, 0098-5589

Chalin, P.; Kiniry, J.; Leavens, G. & Poll, E. (2006). Beyond Assertions: Advanced Specification and Verification with JML and ESC/Java2, In: *Formal Methods for Components and Objects*, de Boer, F.; Bonsangue, M.; Graf, S. & de Roever, W.-P., (Ed.), 342-363, Springer, 978-3-540-36749-9, Heidelberg, Germany

Crocker, D. (2004). Safe Object-Oriented Software: The Verified Design-by-contract Paradigm, In: *Practical Elements of Safety: Proceedings of the Twelfth Safety-critical Systems Symposium, Birmingham, UK, 17-19 February 2004, Redmill*, F. & Anderson T. (Eds.), 19-43, Springer-Verlag, 978-1-852-33800-8, New York, United States

Dhara, K & Leavens, G. (1995). Weak Behavioral Subtyping for Types with Mutable Objects. *Electronic Notes in Theoretical Computer Science*, 1, (1995) 91-113, 1571-0061

Gosling J.; Joy, B.; Steele, G. & Bracha, G. (2005). *The Java™ Language Specification (Third Edition)*, Addison Wesley, 978-0321246783, United States

Leavens, G.; Baker, A. & Ruby, C. (1998). JML: a Java modeling language. In: *OOPSLA '98 Addendum: Addendum to the 1998 proceedings of the conference on Object-oriented programming, systems, languages, and applications (Addendum)*, ACM, 1-58113-286-7, Vancouver, Canada

Leavens, G.; Baker, A. & Ruby, C. (1999). JML: a Notation for Detailed Design. In: *Behavioral Specifications for Businesses and Systems*, Kilov, H.; Rumpe, B. & Simmonds, I. (Ed.), 175-188, Springer, 978-0792386292, Heidelberg, Germany

Liskov, B. & Wing, J. (1994). A behavioral notion of subtyping, *ACM Transactions on Programming Languages and Systems*, 16, 6, (November 1994) 1811-1841, 0164-0925

Lowe, W.; Neumann, R.; Trapp, M. & Zimmerman, W. (1998). Weak subtyping - yet another notion of inheritance, *Technology of Object-Oriented Languages, 1998, Tools 26, Proceedings*, 333-345, 0-8186-8482-8, Santa Barbara, CA, USA, August 1998, IEEE Computer Society, Washington, DC

McCarthy, J. & Hayes, P. (1987). Some philosophical problems from the standpoint of artificial intelligence. In: *Readings in nonmonotonic reasoning*, Ginsberg, M. (Ed.), 26-45, Morgan Kaufmann Publishers Inc., 0-934613-45-1, San Francisco, United States

Meyer, B. (1992). Applying "Design by Contract". *Computer*, 25, 10, (October 1992) 40-51, 0018-9162

Meyer, B. (1997). *Object Oriented Software Construction (2nd Ed.)*, Prentice-Hall, 0-13-629155-4, United States

Mikhajlov, L. & Sekerinski, E. (1998). A study of The Fragile Base Class Problem. In: *ECOOP '98: Proceedings of the 12th European Conference on Object-Oriented Programming*, Jul, E. (Ed.), 355-382, Springer-Verlag, 3-540-64737-6, London, United Kingdom

Ruby, C. & Leavens, G. (2000). Safely creating correct subclasses without seeing superclass code. In: *OOPSLA '00: Proceedings of the 15th ACM SIGPLAN conference on Object-oriented programming, systems, languages, and applications*, Rosson, M. & Lea, D. (Eds.), 208-228, ACM, 1-58113-200-X, New York, United States

Snyder, A. (1986). Encapsulation and inheritance in object-oriented programming languages, In: *OOPLSA '86: Conference proceedings on Object-oriented programming systems, languages and applications*, 38-45, ACM, 0-89791-204-7, New York, United States

Steyaert, P.; Lucas, C.; Mens, K. & D'Hondt, T. (1996). Reuse Contracts: Managing the Evolution of Reusable Assets, In: *OOPSLA '96: Proceedings of the 11th ACM SIGPLAN conference on Object-oriented programming, systems, languages, and applications*, 268-285, ACM, 0-89791-788-X, San Jose, California, United States

Szyperski, C. (1998). *Component software: beyond object oriented programming (2nd Ed.)*, Addison-Wesley Professional, 0-201-17457-20, United States

Vanderkimpen, K.; van Dooren, M. & Steegmans, E. (2007a). Flexible Object Representation using Properties, *Proceedings of the International Multiconference on Computer Science and Information Technology*, 1103-1112, 1896-7094, Wisła, Poland, October 2007, PTI

Vanderkimpen, K.; van Dooren, M. & Steegmans, E. (2007b). Using Customizable Properties to make Object Representation a First-class Citizen. *Computer Science and Information Systems*, 4, 2, (December 2007) 27-46, 1820-0214

8

Application of semantic networks in natural language issues

Wojciech Górka, Adam Piasecki and Łukasz Bownik
Centre EMAG
Poland

1. Introduction

Semantic networks are becoming a more and more popular issue these days. This popularity is mostly related to the idea of the so called Web 3.0. However, the use of ontologies and semantic networks is not limited to the Internet. They can find application in data integration, formal description of a domain, identification of facts, etc. Semantic networks are related to natural language applications.

Natural language analysis is based on understanding the user's question and generating an answer. Within the analysis of the user's question there are solutions based both on full-text analysis and on patterns. Full-text analysis is related mostly to Internet browsers or ready-to-use tools which perform such functions. On the other hand, there are solutions based on question patters developed for chatterbot applications. Semantic networks can provide extra qualities to both these solutions, i.e. the possibility to define hierarchies, dependencies between concepts, which will allow the data search to become a more intelligent process.

Semantic networks make it possible to record certain facts and data related by concepts which give meaning to these facts and data. It is especially evident now with the development of data publication (Linked data) in social network services. The advantages of such knowledge collecting processes are: easy navigation between particular concepts, browsing the data in a cross-sectional manner, flexible data structure, and the possibility to record information about meta-data (data structure). On the other hand, there are situations when the information about a particular element should be available as text - sometimes the text is more understandable and readable for the user than a table or structure. Semantic networks, equipped with tools suitable for a given language, easily enable such functionality.

The first section of this chapter will describe semantic network issues. Then two sample solutions will be shown, which use semantic networks for natural language analysis and for generating texts on the basis of data recorded in semantic networks. In the first section the semantic networks issues will be described. Next, two examples of the adaptation of semantic networks in a natural language will be proposed: search engine and natural language generation engine based on semantic networks. The examples will be based on works and tests performed with the use of the Polish language. Still, it seems that the presented ideas will find applications in other languages too.

1.1 Semantic network

The semantic network concept was introduced as an answer to new requirements connected with the progress of the Internet network (Berners-Lee, 2001). The functionality of the Internet (share files, contents, websites, services made available through a variety of forms) is gradually becoming insufficient. Shared resources are primarily intended for use directly by humans. Poor standardization of contents makes it impossible to precise search and process data in an automated manner. For example, e-mail addresses, contact information, calendar of events on a web page are readable for humans. However, if it had to be automatically imported into the mail, calendar, etc. this will be confusing. So it became necessary to build a formalized standard for describing data, knowledge and relationships between them. Formally described data could be both human readable and easily accessible to programs operating on them. A standardized form of data storage will allow to use them in different systems, applications, etc.

1.1.1 Standards related to semantic networks

World Wide Web Consortium (W3C) started to process a knowledge description standard. In 1997 a standard was proposed, and as early as in 1999 W3C published the Resource Description Framework (RDF) standard[1] . The standard was complemented in 2004 with the RDF Schema (RDF-S) (Brickley, 2004) specification.
RDF allows to record triples of concepts. Each triple is a subject-predicate-object expression. Such a way of concepts recording forms a network of definitions (each object can be a subject in a different triple). RDF-S introduced the possibility to build meta-concepts: classes, sub-classes, features. It also launches a non-standard way of defining the name of the notion (label) and its description (comment).
The next stage to extend the semantic web standards was to increase the expressiveness of languages intended for ontology recording. W3C published the OWL (Web Ontology Language) standard (McGuiness & Harmelen, 2004). The language allows, among others, to express the number of concept sets, to show how one concept belongs to or differs from the other, to identify necessary and sufficient conditions for a given concept. Greater expressiveness of the language allows to verify concepts added to the ontology and to search out certain facts and features indirectly. Additionally, OWL makes it possible to integrate two ontologies by means of associating their identical concepts.

1.1.2 Defined ontologies until now

Standards (defined and well known ontologies) allow describing the concepts and connections between concepts. These standards are currently creating a base for the specific schema-ontologies which introduce certain aspects of reality. Sample ontologies:

- Dublin Core (DC) [2]– ontology defining the schema for describing library collections such as books, photos, videos and other multimedia resources;
- Friend of a Friend (FOAF) [3]– ontology which describes the person and the friends of that person, thereby creating a network of connected people;

---

[1] http://www.w3.org/RDF/
[2] http://dublincore.org/documents/dcmi-terms/
[3] http://www.foaf-project.org/docs/specs

- Semantically-Interlinked Online Communities (SIOC)[4] - ontology which describes social networks;
- DBPedia [5] - ontology which provides data from Wikipedia in the structural way;
- OpenCyc[6] - ontology describing the data collected within the Cyc project. The project aims at mapping the concepts found in the real world and the relationships between them.

Currently, there is also an initiative aimed at linking together different ontologies (Berners-Lee, 2006). This initiative is led by W3C SWEO Linking Open Data. Its purpose is to provide infrastructure for publishing data by means of semantic techniques.

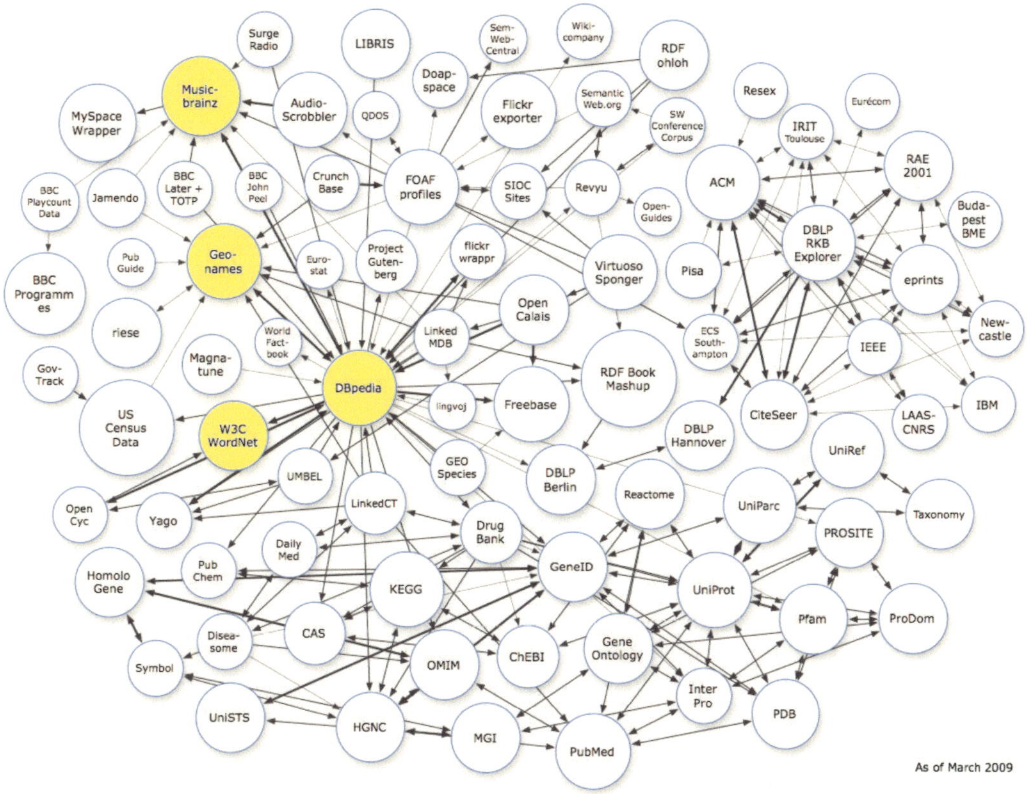

Fig. 1. Existing ontologies and connections between them [source:Linking Open Data Community[7]].

This initiative is primarily concerned with ensuring consistency between existing ontologies (and, therefore, data they describe), so that there would be a smooth transition between the information from different knowledge bases ex. Wikipedia - DBPedia, WordNet, MusicBraintz, Geonames (Figure 1).

---

[4] http://sioc-project.org/ontology

[5] http://dbpedia.org/About

[6] http://www.cyc.com/cyc/opencyc/overview

[7] http://esw.w3.org/topic/SweoIG/TaskForces/CommunityProjects/LinkingOpenData

1.2 Semantic network use cases

Although the idea of semantic networks has been mainly in providing interoperability in the Internet, the work associated with it is also applied in related issues. Currently, semantic networks are seen in the following aspects (Bruijn, 2003):

- as an integrated network of data with different formats;
- as a standard that enables data to define the interface between different fields. As a result, at the intersection of different fields new applications can be produced, benefitting from the recognition of a multi-dimensional issue;
- to support exchange, data sharing, and cooperation on the basis of the same data.

The following areas of application of the semantic network can be highlighted (Saab, 2006):

- linking data with applications (inserting data on a web page and possibility to automatically use them by means of different applications such as: calendar, email, phone etc.) This is due to the standardization of metadata and the implementation of a variety of browser plug-ins that "understand" the data stored in the contents of web pages (e.g. email address, url links, phone numbers, etc.);
- to facilitate filling in the forms. Using ontologies can help to understand the meaning of individual fields in the form;
- combining and integrating data from different sources - the replacement of manual data integration from multiple sources (W3C, 2001). Creating a data bus, the release of data from the application, which allows to create new functionality and easy integration of new systems with the existing ones;
- supporting human cooperation and knowledge acquisition (Davies et al., 2003). Semantic networks facilitate the organization of saving and retrieving knowledge. A sample scenario is the knowledge which is collected by people involved in production and supervision in a factory, etc. They gain knowledge, make decisions, gain experience. However, if it is not recorded, the employees leave it only for themselves. If they do not justify their decisions, a part of their work could be useless in the case they change their jobs. Additionally, in the case of a group of people working on an issue, it is necessary to support the process of saving knowledge, decisions and their justifications. It also permits to track the progress and planning of projects. Other examples of the semantic network application in this area may be as follows:
    - the development of the log of the decisions taken at the stage of production, treatment, evaluation of some facts;
    - maintaining consistency of documentation and informing the service networks about faults;
    - biology, genetics, describing genes, genomes, classification, etc.;
    - description of images and their fragments;
    - customizing therapies with respect to particular patients on the basis of the experience with other cases;
    - integration of research data – different types of data, the structure of the record in the form of troika is more flexible, it is easier to find some "contacts" of data and to view the data multidimensionally;
    - warning about the dangers based on conditions, rules.

- use of semantic networks in the natural language processing (Zaihrayeu et al., 2007), (Jupp et al. 2008);
- integration of geographical data - integration of different data formats, differences in formats and their integration can be assisted by RDF.

As semantic networks are related largely to information processing and organizing, they are also inevitably linked to the issue of natural language. Semantic networks can be used in understanding the text, classification of documents, interpretation of the user's expressions, or to generate dynamic information from the gathered knowledge base. The applications of semantic networks, connected with understanding the users' question and the natural language generation will be described in next sections. The works related to these issues were conducted in the Virtual Consultant for Public Services (WKUP) project, whose objective was to build a service that allows the users to obtain information in the field of competences of the system by means of natural-language communication with the system.

2. Search engine based on semantic networks

The communication with the user is mainly based on understanding the user's question. The issue of interpreting the question can be achieved by text searching as in the case of full-text search engines. On the other hand, there are solutions based on templates related to the user's questions. In the beginning, the existing solutions will be presented. Then, the solution based on semantic networks and ontology Simple Knowledge Organization System (SKOS)[8] will be presented.

2.1 Searching data solutions

In the field of search engines there are widely used solutions as well as those that are not yet applied in production. This section will present the different search solutions available on the market and those which are at the stage of experiments.

2.1.1 Full text search engines

There are many solutions in the realm of information search which allow to index the information contents and search for documents based on the contents. The full-text search solutions are mostly based on statistics and there have been many algorithms developed in order to standardize the search results (Salton & Buckley, 1987). Relatively new solutions are algorithms which allow clustering search results (Manning et al., 2007). The clusterization introduces documents selection with respect to areas of interest (a sort of categorization) based on words used in a given text. A category is, to certain extent, a representation of the document contents determined on the basis of the statistics of words used in the document. Examples of such solutions are Vivismo[9] and Carrot2[10] .

---

[8] http://www.w3.org/2004/02/skos/
[9] http://vivisimo.com/
[10] http://www.carrot2.org/

One of the full-text search products is the Lucene[11] search engine. The engine enables to create a properly compressed index and to efficiently search for documents (even concrete places in documents) which are the answer to the question asked by the user. Additionally, Lucene makes it possible to create adapters which allow browsing different types of documents (Microsoft Office documents, XML documents, PDF documents, etc.)

2.1.2 Solutions based on semantic networks

The application of semantic networks solutions also contributes to improving the search results. Semantic networks allow to describe information in a formal way and to introduce interdependencies between particular pieces of information. This way the information search is broader. The use of semantic webs will allow the search tools developers to design new-quality products. The search tools, equipped with the knowledge about the concepts hierarchy and their interdependencies, will make an impression of intelligent software. Such knowledge allows searching not only for the key words given by the user but also for the related concepts, and shows how this relation is made. On the market, there are search engines which use semantic networks, or at least build results based on the hierarchy of concepts (Hakia[12], Google[13])

2.1.3 Solutions based on language corpora

Irrespective of the development of information technologies, there are works carried out in the realm of text corpora which enable to determine, among others, dependencies between words and the frequency of their occurrence in texts (Przepiórkowski, 2005).
Such works allow creating word nets (WordNet[14]). The works on the word net for the English language have been carried out since 1985. The works on other European languages (Czech, Danish, German, Spanish, Italian, French, Estonian) were carried out between 1996-1999 within the EuroWordNet[15] project.
In Poland the works have been conducted within the plWordNet[16] project. Constructing a word net is done automatically, to a certain extent, thanks to the use of the Polish text corpus. The data from word nets, actually - relations between words, can be used to associate the words which appear in the indexed texts. This way it is possible for the user to find documents on the basis of the question in which the key words included in the document have not been used directly. Thus this solution is similar to proposals derived from the semantic webs concept.
In the realm of information search it is possible to determine the qualities of systems whose objective is to answer the questions. An example is the AnswerBus[17] system based on the knowledge indexed by Internet search tools. The search results are interpreted in an

---

[11] http://lucene.apache.org
[12] http://www.hakia.com
[13] http://www.google.com
[14] http://wordnet.princeton.edu
[15] http://www.illc.uva.nl/EuroWordNet
[16] http://www.plwordnet.pwr.wroc.pl
[17] http://www.answerbus.com

adequate way so that the information looked for by the user could be extracted from the document found by the search tool.

2.1.4 Solutions based on questions templates

The issue how to interpret the user's questions and conduct a dialogue with him/her was a motive to introduce the AIML[18] language. This language makes the way to create solutions enabling conversation with templates based on questions and answers. The AIML language allows to define the templates of the questions asked by the users. The response is generated based on the found templates. AIML enables to reach simple context dialogues, to store personal information about the user with whom the conversation is processed.
This solution, in spite of various constructions which support the management of templates, seems to be difficult to maintain in the context of a large number of predefined templates.

2.2 SKOS ontology

The Simple Knowledge Organization System (SKOS)[19] the specification developed and extended under the auspices of W3C, defines an ontology which allows to express the basic structure and contents of concept diagrams, including thesauruses, thematic lists, heading lists, taxonomies, terminologies, glossaries, and other kinds of controlled dictionaries. The specification is divided into three parts:

- SKOS-Core - defines basic concepts and relations which enable to develop concepts and relations between them;
- SKOS-Mapping - introduces relations which allow to describe similarities between concepts created in different ontologies;
- SKOS-Extensions - introduces extensions of the intensity of hierarchical relations from SKOS-Core.

The SKOS ontology assumes describing "Concepts". Each "Concept" can be labelled. The SKOS ontology extends (compared to RDF-S) labels that can be used:

- prefLabel (chief label of a given concept);
- altLabel (auxiliary label, alternative for a given concept);
- hiddenLabel (hidden label, e.g. for casual words or other words treated as "hidden" due to other reasons).

The concepts can be linked into hierarchies by means of broader and narrower relations. For example the "Car" concept is broader than the "Van" concept. The SKOS-Extensions specification introduces extra semantics of hierarchy relations, among others by the following relations:

- broaderInstantive / narrowerInstantive (express context hierarchies - instances, e.g. Dog and Azorek[20]);
- relatedPartOf / relatedHasPart (express the whole-part semantics, e.g. Car and Wheel).

---

[18] http://alicebot.blogspot.com
[19] http://www.w3.org/2004/02/skos/, http://www.w3.org/TR/2005/WD-swbp-skos-core-guide-20051102/
[20] Popular dog name in Poland

The SKOS ontology also provides the class definition which describes a set of concepts – Collection. Such a set can help to manage the ontology and facilitate its edition by grouping concepts of similar meanings. Possible ways to use the structures of concepts built on the basis of the SKOS ontology were described in use cases (W3C, 2007). What is derived from these use cases is, among others, the application of SKOS to the following:

- to order and formalize the concepts used in a given domain, to search – on the basis on the concepts and a part of relations between them – for resources assigned to the concepts;
- to search for information in different languages (thanks to an easy method of translating labels in the ontology with an unchanged relation structure);
- to label press articles, TV programmes, etc. with key words from a thesaurus recorded in accordance with the SKOS ontology.

The above objectives of the SKOS ontology satisfy, to a large extent, the requirements of the search tool which was build during experiments. Therefore a decision was made to apply this ontology. The application was justified by the possibility to provide the tool with a wide and, at the same time, precise "understanding" of concepts. Thanks to semantics it is possible to record the relations between concepts which, in turn, allows to better interpret the questions. In comparison with the solutions based on AIML language, this solution seems to be more flexible and easier to maintain and managed. It also allows to control and precisely define the search results.

2.3 The applied search algorithm

The use of the SKOS ontology in the built system consists of two stages: edition and production (search tool operations). The way of using the concepts, defined in accordance with the SKOS ontology, with a view to search for certain resources – data – related to these concepts is demonstrated in Figure 2.

At the edition stage (before the system starts) the administrator defines concepts and their mutual relations. Then he/she creates relations of the defined concepts with the data which are to be searched for. The ontologies defined in this manner are used at the search stage (production operations of the system). The user's question is analyzed based on the used concepts. The identified concepts are processed. On the basis of mutual relations between concepts, the best fitting answers of the system are found – the resources the user is looking for.

The analysis algorithm of the user's question was divided into successive stages. The first stage is "cleaning" the user's question from redundant non-alphanumeric signs as well as lemmatization of particular words in the sentence. For the statement prepared in such a way, at the next stage the best-fit concepts are searched for based on their labels (relations prefLabel, altLabel and hiddenLabel). In the case when the found concepts are not related to the resources, the broaderInstantive, broader and relatedPartOf relations are used in order to search the network for the concepts which have certain resources assigned. This allows to find concepts whose meaning is broader than the meaning of concepts used in the sentence.

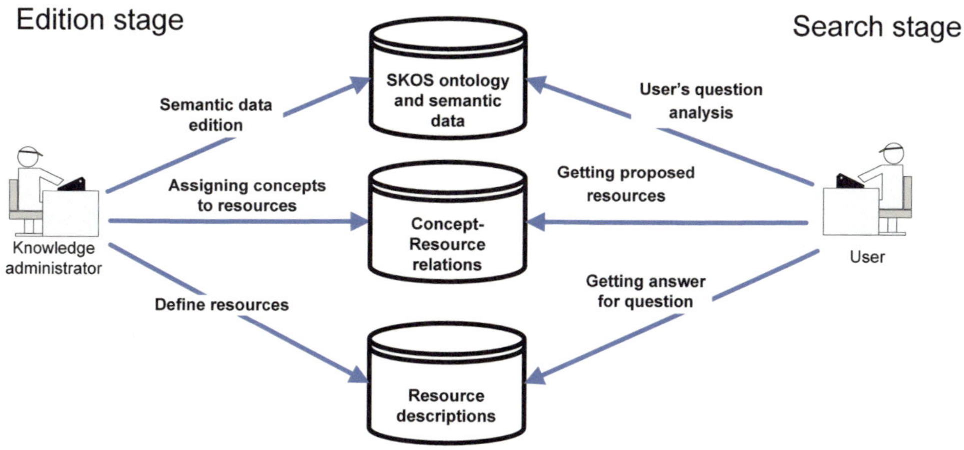

Fig. 2. The use of concepts defined in accordance with the SKOS ontology in the search process. [source: own].

The SKOS ontology has been supplemented by additional structures - sets of concepts which are directly connected to searched resources. The aim of the sets is to model a part of the user's question. The more sets are found in the user's question, the greater significance of the searched resource is. This way it is possible to model connections between concepts, based on the knowledge of a particular domain.

The last stage of the sentence analysis is the use of information about the words location with respect to one another in the user's sentence. The words which are closer to one another and point at the same resource simultaneously raise the priority of the found resource. This results from the prerequisite that, usually, the words which determine the same object are located close to one another in the sentence.

Such analysis allows to present the found resources to the user, according to the assigned search ranking.

Figure 3 shows a sample SKOS concepts structure and its relation to resources that are to be searched for. Three issues (real life situations) have been defined: finding an ID, losing an ID and getting a new ID. Additionally, the following concepts have been defined: finding, loss, theft, getting and issuing. The related relations allow to "strengthen" certain relations other than broader and relatedPartOf. With such defined relationships it is possible to address the questions about "robbery", or about "finding", both using the word "ID card" or "proof of identification".

Building a net of concepts and assigning resources to the concepts allow to model the system answers to the user's questions. This way the data administrator, who defines the system answer by himself/herself, has a clear picture of the system behavior with respect to a given class of questions. Such a solution is more deterministic than full-text search tools which operate on the basis of statistical methods only.

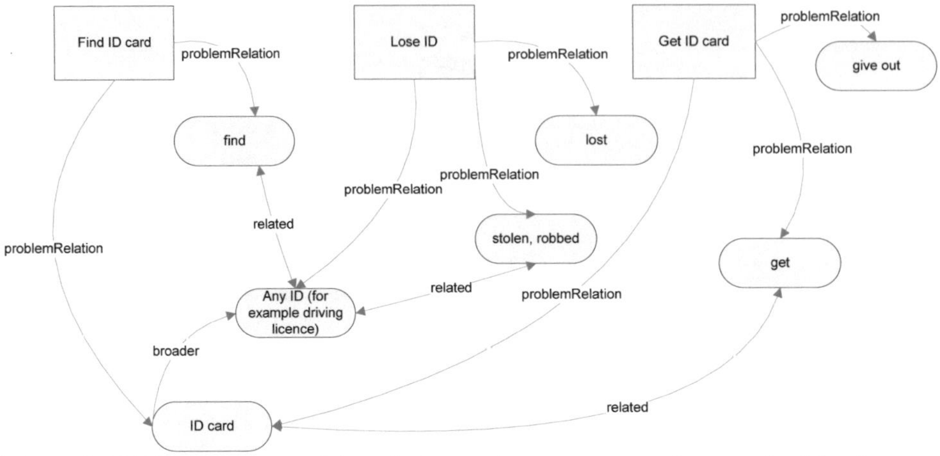

Fig. 3. Sample SKOS structure and its relation to the resources to be searched for [source: own].

Additionally, to improve the data administrator's operations in the system, the mechanisms were introduced which function in traditional search tools solutions, but at the edition stage of the ontology. Thus the possibility of automatic collection of concepts from the indexed elements (descriptions of life cases) was applied, and the process of assigning the concepts to life cases was automated. In order to perform this task, the algorithm was used to calculate normalized words priorities for documents (dt indicator) (Salton & Buckley, 1987). The algorithm allows to calculate the adequacy ranking of a given word for the indicated life case. Therefore the work with the tool can start from automatic indexing of life cases and then can proceed to successive introduction of revisions by means of successive introduction of relations between concepts, changing labels and their classification (pref, alt, hidden), etc.

2.4 Conclusions about search engine based on semantic networks

The presented solution is a proposal to solve a certain issue related to information search. It seems that the solution can improve the search in resources which are limited in terms of the number of indexed documents, and in the situation in which it is assumed that the users will ask "questions" to the search tool. The solution appears especially adequate in the case of the so called FAQ lists. They define ready answers to certain questions and, more importantly, the questions are usually relatively short. In such cases full-text search tools can have problems to properly index the contents.

On the basis of the conducted tests it seems that the efficiency of the search tool operations depends mainly on a well constructed ontology. Therefore the ontology is the key element which affects the functioning of the system. It is necessary to adopt a relevant methodology for building ontologies. The key issue in building an ontology is making it easy to manage in the future.

On the basis of the existing solution it is possible to introduce an extra feature - possibility to clarify the user's question. The proposed solution could be an engine which would control the conversation with the user in a specific manner.. In such a solution, in the first step the issue asked by the user would be found and then the engine should ask some questions (assigned to the chosen issue) to precise the question and give the most correct answer.

3. Natural language text generation

Recording knowledge and facts is related to the introduction of concepts, the features of these concepts, and relationships between concepts. Recording knowledge in the form of a natural-language sentence (descriptive text) contains the above mentioned concepts, dependencies and features. However, due to its nature, this way of recording limits the possibilities to process knowledge as well as to compare and connect similar concepts. Thus it is not possible to automatically combine knowledge from two different sources with the purpose to obtain some extra cross-sectional information based on two separate documents. Such cases refer particularly to the knowledge that resembles data structures where there is focus on certain dependencies between entities. An example is a description of a device and sub-assemblies the device consists of (catalogue of products, catalogue of sub-assemblies). The description will comprise not only typical information on a given sub-assembly but also the dependencies, e.g. which of other sub-assemblies is able to replace the given one, what other sub-assemblies it consists of, what material it is made of, etc. Similarly, scientific research results that contain parameters and their mutual dependencies can be described with the use of such a structure. This kind of solution enables to easily connect data from various sources and to find new dependencies.

Although this way of data description can be easily processed by a computer, it is less readable for the user. An ideal situation for the user would be the possibility to "question" the structural knowledge base with the use of a natural language and obtain answers in the form of grammatical sentences.

In this section the natural language generation will be described. In the first step storing knowledge as a semantic network will be described. Then we will show the state of the art in the natural language generation and specific issues connected with the Polish language. Next, a natural language generation engine based on semantic networks will be presented, which was built in the course of the Virtual Consultant for Public Services project.

3.1 Knowledge stored as semantic networks

As it has been already mentioned, semantic networks allow to describe concepts, their properties, classification of concepts and relationships between concepts. Semantic data can be used to describe documents (assigning tags), or they can be a source of knowledge by themselves. Ontologies which store knowledge have many properties and relationships defined between elements.

Sample ontologies for tagging texts, documents are:

- SKOS ontology[21] which allows to build vocabulary for a particular domain - concepts and relations between them. There are also special relationships between concepts: hierarchy, part-of relation, associations;
- OpenCYC[22] ontology which represents data within the CYC initiative. The main objective of the CYC Project is to collect concepts from real word and build relationships between them.

---

[21] http://www.w3.org/2004/02/skos/

Sample ontologies for knowledge management and storage are:

- FOAF ontology[23] which describes the person and the friends of that person, thereby creating a network of connected people;
- DBPedia[24] - ontology which provides data from Wikipedia in the structural way;
- Ontology for describing photos (Lafon & Bos, 2002);
- Ontology for describing spatial data[25].

Currently, the LikedData[26] initiative is promoting the idea to publish various types of already collected data as semantic data and combining them with each other. There are many tools available that help to publish data over HTTP as semantic data directly from existing relational databases. Thanks to such initiatives, the data published on the Internet will be readable not only for humans but also for different kinds of services, systems, applications. Computer systems will be able to use those data, combine them with each other and perform new functionalities.
Storing knowledge in such a way can be also used by programs that generate texts (readable for humans) from structural data.

3.2 State of the art in natural language generation

The natural language generation has been already described in many publications (Reiter & Dale, 1997), (Paris et al., 1991), (Cole et al., 1997). Some classes of software to generate text have been defined depending on algorithm complexity and quality results of a generated text. Some stages in the generation process were also defined.
The first stage is called text planning. At that stage it should be planned which part of knowledge should be described in a textual form.
In the next stage, the sentence content and order should be stipulated. The last stage is dedicated to generating sentences in a proper grammatical form. This process can be performed in different algorithm complexity, depending on language tools.
Natural language generation systems can be classified into (Cole et al., 1997):

- information systems which produce messages without infrastructure for text planning, sentence order and any language tools;
- systems which base on sentence templates. This solution depends on prepared templates which are filled with changeable elements;
- systems based on phrase templates. This solution depends on a part of sentence templates - phrases which are used recursively up to generate a meaningful sentence;
- systems based on sentences properties. In such solution, sentence templates with defined properties (question sentence, statement) are a starting point. Iterating through the successive stages, these templates are completed with additional details up to generate a meaningful sentence.

---

[22] http://www.cyc.com/cyc/opencyc/overview
[23] http://www.foaf-project.org/docs/specs
[24] http://dbpedia.org/About
[25] http://www.geonames.org/ontology/
[26] http://esw.w3.org

In the natural language generation it is important to use language tools specific for a particular language. They are especially important for inflective languages. It is important to use a proper grammatical form of the word: gender, tense, mode, plural/singular form.

3.3 Polish language specifics and language tools

Natural languages have different ways of building sentences. In English, the position of a word in the sentence is strictly determined. This facilitates the sentence analysis which, in turn, allows to precisely determine the meaning of the sentence. Polish is not a positional language. Verb, subject, attribute, etc. can occur in different positions in the sentence (Vetulani, 2004). However, Polish has fixed connections between parts of speech. These connections determine dependencies between particular parts of the sentence, i.e. the grammatical form of one part of the sentence enforces the grammatical form of the other part (Saloni & Świdziński, 1981). Unfortunately, these dependencies do not have strict character. They depend on the style of the sentences and their types too. For example, questions will have a different word order and different dependencies between forms compared to statements.

Polish language is also inflective. Depending on its gender, case, tense, a particular word is in a different form. Differences in grammatical forms are not manifested only by the endings of words. In comparison with other languages (for example English), there are many more irregular forms in Polish.

Some conclusions:

- Using the rules for sentence building can be very complex, especially for Polish. Formal description of the Polish language is carried out in IPI PAN. The formal description of the Polish language is defined in Gramatyka Świdzińskiego (Świdziński, 1992). There is also an implementation of that formalism, but it is on the experimental stage;
- It is important to use tools for getting a word in its primary form - lemma generation tool - when analyzing a piece of text;
- During the sentence generation it is necessary to use words in appropriate forms (correct case, gender, tense etc.). That is why the tool for generating words in their correct forms is needed.

When developing a natural language generation engine, the UTR tool was chosen for generating lemma and correct word forms. The author of this tool is Jan Daciuk. UTR uses a dictionary which contains words, their forms and form tags. Very good compression and easy browsing through words was achieved thanks to the finite-state automata algorithm. Technical details of the UTR tool have been widely described in the doctoral dissertation of Jan Daciuk (Daciuk, 1999).

3.4 Generator implementation

The described natural language generation engine has been developed as a system which depends on templates. The knowledge base for the generator is the data stored as a semantic network. The engine describes a concept stored in semantic data with the use of its properties and relationships between other concepts. The semantic network naturally provides the text planning stage. Sentence templates are connected to properties defined in the ontology. The lemma tool and the tool for generating forms provide proper forms of the generated text in template gaps.

```
<Flu> <has symptom> <Headache>
<Flu> <has symptom> <Fever>

<Flu> <treatment> <Aspirin>

<Aspirin> <contraindication> <Blood coagulability>
<Aspirin> <indication> <Flu>
```

Relationships between concepts

```
<Aspirin> <description> „Popular medicine. It is antiphlogistic and antithermic. Used in flu and other sicknesses.
```

Textual description

Fig. 4. Semantic data examples [source: own].

Browsing the knowledge base is primarily reviewing the different concepts, reading their properties and navigating between related concepts. The concepts describe some entities, so as a part of speech they are usually nouns. The properties define details about a concept or define relationships between concepts. That is why they are usually verbs or adjectives. Sample data are presented in Figure 4.

```
- for property <has symptom>
            Objawy [[subject gen:sg:]] to [[object]]
        (English: Symptoms …are…)
- for property <treatement>
Możliwe jest leczenie poprzez [[object acc:]]
        (English: Treatement using…)
- for property <contraindication>
Nie może być [[$subject$ stosowany m:|stosowane n:|stosowana f:]]
w przypadku [[object gen:]]
        (English: It can't be used for….)
- for property <indication>
[[$subject$ Używany m: | Używane n:| Używana f:]] jest przy
leczeniu [[object gen:]]
        (English: It is used for…)
```

Fig. 5. Template examples [source: own].

The concept description consist of: textual description, properties (in fig: "has symptom", "treatment", "contraindication", "indication", "description") and relationships. Sentences are generated based on relationships between concepts and templates connected with properties (Figure 5). So the templates consist of the text which should be applied for a particular property and pointers which point where other elements from the RDF triple (subject and object) should be inserted.

In addition, the template contains information about the prescribed form of the expression to be inserted in the template. Information about the prescribed form can contain additional criteria: tense, gender, case, etc. It is not necessary to give each criterion. In such a case the missing criteria will be preserved from the original word. For example, when for a particular field only tense is defined, the inserted words will preserve their gender and case. To achieve some diversity in the generated text it is possible to define more than one template for the same property. In such a case one template will be chosen from the defined set of templates.

Some information may be stored as a text description. Property can point at a broader textual description. In such a situation it is presented as hyperlink.

3.5 Conclusions about natural language generation based on semantic data

The presented solution is an attempt to develop a service providing a universal method of searching and presenting the structural data sources. Not all types of information assets fit this model. Therefore the solution can find application first of all in such cases where the knowledge has an organized, structural character by nature. In the developed engine the most complex stage was choosing an appropriate form for the gaps in the template. Despite the use of markers that point at an appropriate form, there were some ambiguities and confusions. An idea to solve that issue is to use the Google browser to check which version of the phrase or part of sentence is more likely - which option has more results in the Google search engine. For future development it is also possible to build up a phase in which the knowledge is selected for generation and presentation. Currently, for the generation of the text "the nearest environment" of the concept is selected. One can imagine that further relationships are taken into account. It could be done by extending or changing algorithm used by reasoner engine.

4. Summary

The presented solutions combine the knowledge of the semantic networks and natural language processing. They verify the usefulness of the application of network-related issues in the semantic processing of a natural language. Both solutions use the powers of the semantic network in terms of modelling the relationships between concepts. The search engine, through the use of semantics, can better "understand" questions asked by the user. The impact is especially on the ability to define relationships (hierarchy, dependencies, relationships conclusion) between concepts. The mechanism of texts generation shows that semantic networks are a good way to store knowledge in a structural way with a flexible approach to modelling the relationships between properties and concepts. The possibility to describe properties (wide possibilities in metadata description) helps in developing an engine for generating text from the web of relationships. The final result - a generated text based on semantically stored knowledge makes information more readable for humans.

According to the presented solutions one can assume that using semantic networks can have good influence on other issues associated with the natural language. However, it is necessary to identify real needs in each case and define a proper place for using the semantic network in the developed solution.

5. References

Berners-Lee, T. (2001). *The Semantic Web*, Scientific American, (284(5)):34–43

Berners-Lee, T. (2006). *Relational Databases on the Semantic Web*, See: http://www.w3.org/DesignIssues/RDB-RDF

Brickley, D. (2004). *RDF Vocabulary Description Language 1.0: RDF Schema*, W3C

Bruijn, J. (2003). *Using ontologies*, DERI Technical Report, DERI-2003-10-29

Cole, R. & Mariani, J. & Uszkoreit, H. & Zaenen, A. & Zue, V. (1997). *Survey of the State of the Art in Human Language Technology*, Cambridge University Press, ISBN 0521592771

Daciuk, J. (1999). *Incremental Construction of Finite-State Automata and Transducers, and their Use in the Natural Language Processing*,, Politechnika Gdańska

Davies, J. & Fensel, D. & Harmelen F. (2003). *Towards the Semantic Web, Ontology-based Knowledge Management at Work*, John Wiley & Sons, LTD, ISBN 0470848677

Jupp, S. & Bechofer, S. & Stevens, R. (2008). *A Flexible API and Editor for SKOS*, The Univeristy of Manchester

Lafon, Y. & Bos, B. (2002). *Describing and retrieving photos using RDF and HTTP*, W3C

Manning, C.D. & Raghavan, P. & Schütze, H. (2007). *An Introduction to Information Retrieval*, Cambridge University Press, Draft,

McGuiness, D. & Harmelen, F. (2004). *OWL Web Ontology Language Overview*, W3C

Paris, C. & Swartout, W. & Mann, W. (1991). *Natural Language Generation in Artificial Intelligence and Computional Linguistic*, Springer, ISBN 0792390989

Przepiórkowski, A. (2005). *The Potential of The IPI PAN Corpus*, Institute of Computer Science, Polish Academy of Science, Warsaw

Reiter, E. & Dale, R. (1997). Building Applied Natural Language Generation Systems *Natural Language Engineering* Vol. 3, No. 01. pp. 57-87 Cambridge University Press

Saab, S. (2006). *The Semantic Web Revisited*, University of Koblenz-Landau

Saloni, Z. & Świdziński M. (1981). *Składnia współczesnego języka polskiego*, Wydawnictwo Uniwersytetu Warszawskiego, Warszawa

Salton, G. & Buckley, C. (1987). *Term weighting approaches in automatic text retrieval. Information Processing and Management* 32:431–443. Technical Report TR87-881, Department of Computer Science, Cornell University

Świdziński, M. (1992). *Gramatyka formalna języka polskiego*, Wydawnictwo Uniwersytetu Warszawskiego, Warszawa

Vetulani, Z. (2004). *Komunikacja człowieka z maszyną. Komputerowe modelowanie kompetencji językowych*, Akademicka Oficyna Wydawnicza Exit, ISBN 83-87674-66-4, Warszawa

W3C (2001). *Semantic Web Use Cases and Case Studies*, See: http://www.w3.org/2001/sw/sweo/public/UseCases

W3C (2007). *SKOS UseCase*, See: http://www.w3.org/TR/2007/WD-skos-ucr-20070516/

Zaihrayeu, I. & Sun, L. & Giunchiglia, F. & Pan, W. &Ju, Q. & Chi, M. & Huang, X. (2007). *From Web Directories to Ontologies: Natural Language Processing Challenges*, University of Trento - Italy - UNITN-Eprints

9

Towards the Methodological Harmonization of Passive Testing Across ICT Communities

Krzysztof M. Brzeziński
Institute of Telecommunications
Warsaw University of Technology
Poland

1. Introduction

According to its pervasive rôle in Information and Communications Technology (ICT) and science in general, and also in everyday life, *testing* is justly expected to be particularly well understood. Surprisingly, this does not seem to be the case. Unlike measurement science - *metrology*, testing does not (yet) enjoy the status of a scientific discipline. There is no "testology" entry, along with metrology, in general dictionaries and specialized vocabularies (ISO/IEC, 2004).

Yet we claim that there is an identifiable (although still unnamed) science-in-the-making that deals specifically with testing. However, at its conceptual level, it is currently only the evolving set of approaches followed by the particular research groups. On numerous occasions, various authors have noticed that certain communities "*largely failed to inform one another and there was very little interaction between* [them]" (Hierons et al., 2008); this observation is strikingly pertinent to testing. In this setting, testing concepts and solutions are being inevitably re-defined and re-invented, with the ensuing duplication of effort.

Additionally, research communities not dealing with testing as their primary field of study are faced with problems that *could* be recognized as, or mapped onto, the testing problems. The solutions to these problems are often available for potential adoption as *testing* patterns, archetypes, and design paradigms. One of the plausible reasons for the non-recognition of these patterns is the inability or reluctance to transcend a community-specific "language-game". Lamport (2008) notes that "*the obsession with language is a strong obstacle to any attempt at unifying different parts of computer science. . . A recurring theme is the difficulty that arises when necessary concepts cannot be introduced either because the language has no way of expressing them or because they are considered to be politically incorrect*". We wish to think of testing as having some inherent common characteristics, "essence", or higher-level conceptual framework that transcends the results of any particular research community. Establishing "testology" as a science is clearly a formidable intellectual task, not to be undertaken lightly. Our contribution towards this goal is delimited as follows:

- One way to uncover (some portions of) the "essence" of testing is to look at different languages which particular communities use to talk about testing. This *meta-linguistic* approach is similar in vein to (Brzeziński, 2007b). We try to reveal the underlying rules that have become so natural for a given community that they are no longer "seen".

- In order to avoid the premature and simultaneous generalization of *every* aspect of the postulated "essence", we limit the technical scope of this chapter to testing that is applicable to the *behaviour* of *distributed, reactive* systems characteristic of ICT.
- We intentionally focus on one of the most controversial dimensions of the overall concept of testing, namely that of *active* vs. *passive* testing (this controversy itself is what most communities actually agree upon). Whether "passive testing" belongs with testing at all, is subject to debate. Our initial conjecture, for which we seek corroboration, is that passive testing *is* consistent with active testing, does form a part of a wider concept of testing, and is useful as an encapsulated and reusable piece of technology.

Our discussion leads to the decoupling of the elements of (passive) testing methods from their current, fixed place and role. They may then be encapsulated in quasi-independent ("purpose-agnostic") modules of technology, and reused in new combinations, according to the evolving needs. This was the initial rationale for our PMM (*Protocol MultiMeter*) research project (Brzeziński et al., 1996; Brzeziński, 1997, 2005) that led to the development of the family of flexible, modular protocol monitors and testers. The same idea, in a very similar context of formal methods, was later submitted by Rushby (2000) who postulated that "*...the capabilities of monolithic formal methods tools be 'liberated' and be made available as standalone components that can be used inside other tools*".

2. General thoughts on testing

2.1 Extra-technical aspects of testing

Apart from technical aspects of the subject matter, we also consider it necessary to briefly look into its much more general, philosophical aspects (testing as a science is not really conceivable without some epistemological and ontological roots). Testing has not emerged with technical systems. Initially, the concept of testing has been discussed and formalized in the context of philosophy, and in particular one of its branches: epistemology (theory of knowledge). We thus start off with the *Scientific Method* (SM) - a particular paradigm of scientific enquiry, of ancient origins, but elaborated relatively recently by Charles Sanders Peirce and Karl Popper. SM is one of the primary tools of natural (empirical) sciences - those that seek *explanations* and *predictions* of phenomena. The application of SM consists in taking a series of steps, in a generally fixed order (which does not exclude the possibility of backtracking, "looping", and iterating):

- *identifying* a problem - a set of phenomena;
- stating a *hypothesis* about this set of phenomena: a statement p about "the world" (but *not* a valid, trivial, or vacuous logical formula);
- deducing *predictions* - a set of the necessary logical consequences of the hypothesis $p\colon \{p \rightarrow q1, p \rightarrow q2 \ldots\}$. At this stage it is also possible to check (in a purely formal way) if the deduced consequences are mutually consistent, as inconsistency invalidates a hypothesis without the need for any empirical investigation: $(p \rightarrow q) \land (p \longrightarrow \bar{q}) \Longrightarrow \bar{p}$.
- establishing the *empirical content* of the hypothesis, i.e., expressing the selected consequences in terms of predicted phenomena that are *in principle* amenable to experimentation (empirical observation). If this empirical content is empty, then the scientific method simply does not apply. By definition, for each selected consequence q

there is a phenomenon f such that q is **true** iff f exists. The "existence" of a phenomenon may take on diverse forms: the phenomenon may *occur* (as an event), *hold* (as a ratio between two quantities), be *present* (as an entity or quality), but also be *absent* (as the lack of influence or relation).

- *testing* the hypothesis: performing experiments aimed specifically at confirming or denying the existence of pre-stated (predicted) phenomena.

Note that the same method and means of observation could be used in a different way, with a different aim:, e.g., in the initial phase of the scientific method, to "charge" one's intuition as to the phenomena about which one is about to propose an explanation. This activity, although experimental, does not qualify as a test - we would rather call it *monitoring* of some phenomena, with the obvious intention of applying the intuition behind this distinction to technical devices - monitors and passive testers.

Two extreme approaches to how a hypothesis should be tested may be distinguished:

- *verificationism*, which maintains that a hypothesis, to be accepted as true, must be convincingly confirmed - *corroborated*, or *verified* (i.e., "shown to be true"). Careless application of verificationism may lead to the logical fallacy of *affirming the consequent*, i.e., taking the confirmation of q as a proof of the truth of p. Even if this trap is avoided, there is always the dilemma of what is the "convincing level" of corroboration.
- *falsificationism*, which maintains that it is essentially not possible to empirically verify a hypothesis, and the only sensible (meaningful) direction is to try to *falsify* (refute) it. By a simple logical argument (Destructive Dilemma), it is sufficient to deny the existence of a *single* predicted phenomenon to conclusively falsify a hypothesis.

The influence of Popperian falsificationism can be seen in the use of terms: "scientific", "testable" and "falsifiable" as quasi-synonyms. Taken to the ground of telecommunications and computing systems, this is translated to the well known observation by Edsgar Dijkstra that "*testing can only show the presence of bugs* [i.e., falsify the claim of correctness] *but never their absence* [i.e., verify that all the system's properties are as predicted]". However, "pure" approaches are not really advocated - practical applications of the scientific method always combine the elements of verification and falsification, and individual schools of thought differ in their proportions and emphasis. Two sets of experiments: those focused on confirmation, and those focused on refutation, are thus expected.

We now consider the technical setting of testing and draw some analogies. For a predicted phenomenon f, a *method* and *means* (apparatus) for observing it is required. If it is not readily available, then it must be developed. The method and apparatus in which this method is implemented is referred to as a *Test System* (TS). A Test System may be composed of many *Testers* which are related to each other in the framework of a particular *Test Architecture*. The "program" of the operation of a Test System while performing a particular experiment is referred to as a *Test*. Normally, a single Test System is constructed so as to be able to perform all the planned experiments, so that its operation is described by a number of tests: a *Test Suite* consisting of individual *Test Cases*. By convention, the outcome of a test is formalized by a *test verdict*, which values are:

- **Pass**, if a test confirms the predicted phenomenon (thus q = **True**);
- **Fail**, if a test denies the existence of the predicted phenomenon (thus q = **False**);
- **Inconclusive** (**Inc** for short), if a test (this particular execution of a test) does not allow the conclusions to be drawn as to the truth value of q.

The application of a Scientific Method, e.g., for a hypothesis *p="a system is correct"* is shown in fig. 1. In general, **Pass** is not the converse of **Fail** (with the exception of certain formal testing theories). In fig.1(a), tests are divided into two sets (classes): $\{T_m\}$ – tests aiming at falsification (so only able to issue a **Fail** or an **Inc**), and $\{T'_n\}$ – tests aiming at corroboration (so only able to issue a **Pass** or an **Inc**). For some predicted phenomenon, like f_a, tests of both kinds may be conceived, while for other phenomena only falsification tests (as for f_k) or only corroboration tests (as for f_n) will be considered. It may also be possible to combine a falsification and corroboration test into a procedure that, operationally and technically, may be considered as a single experimentation unit, as shown in fig.1(b). Such form of tests is assumed in the telecommunications-oriented methodology of conformance testing (ISO/IEC 9646), and is also inherent in the design of the TTCN-3 testing language (ETSI ES 201 873, 2008).

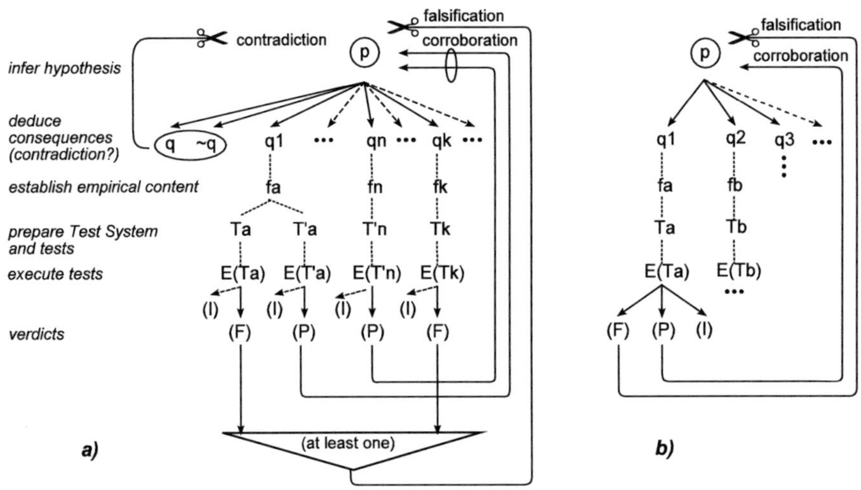

Fig. 1. The Scientific Method: (a) with confirmation and refutation tests; (b) with joint tests

Nowhere in the exposition of the Scientific Method the tests (experiments) are, explicitly or implicitly, described as *active*, i.e., those in which influence is purposefully exerted upon investigated phenomena. This is not to say that philosophers have overlooked this issue: the discussion of the relative merits of active and passive experiments can be found, e.g., in the works of John Stuart Mill (Mill, 1974). As a means of scientific enquiry, Mill distinguishes "pure observation" and "artificial experiments", which allow to, respectively, *"find an instance in nature suited to our purposes, or, by an artificial arrangement of circumstances, make one"*. He goes on to notice *"no difference in kind, no real logical distinction, between the two processes of investigation... as the uses of money are the same whether it is inherited or acquired"*.

2.2 Components of the "testing" concept

In the most general sense, although already focused on technical systems, testing is understood as:

- an activity with at least some empirical, *experimental* elements, i.e., not consisting entirely of calculations;
- with experiments conducted on a particular *Thing Under Test* **(Tut)**. "Tut" is not an established term. We use it here, because more widespread terms, such as **Sut** *(System*

Under Test), **Iut** (*Implementation Under Test*), **Eut** (*Equipment Under Test*) are not general enough. They are related to a particular test architecture or a kind of tests.

- aimed at (here follow the quasi-equivalent formulations which have been adopted by different schools of thought, and differ mainly in the "principal key-word"):
  1. establishing whether a given *relation* holds between a **Tut** and a *reference* **Ref**.
  2. establishing whether a given *hypothesis* concerning a **Tut** is true. This is clearly the language of the Scientific Method, but SM can also be applied, as a kind of a methodological landmark, in engineering (which deals with *creating* rather than *explaining*). For testing, a hypothesis may be formulated as "**Tut** is correct".
  3. obtaining *knowledge* as to whether **Tut** corresponds to a **Ref** in a specific way. Developing knowledge is the subject matter of epistemology. One of the principal notions of knowledge is that of *justified true belief* (JTB) where a subject "knows" proposition *p*, (e.g., *p*="**Tut** is correct") if jointly: (1) *p* is indeed true, (2) the subject *believes* that *p* is true, and (3) the subject is *justified* in believing that *p* is true. The need for testing may be restated as the need to *know* if a system is correct. A valid question is when one accumulates sufficient justification, or - in the context of testing - when one has "tested enough".
- and resulting in evaluating a certain object that partakes in testing - the *object of assessment*, which must be unambiguously identified.

There are many conceivable relations binding a reference and a **Tut**. The intention of defining them is captured in their generic names: "satisfies", "conforms to", "is adequate w.r.t.", or "is correct w.r.t...". In a particular domain ("over programs or systems of programs"), it has become customary to refer to the elements of a set **TUT** as *implementations*, and to elements of a set **REF** as *specifications* (Wing, 1990) The generic correctness relation is then usually called an *implementation relation*, write (**Imp imp Spec**). Here, an "implementation" and a "specification" are used just as *conventional names*.

A *test result* always pertains to a **Tut**. A *test verdict* pertains to an object of assessment, which may, or may not be a **Tut**. It is usually accepted that the domain of verdicts is {Pass, Inc, Fail}, where, conventionally, **Pass** means that the object of assessment is found to be "good enough" for **imp** to hold.

In engineering, and in particular in testing of telecommunications and computing systems, it has been silently accepted that the object of testing (a **Tut**) is also an object of assessment - it is an "implementation" that can be corrected if found to fail the tests, while a reference is given and fixed. Note that **Ref** is arbitrary - it can also express a destructive or chaotic behaviour. The need for the effective and correct development of products that are destructive is obvious, not only in the military domain and the like, but also, e.g., in case of active test systems that should be able to send erroneous or unexpected signals to a **Tut**. An **Imp** that passes tests w.r.t. a destructive **Spec** is correct (in being "destructive enough").

In the primary application area of the Scientific Method, the **Tut** is some physical system, but the object of assessment is a **Ref** - a *hypothesis* that models, explains, and predicts facts about **Tut**. It is not asked whether "the world" is correct, but rather whether our hypothesis about this world is correct (sufficiently and consistently predicts and explains the test outcomes). "Reversing" the direction of assessment is also possible, and is practiced, e.g., in *reverse engineering* (Brzeziński et al., 2008). **Tut** is then considered as given, and a test verdict is used to assess a **Ref** (e.g., a specification being reconstructed). Note that **Tut** and **Ref** cannot be simply swapped, as experiments are still conducted on the same **Tut**.

2.3 Active and passive testing

According to the prevailing intuition of testing as an active experiment, a Test System:

- *generates* stimuli that provoke phenomena to be investigated;
- *observes* phenomena as they appear under the influence of applied stimuli;
- *analyzes* the relation between applied stimuli and observed phenomena, in order to decide if this relation is *as predicted* by a pre-defined *reference.*

However, as in the Scientific Method, a *test* can be simply considered as a synonym of a *pre-designed, purposeful, empirical experiment,* where "being active" is not a part of the essence of the concept. Also in the official terminology of formal testing (ITU-T Z500, 1997), *test cases* (i.e., single tests) are defined simply as *"the experiments that constitute a test suite. . . Each test case specifies the behaviour of the tester in a separate experiment that tests an aspect of the IUT, and that leads to an observation and a verdict"* (no notion of active stimuli here). In this broader understanding, one kind of experiments (let us call them *passive tests*) involves the observation and assessment of phenomena that appear "naturally", i.e., are not invoked (provoked, stimulated, influenced) by a passive tester. The absence of influence exerted upon an investigated phenomenon may be needed, expected, or required due to the test situation (no "input ports"), a phenomenon being "intensive enough" so that any stimulus is actually not needed, or the properties of a system in which investigated phenomena occur - this may be an operational system whose *integrity, safety,* and *performance* critically depends on non-interference with its internal parts and processes.

From the preceding discussion it might transpire that there is nothing unusual in treating active and passive testing as conceptual peers. Yet, passive testing has not been identified as a dimension of the discourse space of testing, nor even mentioned, in any of the following: a recent extensive survey of formal testing (Hierons et al., 2008); the earlier annotated bibliography (Brinksma & Tretmans, 2000); the proceedings of the prestigious Seminar on testing (Brinksma et al., 2005); taxonomies developed to get insight into the notion of testing (Utting et al., 2006; Ryser et al., 1998); standardized glossaries of terms pertaining to testing (BS 7925-1, 1998; ISTQB, 2007) or broader software engineering activities (IEEE Std 610-12, 1990). The telecommunications-oriented standardized methodology of conformance testing (ISO/IEC 9646) openly excludes passive testing from its scope. The standardized test language TTCN-3 (ETSI ES 201 873, 2008) was meant to express active tests, and there have been very few proposals to use it also for passive tests (Brzeziński, 2007a).

Within ICT there is also a body of publications that converge on the concept of passive testing. Some of these publications use the term "passive tester" outright , but most prefer to use "euphemisms" like: observer, trace checker, the oracle, passive monitor, arbiter, supervisor. Tretmans (1999) and Alcalde (2006) refer to passive testing as monitoring. Bochmann & Bellal (1989) treat passive testing as a sub-problem of active testing. Some authors state that active and passive tests are complementary (Chen, Wu, & Chi, 2003), but, save for examples, provide no deeper discussion of the sense of this claim.

According to Netravali et al. (2003), "*the aim of passive testing is to detect faults in a system while observing the system during normal operation, that is, without forcing the system to specialized inputs explicitly for the purposes of testing*". This is a stipulative definition - it intends to convey a particular understanding of a concept. This illustrates the trouble with almost all the definitions to be found in the works on passive testing - they are not the kind of classical, Aristotelian definitions as a "statement of the essence of things". Hopefully, the following discussion will help clarify the doubts.

3. Background

Two very general aspects of a system are: its internal *structure* (which may be hidden), and its *behaviour* exhibited in contact with its environment, which is that part of the universe of discourse that lies outside the system border. Note that a system's border is conventional - in principle it can be moved to contain only those internal components that are "interesting" from some point of view. There is a consensus on defining a behaviour of a system as a "*sequence of observable actions it performs when interacting with the environment*". (Lamport, 1989). Such behaviour is characteristic of *Discrete-Event Systems* (DES). This broad class of systems includes all the systems that we discuss here.

There is a difference between a particular behaviour (a particular sequence, or a *trace*, of actions) and the totality of all such behaviours a system can ever exhibit (execute). The general role of a behavioural specification (a **Spec**) is to state the restrictions on system behaviours so that they stay *safe* and *useful*. Throughout its life-cycle, a system (by convention called an *implementation* - **Imp**) is meant to fulfil such obligations that come from different sources. Checking whether these restrictions (in general - requirements) are actually fulfilled is the essence of *verification* and *validation* (V&V). We understand verification as checking (the behaviour of) a system against a design specification (investigating whether a system has been correctly implemented), and validation as checking a system against an arbitrary reference (also such that a system had no chance to change in order to accomodate its requirements). V&V may proceed by *formal manipulations* on mathematical models of systems, or by *empirical investigation (experimentation)*. Testing belongs to the latter class of V&V techniques.

Testing consists in empirically checking the "correctness" of behaviour. It would be thus useful to develop the understanding of incorrectness. The three crucial notions related to incorrectness are: error, fault, and failure. We understand these notions as follows:

- an *error* is a human action, or lack of action, that (if not remedied) leads to "planting" a fault. It usually results from lack of experience or information, carelessness, neglect, etc.
- a *fault* is a defect (a flaw) in a system, which, when exercised, can lead to a failure. A fault may result from a human error or environmental conditions. A system with a fault is said to be faulty. Faultlessness is one of the generic attributes of correctness.
- a *failure* is a deviation from expected behaviour - *any* visible deviation, as we do not consider the "size" of a failure (this is also assumed in the standardized methodology of conformance testing - ISO/IEC 9646).

The reader should be aware that the meanings of a "fault" and a "failure" are often swapped, and an error may also be understood as an incorrect internal state. The resulting chaos was noted and on occasion dicussed, e.g., by Randell (2003).

The generic function of testing is to *detect failures*. Faced with the very widespread use of the term "fault detection" (also in excerpts that we cite), we interpret it to mean "failure detection with the ensuing inference to the presence of a fault".

4. Overview of research into passive testing

We now briefly survey the main concerns, approaches, and results of research conducted specifically on passive testing. This research may be divided into "epochs" (the list of researchers' names is given for orientation only, and is by far not exhaustive):

- initial (<1980): Ayache, Diaz, Jeron;
- early (ca. 1989): von Bochmann, Dssouli; Chanson et al.;
- early (ca. 1992): Wang, Schwartz, Bouloutas, et al.;
- regular (1997): Lee, Miller et. al.; Bhargavan;
- contemporary (>2000): Cavalli et al.; Petrenko, Hallal et al.; and others.

We strongly focus on the initial and early works, as they are generally more interesting from the meta-linguistic and conceptual point of view. For an alternative view on the history and current state of passive testing, see (Lee et al., 2006).

4.1 The initial epoch

Ayache et al. (1979), and, in a follow-up, Diaz et al. (1994) introduce an *observer* for online, run-time failure detection in a system of concurrent processes. Its intended application is for *self-checking systems*. The proposed architecture is a *worker-observer* system, where a worker is a product (in testing - an **Iut**), and a separate observer contains a representation of a "mission" - the intended behaviour, extracted from the worker's specification. Two different schemes for cooperation between a worker and an observer are considered:

- explicit cooperation (Ayache et al., 1979), in which a worker is modified, or *instrumented*, to inform an observer of selected state changes, at selected checkpoints;
- a "spying" relation (Diaz et al., 1994), in which an observer is able to observe a trace of events execured by a worker, without a worker being aware of that fact.

In fig.2 these modes of cooperation within a self-checking environment are compared with generic passive and active testing scenarios.

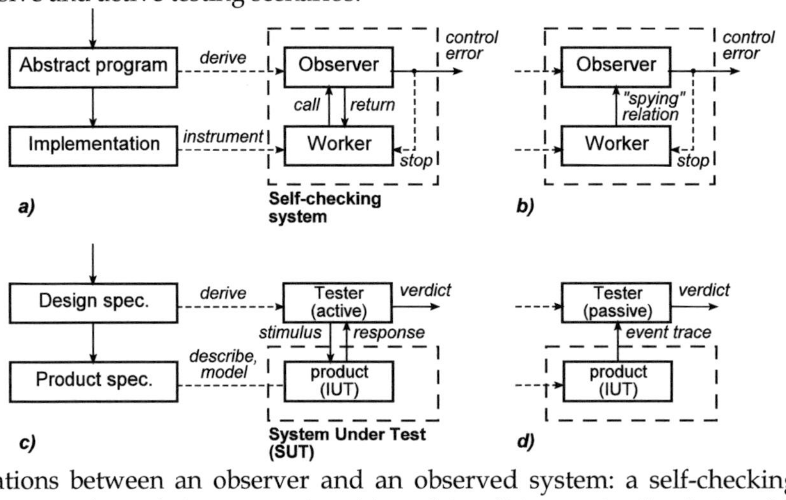

Fig. 2. Relations between an observer and an observed system: a self-checking observer-worker system with explicit cooperation (a) and implicit „spying" relation (b); an active tester (c); a passive tester (d)

In the case of explicit cooperation, the level (granularity) of instrumentation is adjusted to the needs of a particular observer. The calls to an observer serve no other operational purpose, and all the remaining operations of a worker are by definition invisible to an observer - these are two disjoint sets of events, related only by their "closeness" in the local execution sequence. A common-medium Local Area Network is envisaged as a natural environment for the implementation of the "spying" relation (a similar observation is made by Bochmann et al. (1989), in the context of a *trace analyzer* used as an *arbiter*). It is said that in such environment no instrumentation of a worker is necessary (which is a simplification). The capability to detect failures results from detecting a mismatch between the behaviour of two subsystems. As a model of intended behaviour, in both cited works Petri nets have been chosen - this is comparatively rare, and was later almost universally abandoned in favour of state-machine formalisms (FSM, EFSM). Here, the net transitions are fired acording to the occurrence of received observable events, until an event is received that does not correspond to any fireable transition. Only the control part of behaviour is handled (no data). This is essentially a tracking scheme that is also employed, as a homing algorithm, in later state-based passive testers.

The observer may act in three roles: to provide the *audit-trail* (i.e., a sequence of decoded and possibly stamped or counted messages / signals; a function that we would attribute to a generic *protocol monitor*); for *run-time checking*, which amounts to passive testing (i.e., issuing a verdict as to the validity of a trace); and for *performance analysis* based on the existing Petri net scheme, where simple "performance commands" are ascribed to transitions.

Further research problems that have been identified are: observer recovery (re-initialization after messages are lost by the observer), using multiple cooperating observers (which were later proposed to jointly detect a failure, or to individually detect failures of different kinds), and using non-broadcast communication between worker(s) and observer(s) - the non-ideal properties of such communication (loss or reordering of messages) were later addressed both with specialized algorithms and as a general problem of *testing in context*.

Another approach that identifies and proposes solutions to a surprising number of issues related to passive testing is due to Jard & Bochmann (1983). They introduce a *trace checker* - a *"module which observes the execution of a system under test . . . and compares its behaviour with the formal specifications given for that system"*. The contributions have fully retained their appeal.

It is noted that testing may be applied equally well to hardware-software products and to formal objects (implementations of more abstract specifications); this observation makes it clear that testing is not confined to a particular, very late, phase of system development, and may be used to support development activities at *any* stage.

The entirely modern EFSM formalism is used to express the intended behaviour. From the outset it is accepted that a reference specification, or rather the tested behaviour, is *nondeterministic* (some much later works still only assume deterministic behaviour), and that behaviour may be exhibited simultaneously at various ports or interaction points. Input and output events are distinguished, and handled in a different way. The basic trace-checking algorithm over the EFSM specification is of the classical state-tracking type - *"the trace checker ... maintains at all stages of the analysis a list of all states in which the reference specification may possibly be after the interactions already analysed"*. It is remarkable that the algorithm is much more sophisticated than the later approaches. It takes care of partial ordering between the input events (messages seen travelling towards the **Iut**) and output events (messages that must have been already sent by the **Iut**, as they are seen travelling in the opposite direction). Some aspects of the possible observation infidelity are thus handled.

A distinction is made between on-line and off-line operation of a trace checker. The characteristics of on-line operation (e.g., the ability to stop the execution) are discussed, thus establishing the basic conditions for what was later to be known as *Execution Monitoring*.

A trace checker is envisaged as consisting of two parts: reference specification in the form of "loadable" data, and a universal mechanism that is able to traverse the specification. This distinction resembles the division into *oracle information* and *oracle procedure* (see sec. 6.1).

4.2 Early works

Surprisingly, one of the contexts of early research on passive testing was actually *active* testing, in particular - *conformance testing* of telecommunications protocol implementations that was being developed at that time (ISO/IEC 9646). It was taken for granted that the automatic verdict-assignment functionality (the "oracle") was built into conformance test cases, although it was also accepted that some non-standard, *ad-hoc* or "exploratory" tests may not specify any verdicts, being just a specification of vectors of test stimuli (Bochmann et al., 1991). In the TTCN test language (TTCN-2 at the time), test cases are generally specified as trees of events, with leaves decorated with verdicts: **Pass** if the observed behaviour - trace of events is valid (i.e., correct w.r.t. a reference specification) *and* corresponds to a test purpose (i.e., it is as expected by a given test case); **Fail** if a trace is invalid, and **Inc** if a trace is valid, but not expected.

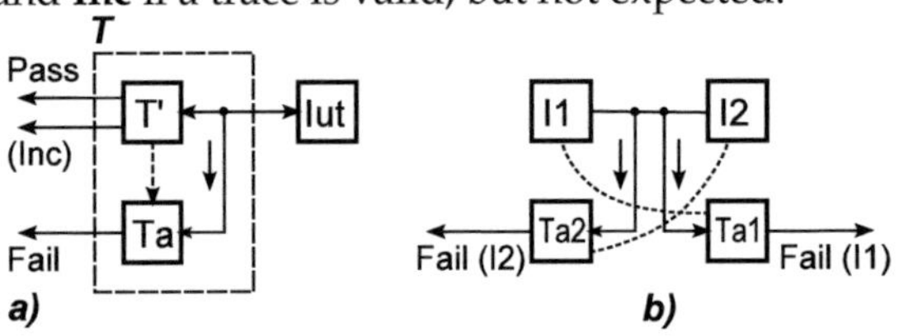

Fig. 3. The trace analyzer approach: (a) for conformance testing; (b) for arbitration testing - symmetric extension of conformance; (c) for arbitration testing - the original formulation

It was noted that the complexity of test cases is, to a large extent, due to the necessity to take into account all the sequences that lead to verdicts other than **Pass**. The solution was sought in separating *some* verdict-assignment functionality (but not *all* such functionality, as in the general oracle problem). An active tester is thus decomposed into a "lean" tester (this quite adequate term has originally not been used), which only drives the **Iut** towards exhibiting an intended correct behaviour up to a **Pass**, and a *trace analyzer*, which issues a **Fail** if an invalid trace is detected (fig.3a). Bochmann & Bellal (1989) "*take the view that the selection* [and application] *of test cases should be separated from the problem of deciding whether the IUT behaves according to the specification for a particular test case*".

In (W vong, 1990; Ziegler & Miskolczi, 1996) two contexts of use of a trace analyzer are identified: as a component of an active tester, and as a stand-alone passive tester. In later works it is often held that "*one of the problems with passive testing is that it is impossible to issue a Pass verdict*" (Tabourier et al., 1999). If "stand-alone" passive testing is considered as a descendant of the trace analyzer approach, then it is easy to see that it was never *meant* to issue such verdicts. Another view on **Pass** and **Fail** verdicts could be "borrowed" from the theories of synchronous active testing, where a verdict is issued at *every* step (after every observation), and the result of testing is a sequence of **Pass** verdicts ending with a single **Fail**. In this interpretation, there is nothing that would prohibit a passive tester from issuing the **Pass** verdicts (meaning: "passed so far").

A trace that corresponds to a test purpose should be *valid*; if not, then a test case is defective. The "bonus" functionality of a trace analyzer coupled with the active test component is to verify, at run-time, whether this is always the case. If, simultaneously, the active component of a tester issues a **Pass** and a trace analyzer issues a **Fail**, then a defect (fault) in a test case is flagged.

Technically, the original von Bochmann's trace analyzer uses a reference specification presented in the process-algebraic form (written in LOTOS), and the mechanism of the analyzer uses the existing LOTOS interpreter. In case of a non-deterministic specification, backtracking is necessary, which makes the approach generally unsuitable for on-line use. In other works from roughly the same period (and also in later works by von Bochmann) automata-based specifications are used, and on-line traversal of these specifications (even nondeterministic ones) poses no unsolvable problems.

A variant of the trace analyzer approach was proposed for arbitration testing (fig.3 b and c) – the simultaneous testing of two interoperating implementations, in order to decide which of the two is faulty. In (Bochmann et al., 1989) arbitration testing was described as a technique of interoperability testing, but interoperability testing has acquired, at least in telecommunications (ETSI EG 202 237, 2007), a particular meaning, not entirely consistent with arbitration testing as it is understood here. The arbiter is envisaged to be composed of two quasi-independent trace analyzers, each equipped with a reference specification of the opposite "side". It provides not only failure detection in a compound system, but also a rudimentary form of *fault localization*, without involving any specialized localization algorithms. A similar structure is also considered by Brzeziński (2005).

Another avenue of early research was taken by Chanson & Lo (1991), who proposed the extension of a conventional monitor (a passive device for decoding, filtering, and presenting messages exchanged at a certain physical interface) with *"the ability to detect protocol violations as they occur (passive testing)"*. The resulting *passive monitor* implements the reference specification for the protocol entities of a hierarchical protocol stack, one FSM machine per entity / layer. The passive testing mechanism is fairly rudimentary. It is implemented directly, as a cascaded switch statement, and requires explicit synchronization with the state of the tested entity (waiting for the period of inactivity or for the restart packet - both methods are protocol-specific, and thus not generally applicable). The idea of a flexible, modular signalling monitor that can be *upgraded* to a passive tester was pursued in (Brzeziński et al., 1996; Brzeziński, 1997, 2005). Recently, the same team developed the idea and a model of a modular tester based on the standardized TTCN-3 technology aimed at active testing (ETSI ES 201 873, 2008), which can be *"downgraded"* to the passive testing functionality and changed into a universal signalling monitor. No traces of similar research could be found elsewhere.

The origin of many early works on passive testing has been fault *management* in complex systems in general, and communications systems in particular. The aim of Bouloutas et al. (1992) has been to construct an *observer* (also called a *supervisor*) that would detect a change of behaviour of a system modelled as a single FSM machine. Both the *correct* behaviour and the anticipated *incorrect* behaviour is given, the *a priori* knowledge of a fault class is thus assumed (which is not the case for von Bochmann's trace analyzer). It was noticed that, in order to detect any possible fault, the observer would need to be the "duplicate of the system".

The specific, distinguishing idea has been to design a simple observer that is *true* (i.e., can indeed detect a failure), but only observes traces restricted to the smallest possible subset of events from the alphabet of **Iut**. A trace observed is thus a restriction, or projection, of the original trace of the **Iut**; the projection operation on traces is often used in modern approaches to formal testing. The projection takes place in a *filter* placed between the observer and the **Iut**. Both the observer and the filter are parts of a "supervisor", or a test system. The rationale for filtering a trace is the minimization of cost and resources (e.g., bandwidth); it is implicitly assumed that the cost of executing the observer on-line is higher than the cost of filtering, and for an efficient and workable observer a most restrictive filter is calculated.

Typically for the FSM model, behaviour is defined as a machine (trace) language: a set of words generated by the **Iut**, and accepted by the observer. Correctness is then defined as language (trace) inclusion.

The proposed test architecture can be translated to *testing in context* (fig.5), but, unlike the standard exposition of the testing-in-context problem (Heerink & Brinksma, 1995), here the context component is not given or assumed – it is intentionally *computed*. Normally, the testing context models or reflects the impairment of the level of control and observability of a **Iut**. A filter is a simple kind of context, which only drops messages according to a predicate, and never re-orders them. No consideration is given to genuine observational infidelity that hits messages before they reach the filter.

The observer executes a *state tracking algorithm*: the state of the observer FSM is updated with each event (symbol), and a failure is reported when a symbol is not acceptable in the current state. Apparently, the algorithm requires the setting of an initial state and requires a deterministic observer FSM; both restrictions were later lifted in the generic homing algorithm – one of the core algorithms of the current passive testing toolbox.

In (Wang & Schwartz, 1993), the FSM observer, of general rationale and features as in (Bouloutas et al., 1992), is decomposed into a number of very small, two-state FSM observers that operate jointly and synchronously. Combinations of states of all the decomposed observers unambiguously correspond to particular states in the original observer. Normally, the mini-observers obtain the copies of all the consecutive events of a trace, e.g., by a broadcast mechanism. However, it is also conceivable to feed the individual observers with differing projections of a trace (different sets of events). A mini-observer issues a **Fail** if it does not accept an event in its current state. A joint verdict is issued by a central decision element, basing on the vector of individual verdicts of all the observers. A word is accepted if it is accepted (i.e., not rejected) by all the mini-observers.

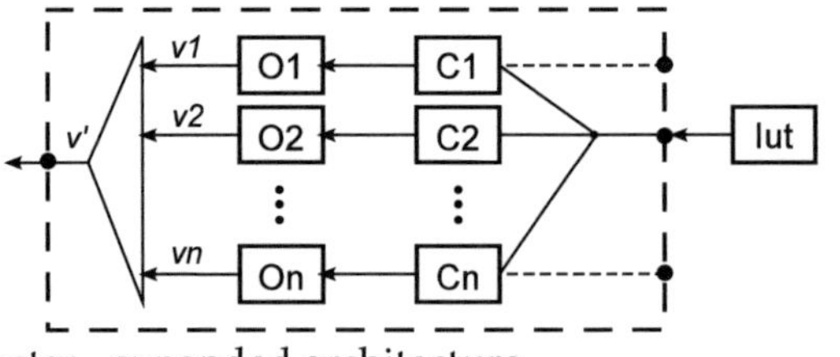

Fig. 4. Generic passive tester - expanded architecture

A set of mini-observers works in parallel, performing sub-tasks that may not be independently meaningful, and their verdicts are composed according to a simple boolean condition, to get a stream of **Accept** / **Reject** verdicts, synchronously with the incoming events. This architecture may be expanded to a building block, or "slice", of a generic passive tester, as proposed in fig.4. In this architecture, each observer may perform a separately meaningful observation (e.g., pertaining to a particular property of behaviour);

alternatively, each observer may result from a technical decomposition, as in (Wang & Schwartz, 1993). Each observer is fed via a separate projection or *context* component, and these components may "read" the same or altogether different traces; in the approach of Wang and Schwartz, the context components are empty and read the same trace (effectively, they implement a broadcast mechanism). The individual verdicts of observers are handled by a decision component. This handling may amount to executing a logical operation upon the verdicts to obtain a single final verdict. However, it may also consist in "packing" or "serializing" the individual verdicts. In both cases, the result of the operation of the "slice" of a passive tester is a sequence of verdicts - a *verdict trace*. This trace may be input to the next "slice" of a hierarchical passive tester, which will issue meta-verdicts: verdicts on verdicts, etc.

5. Sub-problems and their techniques

5.1 Core and additional functionality of testing

The core functionality of both active and passive testing is *failure detection*. The root cause of a failure is a fault (a defect). It *resides* somewhere within a system - the area (a component) in which it resides can in principle be located (*fault localization*), and the fault itself can be pointed to (*fault identification*). What can be located and pointed to ultimately depends on the means of expression - on the available description of the system. For fault localization, a system must be perceived as a collection of separate components / modules that are the domain of a fault localization function: $\{M_i\} \longrightarrow \{True, Possible, False\}$. For a system at the coding stage, a fault may consist in the changed order of operations within a particular line of code. For a system at the requirements stage, this would be meaningless, as the requirements language does not "know" anything about lines of code.

What fault localization and identification belong with, is known under different names, e.g., *debugging*, or *diagnosis*, where *shallow diagnosis* corresponds to fault localization, and *deep diagnosis* - to fault identification (Lamperti & Zanella, 2003). Diagnosis is the example of abductive reasoning, which seeks inferences to the best explanation, given different hypotheses. A localized and identified fault is thus a *possible explanation*.

Diagnosis is different from testing itself - it has different aims and dynamics. This view is corroborated by many authors, e.g., "*the main objective (of testing) is to detect errors. . . Activities like pinpointing and correcting faults are out of scope of testing and are called debugging*" (Machado, 2000); "*The aim of a testing activity is to detect some faults in a program. The use of the verb detect is important here, since locating and correcting the faults are generally regarded as out of the scope of testing: they require different data and techniques*" (Gaudel, 1995). However, the additional functionality of fault localization and identification often gets conflated with testing, because the distinction is immaterial from the point of view of a loop of activities of which testing is a part. As Sunshine (1979) says: "*When an error is found by some verification technique, the cause must still be determined*".

The tests designed particularly with fault localization / identification are called *diagnostic tests* (Belhassine-Cherif & Ghedamsi, 2000). The alternative is to conduct additional abductive reasoning basing on the results of "standard" tests. It is also possible to pre-encode the diagnostic information in a test; a test verdict is then extended to reveal this information.

In line with the common conflation of testing and diagnosis, localization and identification of faults is also researched using passive testing techniques, eg., using backward tracing - usually the off-line procedure of going backwards with the events of a recorded trace (Miller & Arisha, 2001a).

5.2 Continuous vs campaign-oriented testing

Testing (*any* kind of testing), as a particular technique of verification/validation, is necessarily an element of a loop of activities undertaken basing on test results. These activities are generally aimed at achieving or preserving agreed properties. The dynamics of this loop may vary, from an open loop (testing "out of curiosity" or solely for documentation purposes), through a long-term development strategy, redesign or "bug fixes" after failed conformance or interoperability tests, up to real-time on-line control ("reactive monitoring"). The requirements of a particular feedback loop dictate *how often* one should test, and *how fast* should the test results be available, relative to the observation of a particular behaviour. The need for *continuous testing* throughout the operational life-time of a product was one of the driving forces of research into passive testing. Continuous testing, as a concept, is in opposition to a finite *test campaign*, which consists in executing a test suite – a finite set of test cases.

The implicit, and usually neglected assumption of campaign-oriented testing is that the "objective" correctness of the **Iut** *does not change* during the test campaign, which also means that any development activities that could introduce or remove a fault are suspended. This alone (and not any particular model of a system life-cycle) justifies associating a test campaign with a *phase* of a system life-cycle. After the campaign-oriented testing is finished, the verdict is assumed to hold. This is inconsistent with real-life experience, which proves that a product in use, and in particular – a complex component of a larger system, does not preserve its correctness indefinitely. In operation, it may become faulty because of hardware defects, changes in the environment, and accumulated small modifications.

In continuous testing the assumption is that the correctness status of the **Iut** *may* change at any time. If the assumption is that the **Iut** is initially correct (having passed the test campaign), then the ensuing continuous testing is aimed primarily at detecting when the **Iut** *becomes* faulty.

5.3 On-line vs off-line testing

The idea of *on-line* testing is that any execution of a test pertains to behaviour that the **Iut** genuinely exhibits during the test experiment, and the verdicts are issued during that test experiment. In *off-line* testing (also referred to as *post-mortem* testing), the behaviour of an **Iut** is captured and represented by some structure, which can then be assessed by a tester at will, as if this behaviour were exhibited "now".

An entirely different understanding of these terms is also possible, where "on-line" refers to **Iut** being "on-line" (i.e., serving its operational mission) during the testing, and "off-line" – to **Iut** being taken out-of-service for the tests. This latter understanding is sometimes used to characterize the distinction between passive and active testing; however, in this role it is misleading - we have shown that passive testing can serve as an element of active tests (with **Iut** in a fully controlled and "off-line" environment), and some active tests actually require the **Iut** to remain "on-line" (e.g., to "prime" it with some background traffic that would be cumbersome to generate artificially).

Yet another alternative understanding pertains to on-line (or, synonymously, *on-the-fly*) vs off-line *active* testing (Vries & Tretmans, 2000). Off-line refers here to pre-computing (generating) the tests before they are executed, while on-line means that the tests are being generated from a reference specification, event by event, while they are being executed. Such active tests may be performed indefinitely (continuously), which also shows that continuous testing is not the "essence" of passive testing.

Having identified the possible sources of misunderstanding, we stay with the first interpretation. Technically, a "*trace may be immediately analyzed by an observer or stocked in memory for later treatment*" (Dssouli & Fournier, 1991). This corresponds to on-line vs off-line use of a passive tester. To consider the particular aspects of this distinction, we assume a *sequential* passive tester, which reads each event of a trace exactly once, in a strict order of their appearance in a trace, with no look-ahead and no look-back; this seemingly obvious general mode of operation is not the only one - another possibility will also be considered. Operating on-line, a sequential passive tester must be prepared to handle the observed events as they appear, indefinitely. If each event is handled separately, then its processing should end before the next event arrives - a tester should be *fast enough*. "Technical" buffering of events is conceivable, but it should be borne in mind that, in certain extreme cases, a verdict must be issued quasi-immediately, i.e., before the next event occurs. Some testing algorithms, e.g., those dealing with observational infidelity, process an event in relation to other events occurring within a time window or event window (containing a given number of events). In this case, a verdict may be delayed until this (sliding, and bounded) window expires. However, in any case, the on-line tester is not allowed to accumulate any unprocessed tasks. The effectiveness of on-line testing is an important research topic. The general advice, due to Kim (2007), is "*to apply any complex semantic analysis of the specification before testing and minimizing on-line processing work during the passive testing*". Similar observations are made by Brzeziński & Maliński (2006), who explore the possibility of transforming a reference specification to a form that is more efficient at run-time, while preserving the basic testing algorithm.

It is often said that an on-line passive tester is naturally able, without any modifications, to operate off-line. This statement is true for purely logical passive testing, in which the only necessary information is a sequence of events. For those approaches to passive testing that use time-dependent algorithms, e.g., to deal with observational infidelity, it is necessary "*to record, within the trace file, the real time of each interaction in the form of a time stamp*" (Bochmann et al., 1989). To use the on-line tester in the off-line mode, it is then necessary to "replay" a recorded trace. The re-play mechanism would use the timing information to reconstruct the relative moments of presenting events at the interface of a passive tester. However, for a day's or week's trace, its repeated analysis would obviously be impractical (it would take a day, or a week). To overcome this obstacle, the tester should be modified to read the timing information along with the events, and to explicitly use this information in the testing algorithm. The advantage is two-fold: a trace could be analyzed much faster, or a tester could take as long as necessary if a computationally expensive algorithm does not keep up with the dynamics of the original trace.

An entirely different approach to off-line analysis of behaviour is based on modelling the collected (observed) traces as automata, expressing the required properties of an **Iut** as formulae (akin to test purposes), and using traditional model-checking tools to check if properties are *satisfied* in the model of a system. Obviously, the results are meaningful only if the model is *faithful* to the behaviour of a system.

One line of research on model-checking for off-line passive testing was initiated by Hallal et al. (2001). In their approach, a model is constructed using the SDL language, and properties to be checked are represented by an observer expressed in the SDL-like GOAL language. Note that further testing without any stated properties / test purposes is not possible, as the model is constructed with no external reference specification, and does not in itself bear any correctness-related connotations. To ease the formulation of test purposes, pre-defined parameterizable patterns are used. A repository of such patterns, to be used for the general development tasks, has been developed by Dwyer et al. (1999).

A similar, but apparently independent approach was taken by Griffeth et al. (2006). This shows that passive testing and model checking, although entirely different in dynamics and context of use, conceptually have much in common.

5.4 Reference data

A reference specification used by a passive tester may assume different forms. The following variants are most characteristic of research on passive testing to date:

- scope of representation:
  - only control flow (behaviour defined exclusively in terms of atomic, named events), as in Finite State Machines (FSM);
  - control and data (events may carry data values; to define behaviour, predicates on internal data may be used), as in Extended Finite State Machines (EFSM);
- formalism:
  - automata / state machines (FSM, EFSM, CFSM – Communicating FSM);
  - transition system representations, e.g., serving as the underlying semantic model of LOTOS (Bochmann & Bellal, 1989; Bochmann et al., 1989);
  - Petri nets (Ayache et al., 1979; Diaz et al., 1994);
  - logical formulae (where a trace is modelled as an automaton);
- the kind of atomic specification events:
  - pairs of input/output events, in the style of Mealy machines (Lee et al., 1997; Miller, 1998; Miller & Arisha, 2000, 2001; Miller et al., 2005; Alcalde et al., 2004; Tabourier et al., 1999;)
  - individual events of distinguishable kinds: an input, an output, and possibly "silent" transitions τ; in such *event-driven* machines each kind of event may be handled differently (Bochmann & Bellal, 1989; Bochmann et al., 1989, 1991; Lee et al., 2002, 2006; Wvong, 1990; Brzeziński & Maliński, 2006; Brzeziński, 2005);
  - symbols, to which different interpretations may be ascribed outside the model (Wang & Schwartz, 1993; Netravali et al., 2003);
  - "transactions" that consist of autonomous sequences of outputs, sequences of outputs in response to an input, and "silent" transitions (Jard & Bochmann, 1983).

Much effort has been devoted to the handling of both control flow and data (Lee et al., 2002). The EFSM formalism is, arguably, the most popular. The common understanding is that EFSM-based passive testing is closer to reality (and less of an academic exercise), as the behaviour of real systems, described by communication protocols, does involve data (e.g., numerical, and not only enumerated, fields in protocol messages). However, dealing with data enormously complicates all the algorithms. Reservations against the preoccupation with data have also been voiced, e.g., Fecko et al. (2001) argue that the FSM model (derived from the underlying EFSM model of a specification language such Estelle) is *useful* and *viable* even for quite serious tasks.

5.5 Infidelity of observations

In practice, the **Iut** is always embedded in a context - the intervening circumstances that make the access to **Iut** more or less indirect. This is also the rationale for a common distinction between a **Sut** and an **Iut**.

As shown in fig.5(a), in the general test architecture (which was devised for conformance testing, but is also applicable to other types of testing as well), a tester accesses a **Sut** at *Points of Control and Observation* (PCO) for active testing, and *Points of Observation* (PO) for passive testing. The behaviour of **Iut** that is the object of tests is exhibited at *Implementation Access Points* (IAP) between a test context and an **Iut**. A test context is that part of a **Sut** that is not to be assessed in the course of testing, and yet is relevant to the relation between behaviours exhibited at PCO/PO and IAP. The issues of *active* testing in context (including the generation of suitable tests) have been thoroughly researched, e.g., by Heerink & Brinksma (1995). One view on the context as applied to *passive* testing is presented below.

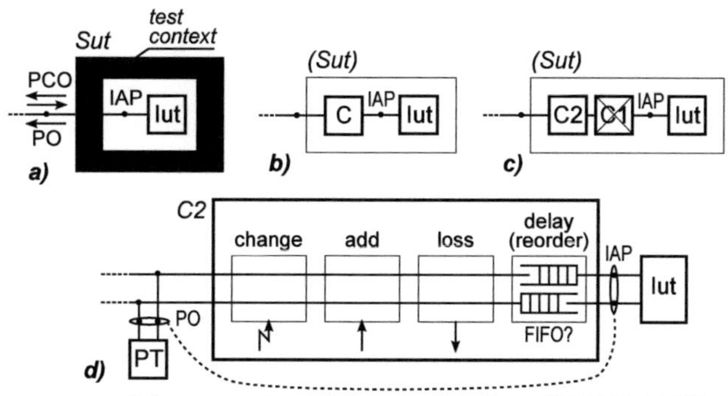

Fig. 5. Testing in context: (a) general architecture, after (ITU-T Z500, 1997); (b) lumped context component; (c) observation and translation contexts; (d) observation infidelity factors

A test context may be envisaged (modelled) as a lumped "context component" (fig.5b), which may be further decomposed into a context component C1 responsible for the translation of alphabets of events and behaviours themselves (it might be envisaged as an interworking protocol entity), and a context component C2 that only represents the degradation of observation fidelity. We now assume that the C1 component is "empty", which means that a passive tester observes what is essentially the behaviour of **Iut** (and not the entirely different behaviour of another component - C1). A trace perceived by a passive tester at a Point of Observation may be *ideal*, i.e., corresponding exactly to what **Iut** perceives (in which case also the context component C2 is empty), or may be degraded by various factors that, together, contribute to the phenomenon of *observational infidelity* or *uncertainty*. Fidelity refers to "*closeness with which the sequence of input and output events seen by the device under test matches the sequence of events observed by the monitor* [passive tester]"

(Bhargavan et al., 2001). The most researched factors of observational infidelity are (fig.5d): losing (dropping), adding, reordering, changing, and delaying the events of a trace.
Research on passive testing has taken various positions on observational infidelity. Ignoring this phenomenon readily leads to the simplistic view on passive testing. As noticed by Alcalde & Cavalli (2006), some authors assume that *"an observation point records the event traces respecting their causal order"* and claim that *"finding the order of these events is a well studied and resolved problem"*. Far from that, this is one of the most intricate, troublesome, and *"surprisingly difficult"* (Bhargavan et al., 2001) sub-problems of passive testing. To dispense altogether with infidelity (which is, of course, not the same as ignoring it), a passive tester might be *co-located* with an **Iut**, virtually "sitting on it", synchronously observing the events of its behaviour as they happen, or might rely on instrumenting the **Iut**. Co-location can also be considered as a kind of instrumentation. Co-location and instrumentation have been identified in the common taxonomy of testing and intrusion detection (Brzeziński, 2007b) as *communicated observability*.
For the testing community, in particular that of telecommunications descent, a co-located tester is an architectural abstraction which is not seriously considered in practice, and instrumenting the **Iut** for testing is "banned for political reasons". Two approaches to dealing with infidelity may be identified:

- to design a trace-checking algorithm so that it expects a non-ideal trace and internally deals with its infidelity (or rather - with particular *classes* of infidelity; deciding on these classes is a kind of a *test hypothesis*);
- to add a functional module that pre-processes a trace, using hypotheses as to its possible classes of infidelity, and presents a trace analysis module with a reconstructed ideal trace, as in a self-tuned passive tester of Brzeziński & Maliński (2007). A passive tester that expects an ideal trace is thus not useless - it may be used as a component of a larger test system, in which a non-ideal trace is conditioned and reconstructed separately.

A number of trace-checking algorithms that explicitly deal with particular classes of infidelity have been proposed. Practically all of them assume that the delaying buffers are FIFO, i.e., that in each direction of communication the partial order of events is retained (there is no reordering of events). The characteristic combinations of infidelity factors are: only loss of messages, only the transmission delay between a passive tester and an **Iut**, both delay and loss. The FIFO buffers may be internal to the physical **Iut** equipment, and may be relatively "short". As noticed by Bhargavan et al. (2001), under various conditions (i.e., heavy traffic load towards a **Iut**, only part of which may be projected upon events visible to a passive tester) such buffers may overflow, leading to what is perceived as loss. Indeed, it is now well known that in modern high-speed packet networks the predominant cause of message loss is input buffer overflow.
We now briefly present the approaches to dealing with combinations of infidelity factors.
Admitting delaying FIFO buffers (with no other infidelity factors) brings about the possibility of *message cross-over* (fig.6a) - the reversal of the order in which events travelling in the opposite directions are observed by a passive tester, in relation to the order in which they are executed by the **Iut**. In the example, message x, travelling towards the **Iut**, is perceived by the passive tester to occur before message y, travelling from the **Iut**. If, basing on this observation, the specification (fig.6b) is consulted with a sequence: $<?x,!y>$, the verdict is **Fail** (trace not accepted - the right branch). Message y was in fact sent before the

reception of x, which corresponds to the acceptable sequence <$!y,?x$> (left branch of the specification), thus a *false fail* was issued. If the passive tester, instead of message y at time 2, observed message y' at time 3 ("a little later"), the fail verdict would have been correct. The difference t between time 3 and time 1 exceeds the *maximum round-trip delay* ($t1 + t2$), while the difference between time 2 and 1 does not.

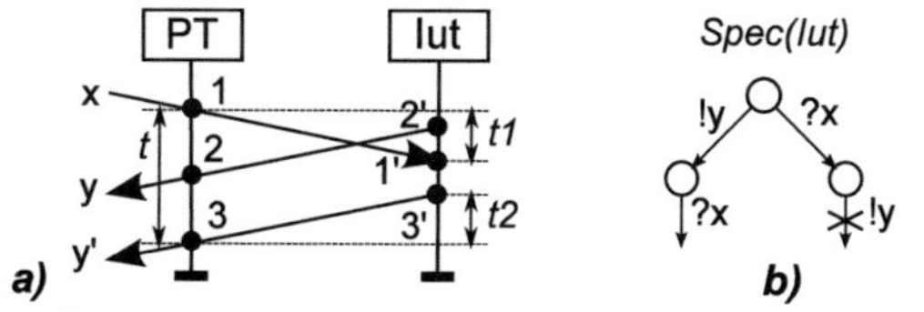

Fig. 6. Message cross-over due to communication delay

Dealing with the possible message cross-over generally involves modifying the basic state-tracking, or homing, algorithm designed for ideal observation - as shown above, this algorithm is incorrect in the presence of communication delays.

In their early work, Jard & Bochmann (1983) treat differently the inputs in a specification (handled when an event corresponding to a message travelling towards a **Iut** is observed) and its outputs (for messages travelling in the opposite direction). The sets of *possible* states of the **Iut** are decorated with the sequences of outputs that could have been sent, but have not been seen by the passive tester yet. These hypothetical past outputs are matched and "consumed" first, when the passive tester sees the output event. It seems that this original algorithm would, correctly, accept y, but it would fail to reject y' (an "optimistic" strategy, with false **Pass** verdicts). The explanation is that the algorithm is purely logical, with no notion of time, so the round-trip delay is assumed to be infinite (it cannot be zero, as this would mean no cross-over effects, and it cannot take any other definite value, as this would require making quantitative decisions on the extra-logical level).

Wvong (1990) extends the FSM-based state tracking (homing) algorithm by keeping not a single set of possible states, but a set of such sets. The sets are calculated in different ways, depending on whether an input or an output message is seen by the tester, and whether within the round-trip delay time other previously observed messages await in internal queues of the algorithm. The algorithm is thus not fully logical - it uses timers.

Bhargavan et al. (2001) consider passive testing (referred to as *passive monitoring*) as a *language recognition* problem. A *co-networked monitor* (as opposed to a *co-located* one) is a passive tester separated from the **Iut** by FIFO queues of *a priori* known lengths. Two variants are discussed - with, and without possible buffer overflow (loss). The proposed universal algorithm is based on the existence of a function that, for a given sequence of events, checks if this sequence belongs to a language of the reference specification. Now, passive testing consists in constructing, for a sequence β observed by a tester at PO, all the sequences α that are consistent with β but occur at the IAP, and checking whether at least one of these sequences is accepted by the specification. The brute-force algorithm is then optimized for various particular properties of the reference specification, which makes these optimized variants non-universal.

Missing observations (possibly after a loss) may be handled as in (Lee et al., 1997). The general idea is to calculate a transitive closure (or "completion") of possible states over the events that could have been lost. This operation is tractable if the exact number, or a bound on the lost events is known. A similar procedure is also given in Wvong (1990).

5.6 Quality of verdicts

A suite of active tests may (and, ideally, should) be:

- *unbiased* (G. Bernot et al., 1991; Gaudel, 1995), *sound* (Hierons et al., 2008; Tretmans, 1996), or *correct* (Jéron, 2006), if it does not reject correct systems; there remains the possibility of "false positives" or "false Pass", i.e., passing also some faulty systems;
- *valid* (G. Bernot et al., 1991; Gaudel, 1995), *exhaustive* (Jéron, 2006; Tretmans, 1996), or *complete* (Hierons et al., 2008), if it does not accept faulty systems (or if it detects / rejects any faulty system); there remains the possibility of "false negatives", or "false Fail", i.e., failing also some correct systems.

A test suite that is both unbiased and valid is said to be *complete* (Tretmans, 1996) or *exhaustive* (Machado, 2000).

For passive testing, the notion of a finite test suite, and also of a single test case, is rather intangible. In active testing, it is an active tester that decides when a particular experiment starts and ends. However, even for active testing, the first event executed by a tester is not necessarily a stimulus. A tester may wait for a particular event (message, signal) from an **Iut** before it starts to send stimuli. Similarly, a passive tester may be thought of as executing a *passive test case*, by deciding when to start listening, how (against what particular reference and with what purpose) to assess a trace, and when to stop listening. Continuous testing might then be envisaged as a process, in which a passive tester executes:

- a single test case that does not normally end;
- a sequence of consecutive test cases: the end of one test case marks the start of another;
- sets of test cases, so that at any time at least one test case is being executed; this interpretation is probably closest to the idea of updating sets of possible states, inherent in the homing algorithm.

Taking into account the peculiarity of passive testing, Netravali et al. (2003) investigate the properties of passive testing algorithms being *sound* and *adequate* (and - jointly - *complete*). It was shown that the standard homing algorithm is complete with respect to any conformance notion that is not weaker than trace-containment. Specifically, every rejected implementation is indeed faulty, but an accepted implementation may still be faulty - the adequacy condition holds because no other sound algorithm could possibly reject such implementation. These fundamental results delimit the "power" of passive testing; however, they have been obtained for the ideal observation conditions (no infidelity effects).

6 Alternative conceptual settings

We now discuss other conceptual settings in which the particular combinations of passive testing technology are clearly present, but are not identified and named as such.

6.1 Test oracles

It is widely accepted (Richardson et al., 1992) that active testing can be decomposed into the following conceptual sub-problems:

- test data selection, usually understood as the selection of vectors of input data;
- test *oracle* creation;
- test execution;

- test execution monitoring, i.e., capturing the events that constitute the behaviour of **Iut**, and transforming them (by mapping, projections, translations) to the level of abstraction of the oracle; here belong various aspects of test architecture and interfaces;
- test result verification - elaboration of a test verdict by an oracle.

A test oracle is a mechanism that "*determines whether a system behaves correctly during test execution*" (Richardson et al., 1992). A test outcome (the behaviour of an **Iut** exhibited during a test experiment) is compared with an expected outcome, and a verdict is issued basing on this comparison. The comparison may be a complex operation, but it is passive by nature, and thus it is tempting to consider the oracle as a passive tester in its own right. Indeed, the "oracle" was used in a number of works as a synonym of a passive tester.

In software engineering there has been a tendency to emphasize the role of test data selection in testing, and to underestimate, or to consider as "straightforward", the problems of checking whether, for selected test data, the system behaves as required. This issue, which is crucial to the assignment of test verdicts, has even been left for human experts to resolve during the testing. For formal testing, the need to "manually" assign a verdict is unacceptable.

In (Richardson et al., 1992), in the tradition of software engineering, a test oracle is envisaged as a distinct functionality. This functionality is further sub-divided into the *oracle information* and the *oracle procedure*. The oracle information corresponds to a reference **Ref**, and the oracle procedure determines how this reference is used (searched, executed) in order to compare the actual outcome with the expected one. Using the general concept of an oracle, the idea and design of active and passive testers can be reconciled as shown in fig.7.

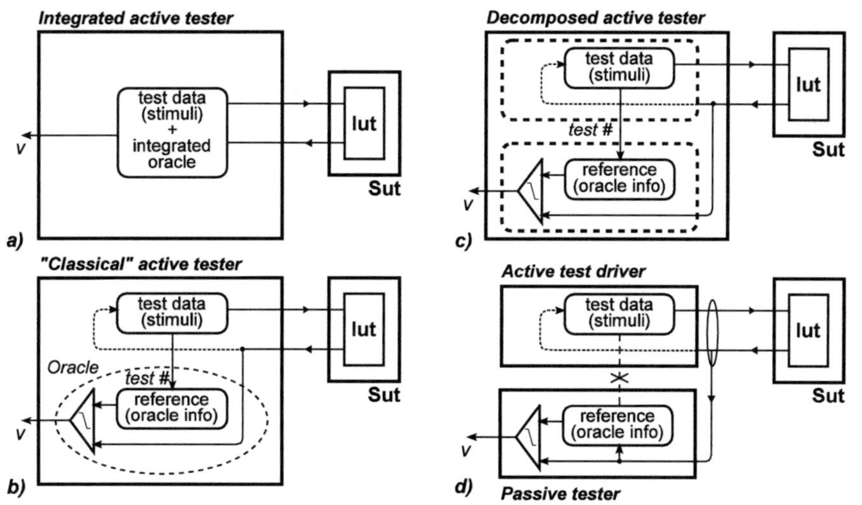

Fig. 7. „Derivation" of a passive tester from the structure of an active tester

In fig.7(a), the mechanisms of sending stimuli and receiving / recognizing responses are not separated at all, and test execution is driven by a tree-like structure (as in TTCN-based testing). In case (b), the oracle is distinguished conceptually. In case (c), this distinction is carried over to the implementation domain, where the oracle is a separate module that, according to the well known "separation of concerns" principle, is related to the construction of a test driver as weekly as possible. Depending on the structure and scope of oracle information, it may be necessary to provide the oracle module with the identification of the test case being executed (so that the oracle may choose the right reference data), and the synchronization information (that a test case was started, that stimulus x has just been sent, that the **Iut** has been reset to the known initial state, etc.). In case (d), the oracle is transformed into a fully independent passive tester.

6.2 Intrusion detection

Intrusions - undesired, hostile, malicious, destructive behaviours of an information system can be regarded as a particular class of behavioural failures. These failures can be, in principle, detected. The cause of such failure - a fault, or defect, may be attributed to the "mutation" caused by an intruder. Such "fault" can be, in principle, located and identified. This interpretation, or translation to the language of passive testing, was presented by Brzeziński (2007b). It is not universally accepted, but its technical implications are obvious in the works by the *Intrusion Detection* (ID) research community, in particular those concerned with specification-based ID techniques. Otherwise, the explicit mutual references between the two communities are rare. Among the few exceptions, we cite an observation from the passive testing community: "*Many network problems that occur due to intrusions and security violations can be addressed by the passive testing approach as well*" (Lee et al., 1997), and the observation from the ID community: "*An alternative is to look at network event recognition as a testing problem*" (Bhargavan & Gunter, 2002).

6.3 Metrology

Establishing the relation between metrology and (passive) testing is a challenging task. It deserves a thorough treatment that is beyond the scope of this chapter. One possible way to proceed is to retrack the approach of Mari (2003), who considers the ways in which measurement differs from general evaluation. For completeness, we will only offer a few observations on the subject.

To be a measurement, determining / assigning a value must be based on observation - similarly for testing. It was postulated (Mari, 1997) that the necessary conditions for calling an evaluation a measurement be: a standard (a reference) adopted for measurement must be well defined and external to any specific measurer, and the operation of comparing a thing to a standard must be well-defined and carried out independently of any specific measurer. These two postulates have always been the cornerstones of formal testing.

Stanley S. Stevens, a prominent psychologist and metrologist, among different types of measurements (or scale types) lists *nominal* measurements, where a "quantity" under measurement (a measurand) is dichotomy (present / absent) or membership in a category (such as colour), and *ordinal* (as for S, M, L, XL). This is very close to admitting test verdicts as the results of a particular kind of measurement.

One particular class of metrological problems concerns measurement errors, or, more generally, uncertainty of measurement. These errors are attributed to the measurement *model* (in testing - the inadequacy or non-fulfilment of test hypotheses, e.g., as to the number of states of an **Iut**), the measurement *method* (in testing - e.g., the limited number of tests), and the measurement *interface* (in testing - dropping or reordering of events in an observed trace). The problems are thus very similar.

7. Concluding remarks

We have surveyed some, but certainly not all, conceptual and technological links of passive testing with other research areas. Among those areas that had to be left out, potentially the most useful and effective in clarifying the essence of passive testing are: *diagnosis* (Sampath, Lamperti, Zanella) and *supervisory control* (Ramadge, Wonham, Arora, Kulkarni, Jeron) of Discrete-Event Systems, and *Execution Monitoring* of safety-critical systems (Ko, Schneider). Surprisingly, also the full and formal treatment of passive testing, e.g., using process calculi, is conspicuously absent; to this end it seems promising to look into Prasad's *Calculus of Broadcasting Systems*. Progress has been achieved in developing a testing theory for broadcasting processes (Ene & Muntean, 2002), while what we need is a passive testing theory that could possibly use the mechanisms of CBS.

Passive testing is a live research subject, with a potential for further theoretical results and practical applications. A large part of its former development went "undercover", with important results hidden rather than shared. It is a fact that after 30 years of development, it still fights its way into becoming a recognized verification / validation methodology and technology - a branch of a wider discipline of testing. The reader will have noticed the similarities of problems related to passive testing, and the differences in languages used to discuss these problems. By making these similarities and differences explicit, and offering their conceptual and technological "translations", or mappings, we hope to have contributed to the better understanding of passive testing.

This work was supported by the Polish Government Research Grant No. N51700831/1429.

8. References

Alcalde, B. (2006). *Advanced techniques for passive testing of communication protocols*. Ph.D. Thesis, INT / Université Pierre et Marie Curie.

Alcalde, B., & Cavalli, A. R. (2006). Parallel passive testing of system protocols - towards a real-time exhaustive approach. In *ICN/ICONS/MCL* (p. 42).

Alcalde, B., Cavalli, A. R., Chen, D., Khuu, D., & Lee, D. (2004). Network protocol system passive testing for fault management: A backward checking approach, *FORTE*, pp. 150-166.

Ayache, J., Azema, P., & Diaz, M. (1979). Observer: a concept for on-line detection of control errors in concurrent systems, *FTCS-9*, pp. 79–86.

Belhassine-Cherif, R., & Ghedamsi, A. (2000). Diagnostic tests for communicating nondeterministic finite state machines, *ISCC*, pp. 424-429.

Bernot, G., Gaudel, M.-C., & Marre, B. (1991). Software testing based on formal specifications: a theory and a tool. *Software Engineering Journal*, *6* (6), pp. 387-405.

Bhargavan, K., Chandra, S., McCann, P., & Gunter, C. (2001). What Packets May Come: Automata for Network Monitoring, *Proc. 28th Symp. Principles of Programming Languages*, pp. 206–219.

Bhargavan, K., & Gunter, C. A. (2002). Requirements for a practical network event recognition language. *Electronic Notes in Theoretical Computer Science*, 70 (4).

Bochmann, G. von, & Bellal, O. B. (1989). Test result analysis with respect to formal specifications. In: *Protocol Test Systems II, pp. 272-294, Berlin.*

Bochmann, G. von, Desbiens, D., Dubuc, M., Ouimet, D., & Saba, F. (1991). Test result analysis and validation of test verdicts. In: *Protocol Test Systems III*, pp. 263-274, North-Holland.

Bochmann, G. von, Dssouli, R., & Zhao, J. R. (1989). Trace analysis for conformance and arbitration testing. *IEEE Trans. Software Eng., 15* (11), pp. 1347-1356.

Bouloutas, A., Hart, G. W., & Schwartz, M. (1992). Simple finite-state fault detectors for communication networks. *IEEE Trans. Communications., 40* (3), pp. 477–479.

Brinksma, E., Grieskamp, W., & Tretmans, J. (2005). Summary - perspectives of model-based testing. In E. Brinksma, W. Grieskamp, & J. Tretmans (Eds.), In: *Perspectives of model-based testing,* E. Brinksma, W. Grieskamp, & J. Tretmans (Eds), IBFI, Schloss Dagstuhl.

Brinksma, E., & Tretmans, J. (2000). Testing transition systems: An annotated bibliography, *MOVEP,* pp. 187-195.

Brzeziński, K. M. (1997). *Testing at LTiV: Research and Application Projects.* Presented at COST247 WG3 MC Meeting and Seminar.

Brzeziński, K. M. (2005). Towards practical passive testing, *Parallel and Distributed Computing and Networks (PDCN '05),* pp. 177-183.

Brzeziński, K. M. (2007a). Intrusion detection as passive testing: Linguistic support with TTCN-3 (extended abstract). In: *DIMVA* (LNCS 4579), pp. 79-88, Springer.

Brzeziński, K. M. (2007b). On common meta-linguistic aspects of intrusion detection and testing. *Int. J. Information Assurance and Security (JIAS), 2* (3), pp. 167–178.

Brzeziński, K. M., Gumieniak, A., & Jankowski, P. (2008). Passive testing for reverse engineering: Specification recovery, *Parallel and Distributed Computing and Networks (PDCN'08)* pp. 27-32.

Brzeziński, K. M., & Maliński, N. (2006). Reference specification issues in on-line verification by passive testing, *Parallel and Distributed Computing and Networks (PDCN'06)* pp. 186-191.

Brzeziński, K. M., & Maliński, N. (2007). Self-tuned passive testers for grey-box distributed systems with indefinite communication delays, *Parallel and Distributed Computing and Networks (PDCN'07)* pp. 126-131.

Brzeziński, K. M., Mastalerz, D., & Artych, R. (1996). *Practical support of testing activities: the PMM family (COST 247 WG3 Report)* (Tech. Rep. No. 965). LTiV IT P.W.

BS 7925-1. (1998). *Software testing. Vocabulary.* British Standards Institution.

Chanson, S. T., & Lo, J. K. H. (1991). Open systems interconnection passive monitor OSI-PM, In: *Protocol Test Systems III,* pp. 423-442, North-Holland.

Chen, D., Wu, J., & Chi, H. (2003). Passive Testing on TCP, *ICCT,* pp. 182-186.

Diaz, M., Juanole, G., & Courtiat, J.-P. (1994). Observer - a concept for formal on-line validation of distributed systems. *IEEE Trans. Softw. Eng., 20* (12), pp. 900–913.

Dssouli, R., & Fournier, R. (1991). Communication software testability, In: *Protocol Test Systems III,* pp.45-55, North-Holland.

Dwyer, M. B., Avrunin, G. S., & Corbett, J. C. (1999). Patterns in property specifications for finite-state verification, *ICSE,* pp. 411-420.

Ene, C., & Muntean, T. (2002). Testing theories for broadcasting processes. *Sci. Ann. Cuza Univ., 11* , pp. 214-230.

ETSI EG 202 237. (2007). *MTS; Internet Protocol Testing (IPT); Generic approach to interoperability testing* (V1.1.2 ed.).

ETSI ES 201 873. (2008). *MTS; The Testing and Test Control Notation version 3.*

Fecko, M., Uyar, M., Duale, A., Amer, P., & Sethi, A. (2001). A formal approach to development of network protocols: Theory and application to a wireless standard, *CPWCSE-2001.*

Gaudel, M.-C. (1995). Testing can be formal, too, *TAPSOFT* pp. 82-96.

Griffeth, N. D., Cantor, Y., & Djouvas, C. (2006). Testing a network by inferring representative state machines from network traces, *ICSEA* p. 31.

Hallal, H., Petrenko, A., Ulrich, A., & Boroday, S. (2001). Using SDL tools to test properties of distributed systems, *FATES (CONCUR)* pp. 125–140.

Heerink, L., & Brinksma, E. (1995). Validation in context, *PSTV* pp. 221-236.

Hierons, R. M., Bogdanov, K., Bowen, J. P., Cleaveland, R., Derrick, J., Dick, J., et al. (2008). Using formal specifications to support testing. *ACM Computing Surveys.*

IEEE Std 610-12. (1990). *IEEE Standard Glossary of Software Engineering Terminology*. IEEE.

ISO/IEC. (2004). *ISO/IEC Guide 2. Standardization and related activities – General vocabulary* (8th ed.). ISO/IEC.

ISO/IEC 9646. (n.d.). *Conformance testing methodology and framework* (Vols. 1-7). ISO/IEC.

ISTQB. (2007). *Standard glossary of terms used in software testing, version 2.0 (December 2007).* ISTQB (Glossary Working Party).

ITU-T Z500. (1997). *Framework on formal methods in conformance testing*. ITU-T.

Jaiswal, S., Iannaccone, G., Kurose, J. F., & Towsley, D. F. (2006). Formal analysis of passive measurement inference techniques, *INFOCOM.*

Jard, C., & Bochmann, G. von. (1983). An approach to testing specifications. *Journal of Systems and Software, 3* (4), pp. 315-323.

Jéron, T. (2006). Model-based test selection for infinite state reactive systems, *DIPES,* pp. 35-44.

Kim, T.-H. (2007). A passive testing technique with minimized on-line processing for fault management of network protocols. *Int. J. Computer Science and Network Security, 7* (3), pp. 7–14.

Lamperti, G., & Zanella, M. (2003). Continuous diagnosis of discrete-event systems. In *Int. Workshop on Principles of Diagnosis (DX'03),* pp. 105–111.

Lamport, L. (1989). A Simple Approach to Specifying Concurrent Systems. *Communications of the ACM, 32* (1), pp. 32–45.

Lamport, L. (2008). *Computation and State Machines.* Available from http://research.microsoft.com/en-us/um/people/lamport/pubs/

Lee, D., Chen, D., Hao, R., Miller, R. E., Wu, J., & Yin, X. (2002). A formal approach for passive testing of protocol data portions, *ICNP,* pp. 122-131.

Lee, D., Chen, D., Hao, R., Miller, R. E., Wu, J., & Yin, X. (2006, April). Network protocol system monitoring - a formal approach with passive testing. *IEEE/ACM Transactions on Networking, 14* (2), pp. 424–437.

Lee, D., Netravali, A. N., Sabnani, K. K., Sugla, B., & John, A. (1997). Passive testing and applications to network management, *ICNP,* pp. 113-122.

Machado, P. D. L. (2000). *Testing from structured algebraic specifications: The oracle problem.* Ph.d. thesis, Univ. of Edinburgh.

Mari, L. (1997). The role of determination and assignment in measurement. *Measurement, 21* (3), pp. 79–90.

Mari, L. (2003). Epistemology of measurement. *Measurement, 34* , pp. 17-30.

Mill, J. S. (1974). Of Observation and Experiment. In: J. M. Robson (Ed.), *The collected works of John Stuart Mill, volume VII – A System of Logic Ratiocinative and Inductive [1843]* (chap. VII). Routledge and Kegan Paul.

Miller, R. E. (1998). Passive testing of networks using a CFSM specification, *IPCCC,* pp. 111–116.

Miller, R. E., & Arisha, K. A. (2000). On fault location in networks by passive testing, *IPCCC,* pp. 281-287.

Miller, R. E., & Arisha, K. A. (2001). Fault identification in networks by passive testing. In *Annual Simulation Symposium,* pp. 277-284.

Miller, R. E., Chen, D., Lee, D., & Hao, R. (2005). Coping with nondeterminism in network protocol testing, *TestCom,* pp. 129-145.

Netravali, A. N., Sabnani, K. K., & Viswanathan, R. (2003). Correct passive testing algorithms and complete fault coverage, *FORTE,* pp. 303-318.

Randell, B. (2003). On failures and faults, *FME* pp. 18-39.

Richardson, D. J., Aha, S. L., & O'Malley, T. O. (1992). Specification-based test oracles for reactive systems, *ICSE,* pp. 105-118.

Rushby, J. (2000, November). Disappearing Formal Methods, *HASE,* pp. 95–96 (invited paper).

Ryser, J., Berner, S., & Glinz, M. (1998). *On the state of the art in requirements-based validation and test of software* (Tech. Rep. No. ifi-98.12). Univ. of Zurich.

Sunshine, C. (1979). Formal Techniques for Protocol Specification and Verification. *IEEE Computer,* 12 (9), pp. 20–27.

Tabourier, M., Cavalli, A. R., & Ionescu, M. (1999). A GSM-MAP protocol experiment using passive testing, *World Congress on Formal Methods,* pp. 915-934.

Tretmans, J. (1996). Test generation with inputs, outputs, and quiescence, *TACAS,* pp. 127-146.

Tretmans, J. (1999). Testing concurrent systems: A formal approach, *CONCUR,* pp. 46-65.

Utting, M., Pretschner, A., & Legeard, B. (2006). *A taxonomy of model-based testing* (Working Paper No. 04/2006). Hamilton, New Zealand: Univ. of Waikato.

Vries, R. G. de, & Tretmans, J. (2000). On-the-fly conformance testing using spin. *STTT, 2* (4), pp. 382-393.

Wang, C., & Schwartz, M. (1993). Fault detection with multiple observers. *IEEE/ACM Trans. Netw., 1* (1), pp. 48-55.

Wing, J. M. (1990). A Specifier's Introduction to Formal Methods. *IEEE Computer, 23* (9), pp. 8–24.

Wvong, R. (1990). *A New Methodology for OSI Conformance Testing Based on Trace Analysis.* Master's thesis, University of British Columbia.

Ziegler, G., & Miskolczi, J. (1996). *Trace analysis method* (COST 247 WG3 Special Seminar No.KFKI-1996-07/M). Hungarian Academy of Sciences.

10

Application of Automata Based Approach for Specification of Model Transformation Strategies

Anna Derezińska and Jacek Zawłocki
Institute of Computer Science, Warsaw University of Technology
Poland

1. Introduction

Model transformation gains the increasing attention in software development and finds application in different areas. Model-to-model transformation can be specified in many different ways, see surveys in (Czarnecki & Halsen, 2006; Ehring at. al., 2005; Mens & van Gorp, 2006). Model transformation languages are developed within the MDA (Model Driven Architecture) initiatives, like QVT languages (MOF QVT Specification, 2008). Other solutions adopt often different, known methods for specification of transformation rules; like graph transformations, term rewriting, algebraic approaches. However, practical application of various types of model transformation, both corresponding to MDA and using other methodologies, is still not fully justified by the experiences gathered in practical projects.

We dealt with manipulation of models describing object-oriented projects. We were interested in the separation of different levels of transformation logic and in the support by a simple transformation engine. Therefore, we combined concepts of meta-modeling graph with extended automata and used for specification of a transformation strategy. The automaton-like graphical models are well understandable by engineers and computer programmers (Hopkroft at al,. 2000).

The main part of a transformation strategy consists of rules. Any rule will be specified by an extended automaton. Transitions between nodes are annotated with enabling conditions and actions. The set of rules is organized in a hierarchical structure. The structure is defined by a graph, conceptually similar to a meta-model graph. Association of the rules to vertices of the graph introduces priorities of the rules. A rule can be executed when its pre-condition is satisfied. We provide the basic definitions of the concepts of a strategy.

An automata-based transformation strategy was applied in the generic framework for traceability in object-oriented designs (Derezinska & Zawlocki, 2007). The framework is aimed at discovering relationships in a given object-oriented model according to a given traceability strategy. Requirements of the framework focus on the generic and highly flexible solutions. It accepts different modeling notations (including UML or its subsets) and

supports adaptation to different strategies according to user needs. The goals of the framework are realized by a chain of three transformations:
1) input transformation - from an object-oriented model to a model in the internal notation (so called Project notation),
2) traceability transformation - from a Project model with a given initial element to the resulting model (in this case so-called Dependency Area),
3) output transformation - from a Dependency Area to a resulting model in a desired notation.
The input and output transformations were realized using QVT approach and presented in (Derezinska & Zawlocki, 2008). This paper is devoted to the second transformation of the framework.
The general idea of Dependency Areas is based on exploration of possible direct and indirect relations among elements of a model. It can be viewed as a kind of traceability when impact relations between model elements are concerned. Identification of a dependency area can be realized as a transformation of an input model into another model.
The design of an executor of rules, used in the framework, is described with its meta-model and a draft of its algorithm. Exemplary strategies were specified for the subsets of UML meta-models. Few examples of the automata defining selected transformation rules will be presented. We show basic implementation of the strategy specification used in the framework and its application. We discuss also the advantages and disadvantages of the approach, its background and related work.

2. Related work

2.1 Model transformation and rule specifications

A model transformation is a mapping of a set of models onto another set of models or onto themselves, where a mapping defines correspondences between elements in the source and target models (Sendall at al., 2004). The description of a transformation is usually concentrated on a set of rules - basic units of the transformation. There can be static and dynamic rules, organized in different structural patterns and scheduled according to different schemata, as summarized in (Czarnecki & Halsen, 2006).
Within the OMG initiative, Query View Transformation (QVT) specification is developed that provides a set of formalisms to transform one object-oriented model into another one (MOF QVT Specification, 2008). QVT supports a relational as well as operational mappings language. The standardization effort triggered development of tools supporting the transformation process, but application of the standard is not yet common in industrial solutions. The QVT operational notation was applied for the input and output transformations of the framework considered in this paper (Derezinska, 2008).
There are many different approaches proposed for the specification of transformations; some of these include: relational/logic, functional, graph rewriting, generator/template-based, and imperative (Czarnecki & Halsen, 2006; Ehring at. al., 2005; Mens & van Gorp, 2006). Transformation rules were also described in specification languages like Object Constraint Language (OCL), Object-Z, B, Maude, etc. Transformations can be also implemented using general-purpose languages such as Java. A developer can access a model directly using any API and is not limited, but also not supported, by any rules. Decomposition of a transformation into a chain of basic units is discussed in (Vanhoof at al.,

2007a). The distinction between specification, implementation and execution of a transformation process is logical and similar to our approach.
Similarly to QVT some other approaches combine also different formalisms, like operational, declarative and hybrid transformation rules in ATL (Jouault & Kurtev, 2005). A transformation mechanism can be general, dealing with different kinds of models, or specialized to a given notation, often a subset of UML. In the USE environment (Buttner, & Bauerdic, 2006) transformations objects are added to the meta-level representations of UML models. The operational semantics is given in transformation meta-classes. Epsilon Wizard Language (EWL) supports update transformation for diverse modeling languages (Kolovos at al., 2007).
One category of transformations is based on graph transformations (Ehring at. al., 2005). A graph transformation rule is specified by two graph patterns - Left Hand Side and Right Hand Side. Graph transformation rules that can be scheduled according to a given state machine specification are, for example, supported in Viatra2 tool (Balogh & Varro, 2006). More examples of graph transformations can be found in (Ehring & Giese 2007).
In our solution we do not propose a new transformation language, but combine different notations on various abstraction levels. Information from a meta-model is stored in a hierarchy and used for prioritization of rules - therefore influences their scheduling. A rule is given in a graph notation, but it is not a rewrite rule. The details of the logic are specified in conditions and actions that can be expressed in a commonly known language, as for example Java in our implementation.
In different domains, rule specifications are also needed, like in knowledge management or business process description. Similarly, as in the case of model transformations, such rules can be specified by any known formalism, e.g. Prolog, Process Algebras, automata, decision tables or graphs, but also model-based notations. Proposal of *Production Rules Representation* dealing with business rules modeling as a part of modeling process is currently under development (W3C Recommendations, 2008). The UML notation, or its variants, like e.g. URML (Wagner at al., 2006), supported by constraints in OCL can be also used for specification of business rules. However, in this paper we do not discuss the problem of usage of the UML notation for rule description, but of automata-based rules used in object-oriented models and these models are illustrated by UML model examples.

2.2 Applications of extended automata

An automaton (Hopkroft at al,. 2000) is a mathematical model of a finite state machine, which definies traversals through a series of states accorging to a transition function. A name of extended automata is applied in many various contexts. It can describe different kinds of extensions of simple automata. These extensions refer usually to data labeling of transitions and mappings of these data. Extended automata can model finite state machines which are enriched with the ability to apply a string operation on a part of the input that has not been consumed yet (Bensh at. al., 2008).
In the context of the UML language, UML statecharts can be described using different kinds of extended automata approaches. For example, in MDA approache presented in (Dayan et al., 2008) standard UML statecharts are transformed into corresponding extended automata called Hierarchical Statechart Automaton (HSA). In this case the main extension refers to the substitution of the hierarchical composite states of statecharts by a combination of simple automata, and parallel execution of orthogonal states using so-called Parallel HSA. The idea

of transformation of UML statecharts into an equivalent format is widely used for the verification methods based on model checking. The models can be, for example, transformed into Extended Hierarchical Automata (Lakhnech, 1997). Further a model is translated into a language accepted by one of model checkers - CadenceSMV (McMillan, 2008).
It should be stressed that transformations of statechart and/or usage of different automata to description of statechart semantics are other application areas than discussed in this paper.

2.3 Traceability strategies

One of the challenges of complex software development is maintaining traceability links among model elements to support model evolution and roundtrip engineering (France & Rumpe, 2007). Automatic recognition of different relations among project elements can be especially important for industrial projects that are usual incomplete and/or inconsistent at different stages of software development. Those relations can be interpreted as a special kind of traceability concepts.
Traceability deals in general with different impact relations between various artifacts created in the process of software development. Traceability can assist in improving the quality of a project and in the project maintenance (Maeder, 2006). It can be used for tracing the requirements and the changes in a design (Spanoudakis, 2004). Traceability links are examined for the UML models at different levels of model abstraction (Letelier, 2002) and in the model refinement process (Egyed, 2004). Different relations are specified directly within the development and evolution process or are automatic (or quasi-automatic) derived basing on the interpretation of information hidden in the software artifacts. In (Walderhaug et al., 2006) the set of services: trace model management, trace creation, trace use and trace monitoring are discussed. The services could support any kinds of artifacts and relations in a heterogeneous MDD (Model Driven Development) environment.
Several other papers described also solutions about traceability within MDD, like in (Vanhooff et. al., 2007b) were generated traces provided information that could be further used in a transformation between models. This problem is therefore opposite to the one presented in this paper and also in (Derezinska, 2008) because we shown an application of MDD in a framework for traceability.

3. Automata-based description of transformation strategy

In this section the general ideas of the model transformation strategy will be presented. The application of these concepts for the traceability strategy in object-oriented designs is shown in the next section.

3.1 Basic concepts of strategy

The core of a strategy is defined by a set of rules. Any rule will be specified as an extended automaton. The rules have their pre-conditions and priorities. The set of rules is organized in a hierarchical structure. The rules are associated to vertices of the hierarchy. An algorithm of a rule execution takes into account a position in the hierarchy. Now, a transformation strategy will be described in more details.

Definition 1. An *extended automaton* is a tuple $EA = <S, \Sigma, DC, C, DO, \Gamma, \delta, iN>$, where
S is a finite set of *states* (*nodes* of the automaton graph),
$iN \in S$ is the *initial state (initial node),*
Σ is a set of *input* symbols,
DC is an n-dimensional linear space,
C is a set of *enabling functions* called *conditions* C_i: DC→{False, True},
DO is an m-dimensional linear space,
Γ is a set of *update functions* called *actions*, $\gamma_i : DO \rightarrow DO$,
$\delta : S \times \Sigma \times DC \times DO \rightarrow S \times DO$ is a *transition* relation.

We will consider as a set of input symbols Σ a subset of non-negative integer numbers {0, 1, 2, ... k}. Input symbols will be interpreted as priorities of the transitions. The extended automaton can be also viewed as a kind of a labeled transitions system with a finite number of states and a finite number of transitions, or as an extended finite state machine.

Definition 2. A rule is a tuple $r = <EA, DC, C_r, p>$, where
EA is an extended automaton,
DC is an n-dimentional linear space,
C_r: DC→{False, True} is an *enabling function* called *precondition* of the rule,
p is a non-negative integer number, a priority of the rule.

Precondition of a rule and conditions of transitions are predicates given in any notation. They evaluates to the Boolean values. Domains DC and DO can be arbitrary chosen for different applications of extended automata. An action can be performed during a given transition only if the appropriate condition is satisfied.
Below, we describe a structure that help organizing the set of rules and identify their priorities.

Definition 3. A *simple, finite graph* is a tuple $G = <V, E, \alpha>$, where
V is a finite set of vertices,
E is a finite set of edges,
$\alpha : V \times V \rightarrow E$ is a function assigning an edge to a pair of verticies

Definition 4. A *model* is a tuple $X = <G, \Psi, \varphi>$, where
$G = <V_G, E_G, \alpha_G>$ is a *simple graph,*
Ψ is itself a *model* (so-called reference model of X) with its graph $<V_\Psi, E_\Psi, \alpha_\Psi>$,
$\varphi : V_G \cup E_G \rightarrow V_\Psi$ is a function assigning elements (vertices and edges) of G to vertices of Ψ (meta-elements).

Model Ψ is a meta-model of the model X. The above definitions are general, as the concepts of meta-modeling. In fact, we would be interpreting the meta-modeling in the similar way as in the specifications of OMG, like UML (Unified Modeling Language, 2008). We assume that dependency graphs between conceptual classes are formed by unidirectional generalisation relationships. Therefore, for example, vertices V of graph G can be interpreted as classes and edges E between nodes represent relations between classes.
Any meta-model is also a model and can have its own meta-model. In special cases, graphs of a model and a meta-model can have the same sets of nodes, like in the MOF (Meta Object Facility, 2006).

Further in the strategy, we will take into account a model, which is a meta-model consisting of classes as graph vertices and a generalization relation as only relation between vertices. In general, we can specify such a model extending its definition with the statement that a graph G is a *directed acyclic graph* (Deo, 1974). Such a model will be called *a hierarchical model.* In strategies, a hierarchical model has usually a tree structure, but it is not limited to such structures.

Definition 5. A *hierarchical model* is a tuple $X = \langle G, \Psi, \varphi \rangle$, where
$G = \langle V_G, E_G, \alpha_G \rangle$ is a *directed acyclic graph,*
Ψ is itself a *model* (so-called reference model of X) with its graph $\langle V_\Psi, E_\Psi, \alpha_\Psi \rangle$,
$\varphi : V_G \cup E_G \rightarrow V_\Psi$ is a function assigning elements (vertices and edges) of G to vertices of Ψ (meta-elements).

Combining a set of rules (Def. 2) with a hierarchical model we can define a strategy.

Definition 6. A strategy is a tuple $\Xi = \langle X, R, \mu \rangle$, where
$X = \langle\langle V_G, E_G, \alpha_G \rangle, \Psi, \varphi \rangle$, is *a hierarchical model* - representing a meta-model
R is a finite, nonempty set of *rules,*
$\mu : V_G \rightarrow R$ is a surjective function, assigning a rule to a vertex of the meta-model.

If a meta-model vertex has assigned a priority, it is also a priority of the corresponding rule. Different vertices may have priorities of the same value.

3.2 Interpretation of rules in transformation process

A transformation process can be understood as the realization of appropriate subsets of rules from a strategy in a desired order. A transformation can be realized by a simple rule executor, because the entire logic is stored in the rules.

Main concepts of a rule executor are shown in Figure 1. The rule executor operates on a collection of rules. Each rule is defined by an automaton. It has a priority specified according to a mapping to the hierarchical model. Any rule has also its precondition. An automaton consists of a set of nodes. For any node a set of outgoing transitions can be specified. A transition has its priority. There is a condition and an action associated with a transition.

The rule executor is responsible for execution of rules. Appropriate operations in the conceptual model represent the execution of rules, the execution of its nodes, evaluation of conditions, and performing of actions. All rules are ordered according to their priorities and executed in the defined order. If two or more rules have the same priority the order of their execution is random.

Before executing a single rule, its precondition is checked. If it is satisfied, the initial node of the rule is considered. In case a node has more than one outgoing transitions, they are ordered according to their priorities. If a condition of a selected transition is satisfied, the transition is followed and its action performed. All nodes of the rule accessible from its initial node can be visited during the rule execution.

The application of the rule executor to the model transformation and its algorithms used in the framework are presented in the next Section.

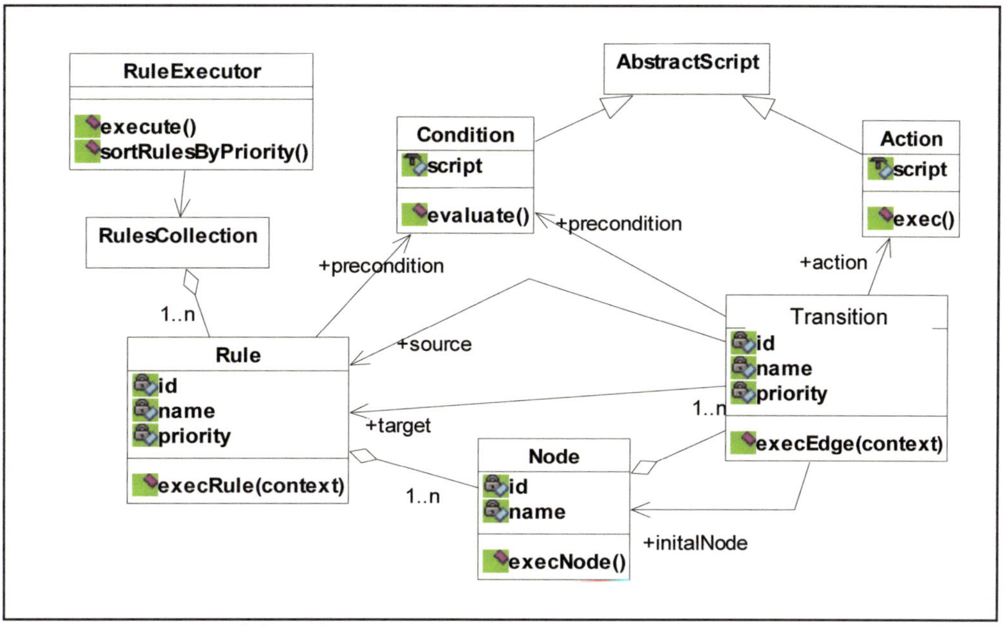

Fig. 1. Main concepts of the rule executor

4. Model transformation in the generic framework for traceability in object oriented projects

4.1 Background

Dependency areas (formerly named dependency regions) were introduced to deal with dependency relationships between subsets of related elements in UML models (Derezinska, 2004). The idea was aimed at the imperfect UML models; because real-world UML projects are often incomplete or inconsistent on different stages of software development. Therefore dependency relationships can be identified on the basis of different explicit relations present in a UML model, as well as reasoning based on supposed developer intentions derived from the model.

The idea of dependency areas was applied in a preliminary system supporting traceability in object-oriented designs (Derezinska, 2004). The system integrated CASE tools for requirements analysis (Rational Requisite Pro), and UML modeling (Rational Rose). Requirements could be associated with corresponding use cases. Dependency areas of a use case could be identified. Elements belonging to a considered dependency area were marked with stereotypes and could be further instrumented during code generation, if necessary. Rules used for identification of dependency areas were specified using structures similar to decision tables. In the tables, possible combinations of UML elements and their relations were taken into account. This solution was precise, but not very flexible, because it was strictly dependent on a given version of the UML specification.

The prototype system was implemented supporting a subset of UML - elements of use case models, class models, components and packages. The subset was limited, but it covered all elements, which were further used in the model to code transformation. The system was used in experiments tracing changes of requirements or model elements to the code of a target application. Such impact analysis was, for example, used for the selection of related code extracts. Next, fault injection experiments were performed only on these selected parts of the code. The impact of changes on fault susceptibility of the application was therefore effectively measured.

The concepts of dependency areas were further generalized (Derezinska & Bluemke, 2005; Derezinska, 2006). Dependency areas were identified using the sets of propagation rules and strategies. Selection strategies controlled application of many, possible rules. Bounding strategies limited the number of elements assigned to the areas. The framework for dependency area identification was specified as a meta-model that extended the UML meta-model (Unified Modeling Language, 2008). Propagation rules were specified using the Object Constraint Language (OCL) (Kleppe & Warmer, 2003).

Based on the framework a new system for traceability in object-oriented projects was developed (Derezinska & Zawlocki, 2008). The system was intended to be a generic one, dealing with different project input and output notations, as well as different strategies for identification of dependency areas among project elements. The high level of flexibility was achieved using different model transformations. The general process realized within the framework consists of three main steps performed as the following model transformations:

1. input transformation,
2. traceability transformation,
3. output transformation.

The transformation engines were not limited to the UML approaches. Input and output transformations were realized using standard QVT (Query/View/Transformation) (MOF QVT, OMG Spec., 2008) developed as a part of MDA approach (Frankel, 2003). The details of input and output transformations were presented in (Derezinska & Zawlocki, 2008). The main model transformation of the system was based on an automata-based approach and its principles are presented in this paper.

4.2 Subjects of transformation

The general idea of Dependency Areas is based on exploration of possible direct and indirect relations among elements of a model. Dependency Area is a subset of all possible elements accessible from an initial element through relations available in the design and selected according to a given strategy. It can be viewed as a kind of traceability when impact relations between model elements are concerned.

Traceability analysis is defined as a transformation that maps a project P with a given initial element IE and traceability strategy Ξ into a resulting dependency area DA

$$\{P, IE, \Xi\} \rightarrow \{DA\} \tag{1}$$

where: P – *Project*

IE – *InitialElement*, $IE \in P$

Ξ – *TraceabilityStrategy* is a strategy $\Xi = \langle X, R, \mu \rangle$ (see Def. 6),

DA – *DependencyArea*

A project is any object-oriented model. It reflects a general model in order to make the idea independent of any specific version of a modeling notation. Any model in other notation can be easily transformed into Project notation. Therefore this assumption does not limit the generality of the concepts.

An initial element is an element of the project that is a starting point of the traceability analysis. A traceability strategy is a strategy comprising a set of transformation rules associated with a given graph of hierarchy. The set of rules can be ordered according to the hierarchy of their priorities.
Dependency area is an output model consisting of elements assigned to a given dependency area. A dependency area can be easily transformed to any notation, which is convenient to a user.

4.3 Meta-model of Project

Any model analyzed in a framework is converted to the internal *Project* notation. This process is realized by the input transformation (Derezinska & Zawlocki, 2008). *Project* notation is a general notation covering a wide range of possible modeling concepts. The basic ideas of the Project notation are shown in its meta-model (Figure 2).

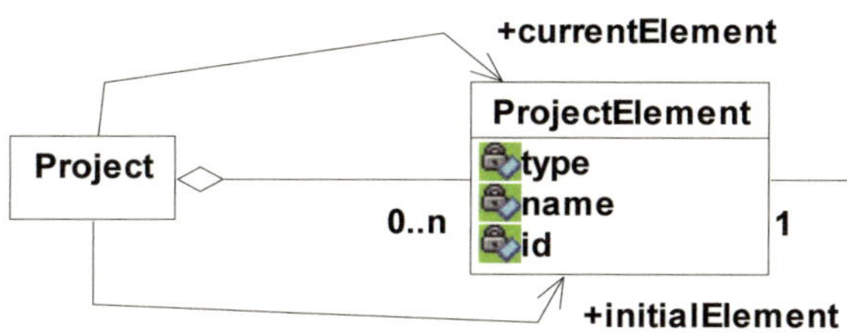

Fig. 2. The core of the Project meta-model

Any project is an aggregation of many elements (class *ProjectElement*). An element has its name, identifier and a type. Using different values of the *type* attribute a variety of different elements can be introduced in Project notation. One of the elements is distinguished as an initial element. An element of a Project can have any number of annotations (class *LinkAnnotation*) referring to a transformation process. Annotations define a set of other elements related in the project, specifying their identifiers, types or names. In a Project model, typical UML relations or properties, like generalization or association between classes, a class attribute or operation, will be converted to objects of class *ProjectElement* with appropriate types.
Transformation strategies are designed to operate on any model consistent with the Project meta-model. Such project can be understood by the executor of traceability rules.

4.4 Dependency Area meta-model

Transformation realized in the traceability framework is a kind of a model-to-model rephrasing. In the traceabilty process a dependency area is created for a model given in *Project* notation and an initial *ProjectElement*. According to Model Driven Engineering paradigma, a transformation is specified by rules dealing with meta-models of a source and target model. Any instance of meta-model *Project* should be transformed to a dependency model. The model is a resulting model of the traceability process and it is an instance of the meta-model of Dependency Area (Figure 3).

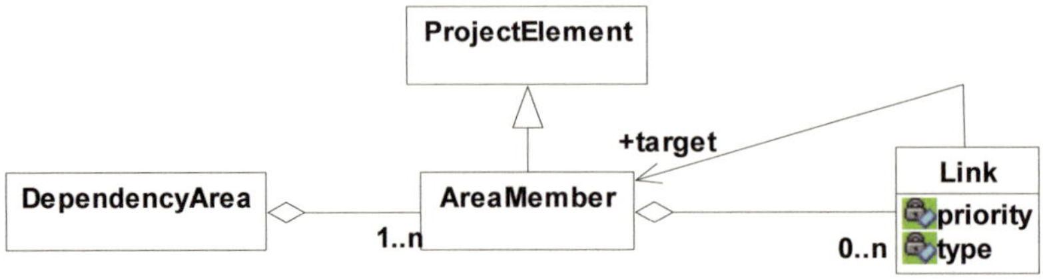

Fig. 3. The core of the Dependency Area meta-model

A dependency area consists of a set of area members. Each area member is a specialization of a *ProjectElement* of the Project meta-model. An area member can have a number of links (class *Link*) to other elements of the dependency area. Links can have their priorities and types.

Definition 7. Two dependency areas DA_1 and DA_2 are *equivalent* if:
1) their initial elements are identical,
2) they consists of the same elements,

$$x \in DA_1 \Leftrightarrow x \in DA_2$$

3) any pair of elements associated with a *Link* in one area is also associated with a *Link* in the second area

$$x \in DA_1 \wedge y \in DA_1 \wedge \exists_L (L=\text{Link}(x,y) \text{ or } L=\text{Link}(y,x)) \Leftrightarrow$$
$$x \in DA_2 \wedge y \in DA_2 \wedge \exists_K (K=\text{Link}(x,y) \text{ or } K=\text{Link}(y,x))$$

In *identical* dependency areas linking elements are of the same direction in both areas (i.e. L=Link(x,y) and K=Link(x,y)) and have the same types and priorities.

4.5 Execution of transformation rules

A strategy specified with an automata-based approach can describe a variety of processes. The general idea of the rule executor was adapted for the traceability process. The goal of the process is identification of a dependency area. An algorithm of the rule execution is shown below in a pseudo-code notation. At the beginning of the model transformation, we should have an input project P with its initial element $IE \in P$ and a strategy $\Xi = <X, R, \mu>$. Using mapping μ, any rule is assigned to a vertex of model X and has its priority. Therefore, the nonempty set of rules R can be ordered according to their priorities. Any rule r from set R is described by its automaton. A rule can be performed in the context of the current *Project* element, it means its conditions and actions of the automaton are evaluated in this context.

```
Map (P, IE , R) {
    create empty DA
    add IE to DA
    WHILE (exist x in DA and x was not considered) {
            get_first x not considered element from DA
            FOR (from first r from R, to last r from R) {
                    execRule (r, x)}
            mark x as  considered
            }
 }
```

Where:

DA - a created dependency area,
x - an element (*AreaMember*) of a given dependency area, and also an element of *Project* (see generalization in the meta-model Figure 3),
r - a rule from the set of rules *R*
get_first from DA - returns the first element from a dependency area according to the order of adding elements to the area,
loop *FOR* in 6th line - visits the set of rules *R* according to the priority order,
execRule(r, x) - calls execution of rule *r* in the context of element *x*.

```
11 execRule(r, x) {
12     IF (precondition of rule r is TRUE)
13          executeNode(r, iN, x)
14 }
15
16 execNode(r, N, x) {
17     sortTransitions (r, N)
18     FOR (from first transition y outgoing node N
19           to last transition y of N) {
20     IF (precondition of transition y is TRUE) {
21          perform_action_of_transition y
22          select node M targeted by transition y
23          execNode(r, M, x)
24     }
25 }
```

Where:

iN - the initial node of the automaton of rule *r*,
execNode(r, N, x) - calls execution of the automaton of rule *r* at node *N* in the context of element *x*,
sortTransitions (r, N) - sorts transitions outgoing node *N* in the automaton of rule *r* according to their priorities,
loop *FOR* in 18th line - visits the set of transitions outgoing the node *N* in the automaton of rule *r* according to the priority order,
y - a transition outgoing the node *N* in the automaton of rule *r*,
M - the node targeted by transition *y*

While performing an action of a transition, a *Project* element can be added to the dependency area. The properties of the identified traceability relation are specified in a *Link* object. The type and priority attributes of the link are defined by the target node and a priority of the transition, accordingly.

Elements assigned to a dependency area are considered by the executor in the order of their addition. The first one is the initial element indicated in the input project. In result of the algorithm, the whole set of rules is executed for any project element assigned to the dependency area. Any element is added only once to the resulting dependency area. If an action specifies assignment of an already existing element, only additional references between elements are added to the output dependency model.

In this solution, the transformation logic is divided between a hierarchy of rules, a structure of automata, predicates of conditions, and actions of transitions. The strategy defines in this way the criteria when and which project elements should be added to the output dependency area. The element added to the area is not removed from it, unless another area is created (e.g. for a different initial element or a different set of rules).

Another way of a strategy definition could be also considered - when some elements once added to the area would be excluded from it in the next step. Such approach was presented in (Derezinska & Bluemke, 2005), where different strategies were discussed. Rules of selection strategies were responsible for selecting and adding elements to a dependency area, whereas rules from bounding strategies decided about removing some, already added elements from the area. This approach was used in our previous framework for traceability. According to our experiences, we decided to use only selection strategies which decide about adding only those elements to an area that should be certainly placed in it. Therefore the algorithm of rule execution can be quite simple. There is a tradeoff between the simplicity of the rule executor realization and a homogenous set of rules on the one hand, and a potential complexity of conditions and actions comprised in the rules on the other hand.

It should be noted, that there are different sources of nondeterminism in the transformation process. Many rules with satisfied preconditions can have the same priorities; different transitions outgoing the same node can be labeled with the same priorities. In such cases the order of rules and operations is random. It means that there could be different transformation processes for the same strategy. In general, we are interested in obtaining unique results. Good strategies should give identical or at least equivalent resulting dependency areas obtained in any transformation processes.

A strategy is *well defined* in respect to the transformation process if for any input project P with an initial element $IE \in P$ any pair of dependency areas DA obtained as a result of two transformation processes are always equivalent (Def. 7).

4.6 Example of rule execution

A model transformation will be illustrated on a simple example. It explains the rule execution process. There is a set of rules defined in an exemplary traceability strategy that are applied for any element of a project. Let assume, that according to these rules two elements alphabetically consecutive to a considered element are assigned to the current Dependency Area.

There are four rules defined in the current strategy *alphabeticRules* (Figure 4), named from *rule1* to *rule4*. The priorities have been already assigned to the rules; therefore no additional hierarchical model is necessary. The rules can be ordered according to their priorities. If two or more rules have the same priority the order of rule execution is not determined. Therefore two orders of the rules are possible {*rule1, rule2, rule3, rule4*} and {*rule1, rule3, rule2, rule4*}.

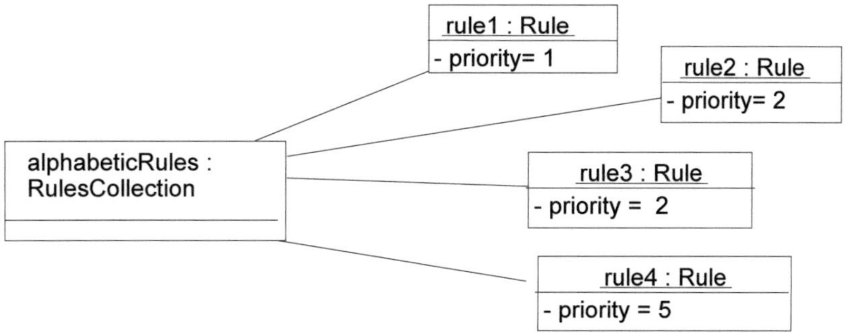

Fig. 4. Exemplary collection of rules.

An input project P1 is shown in an object diagram (Figure 5). The project consists of five elements {a, b, c, d, e}. Element *a* is the initial element and is assigned as a first element to the resulting Dependency Area *DA(a)*.

Fig. 5. A model of an input project - example P1

Next, after considering all rules for element *a,* two elements *b* and *c* will be assigned to the created dependency area *DA(a)* and link to element *a* (Figure 6). For the simplicity, the objects of the corresponding *AreaMembers* are directly connected on the diagram and the objects of *Links* between those elements are omitted. Then, element *b* is considered, because it was assigned first to *DA(a).* Its two consecutive elements are *c* and *d.* Element *c* is already assigned, therefore only *Link* between *b* and *c* is created. Element *d* and a *Link* between *b* and *d* are added to *DA(a).* For element *c,* element *e* and *Links* to *d* and *e* are assigned. Finally, a Link between elements *d* and *e* is added to *DA(a).*
In this case, the given set of rules in respect to the transformation is well defined. An identical dependency area would be obtained if, for example, element *c* were considered before element *b.*

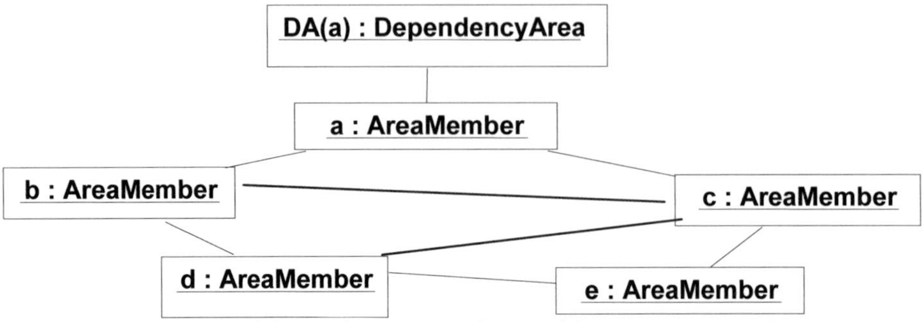

Fig. 6. A simplified model of dependency area obtained for input project P1.

5. Application of strategy specification to traceability of object-oriented projects

The concepts of transformation strategy were applied in the realization of the framework for traceability in object-oriented projects. The principles will be illustrated by examples concerning a subset of UML. The general architecture of the framework was presented in (Derezinska & Zawlocki, 2007). Input and output transformations were realized using QVT approach and existing, supporting it tools (West Team, MDA - Transf User Guide).

5.1 Traceability strategy for a subset of UML

The set of rules can be in general organized in different ways. The main goal of organizing a set of rules in a hierarchical form is identification of rule priorities and specification of their preconditions.

Considering a subset of UML, the basic concepts are described using class models comprising meta-models elements. The rule hierarchy corresponds to a hierarchy of meta-models. It should be noted, that we do not operate directly on a UML meta-model (Unified Modeling Language, 2008) but on a *Project* meta-model. However the necessary elements from the UML meta-model have the corresponding *ProjectElements.* Therefore the nodes contain similar elements as in the UML meta-model. In the UML meta-model one element can be related via generalization to many base elements. Therefore generalizations in the UML meta-model do not create tree-like structures.

A small extract of the hierarchy used in experiments illustrates the idea (Figure 7). A root of the hierarchy is a *ModelElement* with 0 priority (precisely - any rule which is associated with this vertex has priority equal to 0). Two other elements of the graph are *Classifier* and *Package* with rule priorities equal to one. A *ModelElement* can be a *Package* or a *Classifier,* and therefore they constitute the children of this vertex in the graph. A *Classifier* can be, for example, an *Actor,* a *Use Case* or a *Class.* Therefore they are the children of the vertex that corresponds to the *Classifier* rule. The elements lower in the hierarchy have higher priorities. It reflects the idea that any class at the meta level is interpreted at the first place as an actor, a class or a use case. It is less important, that this class is also a classifier. Finally, any class can be also interpreted as an element of a model.

In general, creating such a hierarchy we assign rule priorities, starting from 0 in the root, and incrementing the priority for each hierarchy level. The rules are executed in the order of their priorities. Therefore, for an *Actor* element in a model, firstly its specialized rule will be performed, than a rule characteristic to a *Classifier*, and finally a rule specified for any model element. The similar situation states for a *Class* element and *UseCase* element. A rule associated with a *ModelElement* can be applied to any element of a Project model. It has zero priority i.e. the lowest priority in the strategy. Therefore according to rule executor this rule will be performed as the last rule for any element of a model.

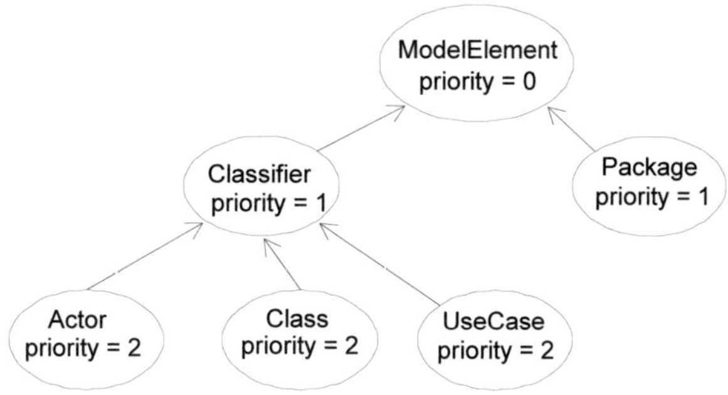

Fig. 7. Hierarchy of rules

The hierarchies of rules used in the traceability framework were created by hand, basing on the meta-model hierarchies given in the UML specification. It seems to be possible to support the construction of a strategy by a tool that analyses a given input meta-model. A graph with ordering of the rules, and description of selected rules could be derived from the meta-model in an automatic way, and further possibly modified by a user.
A traceability rule will be explained on two simple examples. Diagram in Figure 8 shows an automaton specifying a rule of the *Class* - the rule associated with the Class vertex from the hierarchy of rules (Figure 7). The rule has a priority equal to 2 and its precondition. The rule precondition is associated with the initial node of the rule, i.e., the *Class* node in this automaton. According to the precondition the rule is performed only if a current element is an *ProjectElement* of type *Class*.

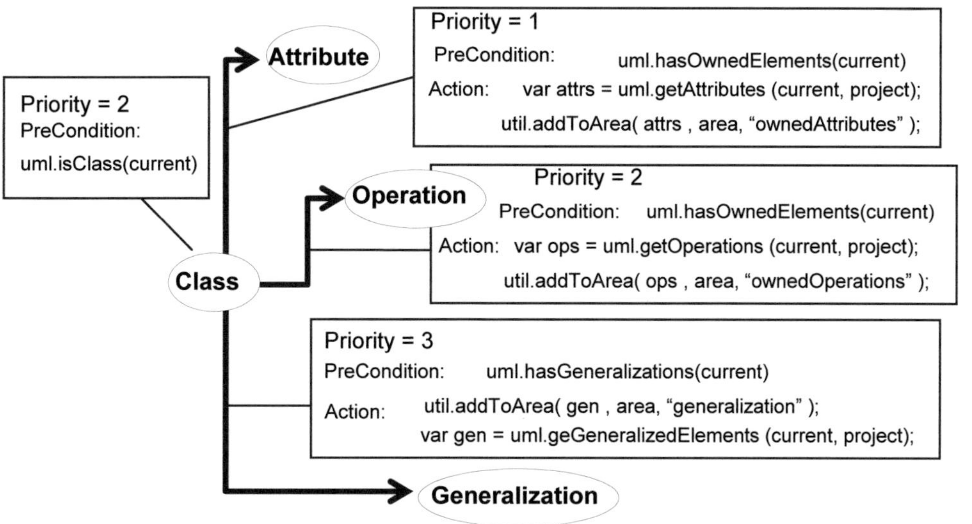

Fig. 8. An example of a traceability rule for metaclass *Class*

In the rule automaton there are three further nodes: *Attribute*, *Operation* and *Generalization*. The *Class* node is connected with transitions to these nodes. Any transition is labeled with a priority, a precondition and an action. For example, a transition to *Attribute* has priority equal 1, which is the lowest in the set of the edges outgoing from *Class* node. The precondition checks whether the current Project element is owned by the class that originates the transition. The action is responsible for adding the targeted attribute(s) to the dependency area of the considered class.
It should be noted, that there is no node corresponding to an association in the rule of the *Class*. A class is in UML specified as a classifier. Therefore in this simple strategy the node of an association will be handled in the rule of the *Classifier* (Figure 9). Such a rule will be performed later for any class, according to the rule priorities.
According to the precondition, the rule shown in Fig 9. can be applied for any initial element of the *Classifier* type. In this example Classifier node is connected to two nodes: *Association* and *ClassifierWithTheSameName*. The first transition with priority equal 1 is responsible for adding elements connected via association with a current project element. The second transition is labeled with an action that inserts to the dependency area an element having the same name as the currently considered classifier. The precondition of the transition is always satisfied (equal true), but the action is an empty operation if no elements with the same names exists. The automaton can be easily extended with other transitions and more complicated actions.

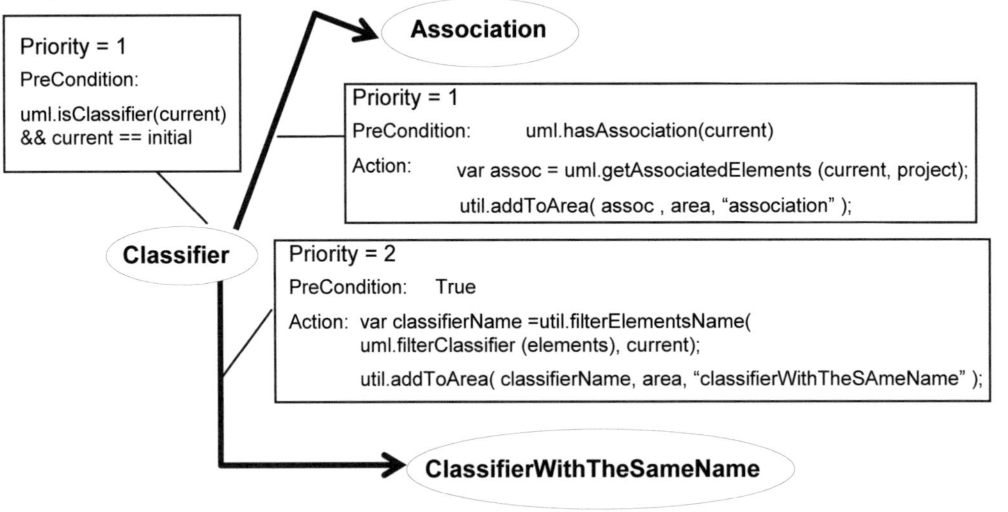

Fig. 9. An example of a traceability rule for metaclass *Classifier*

5.2 Realization of strategies

Any strategy can be specified in the XML format, comprising full descriptions of all automata of the strategy. For any automaton, all its features (identifier, priority, staring node, and the relation to an appropriate element from the meta-model hierarchy), as well as all nodes and transitions are specified with appropriate XML tags. A part of an exemplary specification is shown below. A rule starts with its condition - i.e. a condition of the initial node of the rule automaton. Next, all nodes of the rule are specified. For each node a list of outgoing edges is given.

```
<rules>
<rule id="rule-0" priority="0" initialNode="rule-0.node-1" name="modelElement" >
<condition>
            ...
</condition>
<node id="rule-0.node-1" name="modelElement" rule="rule-0">
        <edge   id="rule0.node-1.edge-1"   target="rule-0.node-2"   source="rule-0.node-1"
priority="1">
                <action>
                                ....
                </action>
                <condition>
                        ....
                /condition>
        </edge>
</node>
<node id="rule-0.node-2" name="alwaysTrue" rule="rule-0">
</node>
</rule>
<rule id="rule-1" priority="1" initialNode="rule-1.node-1" name="classifier">
<condition>
        ....
</condition>
<node id="rule-1.node-1" name="classifier" rule="rule-1">
<edge id="rule1.node-1.edge-1" target="rule-1.node-2" source="rule-1.node-1" priority="1">
        <action>
                ...
        </action>
....
```

Actions and conditions associated with nodes and transitions were written in a script language. In the implemented solution, instances of Project and Dependency Area classes are passed to the context of the script language. Therefore we can call directly those classes in the specification of actions and conditions. The methods of these classes can be executed; as well the values of public attributes can be got or updated. Functionality of the script language can be extended by other objects added to the context.

For this purpose JavaScript and Rhino library were used (Documentation of Rhino). Rhino library enables calling of scripts implemented in JavaScript directly from the Java code. For example, a pre-condition of a rule can be specified in the following way:

```
<condition>
  <script>
        <![CDATA[uml.isClassifier(current) && current == initial]]>
  </script>
</condition>
```

In this JavaScript code we can call the objects passed in the execution context: *uml* - a class supporting selected OCL operations, *current* - a current element of the considered project, *initial* - an initial element of the project.
In the similar way actions associated with transitions can be specified. For example, three actions of a rule are shown below. They used methods of object *log* - to log messages on a console, *uml* - to access model elements according to UML relations, and *util* - to manipulate on a dependency area.

```
<action>
  <script>
        <![CDATA[log.debug("rule1.node-1.edge-1 : start");
        var assoc = uml.getAssociatedElements(current, project);
        util.addToArea( assoc , area, "association");
        ]]>
  </script>
</action>
```

Actions and conditions written in JavaScript are included in XML file. They can be executed directly during a program run, as they are executed in the Rhino engine. Therefore the strategy can be easily changed by rewriting only those scripts. The executed code will be changed without modifying and recompiling the desired application.

5.3 Dependency Area Example

After specifying the input transformation to the model *Project* and the traceability transformation, we can use the framework. Dependency areas were created for a set of projects assuming different initial elements and different traceability strategies.
For the brevity reasons, we illustrate the idea using a simple plug-in for input the subset of UML and an exemplary traceability strategy dealing with this subset. Model elements not considered by the input transformation will be omitted during traceability analysis.
As an example, a simple *Cinema* system will be discussed. An actor of the system - *Client* can review the repertoire of the cinema and buy a ticket of a selected film (Figure 10).

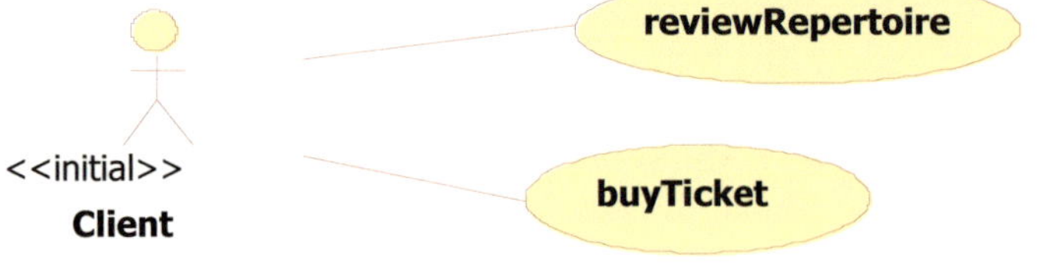

Fig. 10. Use cases of *Cinema* system

The system is divided into several packages. Classes *Client* and *Ticket* are included in *Client* package, and classes *Cinema, Repertoire* and *Movie* belong to *Cinema* package. Selected elements of the project used in this example are shown in Figure 11.

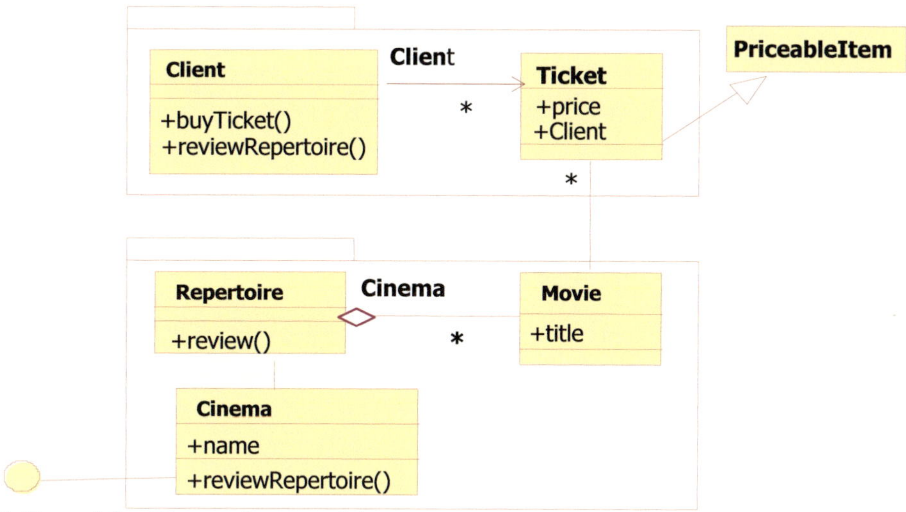

Fig. 11. Part of the *Cinema* class model

Let us assume that actor *Client* is an initial element. After application of a traceability strategy a dependency area is generated. The object diagram of the area is shown in Figure 13. For the simplicity, objects of class *Link* are omitted and the links between objects are labeled by the types of traceability relations. Precisely, the labels are values of the *type* attribute of *Link* objects (see meta-model in Figure 3). We can observe that several objects are related according to the similarity of names, for example, actor *Client* and class *Client*. If relations based on the name similarities were excluded, the resulting dependency area for the actor *Client* would include only its use cases linked via associations.
Another dependency area will be created if *Cinema* package is selected as the initial element (Figure 12). In this case, most of the relations reflect simple ownership relations of the UML meta-model elements. A dependency area is simpler and has a tree-like structure. All elements were included into dependency area according to one unique sequence of rules. In the case of Figure 13 there are several paths connecting the initial element with some elements, like class *Repertoire,* operations *reviewRepertoire, buyTicket,* attribute *Client.* It means that the same element was classified to this dependency area based on different sets of rules.

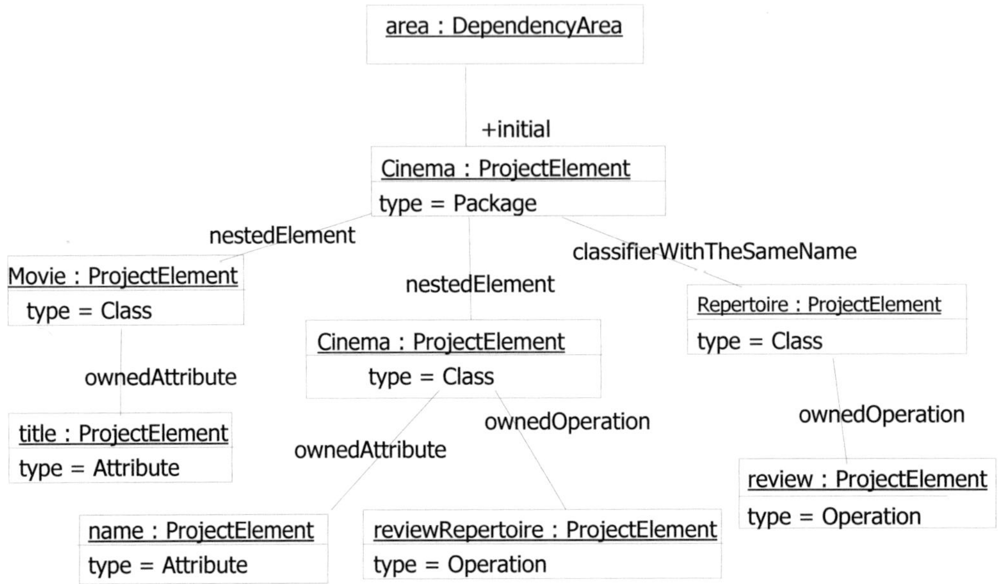

Fig. 12. Dependency relations for initial element associated with package Cinema

6. Conclusions

Automata-based approach for the specification of strategies was presented in this paper. The powerful and flexible mechanism for describing a wide scope of issues was introduced. The approach combines the hierarchy of basic concepts, similar to a meta-model graph, with sets of rules. An automaton defining a single rule is accompanied by conditions and actions that can be specified in a desired notation. In this way a strategy is separated into different abstraction levels, supporting the process of specification refinement and modification.

The automata-based strategy was applied in the generic framework for traceability of object-oriented project. An engine for rule interpretation was realized. The traceability logic can be described in the strategy by selecting appropriate priority levels of the rule hierarchy, creating the set of automata and finally specifying details in conditions and actions. An instance of the framework was implemented. It realized traceability rules based on the dependency area concepts. Exemplary strategies were specified for the subsets of UML models.

Flexibility of the methodology is very beneficial because the same rule execution engine can be used in many cases and strategies can be easily modified. On the other hand, the presented approach faced some problems. Preparation of a detailed specification of a non-trivial strategy requires a lot of work. It could be profitable if a strategy is used many times and the modified strategies are created as, for example, some variants of another, already specified strategy.

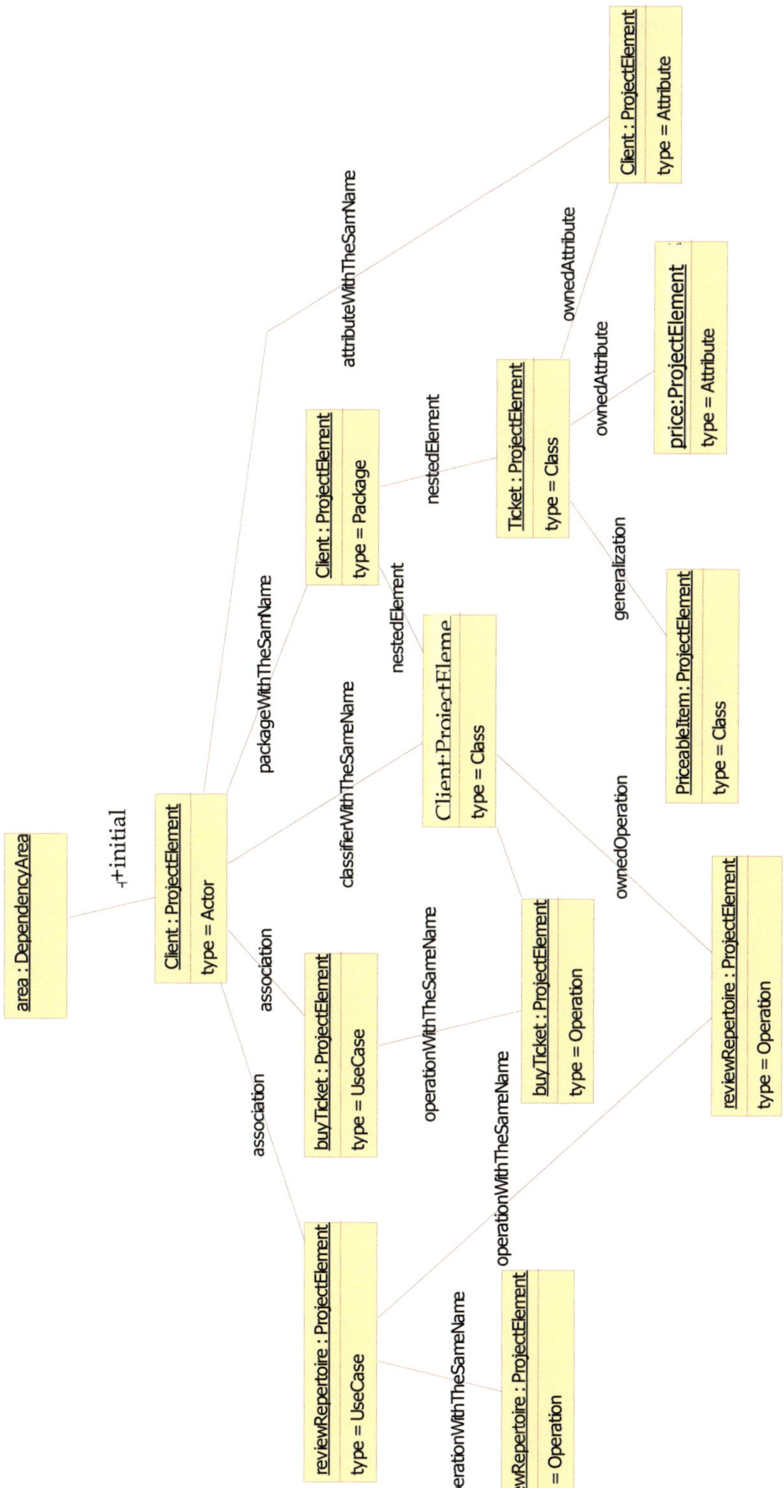

Fig. 13. Dependency relations for initial element associated with actor *Client*

Future work should be aimed at further verification of the approach in different experiments. Specification of various strategies, as well as input transformations for different sets of modeling elements can be applied in experiments using the framework. In the strategies, various intentions of developers can be taken into account, revealing relations between model elements that are not directly expressed in a model.
Another research direction is an application of the automata-based specification of a model transformation strategy in other kinds of model manipulations, like merging of models, weaving of model aspects, model refinement, etc.

7. References

Balogh, A. & Varro, D. (2006). Advanced model transformation language constructs in the VIATRA2 framework, *Proceedings of the ACM symposium on Applied Computing (SAC'06),* pp. 1280-1287, ISBN: 1-59593-108-2, Dijon France, April 2006, ACM Inc. New York, NY, USA

Bensh, S.; Bordhin, H.; Holzer, M. & Kutrib, M. (2008). Deterministic Input-Reversal and Input-Revolving Finite Automata, *Proceedings of International Conference on Language and Automata Theory and Applications (LATA 2008),* LNCS 5196, pp. 113-124, ISBN 978-3-540-88281-7, Tarragona Spain, March 2008, Springer, Berlin Heidelberg

Buttner, F. & Bauerdic, H. (2006). Realizing UML Model Transformations with USE, *Proceedings of Workshop on OCL for (Meta-)Models in Multiple Application Domains* (at Models 2006), pp. 96-110, ISSN 1430-211X, Genova, Italy, Oct. 2006, Technical Report of the Technische Universität Dresden

Czarnecki, K. & Helsen, S. (2006). Feature-based survey of model transformation approaches, *IBM System Journal*, Vol. 45, No 3 pp. 621-645, ISSN 0018-8670

Dayan D., et al. (2008). MDA PIM-to PIM transformation using extended automata, *Computer Modelling and New Technologies*, Vol. 12, No. 1, pp. 65-76, ISSN 1407-2742

Deo, N. (1974). *Graph Theory with Applications to Engineering and Computer Science*, Prentice-Hall Inc., ISBN 0133634736, Upper Saddle River, NJ, USA

Derezińska, A. (2004). Reasoning about Traceability in Imperfect UML Projects, *Foundations on Computing and Decision Sciences*, Vol. 29, No. 1-2, pp. 43-58, ISSN 0867-6356

Derezińska, A. & Bluemke, I. (2005). A Framework for Identification of Dependency Areas in UML Designs, *Proceedings of the 9th IASTED International Conference on Software Engineering and Applications SEA'05*, pp. 177-182, ISBN 0-88986-529-9, Phoenix, Arizona, USA, Nov. 2005, Acta Press, Clagary Canada

Derezińska, A. (2006). Specification of Dependency Areas in UML Designs, *Annales UMCS Informatica,* AI 4, Vol. 4, pp. 72-85, ISSN 1732-1360

Derezińska, A. & Zawłocki, J. (2007). Generic framework for automatic traceability in object-oriented designs, *Annals of Gdańsk University of Technology Faculty of ETI,* No 5, pp. 291-298 , ISBN 978-83-60779-01-9 (in polish)

Derezińska, A. & J. Zawłocki, J. (2008). Towards Model Transformation - A Case Study of Generic Framework for Traceability in Object-Oriented Designs, *IADIS Inter. Journal on Computer Science and Information Systems*, Vol 3, No 1 April 2008, pp. 29-43, ISSN: 1646-3692

Documentation of RHINO, http://www.mozilla.org/rhino/doc.html

Egyed, A. (2004). Consistent Adaptation and Evolution of Class Diagrams during Refinement, *Proceedings 7th Inter. Conf. on Fundamental Approaches to Software Engineering (FASE)*, LNCS 2984, pp. 37-53, ISBN 3-540-21305-8, Barcelona, Spain, March 2004, Springer, Berlin Heidelberg

Ehring, K. & Giese, H. (Eds.) (2007). Proc of the 6th Workshop on Graph Transformation and Visual Modeling Techniques (GT-VMT), Electronic Communications of the EASST, ISSN 1863-2122, vol. 10

Ehring K.; Guerra E. & de Lara, J., at al. (2005) Transformation by graph transformation: a comparative study, *Proccedings of the Model Transformation in Practice Workshop at MoDELS 05*, Montego Bay, Jamaica, October 2005

France, R. & Rumpe, B. (2007). Model-driven Development of Complex Software: A Research Roadmap, Proceedings of Future of Software Engineering (FOSE at ICSE'07), pp. 37-54, ISBN: 0-7695-2829-5, Minneaplois, Minnesota, May 2007, IEEE Comp. Soc. Washington, DC, USA

Frankel, D. S. (2003). *Model Driven Architecture: Appling MDA to enterprise computing*, Wiley Pub. Comp., ISBN 0-471-31920-1, Indianapolis, Indiana

Hopkroft J., Motwani R. & Ullman J. (2000) *Introduction to automata Theory, Languages, and Computation*, 2nd ed., Addison-Wesley, ISBN-10: 0201441241

Jouault F. & Kurtev I. (2005). Transforming Models with the ATL, *Proccedings of the Model Transformation in Practice Workshop at MoDELS 05*, LNCS 3844, pp. 128-138, ISBN 978-3-540-31780-7, Montego Bay, Jamaica, October 2005, Springer, Berlin Heidelberg

Kleppe, A. G. & Warmer, J. (2003). *The Object Constraint Language: Getting your models ready for MDA*, Addison-Wesley 2nd ed, ISBN 0321179366, Boston MA

Kolovos, D.S. at al. (2007). Update Transformations in the Small with the Epsilon Wizard Language, *Journal of Object Technology*, Vol. 6, No. 9, Special Issue TOOLS EUROPE Oct. 07, pp. 53-69, ISSN 1660-1769

Lakhnech, Y.; Mikk, E. & Siegel M. (1997). Hierarchical Automata as Model for Statecharts. *Advances in Computing Science - ASIAN '97, Proceedings of 3rd Asian Computing Science Conference*, LNCS 1345, pp. 181-196, ISBN 978-3-540-63875-9, Kathmandu, Nepal, Dec. 1997, Springer, Berlin Heidelberg

Letelier, P. (2002). A Framework for Requirements Traceability in UML-based Projects, *1st Int. Workshop on Traceability in Emerging Forms of Software Engineering* by IEEE Conf. on ASE, Sept. 2002, Edinburgh UK
http://www.soi.city.ac.uk/~zisman/WSProgramme.html

Maeder P. et al. (2006). Traceability for managing evolutionary change, *Proceedings of 15th Software Engeenierin Data Engeeniering SEDE* (ICSA), pp. 1-8, ISBN: 978-1-880843-59-5, Los Angeles USA, July 2006, ISCA, Cary, North Carolina USA

McMillan, K.: Cadence SMV. http://www.kenmcmil.com/ (visited 2009)

MDA Guide, Ver. 1.0.1, Object Management Group Document omg/2003-06-01 (2003)

Mens, T. & van Gorp P. (2006). Taxonomy of model transformation, *Proceedings of the International Workshop on Graph and Model Transformation (GraMoT 2005)*, Tallin, Estonia, Sept. 2005, *ENTCS*, Vol. 152 , March 2006, pp. 125-142, ISSN: 1571-0661, Elsevier

Meta Object Facility (MOF) , OMG Document, formal/2006-01-01, (2006)

MOF QVT Specification, OMG Document formal/2008-04-03 (2008)

Sendall S. at al. (2004). Understanding Model Transformation by Classification and Formalization, *Proceedings of Workshop on Software Transformation Systems* (part of 3rd International Conference on Generative Programming and Component Engineering GPCE), pp. 30-31, Vancouver, Canada, Oct. 2004, http://www.program-transformation.org/Sts/STS04

Spanoudakis, G. et al. (2004). Rule-based Generation of Requirements Traceability Relations, *Journal of Systems and Software*, Vol. 72, No. 22, pp. 105–127, ISSN: 0164-1212

Unified Modeling Language Superstructure v. 2.2, OMG Document formal/ptc/2008-05-05, (2008), http://www.uml.org

Vanhoof, B. at al. (2007). UniTI: A Unified Transformation Infrastructure, *Proccedings of of 10th International Conference Model Driven Engineering Languages and Systems (Models 2007)*, LNCS 4735, pp. 31-45, ISBN 978-3-540-75208-0, Nashville, USA, Sept-Oct. 2007, Springer, Berlin Heidelberg

Vanhooff, B. et al. (2007). Traceability as Input for Model Transformations, *Proceedings of ECMDA Traceability Workshop*, pp. 37-46, ISBN 978-82-14-04056-2, Haifa, Israel, June 2007

Wagner, G.; Giurca, A. & Lukichev, S. (2006). Modeling Web Services with URML, *Proceedings of Workshop Semantics for Business Process Management*, Budva, Montenegro, June 2006, http://idefix.pms.ifi.lmu.de:8080/rewerse/index.html

Walderhaug S., et al. (2006) Towards a Generic Solution for Traceability in MDD, Proceedings *of 2nd ECMDA Traceability Workshop*. Bilbao, Spain, July 2006, ISBN 82-14-04030, SINTEF Report, http://modelbased.net/ecmda-traceability/index.php?option=com_content&task=view&id=23&Itemid=34

West Team, MDA - Transf User Guide, http://www.lifl.fr/west/modtransf/

W3C Recommendations for rules interchange http://www.w3.org/2005/rules/wiki/RIF_Working_Group (visited 2008)

11

Dissociation of Colloidal Silver into Ionic Form through Membrane under Electric Field

Kuo-Hsiung Tseng[a*], Chih-Yu Liao[a], Der-Chi Tien[b], and Tsing-Tshih Tsung[b]
[a]*Department of Electrical Engineering, NTUT*
[b]*Graduate Institute of Mechanical and Electrical Engineering, NTUT*
Taipei 10608, Taiwan, R.O.C.

1. Introduction

In this study, an electric dissociation system (EDS) for converting colloidal silver (CS) into ionic form through membrane under electric field has been proposed. More specifically, this study was undertaken in order to understand how the silver nanoparticle and ion exerts control over the electric field, and to suggest some theoretical as well as practical implication of this process. This technology will be used to develop a chemical residue-free administration of control-released medical device for iontophoretic application. It is well known that the silver ions can obtain by dissolving the silver salt, for instance, silver nitrate ($AgNO_3$), silver sulfate (Ag_2SO_4), and silver chloride (AgCl), in the aqueous medium. However, the counter-ion of silver salt such as nitrate (NO_3^-), sulfate (SO_4^{--}), and chloride (Cl^-) may cause severe burns or toxicity to body when the silver ion has been consumed. Therefore, conversions of colloidal silver nanoparticles into ionic form are required, but not directly use the silver salts to provide the silver ions. This paper is structured as follows. In the first section of the article, we will start with an introduction to metallic silver and silver nanoparticles, and then present a short literature review of iontophoresis. The second section describes the experimental setup of the electric dissociation system (EDS). The third section summarizes the results and discussions for the various analyses of experimental data. Finally, conclusions are presented and suggestions are made for further research.

1.1 Metallic silver

Metallic silver has been known since ancient times and has long been valued as a precious metal, used to make ornaments, jewelry, currency coins, tableware, and utensils. Today, silver metal is widely used in conductors, switches, contacts, fuses and virtually all electrical appliances. Silver's role as an effective antimicrobial agent has been well established in several studies (Burrell et al., 1999; Thomas & McCubbin, 2003). It can control a wide variety of yeast, fungi, and viruses (Thati et al., 2007). Human health care providers have used silver for diverse purposes for several thousand years (Goodman & Gilman, 1975). Going back to Roman times, silver vessels has been used to preserve drinking water and other liquids fresh from bacteria. In the 18th century, immigrants tracking across America West found that if they placed silver coins in their casks of drinking water, it kept the water safe from bacteria and algae. In the early 1800s, doctors used silver sutures in surgical wounds with very successful results. In 1884, Credé proposed the use of drops of silver nitrate eye solution (1% silver nitrate) to prevent ophthalmia neonatorum in newborns (Rungby, 1986). During World War I, silver foil was used to protect wounds from infection (Lewis, 1909). In the 1970s, the National Aeronautics and Space Administration (NASA) used silver containers to preserve the purity of drinking water (Metodiev & Bozhilova, 1990) on spacecraft. These varied uses demonstrated the bacteriostatic properties of silver. However, at the beginning of the 20th century, the discovery and development of antibiotics has led to a dramatic reduction in deaths from infection. Thus, silver became less used for medicinal purposes. Over the last 50 years, widespread overuse of antibiotics has fueled a growing increase of antibiotic resistance among bacteria. For example, MRSA (methicillin-resistant *Staphylococcus* aureus) (Norrby et al., 2005) and VRSA (vancomycin-resistant *Staphylococcus* aureus) (Tenover, 2005) developed a strong outer wall that prevented antibiotics (penicillin) from penetrating and exerting its effects. But now, the growing ineffectiveness of traditional antibiotics and emergence of nanotechnology have renewed attention in the antibiotic properties of silver. As a result of the rapidly increasing growth of nanotechnology, silver grants a new prospect in 21st century. The development of nano-scale techniques is leading to a resurgence of interest in the medical use of silver.

1.2 Silver nanoparticles

The expression "nanoparticles" is, in general, used in the realm of materials science to represent particles size less than 100 nanometers, ranging between the molecular state and the bulk state. Within these nano-scales, materials in high surface-area-to-volume ratio will create their unique properties (Bawendi et al., 1990) in an extraordinary region, leading to novel and unexpected phenomena. In particular, metal nanoparticles such as silver nanoparticles have become an important target for modern chemistry, physics, and bioscience. Fabrication and characterization of silver nanoparticles has attracted considerable attention as a result of their significant applications in the fundamental sciences and nanotechnology. The potential applications of silver nanoparticles include catalysis (Sun & Seff, 1994), photographic development processes (Huang et al., 1996), nano-detection (Park et al., 1999), electrodes for multi layer ceramic capacitors (MLCC), spectrally selective coating for solar energy absorption, and intercalation material for electrical batteries (Klaus-Joerger et al., 2001). Application of silver nanoparticles depends on the process used to manufacture particles with different size, shape, and chemical composition. Additionally, the products should be chemically and physically stable without undergoing degradation.

The silver nanoparticles suspended in solution as a colloidal suspension is a well-known bacteriostatic and poisonous agent for different bacteria and viruses (Lee et al., 2003). No side effects were observed when using drugs based on metallic nano-silver in clinical trials. Although, silver's exact antimicrobial mechanism is unknown yet. It has been determined, however, that the free silver ion is the active agent, with evidence that silver's antibacterial activity is directly proportional to the amount of silver ions released (Lansdown, 2006). These ions exhibit an oligodynamic effect by denaturing proteins in prokaryotic cells, typical of microorganisms (Feng et al., 2000). Mammalian cells are eukaryotic and so display a strong resistance to silver's effects, making the use of silver in treating human disease safe (Bicanová & Thinschmidt, 1985).

Several methods of silver nanoparticles fabrication exist. Current techniques used to produce silver nanoparticles are usually divided into chemical and physical methods. Reduction of metal ions into neutral metal clusters is a commonly used treatment in chemical synthesis. This includes conventional chemical (one- or two-phase system), photochemical (Huang et al., 1996), sonochemical (Zhang et al., 2004), electrochemical (Starowicz et al., 2006), and radiolytic reduction (Shin et al., 2008). From metal bulk samples are used to generate nanoparticles by physical methods include: lithography (Klein et al., 2008), evaporation (Korchagin et al., 2005), and laser ablation (Bae et al., 2002). Although these conventional methods may successfully produce silver nanoparticles, they require the use of stabilizers or surfactants to protect the silver particles against agglomeration (maintain a colloidal suspension), leaving these undesired chemicals in the solution after fabrication is complete. Additionally, these methods are usually expensive and potentially dangerous for the environment. In order to overcome the problems described above, a novel and easy method for the preparation of silver nanoparticles using the arc-discharge method (ADM) was presented.

The arc-discharge method (ADM) involves pulse direct current (DC) being passed through two silver electrodes which are submerged in deionized water. During discharge the temperature between electrodes can reach several thousand degrees Celsius and the Ag rods are etched in the water medium. Silver vapor condensed in water creates a well-dispersed and thermodynamically stable Ag aqueous suspension. Silver nanoparticles fabricated by ADM in water without any surfactants or stabilizers are characterized as a stable colloid, which can be stored in a glass container for a fairly long time at room temperature without visible sedimentation (no apparent precipitate). The ADM is a good alternative method for silver nanoparticles preparation, and is not only a relatively inexpensive process, but also environmentally friendly. Additionally, any experimental data obtained using these colloids can be confidently established, as there is no interference from any additional chemicals.

1.3 Literature review of iontophoresis

Iontophoresis is a non-invasive transdermal delivery technique, which allows introduction of various ions or other substance into the skin through the use of electricity. It could be considered as a suitable and effective alternative to conventional injection or oral administration. The iontophoresis technique has been developed and modified over the past 260 years. The first suggestions date from the mid 18th century, demonstrated an ongoing relationship between electricity and drug. In 1747, the Giovanni Francesco Pivati reported that the smell of Peruvian balsam preserved in a glass container turned into obvious in the room after connecting electrical source. In 1748, Giovanni Giuseppe Veratti had successfully treated patients with nervous diseases such as deafness, rheumatic afflictions, paralysis, and sciatic pain (Veratti, 1748). In 1800, Bernard Raymond Fabré-Palaprat was interpreted as proof for the electrically assisted transport of iodine ions through the body by using the compress soaked with potassium iodide (KI) and starch solution separately fixed on the both arm. A further significant milestone in the history of iontophoresis was the voltaic narcotism. In 1858, Benjamin Ward Richardson used tincture of aconitine, aconite extract and chloroform which has been used with the assistance of electric current for iontophoresis in dental anaesthesia practice. In the 1870s, the current mediated transport of matter through porous membranes or intact human skin had been extensively studied by the Hermann Musk. To explain his theory, he introduced strychnine hydrochloride into rabbits by means of electricity. After exposure to an electrified strychnine solution, spontaneous cramps were observed in the rabbits. In 1908, Leduc (Leduc, 1908) reported the medical use of iontophoresis for the transport of drugs into the body. He was aware that some chemicals under a direct current which could be carried across an avascular membrane as the transporting agent. The strychnine experiments were also performed by Leduc (Latham et al., 2003). In 1965, Rapperport (Rapperport et al., 1965) achieved a very high level of penicillin in eschar by using iontophoresis. In 1978 and 1980 iontophoresis was clinically used for the treatment of ear chondritis (LaForest & Cofrancesco, 1978). Today, iontophoresis has wide variety of applications, including in ophthalmology, dermatology, ENT (ear, nose, throat), allergic conditions, furthermore in neurological diseases.

The basic components of transdermal iontophoresis consists of a battery, two oppositely charged electrodes, and drug reservoir, as shown in Figure 1. The drug in ionic form in communication with the permeable skin is very susceptible, due to the fact that each ion can be influenced under an electrical field effect formed within the solution. For instance, positively charged ions (cations) like silver will be attracted to the negative electrode (cathode) and repelled from the positive electrode (anode). The electrostatic repulsion of like charges will become the primary driving force for iontophoresis process. In mainly applications, the power source supplies a constant current. As the current drives the ions through the skin barrier walls, the electrical circuit is accomplished whereby the charged molecules. The iontophoretic system offers the following key benefits to improve quality of drug delivery and reduce potential complications. (1) Because the iontophoretic treatment is a non-invasive and simplified therapeutic regimen, it poses minimal tissue trauma, infection risk, and avoids the inconvenience of continuous intravenous infusion. (2) Drug solutions are directly transferred to the treatment or evaluation site without the disadvantage of oral administration. (3) It provides a relatively pain free alternative for patients who are unable or reluctant to receive injections. (4) The therapeutic efficacy can be enhanced due to the hepatic first-pass metabolism is bypassed. (5) Reduce the possibility of over- or under-dosing by continuous drug release at the programmed rate. (6) Permit the administration of a drug with a short biological half-life.

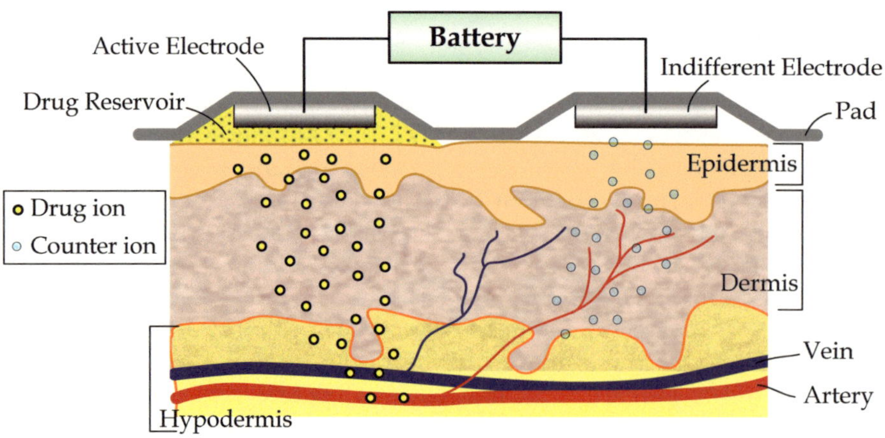

Fig. 1. Basic principle of iontophoresis

2. Experimental Methods

2.1 Preparation of the colloidal silver

An arc-discharge method (ADM) is used to fabricate the colloid silver solution in present work. The ADM system, as indicated in Figure 2, consists of five main parts listed and described below: (1) Two silver electrodes (Gredmann, 99.99%) 1 mm in diameter; (2) A servo control system which maintains a constant distance between the electrodes; (3) A power supply system connected to the electrode, which controls the DC arc-discharge parameters; (4) A glass container with an electrode holder and deionized water (pH = 5.8, conductivity = 0.8 - 0.9 μS/cm) to collect the silver colloids; (5) A stirring system with magnetic stirrer and stirring bar.

The servo control system based on a feedback loop controls the gap between electrodes which is equal to a few microns (20 ~ 40 μm). The glass container with deionized water is stirred by using the magnetic stirrer at room temperature. Silver wires are used as both the positive and negative electrodes. The upper Ag electrode is held by the servo control system and the bottom one is fixed by the electrode holder. The parameters of the control system were chosen for optimal conditions of Ag nanoparticles production.

The power supply system provides a stable pulse voltage of 70-135 V for 2-3 μs and then maintains a pulse of 20-40 V for around 7-8 μs, in order to ionize the aqua medium between the Ag electrodes. In this moment, the etching current can reach 4 A. Well-controlled timing on and off is demonstrated in Figure 3. The governing parameters of this system given in Table 1, such as the working voltage, selected current, pulse duration (on/off-time), electrode gap, and temperature of the deionized water are crucial factors for nanoparticles production. During the spark discharge, the surface layer of the Ag wires is evaporated and condensed in the water. The transparent solution converts to the characteristic pale yellow, and then a stable silver suspension is created. Calculation of the energy is required for system level energy consumption evaluation and optimization. The energy (E) in Joules is the product of the voltage (V), the current (I) and the time (t). By recording this energy level, the corresponding amount of consumed electrode per energy used can be calculated. This in turn, gives information on amount of nanoparticles formed and solution concentration.

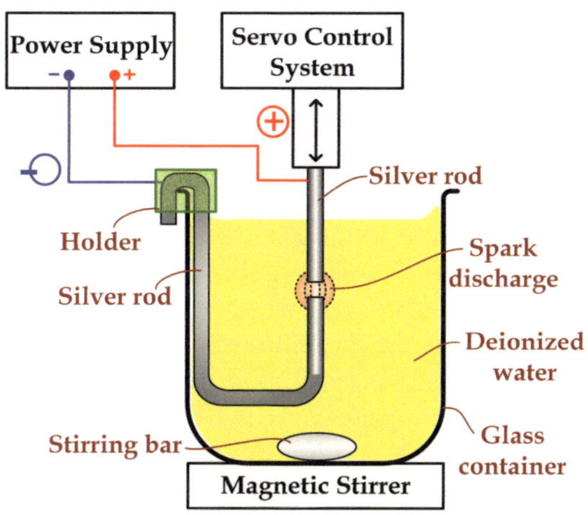

Fig. 2. Schema of the arc-discharge method for colloidal silver production

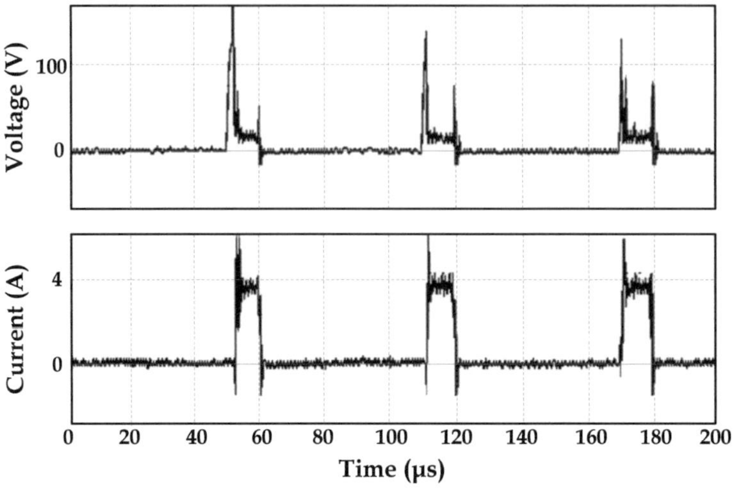

Fig. 3. Current and voltage pulses created by the ADM during etching of the silver electrodes

Parameter	Value
Fabrication pressure	1 atm
Fabrication time	60 s
Initial voltage	135 V
Off-pulse duration	50 μs
On-pulse duration	50 μs
Working current	4 A
Temperature of deionized water	25 °C
Volume of deionized water	500 mL

Table 1. Key parameters for silver nanoparticles suspension production

2.2 Electric dissociation system setup

The complete electric dissociation system (EDS) is shown in Figure 4. The system was performed using two glass bottles (600 cm^3) positioned horizontally with a membrane between them, silicone rings to hold the bottles together, and platinum (Pt) electrode wires (99.99%, Gredmann). Inert Pt was chosen for both electrodes because it was resistant to reaction with the other elements involved and presents no toxicity to any situation. Colloidal silver solution with a yellow tint (400 cm^3) was placed in the anodic chamber with the anode being mounted therein and submerged in the solution. On the other hand, the deionized water (400 cm^3, pH = 6.5, conductivity = 0.7 μS/cm) was placed similarly in the cathodic chamber with the cathode. Cellophane was selected as a membrane between the bottles, and its semi-permeability allows for ions to pass through, but not particles or large molecules. Magnetic spin bars were placed in the bottom of both bottles to ensure the homogeneity of the solutions, and eliminating the concentration variable when monitored by the measuring devices placed within the bottle. Lastly, a direct current (DC) power supply was used to provide constant-voltage (CV) and constant-current (CC) across the electrodes.

The silver ion concentration and light absorbance of the two chambers were collected using, respectively, an ion selective electrode (ISE) and UV-Vis spectrophotometer. Ion selective electrode is a membrane electrode, which responds selectively towards one (or several) ion species in the presence of others, based on the thin membrane property to bind only the intended ion. For instance, the Ag ion selective electrode gives voltage when it is submerged in Ag^+ solution; the voltage is proportional to the ion concentration. A peristaltic pump circulated solution from the chamber to a UV-Vis double-beam spectrophotometer (Helios Alpha 9423UVA1002E) for continuous absorbance measurement during the entire course of the experiment. The spectrum was scanned from 190 nm to 600 nm. The optical properties of a metallic nanoparticle depend mainly on its surface plasmon resonance (SPR), where the plasmon corresponds to the collective oscillation of the free electrons in the conduction band of Ag. According to the Mie theory (Mie, 1908), it is well known that the peaks, intensity, and line-widths of plasmon resonant are sensitive to the nanoparticle size (Tilaki et al., 2006), concentration (Eustis et al., 2005), shape (Sosa et al., 2003), metallic species (Mulvaney, 1996), and the surrounding medium (Kossyrev et al., 2005).

In this investigation, the parameters of EDS such as applied voltage and current were carried out for exploring the properties of this system in detail. A precisely regulated DC power supply can be used to provide either a constant-voltage or constant-current sources. A constant-voltage (CV) source generates a DC voltage that can be set to any determined value in a specific range. On the other hand, a constant-current (CC) source produces a regulated current independent of the voltage over the entire chamber (up to the maximum allowable voltage). As a separate step in the experimental design, the different parameters of constant-voltage (50V, 100V, 150V, 200V) and constant-current (100uA, 200uA, 400uA, 600uA, 800uA) have to be taken into consideration for estimating and optimizing the controlled release of silver ions. An interpretation of these experimental results outlining the main features and phenomena will be presented in detail below.

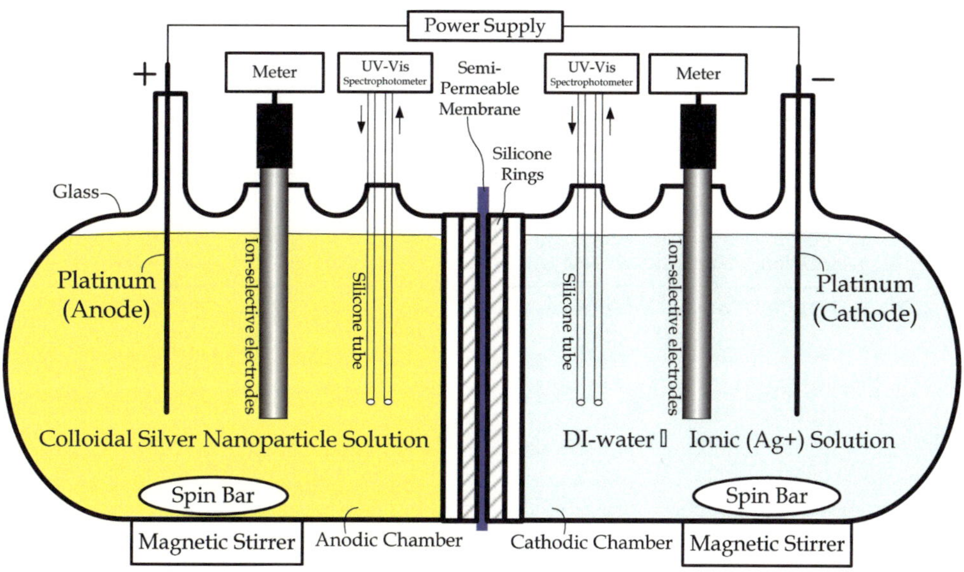

Fig. 4. Schematic of the electric dissociation system (EDS)

3. Results and Discussions

3.1 Characterization of the colloidal silver

The field emission scanning electron microscope (FE-SEM, HITACHI S4700) was used to observe the size distribution and morphology of the silver nanoparticles. Figure 5 show representative SEM image and corresponding size distribution histograms of the Ag particles. As can be seen, a particle size below 30 nm is observed. A titrator (METTLER TOLEDO-DL50), to estimate the concentration of the ionic silver—using NaCl of a predetermined molar concentration that reacts with the ionic silver to form a precipitate, we can calculate the concentration of ionic silver in the colloidal silver (CS) solution. An atomic absorption spectrophotometer (AA, Shimadzu AA-680), to measure the concentration of ionic silver below the threshold of 6 ppm in order to check the accuracy of the estimate made with the titrator. As shown in Table 2, the concentration of the ionic silver in the CS was 19.9 ppm (Titrator) and 26.4 ppm (AA). The measurement taken with the AA is greater than the measurement taken with the titrator because the AA is sensitive to both the ionic silver and the metallic silver nanoparticle, whereas the titrator is sensitive solely to the ionic silver. Using a centrifuge, it was able to separate the ions from the particles and to perform individual qualitative and quantitative analyses in an attempt to explore the nature of the ions. A centrifuge running at 18,000 rpm for 100 minutes is then used to extract the ionic silver (which is contained in the supernatant—Ag^{+}) and the metallic silver nanoparticles (which are contained in the sediment—Ag^{0}). Because ionic silver dissolve only in the supernatant, therefore can determine silver ions concentration of CS through the use of Titration and AA. These gave us measurements of 18.6 ppm and 19.2 ppm respectively. After the sediment (Ag particles) dissolved fully in the nitric acid, the titrator and the AA gave measurements of 11.2 ppm and 11.4 ppm respectively. This suggests that the metallic silver nanoparticle suspended in the CS had a concentration of approximately 11 ppm.

#	Sample	Titrator (ppm)	AA (ppm)
1	Colloidal silver	19.9	26.4
2	Supernatant (Ag^{+})	18.6	19.2
3	Sediment (Ag^{0}) dissolved by HNO_3	11.2	11.4

Table 2. Measurement result of silver concentration

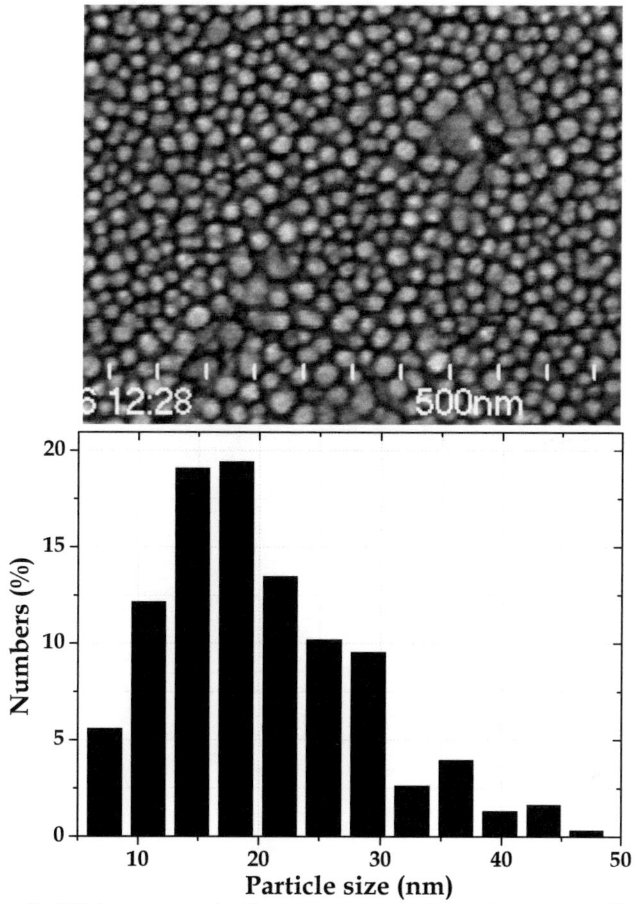

Fig. 5. (Upper panel) SEM image of silver nanoparticles; (lower panel) histogram of size distribution

3.2 UV-visible light absorbance analysis

The UV-visible light absorbance of the both chambers was spectrophotometrically determined detail of silver activity throughout the course of the experiment. Absorption peaks at around 396 nm, characteristic of Ag nanoparticles (Badr et al., 2006), and at around 190 nm, which is assumed to signify silver ions (Matsuoka et al., 2000), are seen in the anodic chamber as shown in Figure 6. These then decrease progressively in absorption peak with increasing time intervals (from 0 to 180 min), indicating loss of both forms (Ag^0 & Ag^+). A corresponding trend towards steadily increasing peak around 190 nm with the migration time in the cathodic chamber indicates the presence of only silver ions, as shown in Figure 7. The anodic chamber shows an unusual increase in absorbance around 435-550 nm region after 60 minutes as shown in Figure 6. This is probably caused by some silver nanoparticle aggregation, due to lacking of Ag^+ in colloidal silver solution. These were visually observed as brown cloud forms billowing outward from the anode in the direction of the cathode. Van der Waal's force causes these to agglomerate together and take on the brown color indicative of high silver nanoparticles concentration. Eventually these dissociate into ions as well, contributing to the silver ion absorbance peak in the cathodic chamber.

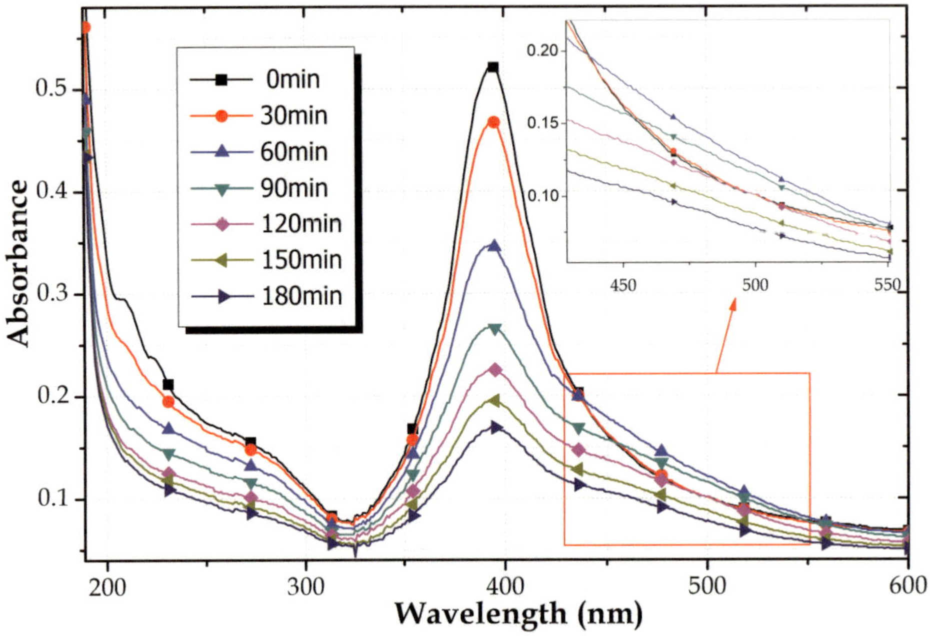

Fig. 6. Typical UV-Vis spectra of anodic chamber during process

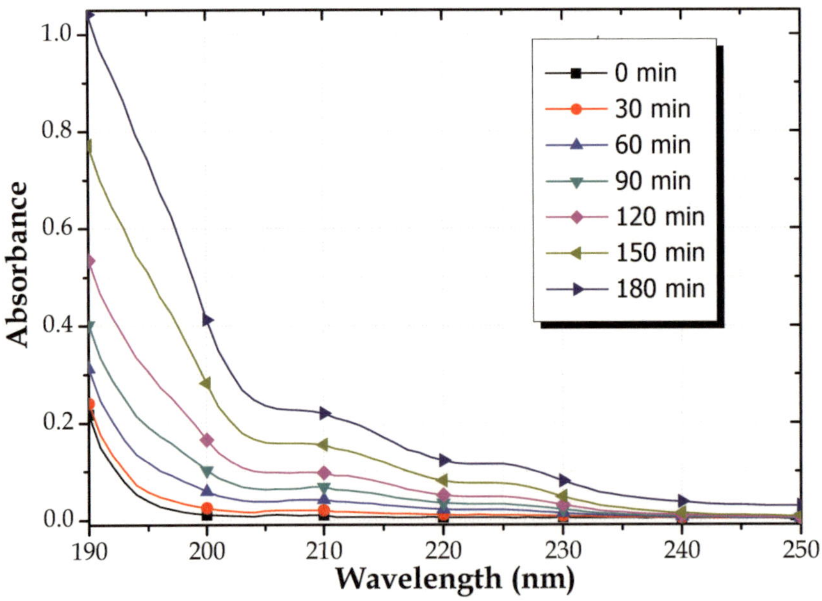

Fig. 7. Typical UV-Vis spectra of cathodic chamber during process

3.3 Time-concentration curve analysis

To consider the processes of electric dissociation system (EDS), the Ag^+ concentration of both chamber have to be measured. Figure 8 illustrates a typical concentration-time profile of anodic and cathodic chamber of using ion-selective electrodes (ISE) to monitor the ionic silver concentration. As can be seen in this figure, the curve reflects two stages of different behaviour. In the stage 1, the process begins when the anodic chamber concentration decreases as the ions move to the cathodic chamber. The cathodic chamber concentration is increased in the first three hours and then reaches a peak. After three hours (second stage), it slowly dropped due to the source of silver at anodic side is fully consumed. As time proceeds, the Ag^+ concentration will decline in the anodic chamber, rise to a maximum in the cathodic chamber, and then decline. It is important to note that the maximum cathodic ion concentration ($C_{\max}^{cathodic}$) is not as same as initial anodic ion concentration ($C_{initial}^{anodic}$) that depend on Ag^+ reduction rate dictated by the cathode. However, the changes in the anodic concentration quantitatively reflect changes in the cathodic. The AUC (area under curve) of both sides indicates that more ions reach the cathodic side than were initially present in the colloidal solution, due to the cathodic ions not only come from the anodic ions but also anodic dissociated Ag particle. However, most of ions in the cathodic side will quickly attach onto the cathode, and rapidly convert to atomic form. Finally, the steady-state Ag^+ concentration gradient in the both chambers tend to zero and the solutions become diluted as water.

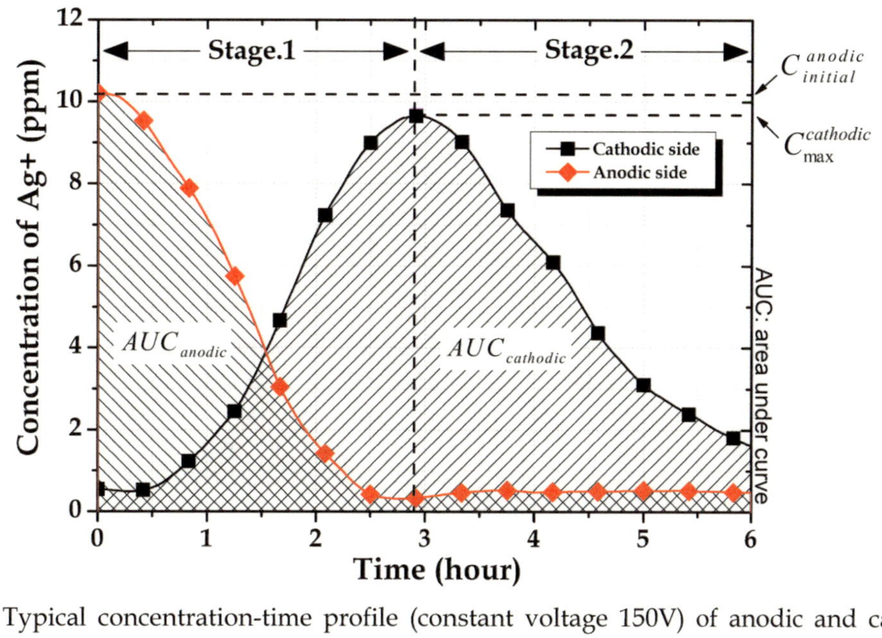

Fig. 8. Typical concentration-time profile (constant voltage 150V) of anodic and cathodic chamber

3.4 CV and CC effects on the properties of EDS

The dissociation experiment tests in constant voltage (CV) mode increased from 50 to 250 VDC in 50V steps had been achieved. All the initial conditions had been pre-determined throughout the entire course, such as the concentration and volume of colloidal silver, the distance between two electrodes, and stirring rate. The concentration-time profiles of anodic and cathodic chamber are shown in Figure 9 and Figure 10, respectively. As observed in Figure 9 (anodic side), it can be clearly found that the magnitude of the applied voltage will correlate with decline in silver ion concentration. That is, the higher the voltage is, the stronger the electric field will be, which will increase the silver consumption rate (ppm/hour). In addition, Figure 10 shows the voltage level will affect the area under curve (AUC), rate of rise and fall of profiles, total dissociation time, as well as the time required to reach peak concentration but not influence the peak level of concentration. The rate of rise is proportional to the ion-flow velocity that correlates to the number of silver ions through the semi-permeable membrane per unit time. The rate of fall indicates the speed of silver ions reduced into atoms by accepting an electron from negative pole. Consecutively, the peak-time was shown on the cathodic chamber, it regarded that the source of silver in anodic side was fully consumed at that particular point. According to the AUC, it can be seen that the lower applied voltage, the higher the AUC. Therefore, in the same initial conditions, a lower voltage can support large AUC with similar peak level of concentration provided by other voltage levels.

The dissociation experiment tests in constant current (CC) mode increased from 100, 200, 400, 600, and 800 uA were also be explored. The experimental results of anodic and cathodic chamber are shown in Figure 11 and Figure 12, respectively. As observed in Figure 11, it can be found that the rise in iontophoretic currents led to an increase in ions transport rate and this effect became larger as the current was increased. These results are compared with results from the CV mode; the performance characteristics of two curves are similar. However, the driving force of ions is relative to the applied current, and as a result, the slope of decline on the anodic side in CC mode is more linear than in CV mode (variable current). Furthermore, Figure 12 shows that applied current can control more operating parameters, such as AUC, rate of rise and fall of profiles, total dissociation time, time required to reach peak, as well as the peak level of concentration. It was evident that the CC mode whether for research purposes or for solving practical problems has more freedom to optimize the performance, particularly in a medical environment.

The quantity of ion transported rate in anodic side and ion received rate in cathodic side for both kinds of modes are shown in Table 3. The release rate of anodic side and cathodic side are calculated by considering the fall- and rise-portion of the curve, respectively. The dissociation rate is a function of current; however, the current always changes over entire course in the CV mode. As a result, the dissociation rate in CC mode is regarded as more stable than that in CV mode. Thus, the maximum dissociation rate in CV mode and average dissociation rate in CC mode of both chambers are listed in this Table. The profiles of release rate versus voltage and current according to the Table 3 are shown in Figure 13 and Figure 14. Therefore, from the above experimental results, it can be inferred that the release concentration of silver ions can be programmed by controlling the magnitude of voltage or current. However, the CC mode is more controllable, due to the premeditated driving force is more precisely rely on the current not voltage.

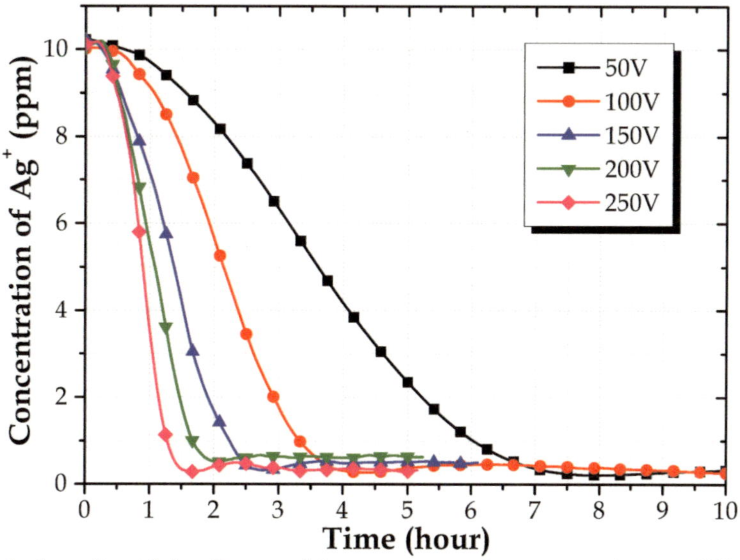

Fig. 9. CV mode (anodic side) - Curve of Ag^{+} concentration versus time at difference voltage

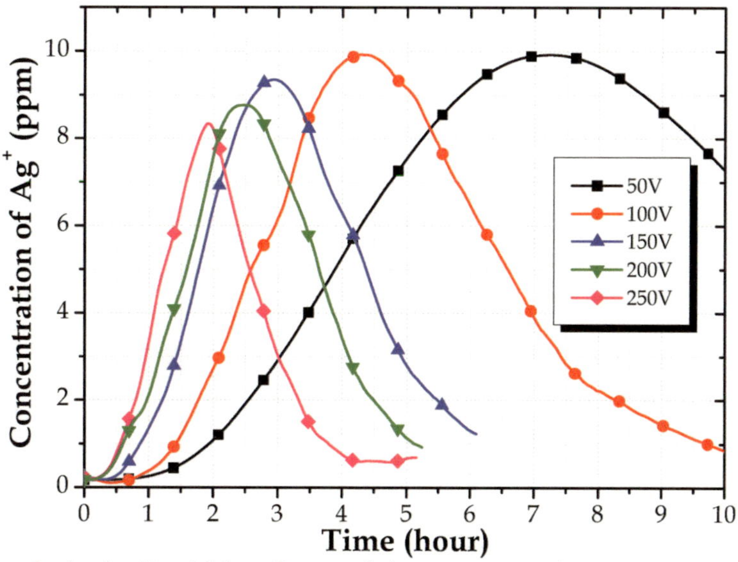

Fig. 10. CV mode (cathodic side) - Curve of Ag^{+} concentration versus time at difference voltage

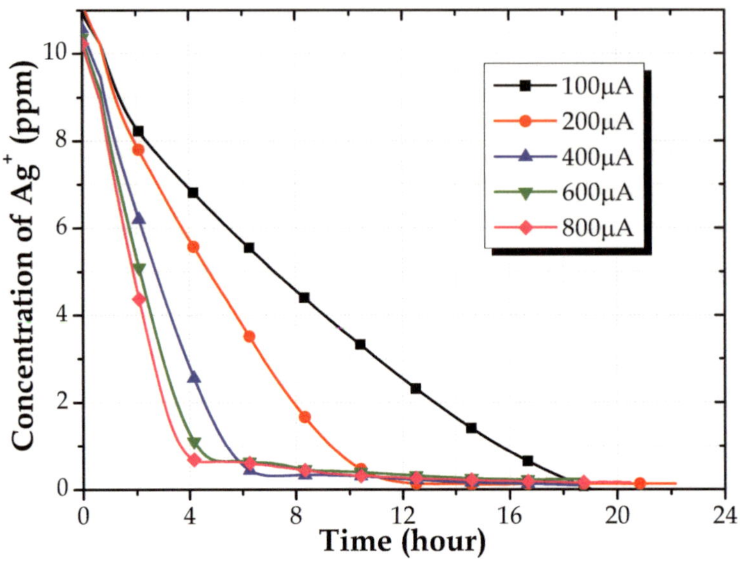

Fig. 11. CC mode (anodic side) - Curve of Ag^+ concentration versus time at difference current

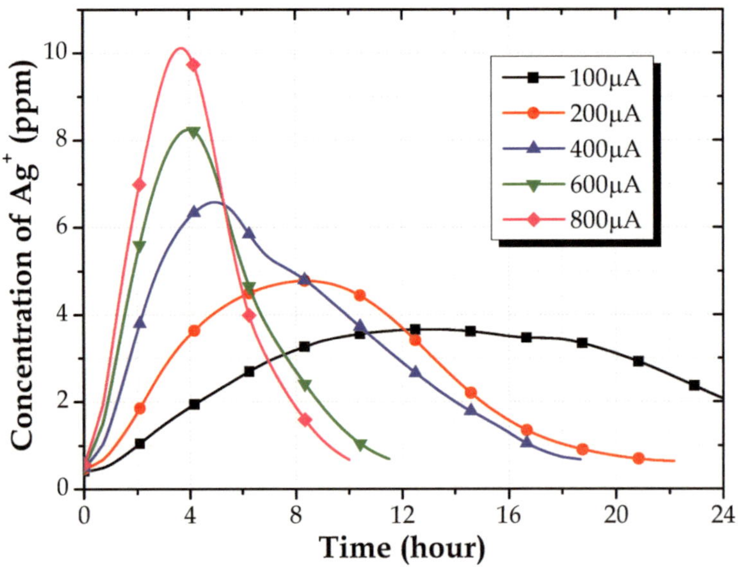

Fig. 12. CC mode (cathodic side) - Curve of Ag^+ concentration versus time at difference current

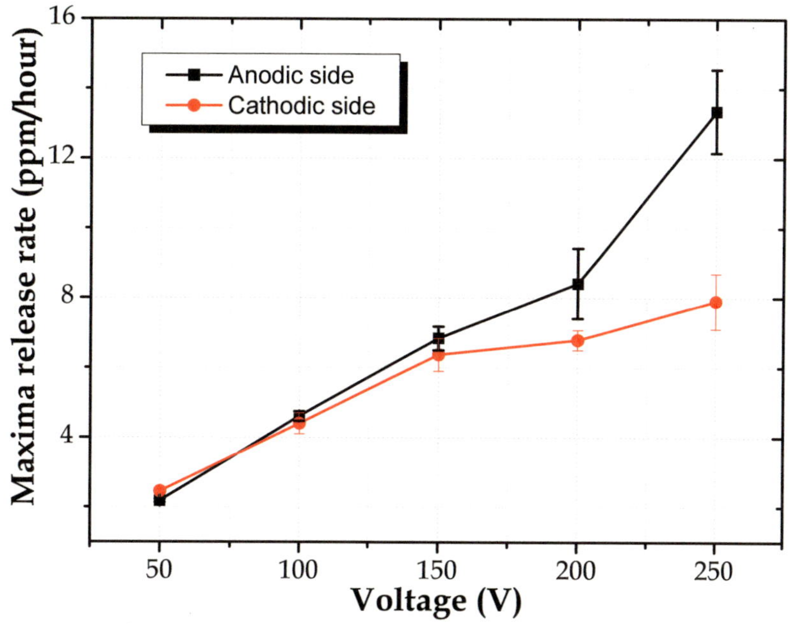

Fig. 13. Maxima ion release rate under different constant voltage

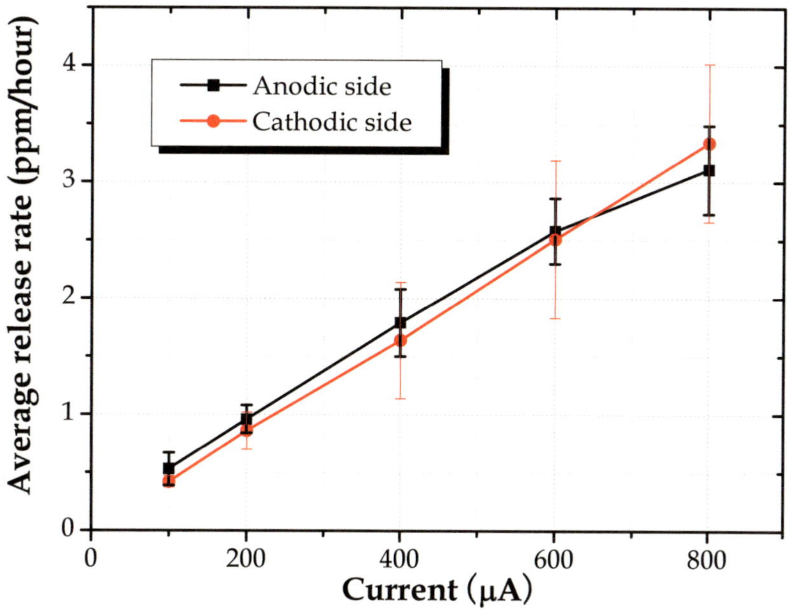

Fig. 14. Average ion release rate under different constant current

Maxima release rate in CV mode (ppm/hour)		
Voltage (V)	Anodic	Cathodic
50	2.18 ± 0.04	2.45 ± 0.07
100	4.61 ± 0.14	4.40 ± 0.30
150	6.84 ± 0.34	6.37 ± 0.47
200	8.42 ± 1.01	6.79 ± 0.29
250	13.35 ± 1.19	7.90 ± 0.79
Average release rate in CC mode (ppm/hour)		
Current (μA)	Anodic	Cathodic
100	0.53 ± 0.14	0.42 ± 0.05
200	0.96 ± 0.12	0.86 ± 0.16
400	1.79 ± 0.29	1.64 ± 0.50
600	2.58 ± 0.28	2.51 ± 0.68
800	3.11 ± 0.38	3.34 ± 0.68

Table 3. Ion release rate under different conditions

3.5 Dissociation mechanism of colloidal silver

Schematic illustration of the colloidal silver dissociation and migration process is illustrated in Figure 15. As soon as power is applied to the primary system (Figure 15a), the first commencement of process commences (Figure 15b). Here, existing Ag^+ are removed from the colloidal solution, as they move rapidly to the negatively charged cathode. Upon contact, the silver ions obtain an electron and convert to atomic form, as seen by the increasing formation of dendrites on the cathode (Figure 15c). In the next stage as demonstrated in Figure 15d, the silver nanoparticles dissociate into ionic form, and likewise migrate towards the cathode, finally leaving a water solution free of silver nanoparticles and ions in the anodic chamber (Figure 15e). In the end, both sides' solutions are turned into pure water as shown in Figure 15f.

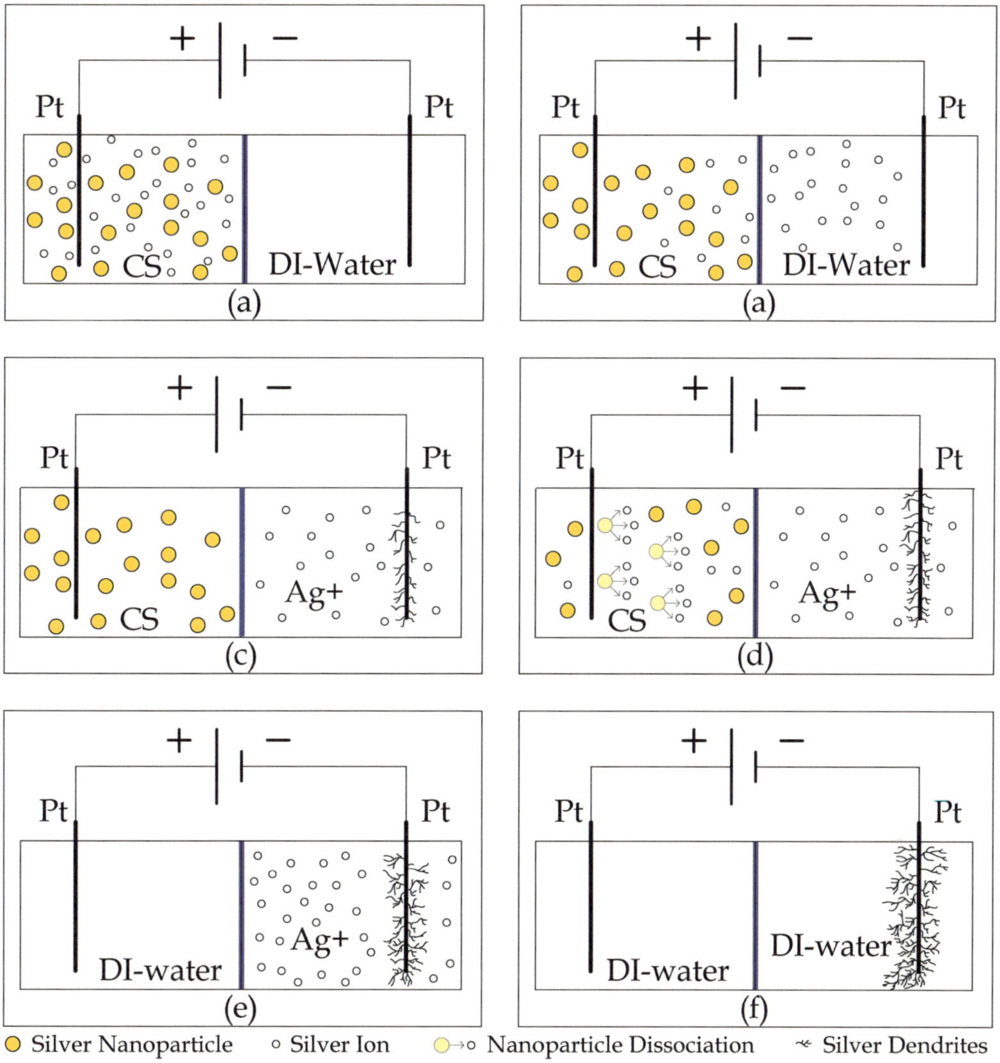

Fig. 15. Schematic illustration of the colloidal silver dissociation and migration process, (a) initial system, (b)(c) existing Ag^+ are removed from the colloidal solution to the negatively charged cathode, (d) silver nanoparticles dissociate into ionic form and migrate towards the cathode, (e) the source of silver at anodic side is fully exhausted, (d) both sides' solutions are turned into pure water.

4. Conclusion

In recent years, there has been a dramatic proliferation of research related to the silver nanoparticle and ion. There is evidence indicating that the antibacterial potency of silver is directly proportional to the concentration of silver ions. Unfortunately, there have been no literature reviews or discussions concerned with the nano-silver suspension as a drug reservoir for iontophoretic application. For medical application, conversion of colloidal silver into ionic form are required, but not directly use the silver salts to provide the silver ions, due to the counter-ion of silver salt may cause severe problems to body as the silver ion has been consumed. The primary goal of this research is to develop a silver nanoparticles electric dissociation system (EDS) which can provide relatively safe silver ion solution with controllable electric field. In this study, the UV-visible spectroscopy and ionic selective electrode (ISE) were used to identify and observe details of the system activity. Both qualitative and quantitative data analyses were performed. The experimental results reveal that the release concentration of silver ions can be programmed by controlling the magnitude of electric power. These results are of great interest both for application and scientific research to develop a chemical residue-free administration of control-released medical device, and will open the doors for further study and application of silver ions. There are four advantages for getting the ionic form of silver via the colloidal solution.

1. The ionic silver is dissociated from metallic silver and will be no interference of counter-ion, as compared with silver salts dissolved in aqueous solution.
2. Under the same power condition, the silver nanoparticle, due to its large surface area per unit mass, may have a higher dissociation rate and efficiency than bulk metal. Thus, it can be drive at lower power for releasing silver ions.
3. Silver nanoparticles suspension prepared by arc-discharge method (ADM) without adding any conventional chemical surfactants is stable and non-toxic, thus there would be no chemical residue after the dissociation process.
4. An electric dissociation system (EDS) exploited in this paper that permits more controllable release rate of silver ion by an electric field for the potential future iontophoretic application.

Future study of this entire process could be integrated into a wound dressing. Its performance is dependent on a continuous controlled rate of silver ion release, which could be achieved by monitoring the current level and using a feedback loop to adjust voltage accordingly.

5. References

Badr, Y.; Wahed, M. G. A. E. & Mahmoud, M. A. (2006). On 308 nm photofragmentation of the silver nanoparticles. *Applied Surface Science*, Vol. 253, No. 5, pp. 2502-2507, ISSN 0169-4332

Bae, C. H.; Nam, S. H. & Park, S. M. (2002). Formation of silver nanoparticles by laser ablation of a silver target in NaCl solution. *Applied Surface Science*, Vol. 197-198, pp. 628-634, ISSN 0169-4332

Bawendi, M. G.; Steigerwald, M. L. & Brus, L. E. (1990). The quantum mechanics of larger semiconductor clusters ("Quantum dots"). *Annual Review of Physical Chemistry*, Vol. 41, No. 1, pp. 477-496

Bicanová, M. & Thinschmidt, G. (1985). Oligodynamic action of silver ions on micro-organisms. *Pharmazie*, Vol. 40, No. 10, pp. 736, ISSN 0031-7144

Burrell, R. E.; Heggers, J. P.; Davis, G. J. & Wright, J. B. (1999). Efficacy of silver-coated dressings as bacterial barriers in a rodent burn sepsis model. *Wounds*, Vol. 11, No. 4, pp. 64-71, ISSN 10447946

Eustis, S.; Krylova, G.; Eremenko, A.; Smirnova, N.; Schill, A. W. & El-Sayed, M. (2005). Growth and fragmentation of silver nanoparticles in their synthesis with a fs laser and CW light by photo-sensitization with benzophenone. *Photochemical & Photobiological Sciences*, Vol. 4, No. 1, pp. 154-159

Feng, Q. L.; Wu, J.; Chen, G. Q.; Cui, F. Z.; Kim, T. N. & Kim, J. O. (2000). A mechanistic study of the antibacterial effect of silver ions on Escherichia coli and Staphylococcus aureus. *Journal of Biomedical Materials Research Part A*, Vol. 52, No. 4, pp. 662-668, ISSN 1552-4965

Goodman, L. S. & Gilman, A. (1975). *The pharmacological basis of therapeutics*, Macmillan Publishing Co., New York, NY

Huang, H. H.; Ni, X. P.; Loy, G. L.; Chew, C. H.; Tan, K. L.; Loh, F. C.; Deng, J. F. & Xu, G. Q. (1996). Photochemical formation of silver nanoparticles in poly(N-vinylpyrrolidone). *Langmuir*, Vol. 12, No. 4, pp. 909-912

Klaus-Joerger, T.; Joerger, R.; Olsson, E. & Granqvist, C.-G. (2001). Bacteria as workers in the living factory: metal-accumulating bacteria and their potential for materials science. *Trends in Biotechnology*, Vol. 19, No. 1, pp. 15-20, ISSN 0167-7799

Klein, M. F. G.; Hein, H.; Jakobs, P.-J.; Linden, S.; Meinzer, N.; Wegener, M.; Saile, V. & Kohl, M. (2008). Electron beam lithography of V-shaped silver nanoantennas. *Microelectronic Engineering*, Vol.In Press, Corrected Proof, ISSN 0167-9317

Korchagin, A. I.; Kuksanov, N. K.; Lavrukhin, A. V.; Fadeev, S. N.; Salimov, R. A.; Bardakhanov, S. P.; Goncharov, V. B.; Suknev, A. P.; Paukshtis, E. A.; Larina, T. V.; Zaikovskii, V. I.; Bogdanov, S. V. & Bal'zhinimaev, B. S. (2005). Production of silver nano-powders by electron beam evaporation. *Vacuum*, Vol. 77, No. 4, pp. 485-491, ISSN 0042-207X

Kossyrev, P. A.; Yin, A.; Cloutier, S. G.; Cardimona, D. A.; Huang, D.; Alsing, P. M. & Xu, J. M. (2005). Electric field tuning of plasmonic response of nanodot array in liquid crystal matrix. *Nano Letters*, Vol. 5, No. 10, pp. 1978-1981

LaForest, N. T. & Cofrancesco, C. (1978). Antibiotic iontophoresis in the treatment of ear chondritis. *Physical Therapy*, Vol. 58, No. 1, pp. 32-4, ISSN 0031-9023

Lansdown, A. B. (2006). Silver in health care: antimicrobial effects and safety in use. *Current Problems in Dermatology*, Vol. 33, pp. 17-34, ISSN 1421-5721

Latham, R.; Linford, R. & Schlindwein, W. (2003). Pharmaceutical and medical applications of polymer electrolytes. *Ionics*, Vol. 9, No. 1, pp. 41-46

Leduc, S. (1908). *Electronic ions and their use in medicine*, Rebman, London

Lee, H. J.; Yeo, S. Y. & Jeong, S. H. (2003). Antibacterial effect of nanosized silver colloidal solution on textile fabrics. *Journal of Materials Science*, Vol. 38, No. 10, pp. 2199-2204

Lewis, J. S. (1909). IX. Note on silver foil in surgery. *Annals of Surgery*, Vol. 50, No. 4, pp. 793-6, ISSN 0003-4932

Matsuoka, M.; Ju, W.-S. & Anpo, M. (2000). Photocatalytic decomposition of N2O into N2 and O2 on the silver(I) ion-exchanged ZSM-5 catalyst. *Chemistry Letters*, Vol. 29, No. 6, pp. 626-627

Metodiev, V. & Bozhilova, N. (1990). The effect of electrochemical silver on the microbiological qualities of drinking water. *Problemi na Khigienata*, Vol. 15, pp. 26-30, ISSN 0323-9179

Mie, G. (1908). Beiträge zur optik trüber medien, speziell kolloidaler metallösungen. *Annalen der Physik*, Vol. 330, No. 3, pp. 377-445, ISSN 1521-3889

Mulvaney, P. (1996). Surface plasmon spectroscopy of nanosized metal particles. *Langmuir*, Vol. 12, No. 3, pp. 788-800

Norrby, S. R.; Nord, C. E. & Finch, R. (2005). Lack of development of new antimicrobial drugs: a potential serious threat to public health. *The Lancet Infectious Diseases*, Vol. 5, No. 2, pp. 115-119, ISSN 1473-3099

Park, S.-H.; Im, J.-H.; Im, J.-W.; Chun, B.-H. & Kim, J.-H. (1999). Adsorption kinetics of Au and Ag nanoparticles on functionalized glass surfaces. *Microchemical Journal*, Vol. 63, No. 1, pp. 71-91, ISSN 0026-265X

Rapperport, A. S.; Larson, D. L.; Henges, D. F.; Lynch, J. B.; Blocker, T. G., Jr. & Lewis, R. S. (1965). Iontophoresis. A method of antibiotic administration in the burn patient. *Plastic and Reconstructive Surgery*, Vol. 36, No. 5, pp. 547-52, ISSN 0032-1052

Rungby, J. (1986). The silver nitrate prophylaxis of Credé causes silver deposition in the cornea of experimental animals. *Experimental Eye Research*, Vol. 42, No. 1, pp. 93-94, ISSN 0014-4835

Shin, J.; Kim, Y.; Lee, K.; Lim, Y. M. & Nho, Y. C. (2008). Significant effects of sodium acetate, an impurity present in poly(vinyl alcohol) solution on the radiolytic formation of silver nanoparticle. *Radiation Physics and Chemistry*, Vol. 77, No. 7, pp. 871-876, ISSN 0969-806X

Sosa, I. O.; Noguez, C. & Barrera, R. G. (2003). Optical properties of metal nanoparticles with arbitrary shapes. *The Journal of Physical Chemistry B*, Vol. 107, No. 26, pp. 6269-6275

Starowicz, M.; Stypula, B. & Banas, J. (2006). Electrochemical synthesis of silver nanoparticles. *Electrochemistry Communications*, Vol. 8, No. 2, pp. 227-230, ISSN 1388-2481

Sun, T. & Seff, K. (1994). Silver clusters and chemistry in zeolites. *Chemical Reviews*, Vol. 94, No. 4, pp. 857-870

Tenover, F. C. (2005). The real vancomycin-resistant Staphylococcus aureus has arrived. *Clinical Microbiology Newsletter*, Vol. 27, No. 5, pp. 35-40, ISSN 0196-4399

Thati, B.; Noble, A.; Rowan, R.; Creaven, B. S.; Walsh, M.; McCann, M.; Egan, D. & Kavanagh, K. (2007). Mechanism of action of coumarin and silver(I)-coumarin complexes against the pathogenic yeast Candida albicans. *Toxicology in Vitro*, Vol. 21, No. 5, pp. 801-808, ISSN 08872333

Thomas, S. & McCubbin, P. (2003). A comparison of the antimicrobial effects of four silver-containing dressings on three organisms. *Journal of wound care*, Vol. 12, No. 3, pp. 101-107, ISSN 09690700

Tilaki, R. M.; Iraji zad, A. & Mahdavi, S. M. (2006). Stability, size and optical properties of silver nanoparticles prepared by laser ablation in different carrier media. *Applied Physics A: Materials Science & Processing*, Vol. 84, No. 1, pp. 215-219

Veratti, G. (1748). *Osservazioni fisico-mediche intorno alla elettricità*, Lelio della Volpe Bologna, Italy

Zhang, J.-P.; Chen, P.; Sun, C.-H. & Hu, X.-J. (2004). Sonochemical synthesis of colloidal silver catalysts for reduction of complexing silver in DTR system. *Applied Catalysis A: General*, Vol. 266, No. 1, pp. 49-54, ISSN 0926-860X

12

SOA and supporting software processes integrated with self-organizing business networks

Francesco Rago
M3 Comp. Llc
USA

1. Introduction

Actual business leverages on software services to improve general firm performance. Software is always more a strategic asset to sustain business, but in meantime business is changing continuously: there is a transition from centralized to distributed and cooperative organizations. For this reason Business Models of firms are changing: there is an evolution toward distributed models better suited for integration into a global economy. This scenario implies a strategic capacity to manage new emerging values, strategies, technologies and products. The enterprise organizational models have to consider a network of internal and external agents (partners) with fuzzy boundaries and continuous exceptions in processes. The Business Model approach help a firm or a network of firms to structure its organization in a way to become more efficient, more flexible and responsive to customer demand, to forecast possible future scenarios and therefore to stay competitive.

This environment is particularly challenging for software maintenance and new "smart" approaches have to be defined. We describe a software development and maintenance process strictly integrated with enterprise evolution. The innovative aspect derives from an agile approach integrated with self-organizing and changing business. It is also based on the basic hypothesis that the service model of software maintenance has to be integrated in the process of define or improve business models at run time and not in a separate step. The shift from centralized to distributed and cooperative organizations needs software with Service Oriented Architecture (SOA) dynamically integrated with business architecture. Software services become the fundamental platform to support products delivery and services management. Their maintenance is becoming a major challenge to guarantee software aligned to business processes.

2. Inter-Organizational Systems (IOS)

The consequence of actual economic and technological scenario is the blurring of boundaries of companies in the field of knowledge, locations, information. This process is amplified by

the so called "ubiquitous computing" fundamentally characterized by the "connection of things" in the world with computation.
Partnering is becoming an alternative to mergers and acquisitions particularly for Subject Matter Experts, as it is cheaper and less capital intensive. The formation of Inter-Organizational Networks has environmental drivers such as technological changes, changing customer behavior and increasing importance of information and knowledge. Motives of the co-operating parties derive from the need to enhance services or products portfolio, to improve the efficiency of processes and to share of risks and development costs. The network strategy is described by an inter-firm strategic planning and a technical configuring networking initiative. ITC is an enabler making collaboration feasible and it supports IOS to coordinate interdependencies or to pool information with the emergence of networked organizations with core business ICT-based (e.g. virtual organizations, value webs, value nets etc.). The different partners offer specialization and focus on core competencies. Firms need clear responsibilities and clear views of contribution of each element of the net defined essentially as groups often belonging to more companies. Forming of groups is Project-dependent and Integration of groups means an Organizational context that facilitates the cohesion.
This scenario is feasible if technical trends are in right focus. The ICT infrastructures become global supported by Standards and Protocols like EDIFACT, XML and Three-tier architecture.
We have different types of interdependencies between firms and their activities: first of all a configuration can be called Pooled. Pooled means the existence of some firms that create pools having a basic set of capabilities to share with others firms. In this case there are infrastructures coordinated by Standards & Rules. Type of Inter-Organizational Systems Pooled are information and resource IOS.
A second type of interdependence is Sequential: it is a chain of companies creating a connection to satisfy specific goals. Value Chain stages are coordinated by Standards & Rules, Schedules & Plans. Types of Inter-Organizational Systems are EDI, SCM Applications and Workflow Systems.
Last but not least, Reciprocal is a "small-world", based on Collaborative project management to produce customer specific product. The Co-ordination mechanism is more complex requiring Standards & Rules, Schedules & Plans and Mutual Adjustments. Inter-Organizational Systems are Groupware and Distributed Project Management. All these organization style requires SOA as a common base of services: Inter-Organizational Systems fit well organizations if services and not application oriented. This generates flexibility and adaptability.
With the extending enterprise, organizational networks arise and information systems cross the firm's boundaries. There is a complex interaction between technology and the Organization generated by IOS driven linkages and networks.

3. Firms and ITC Strategies

"Business strategies specify how a business model can be applied to the market to differentiate the firm from its competitors" (Elliot, 2002).
In the book "Competitive Advantage", Michael Porter introduces the value chain as a tool for developing a competitive advantage. The tool has the goal to define a strategy for

interrelationships between value chains of different firms segments. Value chain analysis describes the activities within and around an organization, and relates them to an analysis of the competitive strength of the organization, starting with the generic value chain and then identifying the relevant firm-specific activities. Process flows are defined and used to isolate the individual value-creating activities. Linkages between activities describe the affects of performance or cost of one activity on another. The linkages are flows of information, goods and services, as well as systems and processes for adjusting activities. These linkages are crucial for corporate success and are the basic point of introduction of appropriate SOA. Competitive advantage may be obtained by optimizing and coordinating linked activities. A result of his approach was the understanding of the role of technology in competitive advantage.

Integration between business planning and ITC planning is one important enabler of business-IT alignment (Teo and King 1997). Teo and King found a significant relationship between the level of business and IT planning integration and the extent of information systems contribution to organizational performance. The role of ITC function has an evolution from technically oriented and non-strategic at first, until resource to support and influence business strategy. ITC becomes critical to long-term survival of organization in a fully inter-operational strategy. In mean time the different stage of business integration have to happen. The purpose of integration begins with administrative and non-strategic as first stage arriving to full integration with joint development of business and ITC strategies. Thompson (1967) describes three types of technology, which are important to the understanding of strategy in organizations: long-linked technology, mediating technology, and intensive technology.

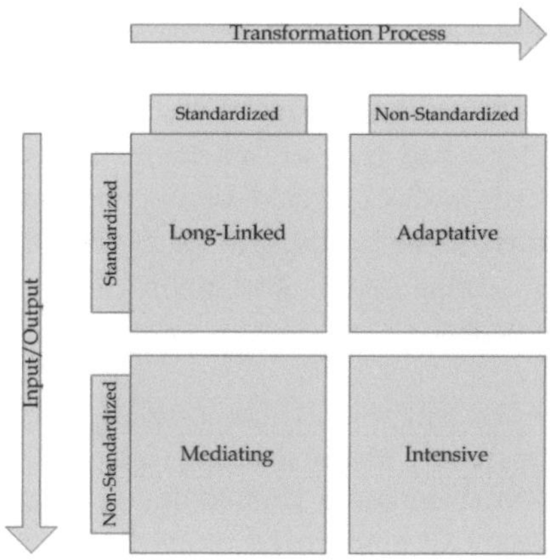

Fig. 1. IT and Business Integration

The classification has importance in the integration approach and in the platforms choice. As the three technology types have distinctive value creation logic, this has an impact in strategic planning.

Long-linked technologies focus on transformation of inputs into outputs having a production process consisting of a fixed sequence of steps to transform standardized inputs into standardized outputs.

Mediating technologies are characterized by a standardized transformation process and unique inputs and outputs. Service providers deliver to unique clients based on a pre-defined delivery process. These technologies often link partners in an exchange that helps them locate appropriate parties to conduct their transactions. Of course this type of technological approach has a meaning when precise and unique chain of firms is defined.
Intensive technologies combined a non-standard transformation process with unique inputs and outputs. This technology focused on the coordination of experts and pooling their expertise to create a unique outcome.
We have had a forth technology: Adaptive. It normalizes the status of transformation process to standard inputs and outputs with the scope to value what it is happening when environmental changes of the net happen.
Having in mind a general strategy, the organization structure and the type(s) of technology the integration of general strategy and IT Planning can be represented using a business model that all Stakeholders share and agree.
Rappa (Rappa 2005) gave the following definition of Business Model:

"In the most basic sense, a business model is the method of doing business by which a company can sustain itself -- that is, generate revenue. The business model spells-out how a company makes money by specifying where it is positioned in the value chain."

A Business Model is a blueprint that describes how a network of cooperating agents intends to create and capture value. In a Business Model one of the main points is the Customer Value: this describes how the firm offering its customers something distinctive or lower cost than its competitors. Another basic issue was the Scope which describes to which customers is the firm offering his value and the range of products/services offered that embody this value. Capabilities are the firm's capabilities and capabilities gaps that need to be filled to sustain the Scope. Something distinctive characterizes capabilities to allow the firm to offer the value better than other firms and that makes them difficult to imitate. The sources of these capabilities can be many and exploited using appropriate SOA and specific ITC infrastructure. For this reason we have to clarify what is the fit between them and how SOA do to the strategy, structure, systems, people and environment of firm. The components of a business value are here summarized:

- Model Ontology Concepts: purpose of the ontology is to improve communication, inter-company interoperability, intra-company interoperability, achieving reliability, enhance business model maintenance, knowledge acquisition, fundament for enabling support tools. The Ontology allows to accurately describe the business model of a firm
- Service domain: it is a description of the service offering, its added value, and the market segment at which the offering is targeted.
- Technology domain: a description of the SOA required to realize the service offering.
- Organization domain: a description of the structure of the multi-agents value network required to create and distribute the service offering (organizational arrangements)
- Finance domain: a description of how risks, investments and revenues are divided over the different actors of a value network (financial arrangements).

Of course Business Models have their dynamics depending on external and internal issue. Any change has a direct impact on business models to continue to give to a firm a competitive advantage. The Model is subject of Technological changes because the natural evolution of IT and of its application in competitors.

4. Business Model Framework

We propose a specific Business Model that we consider well suited to improve IOS and SOA interrelationship. The framework is divided into six principal components:

(1) The agents that agrees the alliance.

(2) The products and services a firm offers represent a substantial value to a target customer (value proposition), and for which he is willing to pay.

(3) The relationship capital the firm creates and maintains with the customer, in order to satisfy him and to generate sustainable revenues.

(4) The infrastructure.

(5) The network of partners that are necessary in order to create value and to maintain a good customer relationship.

(6) The financial aspects such as cost and revenue structures.

There are no interfaces listing Agents and their all processes in a common and agreed open space. The Business Model can be enforced deriving its components from shared value propositions, available capabilities in each forms and business constraints. In an organization based on the described Business Model the SOA permits more easily to organize and use distributed capabilities that may be under the control of different ownership domains.

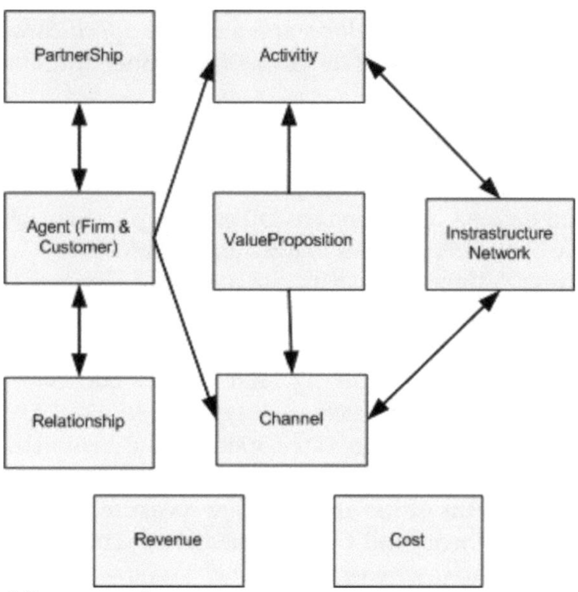

Fig. 2. Business Model Framework

The adaptability is improved if a Business Model is able to provide a systems of values, a shared structure and a SOA input to ITC. ITC loses the role of infrastructure and becomes a component of business organization.
In general, agents create capabilities to solve or support a solution for the problems they face in the course of their business. The needs of a web of firms are met by capabilities offered by net members.
The value of SOA is that it provides a powerful framework for matching needs and capabilities and for combining capabilities to address firms nets. Services are the mechanism by which needs and capabilities are brought together. SOA is a mean of organizing solutions that promotes reuse, growth and interoperability.
Visibility, interaction, and effect are key concepts of the SOA paradigm. In our approach visibility refers to the capacity for those with needs and those with capabilities to be able to see each other. The descriptions need to be in a form (or can be transformed to a form) in which their syntax and semantics are widely accessible and understandable.
The Business Model declares activities based on visible services and interactions are the way of using a capability. At its core, an interaction is "an act" and the result of an interaction is a set/series of effects. This effect may be the return of information or the change in the state of entities that are involved in the interaction. Effects are couched in terms of changes to shared states.
Visibility is promoted through the service description which contains the information necessary to interact with the service and describes this in such terms as the service inputs, outputs, and associated semantics. The service description also conveys what is accomplished when the service is invoked and the conditions for using the service.
Agents offer capabilities and act as service providers. Those with needs who make use of services are referred to as service consumers. The service description allows prospective consumers to decide if the service is suitable for their current needs and establishes whether a consumer satisfies any requirements of the service provider.
A software service specification is the definition of a set of capabilities that fulfil a defined purpose. In model-driven systems development, a service specification can be made using Systems Modelling Language like SysML or UML or any other Specification tool.

5. Software Maintenance of Systems

This environment is particularly challenging for software maintenance and new "smart" approaches have to be defined. Maintenance is becoming a major challenge to guarantee software aligned to the business processes of the Business Model.
The maintenance process designed to satisfy the described scenario has an agile approach integrated with self-organizing and changing business.
The shift from centralized to distributed and cooperative organizations needs software with SOA dynamically integrated with business architecture. Software services become the fundamental platform to support products delivery and services management. There is a paradigmatic changes: from top down development and maintenance to a bottom-up evolutionarily life cycle where software assets maintenance is integrated with organizational assets maintenance. The benefits of the approach are measured reduction of the number of defects on high level requirements and the incremental commitment nature of the process: expenditures tend to be balanced with certainty level. Another advantage is a reduced time to upgrade software assets.

Once a business model is defined and agreed by all agents, we used a method to support software maintenance through advanced iterative and incremental approach. We adopted a process similar to SCRUM because it is not a step-by-step cookbook approach and requires active, thoughtful development and management. The method starts with the premise that maintenance environment is complicated and unpredictable. You can predict or definitively plan what you will deliver, when you will deliver it, and what the quality and cost will be, but you have to negotiate continuously them according to various risks and needs as you proceed. SCRUM method is integrated with the Business Model maintenance to improve the associated SOA model and the software architecture.

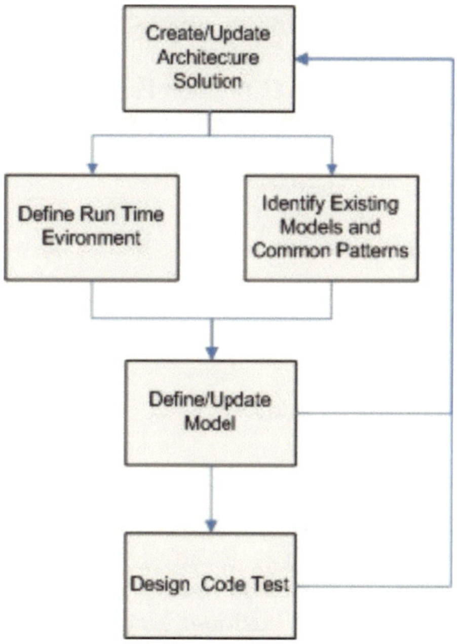

Fig. 3. Self-Organization Business Model Ontology

The fundamental steps of the method follow:

Stage I. Concept

The purpose of the concept stage is to better define exactly how the business model and its context was changed or improved, who is aimed at, how it will be positioned in market segments and how Information Technology assets has to be changed/improved to support business focus on target.

Stage II. Backlog update

The software maintenance begins in earnest. It is used a streamlined, flexible approach to requirements change management reflecting both Extreme Programming (XP)'s planning game and the SCRUM methodology.

Stage III. Technical Cycle

This is an iterative stage where technical operations are accomplished. The structure of the service application is created/maintained. The stage has the following steps:

III.1 Create/Update Solution architecture Definition of Model Technology and its use. Define/Update the conceptual structure of the SOA.

III.2 Define/Update runtime environments
Define the runtime environments in which the Service application should run. This covers all test environments, including unit test and final production environments.

III.3 Identify Existing Models and Common Patterns
The repeating patterns are identified within the service application.

III.4 Define/Update design model

III.5 Design, code, test

Stage IV. Trial

Stage V: Launch

6. Stage I. Concept

The purpose of the concept stage is to better define exactly how the business model and its context was changed or improved, who is aimed at, how it will be positioned in market segments and how Information Technology assets has to be changed or improved to support business focus on target. The Business Model can be analyzed with a process approach using Statistical Process Control results (where applicable) to value the actual status of processes. Processes are at the core of Business Model and the starting point of any innovation, adaptation or integration of firms (Dubray, 2007). There is a clear distinction between business processes and services orchestrations that can be defined in another Stage. Business processes are defined using Business Process Modelling Notation (BPMN) and are modelled from a user point of view. These process models describes user's view of the BM. We now introduce some details on BPMN so that it is more easy to understand how to integrate it with software maintenance process.
BPMN is focused on creating a standard look and feel for process diagrams that is more "business-friendly". By standardizing the semantics of things like tasks, sub-processes, and events, and linking each to specific graphical shapes, icons, and line styles in the process diagram, BPMN allows Agents to understand a process diagram regardless of which vendor's modelling tool created it, and conversely to create process diagrams that other analysts can immediately understand without special training. While the BPMN specification suggests mappings of certain shapes and patterns to specific BPEL code, it's been reduced a bit from the original vision of a standard business-friendly front end for executable process models.

BPMN Diagrams are essentially flowcharts. Process participants are defined by pools, which may be subdivided into swim-lanes, as in many other modelling notations. From the perspective of the executable model, each pool represents a BPEL process. In addition, blank but named pools can also be used to represent other business processes for which the internals are opaque, a black box, as decided in the contract phase. A single business process diagram can be composed of multiple pools, meaning multiple executable processes.
The basic units of a process are tasks, sub-processes, and events. Sub-processes and tasks are represented by rectangles, events by circles. Various icons within those shapes indicate the particular type of event or sub-process. Sub-processes may either be embedded in the calling process or launched as an independent process, running in parallel with the calling process, and synchronizing with it via messages. Solid lines group sequence flows and interconnect the tasks, sub-processes, and events within a single pool. Each sequence flow may be conditional or unconditional. In addition, BPMN offers a diamond Gateway shape that, depending on its icon, can be used for branching, splits, conditional splits, merges, or synchronizing joins.

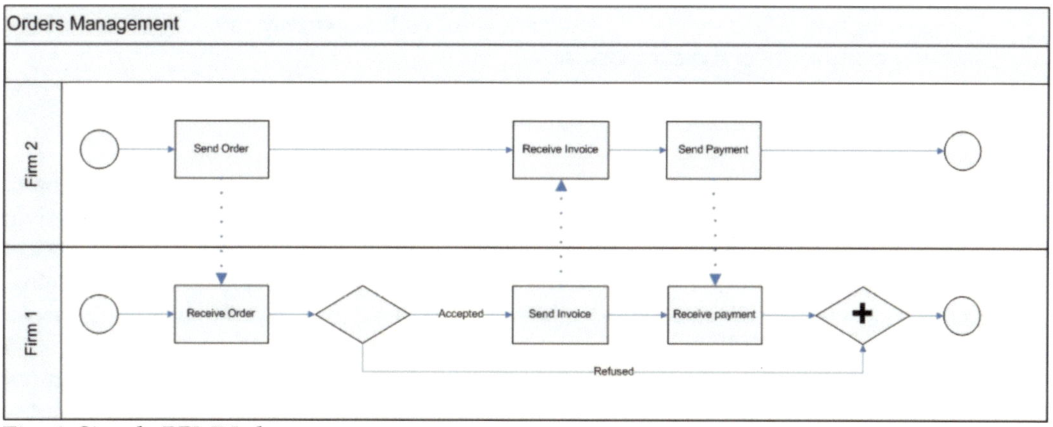

Fig. 4. Simple BPMN chart.

In addition to sequence flows within a pool, BPMN shows message flows exchanged between pools. These indicate the signals the process uses to communicate with invoked services and partner processes. BPMN explicitly shows events, actions triggered by a signal of some sort, such as receipt of a message, expiration of a timer, detection of an error, etc. Each event has a trigger and a resulting action. The various types of triggers and resulting actions are indicated by the placement of the event in the diagram along with its internal icon. Events shown with an incoming sequence flow mean that the process issues the event (i.e., sends the message, waits for a time delay, or throws the error), and those with no incoming sequence flow mean that its outgoing sequence flow is triggered by the event (e.g., receipt of a message, timeout, or exception). Events of the second type placed on the border of a task, sub-process, or pool indicate that the normal flow within that task, sub-process, or pool is to be interrupted and the exception flow connected to the event is to be triggered. Already completed tasks within a process interrupted in this way are reversed by compensation actions defined by a compensation event linked to the task. Thus with BPMN events, exception-handling behaviour and inter-process communications critical to the executable implementation are shown explicitly in the diagram, without requiring the modeller to specify the underlying technical details.

The analysis of a BM permits to decide the implementation or update of SOA. A service will be implemented or updated if it adheres to the following principles (Erl, 2007):

- *Standardized Service Contracts:* services within the same service inventory are in compliance with the same contract design standards.
- *Service Discoverability:* services are supplemented with communicative meta data by which they can be effectively discovered and interpreted.
- *Service Abstraction:* service contracts only contain essential information and information about services is limited to what is published in service contracts.
- • *Service Loose Coupling:* service contracts impose low consumer coupling requirements and are themselves decoupled from their surrounding environment.
- *Service Autonomy:* services exercise a high level of control over their underlying runtime execution environment.
- *Service Composability:* services are effective composition participants, regardless of the size and complexity of the composition.
- *Service Statelessness:* services minimize resource consumption by deferring the management of state information when necessary.

Standardized service contracts, discoverability and abstraction are all about the definition of the interface (or contract) of a service. These general requirements are accomplished in compliance to the chosen BM that different Agents have agreed. The other principles are more technical and are needed to enable the principles of reusability and loose coupling. Loose coupling calls for a messaging system supporting the communication between services. Service composability asks for the concept of assemblies to be introduced as a programming concept. The principle about service statelessness is good to strive for, but not always possible. Therefore the notion of state alignment is crucial to loosely coupled solutions (Dubray, Composite Software Construction, 2007).
From a technical perspective the presented principles can be applied only if an infrastructure is defined and available.
A distinction can be made between two main types of services (Cohen, 2007): those that are infrastructural in nature and provide common facilities that would not be considered part of the application, and those that are part of the application and provide the application's building blocks. Infrastructure services are common facilities that are part of the required infrastructure for the implementation of any business process in a SOA. Infrastructure services can be further divided into (Cohen, 2007): Communication services, which are mainly used for message transportation, and Utility services, which deliver generic (non-application-specific) infrastructural functionality. Application services, on the other hand, are services that take part in the implementation of a business process providing explicit business value. Cohen (Cohen, 2007) divides these services into entity, capability, activity and process services. Dubray (Dubray, Composite Software Construction, 2007) adds two important types of services: delivery and decision services. These classifications are described as follows:

- Entity services, exposing and managing business entities;
- Activity services, implementing a specific application-level business capability;
- Capability services, implementing a generic value-add business capability;
- Process services, implementing a business process by orchestrating other services;
- Decision services, supporting the externalization and reuse of complex and critical decision points within a task, process or business object;
- Delivery services, enabling user interactions with the system, which are always performed within a task.

The main difference between Capability services and Activity services is the scope in which they are used. While Capability services are an organizational resources, Activity services are used in a much smaller scope, such as a single composite application (Cohen, 2007).
The common and shared Business Model generates decision about common SOA. At this point a service contract is agreed on comprehensive of description of the business functionality provided by the service, but also the high-level requirements of the service along with specifications governing its usage service level declarations and key performance indicators. A service contract description develops and catalogues a *uniform* yet multi-dimensional, *enterprise-wide* understanding of the purpose, scope and representation of what this service entails and involves.

Starting from BPMN model the following characteristics will be collected:

Responsibility of the service: This provides the basic description of why the service should exist. In other words, this states the basic business scope of the service. A service "does" something in terms of business significance (in other words, encapsulates business functionality). This also identifies the software component/s which implement(s) the service.

Pre-conditions and post-conditions: Describe the factors that must be in place for this service to be used and the limitations and constraints of the service.

Synchronous or asynchronous conditions: This refers to the call semantics of the service - synchronous or asynchronous.

Identify the consumers of this service: Define the Agents and their roles that need to represent when calling this service.

Other documented requirements: Security, Data, availability and Service Level Agreement governing the service with costs.

7. Stage II. Backlog update

The software maintenance begins in earnest. It is used a streamlined, flexible approach to requirements change management reflecting both Extreme Programming (XP)'s planning game and the SCRUM methodology.
Scrum is a "lean" approach to software development. Scrum is a simple framework used to organize teams and get work done more productively with higher quality. Designed to

adapt to changing requirements during the development process at short, regular intervals, Scrum allows teams to prioritize customer requirements and adapts the work product in time to customer needs.

The output of periodic Concept stage is an input to a plan which includes a Product Backlog. The Product Backlog is a list of functional and non-functional requirements that will deliver the SOA updates when turned into functionality. The Product Backlog is prioritized so that the more value items are top priority. The Product Backlog is divided into proposed releases and the release are reported and validated in periodic Concept Meetings. Changes in the Product Backlog reflect changing requirements and how quickly or slowly the Team can transform the Product Backlog into functionality.

All work is done in Sprints. Each Sprint is an iteration of one month. Each Sprint is initiated with a Sprint Planning meeting, where the Product Owner and Team get together to collaborate about.

8. Stage III. Technical Cycle

This is an iterative stage where technical operations are accomplished. The structure of the service application is created or maintained. The Stage transforms requirements in a technical feasible set of Services and Applications. We have the problem to integrate different realities and technical environments and this cannot be coped with traditional approaches.

According to the Object Management Group (OMG): "Given the continued, and growing, diversity of systems, this will never be achieved by forcing all software development to be based on a single operating system, programming language, instruction set architecture, application server framework or any other choice. There are simply too many platforms in existence, and too many conflicting implementation requirements, to ever agree on a single choice in any of these fields." (OMG, 2003). The solution of the OMG is Model-Driven Architecture (MDA).

OMG generated MDA as the difficulty to manage Enterprise Architecture able to cover distributed multi firms organizations. Organizations are complex and as consequences the design of architecture is difficult even if SOA approach is used. We give some definition to introduce SOA/MDA:

A model of a system is a description or specification of that system and its environment for some certain purpose. The text may be in a modelling language or in a natural language (OMG,2003).

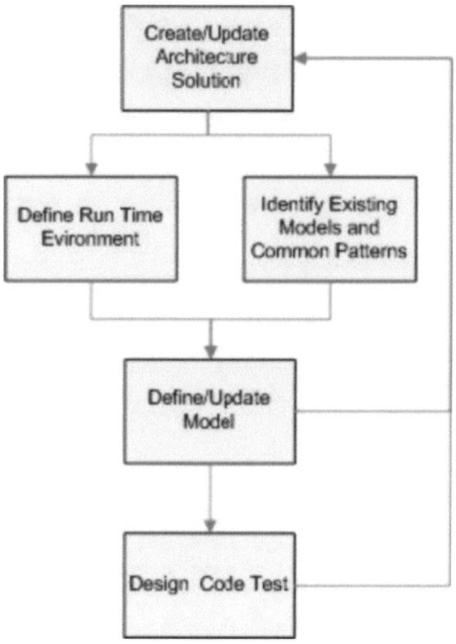

Fig. 5. Technical Cycle

A viewpoint on a system is a technique for abstraction using a selected set of architectural concepts and structuring rules, in order to focus on particular concerns within that system. The word abstraction is used to mean the process of suppressing selected detail to establish a simplified model (OMG, 2003).
A platform is a set of subsystems and technologies that provide a coherent set of functionality through interfaces and specified usage patterns, which any application supported by that platform can use without concern for the details of how the functionality provided by the platform is implemented (OMG, 2003).
MDA is an approach using models in software development. The MDA prescribes certain kinds of models to be used, how those models may be prepared and the relationships of the different kinds of models. The basic concept of the Model-Driven Architecture is the separation of the operations of a system from capabilities details of its platform. The MDA provides an approach in which systems are specified independently of the platform that supports it. It also provides an approach for specifying platforms, for choosing a particular platform for the system and for transforming the system specification into one for a particular platform. The three primary goals of MDA are portability, interoperability and reusability through architectural separation of concerns (OMG, 2003).

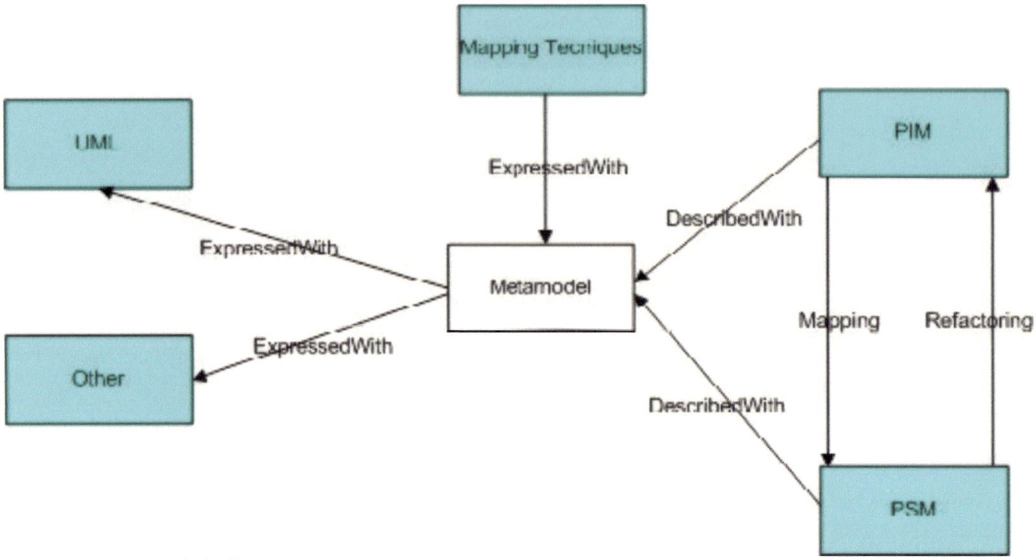

Fig. 6. Meta-model of MDA

MDA specifies three default models of a system:

- The Computation Independent Model (CIM).
- Platform Independent Model (PIM).
- Platform Specific Model (PSM)

The Computation Independent Model (CIM). A computation independent model is a view of a system from the computation independent viewpoint. A CIM does not show details of the structure of systems. A CIM is sometimes called a domain model and a vocabulary that is familiar to the practitioners of the domain in question is used in its specification (OMG, 2003). It is assumed that the primary user of the CIM is the domain practitioner or business consultant. The user of a CIM doesn't have to have knowledge about the models or artefacts used to realize the construction of the application complying to the requirements defined in the CIM. The CIM specifies the function (or external behaviour) of a system without showing constructional details.

An instantiation of a CIM can be an UML or BPMN chart or business functional characteristics (inner and external objects, functional features) by means of noun and verb analysis in the informal problem description. Cause-effect relations form causal chains that are functioning cycles. All the cycles and sub-cycles should be carefully analyzed in order to completely identify existing functionality of the system.

In case of studying a complex system, a CIM can be separated into a series of subsystems according to identified.

A platform independent model is a view of a system from the platform independent viewpoint. A PIM exhibits a specified degree of platform independence so as to be suitable for use with a number of different platforms of similar type (OMG, 2003). A PIM describes the construction of a system on an ontological level, meaning that the construction of the system is specified without implementation details.

A platform specific model is a view of a system from the platform specific viewpoint. A PSM combines the specifications in the PIM with the details that specify how that system uses a particular type of platform (OMG, 2003). In other words: the PSM is a more detailed version of a PIM. Platform specific elements are added. When defining a PSM a target Platform Model has to be available.

8.1 Create/Update Solution architecture

Transition from an initial problem domain model to a CIM "output" model, i.e. a use case model, goes as follows:
1) Acquire the list of Agents and their goals belonging to BPNM charts. Identification of goals is the identification of the set of functional features necessary for the satisfaction of the goal.
2) Identification and refinement of system's use cases that include discovering functional features specified by requirements that are needed to achieve a business goal. An executor of the goal is transformed into an (UML) actor. Identified use cases can be represented in an UML activity diagram by transforming functional features into activities, and cause-effect relations into control flows.
The last step is identification of a conceptual class model. In order to obtain a conceptual class model each functional feature is detailed to the level where it only uses one type objects. This is an architecture solution that can also be retrieved melting or updating existing CIM's in organisation repository.

8.2 Define/Update runtime environments

This step define the runtime environments in which the service application should run. A runtime environments is a platform defined as a set of subsystems and technologies that provide a coherent set of functionality through interfaces and specified usage patterns. Any application supported by that platform can use without concern for the details of how the functionality provided by the platform.
As known, the CIM will be transformed into a Platform Independent Model. The resulting PIM has to be targeted to a platform to complete the build process. Therefore a detailed model of the platform is needed.
Of course all test environments, including unit test and final production, will be defined inside the running environments.

8.3 Identify Existing Models and Common Patterns

The main challenge of the design is the transformation between the different models. In traditional approaches these transformation are mostly very inefficient because no formal models are used. Without formal models it isn't possible to define a formal transformation which can be (partly) automated. In practice the process from CIM to PSM might be a lot more complex. Gaps can exist between models not small enough to perform a direct transformation. In that case many interrelated models may consist on different layers of abstraction. Within this global set of models horizontal transformations may occur within a single layer of abstraction. This happens if models already exists and are identified for reuse and adapted to new requirements.

The repeating patterns are identified within the models. These patterns often occur either because of the consistent use of an architectural style or because of the requirements of the runtime platforms. Common patterns are compared with existing models, making any necessary small adjustment to their architecture to exploit what is already available.

8.4 Define/Update design model

The transformation of a PIM to a PSM will be done by a technical specialist. The resulting PSM can be an implementation if it provides all the information needed to. Between the models gaps can exist not small enough to perform a direct transformation. A transformation is the manual, semi-automatic or automatic generation of a target model from a source model, in accordance with a definition of transformation. It is a collection of transformation rules that describe how to transform a model specified in a source language into another model specified in a target language. Approaches that transform models can be: marking, transformation meta-model, model transformation, and application of patterns merger models (model merging).

Within a set of models horizontal transformations may occur within a single layer of abstraction. By example, a PIM is transformed in a more detailed PIM several times. These horizontal transformations are an addition to the vertical transformation of models across the layers. At the current level of MDA, the model of entry is often the PIM and the target model is often PSM. However, a transformation can have a PSM as a source and a target PSM.

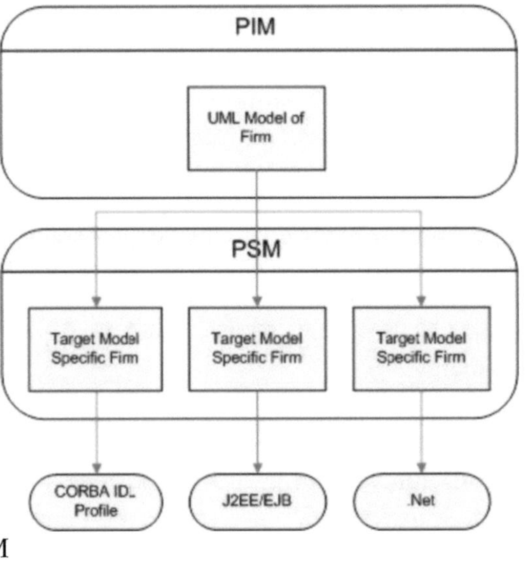

Fig. 7. From PIM to PSM

8.5 Design refinement, code, test

The resulting PSM can be an implementation if it provides all the information needed to construct a system and to put it into operation. The design artefact has the final refinements, if necessary.

Service orchestrations are modelled from a system's point of view and are used to implement new composite services based on other services, if appropriate. The coding and testing activities are executed.

9. Stage IV. Trial

The Trial stage is a validation of the product's design and features in use. Software prototypes are tested within the firm to determine that no technical flaws exist. In parallel, an agent test of the product is conducted. The object is to identify design defects, and, in particular, modifications needed to improve business agents' acceptance. The trial stage represents a "dry run" of all commercial facets of the software. The agents' tests provide the inputs to finalize the business model if issues appear in the new enterprise architecture. This means the identification of needed adjustments to the business model. A final estimate of market share and expected sales are two results of the test market.

10. Stage V. Launch

The launch stage involves startup of full or commercial production and the implementation of infrastructure assets of the business model. Post launch evaluation or control points at pre-designated times after launch provide benchmarks to gauge whether a software product is "on target." Such benchmarks include market share, sales volume, production costs, etc. Post-launch evaluations are essential to control the software product and to signal the implementation of corrective schemes to move the software product back on course.

11. Conclusion

People culture is still not aligned to service approach. Managers think in term of functional black box, with strictly defined boundary following a typical top-down engineering approach. This is a problem in the beginning of the innovation process. It is difficult to reason in term of knowledge and services sharing on common goals in a network. This has a heavy impact on the start-up of software process with an over-cost of 30-40% of effort. The real improvement was measured in the number of defects on high level requirements, giving a positive answer to the basic hypothesis that the software service model has to be integrated in the process of define/improve business model at run time and not after in a separate step.

New software product/service maintenance will never be risk free. Much can be learned about effective new software management from a review of the experiences in past projects. Many of these insights have been incorporated into the method presented. The benefits of the model are many. One result is that the process becomes more multidisciplinary. The balance between the internal versus external orientation becomes obvious. A second payoff is that interaction between agents is encouraged: many evaluation nodes demand diverse inputs from different groups in the company. A third benefit is the incremental commitment nature of the process: expenditures tend to be balanced with certainty level; each stage involves progressively better information and concurrently entails progressively higher expenditures; and risk is managed. Further, decision nodes and bail-out points are provided at each stage. Finally, the process is market oriented, providing for ample market information and marketing planning, not only towards the launch phase, but throughout the entire process.

12. References

Cohen, S, 2007, Ontology and Taxonomy of Services in a *Service-Oriented Architecture,* The Achitecture Journal. MSDN. Journal 11. May 2007.

Elliot. (2002) Electronic Commerce: B2C Strategies and Models. Chichester: Prentice-Hall

TSH Teo, WR King. (1997). Integration between business planning and information systems planning: an evolutionary-contingency, Journal of Management Information Systems I Summer

Erl, T. (2007). SOA Principles. Retrieved June 18, 2007, from *SOA Principles, an introduction to the Service-Orientation paradigm:* http://www.soaprinciples.com, Dubray, J.-J. (2007). *Composite Software Construction.* InfoQ.com: C4Media.

Dubray, J.-J. (2007, December 04). The Seven Fallacies of Business Process Execution. Retrieved April 24, 2008, from InfoQ: http://www.infoq.com/articles/seven-fallacies-of-bpm, Dubray, J. J. (2007). *Composite Software Construction,* Lulu.com

Erl, T. (2007). SOA Principles. Retrieved June 18, 2007, from *SOA Principles, an introduction to the Service-Orientation* paradigm: http://www.soaprinciples.com/

Dubray, J.-J. (n.d.). Automata, State, Actions, and Interactions. Retrieved April 25, 2008, from eBPML: http://www.ebpml.org/pi-calculus.htm

Küster, J. M., Ryndina, K., & Gall, H. (2007). Generation of Business Process Models for Object Life Cycle Compliance. In G. Alonso, P. Dadam, & M. Rosemann (Ed.), *BPM 2007,* LNCS 4714 (pp. 165-181). Berlin Heidelberg: Springer-Verlag OMG. (2003, 06 12). MDA Guide Version 1.0.1. Retrieved from Object Management Group: http://www.omg.org/mda

Rappa, M. (2005). *Managing the Digital Enterprise,* North Carolina State University Thompson, J. D. (1967). *Organizations in action,* McGraw-Hill.

King, W.R., and Teo, T.S.H. (1997a), *Integration between business planning and information systems* planning: *validating a stage hypothesis,* Decision Sciences, Vol 28, Number 2, p 279-308.

King, W.R., and Teo, T.S.H. (1997b), *Integration between business planning and information systems planning: An evolutionary-contingency perspective, Journal of Management Information Systems,* Vol 14, Number 1, p 185-214

13

Algebraic Algorithms for Image Tomographic Reconstruction from Incomplete Projection Data

Nadiya Gubareni
Technical University of Częstochowa
Poland

1. Introduction

Technique of computerized tomography has a wide application not only in medicine but also in different fields of technique. In many applications because of some reasons one cannot obtain the full set of projection data of a reconstructed object, e.g. the projection data are not available at each angle of view or they are very limited in number. Sometimes because of the large size of objects and limitation in the size of the scanners it is not possible to obtain the complete set of required projections. In these cases we deal with the problem of image reconstruction from incomplete projection data. In particular, such kind of problems arise in mineral industries and engineering geophysics connected with acid drainage, the stability of mine workers, mineral exploration and others.

When the projection data available are not limited in number and complete, the transform methods of reconstructions are usually used (Herman, 1980), (Natterer, 1986), (Kak & Slaney, 1988). For incomplete projection data these methods cannot be used directly. In this case there often used different kinds of algebraic iterative algorithms the most well-known from which are algorithms of algebraic reconstruction technique (ART) (Gordon et al., 1970), (Herman et al., 1973), (Eggermont et al., 1981). They are generally simple, flexible and permit to use a priori knowledge of the object before its reconstruction that is very important in many practical applications. Recently algebraic iterative algorithms are also used in magnetic resonance imaging (MRI) (Liang & Lauterbur, 2000), (Harshbarger & Twieg, 1999) and low-contrast 3D-cone-beam tomography (Mueller et al., 1997).

However the application of algebraic iterative algorithms to real practical problems has some important obstacles. The main repellant for using these algorithms are their significantly slow reconstruction speed and so a large time of computations for obtaining the good results, and a large memory space required to store the reconstruction image, projection data and the projection matrix. In order to avoid these difficulties there are often used the algebraic algorithms which can be allowed to parallelize and can be realized on the parallel computing systems (PCS). The main general types of parallel iterative algebraic algorithms for computerized tomography were proposed by Y. Censor (Censor, 1988). The efficient performance of some of the parallel algorithms were described in (De Pierro & Iusem, 1985); (Chen & Lee, 1994); (Chen et al., 1990); (Laurent et al., 1996); (Gubareni, 1998a).

One of the most perspective areas of parallel computations is an elaboration of asynchronous realizations of iterative algorithms. The main characteristic of the organization of asynchronous computations is that the solution is obtained during a non-synchronous interaction of processor elements of a parallel structure. Each processor of this PCS updates the values of corresponding components of the solution using available information about other components of the solution, and it obtains this information from local processors or shared memory without waiting their full update. The researches showed that the asynchronous realizations of parallel algorithms are more efficient from the point of view of their speed of convergence in many important cases (Kung, 1976); (Bertsekas & Tsitsiklis, 1989; 1991); (Savari & Bertsekas, 1996). Note that the convergence of asynchronous algorithms and their synchronous prototypes may be different. Some models of asynchronous iterative methods for image reconstruction are considered in (Baudet, 1978); (Chazan & Miranker, 1969); (Bru et al., 1988); (Elsner et al., 1990); (Kaszkurewicz et al., 1990). Some generalization of these models for image reconstruction were considered in (Baran et al., 1996); (Gubareni et al., 1997b); (Gubareni, 1999).
This chapter is devoted to consider the problem of image reconstruction from incomplete projection data for particular reconstruction systems which arise in engineering geophysics and mineral industry. Besides the well-known algorithms such as ART and MART their chaotic, parallel and block-parallel implementations are considered in this chapter. The use of these algorithms to reconstruct high-contrast objects from incomplete data is examined. The influence of various parameters of these algorithms, such as the relaxation coefficients, the number of iterations, the number of projections, and noise in projection data on the reconstruction quality for different schemes of reconstruction are investigated.
Numerical results of image reconstruction from incomplete projection data for some modeling objects, comparing evaluations of errors and the rate of convergence of these algorithms are presented and discussed. It is shown that for some choice of parameters one can obtain a good quality of reconstruction with these algorithms under the noise and incomplete data.

2. Problem of incomplete projection data

The main goal of computerized tomography is to recover an unknown density function from its line integrals. Let $f(x,y)$ be a density function which represents the spatial distribution of a physical parameter. If $L: \; l = x\cos\theta + y\sin\theta$ is a line (ray) in the plane then the line integral

$$p_L = \int_L f(x,y)dL = \int_{-\infty}^{+\infty}\int_{-\infty}^{+\infty} f(x,y)\delta(l - x\cos\theta - y\sin\theta)dxdy\,, \tag{1}$$

which is called a projection, is usually obtained from physical measurements.
From mathematical point of view the problem of reconstruction from projection data is to find an unknown function $f(x,y)$ by means of a given set of projections p_L for all L. Theoretically it is possible to reconstruct the function $f(x,y)$ from the set of projections p_L by means of the Radon inversion formula (Radon, 1917). The classical inversion formula of Radon requires information of all the line integrals in order to recover the function $f(x,y)$ in each point. Unfortunately, this mathematical problem represents only an idealized abstraction of problems which occur in real practical applications. In practice there is given

only a discrete set of projection data that estimate p for a finite number of rays. Since projection data are obtained by physical measurements with limited precision, they are given with some errors. Therefore all these restrictions do not allow to use the Radon inversion formula directly.

The projection data for computerized tomography is said to be complete if they are obtained from every aspect of view angle. In many practical applications projections are often not available at each direction and may be very limited in number. Moreover, because of the large size of objects it is not possible to obtain the complete set of the required projection data. In these cases one says that there is a problem of image reconstruction from incomplete projection data. In particular, such kind of problems arise in mineral industries and engineering geophysics connected with acid drainage, the stability of mine workers, mineral exploration and others (Patella, 1997), (Williams, et al., 2004).

There exist two fundamentally different approaches for solving the image reconstruction problem. In the first approach the problem is formulated for continuous functions f and p and the inversion formula is derived in this continuous model. This method is called the transform method approach (Censor & Zenios, 1997). The second approach is connected with the discretization of functions f and p at the outset. So the object f and measurements p become the vectors in the finite dimensional Euclidean space. In this case the methods of linear algebra and optimization theory are used for solving the problem of image reconstruction. This approach is called the fully discretized model (Censor & Zenios, 1997).

If the projection data can be obtained from every aspect of view angle and their number can be obtained large enough (in medicine, for example), then it is more preferred to use the transform method approach, e.g. the convolution back projection (CBP) algorithm (Ramachandran & Lakhshminarayanan, 1970) or direct Fourier technique.

In dependence on the obtaining system of projections there are many image reconstruction schemes, the main of them are parallel and beam schemes in the two-dimensional space. Both of them are represented in Figure 1.

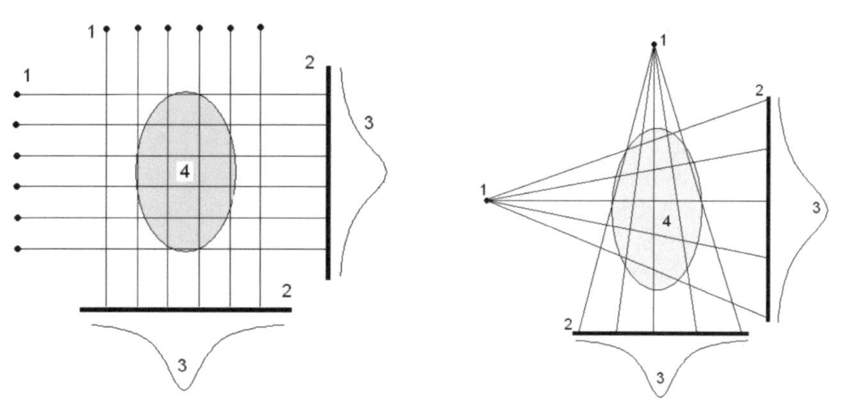

Fig. 1. Parallel and beam schemes of obtaining projection data in image reconstruction. 1- sources; 2- detectors; 3 - projections; 4 - a research object

In some practical problems, in engineering for example, it is impossible to obtain projections from all directions because of the existence of some important reasons (such as situation, size or impossibility of an access to a research object). This situation arises, for example, in the coal bed working. During the preparing process for working in this coal bed the access to longwalls may be very difficult or impossible at all in dependence on the scheme of obtaining projection data. Sometimes it is impossible to access to one or two sides of longwalls, and sometimes it is impossible only to access to the basis but all the longwalls are accessible. Each this situation has its own scheme of obtaining information.

Some examples of the schemes for obtaining projection data is shown in Figure 2. In the first case there is an access to a research object from only two opposite sides. Therefore the sources of rays can be situated only on one side and the detectors are situated on the opposite side of the research part of a coal bed. This scheme will be called the system (1 × 1). And in the second case there is an access to all four sides of an object. Therefore the sources can be situated, for example, onto two neighboring sides, and the detectors can be situated on the opposite sides. So the projections can be obtained from two pairs of the opposite sides.

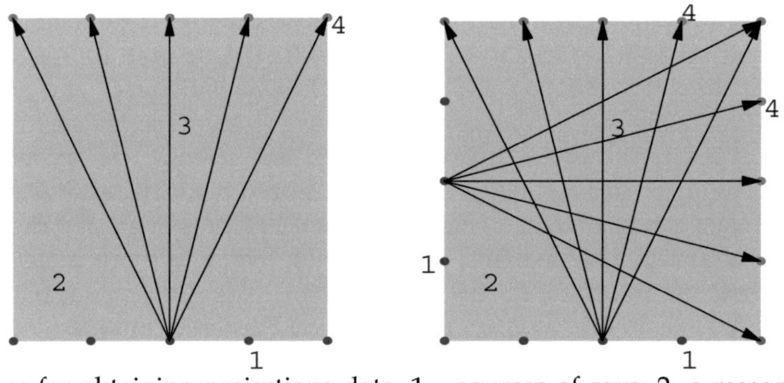

Fig. 2. Schemes for obtaining projections data. 1 – sources of rays; 2- a research object; 3 – rays; 4 – detectors.

3. Algebraic iterative algorithms

The numerical solution of equation (1) using ART requires the discretization of the cross-section of an object. To construct a discretized model, a reconstructed domain $D \subset R^2$ is included into a rectangle E and divided into n small elements (pixels). The full discrete model of the problem of image reconstruction is based on the main principal that a research object has the constant distribution inside each pixel. So for any i-th pixel one can correspond an unknown x_i. Secondly, one can assume that sources and detectors are points and the rays between them are lines. Denote by a_{ij} the length of the intersection of the i-th ray with j-th pixel. The length a_{ij} represents the contribution of the j-th pixel to the total attenuation along the i-th ray. Thus, the discretized model of the problem of image reconstruction is reduced to a system of linear algebraic equations:

$$\mathbf{A} \cdot \mathbf{x} = \mathbf{p} \,, \tag{2}$$

where:

$\mathbf{A} = (a_{ij}) \in \mathbf{R}^{m,n}$ is the matrix of coefficients,

$\mathbf{x} = (x_1, x_2, \ldots, x_n)^T \in \mathbf{R}^n$ is the image vector,

- $\mathbf{p} = (p_1, p_2, \ldots, p_m)^T \in \mathbf{R}^m$ is the measurement vector of projection data.

This system has a few characteristics: it is a rectangular as a rule and it has a very large dimension. For solving this system it is often used different kinds of algebraic iterative algorithms the most well-known of which are the additive algorithm ART (Herman, el. al., 1973), (Herman, 1975), (Herman, 1980), (Eggermont, el. al., 1981). These algorithms are very flexible and allow to apply different *a priory* information about object before its reconstruction that is especially very important when we have incomplete projection data. Denote

$$\mathbf{P}_i(\mathbf{x}) = \mathbf{x} - \frac{(\mathbf{a}^i, \mathbf{x}) - p_i}{\left\|\mathbf{a}^i\right\|^2}\mathbf{a}^i, \tag{3}$$

$$\mathbf{P}_i^{\omega} = (1-\omega)\mathbf{I} + \omega\mathbf{P}_i, \tag{4}$$

where $\mathbf{a}^i$ is the i-th row of the matrix **A**, and ω is a relaxation parameter.

Algorithm 1 (ART-1).

1. $\mathbf{x}^{(0)} \in \mathbf{R}^n$ is an arbitrary vector;
2. The k-th iteration is calculated in accordance with the following scheme:

$$\mathbf{x}^{(k+1)} = \mathbf{C}\mathbf{P}_i^{\omega_k}\mathbf{x}^{(k)} \quad (i = 1,2,\ldots,m), \tag{5}$$

where $\mathbf{P}_i^{\omega_k}$ are operators defined by (4), ω_k are relaxation parameters, **C** is a constraining operator, and $i(k) = k(\bmod m) + 1$.

This algorithm was proposed by Kaczmarz (Kaczmarz, 1937) and independently discovered and investigated by G.T.Herman, A.Lent, S.Rowland in (Herman, el. al., 1973). It was used successfully in application of computerized tomography in medicine. This algorithm runs through all equations cyclically with modification of the present estimate $\mathbf{x}^{(k)}$ in such a way that the present equation with index i is fulfilled.

The multiplicative variant of ART, the algorithm MART, is given by the following form.

Algorithm 2 (MART).

1. $\mathbf{x}^{(0)} \in \mathbf{R}^n$ is an arbitrary vector and $\mathbf{x}^{(0)}>0$.
2. The k+1-th iteration is calculated by the following way:

$$x_j^{(k+1)} = \left(\frac{p_i}{(\mathbf{a}^{i(k)}, \mathbf{x}^{(k)})}\right)^{\omega_k^i a_{ij}} x_j^{(k)} \tag{6}$$

where

- $\mathbf{a}^i$ is the i-th row of the matrix **A,**
- ω_k^i is a relaxation parameter,
- p_i is the i-th coordinate of the projection vector **p**,
- $i(k) = k$ (mod m) +1.

This algorithm was invented and reinvented in several fields. It was shown that it is convergent if 0 < $\omega_k^i a_{ij}$ < 1 for all i, k, j, and its solution gives the solution of the linearly constrained entropy optimization problem (Lent, 1977), (De Pierro, 1990), (Censor & Zenios, 1997).
In practice the vector of projection data is given as a rule with some error. Therefore instead of a system of linear equations (2) there results a system of linear inequalities:

$$\mathbf{p} - \mathbf{e} \le \mathbf{A} \cdot \mathbf{x} \le \mathbf{p} + \mathbf{e} \tag{7}$$

where $\mathbf{e} = \{\varepsilon_1, \varepsilon_2, \ldots, \varepsilon_m\}$ is a non-negative vector. And one can consider that the vector $\mathbf{e}$ is given a priory and defines the errors of projection data.
Introduce the following projection operator:

$$\mathbf{P}_i(\mathbf{x}) = \mathbf{x} - \frac{((\mathbf{a}^i, \mathbf{x}) - p_i - \varepsilon_i)^+ - (p_i - \varepsilon_i - (\mathbf{a}^i, \mathbf{x}))^+}{\left\| \mathbf{a}^i \right\|^2} \mathbf{a}^i, \tag{8}$$

where

$$s^+ = \begin{cases} s, & \text{if } s \ge 0; \\ 0, & \text{otherwise} \end{cases}$$

and

$$\mathbf{P}_i^{\omega} = (1 - \omega)\mathbf{I} + \omega \mathbf{P}_i, \tag{9}$$

where $\mathbf{a}^i$ is the i-th row of a matrix $\mathbf{A}$, and ω is a relaxation parameter.
In this case there results the following additive algorithm which is analogous to the algorithm 1.

Algorithm 3 (ART-3).
1. $\mathbf{x}^{(0)} \in \mathbf{R}^n$ is an arbitrary vector.
2. The k+1-th iteration is calculated by the following way:

$$\mathbf{x}^{(k+1)} = \mathbf{C}\mathbf{P}_i^{\omega_k} \mathbf{x}^{(k)} \quad (i = 1,2,\ldots,m), \tag{10}$$

where $\mathbf{P}_i^{\omega_k}$ are operators defined by (8) and (9), ω_k are relaxation parameters, $i(k) = k(\mathrm{mod}\, m) + 1$, and $\mathbf{C}$ is a constraining operator.

This algorithm was investigated by G.T. Herman (Herman, 1975), and it was used successfully in medicine.

4. Block-parallel iterative algorithms

The convergence rate of algebraic iterative algorithms considered in the previous section is very slow and a lot of iterations should be made to obtain a good reconstruction. It is more efficient to apply the algorithms which use simultaneously all equations (or inequalities) of system (2) (or (3)) at each step of iteration process. The examples of these algorithms are the generalized algorithms of the Cimmino type (Censor, 1988) which can be related to the class of parallel algorithms. Following Y. Censor (Censor, 1988), the iterative algorithm is considered to be parallel if it can be represented in the following form:

$$\mathbf{y}^{k,i} = \mathbf{R}_i(\mathbf{x}^{(k)}, \mathbf{a}^i, p_i) \tag{11}$$

$$\mathbf{x}^{(k+1)} = \mathbf{S}\left(\left\{\mathbf{y}^{k,i}\right\}_{i\in J}\right) \tag{12}$$

where $\mathbf{R}_i$ is an operator of the row type, $\mathbf{S}$ is an algorithmic operator which uses simultaneously information obtained while solving all equations (inequalities) of system (2) (or (7)) and generalizes them, $J=\{1,2,\ldots,m\}$, k is the number of iteration.
Consider the operator $\mathbf{S}$ from $\mathbf{R}^n$ to $\mathbf{R}^n$ in the following form:

$$\mathbf{S}\left(\left\{\mathbf{y}^{k,i}\right\}_{i\in J}\right) = \sum_{i=1}^{m} \mathbf{B}_i^k \mathbf{y}^{k,i} \tag{13}$$

where $\mathbf{B}_i^k$ are $n\times n$-matrices with real nonnegative elements and $\sum_{i=1}^{m} \mathbf{B}_i^k = \mathbf{E}$ ($\mathbf{E}$ is the identity matrix).
Consider the following class of parallel iterative algorithms.

Algorithm 4 (PART).
1. $\mathbf{x}^{(0)} \in \mathbf{R}^n$ is an arbitrary vector;
2. The k+1-th iteration is calculated in accordance with the following scheme:

$$\mathbf{y}^{k,i} = \mathbf{P}_i^{\omega_k} \mathbf{x}^{(k)} \qquad (i = 1,2,\ldots,m), \tag{14}$$

$$\mathbf{x}^{(k+1)} = \mathbf{C}\sum_{i=1}^{m} \mathbf{B}_i^k \mathbf{y}^{k,i}, \tag{15}$$

where $\mathbf{P}_i^{\omega_k}$ are operators defined by (9), ω_k are relaxation parameters, $\mathbf{C}$ is a constraining operator and $\mathbf{B}_i^k$ are matrices of dimension $n\times n$ with real nonnegative elements and

$$\sum_{i=1}^{m} \mathbf{B}_i^k = \mathbf{E}, \qquad \sum_{i=1}^{m} \| \mathbf{B}_i^k \| \le 1, \tag{16}$$

for all $k \in \mathbf{N}$.

Remark 1. Let $\mathbf{B}_i^k = (\gamma_{jj}^i)_{j=1}^n$ be a diagonal matrix with elements $0 < \gamma_{jj}^i < 1$. If $\gamma_{jj}^i = \gamma_i$ for each $j \in J$, $i \in I$, $\omega_k = 1$, $\mathbf{C} = \mathbf{I}$, then there results the Cimmino algorithm (Censor, 1978). If $\gamma_{jj}^i = 1/m$ for each $j \in J$, $i \in I$, $\omega_k = 1$, $\mathbf{C} = \mathbf{I}$, then there results the von Neumann algorithm (Censor, 1978).
The study of different variants of this class of parallel algorithms by analyzing their convergence was conducted by many authors, e.g. (Censor, 1978), (De Pierro & Iusem, 1985a, 1985b), (Censor & Zenious, 1997), (Gubareni, 1997).

For many practical applications $\mathbf{x} \geq 0$, the elements of a matrix $\mathbf{A}= (a_{ij})$ are nonnegative real numbers and $p_i > 0$ for all $i \in I$. In this case one may consider the following parallel multiplicative algorithm for solving system of linear inequalities (7) (Censor, 1974), (De Pierro, 1990).

Algorithm 5 (MARTP).

1. $\mathbf{x}^{(0)} \in \mathbf{R}^n$ and $\mathbf{x}^{(0)} > 0$.
2. The k+1-th iteration is calculated in accordance with the following scheme:

$$x_j^{(k+1)} = x_j^{(k)} \prod_{i=1}^{m} y_j^{k,i}, \tag{17}$$

where

$$y_j^{k,i} = \left(\frac{p_i}{(\mathbf{a}^i, \mathbf{x}^{(k)})} \right)^{\gamma_{ij}^k a_{ij}}, \tag{18}$$

(i=1,2,..., m; j=1,2,..., n), γ_{ij}^k are positive real numbers for every j, k.

These algorithms may be realized on parallel computing structure consisted of m elementary processors and one central processor. On each (k+1)-th step of iteration every i-th elementary processor computes the coordinates of the vector $\mathbf{y}^{k,i}$ in accordance with formula (14) or (18) and then the central processor computes the (k+1)-th iteration of the image vector $\mathbf{x}$ in accordance with formula (15) or (17).

The main defect of parallel algorithms considered above is their practical realization on parallel computational structures because it needs a lot of local processors in an MPCS. In order to reduce the number of required local processors consider block-iterative additive and multiplicative algorithms considered in (Elfving, 1980), (Eggermont et al. 1981), (Censor, 1988), (Gubareni, 1997).

For this purpose decompose the matrix $\mathbf{A}$ and the projection vector $\mathbf{p}$ into M subsets in accordance with a decomposition

$$\{1,2,\ldots,m\} = H_1 \cup H_2 \cup \ldots \cup H_M, \tag{19}$$

where

$$H_t = \{m_{t-1}+1,\ m_{t-1}+2,\ \ldots,\ m_t\}, \tag{20}$$

$0=m_0<m_1<\ldots< m_M=m$, $1\leq t \leq M$.

Algorithm 6 (BPART).

1. $\mathbf{x}^{(0)} \in \mathbf{R}^n$ is an arbitrary vector;
2. The k+1-th iteration is calculated in accordance with the following scheme:

$$\mathbf{x}^{(k+1)} = \mathbf{C} \sum_{i \in H_{t(k)}} \mathbf{B}_i^k \mathbf{P}_i^{\omega_k} \mathbf{y}^i, \tag{21}$$

where $t(k) = k(\text{mod } M) + 1$, $\mathbf{P}_i^{\omega_k}$ are operators defined by (9), $0 < \omega_k < 2$ are relaxation parameters, **C** is a constraining operator and $\mathbf{B}_i^k$ are matrices of dimension $n \times n$ with real nonnegative elements and

$$\sum_{i \in H_{t(k)}}^{m} \mathbf{B}_i^k = \mathbf{E}, \qquad \sum_{i \in H_{t(k)}}^{m} \| \mathbf{B}_i^k \| \le 1, \tag{22}$$

for all $k \in \mathbf{N}$.

The parallel implementation of this algorithm can be described as follows:

$$\mathbf{y}^{k,i} = \mathbf{P}_i^{\omega_k} \mathbf{x}^{(k)} \qquad (i \in H_{t(k)}),$$

$$\mathbf{x}^{(k+1)} = \mathbf{C} \sum_{i \in H_{t(k)}}^{m} \mathbf{B}_i^k \mathbf{y}^{k,i},$$

The block-iterative algorithms represent examples of sequential-parallel algorithms. They may be considered as intermediate version between sequential algorithms and full parallel ones. In each step of an iterative process the block-iterative algorithm uses simultaneously information about all equations concerning to a given block.
Block-iterative algorithms may be also considered in the case of multiplicative algorithms. In this case there results the following algorithm.

Algorithm 7 (BMART).

1. $\mathbf{x}^{(0)} \in \mathbf{R}^n$ and $\mathbf{x}^{(0)} > 0$.
2. The k+1-th iteration is calculated in accordance with the following scheme:

$$x_j^{(k+1)} := x_j^{(k)} \prod_{i \in H_{t(k)}} \left(\frac{p_i}{(\mathbf{a}^i, \mathbf{x}^k)} \right)^{\gamma_{ij}^k a_{ij}}, \tag{23}$$

where γ_{ij}^k are positive real numbers such that

$$0 < \sum_{i \in H_{t(k)}} a_{ij} \gamma_{ij}^k \le 1 \tag{24}$$

for every j, k; $H_{t(k)}$ are defined in accordance with (20) and $t(k)$ is almost cycle control sequence.

If $\gamma_{ij}^k = \gamma_i$ for all k,j and $0 \le a_{ij} \le 1$, $\sum_{i \in H_{t(k)}} \gamma_i = 1$, then there results the block-iterative multiplicative algorithm proposed in (De Pierro & Iusem, 1985).

5. Chaotic and asynchronous algorithms

First chaotic and asynchronous algorithms for image reconstruction were proposed and studied in (Bru et al., 1988), (Elsner et al., 1990). These algorithms are based on the methods of asynchronous iterations introduced first by Chasan and Miranker (Chazan & Miranker, 1969). The further development of these methods and their generalizations for the case of non-linear operators was obtained by Baudet (Baudet, 1978).
Recall some important notions of the theory of chaotic and asynchronous iterations (Chazan & Miranker, 1969), (Baudet, 1978), Bertsekas D.P. (1983), (Bertsekas & Tsitsiklis, 1989), (Bertsekas & Tsitsiklis, 1991).

Definition 1. A sequence of nonempty subsets $I = \{I_k\}_{k=0}^{\infty}$ of the set {1,2…, m} is **a sequence of chaotic sets** if

$$\limsup_{k\to\infty} I_k = \{1,2,...,m\} \tag{25}$$

(another words, if each integer $j \in \{1,2,...,m\}$ appears in this sequence an infinite number of times).
For the first time such sequences were used by Baudet (Baudet, 1978).

Definition 2. If any subset of a sequence of chaotic sets I has the form $I_k = \{j_k\}$, where $j_k \in \{1,2,...,m\}$ (i.e. each set consists of only one element), then the sequence I is called **acceptable** (or **admissible**).

Suppose that PCS (Parallel Computing System) consists of m processors working local independently. In this case the notion of the sequence of chaotic sets has a simple interpretation: it sets the time diagram of work of each processor during non-synchronous work of PCS. So the subset I_k is the set of the numbers of those processors which access the central processor at the same time.
Note, that the definition of the sequence of chaotic sets can be given in the following equivalent form:

Lemma 1. Let $I = \{I_k\}_{k=0}^{\infty}$ be a sequence of nonempty subsets of the set {1,2..., m}. Then the following conditions are equivalent:
1) $\limsup_{k\to\infty} I_k = \{1,2,...,m\}$
2) the set $\{ k \mid i \in I_k \}$ is unlimited for each i = 1,2..., m.
3) for each $j \in \mathbf{N}$ there exists $p(j) \in \mathbf{N}$ such that the following condition satisfies:

$$\bigcup_{i=j+1}^{j+p(j)} I_i = \{1,2,...,m\} . \tag{26}$$

For any sequence of chaotic sets the numbers $p(j)$ depends on a number j. In practice and for researching the convergence of asynchronous implementations of iterative processes there are more important sequences of chaotic sets, for which these numbers do not depend on number j.

Definition 3. If for a sequence of chaotic sets $I=\{I_k\}_{k=0}^{\infty}$ the numbers $p(j)$ defined by (26) do not depend on the choice of number j, i.e. $p(j)=T=\text{const}$ for each $j\in\mathbf{N}$, then this sequence is called **regular**, and the number T is called the **number of regularity of** the sequence I.

Note, that this definition coincides with a concept of a regular sequence, introduced in (El Tarazi, 1984) for the case of an admissible sequence. In this work El Tarazi obtained important results introducing the obvious model for the class of a synchronous algorithms and giving the first correct conditions of convergence in the non-linear case of contraining operators.

Other important concept in the theory of an asynchronous iterations is the concept of a sequence of delays.

Definition 4. A sequence $J=\{\sigma(k)\}_{k=1}^{\infty}$ of m-dimensional vectors $\sigma(k)=\{\sigma_1(k),\sigma_2(k),...,\sigma_m(k)\}$ with integer coordinates, satisfying the following conditions:

$$1)\quad 0\le\sigma_i(k)\le k-1; \tag{27}$$

$$2)\quad \lim_{k\to\infty}\sigma_i(k)=\infty, \tag{28}$$

for each i = 1,2...,m and $k\in\mathbf{N}$, is called a **sequence of delays**.

In the case, when instead of condition 2) it holds the following condition:

2') there exists a fixed number $L\in\mathbf{N}$ such that

$$k-\sigma_i(k)\le L \tag{29}$$

for each $k\in\mathbf{N}$ and i = 1,2...,m, the sequence is called a **sequence with limited delays** and the number L is called a **delay**, or an **asynchronous measure**.

The sequence of delays determines the numbers of using iterations by each fixed processor, and the number L shows a depth of used iterations and actually reflects possibilities of the concrete computing system. For synchronous implementation of the iterative process the difference $k-\sigma_i(k)$ is equal to 0 for $\forall i$ = 1,2..., m and $k\in\mathbf{N}$.

Consider the definition of some generalized model of asynchronous computational process (Robert, et al., 1975), (Baran et al., 1996), (Gubareni et al., 1997b).

Definition 5. Let there exist a set of nonlinear operators $\mathbf{T}_i$: $\mathbf{R}^n \rightarrow \mathbf{R}^n$, $i\in\{1,2,...,m\}$ and an initial value $\mathbf{x}^{(0)}\in\mathbf{R}^n$. A **generalized model of asynchronous iterations with limited delays** for the set of operators $\mathbf{T}_i$, i=1,2,...,m is called a method of building the sequence of vectors $\{\mathbf{x}^{(k)}\}_{k=0}^{\infty}$, which is given recursively by the following scheme:

$$
\begin{aligned}
\mathbf{y}^{k,i} &= \begin{cases} \mathbf{T}_i \mathbf{x}^{(\sigma^i(k))}, & \text{if } i \in I_k \\ \mathbf{y}^{k-1,i}, & \text{otherwise} \end{cases} \\
\mathbf{x}^{(k)} &= \mathbf{S}\left(\mathbf{x}^{(k-1)}, \left\{\mathbf{y}^{k,i}\right\}_{i \in I_k}\right)
\end{aligned} \tag{30}
$$

where $I = \{I_k\}_{k=1}^{\infty}$ is a sequence of chaotic sets such that $I_k \subset \{1,2,\ldots,m\}$ and $J_i = \left\{\sigma^i(k)\right\}_{k=1}^{\infty}$ are sequences of limited delays (i=1,2,...,m).

Apply the generalized model of asynchronous iterations for an implementation of the ART algorithm on a non-synchronous computer structure. In this case there results the following asynchronous algorithm, where the numbers of operators are chosen by a chaotic way.

Algorithm 8.
1. $\mathbf{x}^{(0)} \in \mathbf{R}^n$ is an arbitrary vector;
2. The k+1-th iteration is calculated in accordance with the following scheme:

$$
\begin{aligned}
\mathbf{y}^{k+1,i} &= \begin{cases} \mathbf{P}_i^{\omega_k} \mathbf{x}^{(\sigma^i(k))}, & \text{if } i \in I_k \\ \mathbf{y}^{k,i}, & \text{otherwise} \end{cases} \\
\mathbf{x}^{(k+1)} &= \sum_{i \in I_k} \gamma_i^k \mathbf{y}^{k+1,i}, \quad (i = 1,2,\ldots,m),
\end{aligned} \tag{31}
$$

where $\mathbf{P}_i^{\omega_k}$ are operators defined by (9), ω_k are relaxation parameters, γ_i^k are positive real numbers for each $k \in \mathbf{N}$, $I = \{I_k\}_{k=1}^{\infty}$ is a sequence of chaotic sets such that $I_k \subset \{1,2,\ldots,m\}$, $J_i = \left\{\sigma^i(k)\right\}_{k=1}^{\infty}$ are sequences of delays.

The convergence of this algorithm is given by the following theorem:

Theorem 1. Let system (2) be consistent, $I = \{I_k\}_{k=1}^{\infty}$ a regular sequence of chaotic sets $I_k \subset \{1,2,\ldots,m\}$ with a number of regularity T, $\left\{\sigma^i(k)\right\}_{k=1}^{\infty}$ sequences with limited delays and $\sigma_j^i(k) = \sigma_i(k)$, and let a delay be equal to T. If 0< ω_k <2, γ_i^k are positive real numbers with property $\sum_{i \in I_k} \gamma_k^i = 1$, then for every point $\mathbf{x}^{(0)} \in \mathbf{R}^n$ the sequence $\left\{\mathbf{x}^k\right\}_{k=0}^{\infty}$ defined by the algorithm 8 converges to some point $\mathbf{x}^* \in H$, which is a fixed point of orthogonal projection operators $\mathbf{P}_i$ (i=1,2,...,m).

Consider the particular case of the algorithm 8 when there are no delays and the sequence of chaotic sets is acceptable.

Algorithm 9 (CHART).
1. $\mathbf{x}^{(0)} \in \mathbf{R}^n$ is an arbitrary vector;
2. The k+1-th iteration is calculated in accordance with the following scheme:

$$\mathbf{y}^{k,i} = \begin{cases} \mathbf{P}_i^{\omega_k}\mathbf{x}^{(k-1)}, & \text{if } i \in I_k \\ \mathbf{y}^{k-1,i}, & \text{otherwise} \end{cases}$$
$$\mathbf{x}^{(k)} = \mathbf{C}\sum_{i \in I_k} \gamma_i^k \mathbf{y}^{k,i}, \quad (i = 1,2,...,m), \tag{32}$$

where $\mathbf{P}_i^{\omega_k}$ are operators defined by (9), ω_k are relaxation parameters, γ_i^k are positive real numbers for each $k \in \mathbf{N}$, $I = \{I_k\}_{k=1}^{\infty}$ is an acceptable sequence of chaotic sets such that $I_k \subset \{1,2,...,m\}$ and $\mathbf{C}$ is a constraining operator.

The convergence of the algorithm 9 is given by the following theorem.

Theorem 2. Let system (2) be consistent, $I = \{I_k\}_{k=1}^{\infty}$ be an acceptable sequence of chaotic sets $I_k \subset \{1,2,...,m\}$. If $0 < \omega_k < 2$, γ_i^k are positive real numbers with property $\sum_{i \in I_k} \gamma_k^i = 1$, then for every point $\mathbf{x}^{(0)} \in \mathbf{R}^n$ the sequence $\{\mathbf{x}^k\}_{k=0}^{\infty}$ defined by the algorithm 9 converges to some solution of this system.

6. Block-parallel asynchronous algorithms for computer tomography

Block-parallel asynchronous algorithms with application to tomographic reconstruction from incomplete data were studied by Elsner, Koltracht and Neumann in (Elsner et al. 1990). In this section the generalized model of asynchronous iterations is applied for an implementation of the algorithm BPART on a non-synchronous computer structure. In this case there results the following algorithm, where the numbers of operators are chosen by the chaotic way:

Algorithm 10.

1. $\mathbf{x}^{(0)} \in \mathbf{R}^n$ is an arbitrary vector;
2. The k+1-th iteration is calculated in accordance with the following scheme:

$$\mathbf{x}^{k+1,i} = \mathbf{C}\sum_{i \in H_{t(k)}} \mathbf{B}_i^k \mathbf{P}_i^{\omega_k} \mathbf{x}^{(\sigma^i(k))}, \tag{33}$$

where $\mathbf{P}_i^{\omega_k}$ are operators defined by (9), ω_k are relaxation parameters, $\mathbf{C}$ is a constraining operator, $t(k) = I_k$, $I = \{I_k\}_{k=0}^{\infty}$ is a sequence of chaotic sets such that $I_k \subset \{1,2,...,M\}$ and $\mathbf{B}_i^k$ are matrices of dimension $n \times n$ with real nonnegative elements which satisfy conditions (22), $J_i = \{\sigma^i(k)\}_{k=1}^{\infty}$ are sequences of delays.

Theorem 3. Let system (2) be consistent, $I = \{I_k\}_{k=0}^{\infty}$ a regular sequence of chaotic sets $I_k \subset \{1,2,...,M\}$ with a number of regularity T, $J_i = \{\sigma^i(k)\}_{k=1}^{\infty}$ sequences with limited delays and $\sigma_j^i(k) = \sigma_i(k)$, and let the number of delay be equal to T. Then for every point $\mathbf{x}^{(0)} \in \mathbf{R}^n$ the sequence $\{\mathbf{x}^{(k)}\}_{k=1}^{\infty}$ defined by the algorithm 10 converges to some point $\mathbf{x}^* \in$ H, which is a fixed point of orthogonal projection operators $\mathbf{P}_i$ (i = 1,2,..., M).

Let the particular case of algorithm 10 when there are no delays and the sequence of chaotic sets is acceptable. Decompose the matrix **A** and the projection vector **p** into M subsets in accordance with decomposition (13) and (20). Consider $s_t = |H_t| = m_t - m_{t-1}$ be the cardinality of H_t.

Algorithm 11 (CHBP).

1. $\mathbf{x}^{(0)} \in \mathbf{R}^n$ is an arbitrary vector;
2. The k+1-th iteration is calculated in accordance with the following scheme:

$$\mathbf{x}^{k+1} = \mathbf{C}\sum_{i=1}^{M} \mathbf{B}_i^k y^{(k+1),i}, \tag{34}$$

where

$$y^{(k+1),i} = \mathbf{Q}_i \mathbf{x}^k,$$

$$\mathbf{Q}_i = \mathbf{P}_{i,s_i} \mathbf{P}_{i,s_i-1} \ldots \mathbf{P}_{i,1},$$

$$\mathbf{P}_{i,j} = \mathbf{P}_j^{\omega} \sum_{i=1}^{M} \mathbf{B}_i^k, \quad j \in I_{i(j)},$$

$\mathbf{P}_i^{\omega}$ are operators defined by (9), ω is a relaxation parameter, **C** is a constraining operator, $I = \{I_{i(k)}\}_{k=1}^{\infty}$ is a sequence of chaotic sets such that $I_{i(k)} \subset \{m_{i-1}+1, m_{i-1}+2, \ldots, m_i\} = H_i$ and $\mathbf{B}_i^k$ are matrices of dimension $n \times n$ with real nonnegative elements which satisfy conditions (22) for each $k \in \mathbf{N}$.

Remark 2. If operator $\mathbf{P}_i$ is defined by (3), algorithm CHART, PART, BPART, CHBP will be called CHART-1, PART-1, BPART-1, CHBP-1 respectively, and if $\mathbf{P}_i$ is defined by (8) these algorithms will be called by CHART-3, PART-3, BPART-3, CHBP-3 respectively.

7. Computer simulation and numerical results

In this section there are presented some numerical results of applying the different algorithms considered in the previous sections for reconstruction of high contrast objects from incomplete projection data in the case when they are not available at each angle of view and they are a few-number limited. There are also studied the influence of various parameters of these algorithms such as a pixel initialization, relaxation parameters, number of iterations and noise in the projection data on reconstruction quality and convergence of these algorithms (Gubareni, 1998a), (Gubareni & Pleszczynski, 2007), (Gubareni & Pleszczynski, 2008).

In order to evaluate the goodness of the computer reconstruction of a high-construct image there were tested different kinds of geometric figures and reconstruction schemes. In this

chapter the results of image reconstruction are presented for two different schemes of obtaining projection data (1 × 1) and (1 × 1, 1 × 1), which are described above.
An important factor in the simulation process of image reconstruction is the choice of modeling objects which describe the density distribution of research objects. In a coal bed, where one searches the reservoirs of compressed gas or interlayers of a barren rock, the density distribution may be considered discrete and the density difference of three environments (coal, compressed gas and barren rock) is significant. Therefore for illustration of the implementation of the algorithms working with incomplete data there were chosen the discrete functions with a high contrast.
The first discrete function $f_1(x,y)$ is given in the following form:

$$f_1(x,y)=\begin{cases}1, & (x,y)\in D\subset E\subset \mathbf{R}^2,\\ 0, & \text{otherwise}\end{cases} \tag{35}$$

where E is a square $E=\{(x,y):-1\le x,y\le 1\}$, and D is a subset of E of the following form:

$$D=[-0.4,-0.2]\times[-0.5,0.5]\cup[-0.2,0.2]\times[0.3,0.5]\cup[-0.2,0.2]\times[-0.1,0.1]\cup[0,0.2]\times[0.1,0.3]. \tag{36}$$

The second discrete function $f_2(x,y)$ is given in the following form:

$$f_2(x,y)=\begin{cases}1, & (x,y)\in D_1\subset E\subset \mathbf{R}^2,\\ 2, & (x,y)\in D_2\subset E\subset \mathbf{R}^2,\\ 3, & (x,y)\in D_3\subset E\subset \mathbf{R}^2,\\ 4, & (x,y)\in D_4\subset E\subset \mathbf{R}^2,\\ 0, & \text{otherwise}\end{cases} \tag{37}$$

where E is a square $E=\{(x,y):-1\le x,y\le 1\}$, and D_i are subsets of E of the following form:

$$D_1=[-0.7,-0.4]\times[-0.5,0.2],\ D_2=[-0.2,0.2]\times[-0.1,0.1],$$

$$D_3=[-0.2,0.2]\times[0.3,0.5],\ D_4=[0.4,0.7]\times[0.4,0.7].$$

The three-dimensional view of the plots of these functions are given in Figure 3.

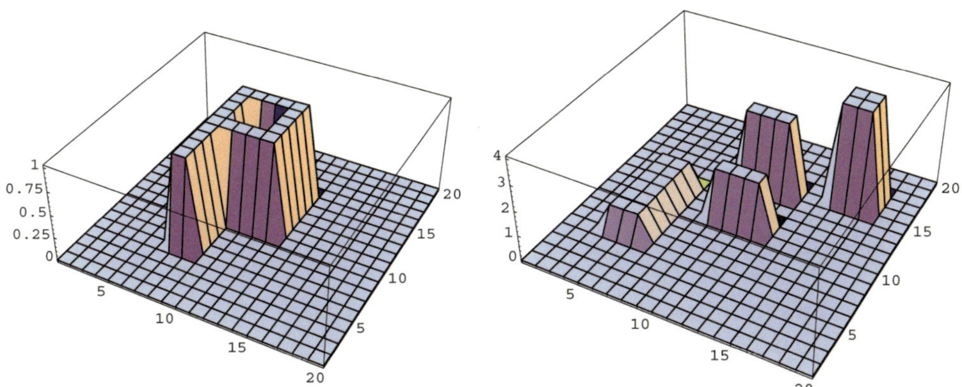

Fig. 3. The original functions $f_1(x,y)$ (on the left side) and $f_2(x,y)$ (on the right side).

As was shown earlier (see, e.g. (Eggermont, el. al., 1981), (Herman, 1980)), the image reconstruction of such objects from complete data gives a good enough results after 6-7 full iterations.
The main criteria which are used to evaluate the quality of reconstruction are the following reconstruction errors: the maximal absolute error, the mean root square error, the maximum relative error, the mean absolute error, the absolute error.
In this paper the convergence characteristics of image reconstruction are presented in a view of plots for the following measures of errors:

- the absolute error:

$$\delta(x,y) = | f(x,y) - \tilde{f}(x,y) |$$

- the maximal absolute error:

$$\Delta = \max_i | f_i - \tilde{f} |$$

- the maximal relative error

$$\delta_1 = \frac{\max_i \left| f_i - \tilde{f}_i \right|}{\max_i | f_i |} \cdot 100\% ,$$

- the mean absolute error

$$\delta_2 = \frac{1}{n} \sum_i \left| f_i - \tilde{f}_i \right|$$

where f_i is the value of a given modeling function in the center of the i-th pixel and $\tilde{f}_i$ is the value of the reconstructed function in the i-th pixel.
In all considered computer simulations it was assumed that **C**= C_1 C_2, where

$$(C_1[\mathbf{x}])_i = \begin{cases} a, & \text{if } x_i < a; \\ x_i, & \text{if } a \le x_i \le b; \\ b, & \text{if } x_i > b; \end{cases} \tag{38}$$

$$(C_2[\mathbf{x}])_j = \begin{cases} 0, & \text{if } p_i = 0 \text{ and } a_{ij} \ne 0; \\ x_j, & \text{otherwise} \end{cases} \tag{39}$$

From the conducted research it follows that the optimal value of a relaxation parameter ω is equal to 1.1 for the system (1 ×1, 1 ×1) and it is equal to 1.3 for the system (1 × 1) in the case where there is no noise in projections. In the case when there is a noise in the projection data the optimal value of ω is changed in dependence on the value of the noise.
In all presented numerical results it was assumed, that

- n - is the number of pixels, i.e. the number of variables,
- m - is the number of rays, i.e. the number of equations,
- M - is the number of blocks,
- *iter* - is the number of full iterations.

In all experiments it was also assumes that

- M is equal to the number of detectors;
- the sequence of chaotic sets I_k has the form { ξ_k }, where ξ_k is an integer random variable in the interval [1,m] with uniform distribution.

- the reconstruction domain $E = \{(x,y): -1 \le x, y \le 1\}$ was divided into n = 20 × 20 pixels.
- the number of projections m in the system (1 × 1) is equal to 788, and in the system (1 × 1, 1 × 1) the number m= 644.

7.1 Reconstruction with algorithms ART-3 and MART-3

The reconstruction of $f_1(x,y)$ with ART-3 after 15 iterations in the scheme (1 × 1, 1 × 1) is presented in Figure 4. The plot of the reconstruction function is shown on the left side, and the plot of the absolute errors for this image reconstruction is shown on the right side.

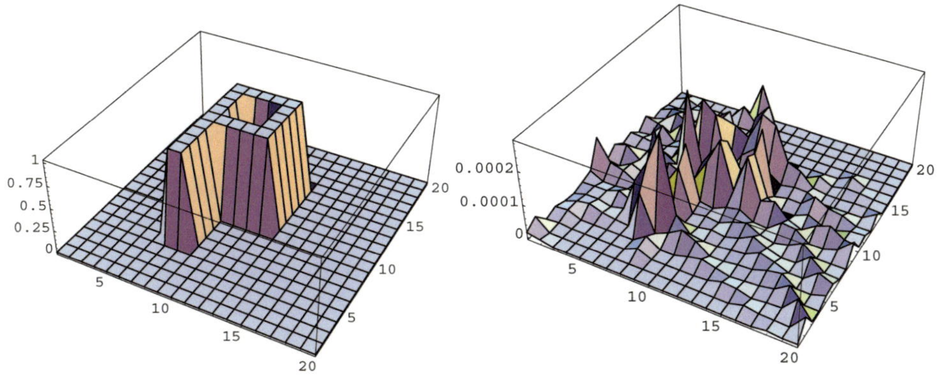

Fig. 4. Reconstruction and the the absolute error $\delta(x,y)$ of $f_1(x,y)$ with ART-3 for n=20 ×20, m= 644, $iter$=15 in the scheme (1 × 1, 1 × 1).

For comparison this function $f_1(x,y)$ was reconstructed with the multiplicative algorithm MART-3 for the same parameters and ω=6.9 and the plots, which are presented in Figure 5, illustrate the dependence of the maximum relative error δ_1 and the mean absolute error δ_2 on number of iterations with ART-3 and MART-3 in the system (1 × 1, 1 × 1).

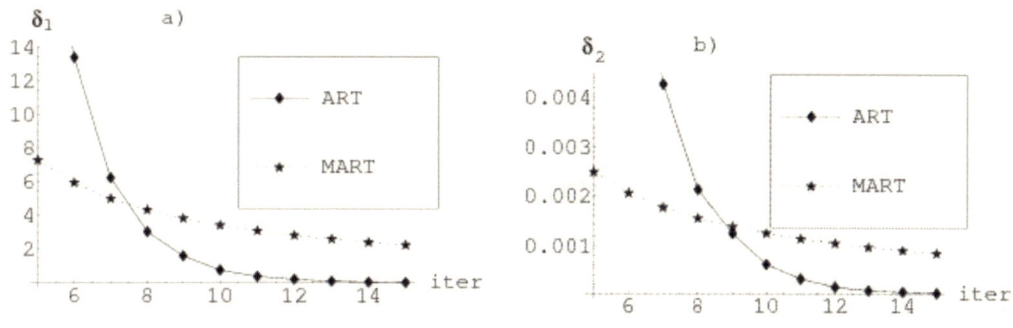

Fig. 5. Dependence of the maximum relative error δ_1 (on the left side) and the mean absolute error δ_2 (on the right side) on the number of iterations for image reconstruction of $f_1(x,y)$ with ART-3 and MART-3 for n=400, m= 644 in the system (1 × 1, 1 × 1).

The same function $f_1(x,y)$ was also reconstructed in the system (1 × 1). The result of this reconstruction with ART-3 for n = 400, m = 788 and 100 iterations is shown in Figure 6.

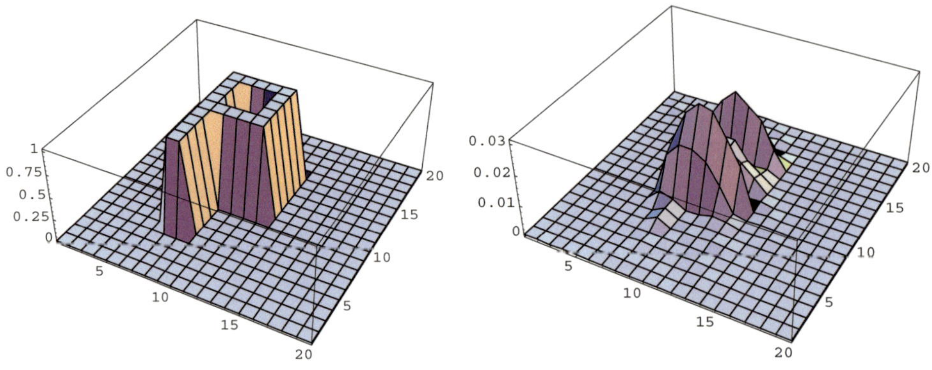

Fig. 6. Reconstruction of $f_1(x,y)$ and the absolute error $\delta(x,y)$ obtained with algorithm ART for n=400, m=788, iter=100 in the system (1 × 1).

The plots, which are presented in Figure 7, illustrate the dependence of the maximum relative error δ_1 and the mean absolute error δ_2 on the number of iterations of image reconstruction of $f_1(x,y)$ with ART-3 in the systems (1 × 1, 1 × 1) and (1 × 1).

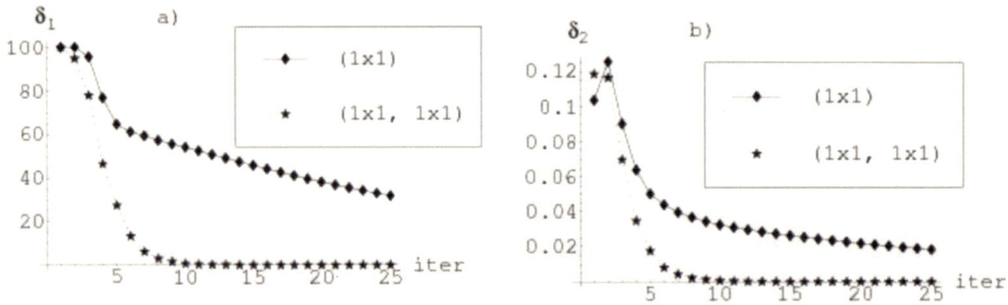

Fig. 7. Dependence of the maximum relative error δ_1 (on the left side) and the mean absolute error δ_2 (on the right side) on the number of iterations of image reconstruction of $f_1(x,y)$ in the systems (1 × 1, 1 × 1) and (1 × 1).

The analogous reconstructions were obtained for the function $f_2(x,y)$. The result of reconstruction of the function $f_2(x,y)$ in the system (1 × 1) is shown in Figure 8.

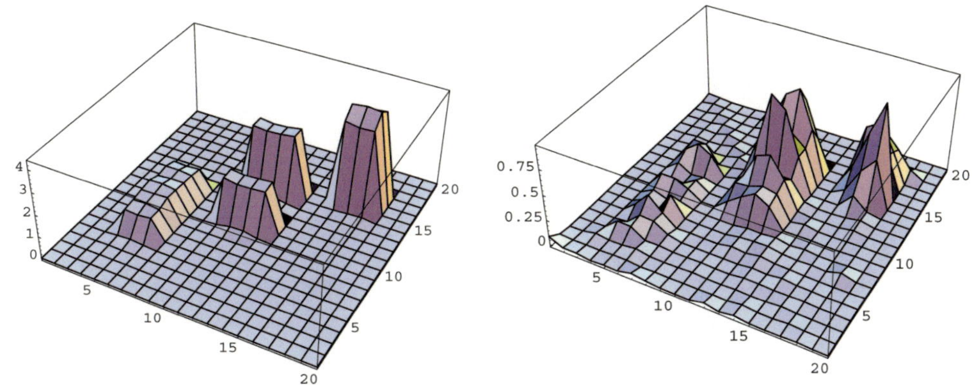

Fig. 8. Reconstruction and the absolute error $\delta(x,y)$ of $f_2(x,y)$ obtained with algorithm ART-3 for n=400, m=788, $iter$=25 in the system (1 × 1).

The plots presented in Figure 9 illustrate the dependence of the maximum relative error δ_1 and the mean absolute error δ_2 on the number of iterations of image reconstruction of $f_2(x,y)$ with ART-3 in the systems (1 × 1, 1 × 1) and (1 × 1).

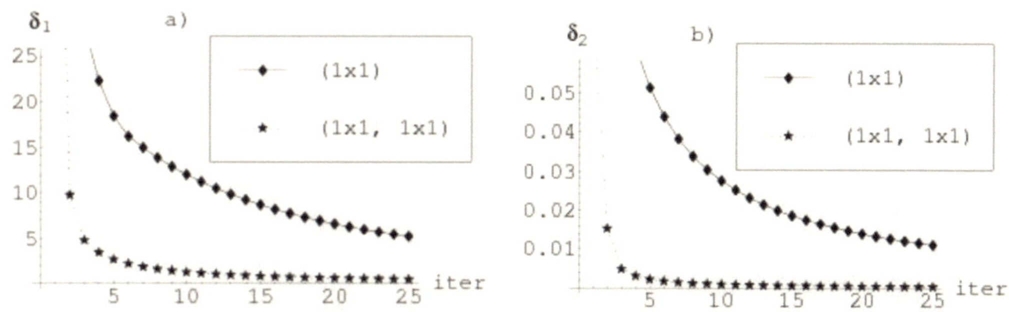

Fig. 9. The dependence of the maximum relative error δ_1 (on the left side) and the mean absolute error δ_2 (on the right side) of image reconstruction of $f_2(x,y)$ in the systems (1 × 1, 1 × 1) and (1 × 1).

Note that the analogous results were obtained for ART-1, MART-1 and MART-3. For the multiplicative algorithms MART-1 and MART-3 the velocity of convergence is considerably less by comparison with the additive algorithms ART-1 and ART-3.

7.2 Reconstruction with chaotic algorithm CHART-1

In this section there are represented some numerical results of reconstructions of the function $f_1(x,y)$ with the chaotic algorithm CHART-1 using the same parameters as in the case of ART-3. The reconstruction result of the function $f_1(x,y)$ with CHART-1 after 100 iterations in the system (1 × 1, 1 × 1) is shown in Figure 10.

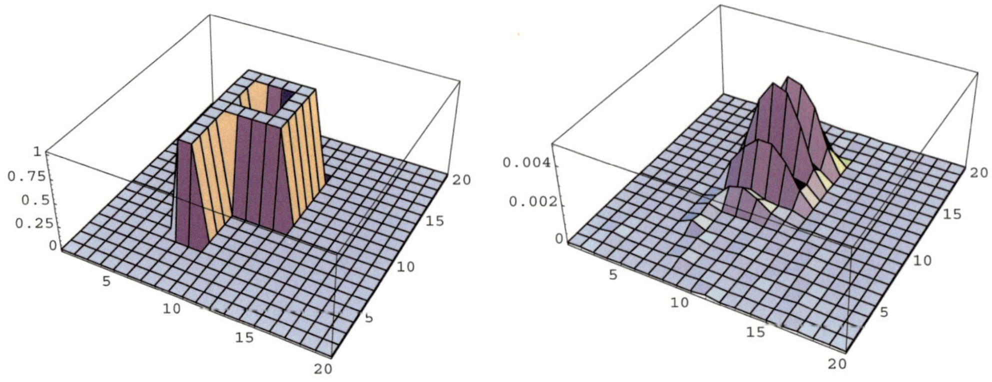

Fig. 10. Reconstruction and the absolute error $\delta(x,y)$ of $f_1(x,y)$ obtained with CHART-1 for n=20 ×20, m= 788, $iter$=100 in the system (1 × 1).

The plots, which are presented in Figure 11, illustrate the dependence of the mean absolute error δ_2 on the number of iterations for image reconstruction of $f_1(x,y)$ with ART-1 and CHART-1 in the systems (1 × 1, 1 × 1) and (1 × 1).

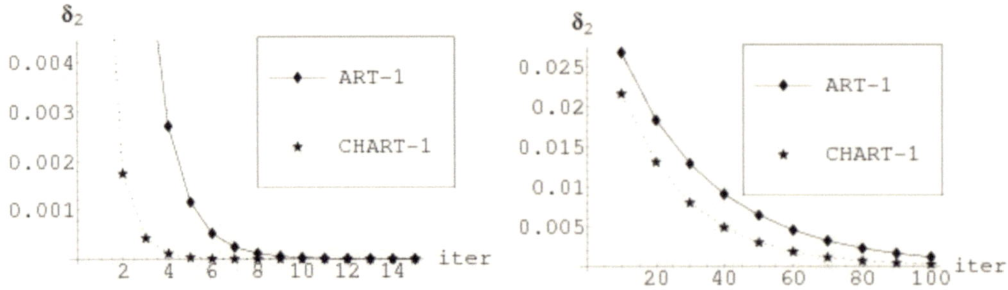

Fig. 11. Dependence of the mean absolute error δ_2 on the number of iterations for image reconstruction of $f_1(x,y)$ with ART-1 and CHART-1 in the system (1 × 1, 1 × 1) (on the left side) and in the system (1 × 1) (on the right side).

The result of image reconstruction of the function $f_2(x,y)$ with CHART-1 after 25 iterations in the system (1 × 1) is shown in Figure 12.

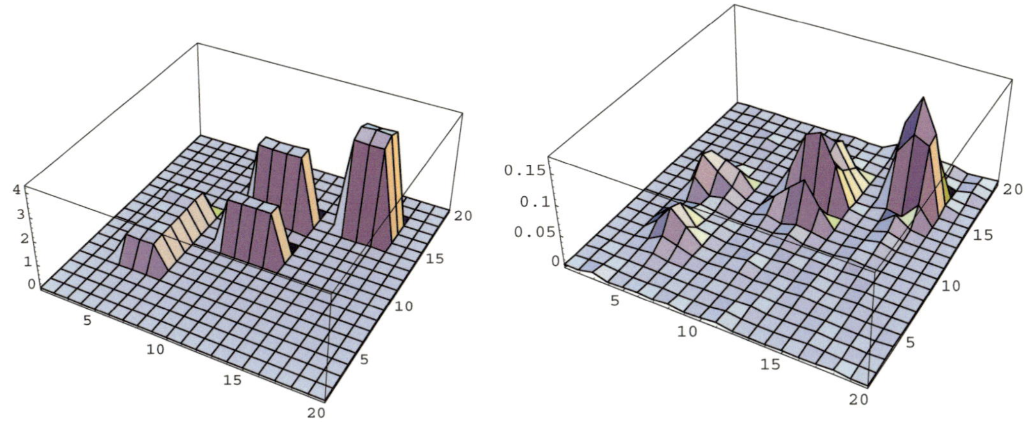

Fig. 12. Reconstruction and the absolute error $\delta(x,y)$ of $f_2(x,y)$ obtained with chaotic algorithm CHART-1 for n=20 ×20, m= 788, $iter$=25 in the system (1 × 1).

Table 1 (resp. Table 2) shows the dependence of the maximum absolute error Δ on the number of iterations for ART-1 and CHART-1 for the system (1 × 1) (resp., the system (1 × 1, 1 × 1)) and the same set of parameters which were chosen above.

iter	ART-1	CHART-1
100	0.0306	0.0073
200	0.00201	0.0001
500	1.209×10^{-6}	4.098×10^{-9}
1000	6.435×10^{-12}	6.328×10^{-15}
2000	5.44×10^{-15}	6.106×10^{-15}

Table 1. The dependence of the maximum absolute error Δ on the number of iterations for ART-1 and CHART-1 in the system (1 × 1).

iter	ART-1	CHART-1
10	0.0077	0.00002
20	9.83×10^{-6}	3.568×10^{-9}
40	3.12×10^{-11}	1.221×10^{-15}
50	3.98×10^{-14}	1.11×10^{-15}
100	8.88×10^{-16}	8.88×10^{-16}

Table 2. The dependence of the maximum absolute error Δ on the number of iterations for ART-1 and CHART-1 in the system (1 × 1, 1 × 1).

The plots, which are presented in Figure 13, illustrates the dependence of the mean absolute error on the number of iterations of image reconstruction of $f_2(x,y)$ with ART-1 and CHART-1 in the system (1 × 1).

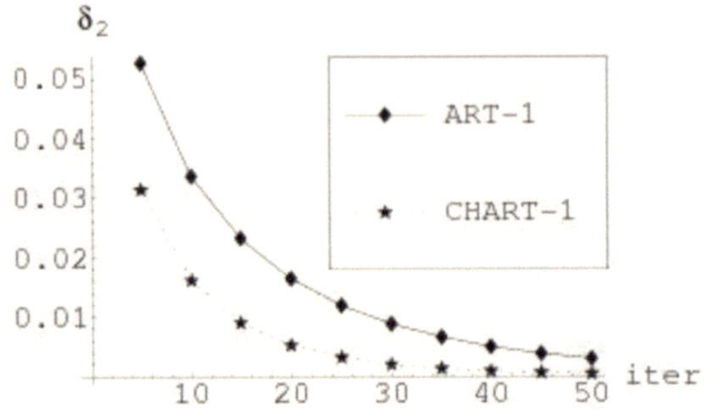

Fig. 13. Comparison between the mean absolute error δ_2 for image reconstruction of $f_2(x,y)$ with ART-1 and CHART-1 in the system (1×1).

7.3 Reconstruction with block-parallel algorithms

In this section there are represented some numerical results of reconstructions of the function $f_2(x,y)$ with the block-parallel algorithm BPART-3 and the chaotic block-parallel algorithm CHBP-3. The reconstruction result of the function $f_2(x,y)$ with BPART-3 and CHBP-3 after 75 iterations in the system $(1 \times 1, 1 \times 1)$ is shown in Figure 14 and Figure 15, respectively.

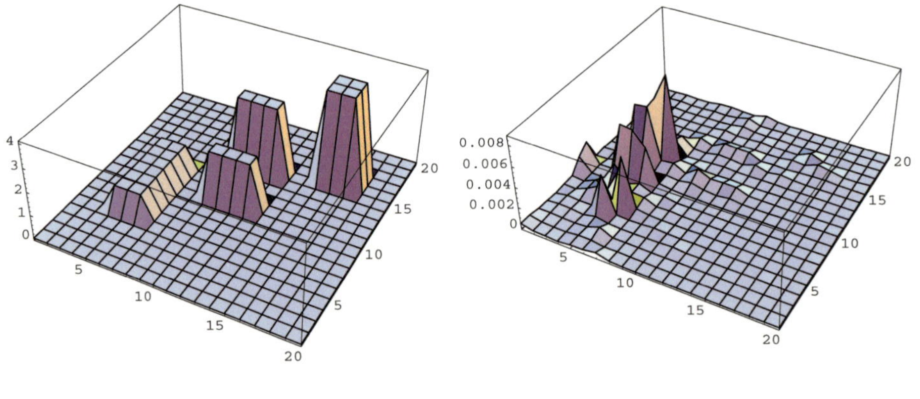

Fig. 14. Reconstruction and the absolute error $\delta(x,y)$ of $f_2(x,y)$ obtained with algorithm BPART-3 for $n = 20 \times 20$, m=644, M=36, $iter$=75 in the system $(1 \times 1, 1 \times 1)$.

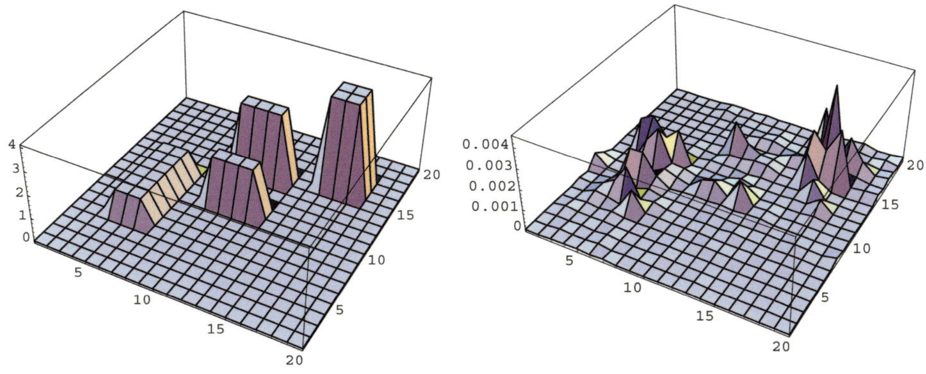

Fig. 15. Reconstruction and the absolute error $\delta(x,y)$ of $f_2(x,y)$ obtained with CHBP-3 for $n = 20 \times 20$, $m=644$, $M=36$, $iter=75$ in the system $(1 \times 1, 1 \times 1)$.

The plots, which are presented in Figure 16, illustrate the dependence of the maximum relative error and the mean absolute error on the number of iterations of image reconstruction of $f_2(x,y)$ with BPART-3 and CHBP-3 in the system $(1 \times 1, 1 \times 1)$:

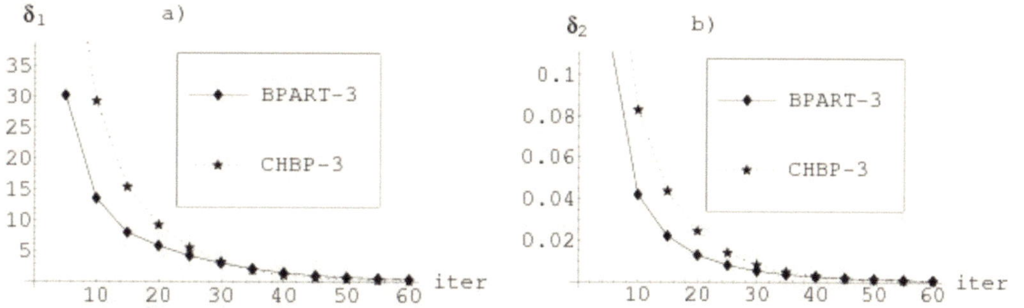

Fig. 16. Dependence of the maximum relative error δ_1 and the mean absolute error δ_2 on the number of iterations for image reconstruction of $f_2(x,y)$ with BPART-3 and CHBP-3 in the system $(1 \times 1, 1 \times 1)$.

Table 3 shows the dependence of the maximum absolute error Δ on the number of iterations for BPART-3 and CHBP-3 in the system $(1 \times 1, 1 \times 1)$.

iter	BPART-3	CHBP-3
10	0.4640	0.2112
20	0.1973	0.0478
40	0.0293	0.0054
50	0.0113	0.0018
100	0.0001	0.000001

Table 3. Dependence of the maximum absolute error Δ on the number of iterations for BPART-3 and CHBP-3 in the system $(1 \times 1, 1 \times 1)$.

The analogous results were obtained for reconstruction of the function $f_2(x,y)$ with BPART-3 and CHBP-3 in the system (1 × 1). The plots presented in Figure 17 illustrate the dependence of the maximum relative error and the mean absolute error on the number of iterations of image reconstruction of $f_2(x,y)$ with BPART-3 and CHBP-3 in the system (1 × 1):

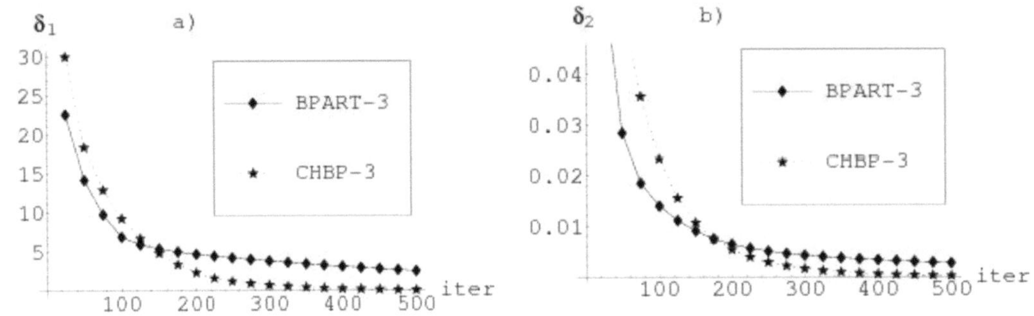

Fig. 17. Dependence of the maximum relative error δ_1 and the mean absolute error δ_2 on the number of iterations for image reconstruction of $f_2(x,y)$ with BPART-3 and CHBP-3 in the system (1 × 1).

Remark 3. The parallel reconstruction algorithms BPART and CHBP were implemented in a simulated parallel environment on a sequential machine. Calculations of all elementary processors that could be run in parallel were times together and the results were stored in temporary arrays. The results of all such calculations were updated into global arrays while all computations were completed.

7.4 Reconstruction with noisy projection data

It is very important for the research of reconstruction quality to consider the effect of noise in projection data on a reconstructed image. For this purpose the various levels of Gaussian (normal) noise are added to projections. The noise model was proposed by Herman (Herman, 1975). In this model the noisy data are simulated by the addition of Gaussian noise. Here each projection is multiplied by a Gaussian distributed random number with mean 1.0 and standard deviation *s*. Usually the noise level is taken less that 10% in computed tomography for non-medical imaging application. In considered experiments the noise level was in the interval from 1% to 5%.

The plots of image reconstruction of the function $f_1(x,y)$ with ART-1 after 10 iterations in the system (1 × 1, 1 × 1) and the normal noise of projection data *s*=2% and s=5% are given in Figure 18.

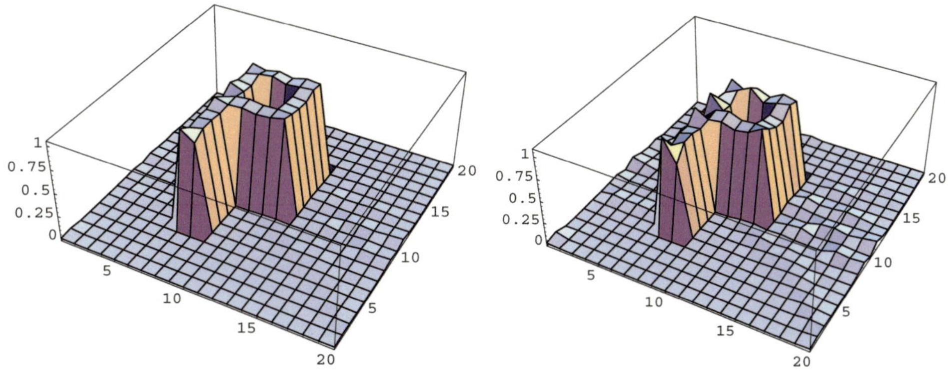

Fig. 18. Reconstruction of $f_1(x,y)$ obtained with ART-1 after 10 iterations in the system (1 × 1, 1 × 1) and the normal noise of projection data s= 2% (on the left side) and s=5% (on the right side).

Analogous results were obtained for the algorithm CHART-1. The plots of image reconstruction of the function $f_1(x,y)$ with CHART-1 after 10 iterations in the system (1 × 1, 1 × 1) and the normal noise of projection data s=2% and s=5% are given in Figure 19.

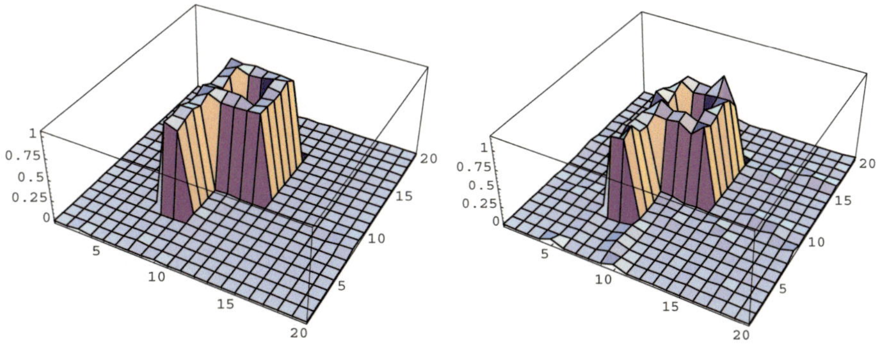

Fig. 19. Reconstruction of $f_1(x,y)$ obtained with CHART-1 after 10 iterations in the system (1 × 1, 1 × 1) and the normal noise of projection data s= 2% (on the left side) and s=5% (on the right side).

The plots, which are represented in Figure 20, show dependence of the mean absolute error δ_2 on the number of iterations for image reconstruction of $f_1(x,y)$ with ART-1 (on the left side) and algorithm CHART-1 (on the right side) in the system (1 × 1, 1 × 1) and the normal noise in projections s= 0% and s= 2%. These results show that both algorithms are stable with regard to noise in projections and they have the same robustness.

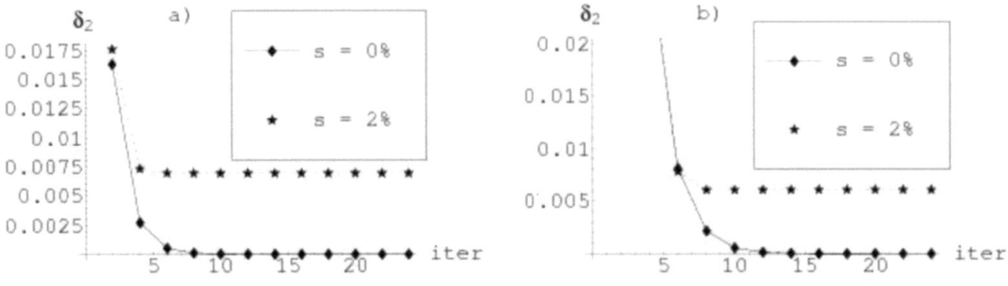

Fig. 20. Dependence of the mean absolute error δ_2 on the number of iterations for image reconstruction of $f_1(x,y)$ with ART-1 (on the left side) and CHART-1 (on the right side) in the system $(1 \times 1, 1 \times 1)$ and the normal noise of projection data $s = 0\%$ and $s = 2\%$.

Remark 4. All algorithms were implemented on IBM/PC (procesor AMD Duron XP, 1600 MHz) by means of C++ and MATHEMATICA 5.1. For reconstruction of examples with small number of pixels (n=20 ×20 and m < 800) one iteration by means of Mathematica 5.1 was implemented approximately 0.5s for all algorithms, and in C++ one iteration for all algorithms is implemented in a real time (< 0.1s).

8. Conclusion

The aim of this paper was to represent and study the different iterative algebraic algorithms for reconstruction of high-contrast objects from incomplete projection data. There were studied the quality and convergence of these algorithms by simulation on a sequential computer.

For each considered system of reconstruction there exist the parameters which allow to obtain a good quality of reconstruction after some number of iterations but this number is considerably larger than for reconstruction with the complete projection data. This number of iterations is approximately 10 times more for the scheme $(1 \times 1, 1 \times 1)$ by comparison with the case of the complete data.

The obtained results show also that for obtaining the good reconstruction quality (with $\delta_1 <$ 1% and $\delta_2 < 0.001$) by means of the chaotic algorithm CHART-1 it suffices 4-6 iterations in the system $(1 \times 1, 1 \times 1)$ and 20-30 iterations in the system (1×1). These results are much better by comparison with algorithm ART-1. The results of reconstruction also show that the chaotic algorithm CHBP-3 gives better results with comparing the block-parallel algorithm BPART-3.

All experimental results show that the errors of reconstruction of considered objects from limited projection data with all considered algorithms are constantly reduced with increasing the number of iterations. It was also shown that all considered algorithms are stable with regard to noise (< 5%) in projections.

It should be note that the parallel and block-parallel algorithms were implemented only on simulated parallel environment on sequential machine. Their implementation on real parallel structure may give some other results. So it will be very interesting to conduct the simulation of these algorithms on such parallel structures.

9. References

Baran, B.; Kaszkurewicz, E. & Bhaya, A. (1996). Parallel Asynchronous Team Algorithms: Convergence and Performance Analysis. *IEEE Trans. on Parallel and Distributive Systems*, Vol. 7, No. 7, (1996) pp. 677-688, ISSN: 1045-9219.

Baudet, G.M. (1978). Asynchronous iterative methods for multiprocessors. *J. Assoc. Comput. Mach.* Vol. 25, (1978) pp. 226-244, ISSN: 0004-5411.

Bertsekas D.P. (1983). Distributed asynchronous computation of fixed points. *Math. Program.*, Vol. 27, (1983) pp. 107-120, ISSN: 0025-5610.

Bertsekas D.P., Tsitsiklis J.N. (1989). *Parallel and Distributed Computation: Numerical Methods*, Prentice-hall, Englewood Cliffs, ISBN: 0-13-648700-9, New York.

Bertsekas D.P., Tsitsiklis J.N. (1991). Some aspects of parallel and distributed algorithms - a survey. *Automatica*, Vol. 27, No. 1, (1991) pp. 3-21, ISSN: 0005-1098.

Bru R.; Elsner L. & Neumann M. (1988). Models of Parallel Chaotic Iteration Methods. *Linear Algebra and its Appl.*, Vol. 103, (1991) pp. 175-192, ISSN: 0024-3795.

Censor, Y. (1988). Parallel application of block-iterative methods in medical imaging and radiation therapy. *Math. Programming*, Vol. 42, (1988) pp. 307-325, ISSN: 0025-5610.

Censor, Y.; Zenios S.A. (1997). *Parallel Optimization. Theory, Algorithms, and Applications*, Oxford University Press, ISBN 0-19-510062-X, New York.

Chazan, D.; W.Miranker, W. (1969). Chaotic relaxation. *Linear Alg. its Appl.*, Vol. 2, (1969) pp. 199-222, ISSN: 0024-3795.

Chen, C.M.; Lee, S. & Cho, Z. (1990). A parallel implementation of a 3-D CT image reconstruction on hypercube multiprocessor. *IEEE Trans. on Nuclear Science*, Vol. 37, (1990) pp. 1333-1346, ISSN: 0018-9499.

Chen, C.M.; Lee, S.Y. (1994). On paralleling the EM algorithm for image reconstruction. *IEEE Transactions on Parallel and Distributive Systems*, Vol. 5, No. 8, (1994) pp. 860-873, ISSN: 1045-9219.

De Pierro, A.R. & Iusem, A.N. (1985b). A parallel projection method of finding a common point of a family of convex sets. *Pesquisa Oper.*, Vol.5, No.1, (1985) pp. 1-20, ISSN: 0101-7438.

De Pierro, A.R. & Iusem, A.N. (1990). On the Asymptotic Behavior of Some Alternate Smoothing Series Expansion Iterative Methods. *Linear Algebra and its Appl.*, Vol. 130, (1990) pp. 3-24, ISSN: 0024-3795.

De Pierro, A.R. (1990). Multiplicative iterative methods in computed tomography. *Lecture Notes in Mathematics*, Vol. 1497, (1990) pp. 133-140, ISSN: 0075-8434.

De Pierro, A.R.& Iusem, A.N. (1985a). A simultaneous projections method for linear inequalities. *Linear Algebra and its Appl.*, Vol. 64, (1985) pp. 243-253, ISSN: 0024-3795.

Eggermont, P.P.B.; Herman, G.T. & Lent, A. (1981). Iterative algorithms for large partitioned linear systems with applications to image reconstruction. *Linear Algebra and Its Appl.* Vol.40, (1981) pp. 37-67, ISSN: 0024-3795.

El Tarazi, M. (1984). Algorithmes mixtes asynchrones. Etude de convergence monotone. *Numer. Math.*, Vol. 44, (1984) pp. 363-369, ISSN: 0006-3835.

Elfving, T. (1980). Block-iterative methods for consistent and inconsistent linear equations. Numerische Mathematik, Vol.35, (1980), pp. 1-12, ISSN: 0029-599X.

Elsner, L.; Koltracht, I. & Neumann, M. (1990). On the Convergence of Asynchronous Paracontractions with Application to Tomographic Reconstruction from

Incomplete Data. *Linear Algebra and its Appl.*, Vol. 130, (1990) pp. 83-98, ISSN: 0024-3795.

Gordon, R.; Bender, R. & Herman, G.T. (1970). Algebraic reconstruction techniques (ART) for three-dimensional electron microscopy and X-ray photography. *J. Theoretical Biology*, Vol.29, (1970) pp. 471-481, ISSN: 0022-5193.

Gubareni, N. & Katkov, A. (1998b). Simulation of parallel algorithms for computer tomography, *Proceedings of the 12-th European Simulation Multiconference*, pp. 324-328, Manchester, United Kingdom, June 16-19, 1998, SCS Publ., ISBN: 1-56555-148-6, Delft.

Gubareni, N. & Pleszczynski, M. (2007). Image reconstruction from incomplete projection data by means of iterative algebraic algorithms, *Proceedings of the Internat. Multiconference on Computer Science and Information Technology*, pp. 503-515, ISSN 1896-7094, Wisla, Poland, 2007.

Gubareni, N. & Pleszczynski, M. (2008). Chaotic Iterative Algorithms for Image Reconstruction from Incomplete Projection Data. *Electron. Model.*, Vol. 30, No. 3, 2008, pp. 29-43, ISSN 0204-3572.

Gubareni, N. (1997a). *Computed Methods and Algorithms for Computer Tomography with limited number of projection data*, Naukova Dumka, ISBN 966-00-0136-3, Kiev. (in Russian)

Gubareni, N. (1999). Generalized Model of Asynchronous Iterations for Image Reconstruction, *Proceedings of the 3-d Int. Conf. on Parallel Processing and Applied Mathematics PPAM'99*, pp. 266-275, ISBN 83-911994-0-1, Kazimierz Dolny, Poland, September 14-17, 1999, Technical Univ. of Częstochowa, Częstochowa.

Gubareni, N.; Katkov, A. & Szopa, J. (1997b). Parallel asynchronous Team Algorithm for Image Reconstruction. *Proceedings of the 15-th IMACS World Congress on Scientistic Computation, Modelling and Applied Mathematics*. Berlin, Germany, 1997, Computational Mathematics, Vol. I (A.Sydow, ed.), pp. 553-558, Achim. Wessenschaft & Technik Verlag, ISBN: 3-89685-551-4, Berlin.

Gubareni, N.M. (1998a). Parallel Iterative Algorithms of Computer Tomography. *Engineering Simulation*, Vol. 15, (1998) pp. 467-478, ISSN: 1063-1100.

Gubareni, N.M. (2001). Asynchronous algorithms for problem of reconstruction from total image, In: *Parallel Computing: Advances and Current Issues*, Joubert, G.R.; Murli, A.; Peters, F.J.; Vanneschi, M. (eds.), pp. 149-156, Imperial College Press, ISBN 1-86094-315-2, London.

Harshbarger, T.B. & Twieg, D.B. (1999). Iterative reconstruction of single-shot spiral MRI with off resonance. *IEEE Trans. Med. Imag.*, Vol. 18, (1999) pp. 196-205, ISSN: 0278-0062.

Herman, G.T. (1975). A relaxation method for reconstructing objects from noisy x-rays. *Math. Programming*, Vol. 8, (1975) pp. 1-19, ISSN: 0025-5610.

Herman, G.T. (1980). *Image Reconstruction from Projections. The Fundamentals of Computerized Tomography*, Academic Press, ISBN: 978-354-0094-173, New York.

Herman, G.T.; Lent, A. & Rowland, S. (1973). ART: Mathematics and application (a report on the mathematical foundations and on the applicability to real data of the Algebraic Reconstruction Techniques). *Journal of Theoretical Biology*, Vol. 43, (1973) pp. 1-32, ISSN: 0022-5193.

Kaczmarz, S. (1937). Angenäherte auflösung von systemn linearer gleichungen. *Bull. Int. Acad. Polon. Sci. Lett. Ser.* A, Vol. 35, (1937) pp. 335-357.

Kak, A. & Slaney, M. (1988). *Principles of Computerized Tomographic Imaging*, IEEE Press, ISBN-13: 978-089-871494-4, New York.

Kaszkurewicz, E.; Bhaya, A. & Siljak, D.D. (1990). On the Convergence of Parallel Asynchronous Block-Iterative Computations. *Linear Alg. and Its Appl.*, Vol. 131, (1990) pp. 139-160, ISSN: 0024-3795.

Kudo, H. & Saito, T. (2007). Tomographic image reconstruction from incomplete projection data by the method of convex projections. *Systems and Computers in Japan*, Vol. 22, No. 2 (2007) pp. 66-75, ISSN: 0882-1666.

Kung, H.T. (1976). Synchronized and asynchronous parallel algorithms for multiprocessors, In: *Algorithms and Complexity* (J. Traub, ed.), pp. 153-200, Acad. Press, ISBN-13: 978-0126975505, New York.

Laurent, C.; Calvin, C.; Chassery, J.M. & Peyrin, F. (1996). Efficient Implementation of Parallel Image Reconstruction Algorithms for 3-D X-Ray Tomography. In: *Parallel Computing: State-of-the-Art and Perspectives,* E.H. D'Hollander, G.R. Joubert, F.J. Peters (Eds.), pp. 109-117, Elsevier Sci. Inc., ISBN: 0444-824-901, New York.

Lent, A., (1977). A convergent algorithm for maximum entropy image restoration with a medical X-ray application. In: *Image Analisys and Evaluation*, R. Shaw (Ed.), pp. 249-257, SPSE, Washington, D.C.

Liang, Z.-P. & Lauterbur, P.C. (2000). *Principles of Magnetic Resonance Imaging*, Piscataway, IEEE Press, ISBN-13: 978-078-034-7236, New York.

Mueller, K.; Yagel, R. & Cornhill, J.F. (1997). The weighted distance scheme: a globally optimizing projection ordering method for the Algebraic Reconstruction Technique (ART). *IEEE Transactions on Medical Imaging,* Vol. 16, No. 2, pp. 223-230, ISSN: 0278-0062.

Natterer F. (1986). *The Mathematics of Computerized Tomography*, John Wiley & Sons, ISBN-13: 978-047-190-9590, New York.

Patella, D. (1997). Introduction to ground surface self-potential tomography. *Geophysical Prospecting*, Vol.45, (1997) pp. 653-681, ISSN: 0016-8025.

Quinto, E.T. (1988) Tomographic reconstructions from incomplete data - numerical inversion of the exterior Radon transform. *Inverse problems*, Vol. 4, (1988), pp. 867-876, ISSN: 0266-5611.

Radon, J. (1917). Über die Bestimmung von Funktionen durch ihre Integralwerte längs gewisser Mannigfaltigkeiten. *Berichte Sächsische Akademie der Wissenschaften*, Leipzig, Math.-Phys. Kl., 69, 1917, pp. 262-267.

Ramachandran, G.N. & Lakhshminarayanan A.V. (1970). Three-dimensional reconstruction from radiographs and electron micrographs: Application of convolution instead of Fourier transforms. *Proc.* Nat. Sci. Acad. USA, Vol. 68, 1970, ISSN: 1091-6490, pp. 2236-2240.

Robert , F., Charnay, M. & Musy F. (1975). Iterations chaotiques serie-parallete pour des equations non lineaires de point fixe. *Aplikace Matematiky*, Vol. 20, (1975) pp. 1-38, ISSN: 0862-7940.

Savari, S.A. & Bertsekas, D.P. (1996). Finite termination of asynchronous iterative algorithms. *Parallel Computing*, Vol. 22, pp. 39-56, ISSN: 0167-8191.

Singh, S.; Muralindhar K. & Munshi P. (2002). Image reconstruction from incomplete projection data using combined ART-CBP algorithm. *Defence Science Journal*, Vol. 52, No. 3, (2002) pp. 303-316, ISSN: 0011-748X.

Smith, B. (1990). Cone-beam tomography: recent advances and a tutorial review. *Optical Engineering*, Vol. 29, (1990) No. 5, pp. 524-534, ISSN: 0091-3286.

Williams, R.A.; Atkinson, K.; Luke, S.P.; Barlow, R.K.; Dyer, B.C.; Smith, J. & Manning, M. (2004). Applications for Tomographic Technology in Mining, Minerals and Food Engineering. *Particle and Particle Systems Characterization*, Vol. 12, No. 2, (2004) pp. 105-111, ISSN: 0934-0866.

14

Templates for Communicating Information about Software Requirements and Software Problems

Mira Kajko-Mattsson
Department of Computer and Systems Sciences,
Stockholm University/Royal Institute of Technology
Sweden

1. Introduction

For years, the need and scope of software system and process documentation has been heavily debated. Questions that have often been raised are whether one should document, what one should document, how much and when. This debate has lasted for more than 30 years. Still, however, we do not have any clear answers. What we claim and what we have always claimed is that both software system and software process documentation are very important for allowing the software systems to live a long life. (Bauer and Parnas, 1995; Briand, 2003; Card et. Al. 1987; Carnegie 1994; Clark et.al., 1989; Connwell, 2000; Cook and Visconti, 1994, El Elman et.al., 1998; Hogan, 2002; Holt, 1993; Kajko-Mattsson, 2005; Kantner, 1997; Kantner, 2002; Martin and McCluer, 1983; Parnas, 2000; Pence and Hon III, 1993; Rombach and Basili, 1987; Saunders, 1989; van Schouwen and Parnas, 1993, Visaggio, 2001; Visconti and Cook, 2000; Visconti and Cook, 2002)

Recently, the debate regarding documentation has intensified. This is because "agile" voices have been raised against extensive documentation (Beck, 2004; Cohn, 2006; Nawrocki, J et.al, Jasinski, M., 2002). These voices advocate its sparse use and production. According to them, documentation should be brief, however, precise enough to be useful within software production. It should be limited to the core parts of the system. In its extreme case, it should encompass only source code and a set of user stories. The remaining system structure may be communicated informally, mainly orally. There may be no requirement specifications nor design documents, or if there are any, then for the purpose of supporting the coding activity.

The agilists' standpoint with respect to documentation has created confusion within the software community. Right now, the software community has a problem of determining the amount and scope of required documentation. Still, it cannot agree on issues such as (1) what one should document, (2) how much, (3) when, and (4) for what purpose. Today, we do not have any concrete answers. We only claim that we should document just enough information for supporting the communication. But, how much enough is enough?

In this chapter, we present two templates of information required for describing and managing software requirements and software problems. We call them *Software Requirements Management Template (SRMT)* and *Problem Management Template (PMT)*. These templates record information about the system to be developed or maintained and the process managing the development or maintenance effort. The templates have been evaluated within the industry in various parts of the world. Our goal is to establish information that is needed for communicating information about software requirements and software problems and the information required for their realization within a software lifecycle.

The chapter is going to be structured in the following. Section 2 motivates why we need to document. Section 3 describes the method taken to evaluate the *SRMT* and *PMT* templates. Section 4 presents the *SRMT* template covering information required for communicating requirements and their realization. Finally, Section 5 provides concluding remarks.

2. Why Do We Need Document?

Documentation, if correct, complete and consistent, has been regarded as a powerful tool for software engineers to gain success. Its purpose is to describe software systems and processes.

Good system documentation thoroughly describes a software system, its components and relationships. It facilitates the understanding and communication of the software system, eases the learning and relearning process, makes software systems more maintainable, and consequently improves the engineer's productivity and work quality (Bauer, 1995; Briand, 2003; Card, 1987; Conwell, 2000; Parnas 2000, Visconti, 2002).

Poor system documentation, on the other hand, is regarded to be the primary reason for quick software system quality degradation and aging (Parnas, 2000; Sousa, 1998; Visconti, 2002). It is a major contributor to the high cost of software evolution and maintenance and to the distaste for software maintenance work. Outdated documentation of a software system misleads the engineer in her work thus leading to confusion in the already very complex evolution and maintenance task.

The purpose of documentation however, is not only to describe a software system but also to record a process. Process documentation is extremely important for achieving (1) insight and visibility into the processes, (2) meaningful process measurement and thereby (3) high process maturity. It should be pervasive in and throughout all the types of lifecycle chores. Proper control and management of development, evolution and maintenance can only be achieved if we have obtained sufficient visibility into the process, its stages and tasks, executing roles, their decisions and motivations, and the results of individual process tasks.

Irrespective of whether documentation supports systems or processes, it constitutes a collective knowledge of the organization. It supports communication and collaboration amongst various groups within the organization such as project managers, quality managers, product managers, support technicians, testers, developers, and other roles (Arthur, 1995). It enhances knowledge transfer, preserves historical information, assists ongoing product evolution and maintenance, and fulfills regulatory and legal requirements.

It provides an efficient vehicle for communication serving a variety of needs. We distinguish between two types of documentation:

- *Self to self*: Software professionals make personal notes. The goal is to remember what they have done, plan for future actions and analyze the results of their own personal processes.
- *Software professional to software professional*: Different roles communicate with one another, such as developers to developers, developers to testers, developers to maintainers, developers and/or maintainers to management, management to developers and/or maintainers, developer and/or maintainer to support personnel, and the like. The goal is to provide feedback to one another.

3. Method

In this section, we present the method taken to create the *PMT* and *SRMT* templates. First, in Section 3.1, we present our method steps. We then in Section 3.2 present the companies involved in creating and evaluating the templates.

3.1 Steps

Our work consisted of two major consecutive phases, starting as early as in 1998. These phases are: (1) *Creation and Evaluation of Problem Management Template (PMT)* and (2) *Creation and Evaluation of Software Requirements and Management Template* (*SRMT*). Below, we briefly describe these steps.

In the years of 1998 - 2001, we did research on problem management within corrective maintenance. This research resulted in a problem management process model, called *Corrective Maintenance Maturity Model (CM³): Problem Management.* It covered the process activities and information required for managing software problems. It is the problem management information that is put into the *PMT* template. *CM³: Problem Management* was created within ABB (Kajko-Mattsson, 2001). The model and the template were then evaluated within fifteen software companies.

PMT is a specialized form of *SRMT*. Problem reports are requirements for change within corrective maintenance. They are generated due to specific software problems and defects. For this reason, we decided to adapt it to the *SRMT* template managing overall software requirements. The *SRMT* template was then evaluated in three consecutive different studies.

First, we evaluated the SRMT template within one Canadian company which practiced both traditional and agile development approach (Kajko-Mattsson, Nyfjord, 2008). We then continued evaluating it within six Chinese companies (Kajko-Mattsson, 2009). Finally, we evaluated it within one major Swedish company together with 60 software engineers. The evaluation was conducted in form of three consecutive workshops.

Due to space restrictions, we cannot describe the evaluation results in this chapter. However, we cordially invite our readers to study our publications in which we report on the documentation status within the industry today (Kajko-Mattsson, 2000; Kajko-Mattsson, 2002, Kajko-Mattsson, 2005, Kajko-Mattsson & Nyfjord, 2008, Kajko-Mattsson, 2009).

3.2 Companies involved in the Evaluation Phase

Two ABB organizations supported us in creating *CM³: Problem Management*. These were *ABB Automation Products* and *ABB Robotics*. In addition, we received scientific support from *ABB Corporate Research.* (ABB, 2009)

Within ABB, we explored the process of problem management within corrective maintenance and the information managed within this process. Here, we interacted with all the possible roles involved within the process such as maintainers, team leaders, testers, support technicians, change control boards, and the like.

CM³: Problem Management and the *PMT* were then evaluated within fifteen non-ABB organisations in 2001. When choosing them, we attempted to cover a wide spectrum of the today's IT state. Deliberately, we chose different sizes and different types of software organisations. Our smallest organisation was a one-person consulting company. Our largest organisation was one major organization having 14 000 employees. The types of products maintained by these organisations varied from financial systems, business systems, embedded real-time systems, consulting services, administrative systems, and different types of support systems.

Regarding the *SRMT*, we first evaluated it within one Canadian organization. We did it in 2007. Here, we interviewed one representative (a process owner). The company develops products ranging from ground stations for satellite radar systems to e-commerce applications. We studied one small and one middle-sized project evolving data transaction systems with high quality and performance requirements.

We then continued to evaluate the *SRMT* template in a Chinese software development context. When visiting Fudan University as a guest professor in fall 2007, we took the opportunity to study the requirements management practice within some Chinese organizations (Kajko-Mattsson, 2009). For this purpose, we used students attending our course on advanced software engineering. The students chose the organizations according to the convenience sampling method (Walker, 1985). These companies practiced both traditional and agile development methods.

Finally, we evaluated the *SRMT* together with 60 software engineers within one big software development company. Due to the fact that the company wishes to stay anonymous, we call it *IT Exchange*. The evaluation was made in form of three consecutive workshops. As illustrated in Figure 1, 65,57% of the workshop participants were involved in programming activities. The remaining 34,43% were involved in other non-programming activities.

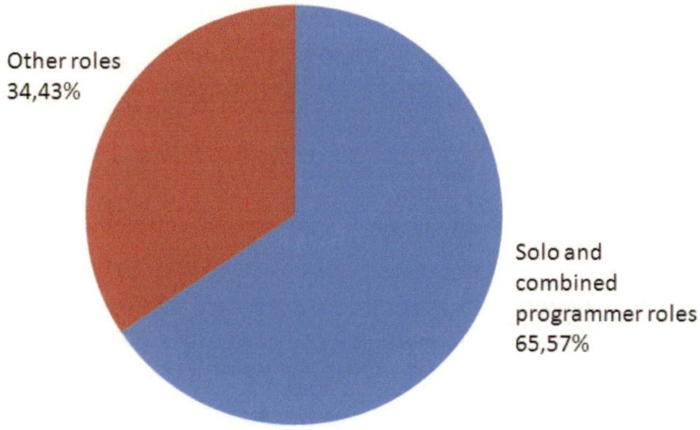

Fig. 1. Distribution of roles at IT Exchange by programmer and non-programmer roles

Figure 2 shows a more detailed distribution of roles involved. Here, we may see that the range of roles involved in the three workshops spanned from programmers, to testers, project managers, technical staff, architects and managers. These individuals were involved both in traditional and agile development and maintenance.

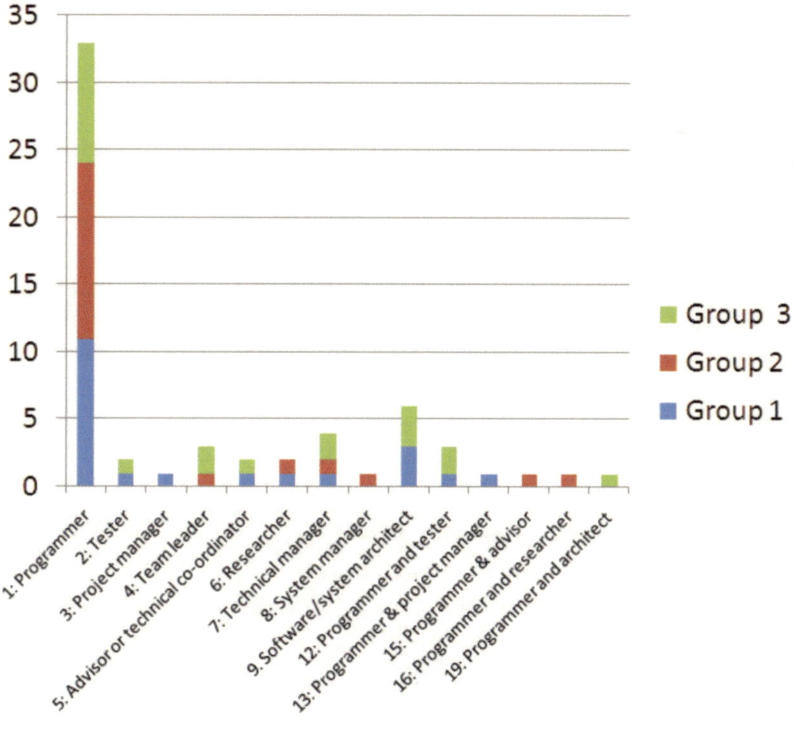

Fig. 2. Roles involved in the workshops at IT Exchange

4. Templates

This section presents and motivates the *SRMT* and *PMT* templates. It first gives an overall view and motivation of the templates in Section 5.1. It then describes the two templates in Section 5.2.

4.1 Overall Presentation of the Templates

The *SRMT* and *PMT* are similar, however, they vary in their contents. Both describe the information about either new requirements or software problems and their management throughout the software lifecycle. However, they require different types of information. This is because the *SRMT* describes new functionality that is going to be created whereas the *PMT* describes old functionality that is going to be changed.

It is difficult to provide a good and clear description of new requirements and software problems. They may be described in several ways using different terms. They can be depicted in different environments and on different system levels (Wedde et.al, 1995).

A proper requirement and problem description is the most important prerequisite for effective implementation. A poor, sketchy, or misleading description may lead to misinterpretation, and thereby, to misimplementation (Kajko-Mattsson, 2000). For this reason, a description of a requirement and a problem should be clear, complete and correct. It has to be communicated in a structured and disciplined way.

To aid in minimising the reporting time for the submitters and in maximising the quality of the reported data, the software organisation should give guidance on how to provide and structure requirement and problem description data. This can be done in form of templates.

The templates should document essential information about all additions and changes made to a system. Since the templates are used to document and communicate information to a wide variety of roles, it is important to include enough information to meet the needs of those roles. At minimum, the information should answer the following questions:

- What is to be implemented/changed?
- Why is it going to be implemented/changed?
- How is it going to be implemented/changed?
- What is the budget?
- Where is it going to be implemented/changed?
- Who is going to make the implementation/change?
- Is the description clear and concise? Are all clues and leads adequately described to allow impact analysis to begin?
- If not, is the submitter available for clarification?
- What information is extraneous to the request?

System Documentation	Process Documentation
General Requirement Description: Requirement ID, Requirement Title, Requirement Description, Requirement Type, Internal/External Req., Rationale, Event/Use Case ID, Related to Requirement(s), Conflicting Requirements, Non-functional requirements, Constraints (Solution, Technical, Budget, Resource), Intended User, Specific user who stated the req., Customer Satisfaction, Customer Dissatisfaction, Assumptions, Reference documents. **Requirements Evaluation Data** Business Value, Other value, Requirements Priority (Rank), Acceptance Criteria, Fit Criteria, Risk **Other Description Data** System Data (System ID, Sub-System ID, Component ID), Adjacent/interfacing Systems ID, Environment	**Requirements Reporting Data** Requirements Reporting Date, Originated by, Reported by, Requirements Owner **Requirements Management Data** Preliminary Implementation Plan, Preliminary outline of activities (Design, Implementation, Testing, other), Change Activities, Planned and Actual Activities(s) (*Activity Description, Activity Start Date, Activity End Date, Expected/Actual Result of Activity Take, Activity Conducted By, Activity Approved By, Effort Spent On Activity, Cost of Action)* **Requirements Management Progress Data** Requirement Management Status, Requirement Mngmt Status Date, Requirement Age, Requirement Changes **Requirements Completion Data** Actual Completion Date, Planned Completion Date, Relation To Tests, Released In, Requirements Completion Approved By, Signed Off Date, Signed Off By, Estimated Total Effort, Actual Total Effort, Estimated Total Cost, Actual Total Cost **Post Implementation Data** Analysis of the Requirements Implementation Process, Lessons learned

Fig. 3. Software Requirement Management Template

System Documentation	Process Documentation
General Problem Description: ProblemID, ProblemTitle, ProblemDescription, Internal/External Problem., Related to Problem(s), Problem Effects and Consequences, Problem Symptoms, Problem Conditions, Problem Reproducibility, Alternative Execution Paths, Assumptions, Reference documents. **Requirements Evaluation Data** Problem Priority (Rank), Problem Severity, Risk **Other Description Data** System Data (System ID, Sub-System ID, Component ID), Adjacent/interfacing Systems ID, Environment, **Problem Reporting Data** Problem Reporting Date, Originated by, Reported by, Problem Owner	**Problem Management Data** Preliminary Resolution Plan, Preliminary outline of activities (Design, Implementation, Testing, other), Change Activities, Planned and Actual Activities(s) (*Activity Description, Activity Start Date, Activity End Date, Expected/Actual Result of Activity Take, Activity Conducted By, Activity Approved By, Effort Spent On Activity, Cost of Action)* **Problem Management Progress Data** Problem Management Status, Problem Mngmt Status Date, Problem Age **Problem Completion Data** Actual Completion Date, Planned Completion Date, Relation To Tests, Released In, Requirements Completion Approved By, Signed Off Date, Signed Off By, Estimated Total Effort, Actual Total Effort, Estimated Total Cost, Actual Total Cost **Post Implementation Data** Analysis of the Problem Resolution Process, Lessons learned

Fig. 4. Problem Management Template

The *SRMT* and PMT consist of two main sections; one dedicated to system documentation and the other one dedicated to process documentation. As listed in Figure 3 and Figure 4, each section covers a set of attributes bearing on coherent information. The attributes concerning the system documentation are (1) *General Requirement/Problem Description,* (2) *Requirement/Problem Evaluation Data,* and (3) *Other Description Data.* The attributes concerning the process documentation are (1) *Requirement/Problem Reporting Data,* (2) *Requirement/Problem Management Data,* (3) *Requirement/Problem Management Progress,* (4) *Requirement/Problem Completion Data,* and (5) *Post Implementation Data.*

4.2 System Documentation

In this section, we describe the tree clusters used for documenting the system. Just because the descriptions of new requirements and problems somewhat differ, we first describe and explain the attributes used for describing the new requirements in the *SRMT* template. For each of the clusters in the *SRMT*, we then describe their correspondences in the *PMT* template.

General Requirement/Problem Description

The *General Requirement Description* describes basic requirement information needed for identifying, understanding, and classifying requirements (Atlantic, 2007; Higgins, 2002). It covers the following attributes:

- *Requirement ID:* Each requirement should be uniquely identified. This allows the requirement to be traced throughout the whole lifecycle process. Usually, its ID corresponds to a numerical value. Some of the requirements may however be identified with an alphanumerical value.
- *Requirement Title:* A title is a short name of a requirement. However, it is not an identifier. It rather corresponds to a mnemonic problem identification. It usually consists of several keywords. It is very helpful in communicating on requirements and in doing manual searches in the tool recording the requirements. It allows one to quickly browse through a requirements list without having to read the whole requirement description.
- *Requirement Desciption:* General information describing the requirement in free text. The requirement orginator describes his own needs and motivates them. This description may be quite comprehensive. Usually, there is no space limit for this field.
- *Requirement Type:* Specification of whether the requirement concerns some new or some existing behavior of the system or whether it concerns some non-functional requirement specifying the characteristics of some functinality.
- *Internal/External Requirement:* Specification of whether the requiement was requested externally by the customer or internally within the development organization. This specification enables priority assignement to the software requirement. Usually, all external requests get higher priority than the internal ones.
- *Rationale:* Motivation of the requirement d'être, that is, the rationale behind the requirement to help the developers understand the requirement and the reason behind it. This helps the developer understand the application domain. Rationale is of great importance in monitoring requirement's evolution during its lifecycle. It disambiguates unclear requirements, and thereby, it prevents from changes leading to unexpected effects.
- *Event/Use Case ID:* List of events and/or use cases descripting the requirement. The use cases, if any, should always be identified. They provide a basis for specifying the requirements.
- *Related To Requirement(s):* Link to other requirements related to the requirement at hand. By following this link, one may achieve an overall picture of groups of requirements and their relationships. In this way, one may discover inconsistencies and duplications among the requirements. One may also record the hierarchies among the major and minor requirements, like the ones presented in Figure 5.

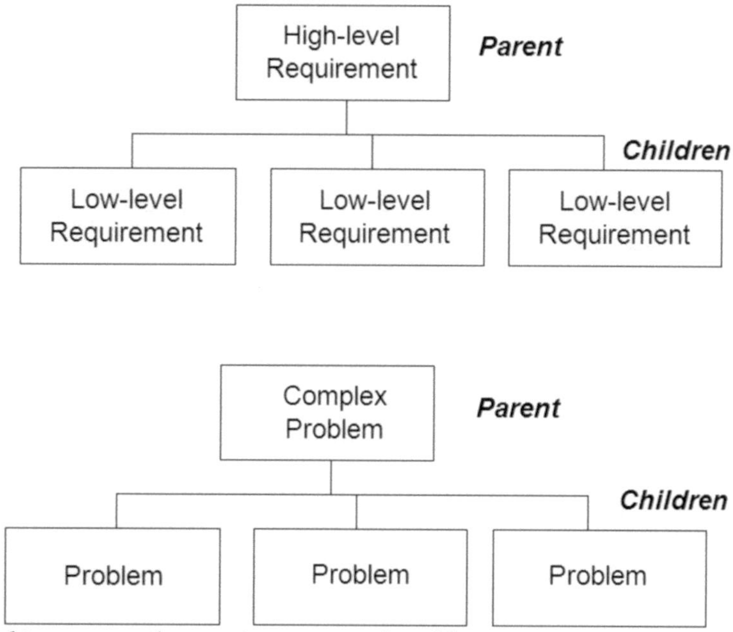

Fig. 5. Hierarchies among the requirements and problems

- *Conflicting Requirements:* Links to conflicting requirements. This information is used for future measures such as negotiations with the customers or provision of extra resources to create an appropriate design that matches these requirements.
- *Non-Functional Requirement(s):* A link to non-functional requirements specifying the criteria to be used when developing the requirement.
- *Constraints:* List of restrictions imposed on resources, budget, technical or solution constraints. These restrictions may lead to a modification of a requirement, and thereby, limit the range of its solutions.
- *Intended User:* Identification of all types of users of the requirement.
- *Customer Satisfaction:* Specification of the degree of satisfaction of how the requirement will meet the customer's needs and expectations.
- *Customer Dissatisfaction:* Degree of customer dissatisfaction, if the requirement is not successfully implemented.
- *Assumptions*: The software system is intrinsically incomplete. The gap between the system and its operational domain is bridged by *assumptions*, explicit and implicit (Lehman, 2000). These assumptions fill in the gaps between the system and the documented and validated requirements of the operational domain.
- *Reference Document(s):* Links to the documentation further describing the requirements.

In the *General Problem Description cluster,* the attributes *ProblemID, ProblemTitle, ProblemDescription, Problem Type, Internal/External Problem, Related to Problem(s),* and *Reference Documents* have their correspondences in *Requirements ID, Requirements Title, Requirements*

Description, Requirements Type, Internal/External Requirement and *Related Requirements,* respectively. Except for *Problem Type* and *Requirement Type,* these attributes connote the same meaning. While *Requirement Type* implies either functional or non-functional requirement, *Problem Type* refers to a specific type of a problem, such as design problem, problem with manuals, and the like.

In addition to the above-mentioned information, one needs to record information that is specific to problem management. This concerns the following attributes:

- *Problem Effect(s) and Consequence(s):* Description of the effects and consequences of the problem. This information is pivotal for assessing the severity and priority of a software problem. Problems implying severe consequences should be attended to as soon as possible.
- *Problem Symptom(s):* A description of an observed manifestation of a problem. Compared to a consequence of a software problem, a symptom may merely indicate a minor system misbehaviour. It does not always directly lead to system failure. This information may greatly help maintenance engineers understand the software problem and localise its cause.
- *Problem Conditions:* Descriptions of the conditions under which a software problem has been encountered. This information must be specified, if deemed relevant. Otherwise, the maintainer will not be able to reproduce the problem.
- *Problem Reproducibility:* a clear description of how to get a software program into a particular erroneous state. It specifies a series of steps that can be taken to make the problem occur. This greatly facilitates the problem investigation process.
- *Alternative Execution Paths:* An identification of all the paths leading to the reproduction of the software problem. This information is pivotal for understanding and resolving the problem.

Requirement/Problem Evaluation Data

The *Requirement Evaluation Data* cluster describes the data essential for evaluating and prioritizing the requirements. It covers the following attributes:

- *Business Value*: Business value is defined for the purpose of meeting some business objectives by implementing the requirement. It is used for prioritizing the requirements.
- *Other Value*: Other values may be specified. Among them are the values of stepping into a new market, attracting new customers, and other opportunities.
- *Requirement Priority*: Evaluation of the urgency of implementing the requirement. Usually, the budget does not allow the companies to implement all requirements. Hence, one needs to prioritize them. The higher the priority, the more urgent it is to implement the requirement.
- *Fit Criterion/Criteria*: A fit criterion describes a condition that a software product must fulfill in order to meet the requirement (Sampayo do Prado Leite 2009). Its purpose is to provide a contextual information so that the requirement will be testable.
- *Risk(s):* Identification of risks related to the requirement. Requirements risks may have major impacts on the success of software projects (Appukkutty et.al, 2005). They may drown the software projects, if they are not properly managed,

In the *Problem Evaluation Data* cluster, the value of *Problem Priority* and *Risk(s)* connotes the same meaning as *Requirements Priority* and *Risk(s)* in the *Requireents Evaluation* cluster. Regarding the attributes such as *Business Value, Acceptance Criteria* and *Fit Criteria,* they are not relevant in the context of problem management. In addition, a new value is added. It is *Problem Severity* measuring the effect of the disruption caused by a software problem.

Other Description Data

The *Other Description Data* cluster provides the context of the requirement and the problem. It covers the attributes identifying the system(s) and its(their) environment and the like. It includes the following attributes:

- *System Data*: To avoid confusion where the requirement/problem must be implemented/resolved, one needs to identify the system, subsystem and component. It is especially imperative in cases when the organizations manage several products with similar functionality.
- *Interfacing System ID*: Identification of the adjacent systems that are or may be impacted by the requirement/problem at hand.
- *Environment*: Specification of the environment in which the requirement/problem will be implemented/resolved. They concern hardware, software, and data environments in which the requirement must function.

4.3 Process Documentation

In this section, we describe the clusters used for documenting the system. Just because the information describing the management of new requirements and software problems does not differ much, we describe and explain the *SRMT* and *PMT* together.

Requirement/Problem Reporting Data

The *Requirement/Problem Reporting Data* cluster records when and by whom the requirement or software problem has been identified and to whom it has been assigned (Kajko-Mattsson, 2001). It covers the following attributes:

- *Requirement/Problem Reporting Date*: The date when the requirement or problem was stated/reported. This date is used for determining the age of a requirement or software problem. In the context of a requirement, a high age is an indicator that the requirement must be revisited so that it does not imply risks to the project. In the context of a software problem, a high age indicates that the software organization has probably neglected its resolution.

- *Requirement/Problem Originator*: The originator of the requirement or problem must be identified. This information is needed for tracking and clarification purposes.

- *Reported By*: Name of the role who reported on the requirement or problem. This individual may be some engineer who reported on the requirement or problem on the *Requirement/Problem Originator's* account.

- *Requirement/Problem Owner*: Role or group of roles (team) responsible for managing the requirement or solving the software problem. The owner makes decisions on the requirement implementation or problem resolution throughout the whole implementation/resolution process. Usually, the owner is the role who originally entered the requirement.
- *Date required*: Date when the requirement must be implemented or the software problem must be resolved.

Requirement/Problem Management Data

The *Requirement Management Data* cluster communicates information about the requirement or problem management process. It covers both planned and actual actions taken to implement the requirement or to resolve the problem, identifies the roles involved in these actions, records the effort required for implementing the requirement or resolvning the problem, and the effectiveness of the implementation activities (Higgins, 2002). The cluster covers the following attributes:

- *Implementation Plan*: The preliminary outline of the activities to be taken to implement the requirement or to resolve the problem.
- *Planned and actual activities*: The activities and their estimated/actual effort and cost. It covers the following information:
  - *Activity Description*: Identification and description of the activity.
  - *Activity Start Date*: Date when the activity started.
  - *Activity End Date*: Date when the activity ended.
  - *Expected/Actual Result*: Description of the expected/actual results of the activity.
  - *Activity Conducted By*: Name of the role responsible for performing the activity.
  - *Activity Approved By*: Name of the role who approved the activity and its results.
  - *Effort Spent on Activity*: Estimated/actual effort spend on the activity.
  - *Cost of Activity*: Estimated/actual cost of the activity.

Requirement/Problem Management Progress

The Requirement Management Progress cluster tracks the status of the requirement implementation or problem resolution process. This status is essential for monitoring and controlling the requirement or problem. It records the status value, the date when the requirement/problem changed status values, the overall requirement implementation or problem resolution progress, and the requirement/problem age. The following attributes are suggested for descring the progress:

- *Requirement/Problem Management Status*: Status value indicating the progress of implementing the requirement or resolving the problem.
- *Requirement/Problem Management Status Date*: Date when the requirement/problem stepped into the particular status state.

- *Requirement/Problem Age*: Time period elapsed from the date when the requirement/problem was recognized and reported. This value is used for assuring that high priority requirements/problems get attended to as soon as possible.
- *Requirement/Problem Change(s)*: Link to change requests concerning the requirement/problem at hand.

Requirements Completion Data

The *Requirement Completion Data* cluster covers information about the completion of the requirement implementation or problem resolution process. It records planned and actual completion date, roles involved in approving and signing off the completion, and the total effort spent on requirement implementation or problem resolution. The cluster includes the following attributes:

- *Planned/Actual Completion Date*: Date when the requirement/problem was or was planned to be completed and tested.
- *Relation to Test(s):* Identification of tests to be used for testing the requirement or problem solution.
- *Released In*: Identification of the release(s) in which the requirement/problem was implemented/resolved.
- *Requirement Completion Approved By*: Name of the role who approved the requirement implementation or problem resolution. Usually, it is the owner.
- *Sign Off Date*: Date when the requirement/problem was signed off by the organizational authority.
- *Signed Off By*: Identification of the roles involved in signing off the requirement/problem completion.
- *Estimated/Actual Total Effort*: Total effort spent/to be spent on implementing/resolving the requirement/problem.
- *Estimated/Actual Total Cost*: Total cost spent/to be spent on implementing/resolving the requirement/problem.

Post-Implementation Data

The *Post Implementation Data* cluster holds the information about the post-mortem analysis of the requirement implementation or problem resolution process. The analysis results should provide an important feedback for improving the future requirements management or problem resolution. The attributes belonging to this cluster are the following:

- *Analysis of the Requirement/Problem Implementation/Resolution Process*: Evaluation of the process used for implementing the requirement.
- *Lessons Learned:* List of experiences as encountered during the implementation/ resolution of the requirement/problem.

5. Final Conclusions

In this chapter, we have presented two templates: the *SRMT* template used for communicating software requirements within development and evolution and the *PMT* template used for communication software problems within corrective maintenance. We then evaluated these two templates within more than 20 software organizations. Due to space restrictions, we cannot describe the evaluation results. However, we cordially invite our readers to study (Kajko-Mattson, 2000; Kajko-Mattson, 2001; Kajko-Mattson, 2002; Kajko-Mattson, 2005; Kajko-Mattson & Nyfjord, 2008; Kajko-Mattson, 2009).

The attributes as suggested in both templates are highly relevant both within heavyweight and lightweight software development. Many of them however, are not explicitly documented. They may however be communicated in an oral form. The rigidity of the documentation is dependent on the type of software systems being developed or maintained. In cases when the software system is not a safety critical or business critical and it is not expected to live a long life, one may compromise on the amount and scope of the information to be documented in favor of oral communication. In case of critical systems, one should not compromise on even one single attribute in both the *SRMT* and *PMT* template. For instance, the engineers within *IT Exchange* claim that they would not be able to survive for long without the information that is listed in the two templates.

So far, very little research has been done on documentation. To our knowledge, there are only a few publications reporting on this subject. Hence, we claim that this domain is strongly under-explored. More research is required for agreeing upon the scope and extent of documentation so that the short-term and long-term benefits may be gained in both the heavyweight and lightweight contexts.

6. References

ABB. (2009) ABB Group Sweden, http://www.abb.com/secrc, Accessed in July 2009.

Atlantic Systems Guild. (2007). Volare Requirements Specification Template, available at: http://www.systemsguild.com/GuildSite/Robs/Template.html, Accessed in December 2007.

Antoniol, G.; Canfora, G.; Casazza, G.; De Lucia. A,. (2000). Information Retrieval models for Recovering Traceability links between code and documentation, *Proceedings of IEEE International Conference on Software Maintenance*, pp. 40-49.

Appukkutty, K.; Ammar, H.H.; Popstajanova, K.G. (2005). Software requirement risk assessment using UML, *Proceedings of International Conference on Computer Systems and Applications*, p. 112.

Arthur, L.J. (1995). Software Evolution: The Software Maintenance Challenge, John Wiley & Sons.

Bauer, B.J. & Parnas, D.L. (1995). Applying mathematical software documentation: An Experience Report, *Proceedings of 10th Annual Conference on Computer Assurance,* pp. 273-284.

Beck K. (2004). *Extreme Programming Explained: Embrace Change,* 2nd Edition. Upper Sadle River, NJ, Addison-Wesley.

Boehm, B.W. (1981). *Software Engineering Economics*, Prentice-Hall.

Briand, L.C. (2003). Software Documentation: How Much is Enough?, *Proceedings of IEEE International Conference on Software Maintenance and Reengineering*, pp. 13-15.

Card, D.; McGarry, F.; Page, G. (1987). Evaluating Software Engineering Technologies, *Journal of IEEE Transactions on Software Engineering*, Vol. 13, No. 7, pp. 845-851.

Carnegie Mellon University and Software Engineering Institute. (1994). *The Capability Maturity Model: Guidelines for Improving the Software Process*, Addison-Wesley.

Chapin, N. (1985). Software maintenance: a different view, *Proceedings of National Computer Conference*, AFIPS Press, Reston, Virginia, Volume 54, pp. 508-513.

Clark, P.G.; Lobsitz, R.M.; Shields, J.D. (1989). Documenting the Evolution of an Information System, *Proceedings of IEEE National Aerospace and Electronic Conference*, pp. 1819-1826.

Cohn M. (2006). *Agile Estimating and Planning*, Pearson Education, Upper Saddle River, NJ.

Conwell, C. L. (2000). Capability maturity models support of modeling and simulation verification, validation, and accreditation. *Proceedings of IEEE Winter Simulation Conference*, pp. 819– 828.

Cook, C. & Visconti, M. (1994), Documentation Is Important, *Journal of CrossTalk*, Vol. 7, No. 11, pp. 26-30.

Delanghe, S. (2000), Using Learning Styles in Software Documentation, *Proceedings of IEEE, Transactions of Professional Communication*, pp. 201-205.

Higgins S.A et. al, (2002). Managing Product Requirements for Medical IT Products. *Proceedings of Joint International Conference on Requirements Engineering*, pp 341-349.

Hofmann, P. (1998). Away with Words! How to create Wordless Documentation, *Proceedings of IEEE International Professional Communication Conference*, pp. 437-438.

Holt, P.O. (1993). System Documentation and System Design: A Good Reason for Designing the Manual First, *Proceedings of IEEE Colloquium on Issues in Computer Support for Documentation and Manuals*, pp. 1/1-1/3.

IEEE Standards Collection. (1999). Software Engineering, The Institute of Electrical and Electronics Engineers, Inc.

Kajko-Mattsson, M.; Forssander, S.; Andersson, G. (2000). Software Problem Reporting and Resolution Process at ABB Robotics AB: State of Practice, *Journal of Software Maintenance and Evolution, Research and Practice*, Vol. 12, No. 5, pp. 255-285.

Kajko-Mattsson, M. (2001). *Corrective Maintenance Maturity Model: Problem Management*, (2001). PhD thesis, ISBN Nr 91-7265-311-6, ISSN 1101-8526, ISRN SU-KTH/DSV/R--01/15, Department of Computer and Systems Sciences (DSV), Stockholm University and Royal Institute of Technology.

Kajko-Mattsson M. (2002). Evaluating CM^3: Problem Management, (2002). *Lecture Notes in Computer Science, Proceedings of Conference on Software Advanced Information Systems Engineering*, Springer-Verlag, Volume 2348, pp. 436-451.

Kajko-Mattsson, M. (2005). A Survey of Documentation Practice within Corrective Maintenance, *Journal of Empirical Software Engineering Journal*, Kluwer, Volume 10, Issue 1, January, pp. 31 - 55.

Kajko-Mattsson M. & Nyfjord, J., (2008). A Template for Communicating Information about Requirements and their Realization, *Proceedings of IAENG International Conference on Software Engineering*, BrownWalker Press: Boca Raton, USA.

Kajko-Mattsson, M. (2009). Status of Requirements Management in Six Chinese Software Companies, *Proceedings of International Conference on Industrial Engineering, IAENG International Conference on Software Engineering*, BrownWalker Press: Boca Raton, USA.

Kantner, L., et.al., (1997). The Best of Both Worlds: Combining Usability Testing and Documentation Projects, *Proceedings of IEEE International Professional Communication Conference*, pp. 355-363.

Kantner, L., et.al., (2002). Structured Heuristic Evaluation of Online Documentation, *Proceedings of IEEE International Professional Communication Conference*, pp. 331-342.

Lepasaar, M.; Varkoi, T.; Jaakkola, H. (2001). Documentation as a Software Process Capability Indicator, *Proceedings of IEEE International Conference on Management of Engineering and Technology*, Vol. 1, p. 436.

Malcolm, A. (2001). Writing for the Disadvanteged Reader, *Proceedings of IEEE International Conference on Professional Communication*, pp. 95-100.

Nawrocki, J.; Jasinski, M.; Walter, B.; Wojciechowski, A. (2002). Extreme Programming Modified: Embrace Requirements Engineering Practicies, (2002). *Proceedings of IEEE Joint International Conference on Requirements Engineering (RE'02)*, pp. 303-310.

Norman, R.L & Holloran, R.W. (1991). How to simplify the structure of administrative procedures to make them easier to write, review, produce, and use, *Proceedings of International Conference on Professional Communication*, Vol.2 pp. 447 – 450.

Parnas, D. L. & Clements, P.C. (1993). A Rational Design Process: How and Why to Fake it, *Journal of IEEE Transactions on Software Engineering*, Vol. SE-12, No. 2.

Parnas, D. L. (1995). Software Aging, *Proceedings of 16th International Conference on Software Engineering*, pp. 279-287.

Parnas, D. L. (2000). Requirements documentation: why a formal basis is essential, *Proceedings of IEEE 4th International Conference on Requirements Engineering*, pp. 81-82.

Pigoski, TM. (1997). *Practical Software Maintenance*, John Wiley & Sons.

Ramsay, J. (1997). Corporate Downsizing: Opportunity for a New Partnership between Engineers and Technical Writers, *Proceedings of IEEE International Professional Communication Conference*, pp. 399-403.

Sampayo do Prado Leite J.C. & Doorn, J.H. (2009). *Perspectives on Software Requirements*, Kluwer Academic Publishers.

Saunders, P.M. (1989). Communication, Semiotics and the Mediating Role of the Technical Writer, *Proceedings of IEEE International Professional Communication Conference*, pp. 102-105.

Sousa, M. & Mendes Moreira, H. (1998). A survey of the software maintenance process. *Proceedings of IEEE International Conference on Software Maintenance*, pp. 265– 272.

van Schouwen, A.J.; Parnas, D.L.; Madey, J. (1993). Documentation of Requirements for Computer Systems, *Proceedings of IEEE International Symposium on Requirements Engineering*, pp. 198-207.

Visconti, M. & Cook, C.R. (2000). *An Overview of Industrial Software Documentation Practices*, Technical Report 00-60-06, Computer Science Department, Oregon State University, April.

Visconti, M. & Cook, C.R. (2002). An overview of Industrial Software Documentation Practice, *Proceedings of 12th IEEE International Conference of the Chilean Computer Science Society*, pp. 179-186.

Walker, R. (1985). *Applied Qualitative Research*, Gower Publishing Company Ltd.

Wedde, K. J.; Stalhane, T.; Nordbo, I.; (1995). A Case Study of a Maintenance Support System, Proceedings of IEEE International Conference on Software Maintenance, pp. 32-41.

15

Ontological description of gene groups by the multi-attribute statistically significant logical rules

Aleksandra Gruca and Marek Sikora
Silesian University of Technology, Institute of Informatics
Poland

1. Introduction

With the beginning of the post-genomic era, the DNA microarray chips became one of the most indispensable tools used in the biological laboratories all over the world to support the genome scale experiments (Baldi & Hatfield, 2002). Development of the DNA chip technologies provided a great opportunity to learn and understand biological phenomena of the world of living organisms better by identifying the genes involved in various biological processes.

A single DNA microarray experiment allows to record simultaneously thousands of gene expression profiles obtained under similar experimental conditions. Such abundance of data needs to be analyzed and processed by means of sophisticated mathematical tools. Nowadays it is impossible for a single person to understand and interpret the experiment results which consist of thousands of numbers describing the expression profiles of all the genes whose probes are located on the DNA microarray chip. Only the cooperation among biologists, mathematicians and computer scientists leads to the complete and profound understanding of the biological phenomena that are recorded in the laboratory.

The analysis of the data obtained in the DNA microarray experiment is a complex and difficult process involving applications of many specialized algorithms. Various methods such as statistical analysis and data mining techniques need to be applied until a final biological conclusions are derived from the spot intensity measurements obtained from a scanner software.

Such complex analysis usually consists of the four main steps: data normalization, identification of the differentially expressed genes, application of the algorithms grouping together genes with similar expression patterns and interpretation of the biological functions of the genes co-expressed together.

Data normalization involves methods for reducing effect of the systematic errors. Differentially expressed genes are identified by applying statistical tests. Unsupervised methods organize genes expression into separate sets (clusters) that co-expressed together, thus the groups obtained are expected to include genes involved into similar biological processes.

One of the most important tasks is the interpretation of the obtained clusters - genes that form the clusters need to be confronted with existing biological knowledge on its classes and functions. The knowledge of genes and their functions included in the analysis supports extracting biological knowledge from the performed experiments. This aspect of data analysis is often done by an expert in the field of the experimental design, frequently manually, what is time consuming for large data sets.
However, the expert work may be supported by specialized systems designed for storing, organizing and extracting the relevant information and the new algorithms incorporating the existing knowledge about genes. These methods, including knowledge discovery, artificial intelligence and automatic reasoning appeared to be very useful and efficient on the field of analyses of specific biological data.

2. Gene Ontology analysis

One of the most popular and widely used sources of information about biological processes and genes involved in these processes is the Gene Ontology database (Ashburner et al., 2002). Gene Ontology consortium provides structured and controlled vocabulary that is used to describe genes and their products independently of the species. The GO database is organized into three disjoint directed-acyclic graphs (DAGs) describing biological process (BP), molecular function (MF) and cellular component (CC). Each node of the graph is called a GO term, and it is a single unit that describes some known biological process or function of the gene. The dependences between GO terms are hierarchical and as the DAG is traversed from the root into its leafs, the terms are inspected from the general ones to the more specific concepts. Figure 1 presents part of the GO directed-acyclic graph structure.

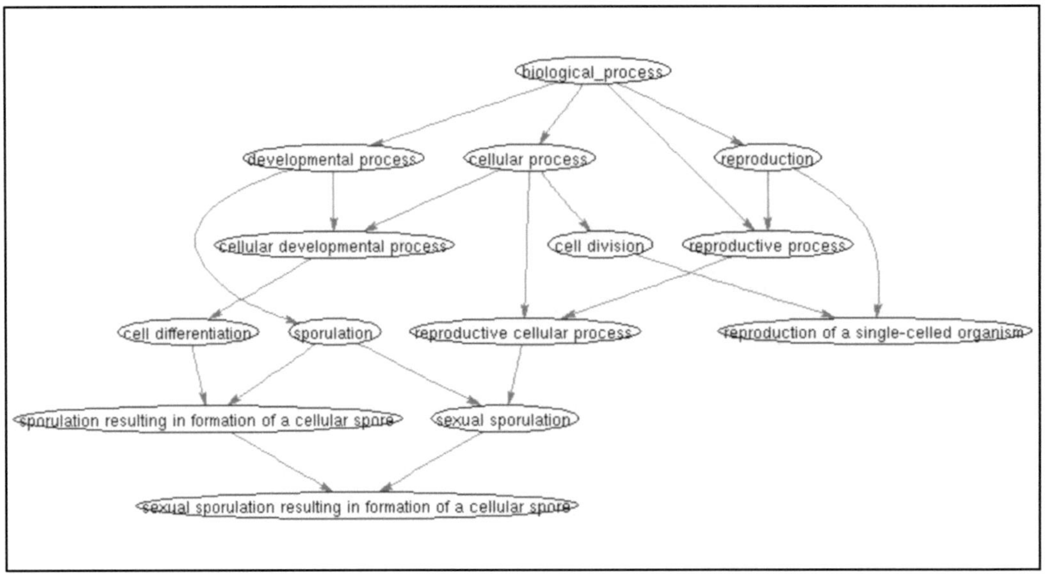

Fig. 1. Gene Ontology directed-acyclic graph structure

Standard approach to the analysis with the use of the GO terms includes performing various statistical tests to detect enrichment or depletion of the GO terms in the analyzed gene group. There is a number of GO processing tools available, based on the same idea of mapping GO terms on the genes composing the cluster and then performing a statistical test to extract over- or underrepresented GO terms in the analyzed set of genes. Thus, a Bingo (Maere et al., 2005), Cytoscape plugin, implements a hypergeometric and binominal test for the over-representation of the GO terms and then visualizes the results by means of Cytoscape network (Cline et al., 2007). Another example of the GO processing tool is a FatiGO (Al-Shahrour et al., 2005), a web-based application which allows to identify over- or underrepresented GO terms by applying Fisher's exact test and performs the analysis separately for each GO level. Most of the tools consider using multiple-testing corrections what reduces the rate of false positives occurring among significant results when testing of thousands hypothesis in the same experiment (Dudoit et al., 2003).

GO browsers such as Bingo or FatiGO usually take as an input two lists of genes: one of them represents investigated gene set, the other - rest of the genes involved in the microarray experiment. Each gene from the both lists is then annotated with the appropriate GO terms and the statistical test is applied to check for significant over or under-representation of GO terms in one of the sets with respect to another one. Thus, the final result obtained from such analysis is the list of the statistically significant GO terms that are enriched or depleted in the investigated gene set. For each term, the p-value of the statistical test corresponding to that term is recorded and by comparing the p-values of all GO terms describing genes belonging to the cluster one can have a good indication about the prominence of a given functional GO category in the gene set.

3. Related work

Knowledge based approaches were used in Gene Ontology analysis mainly for genes grouping with respect to their expression level (Eissen et al., 1998, Iyer et al., 1999) and describing groups of similar genes by means of a set of Gene Ontology terms (Brown et al. 2002; Khatri & Draghici, 2005).

The research strictly connected with Gene Ontology analysis by means of rule induction algorithms were conducted by Hvdistein (Hvidstein et al., 2003) and Midelfart (Midelfart, 2005a, Midelfart, 2005b). In the paper (Hvidstein et al., 2003) conditional rules of the form *"IF conjunction of conditions describing time series of gene expression profile THEN ontological term"* were created. The authors wanted to assign genes with specified expression profiles to a specific gene ontology term. To simplify the analysis process and get more general rules, a set of gene ontology terms was limited in such manner that only terms located on the specified ontology level were considered during the analysis. The ROSETTA (Øhrn et al., 1998) software based on rough sets methodology (Pawlak, 1991) is used for induction of rules. Conclusions of rules with the same conditional parts are joined, thus the rules describing a group of genes with similar expression profiles are obtained. In the conclusions of the rules, the set of gene ontology terms describing the group is included. The research shows that number of the obtained rules is huge and there is a need to apply a rule filtration method (Sikora, 2006) or pointing to a user so-called the most interesting rules (Agrawal & Srikant, 1994).

In the Midelfart paper a similar approach was used, except that there was not defined which terms can be located in the rule conclusions. The induction algorithm considers the fact that terms (what means also rule conclusion) are related (according to the ontology graph). Beginning from the terms lying at the lowest level of the ontology graph, the algorithm generates rules for each term. If the rules generated are recognized as good quality rules, they are added into a result set of rules, and all genes recognizing the rules are removed from the analyzed data set. If the rules describing a given ontology term are not of good quality, they are removed from the description and genes assigned to the analyzed term are moved to higher ontology level, and learning process proceeds again for a new (placed higher) term. Accuracy and generality decide about a rule quality and thresholds values of the both parameters have to be defined by a user. From the experiments performed follows that the method given by Midelfart allows obtaining better results than the method proposed by Hvdistein. Both papers verify quality of obtained results by means of a classification accuracy, that is by rightness of assignment to corresponding GO terms these genes that were not taken into consideration during the analysis. Midelfart also introduces a measure that presents how many ontology terms managed to describe (assign) genes placed in the analyzed data set.

Both of the methods presented above do not allow obtaining an information about influence of co-appearing of some ontology terms on a gene membership to a specified gene group. The methods do not consider statistical aspect of determined rules, that is they do not search whether discovered dependences are statistically significant (Rice, 1995).

None of the published papers include research on describing already defined group of similar genes by means of multiattributes logical rules. Conjunctions of ontology terms are placed in premises of rules and conclusion include a specific group of similar genes - research on one-attribute rules were conducted only (Gruca, 2008).

However, the similar research has been conducted recently by Carmona-Saez and coworkers (Carmona-Saez et al., 2007). The authors propose a method Genecodis, a web-based tool for integrated analysis of annotations from different sources. They applied the classical Apriori algorithm (Agrawal & Srikant, 1994) to discover association rules to extract a sets of annotations (so-called itemsets) that frequently co-occur in analyzed group of genes. In order to reduce the number of possible outcome combinations, and thus the computation time, the authors introduced the threshold, so-called support value, that allows discovering only such combinations of annotations that appear in at least x genes. The algorithm starts by determining a set of single annotations that satisfy the minimal support condition x. Then, combinations of annotations are created on the basis of the set of single annotations obtained in a first step of algorithm. Each combination generated must describe at least x genes. The combinations obtained are further analyzed in order to verify statistical significance of computed concurrencies.

On the basis of this method Hackenberg (Hackenberg & Matthiesen, 2008) developed another web-based application that uses various annotation databases and that allows a user to discover combinations of annotations from many different fields such as functional categories, gene regulation, sequence properties, evolution, conservation, etc.

Association rules are also considered in (Carmona-Saez et al., 2006). The method proposed in this paper combines expression data and biological information. Extracted association rules are of the following form: {*cell cycle* → *[+] condition 1, [+]condition2, [-]condition3*} which means that in the data set a significant number of genes annotated as "cell cycle" are over-

expressed in condition 1 and 2 and under-expressed in condition 3 (Carmona-Saez et al., 2006). Several measures such as support, confidence and improvement are applied to compute the significance of the rule.
In our research we assume that there are the groups of genes with similar expression profiles. The groups were obtained by expert analysis, or by means of clustering method (Eisen et al., 1998; Kustra & Zagdański, 2006). The aim of this paper is to present a method that allow to describe each of obtained group of genes with the use of gene ontology terms. The rules determined have the following meaning:

"if a gene is described by a conjunction of gene ontology terms appearing in a rule premise, then it belongs to a specific group of genes".

Covering all genes belonging to a given group we obtain a set of rules which can be interpreted as follows:

"a given group of genes is described by gene ontology terms appearing in at least one rule indicating the described group".

It is also important that the rules generated have a statistical significance level which can be determined by a user. Obtained rules also consider co-occurrence of the terms in a given gene group and the presented method guarantees that the co-occurrence will not be trivial (for example, resulting from hierarchy of the ontology graph).

4. Description of gene groups by multi-attribute logical rules

4.1 Basic notions

Let there be a set of genes G and a set of descriptions of genes and gene products A. There is a hierarchical relationship among elements from the set A in a form of directed-acyclic graph (DAG) (Fig.1). This graph is interpreted as a database, called Gene Ontology. Each element of the Gene Ontology database is called GO term which is represented by a name and a unique 7-digits identifier. There are three main ontologies describing genes and gene products from three independent biological domains: biological process, molecular function and cellular component. Each of them is represented as a separate DAG. The root of each graph is also the name of the biological domain that is described by that ontology.
Formally, Gene Ontology is a directed acyclic graph GO=$(A,\leq)$, where A is a set of GO terms describing genes and its products and $\leq$ is a binary relation on A such that genes described by GO term a_j are a subset of genes described by GO term a_i, denoted $a_j \leq a_i$, if and only if there exist a path $(a_i,a_{i+1},\ldots,a_{j-1},a_j)$ such that $a_m \leq a_{m-1}$ for $m=i+1,i+2,\ldots,j-1,j$ (we can find here an analogy to the inverse Hasse diagram for ordering relations). Relation $\leq$ is the order relation (reflexive, antisymmetric and transitive). The root of the DAG is the largest element and we assume that the root is on a level zero in the ontology. Each level of the graph is defined in the following way: the i-th level of the graph is formed by all GO terms $a \in A$ for which a path exists $(root,a_1,\ldots,a_{i-1},a_i)$ such that: $a_1 \leq root$, $a_m \leq a_{m-1}$ for m=2,3,...,i-1 and $a_i \leq a_{i-1}$ (in other words there exists a path of length i from the root to that GO term). The hierarchical structure of the ontology database allows representing biological knowledge on the multiple levels of details. Terms at the higher levels (closer to the root) describe more general

function or process while terms at the lower levels are more specific. Each node from the DAG is represented by a single GO term from the set A. These terms are further applied in the annotations of genes or gene products in the biological databases. Each annotation is an association between gene and the GO term describing it, thus for a simplification, we can assume that each node of the Gene Ontology is also annotated by the genes from the set G. A gene can be annotated to zero or more nodes for each ontology, at any level within each ontology. All GO terms that exist in the DAG must follow the true path rule: "the pathway from a child term all the way up to its top-level parent(s) must always be true". The consequence of such approach is that annotating gene to a GO term implies annotation to all parents via any path.
It stems from the definition of the Gene Ontology and from the interpretation of the relation $\leq$ that each gene annotated with GO term $a_j \in A$ is also annotated with a GO term $a_i \in A$ such that $a_j \leq a_i$. The relation $\leq$ is transitive, so if we take into consideration the hierarchical structure of the DAG we may assume that each gene annotated with the particular GO term (that was assigned to that gene by a curator from Gene Ontology consortium), is also annotated with the GO terms that are parents of that particular term. In the other words – the higher is the level of a GO term, the more genes are annotated to that term. Assuming that G_a is a set of genes annotated with the GO term corresponding to the node a, for each node a_i such that $a \leq a_i$, $Ga \subseteq Ga_i$ is satisfied.
To preserve the clarity of the ontology, the annotation files that are available at the Gene Ontology consortium website include only "original" annotations, that is annotations that were assigned to the particular GO terms by a curator. The annotations resulting from the "true path rule" (annotation of that gene to all parent nodes of that term) are not included in the annotation files. In our analysis we consider a graph that is constructed as described above. To increase the number of genes annotated to each node (GO term) of the graph, we assign to each node not only the genes that were directly extracted from the Gene Ontology annotation database but also the genes that are annotated to all descendant terms of that node. We call such a graph GO-Inc (similar approach called inclusive analysis is introduced in GO browser FatiGO).
To summarize, there are given: a set G of genes, a set A of GO terms that create GO-Inc ontology graph and n gene groups with similar expression profiles $\{G(1),G(2),...,G(n)\}$. It is possible to create a decision table $\boldsymbol{DT}=(G,A\cup\{d\})$, where for all $a \in A$, $a:G \rightarrow \{0,1\}$, and $d(g) \in \{G(1),G(2),...,G(n)\}$ for all $g \in G$. Thus, rows in the table $\boldsymbol{DT}$ contain descriptions of the single genes belonging to the set G created by means of GO terms from A. The notation $a(g)=1$ denotes that the gene g is assigned to the term a in the GO-Inc graph. Beside description by the terms from A, each gene is also characterized by a membership to specific group of similar genes (value $d(g)$). In the table $\boldsymbol{DT}$ we try to find all statistically significant relationships in the rules of the form (1)

$$\textbf{IF } a_{i1}=1 \text{ and } a_{i2}=1 \text{ and } \ldots \text{ and } a_{ik}=1 \textbf{ THEN } d=\mathrm{G}(l) \qquad (1)$$

or in the shortened notation:

$$\textbf{IF } a_{i1} \text{ and } a_{i2} \text{ and } \ldots \text{ and } a_{ik} \textbf{ THEN } d=\mathrm{G}(l) \qquad (2)$$

where: $\{a_{i1},a_{i2},...,a_{ik}\} \subseteq A$, $G(l) \in \{G(1),G(2),...,G(n)\}$.

A rule of the form (2) should be interpreted as follows:

IF a gene is described simultaneously by the terms occurring in a premise of the rule THEN it belongs to the gene group G(l)

The above form of the rule representation denotes that descriptors $a_{i1}=0$ are not in our interest now, that is we do not describe gene group by means of the statements "GO term *a* does not describe a given gene group".

A set of rules with identical conclusions we denote by $RUL_{G(l)}$ and call the description of the gene group $G(l)$.

4.2 Rules quality measures

Rules of the form (2) are the special case of so-called decision rules, and several measures that reflect quality of a decision rule can be connected with the rule. These measures are called the rule quality measures and their main purpose is a rule evaluation and/or such steering of induction and/or reduction processes that there are rules of the best quality in the output rule set. Values of most known rule quality measures (An & Cercone, 2001; Sikora, 2006) can be determined based on the analysis of a contingency table, that allows describing rules behavior with relation to the decision table ***DT***.

A set of genes which are described by the terms occurring in a premise of a rule *r* of the form (2) we denote by match(*r*). A set of genes characterized by the terms occurring in the premise of *r* and belonging to a group indicated by the rule conclusion we denote by supp(*r*). If the rule *r* is shortly written as $\varphi\rightarrow\psi$, then the contingency table of the rule has the following form:

$n_{\varphi\psi}$	$n_{\varphi\neg\psi}$	n_{φ}
$n_{\neg\varphi\psi}$	$n_{\neg\varphi\neg\psi}$	$n_{\neg\varphi}$
n_{ψ}	$n_{\neg\psi}$	n

Table 1. Contingency table of the rule $r\equiv\varphi\rightarrow\psi$

In Table 1, $n_{\varphi}= n_{\varphi\psi}+ n_{\varphi\neg\psi}=|G_{\varphi}|$ is the number of genes that recognize the rule $\varphi\rightarrow\psi$; $n_{\neg\varphi}= n_{\neg\varphi\psi}+ n_{\neg\varphi\neg\psi}=|G_{\neg\varphi}|$ is the number of genes that do not recognize the rule $\varphi\rightarrow\psi$; $n_{\psi}= n_{\varphi\psi}+ n_{\neg\varphi\psi}=|G_{\psi}|$ is the number of genes that belong to the gene group described by the rule $\varphi\rightarrow\psi$; $n_{\neg\psi}= n_{\varphi\neg\psi}+ n_{\neg\varphi\neg\psi}=|G_{\neg\psi}|$ is the number of genes that do not belong to the gene group described by the rule $\varphi\rightarrow\psi$; $n_{\varphi\psi}=|G_{\varphi}\cap G_{\psi}|$ is the number of genes that support the rule $\varphi\rightarrow\psi$; $n_{\varphi\neg\psi}=|G_{\varphi}\cap G_{\neg\psi}|$; $n_{\neg\varphi\psi}=|G_{\neg\varphi}\cap G_{\psi}|$; $n_{\neg\varphi\neg\psi}=|G_{\neg\varphi}\cap G_{\neg\psi}|$.

Using the information included in the contingency table and the fact that for a known rule $\varphi\rightarrow\psi$, there are known the values $|G_{\psi}|$ and $|G_{\neg\psi}|$, it is possible to determine the values of quality measures based on the values $n_{\varphi\psi}$ and $n_{\varphi\neg\psi}$. It can be also noticed that for any rule $\varphi\rightarrow\psi$ the inequalities $1\le n_{\varphi\psi}\le|G_{\psi}|$, $0\le n_{\varphi\neg\psi}\le|G_{\neg\psi}|$ hold. Hence, the quality measure is the function of two variables $q(\varphi\rightarrow\psi):\{1,\ldots,|G_{\psi}|\}\times\{0,\ldots,|G_{\neg\psi}|\}\rightarrow\mathbf{R}$.

Two basic quality measures are accuracy (3) and coverage (4) of a rule. Both the measures considered at the same time provide complete objective (referring to ***DT***) evaluation of the rule quality, since according to the principle of induction by enumeration it is known that the rules with a good accuracy and coverage reflect real dependences. The dependences are true also for the objects from outside of the analyzed dataset. It is easy to prove that along with accuracy increasing, rule coverage decreases. Therefore, attempts are performed to define objective quality measures that respect accuracy and coverage of a rule simultaneously (Bruha, 1997; An & Cercone, 2001; Furnkranz & Flach, 2005 ; Sikora, 2006). In the researches quoted some evaluation measures achieved the good results both in a classification accuracy (generalization ability) and a size of classifiers (description ability).

$$\mathrm{acc}(r)=\frac{n_{\varphi\psi}}{n_{\varphi}} \tag{3}$$

$$\mathrm{cov}(r)=\frac{n_{\varphi\psi}}{n_{\psi}} \tag{4}$$

In our research, a rule quality measure is used in filtration process in order to limit a number of determined rules. We applied a modified version of the WS (5) measure proposed by Michalski (Michalski, 1983).

$$\mathrm{WS}(r)=w_1\mathrm{acc}(r)+w_2\mathrm{cov}(r) \tag{5}$$

In a rule induction system YAILS values of parameters w_1, w_2 for the rule r are calculated as follows: w_1=0.5+0.25acc(r), w_2=0.5-0.25acc(r). The WS measure is monotone with respect to each variable $n_{\varphi\psi}$ and $n_{\varphi\neg\psi}$, and assumes values from the interval [0,1] (Fig.2).

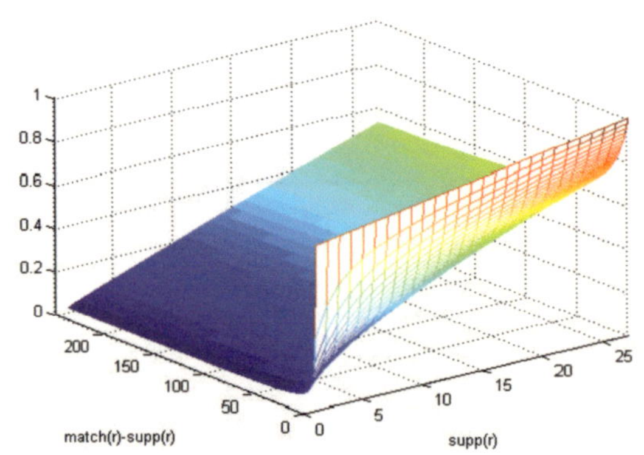

Fig. 2. Graph of WS-Yails measure for the rule $\varphi\to\psi$ depending on $n_{\varphi\psi}\equiv\mathrm{supp}(\varphi\to\psi)$ and $n_{\varphi\neg\psi}\equiv\mathrm{match}(\varphi\to\psi)-\mathrm{supp}(\varphi\to\psi)$. A number of genes described by the rule is n_{ψ}=25, and a number of remaining genes is $n_{\neg\psi}$=250.

We assume, that the rules determined of the form (2), have to be statistically significant rules, with a significance level better then or equal to a level established by a user. To evaluate a statistical significance of created rules we use a hypergeometric test (6). It can be easily noticed that a p-value for the rule r of the form (2) can be determined on the basis of the contingency table (Table 1) and computed using the formula (7). P-values obtained for fixed n_{ψ} and $n_{\neg\psi}$ are presented on a graph in Fig.3. To verify the statistical significance of the rules induced, we also compute false discovery rate (FDR) coefficient (Benjamini & Hochberg, 1995)

$$p(n_{\varphi\psi}, n_{\varphi\neg\psi}, n_{\neg\varphi\psi}, n_{\neg\varphi\neg\psi}) = \frac{\binom{n_{\varphi}}{n_{\varphi\psi}}\binom{n_{\neg\varphi}}{n_{\varphi\neg\psi}}}{\binom{n}{n_{\psi}}} \tag{6}$$

$$p_{val}(n_{\varphi\psi}, n_{\varphi\neg\psi}, n_{\neg\varphi\psi}, n_{\neg\varphi\neg\psi}) = \sum_{k=0}^{n_{\varphi\neg\psi}} p(n_{\varphi\psi}+k, n_{\varphi\neg\psi}-k, n_{\neg\varphi\psi}, n_{\neg\varphi\neg\psi}) \tag{7}$$

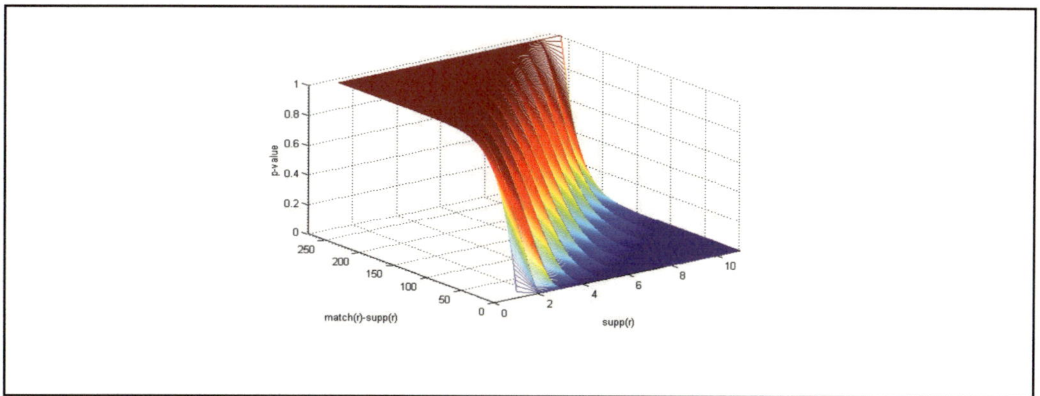

Fig. 3. Graph of p-values depending on $n_{\varphi\psi}$≡supp($\varphi\rightarrow\psi$) and $n_{\varphi\neg\psi}$≡match($\varphi\rightarrow\psi$)-supp($\varphi\rightarrow\psi$). A number of genes described by the rule is n_{ψ}=10, a number of remaining genes is $n_{\neg\psi}$=250.

4.3 Rules induction

Induction of decision rules can be classification or discovery oriented. The purpose of classification-oriented induction is to find, on the basis of the set of learning examples, a set of decision rules that will be used to classify new unknown examples (Michalski et al., 1998; Mitchell, 1997). The purpose of discovery-oriented induction is to discover patterns and regularities (in the form of IF THEN rules) in data which are interesting and useful to different kinds of users. A set of classification rules often contains only a limited part of all possible rules that could be induced from that set. Majority of the classification-oriented algorithms follow the same general scheme using a greedy heuristic strategy. This scheme consists of creating a first rule by choosing sequentially the 'best' elementary conditions according to some quality criteria. Then, learning examples that match this rule are removed from the set considered. The process is repeated iteratively until all the examples are covered by the result rule set. An alternative approach, better from the knowledge discovery point of view, is the induction of all the rules that satisfy some requirements. This approach is implemented among others in the association rules induction algorithm Apriori (Agrawal & Srikant, 1994), and the decision rules induction algorithm Explore (Stefanowski & Vanderpooten, 2001). Another possibility is to induce all rules and then filter them to find the most interesting ones (Klemettinen, 1994; Sikora, 2009).

We generate the rules with p-values less or equal to a threshold established by a user. Therefore to describe given gene group, we must determine all possible combinations of all possible subsets of GO terms. Since we are interested in the premises with descriptors assuming value one (see rule definition (2)), in a pessimistic case we have to determine $\sum_{k=1}^{|A|}\binom{|A|}{k}=2^{|A|}-1$ rules, what is impossible in the case of a big number of considered GO terms. We can model on the heuristic algorithm Apriori used for association rules searching during rules determining. In contrast to association rules, in our case a rule conclusion is already established. Therefore, Explore algorithm proposed by Stefanowski is more suitable for our aims. Using Explore algorithm we can generate all possible conjunctions of GO terms for each gene group. To limit a number of analyzed combinations, a user can provide minimal requirements concerning the quality of determined rules (for example, minimal rule coverage, minimal rule accuracy). In the method proposed, we generate only satistically significant conjunctions of GO terms.

In the standard version of Explore algorithm, rule induction starts from one-condition rules and then next conditions are iteratively added to each rule. After adding a next condition, a created rule is verified whether it satisfies quality criteria defined by a user. If it does, then the rule is added to a result rule set. If it does not, then the algorithm checks whether the created (temporary) rule may satisfy quality criteria introduced by the user (for example, whether the rule of the current form covers enough quantity of objects - minimal coverage requirements). A premise of the temporal rule that has a chance of satisfying minimal requirements of quality is widen by the next conditions, other temporal rules are not widen and are removed. A detailed description of the algorithm can be found in (Stefanowski & Vanderpooten, 2001).

For our purposes, Explore algorithm was put to a few modifications. Searching space of potential candidates for rules is made by means of a procedure that is iteratively repeated for each gene group. The main part of the algorithm generates premises with increasing size, beginning from premises containing one GO term. When a rule created in this way satisfies a p-value criterion established by a user, it is added to the generated rule set and conjunction is widen (assuming that other statistically significant rules can be determined from the conjunction). Motivation of such solution is that more information may be obtained from the statistically significant rule (8) than also significant, but shorter rule (9).

IF primary metabolic process **and**
membrane-bounded organelle **and**
proteasome storage granule **and**
threonine-type endopeptidase activity **and**
proteasome core complex (8)
THEN gene group 2
supp(*r*)=9, match(*r*)=9,
acc(*r*)=1, cov(*r*)=0.33, pVal(*r*)=2.231392e-010

IF primary metabolic process **and**
membrane-bounded organelle
THEN gene group 2 (9)
supp(*r*)=19, match(*r*)=114,
acc(*r*)=0.166, cov(*r*)=0.703, pVal(*r*)=0.00147

If for a given premise all GO terms were already considered, then a new GO term is selected (not chosen yet) and a new rule creation begins.
In order to narrow the searching space the following solutions were applied:

- After adding a GO term a to a rule premise, no terms lying on any path (from ontology leaf to the root) that leads to the term a are considered. Let us notice that for any term $b \in A$ for which $b \leq a$, the conjunction $b \wedge a$ reduces to a, since b lies on lower level than a, so $G_b \subseteq G_a$. Similarly, for $c \in A$ for which $a \leq c$, the conjunction $a \wedge c$ reduces to c, since c lies on a higher level. There is no point to consider the conjunction $a \wedge c$ because the descriptor c will be considered by the algorithm separately. The same reasoning can be presented for a conjunction composed of bigger number of terms to which a new GO term is added.
- If a rule with the premise $a_1 \wedge a_2 \wedge \ldots \wedge a_j$ was added to the result set of rules, then rules with premises being permutations of $\{a_1, a_2, \ldots, a_j\}$ will be no longer considered. The algorithm starts creation of a rule premise by selecting the terms that describe the most genes in the analyzed gene group.
- Assuming that the currently created rule has the form $\varphi \to \psi$, the GO term a will be added to its premise forming the rule $\varphi \wedge a \to \psi$, if $\mathrm{acc}(\varphi \to \psi) \leq \mathrm{acc}(\varphi \wedge a \to \psi)$. The condition limits a number of analyzed combinations by rejecting the terms that do not contribute to improving a rule accuracy, thus improving statistical significance of the rule as well.

The algorithm starts with a parameter characterizing maximal number of terms in the rule premises. However, a number of rules determined in this way is still very large. Therefore, a method of rules evaluation and filtration is required.

4.4 Rules evaluation and filtration

Statistical significance of a rule is the first criterion of its evaluation. A graph of p-value depending on a number of objects recognizing and supporting the rule is presented on the Fig. 3. From the graph follows that evaluating statistical significance only may lead in some cases to prefer hardly accurate rules. A rule describing one of gene group from the YEAST set (Eisen et al., 1998) is such example (10):

IF cellular metabolic process **and**
macromolecule metabolic process
THEN gene group 2 (10)
acc(r)=0.116,cov(r)=1, pVal=0.0077, FDR(r)=0.00872

The group consists of 27 genes, and there are 274 genes in the analyzed set. The presented rule covers the whole group, and recognizes 231 genes. Thus it is very inaccurate one. The rule is low-quality rule, however, significance level of the rule is good. This follows from the fact that the rule concentrates probability of selecting genes from the group described by the rule with relation to whole data set. The presented example shows that we need other rule quality evaluation criteria in order to select the best rules from the analyzed set of rules. Thus, the next criterion evaluating rule quality is a modified measure WS (11):

$$\mathrm{mWS}(r)=[0.5+0.25\,\mathrm{acc}(r)]\mathrm{acc}(r)+[0.5-0.25\,\mathrm{cov}(r)]\mathrm{cov}(r) \qquad (11)$$

It can be easily noticed that the measure mWS differs from the measure applied in the system YAILS (5) by a manner of calculation a value of the parameter w_2. In the modification presented in the formula (11) the rule coverage was used for establishing the value of the parameter w_2 unlike the rule accuracy used for the measure (5). The change is justified by the fact that for general, inaccurate rules the modified version of WS (11) assumes less values than original WS measure. Differences in rule evaluation between measures (5) and (11) can be clearly seen by comparing graphs of the both measures (Fig. 4).

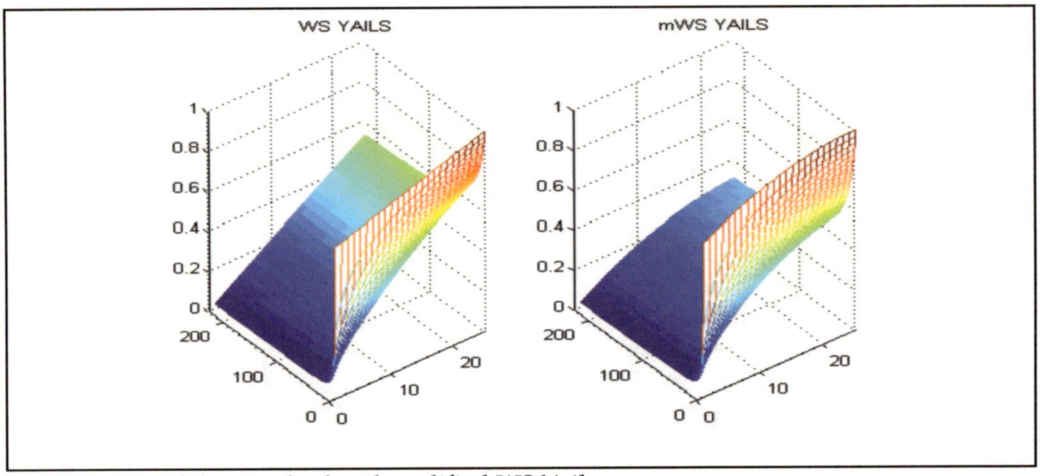

Fig. 4. Graphs of the standard and modified WS Yails measure

Another criterion of a rule quality evaluation is a number of GO terms included in a rule premise (12). We assume that the bigger number of terms is in the rule premise, the more information is represented by rule (we remind that terms occurring in a premise do not lie on a common path in ontology graph).

$$\text{length}(r) = \frac{\text{NoGOterms}(r)}{\text{MaxGOterms}} \tag{12}$$

where NoGOterms(r) is the number of GO terms in the r rule premise, MaxGOterms is the maximal number of descriptors in the longest rule that describes the same gene group as the rule r.

The last rule quality evaluation criterion is the level of GO terms occurring in the rule premise (13). From a description point of view we should prefer rules with premises including terms from as low level of the GO graph as possible.

$$\text{depth}(r) = \frac{\sum_{i=1}^{\text{NoGOterms}(r)} \text{level}(a_i)}{\sum_{i=1}^{\text{NoGOterms}(r)} \text{max\_path}(a_i)} \tag{13}$$

where: level(a_i) is the level of GO term a_i that occurs in the rule premise, max_path(a_i) is the longest path leading form the root to leaf of GO-Inc that pass trough the node a_i.

Finally, a measure that incorporates all aspects of rule quality evaluation presented above, is a product of all component measures (14):

$$Q(r)=\text{mWS}(r)\times\text{length}(r)\times\text{depth}(r) \quad (14)$$

The measure Q is monotone with respect to each component of the product, i.e. when values of any two factors are fixed, the measure value is non-decreasing function with respect to the third factor. This feature fulfills assumptions of quality measures that were given by Piatetsky-Shapiro (Piatetsky-Shapiro, 1991).
The compound quality measure Q allows creating a ranking of rules describing each gene group. Below we present a filtration algorithm that uses obtained rules ranking:

Rules filtration algorithm
Input: G – a genes set, RUL_G a set of rules describing the gene group G.
Output: RUL_G^F – filtered rule set covering the same objects from the set G as the set RUL_G.

```
Begin
  RUL_G^F:=∅;
  Create a ranking RANK_RUL of rules from the set RUL_G according to decreasing value of
  an evaluation measure Q;
  While RANK_RUL≠∅ or G=∅ do
    Begin
      Take a first rule r from the set RANK_RUL;
      RANK_RUL:= RANK_RUL - {r};
      RUL_G^F := RUL_G^F ∪{r};
      For all rr∈RANK_RUL do
        Begin
          If supp(rr)⊆supp(r) then
            Begin
              If sim(rr,r)≤ε then RUL_G^F:= RUL_G^F∪{rr};
              RANK_RUL:=RANK_RUL-{rr}
            End if
      End for
      Renumber the set RANK_RUL taking into account removed rules;
      G:=G-supp(r);
    End while
End
```

The presented filtration algorithm creates a coverage of the set G (or part of the set G which is covered by rules from the set RUL_G) beginning from the best rules with respect to the value of measure Q. If the rule rr covers the same objects as currently the best rule r, but contains other biological knowledge, then rule rr is not removed but remains in the result set of rules. It is worth to notice that the filtration algorithm defined in such way does not guarantee that filtered rule set RUL_G^F includes only dissimilar rules containing different biological knowledge. If we assume that there are three initial rules in the ranking $r1,r2,r3$ such as: $\text{supp}(r3)\subseteq\text{supp}(r1)$, $\text{supp}(r2)\subseteq\text{supp}(r1)$ and $\text{sim}(r1,r3)\leq\varepsilon$, $\text{sim}(r1,r2)\leq\varepsilon$, then the rules

$r2,r3$ will be included in the result data set. Meanwhile, it may appear that sim($r2,r3$)>ε which means that rules $r2,r3$ include similar biological knowledge. However, the presented filtration algorithm do not remove neither the rule $r2$ nor $r3$. Therefore, after the first part of the filtration, the second part consist in verification of rules similarity in pairs. If rules are similar, then a rule covering more objects always remains in the filtered rules set.
The similarity of rules is determined by the formula (15). If a rule is similar to the reference rule to degree greater than 50% (ε=0.5), then it is finally removed from the set of determined rules, otherwise it remains in an output rule set.

$$\text{sim}(r_i, r_j)=\frac{\text{uGOterms}(r_i,r_j)+\text{uGOterms}(r_j,r_i)}{\text{NoGOterms}(r_i)+\text{NoGOterms}(r_j)} \tag{15}$$

where: uGOterms(r_i,r_j) is a number of unique GO terms occurring in the rule r_i and not occurring in the rule r_j; the GO term a from the rule r_i is unique if it does not occur directly in the rule r_j and there is no path in GO-Inc graph that includes both term a and any term b from rule r_j premise; NoGOterms(r) is the number of GO terms in the rule r premise.

4.5 Evaluation of significance of GO terms appearing in induced rules

Based on induced rule set we can also determine which of GO terms occurring in rule premises are characterized by the highest significance. A statistical significance is not the thing here but a significance (influence) of a given GO term for a quality of rule that include this term. A problem of evaluation a significance of conditions appearing in rules premises was considered in (Greco et al., 2007) where the authors applied indexes used in games theory for evaluation a quality of coalition. In conducted researches, the Banzhaf index (Banzhaf, 1965) and the modified version of the approach presented in (Greco et al., 2007) were applied to evaluate a significance of GO terms occurring in rules premises.
Let be given a rule r of the form (2). A set of GO terms occurring in the rule premise we denote by W, that is $W=\{t_1,t_2,\ldots,t_n\}$. In the standard form presented in (Greco et al., 2007), the Banzhaf measure that evaluates contribution of elementary condition (a single GO term t_i here) to the rule r accuracy is calculated according to the following formula (16):

$$\phi_B(t_i, r)=\frac{1}{2^{n-1}}\sum_{Y\subseteq W-\{t_i\}}\left[\text{acc}(Y\cup\{t_i\},r)-\text{acc}(Y,r)\right] \tag{16}$$

where acc(Y,r) denotes the accuracy of r in premise part of which only GO terms included in the set Y occur; acc($\emptyset,r$)=0; acc(W,r)=acc(r).

To evaluate a quality (significance) of a GO term in whole set of rules that create a description of analyzed gene group, it is necessary to compute its significance in each rule from the description (in each rule that include a considered GO term) and verify whether, by any chance, the GO term occurs also in rules from other gene groups descriptions. We can represent above requirements as a formula which allows evaluating GO term significance for the description of a given gene group (17):

$$G(t_i, RUL_G) = \sum_{r \in RUL_G} \phi_B(t_i, r)\mathrm{cov}(r) - \sum_{r \notin RUL_G} \phi_B(t_i, r)\mathrm{cov}(r) \quad (17)$$

where cov(r) is the coverage (4) of the rule r, and RUL_G is the set of rules that create the description of the gene group G.

In described method of GO terms significance evaluation, contribution of each term to a rule accuracy is evaluated, while its contribution to the rule coverage is not evaluated (the coverage is considered for the whole rule only). For the purpose of a significance evaluation of GO terms describing a gene group it would be better to evaluate contribution of analyzed GO term to both accuracy and coverage. Such evaluation can be obtained by using mWS measure in formula (11) instead of the accuracy. Using mWS measure in the formula allows considering the contribution of the GO term to accuracy and coverage of all 'subrules' which can be created from the rule r. Finally, to evaluate a significance of the GO terms occurring in rule premises, a modified measure ϕ_B was applied:

$$\phi_B(t_i, r, \mathrm{mWS}) = \frac{1}{2^{n-1}} \sum_{Y \subseteq W - \{t_i\}} [\mathrm{mWS}(Y \cup \{t_i\}, r) - \mathrm{mWS}(Y, r)] \quad (18)$$

where: mWS(Y,r) denotes a value of the mWS measure determined for the rule r, in premise part of which only GO terms included in the Y occur; mWS($\varnothing$,r)=0; mWS(W,r)=mWS(r).

As a consequence of the introduced modification, the measure G that evaluates quality (significance) of a GO term in whole set of rules describing analyzed gene group (19) was also modified:

$$G(t_i, RUL_G, \mathrm{mWS}) = \sum_{r \in RUL_G} \phi_B(t_i, r, mWS(r)) - \sum_{r \notin RUL_G} \phi_B(t_i, r, mWS(r)) \quad (19)$$

Instead of mWS measure any rule quality evaluation measure can be substituted.

It is worth to mention that acc(Y, r) is monotonic measure which means that if $Y \subseteq X \subseteq W$, then acc($Y$,$r$)≤acc($X$,$r$). It can be easily proved that, at the worst case, adding next conjunction may not improve the rule accuracy. Moreover, it is also easy to prove that mWS measure is not monotonic, because removing the condition from the premise, though can decrease accuracy of the rule, may also increase the rule coverage which can finally increase a value of mWS measure. A consequence of the reasoning is the fact that a value of the measure (18) may be negative (then (18) is the function but not the measure), while a value of the measure (16) is always nonnegative. The negative value of (18) means that 'subrules' have, at the average, better quality without the GO term t_i than 'subrules' with the term, since in such case the term t_i should be considered as unimportant (causing noises). The presented property of the measure (18) is consistent with the idea of significant descriptor, therefore lack of monotonicity is not a problem in our case.

5. Data analysis

5.1 Data description

Experiments were conducted on two freely available data sets: YEAST and HUMAN. The data set YEAST contains values of expression levels of budding yeast *Saccharomyces cerevisiae* measured in several DNA microarray experiments (Eisen et al., 1998). Our analysis were performed on 274 genes from 10 top clusters presented in the paper (Eisen et al., 1998). The data set HUMAN contains values of expression levels of human fibroblasts in response to serum (Iyer et al., 1999). In the paper (Iyer et al., 1999), 517 EST sequences were reported and divided into 10 clusters. After translation of the sequences for unique gene names and removal sequences that are duplicated or that are currently considered to be invalid, we obtained set of 368 genes. Then, each gene from YEAST and HUMAN data sets were described by GO terms from biological process ontology (BP) and from all three types of ontologies (ALL).

There were some genes in the HUMAN data set that had no GO terms assigned, thus we removed them from further analysis. After that step we obtained set consisting of 319 objects for BP ontology and 364 for all three types of ontology. To induce decision rules we created decision tables on the basis of the GO-Inc graphs for BP, CC and MF ontology. We used GO terms from at least second ontology level and describing at least three (for HUMAN data set, genes described by all three types of ontologies) or five genes from our data sets (for other data sets).

After removing from gene description GO terms that did not fulfilled the above conditions we finally obtained four decision tables. Number of genes and GO terms for each decision table are presented in Table 2.

Decision table	Number of genes	Number of GO terms
YEAST BP	274	249
YEAST ALL	274	418
HUMAN BP	310	625
HUMAN ALL	364	588

Table 2. Number of genes and GO terms obtained for each decision table.

5.2 Results of analysis

For each decision table we computed decision rules using the following criteria for Explore algorithm:

- statistical significance of the rules: 0.01,
- maximal number of descriptors in premise of the rule: 5.

The results of the analysis: number of the rules obtained (before and after filtration) and the coverage for each gene group are presented in Table 3 (for YEAST data set) and in Table 4 (for HUMAN data set).

Gene group	Decision table	Coverage	No of rules before filtration	No of rules after filtration
1	BP	100%	377	6
	ALL	100%	9625	25
2	BP	100%	1447	4
	ALL	100%	50356	14
3	BP	93%	4308	12
	ALL	100%	31708	20
4	BP	100%	43083	22
	ALL	100%	254289	50
5	BP	41%	307	4
	ALL	100%	13457	13
6	BP	93%	20225	11
	ALL	100%	4982663	25
7	BP	100%	6645	12
	ALL	100%	61361	18
8	BP	100%	3842	12
	ALL	100%	76963	18
9	BP	100%	54426	12
	ALL	100%	737049	31
10	BP	94%	810	8
	ALL	94%	124486	19

Table 3. Number of decision rules and coverage obtained for YEAST data set.

Gene group	Decision table	Coverage	No of rules before filtration	No of rules after filtration
1	BP	27%	6	6
	ALL	58%	1547	23
2	BP	53%	1204	15
	ALL	67%	16344	38
3	BP	44%	5030	11
	ALL	71%	3639	20
4	BP	88%	3937	26
	ALL	91%	87610	70
5	BP	80%	7134	8
	ALL	100%	68714	23
6	BP	90%	58263	42
	ALL	62%	84759	75
7	BP	46%	11763	8
	ALL	92%	29954	27
8	BP	26%	27	4
	ALL	37%	129	9
9	BP	43%	147	6
	ALL	86%	3875	24
10	BP	81%	16208	31
	ALL	88%	119917	48

Table 4. Number of decision rules and coverage obtained for HUMAN data set.

5.3 Interpretation of the obtained decision rules

Decision rules are generated mainly for description purposes to support drawing biological conclusions from the DNA microarray experiments. Thus, the real verification of the rule quality is its ability to provide biological interpretation of the genes composing the analyzed groups.
Below, we present two exemplary decision rules from YEAST and HUMAN data sets. We also provide their short, biological interpretation.

IF generation of precursor metabolites and energy **and**
glucose metabolic process **and**
hexose catabolic process **and**
pyruvate metabolic process **and**
hexose biosynthetic process
THEN gene group 4 (20)
acc(r)=1.0,cov(r)=0.47, pVal=3.42e-11, FDR(r)= 1.79e-10

genes supporting the rule:
TPI1,GPM1,PGK1,TDH3,TDH2,ENO2,TDH1,FBA1

The above rule was generated from YEAST data set, for gene group number 4, which was described as *glycolisys* in the original paper (Eisen et al., 1998). This rule is supported by 8 genes which encode proteins that are active in energy metabolism processes. The names of some of these processes can be obtained directly from GO terms that compose a conditional part of the rule. We also searched trough available internet databases of publications in order to find papers that include information about all of the genes supporting the rule. One of the results of our analysis is a paper (Bruckman et al., 2007) where all genes supporting the rule are mentioned and described as the genes encoding proteins active in the glucogenesis process which is part of the glycolisys.
Another exemplary interpretation of decision rule is presented for the rule from HUMAN data set and was generated for gene group number 6.

IF protein binding **and**
system development **and**
cell proliferation **and**
extracellular space **and**
transmembrane receptor protein tyrosine kinase signaling pathway
THEN gene group 6 (21)
acc(r)=1.0,cov(r)=0.16, pVal=0.3.3e-04, FDR(r)= 0.13

genes supporting the rule:
FGF2,FLT1,VEGFA

The above rule is supported by three genes which encode proteins involved in the process of angiogenesis. VEGFA is one of the most important proteins from the VEGF (vascular endothelial growth factor) sub-family of growth factors. VEGFA stimulate cellular responses by binding to tyrosine kinase receptors Flt-1 and KDF/Flk-1. A VEGFA and fibroblast growth factor 2 (FGF2), both are well-investigated pro-angiogenic molecules (Kano et al.,

2005). There are evidences that VEGFA regulates expression of FLT1 (Mata-Greenwood et al., 2003) and FGF2 (Seghezzi et al., 1998).

5.4 Comparison of our method with results from Genecodis tool

We also compared results from our analysis with the results obtained from Genecodis - an Internet service for discovering co-occurrences of the annotations in the analyzed group of genes. The rule generation method provided by the authors of Genecodis is based on the Apriori algorithm for discovering frequent itemsets of attributes that describe analyzed set of objects. To generate the rules we used the following values of algorithm parameters:

- GO level: lowest level,
- Minimum number of genes: 2.

The results of a comparison: number of the rules and coverage are presented in Table 5.

Both methods, Genecodis and Explore, are based on the similar idea of searching for frequent co-occurrences of combinations of annotations, however the process of selection of attributes differs significantly in both methods. Genecodis algorithm do not perform any initial selection of the attributes that are added to the premise of created rule - it simply generates all possible combinations of GO terms. As a result of such approach one may obtain the rules that include redundant information in their premises, i.e. GO terms that are in relation ≤ with other GO terms composing the rule. With the Explore method, rules obtained include smaller number of GO terms, but each of the term describe different biological process.

Below we present an exemplary list of descriptors form the rule obtained from the Genecodis. This rule was generated for the objects form gene group number 6, from YEAST data set for GO terms from BP ontology:

IF transport **and**
ion transport **and**
ATP synthesis coupled proton transport **and**
proton transport **and** (22)
ATP metabolic process **and**
ATP biosynthetic process **and**
THEN gene group 6

The analysis of the structure of GO graph for BP ontology, revealed that there are following relations among GO terms composing the above rule:

ATP synthesis coupled proton transport ≤ proton transport ≤ ion transport ≤ transport,
and
ATP synthesis coupled proton transport ≤ ATP biosynthetic process ≤ ATP metabolic process.

Gene group	Method of analysis	Coverage	Number of rules
1	Genecodis BP	45%	4
	Explore BP	100%	6
	Genecodis ALL	45%	2
	Explore ALL	100%	25
2	Genecodis BP	100%	6
	Explore BP	100%	4
	Genecodis ALL	100%	37
	Explore ALL	100%	14
3	Genecodis BP	0%	0
	Explore BP	93%	12
	Genecodis ALL	57%	5
	Explore ALL	100%	20
4	Genecodis BP	88%	23
	Explore BP	100%	22
	Genecodis ALL	100%	115
	Explore ALL	100%	50
5	Genecodis BP	0%	0
	Explore BP	41%	4
	Genecodis ALL	63%	10
	Explore ALL	100%	13
6	Genecodis BP	60%	3
	Explore BP	93%	11
	Genecodis ALL	93%	23
	Explore ALL	100%	25
7	Genecodis BP	100%	5
	Explore BP	100%	12
	Genecodis ALL	100%	5
	Explore ALL	100%	18
8	Genecodis BP	25%	2
	Explore BP	100%	12
	Genecodis ALL	92%	41
	Explore ALL	100%	18
9	Genecodis BP	80%	4
	Explore BP	100%	12
	Genecodis ALL	100%	8
	Explore ALL	100%	31
10	Genecodis BP	75%	12
	Explore BP	94%	8
	Genecodis ALL	81%	52
	Explore ALL	94%	19

Table 5. Comparison of the rules obtained from Genecodis and Explore

5.5 Significance of descriptors

The evaluation of rule descriptors significance was performed after filtration. Numbers of the rules and descriptors obtained for each gene group are presented in Table 6.

Gene group	Yeast		Human	
	Rules	$\sum$GO terms	Rules	$\sum$GO terms
1	6	17	6	11
2	4	12	15	20
3	12	25	11	21
4	22	31	26	40
5	4	7	8	18
6	11	11	42	63
7	12	19	8	18
8	12	22	4	8
9	12	17	6	19
10	8	12	31	56

Table 6. Number of the rules and descriptors obtained for descriptions of each gene group

Detailed results for each gene group are presented in Table 7 and Table 8, and the names of the most important and the least important GO term describing the considered group are given. Values of the significance coefficient defined by the formula (19) are also given. A ranking of the considered GO term specified by the standard method defined by formulas (16), (17) is presented in the column *Std. ranking*. Moreover, a number of descriptors describing each group are given additionally for the worst term.

As it can be noticed, there are some differences between rankings created by the standard and modified methods. We will not provide more detailed analysis of the differences as is not in the field of this paper.

The analysis of obtained results shows that establishing a ranking of GO terms that describe a given gene group provides additional knowledge about the group. Analysis of the rules and the results presented in Tables 7 and 8 leads to the conclusion that the best GO terms describing a given gene group usually occur in the best rules describing the group and do not occur in rules describing other groups (even if they occur, then they are recognized as the worst or almost the worst terms and are placed at the bottom of the other group rankings). The least significant terms usually have negative values of the coefficient (19) and are considered as the worst terms in two or more gene groups in an analyzed data set. This result is consistent with intuition and can be justified by the fact that such terms introduce a noise into gene groups description. Thus, application to the analysis some methods of postprocessing, such as rule shortening, may significantly improve the quality of obtained description. There is also interesting to verify the similarity of the groups (or at least part of genes belonging to these groups) which are described by the same, the least significant, GO terms.

Gene group	The best GO terms name (significance)	Std. ranking	The worst GO term name (significance)	Std. ranking
1	protein ubiquitination (0.78)	4	cellular macromolecule metabolic process (-0.49)	worst
2	reproductive process in single-celled organism (0.31)	5	cellular catabolic process (-0.56)	9/12
3	RNA splicing, via transesterification reactions (0.98)	2	biopolymer biosynthetic process (-1.01)	15/25
4	pyruvate metabolic process (1.53)	best	gene expression (-0.92)	worst
5	cellular respiration (1.46)	best	biopolymer biosynthetic process (-0.80)	4/7
6	purine nucleoside triphosphate biosynth. process (1.30)	best	oxidation reduction (-0.48)	worst
7	negative regulation of nucleobase, nucleoside, nucleotide and nucleic acid metabolic process (1.63)	4	regulation of macromolecule biosynthetic process (-1.04)	18/19
8	ribosomal small subunit biogenesis (0.98)	8	biopolymer biosynthetic process (-0.64)	worst
9	S phase (2.13)	best	biopolymer metabolic process (-0.53)	worst
10	respiratory electron transport chain (0.90)	best	generation of precursor metabolites and energy (-0.17)	11/12

Table 7. Results of evaluation of GO term significance for YEAST dataset

Gene group	The best GO terms name (significance)	Std. ranking	The worst GO term name (significance)	Std. ranking
1	cognition (0.93)	best	biopolymer metabolic process (-0.88)	worst
2	RNA biosynthetic process (0.76)	2	regulation of cellular process (-0.54)	18/20
3	innate immune response (0.59)	2	cellular alcohol metabolic process (-0.90)	worst
4	cell cycle checkpoint (1.64)	3	biopolymer metabolic process (-0.97)	39/40
5	cellular alcohol metabolic process (0.90)	best	regulation of cellular process (-1.19)	17/18
6	leukocyte migration (2.80)	best	response to stress (-0.93)	62/63
7	androgen receptor signaling pathway (1.85)	best	response to biotic stimulus (-0.49)	10/18
8	blood circulation (0.58)	best	regulation of cellular process (-1.10)	worst
9	lipid biosynthetic process (0.56)	best	regulation of cellular process (-1.29)	worst
10	skeletal system development (1.65)	best	regulation of cellular process (-1.19)	worst

Table 8. Results of evaluation of GO term significance for HUMAN dataset

6. Conclusions

Issues of gene groups description by means of GO terms were presented in the paper. Logical rules were used as a language of the description. Work connected with gene groups description by means of rules with various representations were presented. A novel method of induction, evaluation and filtration of logical rules describing gene groups was shown in the fundamental part of the paper. A method of significance evaluation of a single GO term occurring in the premises of the rules determined was also introduced. The presented method of rules induction, evaluation and filtration appeared to be very effective. After filtration we obtained small rule sets having average statistical significance better than for the unfiltered rule set.

The presented method of rules induction guarantees that all statistically significant rules are determined. Features that distinguish the proposed approach from other methods are: the way of evaluation and filtration of the rules and the fact that terms lying on the same path in Gene Ontology graph do not occur in the rule premises simultaneously (like, for example, in Genecodis system). Both, objective factors (accuracy and coverage) and subjective factors that express what is interesting for a user (premises composed of many GO terms assigned to the lowest possible level in the ontology graph) are involved in a rule evaluation. Additionally, the filtration allows the user to extract the most interesting information that can be derived from the huge number of rules.

The algorithms presented may be a useful tool that helps biologists to understand and interpret the DNA microarray experiment results. Results of the experiments presented show that the proposed method of rules induction and postprocessing is useful. In particular, the method enables to discover automatically the dependences which were found during the researches published by biologists (Bruckman et al., 2007; Mata-Greenwood et al., 2003, Kano et al., 2005; Seghezzi et al., 1998)

The algorithms described in the paper are available for the users through RuleGO Internet service (http://rulego.polsl.pl) (Gruca et al., 2009). The service is continuously and intensively developed. In particular, research on developing algorithms that enable rules induction in much faster way are conducted. Explore algorithm allows obtaining all statistically significant rules but, depending on the data set, calculation time may vary from several minutes to several hours, even after introducing modifications described above. Long calculation time should be regarded as the disadvantage of the presented method, thus users submitting the computational task to RuleGO service are notified by an email when their calculations are finished.

Future research will concentrate on determining the rules including descriptors referencing GO terms which does not describe the analyzed genes. In such case we will be interested in occurrence of this type of descriptors on the highest possible level of the ontology. The appropriately modified version of heuristics rules induction algorithm LEM (Grzymała-Busse & Ziarko, 2003) will be implemented in order to improve the algorithm performance.

7. References

Agrawal, R. & Srikant, R. (1994). Fast Algorithms for Mining Association Rules. Proc. of the 20th VLDB Conference, Santiago, Chile.

Al-Shahrour, F.; Minguez, P.; Vaquerizas, J.M.; Conde, L. & Dopazo, J. (2005). BABELOMICS: A Suite of Web Tools for Functional Annotation and Analysis of Groups of Genes in High-Throughput Experiments. *Nucleic Acid Research*, 33, W460–W464.

An, A. & Cercone, N. (2001). Rule quality measures for rule induction systems: Description and evaluation. Computational Intelligence, 17(3).

Ashburner, M.; Ball, C.A.; Blake, J.A.; Botstein, D.; Butler, H.; Cherry, J.M. et al. (2005). Gene Ontology: Tool for the Unification of Biology. The Gene Ontology Consortium. *Nature genetics*, 25, 25–9.

Baldi, P. & Hatfield G.W. (2002). *DNA Microarrays and Gene Expression*. Cambridge University Press, Cambridge.

Banzhaf, J. F. (1965). Weighted voting doesn`t work : A mathematical analysis. *Rutgers Law Review* 19, 317-343.

Benjamini, Y. & Hochberg, T. (1995). Controlling the false discovery rate : a practical and powerful approach to multiple testing. *J. Roy. Statist. Soc. Ser. B*, 59, 289-300.

Brown, M.P.S.; Grundy, W.N.; Lin, D.; Cristianini, N.; Sugnet, C.W.; Furey, T.S.; Ares, M. & Haussler, D. (2000). Knowledge-based analysis of microarray gene expression data by using support vector machines. *Proc. Natl. Acad. Sci. USA*, 97, 262-267.

Bruckmann, A. ; Hensbergen, P.J. ; Balog, C.I. ; Deelder, A.M. ; de Steensma, H.Y. & van Heusden G.P. (2007). Post-transcriptional control of the saccharomyces cerevisiae proteome by 14-3-3 proteins. *J. Proteome Res.* 6, 1689–1699.

Bruha, I. (1997). Quality of Decision Rules: Definitions and Classification Schemes for Multiple Rules. In *Machine Learning and Statistics*, Nakhaeizadeh G., Taylor C. C. (ed.), John Wiley and Sons.

Carmona-Sayez, P.; Chagoyen, M.; Rodriguez, A.; Trelles, O.; Carazo, J.M. & Pascual-Montano, A. (2006). Integrated analysis of gene expression by association rules discovery. *BMC Bioinformatics*, 7.

Carmona-Saez, P.; Chagoyen, M.; Tirado, F.; Carazo, J.M. & Pascual-Montano, A. (2007). Genecodis: a web based tool for finding significant concurrent annotations in gene list. *Genome Biology*, 8.

Cline, M.S.; Smoot M.; Cerami E. et al. (2007). Integration of biological networks and gene expression data using Cytoscape, *Nat. Protoc.*, 2, 1, 2366-82.

Dudoit, S.; Shafer, J.P. & Boldrick, J. (2003). Multiple hypothesis testing in microarray experiments. *Statistical Science*, 18, 71–103.

Eisen, M.B.; Spellman, P.T.; Brown, P.O. & Botstein D. (1998). Cluster analysis and display of genome-wide expression patterns. *Proc. Natl. Acad. Sci. USA.*, 95, 14863–14868.

Furnkranz, J. & Flach, P.A. (2005). ROC 'n' Rule Learning – Towards a Better Understanding of Covering Algorithms. *Machine Learning* 58, 39-77.

Greco, S.; Słowiński, R. & Stefanowski, J. (2007). Evaluating importance of conditions in the set of discovered rules. (*RSFDGrC 2007*) *Lecture Notes in Artificial Intelligence* 4482, 314-321.

Gruca, A. (2008). Analysis of GO composition of gene clusters by using multiattribute decision rules. *Biocybernetics and Biomedical Engineering*, 28, 4, 21-31.

Gruca, A.; Sikora, M.; Chrost L. & Polanski A. (2009). RULEGO. Bioinformatical Internet Service - System Architecture. Proc. of the 16th Conference CN'09. Communications in Computer and Information Science, Wisla, Poland

Grzymała-Busse, J.W. & Ziarko, W. (2003). Data mining based on rough sets. In: Wang J. (eds.) *Data Mining Opportunities and Challenges*. IGI Publishing, Hershey, USA, 142-173.

Hackenberg, M. & Matthiesen, R. (2008). Annotation-modules: a tool for finding significant combinations of mulitsource annotations of gene lists. *Bioinformatics*, 24.

Hvidstein, T. R.; Legreid, A. & Komorowski, J. (2003). Learning rule-based models of biological process form gene ontology expression time profiles using Gene Ontology. *Bioinformatics*, 19, 9, 1116-1123.

Iyer, V.R.; Eisen, M.B.; Ross, D.T.; Schuler, Moore, G. T.; Lee, J.C.; Trent, J.M.; Staudt, L.M.; Hudson, J.; Boguski, M.S.; Lashkari, D.; Shalon, D.; Botstein, D. & Brown, P.O. (1999). The transcriptional program in the response of human fibroblasts to serum. *Science*, 283, 83–87.

Kano, M.R. ; Morishita, Y. ; Iwata, C. ; Iwasaka, S. ; Watabe, T. ; Ouchi, Y. ; Miyazono, K. & Miyazawa, K. (2005). Vegf-a and fgf-2 synergistically promote neoangiogenesis through enhancement of endogenous pdgf-b-pdgfrbeta signaling. *J. Cell Sci.*, 118, 3759–3768, 2005.

Khatri, P. & Draghici, S. (2005). Ontological analysis of gene expression data: current tools, limitations and open problems. *Bioinformatics* 21, 3587-3595.

Klemettinen, M. ; Mannila, H. ; Ronkainen, P. ; Toivonen, H. & Inkeri-Verkamo, A. (1994). Finding interesting rules form large sets of discovered association rules. In *The third international conference on information and knowledge management*. 29.11-02.12.1994, Gaithersburg, Maryland, USA.

Kustra, R. & Zagdański, A. (2006). Incorporating Gene Ontology in Clustering Gene Expression Data. In *Proc. of the 19th IEEE Symposium on Computer-Based Medical Systems* (CBMS'06).

Maere S.; Heymans, K. & Kuiper, M. (2005). BiNGO: a Cytoscape plugin to assess overrepresentation of Gene Ontology categories in biological networks. *Bioinformatics*, 21, 3448-3449.

Mata-Greenwood, E.; Meyrick, B.; Soifer, S.J.; Fineman, J.R. & Black, S.M. (2003). Expression of vegf and its receptors flt-1 and flk-1/kdr is altered in lambs with increased pulmonary blood flow and pulmonary hypertension. *Am. J. Physiol. Lung Cell Mol. Physiol.*, 285, L222–L231.

Michalski, R. S. (1983) A Theory and Methodology of Inductive Learning, In: *Machine Learnig: An Artificial Intelligence Approach*, 83–129, Tioga, Palo Alto, Calif.

Michalski, R. S. ; Bratko, I. & Kubar, M. (1998). Machine learning and data mining. John Wiley and Sons.

Midelfart H. (2005a). Supervised Learning in Gene Ontology Part I: A Rough Set Framework. *Transaction on Rough Sets IV LNCS*, 3700, 69-97.

Midelfart H. (2005b). Supervised Learning in Gene Ontology Part II: A Bottom-Up Algorithm. *Transaction on Rough Sets IV LNCS*, 3700, 98-124.

Mitchell, T. (1997). Machine learning. McGraw Hill.

Øhrn, A.; Komorowski, J.; Skowron, A. & Synak, P. (1998). The ROSETTA software system. In *Rough Sets in Knowledge Discovery 1: Methodology and Applications*, Polkowski, L. & Skowron, A. (Ed,), 572–576. Physica-Verlag, Heidelberg, Germany.

Pawlak, Z. (1991). *Theoretical aspects of reasoning about data*. Kluwer Academic Publisher, Dordrecht.

Piatetsky-Shapiro, G. (1991). Discovery, analysis and presentation of strong rules. *Knowledge Discovery in Databases*, 229-248, Melno Park, CA:AAAI Press.

Rice, J.A. (1995). Mathematical Statistics and Data Analysis. Duxbury Press, Belmont, ed. 2

Seghezzi, G.; Patel, S.; Ren, C.J.; Gualandris, A.; Pintucci, G.; Robbins, E.S.; Shapiro, R.L.; Galloway, A.C. ; Rifkin, D.B. & Mignatti, P. (1998). Fibroblast growth factor-2 (fgf-2) induces vascular endothelial growth factor (vegf) expression in the endothelial cells of forming capillaries: an autocrine mechanism contributing to angiogenesis. *J. Cell Biol.*, 141, 1659–1673.

Sikora, M. (2006). Rule quality measures in creation and reduction of data rule models. *Lecture Notes in Artificial Intelligence*, 4259, 716–725.

Sikora, M. (2009). Decision rules-based data models using TRS and NetTRS - methods and algorithms. *Transaction on Rough Sets*, LNCS, Springer (in press).

Stefanowski, J. & Vanderpooten, D. (2001). Induction of Decision Rules in Classification and Discovery-Oriented Perspectives. *Internatinal Journal of Intelligent Systems*, 16, 13-27.

16

Mathematical modeling of the Internet survey

Getka-Wilczyńska Elżbieta
Warsaw School of Economics
Poland

1. Introduction

Recently statistical research as for as sampling selection can be divided into representative surveys based on the probability sample and surveys based on the non-probability sample, e.g. the Internet surveys. After choosing the kind of the sample selection next stage of the survey is data gathering. In all surveys, the data is collected using an immediate interview, a telephone interview or a post and in recent years an interview over the Internet (Internet, 2001, Dillman, 2000).

Surveys over the Internet (Internet mediated research: online surveys, Internet surveys, Web surveys (Vehovar, 2007)) are in a process of intensive development and key of characteristic of it is their diversity. Collecting data through the Internet surveys is useful either for marketing and other private research societies either statistical agencies. The first graphic browser (NCSA Mosaic) was released in 1992, with Netscape Navigator following in 1994 and Internet explore in 1995. The first publishes papers on Web surveys appeared in 1996. Since then, there has been a virtual increasing tendency of interest in the Internet generally, and World Wide Web specifically, as a tool of data collection (www.WebSM.org). A special portal WebSM - Web survey methodology web site is a website dedicated to the methodology of Web surveys. It supported by EU since 2002 and it includes bibliography lists and software database.

Generally, difference between these researches rely on following aspects. In representative surveys based on the probability sample the frame of sampling is known, respondents are drawn to the sample by a statistician in accordance with sampling design (sampling scheme) and the methods of theory sampling are applied to data analysis (Bracha, 1996; Kordos, 1982; Tille, 2006; Särndal et al., 1992; Steczkowski, 1988; Wywiał, 1992). If in these surveys an electronic questionnaire is used, it is only one of modes of data collection and then the correct use of this data collection tool requires the suitable survey methodology (Biffignandi & Pratesi, 2000).

The Internet survey has several advantages, such as low costs of collecting information, the speed of the data transmission and a possibility to monitor it. Moreover, the computerized nature of Web surveys facilitates conducting experiments. The usage of the electronic questionnaire in the Internet survey makes the interview more efficient, lowers the workload of the respondents and controls the responds' quality.

But the basic problem in the surveys over the Internet is concerned with collecting data sets according to classical methods of the sampling theory. In the Internet surveys drawing the sample is not possible and respondents are not randomly selected to the sample, but they participate in the survey with a subjective decision and they form an uncontrolled sample (the Internet sample). The methods of the sampling theory can not be used immediately for the data from such the sample because the probability inclusions are not known and statistics are calculated usually on the basis Internet data refer usually to the population surveyed (Getka-Wilczyńska, 2003). In theory and practice of Internet survey two approaches to dealing with this problem are identified (Couper & Miller, 2008). The first - the design based approach, attempts to build probability – based Internet panels by using other methods for sampling and recruitment and – if it is necessary- providing Internet access to those without. This approach is applied e.g. by Knowledge Networks in the USA and CentERdata's MESS panel in the Netherlands. The second – the model based approach begins with a volunteer or opt - in panel of Internet users, and attempts to correct for representation biases using e.g. propensity score adjustment (Lee, 2006) or some other weighting method for assessing Web panel quality (Callegaro & Disogra, 2008, Toeppoel et.al., 2008). In both approaches usually are used methodology of sampling theory to data analysis. Other an interesting proposition is an application of a dynamic theory of decision making and the decision field theory to theoretical explanation of survey behavior (Galesic, 2006).

In this study are proposed certain conceptions of modelling of the Internet survey as a random experiment or a life testing experiment by using notions and methods of the stochastic processes and the reliability theory (Kingman, 2002; Kopociński, 1973; Barlow & Proschan, 1965 (1996), 1975; Sołowiew, 1983). Generally this approach is presented in following way.

At the first, the process of the Internet data collection is considered as a process of registering questionnaires on the server at fixed interval of the time, the time of the survey conducted. An events appear in the Internet survey are interpreted as the moment of an arrival, a birth, a death of the population elements or a waiting time for these events. In this case the random size of the uncontrolled sample (Internet sample, a random set of the moments in which questionnaires - from respondents who participate in the Internet survey - are recorded on the server) is defined as a counting process by using Poisson processes (Getka-Wilczyńska, 2004 (in Polish), 2005, 2008).

At the second, the Internet survey is considered as a life test of the population surveyed by using the notions and methods of the reliability theory, (Getka-Wilczyńska, 2007). In this case the events which appear in the Internet survey are interpreted as the moment of failure, renew or functioning time of the population elements, when the population is treated as a coherent system of finite number of elements or as the lifetime of the population elements, when the length of the population lifetime is considered. The length of the population lifetime is defined by using the structure function of the population and the reliability function of the length of the population lifetime is defined for the series, parallel and partial structure of the population. Then the basic characteristics of the reliability function are described, calculated and estimated by using path and cut method (Barlow & Proschan, 1965).

More interesting is the life testing experiment, if different models of elements' dependence are considered, e.g. dependence on initial parameters of the population (the system), external conditions, as well as on the states of other elements. In this study is described a general model of functioning of the population (the system), when exist the dependence of the reliability of one element on the states of the other elements, (Sołowiew, 1983). Then the changes in time of the population states (the system states) are determined by multidimensional stochastic process which is chosen in such a way that the state of the population can be explicitly defined in each moment (whether the population is in the state of life or in the state of death). As an example are considered the particularly cases of stochastic processes - a general death process (when the rate of the state change of the element depend only on the states of the elements) and a pure death process (when in the general death process the elements of the population are symmetrical), (Sołowiew, 1983). In an aspect of the Internet survey three characteristics are important: the time until the first change of state of the population, the length of the lifetime of the population per one change of the state and the residual time of the population lifetime.

2. Assumptions

We generally assume, that Internet survey begins at the moment $t=0$, when the electronic questionnaire is put on the website and the survey is conducted for the time $T>0$.
A set $\{u_1, u_2, ...,\}$ denotes the population of potential respondents. For each $n \geq 1$, the population of n units is surveyed and the respondent sent the questionnaires independently.
By $X_j, j=1,2,...,n, n \geq 1$, we denote a moment of questionnaire record on the server after an initial moment $t=0$, from each respondent $u_k, t=1,2,...,n$, $n \geq 1$, belonging to the population of the size $n \geq 1$, who took part in the survey as j-th.
The moment of the questionnaire record is an event that can be interpreted

- as the moment of arrival or the respondent, who took part in the survey as j-th, when the size of the uncontrolled sample is defined,
- as the moment of failure or renew of j-th element of the population, when the population is treated as a coherent system,
- as the waiting time for the j-th questionnaire record after the initial moment $t=0$ equal the length of lifetime of j-th element of the population until the moment $t \geq 0$
- the moment of death or birth of the j-th element of the population, when the length of the population lifetime is considered.

Theoretically, four cases which describe the relation between the time of the survey conducting, $T>0$, and the size of the uncontrolled sample can be considered.
In the first case, the registering the questionnaires ends at the moment $T>0$ specified in advance, independently of the questionnaires' number recorded. The size of the uncontrolled sample is then a random value in the interval $[0,T]$ and depends on the length of time of the survey and on a selection procedure applied in the survey (if it is used in the survey). An extreme situation occurs when no data was collected (an arrival set is empty or the questionnaire, which arrived were rejected by the selection procedure used in the survey).
In the second case the sample size is specified in advance and the survey ends when the assumed number of responses has arrived, independently of the length of time of the survey (a random value in this case). An extreme situation occurs when the length of time of the survey is infinite.

In the third case, both the length of time of the survey and the sample size are specified in advance and the survey ends in earlier of the assumed moments.
In the fourth case, the final moment of the survey is not specified in advance. The process of registering questionnaires lasts at the moment when the collected data set meets the demands of the survey organizers.

3. The random size of an uncontrolled sample

If the process of Internet data collection is considered as a process of registering questionnaires on the server in a fixed interval of the time $T > 0$ (the time of the survey conducting) then the size of the uncontrolled sample at the moment $t \ge 0$ equals the total number arrivals until the moment $t \ge 0$ and is defined as a counting process - Bernoulli, Poisson or compound Poisson process (Kingman, 2001).
In this part of the study paper we describe the two cases, the first and the second of the dependence between the time of the survey conducting and the size of the Internet sample (Getka-Wilczyńska, 2008).

3.1 The size of the uncontrolled sample as Bernoulli process

Definition 2.1. For fixed $n \ge 1$ the size of uncontrolled sample until the moment $t \ge 0$ is given by

$$N(t) = \text{card}\,\{1 \le k \le n : X_k \in [0,t]\}$$

and is equal to a sum

$$N(t) = N_1(t) + \ldots + N_n(t),$$

where

$$N_k(t) = \begin{cases} 0 & \text{if} \quad X_k > t \\ 1 & \text{if} \quad X_k \le t \end{cases}, \quad X_k, k = 1,2,\ldots,n\ ,\ n \ge 1,$$

are independent random variables with uniform distribution over $[0,T]$, $T > 0$, $X_{k-1} \le X_k$ for $j \ge 1$, $X_0 = 0$ and at the initial moment $t = 0$ no arrivals occur.
The value of the random variable $N(t), t \ge 0$ equals the total number of arrivals until the moment $t \ge 0$ and the process $\{N(t), t \ge 0\}$ can be described in a following way. Each of n respondents, independently of others send only one questionnaire with the probability 1 in the interval $[0,T]$ for $T > 0$ (the time of the survey conducted). The probability of sending the questionnaire by the certain respondent in the interval of the length $\Delta \subset [0,T]$ is equal to ratio $\frac{|\Delta|}{T}$.
In this way, each respondent generates a stream consisted of only one arrival. A summary stream obtained by summing these streams is called a bound Bernoulli stream, that is, it consists of finite number of events.
To complete the definition of the counting process it remains to compute the distribution of $N(t)$ and the joint distribution of $N(t_1), N(t_2), \ldots, N(t_n)$ for any non-negative $t_0, t_1, \ldots, t_n$.

Let

$$P_k(t) = P\{N(t) = k\},\ k = 1,...,n$$

be the probability of event, that at the moment $t \geq 0$ the total number of arrivals $N(t)$ equals k.

Since the probability of arrival of the given respondent in the interval $[0,t] \subset [0,T]$ is equal to ratio $\frac{t}{T}$ and the arrivals came independently, hence the total number of arrivals $N(t)$ at the moment $t \geq 0$ is random variable with Bernoulli distribution

$$P_k(t) = \binom{n}{k}\left(\frac{t}{k}\right)^k\left(1 - \frac{t}{k}\right)^{n-k}$$

If the intervals $\Delta_1,...,\Delta_n$ are disjoint pairs and the interval $[0,T] = \Delta_1 \cup ... \cup \Delta_n$ is a sum of $\Delta_1,...,\Delta_n$, then for any non-negative integers $k_1,...,k_n$ such that $k_1 + ... + k_n = n$ holds

$$P\{N(\Delta_1) = k_1,...,N(\Delta_n) = k_n\} = \frac{n!}{k_1!...k_n!} p_1^{k_1}...p_n^{k_n},$$

where $N(\Delta_i)$ is the number of arrivals which occur in the interval Δ_i, $p_i = \frac{|\Delta_i|}{T}$ for $i = 1,...,n$, and $|\Delta_i|$ is the length of the interval $\Delta_i = t_i - t_{i-1}, i = 1,...,n$.

3.2 The size of the uncontrolled sample as Poisson process

***Definition** 2.2.* For fixed $n \geq 1$ the size of uncontrolled sample until the moment $t \geq 0$ is given by

$$N'(t) = \text{card}\,\{n: X_n \in [0,t]\} = \max\{n \geq 0: S_n \leq t\},$$

where $X_1, X_2, ...,$ denote as before the successive moments of questionnaires record, $X_{k-1} \leq X_k$ for $k \geq 1$ and $X_0 = 0$,

$(Y_k)_{k=1}^{\infty}$ is a sequence of independent and identically distributed random variables $Y_k = X_k - X_{k-1}$ with exponential distribution

$$G(t) = 1 - e^{-\lambda t}, t \geq 0,\ \lambda > 0 \text{ and } Y_k = X_k - X_{k-1} \text{ for } k \geq 1$$

denotes $k-$th spacing between $k-$th and $(k-1)-$th arrivals, $S_n = \sum_{k=1}^{n} Y_k$ is a random variable with Erlang distribution given by

$$P(S_n \leq t) = 1 - \sum_{i=0}^{n-1} \frac{(\lambda t)^i}{i!} e^{-\lambda t} \text{ for } t \geq 0 \text{ and } \lambda > 0,$$

Then

$$P\{N'(t)=k\}=P\{N'(t)\leq n+1\}-P\{N'(t)\leq n\}=P\{S_{n+1}>t\}-P\{S_n>t\}=\frac{(\lambda t)^n}{n!}e^{-\lambda t}\ ,t\geq 0\ ,$$

the total number of arrivals until the moment $t\geq 0$, is a random variable with Poisson distribution with the parameter $\lambda>0$ and $\{N'(t):t\geq 0\}$ is Poisson process.

Moreover, if in the Poisson process (stream) in the interval $[0,T]$, $T>0$, n arrivals occur, then process (stream) of arrivals in this interval is the Bernoulli process (stream), (Kingman, 2001). This fact is shown below.

If $0\leq t\leq T$ and $0\leq k\leq n$, then

$$P\{N'(t)=k|N'(T)=n\}=\frac{P\{N'(t)=k,N'(T)-N'(t)=n-k\}}{P\{N'(t)=n\}}=\frac{P\{N'(t)=k\}P\{N'(T-t)=n-k\}}{P\{N'(T)=n\}}=$$

$$=\frac{\frac{(\lambda t)^k}{k!}e^{-\lambda t}\frac{(\lambda(T-t))^{n-k}}{(n-k)!}e^{-\lambda(T-t)}}{\frac{(\lambda T)^n}{n!}e^{-\lambda(T-t)}}.$$

Hence

$$P\{N'(t)=k|N'(T)=n\}=\binom{n}{k}\left(\frac{t}{T}\right)^k\left(1-\frac{t}{T}\right)^{n-k}.$$

If the intervals $\Delta_1,...,\Delta_n$ are disjoint pairs and $[0,T]=\Delta_1\cup...\cup\Delta_n$, then for any nonnegative integers $k_1,...,k_n$ such that $k_1+...+k_n=n$ holds

$$P\{N'(\Delta_1)=k_1,...,N'(\Delta_n)=k_n|N'(T)=n\}=\frac{P_k\{N'(\Delta_1)=k_1,...,N'(\Delta_n)=k_n\}}{P\{N'(T)=n\}}=\frac{\prod_{i=1}^{n}P\{N'(\Delta_i)=k_i\}}{P\{N'(T)=n\}}=$$

$$=\frac{\prod_{i=1}^{n}(\lambda|\Delta_i|)^{k_i}e^{-\lambda|\Delta_i|}}{\frac{(\lambda T)^n}{n!}e^{-\lambda T}}.$$

Therefore

$$P\{N'(\Delta_1)=k_1,...,N'(\Delta_n)=k_n|N'(T)=n\}=\frac{n!}{k_1!...k_n!}p_1^{k_1}...p_n^{k_n}.$$

3.3 The size of the uncontrolled sample with a selection procedure as compound Poisson process

In the Internet surveys the electronic questionnaire is available to all Internet users and a part of the registered arrivals came from respondents who do not necessarily belong to the surveyed population.

In this case only the arrivals of these respondents whose questionnaires qualified for the data set based on the selection procedure are included in the sample. By this assumption and the assumptions made in case 2 the size of the uncontrolled sample is defined as a compound Poisson process (Kingman 2001).

***Definition* 3.3.** For fixed $n \geq 1$ the size of uncontrolled sample until the moment $t \geq 0$ is given by $Y(t) = S_{N'(t)}$,
where

$$N'(t) = \text{card}\{n : X_n \in [0,t]\} = \max\{n \geq 0 : S_n \leq t\}, \; S_{N'(t)} = \sum_{j=1}^{N'(t)} U_j,$$

a sequence $(U_n)_{n=1}^{\infty}$ of independent and identically distributed random variables and the Poisson process $\{N'(t) : t \geq 0\}$ are independent.
The arrivals $X_n, n = 1,2\ldots$, are selected for the uncontrolled sample in the following way (the sequence of arrivals $X_n, n = 1,2\ldots$ is thinned): the arrival $\tau_n, n = 1,2\ldots$., is omitted with the probability p, $p \in [0,1]$ (independently of the process taking place), if the respondent does not belong to the population and the arrival $X_n, n = 1,2\ldots$., is left with the probability $1-p$, otherwise.
The random variable U_i is equal to 1, if the arrival X_i remains, and 0, if the arrival X_i is omitted.
The probability p, $p \in [0,1]$ is defined by the procedure of selection used in the survey and consequently, process $\{Y(t), t \geq 0\}$ is compound Poisson process with expected number of the arrivals $\lambda(1-p)$.

4. Length of the population lifetime

In the remaining part of this study we assume that the population of n units for $n \geq 1$ is treated as a finite coherent system of n components (Barlow & Proschan, 1965) and the Internet survey begins at time $t = 0$ and it is conducted for the time $T, T > 0$. In this case the process of Internet data collection can be considered as a random experiment or a life testing experiment in which the basic characteristics of length of the population lifetime are analysed by using the methods of reliability theory (Barlow & Proschan, 1965 (1996), 1975; Kopociński, 1973, Sołowiew, 1983).
We assume that a non-negative independent random variables $X_k, k = 1,2\ldots, n, n \geq 1$ with distribution function

$$F_k(t) = P(X_k \leq t), \text{ for } t \geq 0, \; k = 1,2,\ldots,n, \; n \geq 1,$$

and probability density function

$$f_k(t) = F_k'(t) \quad \text{and} \quad F_k(t) = \int_0^t f_k(x)dx$$

are interpreted as the length of lifetime of k-th element of the population until the moment $t \geq 0$ or the moment of death of k-th element of the population until the moment $t \geq 0$ or the waiting time of arrival of k-th element of the population until the moment $t \geq 0$.
The probability

$$\overline{F}_k(t) = 1 - F_k(t) \text{ for } t \geq 0, \; k = 1,2,\ldots,n, \; n \geq 1$$

is the reliability function of the length of lifetime of k-th element at the moment $t \geq 0$, (the reliability of the k-th element in short) and equal to the probability of the length of lifetime of k-th element at least $t \geq 0$ or the probability of event that k-th respondent is in the state of life at least $t \geq 0$.
The conditional probability density function

$$\lambda_k(t) = \frac{f_k(t)}{\overline{F}_k(t)} \quad \text{for } t \geq 0,\ k = 1,2,\ldots,n,\ n \geq 1$$

is called arrival or failure rate of k-th element of the population, (Kopociński, 1973).
The elements of the population are not renewed - each record of questionnaires decreases the size of the population in one and the element which arrived is not replaced by a new one. This way of selection is called random sampling without replacement.
The length of the population lifetime and is defined by using the structure function of the population as follows (Sołowiew, 1983).

4.1 States of elements of the population

The state of i-th elements of the population (as the system) is defined by the values of the binary function

$$Y_i(t) = \begin{cases} 0 & \text{if } i\text{-th element is in the state of life or } i\text{-th element did not arrive until the moment } t \\ 1 & \text{if } i\text{-th element is in the state of death or } i\text{-th element arrive until the moment } t \end{cases}$$

where $Y:[0,\infty)\times\{1,2,\ldots,n\}\to\{0,1\}$ and $Y(t,i) = Y_i(t)$ for $i \in \{1,\ldots,n\}$, $t \in [0,\infty)$.
Then the state of all elements of the population of size n, for $n \geq 1$, is determined by n-dimension vector $\underline{Y}(t) = (Y_1(t), Y_2(t),\ldots, Y_n(t))^T$ and we assume that at the initial moment $t = 0$ all elements of the population of size n, for $n \geq 1$, are in the states of life. This assumption means that at the moment $t = 0$ no arrivals occurred.

4.2 States of the population

The state of the population of the size n, for $n \geq 1$, at the moment $t \geq 0$ is defined by the values of the binary function

$$\varphi_0(t) = \begin{cases} 0 & \text{if the population is in state of life (the survey (test) is conducted) at the moment } t \\ 1 & \text{if the popualtion is in the state of death (the survey (test) ended) until the moment } t \end{cases}$$

and at each moment $t \geq 0$ it depends on the states of the elements through the values of the function $\varphi_0(t) = \varphi(Y_1(t),\ldots, Y_n(t)) = \varphi(\underline{Y}(t))$.
In the process of Internet data collection treated as a life test of the population of size n, for $n \geq 1$, the population can be found at the moment $t \geq 0$ in the state of life during the conducting of the survey in following cases.

In the first case, at the moment $0 \le t \le T$ where T is the time of the survey conducting specified in advance and the number of death (arrivals) in interval of the length $t \ge 0$ is a random value but it is less than the size of the population. Otherwise, until the moment T specified in advance.
In the second case, until the moment $t \ge 0$, in which the number of death (arrivals) is equal to the size of the sample specified in advance (it is equals or less than the size of the population) and the time of the survey conducting T is not specified in advance.
In the third case, until the earlier of the time of the survey conducting T and the moment $t \ge 0$, when the number of death (arrivals) is equal to the sample size, where both the length of time of the survey T and the sample size are specified in advance.
In the fourth case, until the moment $t \ge 0$, when the collected data set (it can be a subset of the population or the population surveyed) meets the demands of the survey organizers and the final moment of the survey is not specified in advance.

4.3 Properties of the structure function

The structure function $\varphi(\underline{Y})$ is increasing, if for any two vectors $\underline{Y}^{(1)}$ and $\underline{Y}^{(2)}$ is satisfied the condition:

$$\text{if } \underline{Y}^{(1)} \le \underline{Y}^{(2)}, \text{ then } \varphi\left(\underline{Y}^{(1)}\right) \le \varphi\left(\underline{Y}^{(2)}\right),$$

where $\underline{Y}^{(1)} \le \underline{Y}^{(2)}$, if for all $i = 1,\dots,n$, $Y_i^{(1)} \le Y_i^{(2)}$.
This property of the structure function introduce a partial order in a set of the binary vectors and means that additional death of the element can not change the state of the population from the state of death to the state of life.
The function $\varphi(Y(t))$ define a division of a set $E = \left\{\underline{Y}: \ \underline{Y}: Y^n \to \{0,1\}^n\right\}$ of all n - dimension and binary vectors which describe the state of the population to two sets:

$$E_+ = \{\underline{Y} : \varphi(\underline{Y}(t)) = 0\}, \text{ a set of states of life of the population and}$$
$$E_- = \{\underline{Y} : \varphi(\underline{Y}(t)) = 1\}, \text{ a set of states of death of the population.}$$

If the structure function is increasing, then the division of the set E to two sets E_+ and E_- is called a monotonic structure (Barlow & Proschan, 1965).

4.4 Length of the population lifetime

Let us denote by X the length of the population lifetime and

$$X = \inf\{t : \varphi(\underline{Y}(t)) = 1\}.$$

Then

$$F(t) = P(X \le t)$$

is the probability of ending of the survey (test) until the moment $t \ge 0$ or the probability of the event that the population is in the state of death until the moment $t \ge 0$
and

$$\overline{F}(t) = P(X > t)$$

is the probability of the conducting survey (test) at least $t \geq 0$, the probability of the event that the population is in the state of life at least $t \geq 0$ or the reliability function of the X, the length of the population lifetime at the moment $t \geq 0$, (the reliability of the population in short).

4.5 Calculation of the reliability of the length of the population lifetime

The formula which expresses the relation between X, the reliability of the length of the population lifetime and $X_k, k = 1,2...,n, n \geq 1$ reliabilities of elements at the moment $t \geq 0$ is given by

$$\overline{F}(t) = \sum_{\underline{Y}(t) \in E_+} p(\underline{Y}(t)),$$

where

$$p(\underline{Y}(t)) = \prod_{k=1}^{n} \overline{F}_k^{1-Y_k}(t) F_k^{Y_k}(t),$$

(there is adopted the convention $0^0 = 1$) is a probability of event that the population is in the state $\underline{Y}$.

If $X_k, k = 1,2...,n, n \geq 1$ are non-negative independent random variables, the elements are not renewed and the function $\varphi(e)$ is increasing, then the reliability function of the length of the population lifetime $\overline{F}(t)$ is increasing respectively to each coordinate of the reliability function of the length of the element lifetime $\overline{F}_k(t)$.

Thus an upper or a lower bound on the reliability of X, the length of the population lifetime may be obtained from the upper or lower bounds on the reliabilities of the elements.

When the number of the states is large (the number of all states is equal to 2^n) and the function $\varphi(\underline{Y})$ is very complicated, then a formulae given above is not efficient and the other methods of calculation are applied e.g. the method of path and cut (Barlow & Proschan, 1975; Koutras et al.,2003) or the recurrence method of Markov chain or generally, the Markov methods (Sołowiew, 1983).

5. Basic structures of the population

5.1 Length of the population lifetime for the series structure

The population (as the system) of n - elements for $n \geq 1$ is called a series structure, when the population is in the state of life if and only if each element is in the state of life.

In this case, the change of the state of any element causes the change of the population state. The length of the population lifetime is equal to the waiting time of the first death and the size of the uncontrolled sample equals zero for the first death. Then the basic characteristics of the reliability function of the series structure are given as follows.

From definition of the series structure follows that the length of the population lifetime is equal

$$X_{1,n} = \min(X_1, X_2, ..., X_n)$$

and the probability of it (duration of the survey) at least $t \geq 0$ is equal to

$$\overline{F}(t) = \prod_{i=1}^{n} \overline{F}_i(t).$$

From inequality (Hardy, et. al, 1934)

$$1 - \sum_{i=1}^{n} F_i \leq \prod_{i=1}^{n}(1 - F_i) \leq 1 - \sum_{i=1}^{n} F_i + \sum_{i<j} F_i F_j \leq 1 - \sum_{i=1}^{n} F_i + \frac{1}{2}\left(\sum_{i=1}^{n} F_i\right)^2$$

it follows that

$$\left|F(t) - \sum_{i=1}^{n} \overline{F}_i\right| \leq \frac{1}{2}\left(\sum_{i=1}^{n} F_i\right)^2.$$

The change rate of the population equals the sum of the change rate of the elements

$$\lambda(t) = -\frac{\overline{F}'(t)}{\overline{F}(t)} = -\left[\ln \overline{F}(t)\right]' = -\sum_{i=1}^{n}\left[\ln \overline{F}_i(t)\right]' = -\sum_{i=1}^{n} \frac{\overline{F}_i{}'(t)}{\overline{F}_i(t)} = \sum_{i=1}^{n} \lambda_i(t).$$

The expected time of the length of the population lifetime is equal to

$$E(X) = \int_0^{\infty} \overline{F}(t)dt.$$

5.2 Length of the population lifetime for the parallel structure

The population (as the system) of n - elements for $n \geq 1$ is called a parallel structure, when the population is in the state of death if and only if all elements are in the state of death.
In this case, the change of the state of the population (death of the population) takes places only if changes of all population elements occur - all elements of the population died and the size of the uncontrolled sample is equal to the size of the population (all elements of the populations arrived).
From definition of the parallel structure follows that the length of the population lifetime is equal to

$$X_{n,n} = \max(X_1, X_2, ..., X_n)$$

and the probability of the length of the population lifetime (duration of the survey) at least $t \geq 0$ is equal to

$$F(t) = \prod_{i=1}^{n} F_i(t) \text{ or } F(t) = F_0^n(t)$$

and the expected time of the length of the population lifetime is equal to

$$E(X) = \int_0^{\infty}[1 - F(t)]dt \text{ or } E(X) = \int_0^{\infty}[1 - F_0^n(t)]dt, \text{ when } F_i(t) = F_0(t), i = 1,2,...,n.$$

5.3 Length of the population lifetime for the partial structure

The population (as the system) of n - elements for $n \geq 1$ is called a partial structure if all elements of the population are identical and the population is in the state of life if at least m elements of the population are in the state of life (that is, at most $n-m$ death occur) and the size of the uncontrolled sample equals $n-m$.

The reliability function of the length of the population lifetime is equal to

$$\overline{F}(t)=1-P\left(X_{n-m+1,n} \leq t\right)=\sum_{k=m}^{n}\binom{n}{k}\overline{F}_0^k(t)F_0^{n-k}(t).$$

6. Estimate of the reliability of the length of the population lifetime - the method of path and cut

In this method are defined notions of minimal path minimal cut that used to estimate the reliability function of the length of the population lifetime, (Barlow & Proschan, 1965).

Definition 6.1. The set of elements $A=\{u_1,\ldots,u_k\}$ of the population of the size n, $n \geq 1$, is called a minimal path if all the elements of this set are in the state of life (the population is in the state of life, the survey is being conducted) and no subset of the set A has this property.

From the monotonic property of the structure function, the set $A=\{u_1,\ldots,u_k\}$ is a minimal path if and only if $\underline{Y} \in E_+$, where e is a vector in which coordinates $i_1,\ldots,i_k$ take on the value zero and the remaining coordinates take on the value one, with any state greater than $\underline{Y}$ belonging to E_-.

Therefore, every minimal path determines a bordering state of the life of the population in which the occur of death of any element causes a change of the state of the population into the state of death one (ending of the survey (test)).

In term of the size of the uncontrolled sample, it means, that the number of arrivals is equal to the number of elements of the minimal path is smaller per one than the size of the sample assumed in the survey.

Let $\{A_1,A_2,\ldots,A_m\}$ be a sets of all minimal paths with the corresponding bordering states $\underline{Y}^{(1)},\underline{Y}^{(2)},\ldots,\underline{Y}^{(m)}$.

A_s is an event in which all elements of the minimal path A_s are in the state of life. Since $E_+=\bigcup_{s=1}^{m}A_s$, (Sołowiew, 1983), the reliability function of the length of the population lifetime is calculated from the formula

$$\overline{F}(t)=P\left(\bigcup_{s=1}^{m}A_s\right)=\sum_{i=1}^{m}P(A_i)+\sum_{i,j}P\left(A_iA_j\right)+\sum_{i<j<k}P\left(A_iA_jA_k\right)+\ldots+(-1)^{m+1}P(A_1A_2\ldots A_m)$$

The number of the elements of the sum on the right is equal to 2^m-1 and the probability of any event which is given by $A_{i_1}A_{i_2}\ldots A_{i_k}$, where $i_1<i_2,\ldots<i_k$ is equal to

$$P(A_{i_1}A_{i_2}\cdots A_{i_k}) = \overline{F}_{s_1}(t)\overline{F}_{s_2}(t)\ldots\overline{F}_{s_l}(t),$$

where s_1, s_2,. s_l are different indices of elements of the minimal paths (that is, in the case of the elements belonging to overlapping parts of different paths, each element is calculated only once).

In the order to lower the number of calculation are introduced the following notions.

The two minimal paths are called crossing, when they have at least one common element.

The two minimal paths are called relevant, if there exists a chain of crossing paths which connects them.

The relevant relation is the equivalent relation which divides a set of all minimal paths into classes of relevant minimal paths.

Let $\{A_1 \ldots A_{k_1}\}, \{A_{k_1+1} \ldots A_{k_2}\}, \ldots$ be the successive classes of the relevant minimal paths.

Because

$$F(t) = 1 - \overline{F}(t) = P\left(\prod_{i=1}^{m} \overline{A}_i\right),$$

(the symbol $\prod_{i=1}^{m} \overline{A}_i$ means an intersection of sets $\overline{A}_i$ for $i = 1, \ldots, m$) and the events belonging to different classes are independent, then

$$F(t) = P\left(\prod_{i=1}^{k_1} \overline{A}_i\right) P\left(\prod_{i=1}^{k_2} \overline{A}_{k_1+1}\right) \ldots .$$

A dual notion of the minimal path is a minimal cut (a critical set).

Definition 6.2. A set of elements $B = (j_1, j_2, \ldots, j_l)$ is called a minimal cut, if all elements of this set are in the state of death (the population is in the state of death, the survey (test) ended) and no subset of the set B has this property.

In this case we are interesting in those cut set in which the number of elements is equal to the size of the uncontrolled sample specified in advance (all elements belonging to the set B arrived).

If $\{B_1, B_2, \ldots, B_s\}$ is a set of all the minimal cuts, then the probability of an event that the survey (test) ends until the moment $t \geq 0$ is equal to

$$F(t) = P\left(\bigcup_{i=1}^{s} B_i\right) = \sum_{i=1}^{s} P(B_i) + \sum_{i<j} P(B_i B_j) + \sum_{i<j<k} P(B_i B_j B_k) + \ldots + +(-1)^{m+1} P(B_1 B_2 \ldots B_m) =$$

$$= S_1 - S_2 + S_3 + \ldots + (-1)^{s+1} S_s$$

From this formula the estimation of the length of the population lifetime (during the survey) as the estimation of the reliability function of the population can be obtained.

In this case the number of elements in the successive minimal cuts is interpreted as the possible sample sizes which can be collected in the survey on condition that the survey ends after collection of the sample of the assumed size.

From proof of this formula for the non-crossing minimal cuts holds

$$S_2 \leq \frac{S_1^2}{2}, \quad S_3 \leq \frac{S_1^3}{6},$$

and so on, and in the case of the crossing minimal cuts the partial sums maintain an order $S_k = O(S_1^2)$.

Moreover, for any k,

$$S_1 - S_2 + \ldots - S_{2k} \leq F(t) \leq S_1 - S_2 + \ldots - S_{2k} + S_{2k+1}.$$

Thus there exists the possibility of the estimation of the probability of length of the population lifetime with assumed precision because partial sums on the right of the last formula are the interchangeable upper and the lower bounds of the reliability function.

7. Reliability of the length of the population lifetime – Markov methods

So far we have assumed that the length of the lifetime of the population elements (the waiting time for arrival) are independent distributed random variables. In literature devoted to research of reliability of the system of order n considered dependence on initial parameters of the system, external conditions, as well as on the states of other elements. Let us consider the last dependence.

7.1 Model of dependence of the element of the population

In the most general way, if no dependence of initial parameters exists and there is no dependence of the lifetimes of the elements on the common external conditions, then the only type of dependence is the dependence of the reliability of one element on the states of the other elements. This dependence is described as follows (Sołowiew, 1983).

Let the states of the population of n - elements for $n \geq 1$ are defined by the binary vector

$$\underline{Y}(t) = (Y_1(t), Y_2(t), \ldots, Y_n(t))^T$$

and by Γ_t is denoted a realisation of the process $\underline{Y}(x)$ in interval $[0,t]$.

If the realisation Γ_t of the process $\underline{Y}(x)$ is determined until the moment t, then the transition probability in the time Δt to the state $\underline{Y}$ equals

$$\lambda(\Gamma_t, \underline{Y})\Delta t + o(\Delta t) \tag{7.1.1}$$

There are can be considered the following cases:

1) at the same time the change of the states of a few elements occur,

2) in each moment the change of the state of only one element occurs (failure, arrival).

If case 2 is considered, then the process $\underline{Y}(t)$ is described by the arrival (failure) rates of the elements and $\lambda_i(\Gamma_t)$ is the conditional arrival (failure) rate of the i -th element, on condition that the realisation of the process is determined until the moment t.

If the arrival (failure) rate of the element given by formulae $\lambda_i(\Gamma_t) = \lambda_i[t, \underline{Y}(t)]$, depends only on the moment t and the state of the process in this moment then the process $\underline{Y}(t)$ is non-homogeneous Markov process with a finite number of states.

If the arrival (failure) rate of the element does not depends on time, but depends only on the states of the elements $\lambda_i(t,\underline{Y})=\lambda_i(\underline{Y})$, then such a homogeneous Markov process is a generalised pure death process.
If in the generalised pure death process the elements of the population are symmetrical, then all arrival (failure) rates of elements are equal to $\lambda_i(\underline{Y})=\lambda(\underline{Y})$ and the arrival (failure) rate of the population not depend on the vector $\underline{Y}$, but depends only on the number of states changes (arrivals, failures) of the elements $\lambda(\underline{Y})=\lambda\|\underline{Y}\|$, where $\|\underline{Y}\|=\sum_{k=1}^{n} Y_k^2$. The process $\|\underline{Y}(t)\|$, in which the transition from the state $\|\underline{Y}\|=i$ is possible only to the state $i+1$ with the rate $(n-1)\lambda(i)$ is a pure death process.
The pure death process describes functioning of the non-renewable the system consisting of identical elements while the generalised one describes functioning of the system consisting of different elements. It seems to me that the application of the Markov methods for the research of the length of the population lifetime when the population is treated as a system of n, $n \geq 1$ elements is natural.
Namely - changes in time of the population states (as the system of n, $n \geq 1$ elements) are determined by multidimensional stochastic process. This process is chosen in such a way that when we investigate the reliability of the population and we know the state of the process, we can in each moment explicitly define the state of the population (whether the system is functioning or failed, whether the population is in the state of life or death).
Bellow is presented a general model of functioning of that population (as the system of n, $n \geq 1$ elements), (Sołowiew, 1983).

7.2 General model functioning of the population

Let $\xi(t)$ denote the stochastic process chosen in the way described above.
A set E of this process states decomposed into two disjoined subsets $E = E_+ \cup E_-$.
If $\xi(t) \in E_+$, then the population is in state of life at the moment t and if $\xi(t) \in E_-$, then the population is in state of death at the moment t.
The transition of the process from the set E_+ to the set E_- is called death of the population, and a reverse transition from the set E_- to the set E_+ is called a renewal of the population.
The process observed in time changes the state E_+ into the state E_- and reverse.
Let

$$Z_0', Z_1', \ldots, Z_k', \ldots \text{ and } Z_0'', Z_1'', \ldots, Z_k'', \ldots$$

denote successive intervals respectively, in which the population is in the state of life or death.
If there exists a stationary distribution for the process $\xi(t)$, which describes the functioning of the renewable population, then there exist limits $Z_k' \xrightarrow{P} Z'$ $Z_k'' \xrightarrow{P} Z''$.
A random variable
Z_0' - is called the time until the first change of the state of the population
Z' - is called the length of the lifetime of the population per one change of the state

$Z(t)$ - is the lifetime of the population from the moment t until the first moment after the change of the state of the population, residual time of the population lifetime.
As before, if there exists a stationary distribution for the process $\xi(t)$, then there exists the limit $Z(t) \xrightarrow{P} Z$.
Distributions of random variables $Z_0', Z_k', Z_k'', Z(t), Z', Z'', Z$ and their an expected values $E(Z_0')$, $E(Z_k')$, $E(Z_k'')$, $E(Z(t))$, $E(Z')$, $E(Z'')$, $E(Z)$) are basic characteristics of the reliability function.
One of the simpler type of the processes used in the reliability calculations is the class of Markov processes with a finite or uncountable number of states. In this sense the pure death or general death process could be a model describing the changes of the population states.

In aspect of Internet survey three characteristics are important:
Z_0' - the time until the first change of the state of the population,
Z' - the length of the lifetime of the population per one change of the state,
$Z(t)$ - the lifetime of the population from the moment t until the first moment after the change of the state of the population, residual time of lifetime of the population.

Below the probability distribution of these random values and their the expected values are derived.

7.3 Formulae of characteristics of Markov process

Assume that the process $\xi(t)$ is a homogeneous Markov process with a finite number of the states which is assigned $1,2,...,N$.
Let the set $E_+ = \{0,1,2,...,n\}$ denote a set of the functioning states of the system (life states of the population) and $E_- = \{k+1, k+2,...,n\}$ a set of the failed states of the system (a set of death states of the population which is interpreted as break between repeated surveys).
The Markov process is analysed in following steps.

1. The Markov process has two properties which are equivalent to the definition the Markov process:

- the interval in which the process finds itself in the state i, does not depend on the process taking place outside the interval and it has exponential distribution

$$P\{t_i > t\} = e^{-\lambda_{i,i} t} \text{ , where } \lambda_{i,i} = -\sum_{j \neq i} \lambda_{i,j} ,$$

- a sequence of the states through which the process passes is the homogenous Markov chain with transition probabilities $\pi_{i,j} = -\frac{\lambda_{i,j}}{\lambda_{i,i}}$. At the same time, if $\lambda_{i,i} = 0$, then the state i is called an absorbing state, because when the process has entered the state, it will remain in it forever. In this case we assume that $\pi_{i,j} = 0$.

2. Solution of the Kolmogorov equations

Let

$$p_i(t) = P\{\xi(t) = i\}.$$

The probabilities of the states $p_i(t)$ satisfy the Kolmogorov equations

$$p_j'(t) = \sum_{i=0}^{N} \lambda_{i,j} p_i(t), \quad j = 0, 1, \ldots, N \tag{7.3.1}$$

These equations are rewritten in a matrix form

$$p'(t) = p(t)\Lambda,$$

where $p(t) = \lfloor p_0(t), \ldots, p_n(t) \rfloor$ is the vector of the states probabilities, $\Lambda = \lfloor \lambda_{i,j} \rfloor$ is the matrix of the transition rate with the properties:
a) all elements of the matrix $\Lambda = \lfloor \lambda_{i,j} \rfloor$ satisfy the condition $\lambda_{i,j} > 0$,

b) $\sum_{j=0}^{N} \lambda_{i,j} = 0$.

After assuming the initial distribution of the process $p_i(0) = p_{i0}$ the system of the Kolmogorov equations (7.3.1) has the explicit solution

$$p_i(0) = p_{i0}.$$

The system of the Kolmogorov equations (7.3.1) is solved by means of Laplace transform.
Let

$$a_i(z) = \int_0^{\infty} e^{-zt} p_i(t) dt.$$

Taking the properties of Laplace transform is obtained

$$-p_{j0} + z a_j(z) = \sum_{i=0}^{N} a_i(z) \lambda_{i,j}, \quad j = 0, 1, 2 \ldots, N,$$

and from the Cramer's formulae the solution of the system is given by

$$a_i(z) = \frac{\Delta_i(z)}{\Delta(z)} \tag{7.3.2}$$

where $\Delta(z) = \left\| z \delta_{i,j} - \lambda_{i,j} \right\|$, the determinant in the numerator is calculated from the determinant in the denominator by the replacement of the i- th line with the line of the initial probabilities p_{j0}, $\delta_{i,j}$ is a Kronecker's symbol. After inversion of the Laplace transform the formulae of the probability of the process states is obtained.

3. Conditions of existing of the stationary distribution of the process.

Two states are called communicating, if there exist such indices $i_1, \ldots, i_k$ as well as $j_1, \ldots, j_l$, that $\lambda_{i,i_1}, \lambda_{i_1,i_2}, \ldots, \lambda_{i_k,j} > 0$ and $\lambda_{j,j_1}, \lambda_{j_1,j_2}, \ldots, \lambda_{j_l,i} > 0$. We also assume that each state communicates with itself.

The communication relation is an equivalence relation and introduce the decomposition of the set of the states into the classes of communicating states $A_1,\dots,A_m$.

The class A_s follows the class A_r, if there exist the states $i \in A_r$ and $j \in A_s$ such that $\lambda_{i,j} > 0$.

A class is called ergodic, if it is not followed by any class. By compliance with or satisfaction of these conditions the proposition holds:

The stationary distribution of the process, $\lim_{t\to\infty} p_i(t) \xrightarrow{P} p_i$, which is independent of the initial distribution exists if and only if there exists exactly one ergodic class, whereas the stationary probabilities satisfy the system of equations:

$$\sum_{i=0}^{N} p_i \lambda_{i,j} = 0, \quad j = 0,1,2,\dots,N, \quad \sum_{i=1}^{n} p_i = 1 \tag{7.3.3}$$

4. Basic characteristics of the reliability function

Let A be a set of the states and let $i \in A$.

The transition time to the set A is defined as a random variable

$$X_i(A) = \inf\{t : \xi(t) \in A | \xi(0) = i\}.$$

Its probability distribution is obtained by means of Laplace transform

$$\varphi_i(z) = E[\exp(-z X_i(A))].$$

From the formula of the total probability for the expected value

$$\varphi_i(z) = \frac{-\lambda_{i,i}}{z-\lambda_{i,i}}\left(\sum_{j\in A}\frac{\lambda_{i,j}}{-\lambda_{i,i}} + \sum_{j\notin A, j\neq i}\frac{\lambda_{i,j}}{-\lambda_{i,i}}\varphi_j(z)\right)$$

is computed in the following way.

In the state i the process is for the time ξ_i which is the random variable with exponential distribution and Laplace transform $\frac{-\lambda_{i,i}}{(z-\lambda_{i,i})}$, next, from this state it passes with the probability $\frac{-\lambda_{i,j}}{(-\lambda_{i,i})}$ to the state j.

If $j \in A$, then $X_i(A) = \xi_i$, and if $j \notin A$, then $X_i(A) = \xi_i + X_j(A)$ and both components are independent.

The solutions of the equations system

$$\begin{cases} \sum_{j\notin A} (z\delta_{i,j} - \lambda_{i,j})\varphi_j(z) = \lambda_i(A) \\ i \notin A, \lambda_i(A) = \sum_{j\in A} \lambda_{i,j} \end{cases} \tag{7.3.4}$$

are rational functions and after inversing them the probability distribution of the random variable $X_i(A)$ is obtained.
Differentiating the equation system (7.3.4) as regards to z and substituting $z=0$, the expected transition times

$$E(X_i(A)) = -\varphi_i'(0)$$

are obtained and they are satisfying the equations system

$$\sum_{j \notin A} \lambda_{i,j} E(X_j(A)) + 1 = 0, i \notin A .$$

Let $q_{i,j}(A)$ denote probability of an event, that in the moment of the first entrance of the process to the set *A*, the process will enter the state $j \in A$, on condition that at initial moment the process was in the state $i \notin A$.
In the analogical way as above are obtained the forward equations for these probabilities

$$q_{i,j}(z) = \frac{\lambda_{i,j}}{-\lambda_{i,i}} + \sum_{k \notin A, k \neq i} \frac{\lambda_{i,k}}{-\lambda_{i,i}} q_{k,j}(A).$$

Transforming the equations we have

$$\sum_{k \notin A} \lambda_{i,k} q_{k,j}(A) = -\lambda_{i,j}, \; i \notin A, j \in A \tag{7.3.5}$$

5. Transcription of the characteristics from the point 4 by means of $X_i(A)$ and the probability $q_{i,j}(A)$.
Let at the initial moment $\xi(0)=0$, that is at the initial moment all the elements of the system are functioning (all the elements of the population are in the state of life).
Then

$$Z_0' = X_0(E_-).$$

The probability $q_{0,j}(E_-)$ is computed from the equations system of (7.3.5) and from the formula of the total probability is derived

$$P\{Z_i'' \le t\} = \sum_{j \in E_-} q_{0,j}(E_-) P\{X_j(E_+) \le t\} .$$

Probability of the event that in the moment of the first renewal the process enters the state $k \in E_+$ from the formula of the total probability is equal to

$$\sum_{j \in E_-} q_{0,j}(E_-) q_{j,k}(E_+) .$$

If these probabilities are known, then the probability distribution Z_1' and the probabilities of entrance to given states at the moment of the second failure (at the moment of the second change of the population state) can be computed. This in turn makes it possible to compute the probability distribution Z_2' and so on.

To compute the stationary distributions of the random variables Z' and Z'' let us introduce the following probabilities:

- $q_i(E_+)$ - probability of an event that in the moment of the renewal of the population (as the system) in stationary conditions the process enters the state $i \in E_+$,
- $q_i(E_-)$ - probability of an event that in the moment of the death of the population (the failure of the system) in stationary conditions the process enters the state $i \in E_-$.

$q_i(E_+)$ is the probability of the event that in the time dt the process will pass from the set E_- to the state $i \in E_+$ on condition that in this time the process passed from the set E_- to the set E_+.

Formally, it is transcribed by formulas

$$q_i(E_+) = \frac{\sum_{j \in E_-} p_j \lambda_{j,i}}{\sum_{i \in E_+} \sum_{j \in E_-} p_j \lambda_{j,i}} \tag{7.3.6}$$

and analogically

$$q_i(E_-) = \frac{\sum_{j \in E_+} p_j \lambda_{j,i}}{\sum_{i \in E_-} \sum_{j \in E_+} p_j \lambda_{j,i}} \tag{7.3.6}$$

where p_j are the stationary probabilities of the process.

The probability distributions of the random variables Z', Z'' and Z - residual time of the system life are given by

$$P\{Z' \le t\} = \sum_{i \in E_+} q_i(E_+) P\{X_i(E_-) < t\} \tag{7.3.7}$$

$$P\{Z'' \le t\} = \sum_{i \in E_-} q_i(E_-) P\{X_i(E_+) < t\} \tag{7.3.8}$$

$$P\{Z > t\} = \sum_{i \in E_+} p_i P\{X_i(E_+) > t\} \tag{7.3.9}$$

The expected values of the basic reliability characteristics are given by

$$E(Z_0') = E(X_0(E_-)),$$

$$E(Z') = \sum_{i \in E_+} q_i(E_+) E(X_i(E_-)),$$

$$E(Z'') = \sum_{i \in E_-} q_i(E_-) E(X_i(E_+)),$$

$$E(Z) = \sum_{i \in E_+} p_i E(X_i(E_-)),$$

8. The pure death process

The pure death process is a homogenous Markov process $\xi(t)$ with the space of states 0,1,2,...,n,..., for which

$$\lambda_{i,j} = \lambda_i = 0 \text{ as well as } \lambda_{i,j} = 0 \text{ for } j \neq i+1 .$$

That is, the pure death process passes successively through the states $0 \to 1 \to 2 \to ... n \to ...$ and in the state k it is for the time t_k with exponential distribution

$$P\{t_k > t\} = e^{-\lambda_k t}$$

and next it passes to the state $k+1$ with the probability one.

Let $E_+ = \{0,1,2,...,n\}$ be a set of the functioning states of the system (the set of the states of the life of the population), $E_- = \{n+1, n+2,...\}$ is a set of the failed states of the system (the set of the states of death of the population), and $\xi(0) = 0$.

Because the pure death process describes behaviour of the non- renewable system, we assume that a basic characteristic of the pure death process is the time until the first failure of the system (the time until the first change of the state of the population, the time until the first of death of the population)

$$Z_0' = X_0(E_-) .$$

And as before

$$X_i(A) = \inf\{t : \xi(t) \in A | \xi(0) = i\} \quad \text{and} \quad E[\exp(-zX_i(E_-))] = \varphi_i(z)$$

are introduced.

Then the equations system (7.3.4) takes on the form

$$\begin{cases} -\lambda_i \varphi_{i+1}(z) + (z + \lambda_i)\varphi_i(z) = 0, i < n \\ (z + \lambda_n)\varphi_n(z) = \lambda_n \end{cases}$$

from which it follows that

$$\varphi_0(z) = E\left(e^{-z\tau_0'}\right) = \frac{\lambda_0 \lambda_1 \cdots \lambda_n}{(z + \lambda_0)...(z + \lambda_n)} ,$$

$$\overline{F}(t) = P\{Z_0' > t\} = \lambda_0 \lambda_1 \cdots \lambda_n \sum_{k=0}^{n} \frac{e^{-\lambda_k t}}{\lambda_k w'(-\lambda_k)} \tag{8.1}$$

where $w(x) = (x + \lambda_0)(x + \lambda_1)...(x + \lambda_n)$.

Because the time until the first moment of the failure of the system (the time until the first change of the state of the population, the time until the first death of the population) is a sum of the random variables

$$Z_0' = \xi_0 + \xi_1 + ... + \xi_n$$

hence the expected time until the first failure of the system (the time until the first change of the state of the population, the time until the first death of the population) is equal to

$$E(Z_0') = \frac{1}{\lambda_0} + \frac{1}{\lambda_1} + \ldots + \frac{1}{\lambda_n} \tag{8.2}$$

9. The general pure death process

The general pure death process is a homogeneous Markov process $\xi(t)$ with the number of states $E = \{\underline{Y}: \ \underline{Y}: Y^n \to \{0,1\}^n\}$, where $\underline{Y} = (Y_1,\ldots,Y_n)^T$, $Y_i = 0$ or $Y_i = 1$, for which only immediate transitions in the form

$$\underline{Y} = (Y_1,\ldots,Y_{i-1},0,Y_{i+1},\ldots,Y_n) \to \underline{Y}' = (Y_1,\ldots,Y_{i-1},1,Y_{i+1},\ldots,Y_n), \quad i = 1,\ldots,n,$$

with the transition rates $\lambda_i(\underline{Y})$ are possible.

Such a transition denotes a change of the state of one element of the population and can be interpreted in the research of the population lifetime as a failure, an arrival or a death of the i-th element.

By the previous denotations E_+ is a set of the states of life of the population (a set of the functioning states of the system), E_- is a set of the states of death of the population (a set of the failed states of the system).

We assume that in the initial moment all the elements are in the state of life that is $\underline{Y}(0) = \underline{0}$.

The notion of the way π is defined as class of the realisation of the process $\underline{Y}(t)$ with an assumed sequence of the states, through which the process passes. This sequence begins from the state at the initial moment zero and ends with the state at the moment of the change of the state of the system (the failure of the system, the death of the population)

$$\pi = (\underline{Y}^{(0)}, Y^{(1)},\ldots, Y^{(m)}),$$

$$\underline{Y}^{(0)} = (0,0,\ldots,0), \ \underline{Y}^{(k)} \in E_+ \text{ for } k < m, \ Y^{(m)} \in E_-.$$

Each transition from a state to a state described by the way $\pi = (\underline{Y}^{(0)}, Y^{(1)},\ldots, Y^{(m)})$ is the change of the state of the system element (which is the failure of the system element or arrival or death of the element of the population of the size n, $n \geq 1$).

Summary rate is defined then as

$$\lambda(\underline{Y}) = \sum_{i=1}^{n} \lambda_i(\underline{Y}),$$

where $\lambda_i(\underline{Y}) = 0$, if in the state $\underline{Y}$ i-th element is already failed (i-th element of the population has arrived).

Then from the properties of the Markov process

$$p_i(\underline{Y}) = \frac{\lambda_i(\underline{Y})}{\lambda(\underline{Y})}$$

is the probability of the event that the process passes from the state $\underline{Y}=(Y_1,...,Y_{i-1},0,Y_{i+1},...,Y_n)$ to the state $\underline{Y}'=(Y_1,...,Y_{i-1},1,Y_{i+1},...,Y_n)$, that is i-th element changes its state (fails, arrives or dies).

Let i_k denote the number of the element changing the state (failing, arriving or dying) when it passes from the state $Y^{(k-1)}$ to the state $Y^{(k)}$ during the passage of the way π.

Then from the formula of the total probability the probability of the change of the system state (failure of the system, death of the population) equals

$$F(t)=P\{Z'_0 \le t\}=\sum_{\pi} F(t|\pi)p(\pi) \tag{9.1}$$

where sum is calculated for all the possible ways π,

$$p(\pi)=p_{i_1}\left(e^{(0)}\right)p_{i_2}\left(e^{(1)}\right)...p_{i_m}\left(e^{(m)}\right)$$

is the passage probability of the way π, and $F(t|\pi)$ is the conditional probability of the change of state of the system (failure of the system, death of the population) on the condition of the passage of the way π.

Since in each state $\underline{Y}^{(k)}$ the process remains for the time with the exponential distribution with the parameter $\lambda\left(\underline{Y}^{(k)}\right)$, hence the conditional process $\underline{Y}(t)$ on the condition of the passage of the way π is the pure death process with transition rates being given by $\lambda\left(\underline{Y}^{(k)}\right)$.

Substituting to the form (9.1) the expression (8.1) the probability of the first death of the population (the first failure of the system) is obtained.

The expected time of the first death of the population (the first failure of the system) from the equality (8.2) is derived and equals

$$E\left(Z'_0\right)=\sum_{\pi} p(\pi)\left[\frac{1}{\lambda\left(\underline{Y}^{(0)}\right)}+...+\frac{1}{\lambda\left(\underline{Y}^{(m-1)}\right)}\right].$$

10. Conclusions

In this study the process of Internet data collection is interpreted and analysed as a random experiment or the life test of population surveyed by using the notions and methods of the probability and reliability theories. A random set of respondents who participate in Internet survey is called the uncontrolled sample and defined as the counting process by using Poisson processes. The proposed approach allows to study some stochastic properties of the process of the Internet data collection, the calculation and the estimate of the basic characteristics by the assumed assumptions. Moreover, the Markov methods are applied to description of a life testing experiment in which the basic characteristics of a reliability of the length of the population lifetime are derived, when the finite population is interpreted as a system with the monotonic structure function and the changes of the population states are described through the death and the general death processes.

11. Acknowledgments

The research was partially supported by the Ministry of Science and Higher Education programs 03/S/0063/04, 03/S/0059/07 and 03/E/0015/08, Warsaw School of Economics.

12. References

Barlow, R.E. & Proschan, F. (1965, 1996). *Mathematical theory of reliability*. J. Wiley and Sons, Inc. New York or Philadelphia SIAM, ISBN 0-89971-369-2

Barlow, R.E. & Proschan, F. (1975). *Statistical theory of reliability and life testing*, Holt, Reinhart and Winston INC. New York

Biffignandi, S. & Pratesi, M. (2000). Modelling firm response and contact probabilities in Web surveys, *Proceedings of the "Second International Conference on establishment surveys"*, USA, June 2000, Buffalo

Bracha, Cz. (1996). *Theoretical foundation of survey sampling* (in Polish), Polish Scientific Publisher, ISBN 83-01-12123-8, Warsaw

Callegaro, M. & Disogra, CH. (2008). Computing response metrics for online panels, *Public Opinion Quarterly*, Vol. 72, No. 5, 2008, Special Issue, pp. 1008-1032, ISSN 0033-362X

Couper, M.P. & Miller, P.V. (2008). Web survey methods, *Public Opinion Quarterly*, Vol. 72, No. 5, 2008, Special Issue, pp. 831-835, ISSN 0033-362X

Dilman, Don A.; Smyth, J. & Christian, L.M. (2008). *Internet, Mail and Mixed-Mode Surveys: The Tailored Design Method, 3rd ed.*, Hoboken, NJ: John Wiley Co., ISBN 978-0-471-69868-5, New York

Galesic, M. (2006). Dropout on the Web: effects of interest and burden experiences during an online survey, *Journal of Official Statistics*, Vol. 22, No. 2, June 2006, pp. 313-328, ISSN 0282-423X

Getka-Wilczyńska, E. (2003). Using WWW for data collection in a national survey on scholarship granted to young researches, *Statistics in Transition, Journal of the Polish Statistical Association*, Vol. 6, No. 1, June 2003, pp. 33-55, ISSN 1234-7655

Getka-Wilczyńska, E. (2004). About random properties of an uncontrolled sample (in Polish, O losowych własnościach próby niekontrolowanej), *Annals of College of Economic Analyses*, Vol. 13, 2004, pp. 59-69, ISSN 1232-4671

Getka-Wilczyńska, E. (2005). Stochastic properties of Internet data collection process, *Proceedings of the 55th Session of the International Statistical Institute*, CD-ROM, paper No. 998, ISBN 1-877040-28-2, Australia, April 2005, International Statistical Institute, Sydney

Getka-Wilczyńska, E. (2007). Markov methods in test of the population lifetime, *Proceedings of the 56th Session International Statistical Institute 56th Session*, CD-ROM, papers No. 1708, ISBN 978-972-8859-71-8, Portugal, July 2007, Centro de Estatística e Aplicacões (CEAUL), Instituto Nacional de Estatística (INE) & International Statistical Institute(ISI), Lisbon

Getka-Wilczyńska, E. (2008). The Internet sample, *Statistics in Transition – new series, Journal of Polish Statistical Association*, Vol. 8, No. 3, December 2008, pp. 553-560

Hardy, G.H.; Littlewood, J.E. & Polya, G. (1934). *Inequalities.* Cambridge University Press, Cambridge Internet and Innovative Data Collection (2001). *Bulletin of the International Statistical Institute, 53rd Session, Proceedings, Tome LIX, Three books, Book 1,* Topic 16, pp. 229-253, ISBN 90-73592-20-8, South Korea, August 2001, International Statistical Institute, Seoul

Kingman, J.F.C. (2002): *Poisson' processes* (in Polish), Polish Scientific Publishers, ISBN 83-01-13534-4, Warsaw

Kopociński, B. (1973). *Outline of the renewal and reliability theory,* (in Polish), Polish Scientific Publishers, Warsaw

Kordos, J. (1982). *Quality of statistical data* (in Polish), Polish Economic Publisher, Warsaw

Koutra, M. V.; Tsitmidelis, S. & Zissmopoulos, V. (2003). Evaluation of reliability bounds by set covering models, *Statistics and Probability Letters,* 61, 2003, pp. 163-175, ISSN 0167-7152

Lee, S. (2006). Propensity score adjustment as a weighting scheme for volunteer panel Web surveys, *Journal of Official Statistics,* Vol. 22, No. 2, June 2006, pp. 329-349, ISSN 0282-423X

Särndal, C.E.; Swensson, B. & Wretman, J. (1992). *Model assisted Survey Sampling,* Springer-Verlag New York Inc., ISBN 0-387-97528-4, New York

Sołowiew, A.D. (1983). *Analytical methods in reliability theory* (in Polish), Technical - Scientific Publisher, ISBN 83-204-0473-8, Warsaw

Steczkowski, J. (1988). *Application of survey sampling in social-economics research* (in Polish), Polish Economic Publisher, Warsaw

Tillě, Y. (2006). *Sampling algorithms,* Springer Science-Business Media, Inc., ISBN 10:0-387-30814-8; ISBN 13:978-0387-30814-2, New York

Toepoel, V.; Das, M. & Van Soes, A. (2008). Effects of design in Web surveys, *Public Opinion Quarterly,* Vol. 72, No. 5, 2008, Special Issue, pp. 985-1007, ISSN 0033-362X

Vehovar, V. (2007). Workshop on Internet Survey Methodology, Ullehammer, September 2007, http://vv.ris.org

www.WebSM.org

Wywiał, J. (1992). *Statistical survey sampling in economics research* (in Polish), Economic Academy, Katowice

17

Toward Personalized RSS Retrieval Service: The Effect of Using User's Context

Haesung Lee[1] and Joonhee Kwon[2]
Dept. Computer Science, Kyonggi University
Republic of Korea

1. Introduction

Web 2.0 is a new way to find, save, and share information generated on the web. The goal of Web 2.0 is to facilitate forming network and sharing knowledge between users. Useful techniques that allow users easily to edit, store and publish contents on the web have been created. After that, multiple personal contents platform or personal media platform such as blog have developed. Using those platforms, a private individual publishes and shares his or her useful knowledge with others on the web very easily (Tim Oreilly. 2007). In addition, personalization is very critical concept to Web 2.0. Multiple personal contents platform or media platforms such as a blog or YouTube [www.youtube] allow users easily to edit, store and publish contents on the web. Moreover, those techniques help people publish and share his or her useful knowledge with others on the web very easily (Maged N Kamel Boulos et al. 2006). Web rapidly enlarges with explosively and newly increased information formed in UCC (User Created Contents). More that 513 million people around the world now have access to this global information resource (Lyman et al. 2000). However, how do all of these people find the information they are most interested in from among all of those terabytes? One among the most time-consuming human activities in modern times is keeping up updated and useful information with a huge amount of continuously generated information. The need of quickly obtaining and effectively sharing that information should be more concerned.

In Web 2.0, it is very important that useful information should be found, acquired and consumed efficiently. It is no longer the user who searches the information he or she is looking for, but it is the information that reaches directly its consumers. Also, each user is provided with the different information what he or she interests individually and shares his or her own worth knowledge with others (Tim Oreilly. 2007).

After appearance of the World Wide Web, initial search engines possessing only 1000 Web page indices, the method of acquiring information and ranking mechanisms have repeated a numerous change to provide more satisfactory services to users (Sergey Brin et al. 1999). In spite of dazzling technical development, the expansion of the web continually has demanded new and epoch-making techniques relevant the mechanism through which a search engine efficiently acquires information generated on the web and effectively provides each user with useful information.

The RSS is considered as the next generation information delivery technique, which deliveries newly created information to users simultaneously and frequently without asking them to visit the site every time when new content is published. Practically, many services in Web 2.0 provide useful information in RSS feed format and a great many RSS feeds has risen in quite short term (Don E. Descy. 2004).
Although there are actually millions of feeds available, finding those that are appealing and relevant to user's interests is not always easy. By rising RSS feed, consequently, many RSS feed search services have appeared. Those RSS feed search service provide useful information such as the best favorite feed or blog (A. Gulli. 2005). However, those RSS feed search services are all tiptoeing around RSS search, but none have yet to launch a full-blown personalized RSS search service.
As the scope of the internet gets larger and larger, the need for personalization to bring it within our scope becomes more and more important. Nevertheless, typically existing RSS retrieval systems offer user RSS feeds as results using mainly keyword based matching mechanism or statistical approach such as favorite RSS feeds with many persons (Chris Sherman. 2005). Therefore, existing RSS feed retrieval services have limitations to answer efficiently to user's need to obtain useful and appropriate RSS feeds. In other words, because of this limitation, those services are not useful to many users.
To provide more useful and personalized RSS feed retrieval service to each user, it is important to incorporate the feed characteristics and the user's context. We describe this corporation in this article later.
Contexts are any information that can be used to characterize the situation of an entity such as a person, place or object (Jong-yi Hong et al. 2009). To provide each user or searcher more personalized and useful information, number of applications or web services takes the advantage of various contexts such as user's preference (Haveliwala et al. 2003). For realizing completely personalization in Web 2.0, the user's preference is very efficiently used to find and to acquire useful information among overexposure of information (Diane Kelly et al. 2003). That is, user's context has a large influence on the interest and intent of one particular user.
Considering those described above, we introduce personalized RSS feed retrieval system in which two factors are mainly considered, which are user's context and existing information retrieval techniques based on RSS characteristics.
In detail this article is organized as follows: Section 2 explores conceptual personalization in Web 2.0 and important challenges to implementation of personalized application in Web 2.0; Section 3 introduces RSS's potential ability to deriver personalized information to each user. Also, in this section, we explore the existing RSS services or applications and their limitations and introduce some solutions; Section 4 focuses on the use of user's context in personalized RSS retrieval through the case of previous study; Section 5 outlines our design of personalized RSS feed retrieval. For new and efficeint personalized RSS feed retrieval, we describe some algorithms for incorporating information retrieval techniques and characteristic of RSS. And we introduces each module of designed personalized RSS retrieval system in detail and an equtation for ranking RSS feeds based on user's preference. Section 7 looks at future possibilitof our proposed personalized RSS feed service in ubiquitous computing environment and tha way of our research in the future.

2. Personalization in Web 2.0

Web personalization can be described as any action that can customize the content or structure of a web site to the user's taste or preferences. Personalization has widely been utilized by e- commerce organizations to better serve their customers (Bamshad Mobasher et al. 2000).

Fig. 1. A person who has attributes

For personalization of Web 2.0, there are two important things: people, and content objects. People are represented by identities (Ryan Turner, 2007). Most of people have many attributes. Identities have information attached to them. In Fig. 1, there is a person. The person has attributes.

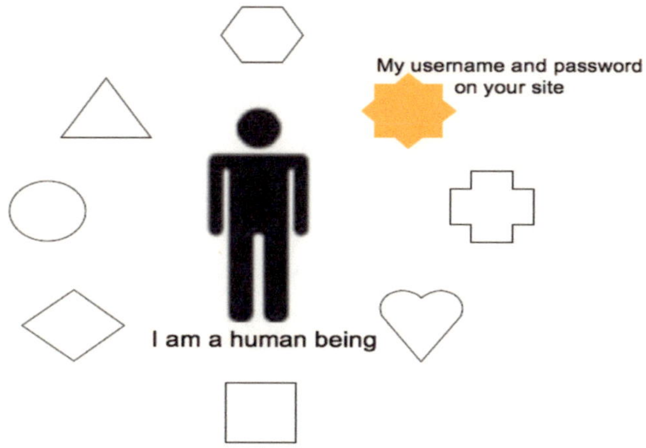

Fig. 2. The user who has some account attributes

When a person comes to your web site, you often know a few things about them, like their referring URL, their browser, etc. This isn't much. An early goal for conversion on Web 2.0 sites is account creation. In Figure 2, there is a person with a brand-new account. You know their account information, but not much else. The person has many attributes, but you don't know what they are. A web site is made of contents objects, and the content objects have attributes. In Web 2.0, you know what some of the attributes are. Other attributes, like user-generated tags, might not yet be knowable. One of the most basic kinds of personalization is access control. Based on the person's account information, they can access some content objects and not others.

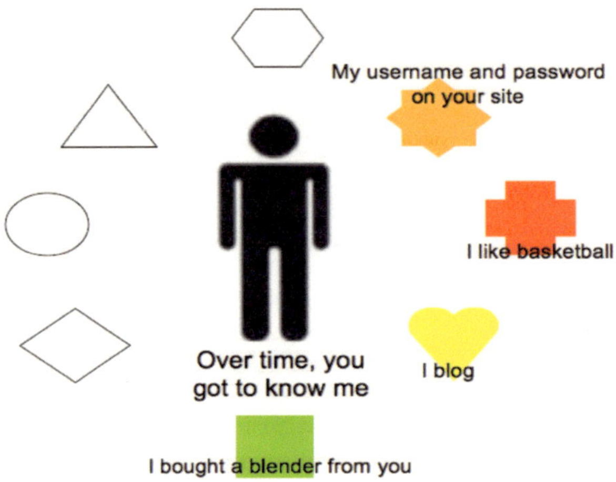

Fig. 3. A person frequently using your web site

Like the case saw in Figure 3, as a person uses your web site, you learn more about their attributes. Sometimes they tell you ("subscribe to newsletter") and other times you learn about people by knowing what they do ("I bought Scoble's book about blogging").
Different content objects have different attributes. Some, like content type (photo, video, downloadable document, product info) are structured, and others, like title, are unstructured. Some, like tags on a Flickr photo, are added by users.

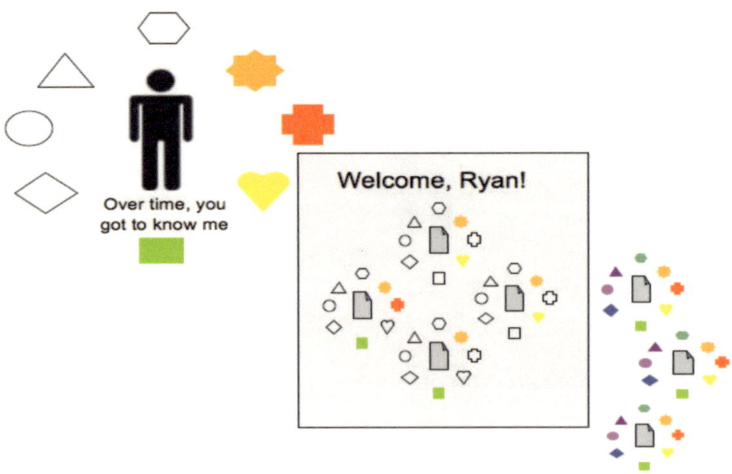

Fig. 4. Personalized information for an user

Like Figure 4, basic content personalization is a matter of matching up the attributes of a person with the attributes of a content object. You know the person likes basketball because they bought a Duke Basketball jersey, so you show them a content object that has to do with March Madness.

On the UK's Guardian newspaper site, writer Jemina Kiss suggested that web 3.0 will be about recommendation. "If web 2.0 could be summarized as interaction, web 3.0 must be about recommendation and personalization." she wrote (Jemima Kiss. 2008). We don't think whether this day is web 2.0 or web 3.0, but we know that the personalized information service is very important and needed service for information providers and information consumers in both two generations.

Fig. 5. Amazon's personalization service

Like figure 5, Amazon (http://www.amazon.com) has been the early adopter of personalization technology to recommend products to shoppers on its site, based upon their previous purchases (Linden, G. Et al. 2003). Amazon makes extensive use of collaborative filtering in its personalization technology.

Google provides a personalized service shown in figure 6, the gadget maker, which allows users to make their personalized web page by themselves reflecting their preference.

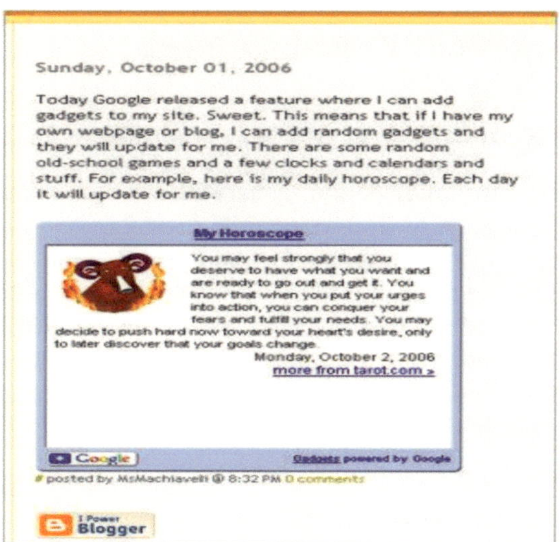

Fig. 6. Gadget Maker

Another example providing personalized service on the web is Pandora's music genome project offering users music streaming service based on their preference for music (Shane et al. 2007). This provides very useful service that allows users not to take the time of searching music related their preferences. With this service, user listens music related their preferences continually. The use of those contexts in user-centered service makes it possible to provide more useful and personalized information satisfying each user.

In Web 2.0, the concept of personalization is very important. As the scope of the Internet gets larger and larger, the need for personalization to bring it within our scope becomes more and more important (Udi Manber et al. 2000). But, any online examples where personalization was really well integrated with the user experience currently are very few. The best example we can come up with was Amazon's personalization engine. However this case is just scratching the surface of what's possible.

Most application or studies about personalized information service mainly focus on statistical or artificial intelligence techniques related with the semantic web. In this article, however, we focus on the use of user's contexts. Using user's context in information deliveries process is to satisfy user's need for information than other computational approaches.

There are currently many projects underway exploring methods of personalization for information seeking. The general starting point is to represent the interests of a user by means of one or more keyword profiles expressing aspects of the user's interest. In a very simple approach incoming information is compared with the profiles and is possessed to the user if there is a sufficiently high match (Stephen S. Yau et al. 2003). This case is very simple to standard information filtering techniques where the profiles represent topics of interest to the users. The most important issue in personalized information retrieval is how the interests of the user are captured. Various options are available; the user selects from a number of preset topics, the user enters sets of keywords which they believe represent topics that they are interested in, or the personalization system monitors the user's behavior and learns profiles from this.

It is sure that personalization in Web 2.0 and future Web is very important thing. So, we use user's context to provide personalized information to each user.

3. The next generation information delivery technique, RSS

The amount of the different information generated on the broad-scale web increases explosively. In Web 2.0, it is very important that useful information for each consumer should be found, acquired and consumed effectively. It is no longer the user that searches the information she is looking for, but it is the information she values that reaches directly its consumers. RSS (Really simple syndication) is a very useful technique in Web 2.0 providing users a efficient new way to share content on their website with other users and makes it available to offer them various information without asking them to visit the site every time when new content is published (S. Jeff Cold. 2006).

```
- <rss version="2.0">
 - <channel>
     <title>Information Retrieval Gupf</title>
     <atom:link href="http://irgupf.com/feed/" rel="self" type="application/rss+xml"/>
     <link>http://irgupf.com</link>
   - <description>
       Information Retrieval Research, Issues, and Discussion
     </description>
     <pubDate>Thu, 16 Apr 2009 21:11:40 +0000</pubDate>
     <generator>http://wordpress.org/?v=2.7</generator>
     <language>en</language>
     <sy:updatePeriod>hourly</sy:updatePeriod>
     <sy:updateFrequency>1</sy:updateFrequency>
   - <item>
       <title> "Improving Findability" Falls Short of the Mark</title>
     - <link>
         http://irgupf.com/2009/04/16/improving-findability-falls-short-of-the-mark/
       </link>
     - <comments>
         http://irgupf.com/2009/04/16/improving-findability-falls-short-of-the-mark/#comments
       </comments>
       <pubDate>Thu, 16 Apr 2009 21:08:23 +0000</pubDate>
       <dc:creator>jeremy</dc:creator>
       <category>Exploratory Search</category>
       <category>Social Implications</category>
       <guid isPermaLink="false">http://irgupf.com/?p=502</guid>
     - <description>
         Via Tim O&#8217;Reilly on Twitter, I came across this article by Vanessa Fox on how go
         better informed and government to be more transparent. Fox writes: In an earlier post, I sa
       </description>
     - <content:encoded>
         <p>Via <a href="http://twitter.com/timoreilly">Tim O&#8217;Reilly on Twitter</a>, I cam
```


Fig. 7. RSS Feed

RSS can literally be used with just about any kind of web-based content. RSS fundamentally is a simple specification that uses XML and a format for web-based content in a standard way. RSS is a form of XML. An example of RSS feed is shown in Figure 7. A big advantage of XML is that the data can be self-contained. Inside of XML, there's an opportunity to include a description of the methods required to use the data, along with the data itself. Because RSS uses XML to glean relevant information, RSS may well become the universal method people use to mine information from the Internet (Ronald J. Glotzbach et al. 2007). Figure 9 shows a RSS format with number of tags. Those tags are composed structurally and expressed in the tree as viewed at Figure 8.

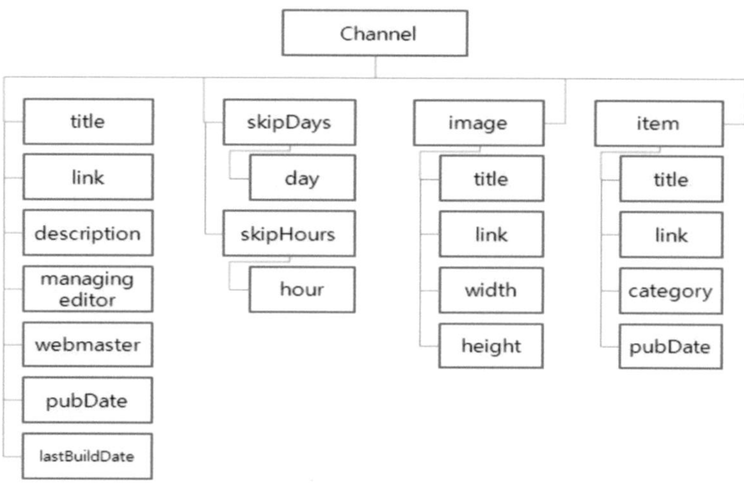

Fig. 8. RSS feed structure

RSS feeds are increasingly being used for other types of content. For example, you can get RSS feeds with weather forecasts, company news and financial information, package tracking and lots of others. RSS completely revolutionizes the paradigm according to which people collect information generated at number of information sources. A recent Pew Internet & American Life Project poll shows that only 9% of Americans understand what RSS feeds can do, and according to Forrester Research, only 2% of households with Internet access use RSS (Overhole et al. 2005)
Although there are actually millions of feeds available, finding those that are appealing and relevant to a user isn't always easy. While RSS is not a widely used internet tool today, a simple-to- use software client can make its use widespread in the near future. Email didn't go mainstream because people understood how data packets made their way around the Net. It happened when an email client made that technology invisible and easy to use. RSS will likely follow a similar path. Microsoft has already pledged to support all forms of RSS in its new browser: Internet Explorer 7 (Langley. 2005). RSS will be used increasingly as a way to cope with information overload.
News Aggregators (aggregators) or feed collectors download information from RSS feeds to which you subscribe based on key. Increasingly, publishers are providing RSS feeds for aggregation. This makes it easy to search their publications for research purposes. For example, the New York Times provides a free RSS feed (http://www.nytimes.com/services/xml/rss/). The range of current events and even topic-specific research that researchers can collect by subscribing to several RSS feeds is significant (Richardson. et al). Using a web-based aggregator, users can access their feeds from any place they have an internet connection. Once users create a free account on web-based aggregator, they can add the RSS URL of any information resource to begin the feed. But, this simple and efficient RSS aggregator (or reader) services have some limitations to satisfy user's underlying need for information. To provide each user RSS feeds automatically and periodically, these services request users to input RSS feed URLs themselves. However those RSS feed search engine annoy users with those requests. Because, it is very difficult to users to find which RSS channels publish useful RSS feeds satisfying them.
Although there are actually millions of feeds available, finding those that are appealing and relevant to a user isn't always easy. By rising necessity of RSS, consequently, RSS feed search engines mainly dealing with RSS feed appear.

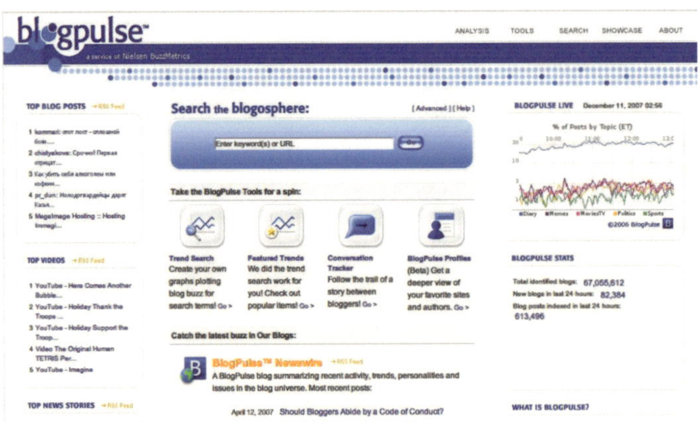

Fig. 9. Blogpulse

Blogpulse (www.blogpulse.com) viewed at Figure 9 is known primarily as a tool for tracking trends and hot topics in the blogosphere. Also, it has the largest indexes of feed-based search engine. Blogpulse's search service provides phrase search, all the words or any of the words filters, and even allows a user to create her or his own free-form boolean queries.

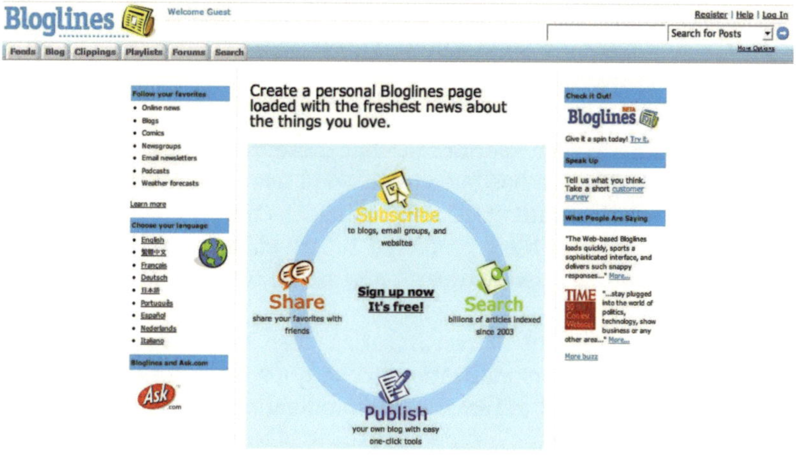

Fig. 10. Bloglines

Figure 10 shows Bloglines(www.bloglines.com). It is both a feed search tool and a feed reader/aggregator. A drop-down menu next to its search form allows a user to search all of the indexed blogs or to add a feed to user's subscription.

They are all tiptoeing around RSS search, but none have yet to launch a full-blown RSS search service. While there are a number of smaller, specialized blog and feed search engines, their lack of resources and the problem of blog and feed spam mean their search results are often useless. So finding relevant feeds, at least for the time-being, often remains a hit-or-miss affair. Also, those RSS feed search engines cannot provide effectively and quickly useful results related each user's need for some information.

To provide more relevant information to the user in RSS retrieval service, it is important to incorporate the feed characteristics and the user's contextual information into the retrieval process. Because the previous retrieval services have not taken into account them, however, they provide no personalized information to each user.

Using RSS techniques, information delivery service to each user is very efficient way for implementing personalization in Web 2.0. We focus on this RSS potential. Also, we expand its techniques to integrate user's context providing each users with their underlying needing information. Later, we describe the integration of RSS and user's context in follow sections.

4. The potential ability of user's context

In this section, we describe user's contexts in ubiquitous computing area and introduce some applications to see potential ability of using user's context in our approach.

Contexts are any information that can be used to characterize the situation of an entity (Gregory D.Abowd et al. 1999). An entity is a person, place, or object that is considered

relevant to interaction between a user and an application. When humans talk with humans, they are able to use implicit situational information, or context, to improve more communicational functionalities. Unfortunately, this ability to convey ideas does not transfer well to humans interacting with computers. By improving the application's access to context, it is available to increase the richness of communication in human-computer interaction and make it possible to produce more useful computational services. There are various human factor related context such as knowledge of habits and emotional state of each user (Anind K. Dey. 2001).
That is an especially favorable case to use context to help select the information that is needed by a user. To provide each user or searcher more interesting and useful information, number of application or solution has been developed using many various contexts such as user's preference (Albrecht Schmidt et al. 1999). A user's context consists of the their present state, their previous history and their predicted future states; this can be enhanced by the contexts of other, similar or related, humans and other objects, or even by the context of information itself.
Currently, a considerable amount of research has been done on providing personalized information service. Existing personalization techniques on information retrieval can be either manual personalization or automatic personalization. Manual personalization, such as MyYahoo (http://my.yahoo.com), allows a user to select the user's own interests from a predefined list. In these services, an account is created on the web page, and the user selects checkboxes to determine what types of content are of interest to the user. There are some problems in manual personalization; (1) It is inconvenient for users to specify many options, (2) The provided options may be too coarse-grained to reflect users' preferences, (3) It is static and requires users to update their profile after their preferences change. Perkowitz, et al. demonstrated the feasibility of automatic personalization for desktop access to the Web (M. Perkowiz et al. 1997). Different from manual personalization, automatic personalization does not require explicit effort from users to customize their profiles. It automatically does the personalization based on access logs using some machine learning, such as Daily Learner, or data mining techniques, such as usage-based Web personalization (D. Billsus et al. 2000 and M. Perkowitz et al. 1999). Widely used data mining techniques include clustering, classification, association rules, etc. Clustering plays an important role in Web mining and has found numerous applications, such as Web search engines, Web directories, decision making assistance, and Web personalization. However, these techniques do not adapt quickly to changing user interests along with the changes in various useful contexts, such as time and location.
In conclusion, the existing systems that can provide personalized information either require users to provide a lot of personal information through questionnaires or to use data-mining techniques to gather and analyze information about users to generate user profiles. These systems cannot effectively reflect the actual needs of users because the actual needs of users may change according to current situation of users and many user actions (e.g. the most recently visited web page) are not considered by this type of systems. So, we seek to more useful user's context and different approach with existing studies to feed each users the information that she want, when she want it. We know that retrieval is much more effective if the context is richer than just location, and includes fields such as temperature, objects nearby, user's current interests, even her emotional state and etc. A context used to aid

retrieval can also usefully include fields that may be considered as aspects of the user model.

Context can also be associated with each of the documents that are candidates for retrieval. Thus a document may have contextual fields representing an associated preference or user's current location. Sometimes these contextual fields are part of the explicit mark-up of a document such as XML based RSS.

In later sections, we introduce related techniques for integrating information delivery technique and user's context to provide each user with personalized information.

5. Personalized RSS Feed Service Using User's Context

In the future, we will be provided information that we want, when we want it. But, there are no tries to integrate next generation syndication technique, RSS and user's context to provide personalized information to each user. In this section, we attempt to look beyond the needs of current personalization of Web 2.0.

In order to locate documents of interest users frequently make use of search engines such as Google. However, current retrieval engines take no account of the individual user and their personal interests or their physical context. We refer to extension of established information retrieval as personalized information retrieval.

IR (Information Retrieval) and the related technology of IF (Information Filtering) are concerned with the finding of information, often in the form of text documents, which are in some sense about a topic that a user is interested in. But, both are not concerned with satisfying the user's underlying information need. Typically, the user expresses their information need as a query, which is then matched against the available documents. Then, information is retrieved from a collection of discrete documents.

In a different way of typical RSS search engine, we subdivide each RSS feeds by feed tags into fields. So, our proposed RSS retrieval service can match user's query with not only contents but also RSS tags. This is useful for users, because they can limit search range to specific content of RSS feeds.

Name of Field	**Description**	**Example**
Title	The title of content	Information Retrieval Gupf
PubDate	The publishing date of content	Thu, 16 Apr 2009 21:11:40 +0000
Author	The author of content	jeremy
link	URL of content	http://www.irgupf.com/2009/04/16/improving-findability-falls-short-of-the-mark/
Description	The content of feed	I came across this article by Vanessa Fox on how government can improve the findability of their web pages, and thereby allow citizens to become better informed and government to be more transparent.

Table 1. Subdivided fields

These fields may be textual, such as title, author, keywords, and full text of content. Table 1 shows subdivided fields by RSS tags. The objective of incorporating contextual information into the retrieval process is to attempt to deliver information most relevant to the user within their current context. Use of context for retrieval within personalized information retrieval is to determine the manner and timing of any information passed to the user. An issue is that, since the information is based on the user's context, it should be delivered in a timely fashion. So, for this consideration we take advantage of simple RSS techniques to deliver information to each user in time when her or his interest changed.

We think to provide more relevant information to the user in RSS retrieval service, it is important to incorporate the feed characteristics and the user's contextual information into the search process. However, the previous retrieval services have not taken into account them. This seriously limits to offer users with useful information in RSS retrieval service.

To provide most relevant contents formed in RSS such as blog or news contents to the users within their context, we incorporate user's contextual information into retrieval process. We consider the following we use the RSS tag structure in query processing. It enables users or search engine to limit retrieval range in a specific RSS feed tag, not searching full RSS documents. Secondly, we consider both the query term frequency and the update frequency in RSS channel. It enables users to get more useful RSS channel by considering multiple RSS channel features. Thirdly, we use the user's context in retrieval service. To provide a personalized retrieval service, it is needed to understand the user's interest or preference. The context has a large influence on the interest and intent of one particular user.

The retrieval task is to deliver the RSS feed that best match the current user's context such as the latest topic which is subscribed by the user. As the user's preference or interest changes, new information may need to be retrieved.

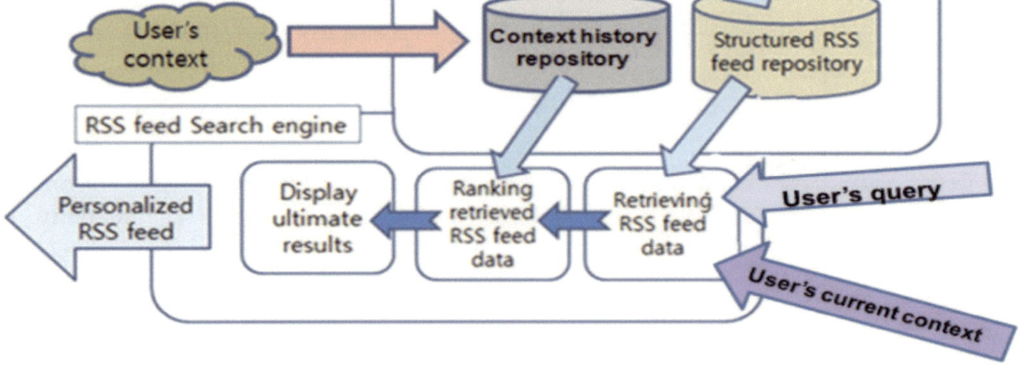

Fig. 11. System Architecture

Considering those described above, we introduce personalized RSS feed retrieval system in which two factors are mainly considered, characteristic of the RSS and user's context. It is a new RSS feed retrieval system that uses user's context for matching retrieval results to their interests.

Figure 11 shows the new architecture of the personalized RSS retrieval system. The architecture is composed of RSS feed crawler, RSS feed repository, and RSS feed retrieval engine. RSS feed crawlers visit RSS feed sites on the Web, down their RSS channels. After duplicated RSS feed elimination processing, captured RSS feeds are indexed in structured RSS feed repository. Historical repository is for storing user's previous context and current context from user's behavior such as web search. From this historical repository, RSS feed retrieval engine capture user's current interest or preference. Matching captured user's interest with indexed RSS contents deliver personalized RSS feed to each user. User's context history data can also associate with each of the RSS feeds in RSS feed repository. The RSS feeds in RSS feed repository are candidates for retrieval.

5.1 Collecting and Updating User's Context

Traditional information retrieval techniques usually require the users to spend much effort to repeatedly refine their request making their requests more specific to eliminate irrelevant results to obtain the result they want. However, those request cause annoyances to each user. And those techniques not provide related information with user's preference.

In order to get personalized RSS feeds based on user's preference, user's context data is needed. So, we store user's context data in a context history tuple. Historical repository showed in Figure 13 consists of a set of context history tuples. A context history tuple has the following structure.

Context History Schema		
Context Type	Context Value	RSS channel

Table 2. A context history schema

A tuple consists of context type, context value and context related data. The context type is to record context attributes such as time, location. Context value data can describe user's context such as time or location. RSS channel data express URL of RSS channel in which the user visit with some context value.

5.2 RSS feed crawler

Called periodically, RSS feed crawlers wander about on the web through the link to find RSS feed link. When accessing corresponded URL address, RSS feed crawlers judge whether the URL present RSS feed address or not. It is very important to acquire valid RSS feed address promptly. Our each RSS feed crawler include feed information cash with which RSS crawlers directly check whether acquired RSS feed URL is duplicated to elevate the whole system's performance. If acquired RSS feed URL is verified as new RSS feed URL, RSS feed crawlers get the RSS feed URL to structured RSS feed database. Otherwise, RSS feed crawlers extract new contents from the RSS feeds.

Figure 13 shows the operation flowchart of RSS feed crawler. By periodical calls which generate the crawler instance, the RSS feed crawler accesses site along hyperlink in the site and then downs web page to determine whether this page is RSS channel or not. If accessed page is RSS channel, RSS feed crawler checks duplicated accesses. RSS feed crawler acquire RSS feeds, and then insert it into structured RSS feed database. RSS feed crawlers use depth-first retrieval algorithm (DFS), which is used typically by many web crawlers (Allan Heydon et al. 1999). Proposed RSS feed crawlers input links acquired from web pages to queue and draw each links out orderly to judge whether the link is RSS channel link or not.

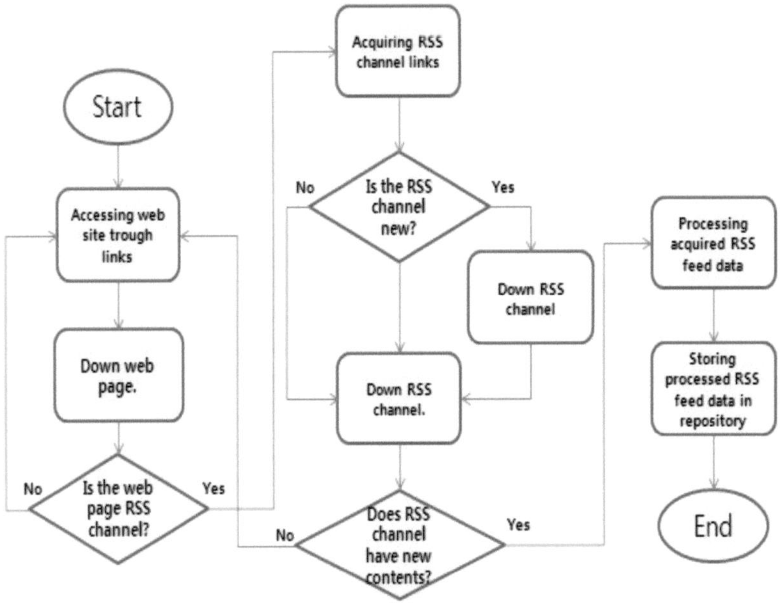

Fig. 12. Operation Flowchart of RSS Feed Crawler

The use of those structural characteristic of RSS not makes it very simple to express the web contents but also makes the RSS feed data to be accessed by crawlers and retrieval engine efficiently. The RSS feed data are structured by sub tags of item and stored in structured RSS feed database. Structured RSS feed enables users to limit retrieval in a specific feed tag, not searching all RSS feeds. This method can provide more useful RSS channel to users. For example, it allows retrieval engine to limit results to content published within a particular date range, and sort results by date reflecting user's context more efficiently.

5.3 RSS feed retrieval engine

In our proposed system, RSS feed retrieval engine takes important key role. The goal of proposed RSS feed retrieval engine is to offer users more useful information. We consider RSS feed characteristics and user's contextual information. The proposed retrieval method is comprised of four main tasks.

First, retrieval engine initiates the query and user's context from each user. Then, RSS feed retrieval engine accesses RSS feed repository and look up related contents using a Term

Frequency (TF) algorithm that retrieves RSS feeds on a similar topic (MJ Pazzani et al. 1996). It is commonly used method in traditional search engines. Second, we consider the publishing rate in RSS channel. The reason of considering the publishing frequency of RSS channel is to conclude whether those RSS channels publish useful contents continually. So, we use the pubDate tag of all feeds of each RSS channel to calculate update frequency. Calculating publishing frequency of each RSS channel can make it possible to filter out the spam RSS channel. Third, we conclude which content includes user's preference. By using user's context, it is possible to provide information with user's preference. Our RSS feed search engine takes the step in providing personalized search results based on user's preferences specifying what interests each users. By using a set of user's context history tuples in the historical repository, we can assume information that the user prefer. Finally, our method ranks RSS feeds using three tasks. Our ranking score is computed by (1) and (2). The RS_{uki} denotes the ranking score with respect to RSS feed i and term T_k of user u. It is possible to compute RS_{uki} with adjustable parameters α, β and $\gamma\ (\alpha + \beta + \gamma = 1)$:

$$\begin{aligned} & RS_{uki} = \alpha \frac{tf_{ik}}{tf_{\max}} + \beta \frac{uf_i}{uf_{\max}} + \gamma pd_{ui} \\ & tf_{ik} = \text{frequency of term } T_k \text{ in RSS channel } D_i \\ & tf_{\max} = \text{maximum frequency of term} \\ & uf_i = \text{updatae frequency pf RSS channel } D_i \\ & uf_{\max} = \text{maximum feed update frequency of RSS channel} \\ & pd_{ui} = \text{preference degree of user } u \text{ in RSS channel } D_i \end{aligned} \quad (1)$$

Equation (2) computes the preference degree of user u in RSS channel D_i. In equation (2), n is the number of context types and C_{uj} is the current context value with respect to context type j of user u.

$$pd_{ui} = \sum_{j=1}^{j \le n} \delta_j \cdot C_{uj}, \ Where \left(\sum_{j=1}^{j \le n} \delta_j = 1 \right) \quad (2)$$

After ranking RSS channels, RSS search engine provides result set of RSS channels in descending order by the computed ranking score.

6. Conclusion

Web 2.0 is a new way to find, save, and share information on the Web. The goal of Web 2.0 is to facilitate forming network and sharing knowledge between users. In Web 2.0, RSS is a one of the most important techniques and a new way to provide a simple way for user to share contents on their website and make it available to users without asking them to visit the site every time when new contents are added. Although there are a lot of RSS feeds available, finding which information are appealing and relevant to user's underlying information need is not easy. Therefore, it is important to incorporate the user's contextual

information and traditional information techniques based on RSS feed characteristics into the retrieval process to get relevant information to user. However, the previous search system have not taken into account them when provide retrieved information as a result to user. This seriously limits to offer users with reliable and useful information automatically.
Personalized RSS feed retrieval needs to bring together a number of disparate technologies. We have discussed related issues in personalized RSS feed retrieval. In this article, we proposes a new RSS feed retrieval system using user's context and traditional information techniques based on the characteristics of RSS feed. The proposed RSS feed search system efficiently collects the data from RSS service site by categorizing RSS feed structure and then rank RSS channel using user's context and relevant tag value.
Using user's context, it does provide personalized RSS feeds that automatically find RSS service site for user based on her or his interests and other RSS service site he or she read. That is, our proposed RSS feed search system uses personal preferences to deliver custom search results based on interests selected by users. Being different with the previous works, our proposed system acquires RSS feed on various web sites more efficiently using RSS feed structure and ranks information more reliably considering user's context such as preference, or predefined profile.
Consequently, RSS feed search engines can learn from what a user do to help him or her find what he or she need. With integration of processes for each factor, we can effective rank the retrieval set of searching result by reliable RSS channel, the source of RSS feed. It makes it possible to provide users with more personalized contents generated on reliable RSS feeds.

7. Future Work

Recent rapid advances in Internet-based information systems and handheld devices make it possible for users to retrieve information anytime and anywhere. Mobile and ubiquitous computing environments provide a challenging and exciting new domain for information retrieval. Some of the challenges are related with providing relevant and reliable information to users often engaged in other contexts of ubiquitous computing environment or to agents acting on behalf of the users.
Through our study described in this article, we know that identification of relevant information can be achieved by integration of existing methods from information retrieval and user's context. In the future work, we take advantage of contributions of human - computer interaction, mobile computing and context-awareness technologies to determine how and when to deliver the information to the user or how best to act on their user's behalf in ubiquitous computing environments. So, we will extend those techniques to meet the challenges and opportunity of ubiquitous context-aware environment. We will focus on context-awareness RSS feed retrieval mobile service in the ubiquitous computing environments in the future.

8. Acknowledgement

This work was supported by the Gyonggi Regional Research Center (GRRC) and Contents Convergence Software (CCS) Research Center.

9. References

A. Gulli.; (2005). The anatomy of a news search engine, *proceedings of international World Wide Web Conference,* pp.880 - 881, ISBN: 1-59593-051-5.

Albrecht Schmidt.; Michael Beigl.; Hans-W. Gellersen.; (1999), There is more to context than location, *Computers & Graphics,* pp. 893-901, Vol. 23, No. 6.

Allan Heydon.; Marc Najork.; (1999). Mercator: A scalable, extensible Web crawler, *World Wide Web,* pp. 219-229, Vol. 2, No. 4, ISBN: 1573-1413.

Anind K. Dey.; Understanding and Using Context, *Personal and Ubiquitous Computing, Springer-Verlag,* pp.4 – 7, Vol. 5, No. 1, ISSN:1617-4909

Bamshad Mobasher.; Robert Cooley.; Robert Cooley.; (2000). Automatic personalization based on Web usage mining, *Communications of the ACM,* pp. 142 – 151, Vol. 43, NO. 8.

Chris Sherman.; (2005), RSS Search Engines, *Search Engine Watch,* http://searchenginewatch.com/3 531191.

D. Billsus.; J. Pazzani.; J. Chen.; A learning agent for wireless news access, *Intelligent User Interfaces,* pp. 33-36, ISBN:1-58113-134-8

Diane Kelly.; Jaime Teevan.; (2003). Implicit feedback for inferring user preference: a bibliography, *ACM SIGIR Forum, pp. 18 – 28,* Vol. 37, No. 2, ISSN:0163-5840

Don E. Descy.; (2004). All aboard the internet: Introducing rss: your one stop for news and information!,*Jounal of TechTrends,* pp. 3-5, Vol.49, NO. 3.

Gregory D.Abowd.; Anind K. Dey.; Peter J. Brown.; Nigel Davies.; Mark Smith.; Pet Steggles.;(1999). Towards a better understanding of context and context- awareness, *Proceedings of the 1st international symposium on Handheld and Ubiquitous Computing,* pp. 304-307, ISBN:3-540-66550-1.

Haveliwala.; T.H.; (2003). Topic-sensitive PageRank: a context-sensitive ranking algorithm for Web search, *Knowledge and Data Engineering, IEEE Transactions,* pp. 784- 796, Vol.15, No.4, SSN: 1041-4347.

Jemima Kiss.; (2008). Web 3.0 is all about rank and recommendation, *Article history,* http://www.guardian.co.uk/media/2008/feb/04/web20?gusrc=rss&feed=media

Jong-yi Hong.; Eui-ho Suh.; Sung-Jin Kim.; (2009). Context-aware systems: A literature review and classification, *Expert Systems with Applications: An International Journal,* pp. 8509-8522, Vol.36, No. 4, ISSN:0957-4174.

Langley.; Nick.; (2005). Explorer 7 and Window Vista set to drive demand for RSS skills. *Computer Weekly (Septemper 6, 2006),* pp. 40.

Linden, G.; Smith, B.; York, J.; (2003). Amazon.com recommendations item-to-item collaborative filtering, *Industry report of Amazon.com,* pp. 76-79.

Maged N Kamel Boulos.; Inocencio Maramba.; Steve Wheeler.; (2006). Wikis, blogs and podcasts: a new generation of Web-based tools for virtual collaborative clinical practice and education, *BMC Medical Education 2006,* http://www.biomedcentral.com/1472-6920/6/41.

M. Perkowitz.; Etzioni.; (1997). Adaptive web sites: an AI challenge, *Proceedings of 15th International Joint Conference on Artificial Intelligence,* pp. 16-23, ISBN 1-55860-480-4

M. Perkowitz.; O. Etzioni.; (1999). Towards adaptive Web sites: conceptual framework and case study, *Computer Networks,* pp. 1245-1258, Vol. 31, No. 11-16.

MJ Pazzani.; J Muramatsu.; D Billsus.; (1996). Syskill & Webert: Identifying interesting web sites, Proceedings of the National Conference on Artificial Intelligence, pp. 69-77.

Overholt.; Alison.; (2005). Learning to Love RSS. *Fast Company*, 99 (October, 2005), pp. 43.

Peter Lyman.; Hal R. Varian.; (2000). How Much Information?, *Counting the Numbers,* Vol. 6, No. 2.

Richardson.;Will.; (2005). RSS: A Quick Start Guide for Educators, *http://www.weblogg- ed.com/rss_for_ed*, Updated march 29, 2005.

Ronald J. Glotzbach.; James L. Mohler.; Jaime E. Radwan.; (2007). RSS as a course information delivery method, *International Conference on Computer Graphics and Interactive Techniques,* No. 16, ACM

Ryan Turner.; (2007). The Basic of Web 2.0 Personalization, http://www.websocial architecture.com/community/2007/03/the_basics_of_w.html

Sergey Brin.; Lawrence Page.; (1999). The anatomy of a large-scale hypertextual Web search engine, *Proceedings of the Seventh International World Wide Web Conference*, pp. 107-117,Vol. 30, No. 1-7.

S. Jeff Cold.; (2006). Using Really Simple Syndication (RSS) to enhance student research, *ACM SIGITE Newsletter,* pp. 6 – 9, Vol. 3, No. 1, ISBN: 1550-1469.

Stephen S. Yau.; Huan Liu; Dazhi Huang,; Yisheng Yao.; (2003). Situation-Aware Personalized Information Retrieval for Mobile Internet, *Proceedings of the 27th Annual International Conference on Computer Software and Applications,* pp. 638, ISBN:0-7695-2020-0.

Tim Oreilly.; (2007). What is the Web 2.0, *Communications & Strategies,* pp. 17, No. 1, First Quarter 2007.

Tim Oreilly.; (2007). What is Web 2.0: Design Patterns and Business Models for the Next Generation of Software, *Communications & Strategies*, pp. 17, No. 1, First Quarter 2007 collaborative filtering, *Internet Computing, IEEE*, pp. 76- 80, Vol. 7, No. 1

Udi Manber.; Ash Patel.; John Robison.; (2000). Experience with personalization of Yahoo!, *Communications of the ACM,* Vol.43, No. 8, ISBN: 0001-0782.

18

Client-based Relay Infrastructure for WiMAX MAN Networks

Gierłowski, Woźniak and Nowicki
Gdansk University of Technology
Poland

1. Introduction

New WiMAX technology, based on IEEE 802.16 (IEEE, 2004) standards family, offers several advantages over currently available metropolitan-area wireless access solutions, which are mainly GSM or UMTS-based. It is cost effective, evolving, and robust - able to provide reliable, fast and Quality of Service (QoS) aware transmissions over significant distances. WiMAX technology provides both line-of-sight (LOS) and no-line-of-sight (NLOS) solutions. The LOS solution allows transmissions with rates over 70 Mbps over distances up to 50 kilometers (or even more), as long as antennas of both devices have straight (not shaded) view of each other. The second one supplies a connectivity using reflected signals when a path between antennas is shaded by various obstacles. In such case the range is limited to about 5 kilometers. The technology also supports different modulation and coding schemes coupled with their adaptive adjustment in order to maximize stable coverage area.

Other strong advantages of WiMAX systems include high security, reliability and integrated QoS support, which jointly allow operators to guarantee their users a required level of network services.

The most popular WiMAX system architecture follows a point-to-multipoint (PtMP) data communications model with a coordinating base station (BS) and participating client terminals (subscriber stations - SSs). Such architecture has undisputed advantages of easy monitoring and management, relatively simple (and cheaper) client terminals and well developed methods of deployment. It also proves adequate for most real-world scenarios.

Unfortunately, measurements conducted in our WiMAX test-bed installation uncovered the "coverage white spots" effect - small areas lacking satisfactory signal quality, located within otherwise well covered area. This effect strongly undermines the popular beliefs concerning excellent performance of WiMAX NLOS mechanisms and can significantly raise cost of network deployment - about the only solution, if we want to provide good coverage (especially for nomadic and mobile users) in PtMP environment, is to install additional base stations.

As the alternative to PtMP mode, the standard also specifies a foundation of a mesh-mode in which peer stations participate in self-organizing network structure by creating logical links between themselves and utilize multihop transmission mode. Such infrastructure provides many unique advantages, including better coverage, as any connecting client will serve as

BS and provide service to others. Scalability of properly configured mesh network is also very good, as any connecting client extends available network resources and massive redundancy makes it extremely resistant to malfunctions.
Regrettably WiMAX mesh mode is currently at very early stage of development while mechanisms necessary for it to function trend to be both numerous and complicated. Because of these reasons the idea of WiMAX mesh network receives at best limited support of hardware manufacturers and we will probably wait for a long time to see it in fully functional, standardized form. Instead, a relay-based approach is gaining momentum and we should expect operational solution very soon.

In the following chapter we describe difficulties encountered in estimating the WiMAX installation coverage by either theoretical or empirical methods. We propose our original approach to fast WiMAX coverage estimation with use of standard subscriber equipment.
Moreover, we describe characteristics of existing WiMAX architectures and propose an alternative, original solution based on both classical point to multipoint (PtMP) and mesh/relay architectures, intended to offset aforementioned "coverage white spot" effect. Our solution extends WiMAX subscriber station functionality to provide it with an ability to act as relay and provide access to other clients. Furthermore, the relay architecture may consist of several levels of relays, forming easily reconfigurable tree-like structure.
The proposed solution was designed to be as uncomplicated as possible and provide maximum compatibility with existing installations. Therefore there is no deed for client terminal modification to provide it with an ability to use our relaying clients for communication. Moreover, in compatibility mode (one of our extension's two basic modes of operation), BS requires no modification and is not even aware that relay nodes are present in the system.

Simulation tests proved that described system can provide solid coverage in vast majority of difficult scenarios including countering the "coverage white spots" effect and can also be used to extend range of a WiMAX system without need for additional, costly BSs. Automatic tree reconfiguration ability makes it resistant to wide range of malfunctions, if sufficient number of relay nodes is present. It is also simple, cost effective and retains most advantages of a mesh mode, while the necessary mechanisms are much easier to design, implement, operate and maintain.

2. Theoretical coverage models

In all types of wireless systems, including WiMAX, prediction of their coverage area is a very challenging task, especially when we want to mark out the coverage with a required accuracy. Because of this there is a need for methods to verify provisional results, obtained via theoretical calculations. There are two basic methods used for current design practices. The first one requires a test-bed installation and depends entirely on empirical measurements. The second one includes software tools able to estimate system coverage with use of one of available propagation models. As the first method is rather time consuming and costly, the software tools are widely used to support coverage calculation for wireless systems, such as short range local area systems (WLANs) or more complex wide area networks, consisting of multiple BSs (WMANs, WWANs).

There are two basic types of propagation models employed in wireless systems design [2,3]:

- empirical (or statistical) models, which are based on a stochastic analysis of series of measurements conducted in the area of interest. They are relatively easy to implement but not very sensitive to environment's geometry,
- site-specific (or deterministic) models, which are far more accurate and do not need signal measurements. However, they require huge amounts of data concerning environment geometry, terrain profile, etc. and high computational efforts.

WiMAX systems should usually provide effective coverage in highly urbanized environments. Following this requirement we are mostly interested in deterministic models, as they can give us results sufficiently accurate for such areas.

Of course, there is always a theoretical possibility to calculate exact propagation characteristics solving sets of Maxwell's equations. However, this method would require very complex data processing and very high computational power, causing such solution to be very inefficient. Due to this fact, current software tools, based on a deterministic propagation model, usually employ simplified simulations: mainly ray-tracing or ray-lunching techniques, based on Uniform Geometrical Theory of Diffraction (UTD) (Sarkar T. K. et al., 2003). Such approach enables significant simplification in calculations, making the model an efficient design tool, but with a loss of accuracy.

WiMAX technology coverage characteristics differ significantly from other wireless network technologies that are employed in similar environments (mainly due to its NLOS capability - see Figure 1), thus a dedicated software model is required to give exact results (ATDI, 2007).

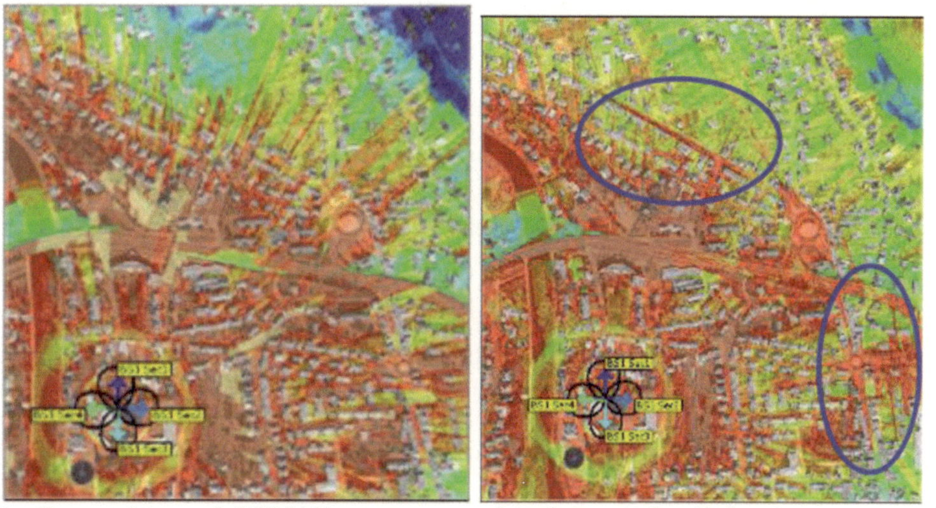

Fig. 1. Comparision of WiMAX coverage estimation results. Left picture - standard propagation model, right picture - specialized, WiMAX propagation model.

Regardless of employed theoretical models and their accuracy, experience in wireless systems design and implementation suggests a necessity of conducting empirical measurements in order to confirm that the system design and theoretically obtained parameters are correct (Olejnik R., 2007). In accordance with a good design practice we implemented a test-bed installation of WiMAX with one base station, and conducted extensive measurements and tests of its coverage and transmission parameters (Gierłowski K. & Nowicki K., 2006).

3. Test-bed installation and example measurements

From both modeling procedures and hardware manufacturers' tests it is clear that WiMAX technology is indeed very well suited for metropolitan environment and generally offers good coverage, even in highly urbanized areas (WiMAX Forum, 2007). To verify these statements and prove accuracy of available software design tools as well as to gather practical design experience, we prepared a study test-bed installation consisting of a single WiMAX BS located at Gdansk University of Technology.

We employed a BreezeMAX Micro Base Station (Alvarion, 2006) provided by Alvarion company and using 3.5 GHz licensed frequency band.

We also developed a dedicated software package consisting of a number of control and monitoring tools. They communicate with BS, client terminals, GPS receivers and are able to automate the experiments to a significant degree.

Moreover, we are currently monitoring long term operation parameters of WiMAX installation, with use of SNMP-based monitoring system developed especially for this purpose. It allows gathering and presentation of over 200 parameters concerning BS, SSs and provided services.

One of our main points of interest was the coverage of WiMAX services in a densely populated metropolitan environment. We performed a variety of tests including:

- measurements of BS signal strength in physical layer,
- modulation and coding profile usage as function of signal quality,
- efficiency of transmission in media access control layer (BER, PER),
- quality of service contract adherence for transport layer services.

The tests were performed with use of hardware spectrum analyzer, equipped with an omnidirectional antenna, BreezeMAX PRO BS, SS subscriber stations (PRO and Si models) (Alvarion, 2006) and transmission performance counters of the base station.

Overall test results confirmed that, in case of LOS, using the equipment mentioned above, we could expect a reliable communication up to 30 km, and 5 km in majority of cases related to NLOS scenarios (Gierłowski K. & Nowicki K., 2006).

Such general statements sound promising. However, we also made quite unexpected observations. It turned out that in case of NLOS communication the network did not cover entirely the tested area. We were able to find multiple small areas not covered by our BS ("coverage white spots"). In some cases, using WiMAX specific propagation models, it would be possible to predict such areas - taking into account terrain profiles and buildings layout.

At the same time, we also detected that there are many locations at which the measured coverage (signal parameters) differs significantly from theoretical estimates. In some places the coverage was a result of repeatedly reflected signals or signals reflected by various objects either improbable or difficult to map, like trees, billboards, trains, trucks, etc. Other places showed a lack of the coverage despite of relatively minor obstacles between BS and a client terminal, thus creating coverage white spots (Figure 2). Our measurements also showed that even a very small displacement (20 m horizontal and/or 3 m vertical) of a client station can result in a dramatic degradation of the transmission parameters - from the best possible modulation and coding profile (QAM64 3/4) to the complete loss of connectivity. This effect makes a WiMAX system design a very difficult task, requiring empirical measurements to validate the project.

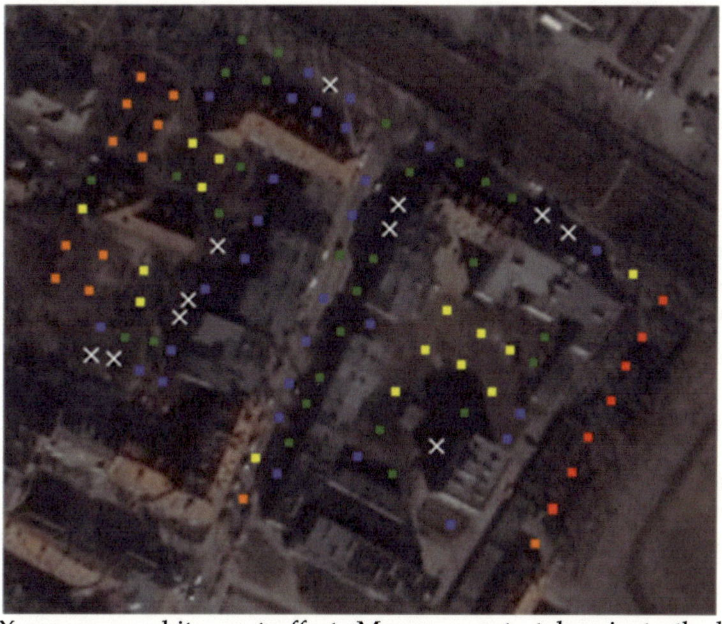

Fig. 2. WiMAX coverage white spot effect. Measurements taken in testbed employing a single BS working in 3.5 GHz band. Colors show stable modulation chosen by a terminal: x - no connectivity, blue - BPSK, green - QPSK, yellow - QAM16, orange - QAM64 1/2, red - QAM64 3/4.

The described "coverage white spots" effect shows difficulties in precise prediction of a real system coverage and system parameters. If a service provider is interested in a complete and continuous coverage of an area it can lead to higher system deployment costs. Also, there is no efficient way to validate this kind of coverage.

In case of a mobile operator the problem becomes even more serious, because mobile terminals can loose and regain connectivity as they move. Such effects can be especially laborious in WiMAX, because in this technology each network entry procedure is complicated and consumes significant network (bandwidth, BS processing power) and client terminal (battery) resources.

Summarizing measurement results we can state, that while WiMAX NLOS capability indeed makes it fit for highly urbanized areas, it is not without disadvantages and requires a careful design and troublesome practical validation.

4. Empirical coverage assessment

The above theoretical analysis and practical measurements clearly show, that an empirical coverage assessment should be performed to verify and supplement simulation modeling.

In case of WiMAX network however, such coverage measurements can be difficult, time consuming and not very precise.
The problem originates in WiMAX ability to function in strictly NLOS environment and to very efficiently utilize reflected signals. This characteristic causes WiMAX coverage area to be a rather abstract concept - in densely urbanized areas the coverage area consists of many small separate regions where good quality signal is present, neighboring regions where there is none available (aforementioned "white spots"). Up to 30 dB of SNR difference has been observed over distances of about 20 m.
To accurately measure coverage in such environment, we require a specialized equipment - for example:

- a spectrum analyzer equipped with an omnidirectional antenna, both able to support an RF band correct for our WiMAX installation,
- a sensitive GPS receiver (in case of densely urbanized area equipped with external antenna),
- a hardware or software analysis solution, able to calculate coverage based on readings from the above devices.

Such equipment tends to be costly (with a possible exception of a GPS receiver) and thus available mostly to larger, commercial network operators. However in case of small installations where specialized equipment is unavailable, we can still employ standard WiMAX subscriber station hardware to obtain a rough assessment of our BS coverage. During our research, we have developed an original method of assessing WiMAX coverage in such way.
Each WiMAX subscriber station must be able to precisely measure BS signal in order to support WiMAX mandatory physical layer control mechanisms, but there are two difficulties which can prevent us from easily exploiting this SS ability to conduct coverage measurements:

- user interface of a particular SS model may not allow access to signal measurement results,
- most of WiMAX client hardware available on the market is intended for use a stationary equipment and thus outfitted with directional antennas.

If user or installer interface of SS provides access to measured values of BS signal quality, we can utilize a laptop with a local application, which captures measured values from SS, geographic location from GPS receiver and records them in database. Such measurements can later be used to create coverage map, provided that enough measurements were made and their spatial layout adequately covered our area of interest - ideally measurement points should form a dense (about 10-20 meters apart) grid. In a real situation we should approximate such grid as closely as possible. Such high density of necessary measurements is a result of unpredictability of WiMAX coverage (discussed earlier).
To help with the task we have developed our original application, which is able to perform the function described above in fully automatic manner. It obtains signal quality measurements from WiMAX client equipment with use of SNMP protocol or, if it is unavailable, by parsing www/telnet output of user/installer interface. In our measurements we decided to use signal to noise ratio (SNR) as it directly influences modulation scheme choice for a given SS. Geographic location is obtained from a standard GPS receiver with use of NMEA protocol.

In case when our WiMAX client equipment is unable to provide us with measured values of signal quality, our application can still be employed in its alternate mode of operation. In this mode it works in cooperation with our second software product - WiMAX base station monitoring system.
The monitoring system is able to gather and record in database over 200 of performance parameters reported by base station, which can be used for both short term monitoring and long term performance tuning. Ability to analyze data in varied time-frames makes it a useful tool in both didactic/research testbed (second by second monitoring) and commercial installation (both short and long term analysis) environment.
Based on gathered data system administrator can create any number of different graphs (Figure 3), by choosing BS parameters to include and additional characteristics such as graph type, X/Y scale, time period, colors, size etc. Defined graphs are then organized in "profiles" - pages which can be configured as a whole - for example: a change of profile time period changes time period of all included graphs.

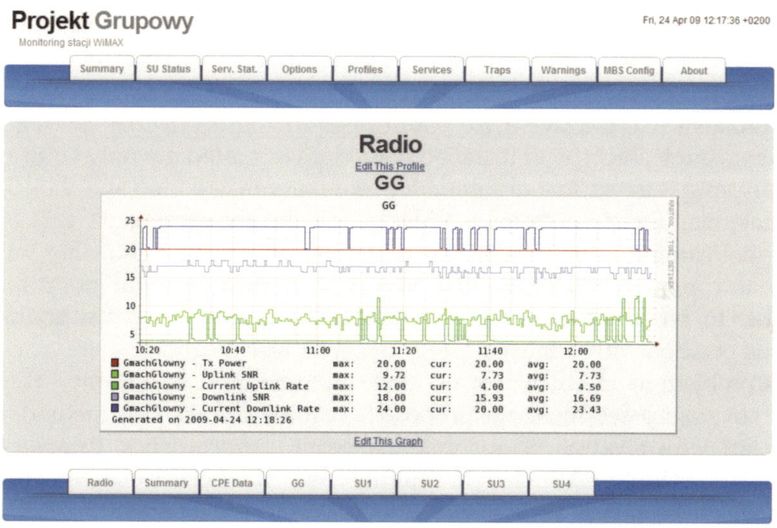

Fig. 3. WiMAX monitoring system - "GG" terminal RF parameters graph.

Such approach allows administrator to customize the visualization for his needs in various situations, for example a dedicated profile can be created to monitor: a given set of subscriber stations, overall RF environment of BS or statistics of transmitted network traffic, system's conformance with its traffic contracts etc.
The system is also able to automatically monitor configured parameters and issue alerts in a number of forms: visual, audio, email, script execution etc.
With such functionality, the monitoring system is a comprehensive solution, able to fulfill most of the monitoring-related tasks necessary in case of a small WiMAX installation.
To further expand system's capabilities, we are currently developing a number of additional modules able to take action in case of WiMAX installation failure or inefficiency to automatically solve the problem by altering configurable BS configuration parameters.
The monitoring system is also able to assist in WiMAX coverage assessment, especially in case when client terminal equipment is does not allow access to measured values of signal

quality parameters. In that case the remote (client side) software package of our design does not perform any signal measuring or analysis tasks – the only function it performs is gathering location data from GPS receiver and transmitting it, accompanied with appropriate timestamps, to the monitoring system by any network link supporting IP traffic. Apart from independent connectivity providers, the measured WiMAX link can be used for this purpose, as the application is able to buffer the data for extended periods of time in case of link failure. There is even a possibility of conducting a completely offline measurement with no network connectivity whatsoever, and then sending data to the monitoring system as a standard file.

It is a straightforward task for the monitoring system to correlate location data from the remote application with its own (BS provided) measurements of link quality to a given terminal, to calculate coverage data.

This method allows us to conduct measurements even in case of a very simple terminal, unable to provide user with measured values of signal quality, but it has its limitations. The most important one is its inability to record signal quality parameters that are below the level necessary for a client terminal to successfully connect to BS, as BS can provide the monitoring system only with performance parameters of active terminals.

The second problem that we face if we plan to use standard WiMAX client equipment for coverage assessment is the type of installed antenna. Very often the only equipment that we have at our disposal is a terminal designed for stationary installation and thus outfitted with directional antenna. This is a serious difficulty, as the measurements will only describe quality of signal coming from a particular direction, which most probably will not be the optimal one and manual reorienting antenna at each measurement point is impractical. Moreover, due to NLOS characteristics of WiMAX operation, we are unable to predict which antenna position will be most appropriate at a given location.

To solve this problem in an efficient way, while still retaining an accuracy of measurement sufficient for coverage assessment, we propose to employ a multi-pass method.

We should start with analysis of our antenna beam characteristics, to assess how many separate orientations will be sufficient to roughly cover all angles (relative to our movement vector) from which we expect the signal at any of measurement points.

Then we set antenna to first of these orientations and perform measurements along our patch through a grid of measurement points. When this first pass is finished, we set antenna to second orientation and repeat the same exact patch through the grid. We repeat this process for each antenna orientation. As a result, we have a set of grid measurements, which can be aggregated to provide an assessment of signal quality at measurement points.

In our experiments we employed a simple maximum as aggregating function, which resulted in ample approximation of our installation's coverage, which we verified by comparing the results with detailed measurements conducted with use of dedicated, physical layer measuring equipment.

Our test measurements covered Wrzeszcz district of the city of Gdansk (Poland). It is a district with dense concentration of 5-6 floor buildings, with a number of small open areas present (city squares). Such terrain is a very complex environment for WiMAX coverage assessment.

In our measurements we have often encountered areas where SNR changes reached 30dB at 20 meter distance. It clearly shows that precise statements declaring WiMAX transmission range in urbanized environment should be threaded as a very rough approximation and the real coverage area is by no means uniform or even continuous. A good illustration of this unpredictability is presented in Table 1, which shows SNR value for a number of measurement points located in a straight line from the BS.

Distance from BS [km]	SNR [dB]
0.30	20
0.70	32
1.23	3
1.37	24
1.64	0
2.30	20

Table 1. WiMAX base station signal SNR at measurement points located in a straight line from base station.

An example visualization (created in Google Earth environment) of measurements obtained with use of our software and described method of employing WiMAX client equipment with directional (90 degree) antenna is shown below (Figure 4).

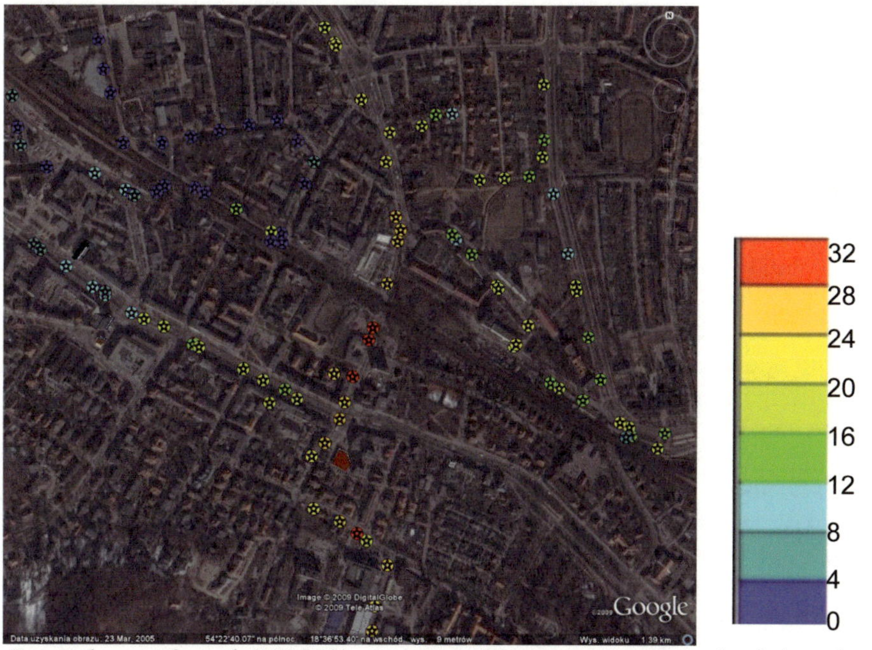

Fig. 4. Example results of WiMAX coverage fast assessment method (results in dB). Standard client equipment with 90 degree directional antenna, 4 measurement passes.

Comparison of results obtained with our method and measured with use of dedicated equipment with omnidirectional antenna shows up to 10 dB (after taking into account different antenna gains) differences. In majority of the measurement points (over 85%) this

error is below 4 dB (accuracy strongly depends on proper selection of employed antenna orientations).
Moreover, our method tends to underestimate measured signal quality, so the assessment can be considered a worst case scenario while assessing BS coverage. It should be clear however, that our method is only intended as a very rough, fast assessment solution, to be used when dedicated equipment is not available.

5. Network design considerations

In the case of simple WiFi (IEEE 802.11) (IEEE, 1999) - wireless local area network - we use test measurements to appropriately design a system. Its usual 50-300 m range makes such approach possible. In case of WiMAX technology, where the range is counted in kilometers such solution seems to be highly impractical, as it is almost impossible to compile a full, detailed, empirical coverage map, by measuring all meaningful points within system's range. In a dense metropolitan area with WiMAX NLOS capability we would have to measure an extremely thick layout of measurement points. Also as we pointed out in the previous section we would need a resolution of about 10-20 m horizontally. Moreover we should not limit such measurements to a 2-dimensional case, because there are significant variations of effective signal strength related to a client station vertical placement, especially prominent near ground level.
Computational propagation models can help us in highlighting potential trouble-spots and suggest important measurement points. They offer a great support during the design process. Regrettably, their application can be costly, because they usually require detailed 3-dimensional digital maps, which may be expensive or even unavailable for the area of interest (Hewitt M. T., 1993).
Furthermore, commercial products, based on ray-tracing and ray-launching models (Sarkar T. K. et al., 2003), are not well suited to detect coverage anomalies as small as the described "coverage hole effect". Our research shows that in order to detect them we must employ a very high resolution of modeling – often higher than popular 3-dimensional map resolution (Rossi J. P. & Gabillet Y., 2002). In case of modeling at such resolution, the simplifications common for these models no longer work in our favor. This leads to the need for much higher computational power and longer modeling time and still does not guarantee detection of all significant anomalies.
Wherever we are able or not to detect the coverage holes, to provide consistent coverage of the area we need much higher number of BSs than we can expect from theoretical modeling. Also, in many places such coverage holes are almost impossible to eliminate without installation of economically impractical number of BSs.
There are at least two basic approaches that could be proposed as possible solutions to this problem:

- heterogonous approach - a number of different connectivity technologies are used in order to provide services for the user,
- homogenous approach - only one wireless technology, i.e. WiMAX is employed.

Currently there is a strong trend towards creation of heterogeneous systems, where users can use a variety of connectivity technologies (Matusz P. et al., 2005).
The emerging IEEE 802.21 standard (IEEE, 2007) is devoted to a seamless handover between networks of the same or different types. In this case the best connection (ABC strategy –

Always Best Connected) is automatically selected at a given user location and the handover is performed without losing quality of service, if possible (Machań P., 2007).
This approach takes into account several different wireless technologies and we will not consider it here. We will concentrate on the homogenous approach, limited to WiMAX technology, considering WiMAX mesh architecture, as a promising solution for coverage issues.

6. WiMAX Mesh Mode

In WiMAX-Mesh mode, there is no prominent BS, but SSs communicate directly with their neighbors forming a dynamic, self-organizing, multi-hop network. In this way a client station does not need to be in range of one of relatively few BSs, but it is sufficient to be in range of any other participating client station and number of these devices is usually much higher (Figure 5). Moreover, with correctly designed control protocols and effective methods of joining the network by new stations, its available capacity can be increased instead of going down.

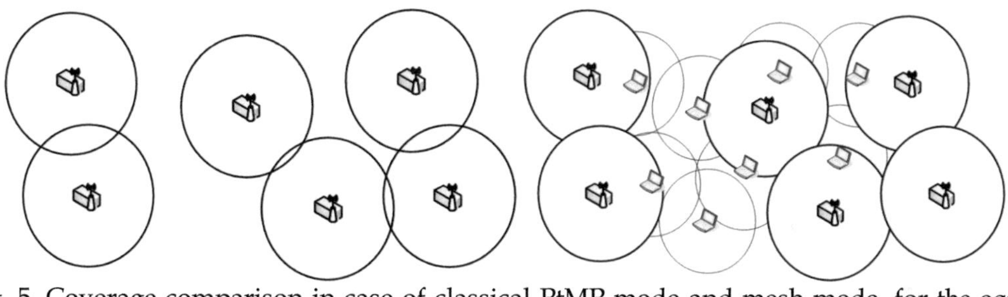

Fig. 5. Coverage comparison in case of classical PtMP mode and mesh mode, for the equal number of operator-provided nodes.

Unfortunately such network architecture requires much more advanced support mechanisms than a simple PtMP setup, where a single entity (BS) sees and controls all the network activity. In case of wireless ad-hoc mesh architecture, these mechanisms (medium access control, security…) have to be significantly extended and be able to operate in a distributed environment. Also new mechanisms (listed below) not required in PtMP setup (which utilizes star architecture), are necessary:

- Topology control - selects logical network node neighborhood based on its physical neighborhood. Running in all network nodes, it is responsible for overall network topology and vast number of derived characteristics (path lengths, bandwidth available, network capacity, transmission delay, error rates…).
- Route discovery - set of mechanisms able to find a route through network nodes to any required destination within and outside wireless mesh. In case of WiMAX, it should be able to provide paths that able to provide specified QoS guarantees.
- Data forwarding - responsible for retransmitting received traffic addressed to remote nodes, with accordance to routing information obtained from discovery mechanisms and QoS guarantees.

In majority of research works and test implementations a mesh network utilizes short range wireless technologies (WLANs or sensor networks) to ensure wide area coverage and high reliability. We claim that, also in case of a wireless metropolitan network (WMAN) of much higher basic range WiMAX-based ad-hoc mesh architecture can provide required functionalities and become practical and economically viable solution (Gierłowski K. & Nowicki K., 2007).

Due to relatively high complexity the WiMAX-mesh mode is not yet specified in the IEEE 802.16 standard. This fact (lack of detailed specification) gives us a possibility to incorporate into the created standard new mechanisms which will make 802.16 especially attractive for metropolitan environments - being definitely its prime areas of deployment.

Our research related to IEEE 802.16 and measurements in the test-bed shows that mesh architecture based on WiMAX metropolitan area network is likely to solve the coverage-hole problems, as long as sufficient number of client stations will participate in the network. In such case it will provide much better terrain coverage than reasonably designed PtMP WiMAX installation. Also the costs of infrastructure will be significantly lower.

We predict that in metropolitan environment the number of client station will not pose a problem, with currently observable user demand and manufacturers' support for the technology. It should also be possible to keep prices of mesh-capable subscriber stations similar to classical PtMP WiMAX terminals.

WiMAX-based ad-hoc mesh network can provide much better terrain coverage and its development costs are significantly lower than in corresponding coverage scenario supported only by classical BSs in PtMP mode. Of course, there is still need for a number of operator-provided network nodes as a foundation of the network.

Moreover, mesh architecture can provide high reliability due to high number of redundant network devices, wireless links and paths to most destinations. It will also scale well, because any participating node brings additional resources to an overall network poll.

The coverage hole problem can be solved by sufficiently dense network of mesh nodes and their redundant links, but network control mechanisms need to be able to deal with rapidly changing mesh topology. In a static mesh configuration (as in static PtMP scenario), the problem is not dangerous, as in most cases the placement of network nodes can be optimized, but in case of mobile mesh nodes even small movement (as mentioned before) can lead to unpredictable breakdowns and reappearances of inter-node links.

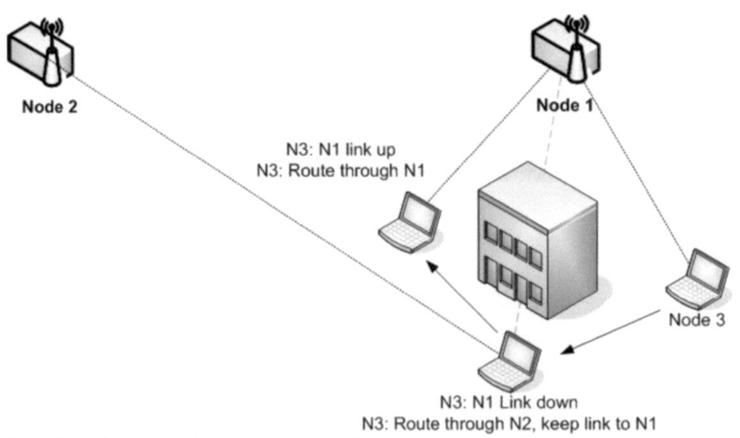

Fig. 6. Use of redundant path routing and coverage hole aware topology control as a solution for short-period link losses at mobile stations.

Such environment greatly lowers efficiency of network mechanisms leading to, for example, frequent activation of ad-hoc routing protocol's discovery mechanisms, which flood the network with control traffic. Also QoS guarantees are extremely difficult to maintain in such environment as fast and frequent, short-term connectivity losses can occur.
Fortunately massive redundancy which exists in a sufficiently dense mesh network can be used to offset the effect without losing transmission reliability and QoS guarantees. Furthermore, our observations and measurements tell us, that signal losses and corresponding link breakdowns caused by coverage hole effect are mostly short term events and as such can be efficiently countered with properly designed network control mechanisms.
Our present research leads us to believe, that efficient topology control, taking into account possibility of short-time disappearance of network links, coupled with redundant path routing and stability-aware routing metric can solve the described problem (Figure 6). We are currently working on a simulation model of WiMAX-based self-organizing mesh network, resistant to the topology stability issues, described above.

7. WiMAX Relay Usage

As the full WiMAX mesh architecture is far from completion and the advantages of having multiple network nodes supporting BS functionality scattered through our area of interest are undisputed, a less complicated solution has been proposed. Instead of creating a dynamic network of mesh-capable subscriber stations, a number of relay stations is to be deployed by network operator.
Relay station (RS) is a simplified version of a full base station, which can provide similar functionality to subscriber stations, but only in cooperation with a fully capable BS.
Due to significant simplifications in its functionality RS is much cheaper than full BS. It also does not require a direct connection to a network backbone, because RS connects to its parent BS via a WiMAX connection. The only external resource required is electrical power.
These characteristics make RS an economical solution, when we are interested in extending range of our WiMAX installation (Figure 7), especially in areas lacking decent communication infrastructure (for example: rural areas). Moreover, such regions do not have a high user density, so the controlling BS should have no problem with allocating enough resources to support its connected RSs.

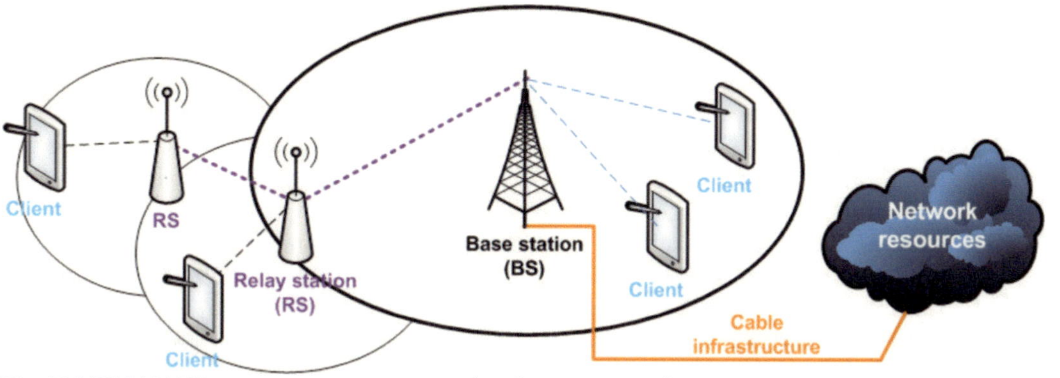

Fig. 7. WiMAX BS coverage extension with relay station infrastructure.

While coverage range extension is very desirable in areas of sparse user density, for example rural ones, it has limited utility in case of densely urbanized areas. In this case we are often interested in limiting the range of a single BS, as such approach allows the network to support a higher number of users. It is possible mainly due to division of area into independent cells in which radio-frequency resources can be reused and by dividing medium access control mechanisms workload between multiple controlling BSs.
In such environment, we can also profit from deploying RS, as they allow us to divide area maintained by a single BS into smaller regions, at least partially controlled by dedicated RSs. A higher number of entities able to provide coverage and service to users (BSs and RSs) helps to eliminate coverage white spots and can also allow a higher number of subscriber stations to connect (Figure 8), due to transference of a part of BS's management functions to cooperating RSs.

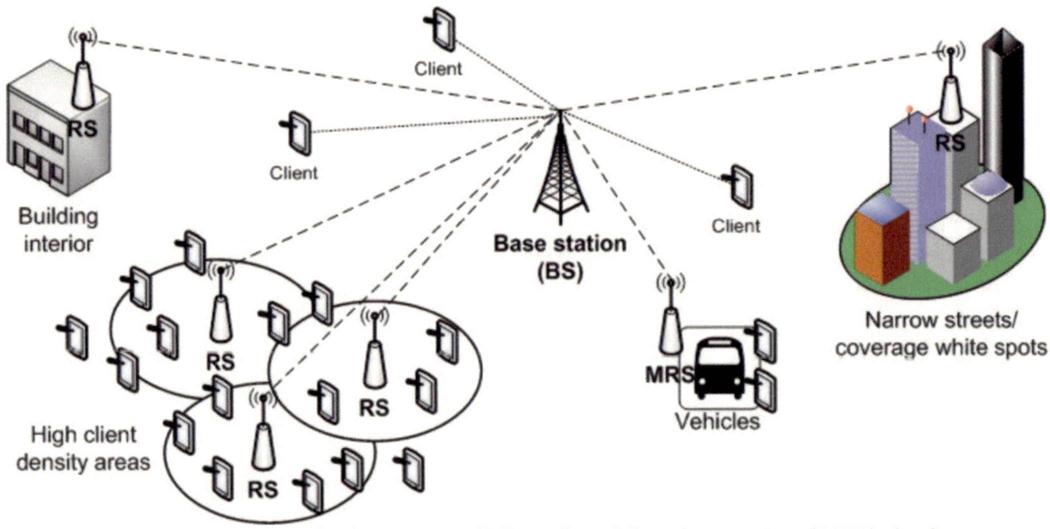

Fig. 8. Different scenarios of relay station (RS) and mobile relay station (MRS) deployment.

The advantages of employing relay stations in WiMAX environment are considerable. The complication of necessary mechanisms and their number is much lower than in case of fully capable mesh architecture. Despite this relatively low complication, there are two main tasks which must be addressed: BS-RS communication and resource management.
There are two basic methods of BS-RS communication, each providing certain advantages and bringing specific complications:

- In-band communication – in this scenario RS communicates with BS using the same physical channel that it uses to provide service to connected clients. Such RSs are significantly cheaper, but their efficiency is limited, especially if deployed in areas of high user density.
- Out-of-band communication – links that connect RSs and BS (thus creating local "backbone") are established using physical channel different from the one utilized for RS-client communication. The gain in efficiency is obvious and considerable, but the costs of equipment (processing power, multiple radio modules, etc.) and

operation (multiple licensed RF bands, etc.) are also significantly higher than in case of in-band communication scenario.

The second, even more important and complex problem in implementing relay station infrastructure is network resource management organization. One of the main advantages of WiMAX system is its ability to provide QoS guarantees to users, by means of careful resource monitoring, management and access scheduling. At the same time, such approach makes advanced reservation and physical medium access control mechanisms strictly necessary. As we are interested in minimizing complexity and cost of relay stations, there are two popular approaches to implementing resource reservation and medium access control mechanisms in BS-RS architectures:

- Centralized scheduling - relay stations tunnel requests from clients to BS and BS's responses to clients in a transparent manner. All monitoring, scheduling and control mechanisms are located at BS. Such approach allows us to employ very simple and cheap relay stations. Unfortunately, we do not gain any additional system capacity or performance, because BS is unable to offload its tasks to RSs. Moreover, it must handle additional load due to a need to coordinate RS infrastructure. There is also a necessity to maintain a low latency communication between client and BS, which is still the only control entity in the system. This requirement drastically limits number of consecutive RS which can be chained (see Figure 7) and creates a likely point of failure.
- Distributed scheduling - relay stations are fully capable of receiving clients' requests and performing scheduling / medium access control tasks for their clients. Relay stations coordinate their actions with BS, which performs overall resource management tasks across its entire controlled area, but does not need to handle work-intensive client-related work. In this scenario BS workload is drastically lower and there is no latency in interpreting client's requests as they are handled by its serving RS. This solution allows easy extension of both system's coverage area and its capacity. Moreover, relay stations can be safely chained, due to their relatively infrequent and not time-critical control communication with BS.

Relay architecture seems to be a promising solution for WiMAX networks. While it does not have the remarkable and diverse advantages of fully capable mesh architecture, it is much easier to implement. As such we should expect its rapid standardization (currently in progress as IEEE 802.16j amendment to a base IEEE 802.16 standard) and appearance in production grade systems. At the same time we hope, that popularity of relay architecture will not hinder standardization work on the full WiMAX mesh mode, concurrently planed as an optional part of IEEE 802.16m specification.

8. Client-based Relay Infrastructure

Relay-based WiMAX architecture is an economical and easy to deploy alternative for utilizing a high number of expensive base stations, which would otherwise be necessary to provide (more or less) continuous coverage in dense urban environment. However, these relay stations are still financed, deployed and maintained by a network operator. As such they are deployed in limited numbers, according to operator's coverage plan.

We would like to propose a slightly different solution, which we call WiMAX support-mesh mode (SMM). It is a relay-based solution designed to utilize modified client equipment to create simple relay stations, while maintaining compatibility with a standard WiMAX system. The solution can be deployed by clients on their own initiative (for example: to provide indoor WiMAX coverage) and should not negatively impact network access experience of other clients.

Our main priority in creating this solution was keeping necessary modifications of existing systems to minimum. Unfortunately, this goal is in contradiction with resulting system's efficiency, as WiMAX PtMP environment is strictly controlled by BS and without modification of functions obtaining efficient solution is very difficult. In this situation we decided to take two approaches:

- Variant 1 - a completely transparent one, which requires no alternations to BS hardware or software, only slight modifications in functionality of SS that is to function as a relay-station.
- Variant 2 - requires slight modification of BS software, but promises higher system efficiency and robustness.

Both variants allow seamless coexistence of standard and modified subscriber stations, which significantly raises practicability of the solution.

In most circumstances the operation of support-mesh mode enabled installation does not differ from classic WiMAX PtMP system. Only in case of low quality link or connectivity loss between SS and BS the new functionality is utilized (Figure 9).

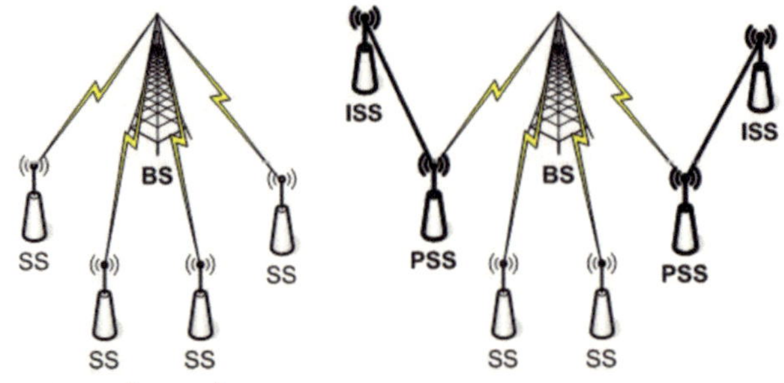

Fig. 9. WiMAX support mesh mode.

In such case support-mesh mode enabled subscriber station (SMM-SS) can connect to another SMM-SS instead of BS and use it as a proxy to maintain its presence in WiMAX PtMP system. The SMM-SS used as a proxy (PSS) is then responsible for providing communication between BS and its connected SMM-SSs (Indirectly connected SS - ISS).

It is even possible to create multiple layers of proxying in case when PSS loses connectivity to BS and becomes an ISS itself, without abandoning its PSS role (Figure 10).

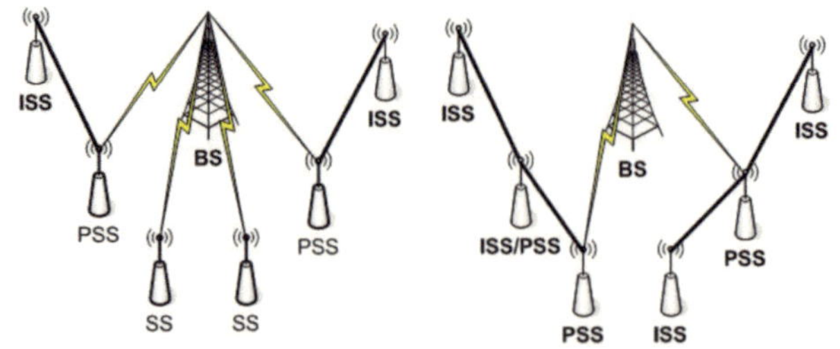

Fig. 10. Multilayer proxying in WiMAX support mesh mode.

Such multilayer network layout is not especially efficient and should be avoided by ISSs by finding alternative (directly connected) PSS, but it is possible which can be useful in case of low-bandwidth, high-reliability applications.

For the system to function effectively it is advisable for the stations (most importantly PSSs) to utilize omnidirectional antennas - in case of directional antennas their field of coverage will be very limited and advantage of employing such PSS is questionable. This requirement is currently in contrast with a large percentage of WiMAX hardware available on the market, but the situation in going to change as there is a strong trend towards omnidirectional antennas.

Proxy-capable subscriber stations work in the same frequency channel as their main BS, and need to perform all operations in their allocated (by BS) transmission times. That includes:

- their own traffic to/from BS,
- receiving transmissions form ISS and retransmitting them to BS,
- receiving transmissions from BS and retransmitting them to ISS,
- maintenance of their own proxy-WiMAX cell.

PSSs will advertise their capabilities by emulating BS frame structure inside their allocated transmission times, which will allow potential ISSs to detect them, connect and transmit traffic. This task may seem highly hardware intensive, as the PSS need to conduct network maintenance tasks similar to that of BS, but there are many simplifications that can be made, taking into account a small expected number of ISSs and small range. Advanced physical transmission control, QoS, network control mechanisms can be radically simplified or, in some cases, removed. If we will allow only SMM-capable SS to connect to proxy stations (in contrast to allowing even unmodified SSs to connect to PSS), the simplifications can be even greater. The exact degree of simplification is currently a subject of our research.

Connecting ISSs can choose PSS according to a number of factors and it is possible use multiple simultaneous links to many PSSs (as described in earlier chapter) to perform dynamic, soft-handover for mobile ISS.

8.1 SMM infrastructure – Variant 1

In this variant our main priority is compatibility with existing, unmodified WiMAX systems. Because of this requirement PSS makes all request to BS - both to accommodate its own needs and needs of ISSs it serves.

Because ISSs are not visible to BS, it is responsibility of PSS to:

- Authenticate connecting ISSs and grant them resources using its own authentication and access control mechanisms.
- Obtain bandwidth grants from BS, necessary to: service its own traffic, communicate with its connected ISSs, retransmit ISS traffic to and from BS.
- Handle PSS-ISS communication and correctly retransmit unidirectional ISS-BS traffic.

Detailed aspects of authentication and access control we consider out of scope of this paper, because there are many appropriate solutions (both strictly local and centralized or distributed) which can be employed.

The remaining problem is conducting PSS-ISS communication within constraints of strictly controlled WiMAX PtMP environment.

The WiMAX downlink phase is exclusively controlled by BS according to both connections' traffic contracts and level of currently buffered traffic waiting transmission - when BS does not have traffic to transmit through a particular connection, there is no downlink transmission time allocated for it. In this situation it is impossible to use WiMAX downlink phase for communication with ISS - all such communications need to be conducted during uplink phase (Figure 11).

Transmission time in WiMAX uplink phase is also granted by BS according to SSs' traffic contracts, but there are no optimizations made by BS. That makes it possible for PSS to obtain necessary transmission time.

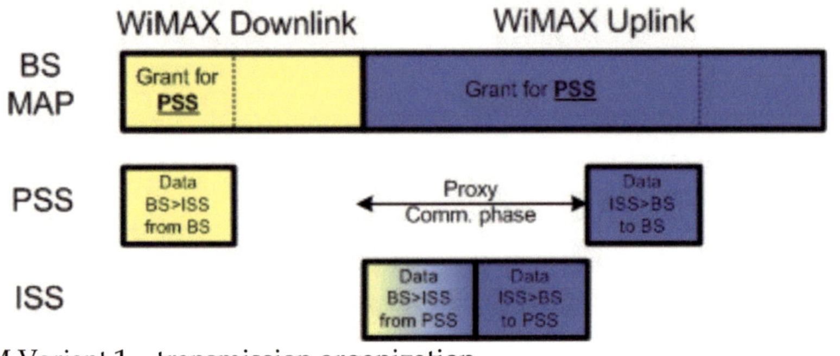

Fig. 11. SMM Variant 1 - transmission organization.

In variant 1 of SMM, PS reserves uplink time to handle (Figure 11):

- Its own uplink traffic to BS,
- Retransmission of ISS uplink traffic from PSS to BS,
- ISS uplink traffic to PSS,
- PSS downlink traffic to ISS.

In presented SMM variant 1 the only stations which require software modification and are aware of SMM operation are indirectly connected subscriber stations (ISSs) and their respective proxy subscriber stations (PSSs). Base station and other subscriber stations are not modified nor aware of SMM operation.

8.2 SMM infrastructure – Variant 2

In event of SMM variant 2 we extend WiMAX BS functionality making it aware of indirectly connected subscriber stations. While it requires BS software modification, it also provides vast advantages in terms of efficiency and system control.

In this case ISS communicate with BS with proxy stations acting as repeaters by retransmitting both control and user traffic between ISS and BS. This allows ISSs to participate in standard network entry procedure, establish WiMAX connections and make their own bandwidth requests (Figure 12).

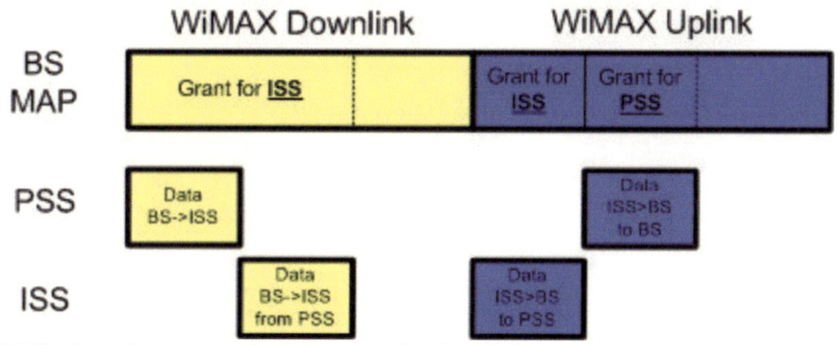

Fig. 12. SMM Variant 2 – transmission organization.

This approach allows us to retain security and management capabilities of classic PtMP WiMAX system, as ISS stations are fully recognized by BS. It also brings us an ability to utilize both downlink and uplink phases for communication with ISS, resulting in their much more balanced usage. Such balance improves system reliability and can provide a big increase in efficiency in case of WiMAX hardware implementations which does not support a dynamic change of WiMAX uplink and downlink phase duration ratio.
In this variant there is also a possibility of utilizing a spatial division multiple access (SDMA) to allow utilization of a single frequency channel by many PSSs and ISSs at the same time (Figure 13). This can be done due to BS's complete knowledge of its network structure (including ISSs), by utilizing additional raging phase to gather additional information about spatial separation of nodes.

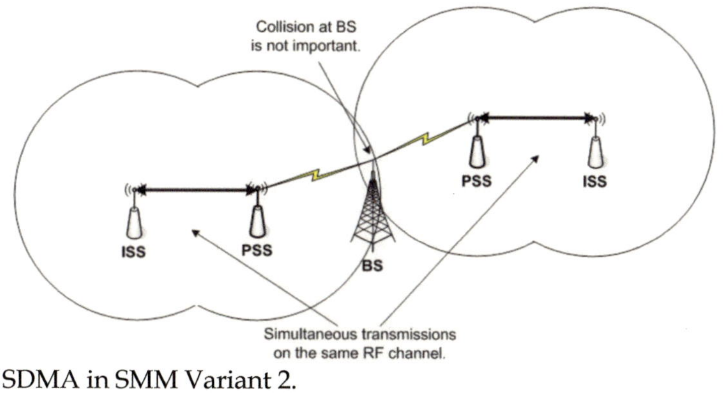

Fig. 13. Use of SDMA in SMM Variant 2.

Ranging is the process of measuring quality of link between BS and SS, conducted during a time period especially reserved for this purpose in each WiMAX frame. This time period can be used by BS to locate SSs which are unable to interfere with each other, by conducting measurements of link existence and quality between pairs or groups of SSs. This task could be also accomplished by SS passive measurements of normal traffic generated by other stations, but the use of ranging mechanisms makes the process independent of station activity and their physical transmission characteristics, such as dynamically adjusted power and modulation.

9. Simulation results

To verify usefulness of our solution we conducted a series of coverage tests, using a modified, WiMAX NLOS-compatible propagation model.
As stated before, the classical propagation models are inefficient in detecting anomalies as small as "coverage white-spots" and thus unfit for the task, we developed and employed a modified version. Its operation is supplemented by a data file containing real-world coverage measurements, which allows localized increase of modeling accuracy. That way the model is able to check the presence of small "white-spots", while still keeping calculation costs within acceptable limits.
We considered two urbanized area types:

- Terrain A: dense urbanized area with blocks 5-6 floor buildings, 3.5 km^2 – Gdansk-Wrzeszcz area.
- Terrain B: sparse residential area with 12 story buildings (building length 30-300 m) and a limited number of smaller buildings and objects, 4 km^2 – Gdansk-Zaspa area.

In these areas we randomly distributed 30 SMM-SS in two scenarios:

- Scenario 1: 30 stationary SMM-SS on rooftops and building walls.
- Scenario 2: 20 stationary SMM-SS on rooftops and building walls, 10 mobile SMM-SS slowly moving at street level.

Below we include results of coverage modeling in percent of previously uncovered area which is now covered by SMM-capable subscriber stations.

- Area A, scenario 1: 80%
- Area A, scenario 2: 85%
- Area B, scenario 1: 95%
- Area B, scenario 2: 100%

Form these scenarios it seems evident, that support-mesh mode subscriber stations can provide significantly better coverage in urbanized areas, that strictly PtMP setup. It vast advantage is a distributes layout of PSSs, which cover target area from varied angles, maximizing chances of archiving through coverage. The result is especially promising in case of relatively small number of large obstacles (area B).

The results above convinced us that WiMAX SMM can efficiently solve coverage issues, so we prepared simulation model of both its variants. We employed a relatively simple WiMAX simulation model, covering in detail only ISO-OSI layer 2 network mechanisms, with very simplified layer 1 modeling, as that was the only such model available to us. We are currently working on development of more through simulation tool.
Simulation test confirmed basic operation principles of WiMAX support-mesh mode, but also uncovered some limitations.
Variant 1 of SMM, from the beginning designed as temporary, low-efficiency, emergency solution proved operable for up to 2 layers of proxying. Additional layers refuse to function due to strict timing constraints of the system. Moreover there is an additional, up to 8 % per layer, performance degradation over one expected from the need for repeated retransmission of data. This degradation applies only to indirectly connected stations and does not impact SSs in classical PtMP setup.
Variant 2 provides better service and was tested for up to 5 layers of proxy stations, at which point it still remained operable. The loss of performance for indirectly connected stations is

about 5% for level of proxying, but in this case BS can compensate for it, and provide given ISS with suitably higher bandwidth.
In both cases (variant 1 and 2) there is also need for retransmission of data by PSSs, which is a main source of performance degradation, halving bandwidth with each level of proxying. Because of that, performance of variant 2 SMM with SDMA mechanisms is in vast majority of cases drastically better, as it allows to conduct multiple retransmissions simultaneously. The exact results depend on station locations and terrain layout.

10. Conclusions

Based on our theoretical research and practical experiments, we observed a possibly dangerous effect present in wireless networks based on WiMAX technology, resulting in small coverage holes in areas of otherwise good coverage. Such white spots are difficult to predict, even with the use of deterministic propagation models, which are amongst the most popular wireless network design support tools, used today.
Such situation can lead to lower than expected service level, requiring repositioning or installation of additional hardware in case of stationery users and can be especially harmful for mobile users that will experience periodic losses of connectivity.
Despite the fact that the same coverage problem would affect mesh nodes (especially in case of mobile nodes) potentially leading to topology instability, it is possible to design network control mechanisms to counter the effect. That would allow WiMAX mesh networks to provide continuous coverage of a given area eliminating "coverage holes", which is very difficult in classical BS-based architecture without large additional hardware costs.
We propose WiMAX mesh networks as viable method of dealing with coverage difficulties in metropolitan areas as they are simultaneously providing additional crucial advantages, such as: well-scaling high network capacity, high reliability based on multiple redundancy, low cost of deployment etc.
As a fully-functional mesh mode requires a significant number of additional, advanced mechanisms and in case of WiMAX network is still in very early stage of research and development, we developed a client-based relay solution (support-mesh mode). It provides subscriber stations with proxying capabilities thus providing many of mesh mode advantages (including coverage and reliability) with use of considerably simpler mechanisms. Both variants of our solution require only limited modification to subscriber station software and only in case of more advanced variant 2 there is a need for modification of base station software.
Operation of both variant of our solution have been confirmed by simulation test and yielded satisfactory results. Variant 1 should be treated as a temporary/emergency solution for currently available systems, while variant 2 can be considered for further development and incorporation as an option in upcoming versions of WiMAX hardware.

11. References

Alvarion (2006). BreezeMAX Whitepapers and Manuals, http://www.alvarion.com/

ATDI, (2007), The WiMax technologies with ICS telecom: Fixed, Nomadic and Mobile! http://www.atdi.com/

Gierłowski K. & Nowicki K. (2006). Test Installation of WiMAX-based Wireless Network on Gdansk University of Technology (in Polish), In: Multimedia in economy and education, L. Kiełtyka (Ed.), pp. 269-277, DIFIN, ISBN 83-7251-673-1, Warszawa.

Gierłowski K. & Nowicki K. (2007). Wireless Networks as an Infrastructure for Mission-Critical Business Applications, Notes in Computer Science Vol. 4658, pp. 49-58, ISBN 3-540-74572-6, Regensburg, September 2007, Springer-Verlag, Berlin

Hewitt M. T. (1993). Surface feature data for propagation modeling, Proceedings of IEEE Colloquium on Terrain Modelling and Ground Cover Data for Propagation Studies, pp. 4/1 - 4/6

IEEE (1999), IEEE 802.11-1999: IEEE Standard for Information Technology - Telecommunications and Information Exchange between Systems - Local and Metropolitan Area Networks - Specific requirements - Part 11: Wireless LAN Medium Access Control (MAC) and Physical Layer (PHY) specifications, IEEE Explore.

IEEE (2007). IEEE P802.21/D05.00: Draft IEEE Standard for Local and Metropolitan Area Networks: Media Independent Handover Services, IEEE Explore.

IEEE, (2004). IEEE 802.16-2004: IEEE Standard for Local and Metropolitan Area Networks Part 16: Air Interface for Fixed Broadband Wireless Access Systems, IEEE Explore.

Machań P. et al. (2007). IEEE 802.21 Standard - mobility support mechanisms, Telecommunication Review and Telecommunication News, No 7/2007, July 2007, pp. 211-216

Matusz P. et al. (2005). Heterogeneous wireless networks - selected operational aspects, Telecommunication Review and Telecommunication News, No. 8-9/2005, August 2005, pp. 284-295, ISSN 1230-3496

Olejnik R. (2007). Methods of designing wireless networks and parametric design method (in Polish), Computer Networks - T. 1: New technologies, pp. 347-356, Wydawnictwo Komunikacji i Łączności, Warszawa.

Rossi J. P. & Gabillet Y. (2002). A mixed ray launching/tracing method for full 3-D UHF propagation modeling and comparison with wide-band measurements, IEEE Transactions on Antennas and Propagation, Vol. 50, Issue 4, April 2002, pp. 517 - 523, ISSN 0018-926X

Sarkar T. K. et al. (2003). A Survey of Various Propagation Models for Mobile Communication, IEEE Antennas and Propagation Magazine, Vol. 45, No. 3, ISSN 1045-9243

WiMAX Forum (2007). WiMAX Forum Whitepaper Library, http://www.wimaxforum.org/

The Decoding Algorithms as Techniques for Creation the Anomaly Based Intrusion Detection Systems

Evgeniya Nikolova and Veselina Jecheva
Burgas Free University, Faculty for Computer Science and Engineering
Bulgaria

1. Introduction

Since information and related infrastructure have become a very important part of today's companies and public organizations' networks, increasing attention has been given to security policies and mechanisms, that can help minimize the risk of unauthorized access and availability threats. Intrusion Detection Systems (IDS) are among the most disseminated security tools usually applied in order to detect attacks. These systems are categorized into misuse detection and anomaly detection systems (Ghosh et al., 1999). Misuse IDSs detect known attacks using preliminarily defined intrusion patterns and signatures in the system activity data. This method is similar to the approach most antivirus programs detect malware.

Anomaly-based approaches in IDS have the advantage of being able to detect unknown attacks since they look for patterns that deviate from the normal behavior (Bahrololum&Khaleghi, 2008). These systems lie on the assumption that an intrusion can be detected by observing a deviation from the normal or expected behavior of the system or network. They monitor network traffic and compare it against a preliminarily established baseline. The baseline describes what behavior is considered to be "normal" for that system and any activity, which deviates significantly from this baseline, is considered to be anomalous. The anomaly IDS have the following advantages over misuse detection approaches: can detect attempts to exploit new and unforeseen vulnerabilities without specific knowledge of details; can detect 'abuse-of-privilege' types of attacks, which usually do not exploit any security vulnerabilities and can recognize unusual network traffic based on network packet characteristics. The major challenges that anomaly IDS have to solve are the improvement of the detection process and the reduction of the number of the false alarms (Dagorn, 2008).

2. Outline of the methodology

The task of an intrusion detection system (IDS) is modelled as a classification problem in a machine-learning context. A typical anomaly recognition model will analyze data, compare to a known profile, run statistical analysis to determine if any deviation is significant, and flag the event(s) as a normal activity or an attack. This problem is very similar to the problem of decoding in the coding theory, that's why we consider this recognition as a decoding problem and we apply the well-known techniques as the Bahl-Cocke-Jelinek-Raviv (BCJR or the MAP) decoding algorithm or the max log MAP algorithm and the junction tree algorithm (JTA). First, we described the system using an oriented graph with nodes - the system state and edges - the system states transitions and applied BCJR algorithm as a method for intrusion detection during the system work. The second present method consists of two stages – the first contains the HMM creation and its adjustment using the gradient method, and the second one includes the intrusion recognition using the decoding algorithm – BCJR or the max-log-MAP algorithm. The forwards-backwards algorithm, also known as the BCJR, for HMM is equivalent to the JTA. The third presented method applies the JTA for the intrusion detection. More details about the results, which are obtained by the methodology based on the enumerated algorithms, are presented in our previous works (Jecheva& Nikolova, 2007, Nikolova&Jecheva, 2007, Nikolova& Jecheva, 2008).

2.1 The system model

As it was already outlined in the introduction, anomaly IDS models operate by building a model of "normal" system behavior. Normal system behavior is determined by observing the standard activity of the system, which has to be protected. In anomaly intrusion detection, how to model the normal behavior of activities performed by a user is an important issue. To extract the normal behavior as a profile, conventional data mining techniques are widely applied to a finite audit data set.

There are various methods for describing the legal user activities. One of them is the Hidden Markov Model (HMM) (Rabiner 1989, Qiao et al., 2002, Vigna 2003, Joshi 2005; Tan 2008), which provides a unifying framework for many tasks, where a measure of uncertainty is needed. The formal definition of a HMM is as follows: $\lambda = (A, B, \pi)$, where A is the state transition probability matrix, B is the observation probability distribution and the vector $\pi = (\pi_1, \pi_2, ..., \pi_N)$ is the initial probability distribution.

Let $S=(S_1, S_2, \ldots, S_N)$ be our state alphabet set, and $V= (v_1, v_2, \cdots, v_M)$ is the observation alphabet set. We define $Q=(q_1, q_2, \ldots, q_T)$ to be a fixed state sequence of length T, and corresponding observations $O=(O_1, O_2, \ldots O_T)$, where each O_t is a certain element $v_k \in V$. The square matrix $A=\{a_{ij}, 1 \le i \le N, 1 \le j \le N\}$, $0 \le a_{ij} \le 1$ and $\sum_{j=1}^{N} a_{ij} = 1$ contains elements, which represent the probability of transitioning from a given state to another possible state. The observation probability distribution is a non-square matrix $B=\{b_j(O_k), 1 \le j \le N, 1 \le k \le M\}$, with dimensions number of states by number of observations. It represents the probability that a given observable symbol will be emitted by a given state.

We consider those processes only in which the state transition probabilities do not change with time, i.e. $P(q_t = S_j \mid q_{t-1} = S_i) = a_{ij}$ the probability of transiting from state S_i to state S_j does not depend on the moment of time t (stationarity assumption) and depends on the previous state only (first-order HMM).

The main goal of the HMM is to describe the system behavior during specific period of time. In order to achieve this goal we determine the model parameters A, B and π for given

HMM λ such that $L = P(O|\lambda)$ takes the maximal value for the observation sequence O. This problem is known as learning problem. There are several optimization criteria for learning, out of which a suitable one is selected depending on the application. We apply the Maximum Likelihood (*ML*) as optimization criteria.

2.2 ML criterion

The ML criterion is based on the gradient based method, in which any parameter Θ of the HMM λ is updated according to the standard formula

$$\Theta_{new} = \Theta_{old} - \eta \left[\frac{\partial J}{\partial \Theta} \right]_{\Theta = \Theta_{old}}, \tag{1}$$

where *J* is a quantity to be minimized. In our case we set $J = -\log p(O|\lambda) = -\log L$. The minimization of *J* is equivalent to the maximization of *L*. We have

$$L = \sum_{i=1}^{N} p(O, q_t = i|\lambda) = \sum_{i=1}^{N} \alpha_t(i)\beta_t(i), \tag{2}$$

where the forward variable $\alpha_t(i)$ can be calculated using the following recursive steps:

$$\begin{aligned} \alpha_1(j) &= \pi_j b_j(O_1),\ 1 \le j \le N, \\ \alpha_{t+1}(j) = p(O_1, O_2, \ldots, O_t, q_t = S_i \mid \lambda) &= b_j(O_{t+1}) \sum_{i=1}^{N} \alpha_t(i) a_{ij},\ 1 \le j \le N,\ 1 \le t \le T-1 \end{aligned} \tag{3}$$

and the backward variable $\beta_t(i)$ can be calculated efficiently recursively as follows:

$$\begin{aligned} \beta_T(i) &= 1,\ 1 \le i \le N, \\ \beta_t(i) = p(O_{t+1}, O_{t+2}, \ldots, O_T, q_t = S_i \mid \lambda) &= \sum_{j=1}^{N} \beta_{t+1}(j) a_{ij} b_j(O_{t+1}),\ 1 \le i \le N,\ 1 \le t \le T-1 \end{aligned} \tag{4}$$

Since there are two main parameter sets in the HMM, transition probabilities a_{ij} and observation probabilities $b_j(O_k)$, we can find the gradient $\frac{\partial J}{\partial \Theta}$ for each of the parameter sets.

- Gradient with respect to the transition probabilities

$$\frac{\partial J}{\partial a_{ij}} = -\frac{1}{L} \sum_{t=1}^{T} \beta_t(j) b_j(O_t) \alpha_{t-1}(i). \tag{5}$$

- Gradient with respect to the observation probabilities

$$\frac{\partial J}{\partial a_{ij}} = -\frac{1}{L}\frac{\alpha_t(j)\beta_t(j)}{b_j(O_t)}. \tag{6}$$

2.3 The BCJR algorithm

The BCJR decoding algorithm estimates random parameters with prior distributions. In the case examined the algorithm scans the traces of the system activity and compares the current activity with the patterns of normal user activity (Bahl et al., 1974). If the deviation from the normal data of system activity is above the preliminarily defined threshold, then the current system call is marked as abnormal, i.e. an intrusion is detected. The description of the BCJR algorithm can be performed based on log-likelihood ratios (*LLR*). The *LLR* are represented as follows:

$$LLR = \ln\frac{P(m_i = 1|O_i)}{P(m_i = 0|O_i)} \tag{7}$$

where m_i is the message bit associated with the state transition q_i to q_{i+1} and $P(m_i = 1|O_i)$ is the a posteriory probability in which the bit, determining the presence of attack, is equal to 1. If the *LLR* of an observation is positive, it implies that m_i is most likely to be a 1 and if it is negative, m_i is most likely to be zero. The algorithm consists of three steps:

- Forward recursion. The forward state metrics $\alpha_t(s_t)$ represent the probability that the current state is s_t given the noisy observation vector $(O_1,\ldots,O_t)$ and are recursively calculated

$$\alpha_0(s_0) = \begin{cases} 1, & s_0 = 0 \\ 0, & otherwise \end{cases},$$
$$\alpha_t(s_t) = \sum_{s_{t-1},i=0,1} \alpha_{t-1}(s_{t-1})\gamma_i(O_t, s_{t-1}, s_t). \tag{8}$$

- Backward recursion. The backward state metrics $\beta_t(s_t)$ represent the probability that the final state is s_{t+1} and are recursively calculated

$$\beta_M(s_M) = \begin{cases} 1, & s_M = 0 \\ 0, & otherwise \end{cases},$$
$$\beta_t(s_t) = \sum_{s_{t+1},i=0,1} \gamma_i(O_{t+1}, s_t, s_{t+1})\beta_{t+1}(s_{t+1}). \tag{9}$$

- Log-Likelihood Ratios

$$LLR(m_t) = \ln \frac{\sum\limits_{s_t, s_{t-1}} \alpha_{t-1}(s_{t-1}) \gamma_0(O_t, s_{t-1}, s_t) \beta_t(s_t)}{\sum\limits_{s_t, s_{t-1}} \alpha_{t-1}(s_{t-1}) \gamma_1(O_t, s_{t-1}, s_t) \beta_t(s_t)}, \tag{10}$$

$$\gamma_i(O_t, s_{t-1}, s_t) = q(m_t = i | s_t, s_{t+1}) P(O_t | m_t = i, s_{t-1}, s_t) P(s_t | s_{t-1}). \tag{11}$$

2.4 Max log MAP algorithm

The $\alpha_t(s_t)$ and $\beta_t(s_t)$ parameters in the MAP algorithm are approximated in the max-log-MAP algorithm by maximization operation (Robertson et al., 1995, Benedetto et al., 1997). The estimated *LLRs* are computed by exhaustively exploring all possible state transitions from s_{t-1} to s_t using forward and backward recursion.

- Forward recursion. The forward state metrics $\alpha_t(s_t)$ are recursively calculated

$$\alpha_0(s_0) = \begin{cases} 1, & s_0 = 0 \\ 0, & otherwise \end{cases}, \\ \alpha_t(s_t) = \max_{s_{t-1}, i=0,1} \alpha_{t-1}(s_{t-1}) \gamma_i(O_t, s_{t-1}, s_t). \tag{12}$$

- Backward recursion. The backward state metrics $\beta_t(s_t)$ are recursively calculated

$$\beta_M(s_M) = \begin{cases} 1, & s_M = 0 \\ 0, & otherwise \end{cases}, \\ \beta_t(s_t) = \max_{s_{t+1}, i=0,1} \gamma_i(O_{t+1}, s_t, s_{t+1}) \beta_{t+1}(s_{t+1}). \tag{13}$$

- *LLR* computation. The output for each bit at time t is computed by using the backward state metrics $\beta_t(s_t)$ and the corresponding forward state metrics $\alpha_t(s_t)$ as follows

$$LLR(m_t) = \ln \frac{\max\limits_{s_t, s_{t-1}} \alpha_{t-1}(s_{t-1}) \gamma_0(O_t, s_{t-1}, s_t) \beta_t(s_t)}{\max\limits_{s_t, s_{t-1}} \alpha_{t-1}(s_{t-1}) \gamma_1(O_t, s_{t-1}, s_t) \beta_t(s_t)}. \tag{14}$$

2.5 The junction tree algorithm

The JTA is an inference algorithm for any graphical model, which gives a solution for the following problem: calculating the conditional probability of a node or a set of nodes, given the observed values of another set of nodes. The idea of this algorithm is to find ways to decompose a global calculation on a joint probability into a linked set of local computations. The algorithm consists of the following steps (Lauritzen at al., 1988, Lauritzen , 1996):

- Given directed graph is converted into an undirected graph G, so an uniform treatment of directed and undirected graphs is possible.
- Form a triangulated graph $\widetilde{G}$ by adding edges as necessary. (Chord is a link joining two non-consecutive vertices of a loop. An undirected graph is triangulated if every loop of length 4 or more has a chord.)
- Given a triangulated graph, a junction tree is constructed by forming a maximal spanning tree from the cliques in that graph. A clique is a subset of vertices containing only one vertex or such that any two vertices are neighbours. A clique tree (in which nodes are cliques of the triangulated graph) will be constructed with separators.
- Extract a junction tree. A clique tree is a junction tree if it has the following two properties:
  - singly connected: there is exactly one path between each pair of nodes;
  - running intersection: all nodes on the path between v and w contain the intersection $v \cap w$.
- Run sum-product, which is the basic decoding algorithm for nodes on graphs, on the resulting junction tree.

Except finding marginal probabilities, JTA helps to answer another natural question: what is the most likely state of the distribution? In our case the considered junction tree is presented in Figure 1:

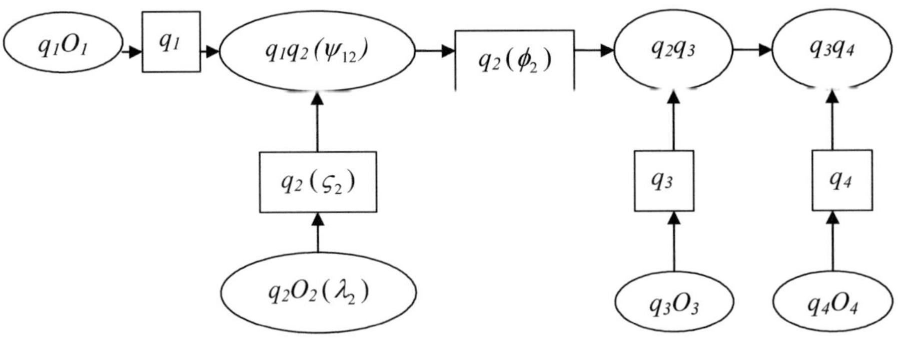

Fig. 1. The junction tree representing the system work

where the vector $O=(O_1, O_2, \ldots, O_T)$ is the current observation sequence and $Q=(q_1, q_2, \ldots, q_T)$ is the state sequence at the moments $t=1, 2, \ldots, T$. Each q_t is one of the elements of the set $S=\{s_1,\ldots,s_N\}$.

As a first step, all clique and separator potentials have been initialized with 1s. Then the conditional probability of each node in the original graph is multiplied onto the clique to which it is assigned. If we assume initially that the nodes, containing observations O_t, are hidden, the λ potentials at the node q_tO_t will be all 1s and the potentials along the node q_tq_{t+1} will be as follows:

$$\Psi_{1,2}(i,j) = P(q_2 = s_j | q_1 = s_i) P(q_1 = s_i) \quad (15)$$

$$\Psi_{t,t+1}(i,j) = P(q_{t+1} = s_j | q_t = s_i) \quad (16)$$

- Forward steps. The potentials were initialized with evidence

$$\lambda_t^*(i) = P(O_t | q_t = s_i) = \varsigma_t^*(i) \quad (17)$$

Running the forward algorithm, the following potentials were obtained:

$$\psi_{t-1,t}^*(i,j) = P(q_{t-1}, q_t, O_{1:t}) = \psi_{t-1,t}(i,j)\phi_{t-1}^*(i)\varsigma_t^*(j). \quad (18)$$

Marginalizing yields:

$$\phi_t^*(j) = P(q_t = s_i, O_{1:t}) = \sum_i \psi_{t-1,t}^*(i,j). \quad (19)$$

- Backward steps. In the backward steps, the potentials are

$$\psi_{t-1,t}^{**}(i,j) = P(q_{t-1} = s_i, q_t = s_j, O_{1:T}) = \frac{\psi_{t-1,t}^*(i,j)}{\phi_t^*(j)} \phi_t^{**}(j). \quad (20)$$

Marginalizing yields:

$$\phi_t^{**}(j) = P(q_t = s_j, O_{1:T}) = \sum_i \psi_{t-1,t}^{**}(i,j). \quad (21)$$

If the messages were propagated from children to their parents in the rooted junction tree, the result of the induction after the forwards steps (after collecting to root) will be $\psi_{t,t+1}^*(i,j) = P(q_t = s_i, q_{t+1} = s_j)$, $\phi_t^*(i) = P(q_t = s_i)$ and all the other potentials will be unchanged (all 1s). After the backward steps we have $\psi_{t-1,t}^{**}(i,j) = P(q_{t-1} = s_i, q_t = s_j)$, $\varsigma_t^{**}(i) = \lambda_t^{**}(i) = \phi_t^{**}(i) = P(q_t = s_i)$. The result from the JTA is the most likely state sequence during the examined period of time, whereupon the state transition probabilities can easily be computed from the result state sequence.

3. Simulation experiments and statistical methods of evaluating the effectiveness of IDS

3.1 Simulation experiments

A large number of simulation experiments, which were based on the described model, were carried out in order to test the proposed methodology. The experimental data were

obtained from Computer Immune Systems Project (University of New Mexico), performed by the researches in the Computer Science Department, University of New Mexico.
The simulation data are collected from Unix system examination during a period of time and consist of system call sequences, which were obtained from observation of some privileged processes executed on behalf of the root account as well some anomalous data. Each data file contains sequences of system call numbers, obtained by the examined process activity. The input data files are sequences of ordered pairs of numbers, where each line consists of one pair. The first number in each pair is the process ID (PID) of the process executed, and the second one is the system call number. Forks are taken into account as separate processes and their execution results are considered as normal user activity.
The privileged processes are among the major targets of the attacker as they are granted access to system resources that are inaccessible to ordinary users. The methods for pattern generation are described in (Forrest at al., 1996, Forrest at al., 1998). They prove the short sequences of system calls can be successfully applied for discriminating between normal and anomalous activities in the system.
The normal activity data patterns compose the system states set S and the intrusion activity patterns compose the set V. The system model, which contains the transition probabilities, was created according to the normal and anomalous data sets. This model is considered as a database, describing normal system activity. Each of the decoding algorithms, which were described in section 2, was applied during the detection stage in order to distinguish normal traces from abnormal ones.

3.2 The results obtained by the BCJR algorithm

The experimental data include normal user activity traces as well as intrusion data. A slide window with length T was applied in order to cross the traces of current user activity, i.e. the system observations, which compose the set O. The experiments were accomplished with the values of T=10, 15 and 20. The *LLR*s which represent the probability of intrusion occurrence at the given moment of time were obtained as a result of BCJR algorithm. Each *LLR* is the logarithmic ratio of the probability of attack presence and the probability of normal activity at specific moment t. Figure 2 presents some of the results of the *LLR*s for the process synthetic sendmail for T=20. The positive values of *LLR* denote an attack presence, while the negative values imply that the examined system call is a pattern of normal activity.

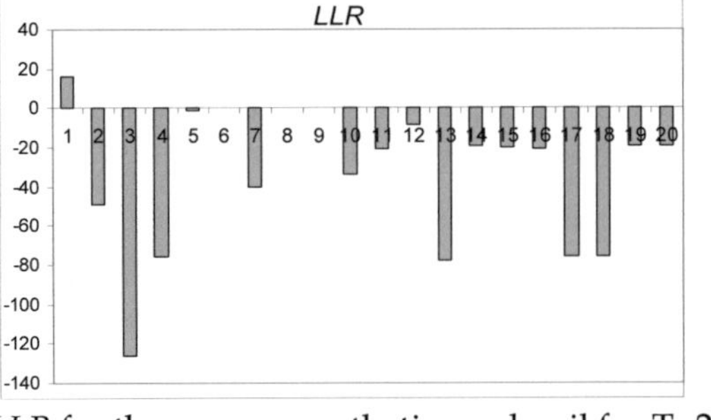

Fig. 2. Some results for *LLR* for the process synthetic sendmail for T=20

Another strategy for checking whether the particular activity data is normal or anomalous is prior to determine the model parameters A, B for given HMM λ and given sequence of observations O using standard gradient method and then to apply the BCJR decoding algorithm. Given an unknown observation sequence, the *ML*-criterion finds the model λ which maximizes the value of $L = P(O|\lambda)$. For standard gradient descent learning rate η were used the following values: from 0,000001 to 0,000009 with step 0,000001, from 0,00001 to 0,00009 with step 0,00001 and from 0,0001 to 0,0009 with step 0,0001 for both observation and transition probabilities. Some of the results for the process synthetic sendmail are summarized in Table 1, which present the number of iterations and the values of L for η=0,0001-0,0005 and η=0,00001-0,00005 and T=10 or 15.

T=10			*T*=15		
η	Number of iterations	*L*	η	Number of iterations	*L*
η=0,0001	322	4.20353e-13	η=0,0001	322	2.88298e-17
η=0,0002	161	3.41980e-13	η=0,0002	162	1.88268e-17
η=0,0003	107	3.21028e-13	η=0,0003	108	4.77443e-18
η=0,0004	80	7.60207e-14	η=0,0004	82	8.53916e-18
η=0,0005	64	1.15635e-13	η=0,0005	65	5.47520e-19
η=0,00001	3224	3.94035e-13	η=0,00001	3207	2.54814e-17
η=0,00002	1611	3.78713e-13	η=0,00002	1604	2.47694e-17
η=0,00003	1074	3.87351e-13	η=0,00003	1070	2.46345e-17
η=0,00004	805	3.58734e-13	η=0,00004	802	2.22364e-17
η=0,00005	644	3.58219e-13	η=0,00005	642	2.21205e-17

Table 1. Numbers of iterations and the values of L depending on the values of η

The algorithm exhibits a tendency to growth of the number of iterations when we increase the number of observations and decrease the learning rate η. The number of iterations necessary for the model training is similar when T=10 and 15. One of the greatest problems in training large models with gradient descent is to find an optimal learning rate. A small one will slow down the speed and significantly increase the number of iterations. On the other hand, a large one will probably cause oscillations during training and finally leading to no useful model would be trained.

Anomalous data was examined using the BCJR decoding algorithm which compares the traces of the system activity for T=10, 15 and 20 with the patterns of normal user activity. The intrusion detection problem is considered as a decoding problem. The results of the algorithm are the values of *LLR*, where each *LLR* is the logarithmic ratio of the probability of attack presence and the probability of normal activity at specific moment t. We assume that the values of *LLR* greater than 0 denote an attack presence. Some of the results for T=10, η=0,00001-0,00009 and the input files: synthetic ftp, named and xlock are summarized in the Figures 3, 4 and 5. For instance, from Figure 3 one can see that the method registers O_2 and O_4, as possible attacks.

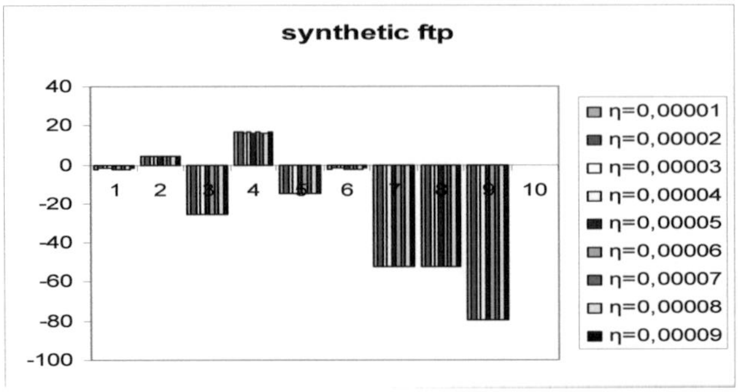

Fig. 3. Values of LLR depending on the value of η when T=10 for synthetic ftp

Fig. 4. Values of LLR depending on the value of η when T=10 for named

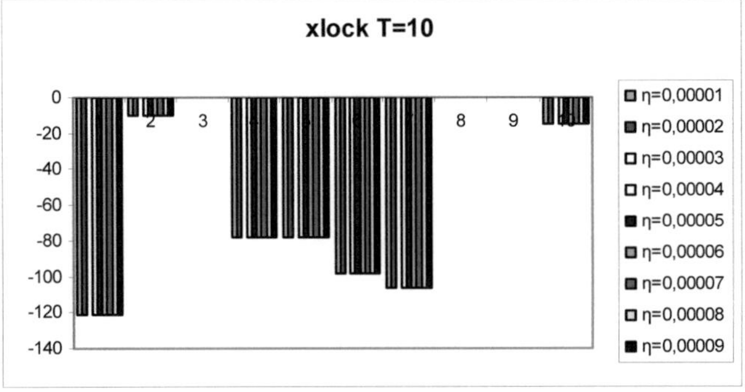

Fig. 5. Values of LLR depending on the value of η when T=10 for xlock

The results of BCJR algorithm were compared against its results over training which was performed using the gradient based method. Figures 6, 7 and 8 present the values of the *LLR*s for the process synthetic sendmail, obtained by applying the above presented two methods - BCJR algorithm and BCJR algorithm over gradient training for T=10, 15 and 20 and η=0,00005. From Figure 8 one could see that the second method registers O_6, O_8, O_{14}, O_{19} and O_{20} as possible attacks, while the first method registers these patterns as results of normal system work. It is worth to mention that the decoding based on BCJR algorithm is more consistent with preceding gradient training.

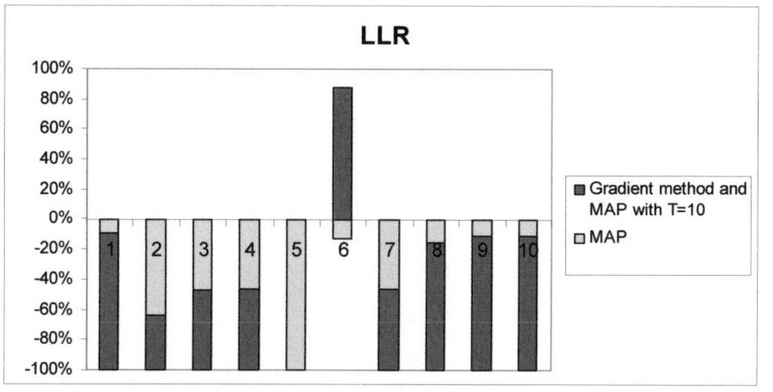

Fig. 6. The *LLR*s for the process synthetic sendmail for *T*=10

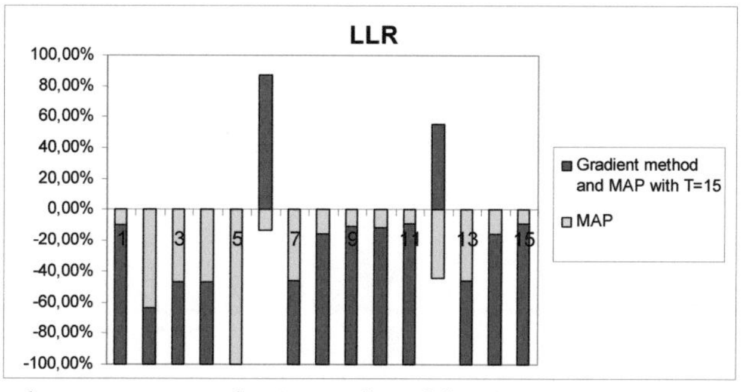

Fig. 7. The *LLR*s for the process synthetic sendmail for *T*=15

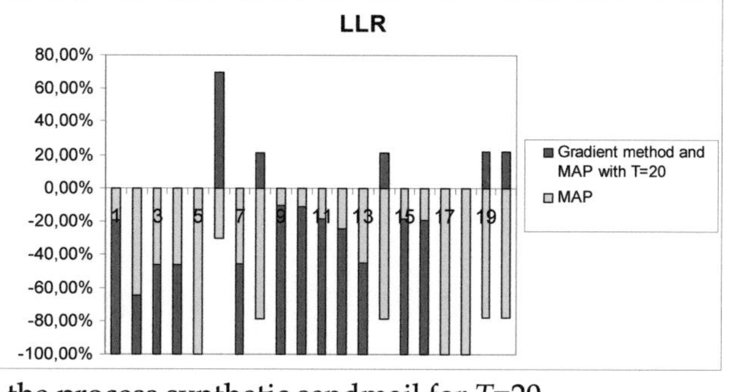

Fig. 8. The *LLR*s for the process synthetic sendmail for *T*=20

3.3 The results obtained by the Max-log MAP algorithm

The initial HMM was created according to the system states set *S*, whereupon it was tuned up using the gradient method. The result model was utilized as a normal user activity description. Then the Max log-MAP decoding algorithm was applied in order to distinguish normal activities from abnormal ones. The results of this algorithm are *LLRs*, which represent the probability of intrusion occurrence at a given moment of time. As in the previous case, the intrusion data were examined consequently with sliding window with length *T*: 10, 15 and 20. For standard gradient descent learning rate η was applied with the values from 0,00001 to 0,00009 with step 0,00001 for both observation and transition probabilities.

Figures 9, 10 and 11 contain the result values of *LLRs* in the case of T=10, when η takes the values between 0.00001 and 0.00009, for the processes synthetic ftp, named and xlock. As the Max log-MAP algorithm follows only the path that maximizes the transition probabilities, this may cause a lack of precision in the intrusion detection. In contrast, the MAP algorithm takes into account the whole trellis of possible system paths.

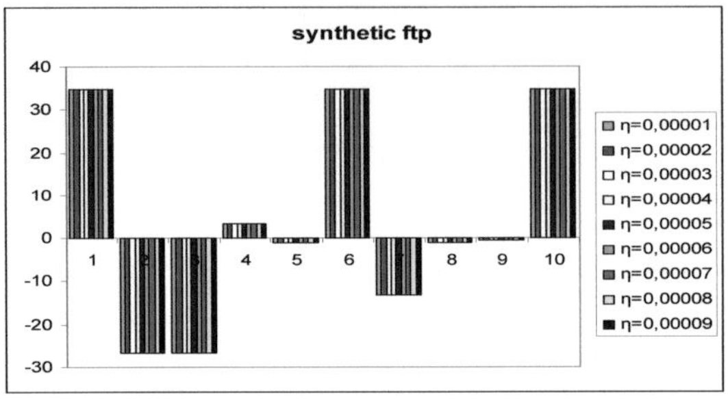

Fig. 9. Values of LLR depending on the value of η when T=10 for synthetic ftp

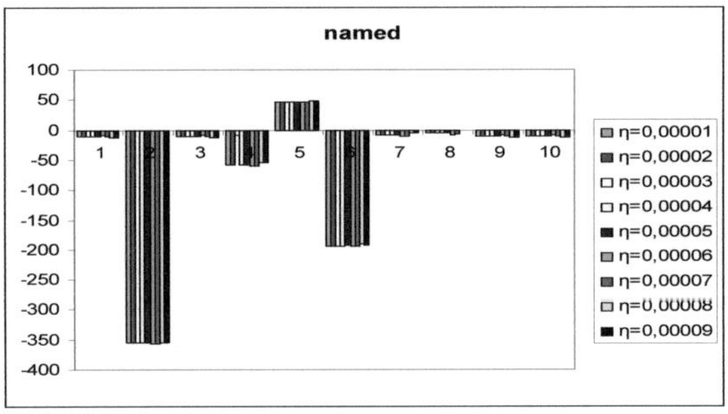

Fig. 10. Values of LLR depending on the value of η when T=10 for named

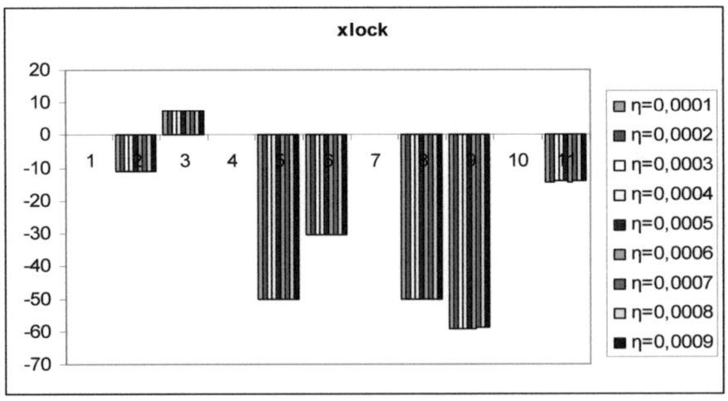

Fig. 11. Values of LLR depending on the value of η when T=10 for xlock

3.4 The results obtained by the JTA

The state transition probabilities were evaluated based on the normal user activity patterns during the system work in attack absence. A slide window with length T=10 was used in order to cross the traces of current user activity. The most likely states sequence and the corresponding state transition probabilities were obtained for each unknown observation sequence. Comparing the obtained state transition probabilities with the state transition probabilities of the normal user activity patterns the intrusions presence or absence was determined. Some of the results from the distribution of anomaly signal for the processes synthetic ftp, named and xlock are presented in Figures 12, 13and 14:

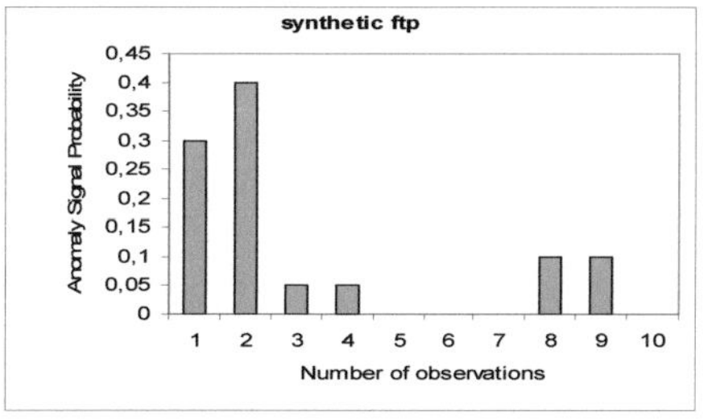

Fig. 12. The distribution of anomaly signal

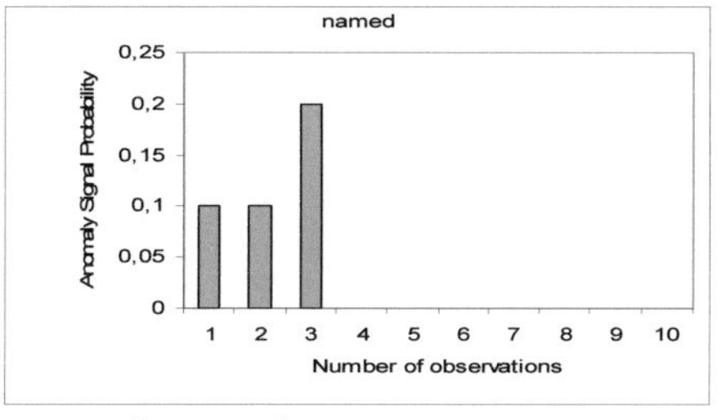

Fig. 13. The distribution of anomaly signal

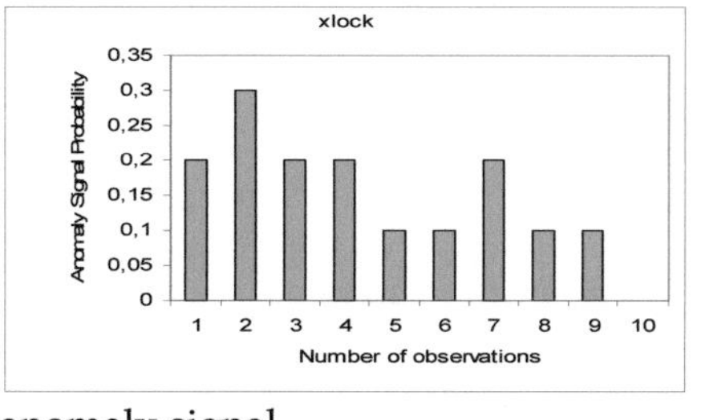

Fig. 14. The distribution of anomaly signal

4. Evaluation of the obtained results

4.1 Statistical methods of evaluating the effectiveness of IDS

The goal of the hypothesis testing is to determine whether a variation between two sample distributions can be explained by chance or not. For every possible criterion value we select to discriminate the two sets, there will be some cases with the intrusion correctly classified as positive (*TP* – True Positive), but some cases with the intrusion will be classified negative (*FN* - False Negative). On the other hand, some cases without the intrusion will be correctly classified as negative (*TN* - True Negative), but some cases without the intrusion will be classified as positive (*FP* - False Positive).

$$FP = Condition\ absent + Positive\ result$$

$$FN = Condition\ present + Negative\ result$$

As are measure of the quality of binary classification can be used the Matthews correlation coefficient (*MCC*) (Matthews, 1975):

$$MCC = \frac{TP.TN - FP.FN}{\sqrt{(TP+FP)(TP+FN)(TN+FP)(TN+FN)}},$$

MCC takes into account true and false positives and negatives and is generally regarded as a balanced measure which can be used even if the classes are of very different sizes. *MCC*=+1 represents a perfect prediction, while *MCC*=-1 represents the worst possible prediction. It considers both the true positives and the true negatives as successful predictions.
The false positive rate (*FPR*) is the frequency with which the IDS reports malicious activity in error. The probability that an observed positive result is a false positive may be calculated using Bayes's theorem, whose basic concept is that the true rates of false positives and false negatives are not a function of the accuracy of the test alone, but also the actual rate or frequency of occurrence within the test set.

$$FPR = \frac{number\ of\ false\ positives}{total\ number\ of\ negative\ instances}$$

The true danger of a high *FPR* lies in fact that it may cause to ignore the system's output when legitimate alerts are raised. The false negative rate (*FNR*) is the frequency with which the IDS fails to raise an alert when malicious activity actually occurs, i.e. they represent undetected attacks on a system.

$$FNR = \frac{number\ of\ false\ negatives}{total\ number\ of\ positive\ instances}$$

FNR changes in an inverse proportion to *FPR*.
The crossover error rate (*CER*) is defined as adjusting the system's sensitivity until the *FPR* and the *FNR* are equal. In order to achieve a balance between *FPR* and *FNR*, we may select the *IDS* with the lowest *CER*.
Sensitivity is a probability that a test result will be positive when the intrusion is present (true positive rate - *TPR*).

$$FNR = 1 - Sensitivity$$

A sensitivity of 100% means that the test recognizes all intrusion as such. In the language of statistical hypothesis testing, it is called the statistical power of the test. Specificity is a probability that a test result will be negative when the intrusion is not present (true negative rate - *TNR*).

$$FPR = 1 - Specificity$$

A specificity of 100% means that the test recognizes all normal activity as normal activity.
The receiver operating characteristic (*ROC*) curve (Ferri et al., 2005, Hanley&McNeil, 1982) is a method of graphically demonstrating the relationship between sensitivity and specificity. An *ROC* space is defined by *1-specificity* and *sensitivity* as x and y respectively, which depicts relative trade-offs between *TP* and *FP*. As the decision threshold moves to the right along the x-axis, sensitivity ranges from one, when all tests are read as abnormal (no *FN*), to 0, when all are normal (no *TP*). Maximal sensitivity is realized when all tests are reported as abnormal. Specificity moves in concert from 0 (no *TN*) to one (no *FP*). Maximal specificity is achieved by reporting all tests as normal. The best possible prediction method would yield a point in upper left corner (0,1) of the *ROC* space, representing 100% sensitivity (all *TP* are found) and 100% specificity (no *FP* are found). This point is called a perfect classification. The diagonal line (from the left bottom to the right corner) divides the *ROC* space in areas of good and bad classification. Points above this line indicate good classification results, while points below the line indicate wrong results. Accuracy is measured by the area under the *ROC* curve. An area from 0.9 to 1 represents an excellent result; an area from 0,8 to 0,9 represents a good result, form 0,7 to 0,8 - a fair result, from 0,6 to 0,7 - a poor result and from 0.5 to 0,6 - a fail result.
The positive predictive value is the probability that the intrusion is present when the test is positive. It is applied to evaluate the usefulness of a recognizable test.

$$PPV = Positive\ Predictive\ Value = \frac{number\ of\ True\ positives}{Number\ of\ True\ positives + number\ of\ False\ positives}$$

The negative predictive value is the probability that the intrusion is not present when the test is negative.

$$NPV = Negative\ Predictive\ Value = \frac{number\ of\ True\ negatives}{number\ of\ True\ negatives + number\ of\ False\ negatives}$$

Accuracy is degree of conformity of a calculated quantity of the anomaly detection method accurately verify a given unknown sequence to be normal or anomalous (Taylor, 1999).

$$Accuracy = \frac{number\ of\ True\ positives + number\ of\ True\ negatives}{number\ of\ True\ positives + False\ positives + False\ negatives + True\ negatives}$$

An accuracy of 100% means that the test identifies all anomalous and normal activity correctly.

4.2 The effectiveness of IDS based on the BCJR decoding algorithm

In order to evaluate the *FPR* we applied a method used by Hoang (Hoang et.al., 2003). This approach is based on the assumption that as a normal traces sequence does not contain any intrusions, any reported alarms could be considered as false alarms. From the normal traces we generated a list of n consecutive short sequences of system calls, using a sliding window of length T. Then, each short sequence of the list is evaluated by the detection method to determine if it is normal or abnormal. We counted all abnormal sequences for the whole list as m. The *FPR* is calculated as m/n.

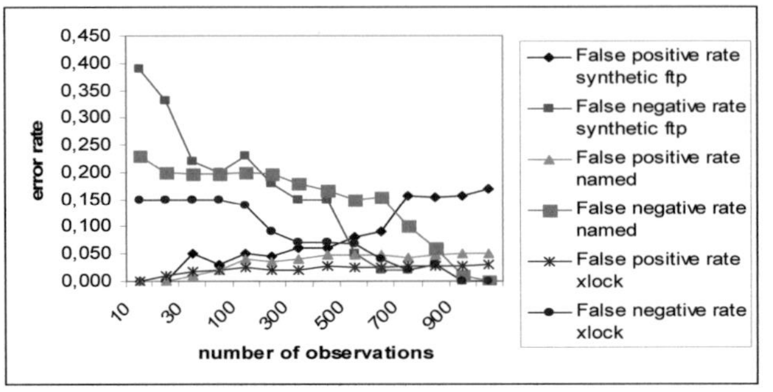

Fig. 15. The *FNR* and the *FPR* for the examined processes

Figure 15 contains graphs of the *FNR* and the *FPR* for the input processes. Table 2 contains the values of the *FPR, FNR, CER,* the accuracy and *MCC* for processes synthetic sendmail, synthetic ftp, named and xlock.

Process	*FPR*	*FNR*	*CER*	Accuracy	*MCC*
synthetic sendmail	5%	21%	0,04	83%	0,67
synthetic ftp	17%	39%	0,07	72%	0,41
named	5%	23%	0,05	86%	0,72
xlock	3%	15%	0,03	91%	0,82

Table 2. The false alarms rate and the algorithm accuracy

The proposed methodology achieves low level of the false positive rate values for the processes xlock, synthetic sendmail and named. The obtained value of 17% for synthetic ftp and the relatively high false negative rates should be further examined. As *FPR* and *FNR* are interrelated, we can reduce one at the expense of increasing the other. *CER* is the point at which the system is tuned so that both kinds of false responses occur with the same frequency. So the obtained values of *CER* could be applied as points of trade-off between *FPR* and *FNR*. Since the *CER* is the point at which these rates are equal, from Table 2 could be seen that for the examined processes the obtained values of *CER* are between 0,03 and 0,07, which implies low error and high accuracy rate of the proposed methodology.
The conducted experiments indicate the proposed methodology produces results with high level of accuracy, since all obtained values are between 72% and 91% for all examined processes. The obtained values of *MCC* are between 0.41 and 0.82, which indicate significant correlation between the current activity data and the data from the normal activity description, as the value of 1 denotes a perfect correlation.
In a *ROC* curve each sensitive value can be plotted against its corresponding specificity value to create the diagram for the examined processes in Figure 16. A methodology with perfect discrimination has a *ROC* plot that passes through the upper left corner, consequently the closer the *ROC* plot is to the upper left corner, the higher the overall accuracy of the test (Zweig&Campbell, 1993). The points in the upper left corner of the *ROC* space, which are produced by the proposed methodology for the processes synthetic ftp, named and xlock are (0,09; 0,97), (0,05; 0,98), (0,03; 0,99) respectively.

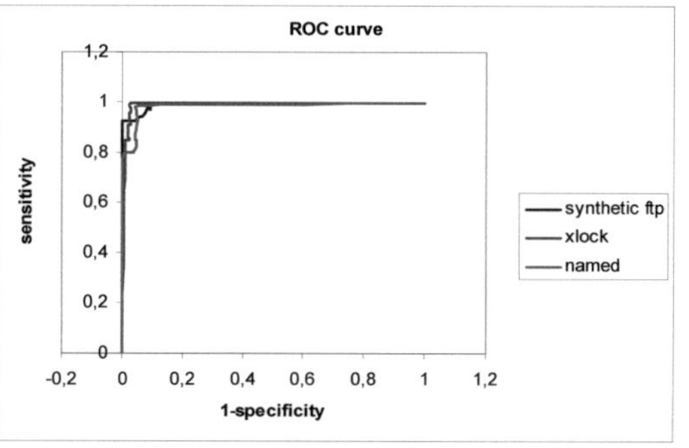

Fig. 16. The *ROC* curve for IDS based on BCJR algorithm

4.3 The effectiveness of IDS based on the Max-log MAP algorithm

In order to evaluate the effectiveness of *IDS* based on the Max-log MAP algorithm we determine the sensitivity, specificity, *PPV, NPV* and accuracy for the processes named, synthetic sendmail, synthetic ftp and xlock, which results are presented in Tables 3, 4, 5 and 6 respectively.

synthetic sendmail	true	false	
positive	True positive=12	False positive=125	PPV=8,7%
negative	False negative=9	True negative=1223	NPV=99,3%
	Sensitivity=57,1%	Specificity=90,7%	Accuracy=90,2%

Table 3. The sensitivity, specificity, *PPV, NPV* and accuracy for the process synthetic sendmail

synthetic ftp	true	false	
positive	True positive=8	False positive=154	PPV=4,9%
negative	False negative=6	True negative=1140	NPV=99,5%
	Sensitivity=57,1%	Specificity=88,1%	Accuracy=87,8%

Table 4. The sensitivity, specificity, *PPV, NPV* and accuracy for the process synthetic ftp

named	true	false	
positive	True positive=11	False positive=135	PPV=7,5%
negative	False negative=7	True negative=1244	NPV=99,4%
	Sensitivity=61,1%	Specificity=90,2%	Accuracy=89,8%

Table 5. The sensitivity, specificity, *PPV, NPV* and accuracy for the process named

xlock	true	false	
positive	True positive=9	False positive=104	PPV=7,9%
negative	False negative=7	True negative=1125	NPV=99,4%
	Sensitivity=56,2%	Specificity=91,5%	Accuracy=91,1%

Table 6. The sensitivity, specificity, *PPV, NPV* and accuracy for the process xlock

The *CER* and the *MCC* for the examined processes are represented in Table 7. As the smaller value of *CER*, the better the intrusion detection performance, the presented results show the proposed method gives its best results for processes named, synthetic ftp and synthetic sendmail and satisfactory value for xlock. Since the *CER* value indicates that the proportion of false acceptances is equal to the proportion of false rejections, the lower the equal error rate value is, the higher the accuracy of the proposed methodology is.
As a single measure of the performance of the test, the values of the *MCC* in Table 7 indicate that the proposed method gives feasible results during the recognition stage. The *MCC* values for all processes are between 0.44 and 0.63, which indicate significant correlation between the examined data and the data from the normal activity description.

Process	*CER*	*MCC*
synthetic ftp	0,05	0,44
synthetic sendmail	0,04	0,63
named	0,03	0,57
xlock	0,12	0,59

Table 7. The value of *CER* and *MCC* for the examined processes

The sensitivity, also referred to as recall rate, reveals how good the methodology is at correctly identifying anomalous patterns. The obtained sensitivity values, presented in Tables 3-6, indicate the proposed methodology produces good sensitivity rates, since all calculated values belong to the interval (56%, 62%). Specificity, on the other hand, is concerned with how good the methodology is at correctly identifying patterns of normal system activity. Both of them may range from 0 to +1 and the latter value is associated with perfect predictions. The proposed methodology achieves high specificity rates, as the obtained values for all processes are between 88% and 92%.
Considering the obtained predictive values, we see in Tables 3-6 that all *PPV* are between 4,9% and 8,7%, while all *NPV* are between 99,3% and 99,5%. Since the positive predictive values refers to the chance that a positive test result will be correct, the obtained results show that the proposed method correctly classifies the patterns with high degree of probability. On the other hand, negative predictive value is concerned only with negative test results. From the Tables 3-6 we see that the proposed methodology produces results with excellent negative predictive values. The both predictive values depend on the prevalence of the intrusions, since they depend on the number of true positives and false negatives and true negatives and false positives, respectively.
Since the accuracy values for all processes belong to the interval (87%, 92%), we can conclude that the proposed methodology produces precise and reliable detection results.

4.4 The effectiveness of IDS based on the *JTA*

Figure 17 contains graphs of the *FNR* and the *FPR* for the processes synthetic sendmail, synthetic ftp, named and xlock. From the graphs could be seen that the *CER* values as trade-offs between the *FPR* and the *FNR* are between 0,02 and 0,18 for the examined processes. Since the *CER* is the point at which *FPR* and *FNR* are equal, the obtained results imply low error and high accuracy rate of the proposed methodology.

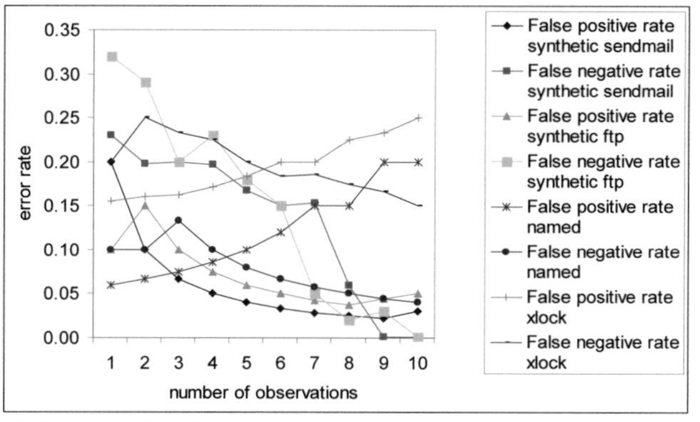

Fig. 17. The *FPR* and the *FNR* for the examined processes

A *ROC* curve is a non-parametric approach to evaluate a binary classification method. It is a two-dimensional depiction of the results, where each sensitive value can be plotted against its corresponding specificity value to create the diagram for the examined processes in Figure 18. The points in the upper left corner of the *ROC* space for the processes synthetic sendmail, synthetic ftp, named and xlock are (0,06; 0,94), (0,05; 0,99), (0,55; 0,95) and (0,25; 0,85) respectively. As the point (0, 1) denotes the perfect detection, the proposed methodology produces reliable and qualitative results while distinguishing the normal activity from abnormal one.

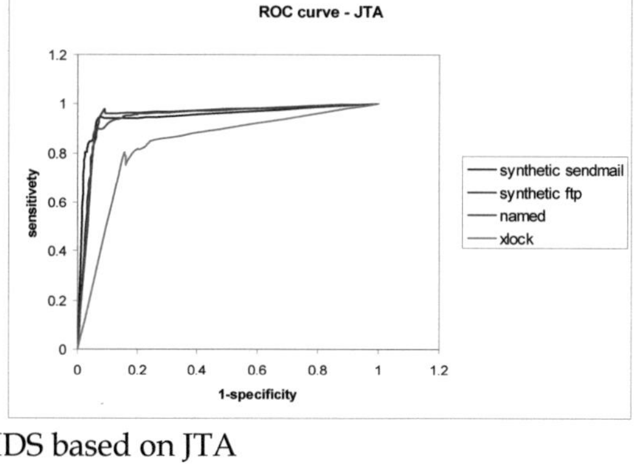

Fig. 18. *ROC* curve for IDS based on JTA

Table 8 contains the values of the *FPR*, the *FNR*, the accuracy and *MCC* for the following processes: synthetic ftp, synthetic sendmail, named and xlock.

Processes	*FPR*	*FNR*	Accuracy	*CER*	*MCC*
synthetic ftp	5%	1%	94%	0,04	0,85
synthetic sendmail	16%	6%	78%	0,02	0,60
named	11%	3%	87%	0,09	0,70
xlock	7%	2%	90%	0,18	0,69

Table 8. The false alarms rate and the algorithm accuracy

The methodology, which applies JTA during the detection stage, achieves low level of the *FPR* values for the processes synthetic ftp and xlock and low level of the *FNR* for all examined processes. The reasons of obtaining values of 16% for synthetic sendmail and 11 % for named should be further examined.
The accuracy is a key feature of each diagnostic algorithm. Analyzing the obtained accuracy values, presented in Table 8, we see that the proposed methodology produces precise and reliable results, since all accuracy values are between 78% and 94 %. The highest accuracy is achieved for the process synthetic ftp; the balanced accuracy results are obtained for the processes xlock and named; and the lowest, but still satisfactory result is obtained for the process synthetic sendmail.
One can observe that the values of *MCC*, presented in Table 8, are between 0,69 and 0,85, which reveals that there is a substantial correlation between the normal activity sequences from the created database and the observed sequences of current system activity.

4.5 Discussions

Let designate with A the methodology, based on the BCJR decoding algorithm during the detection stage, with B the methodology, based on the Max-log MAP decoding algorithm during the detection stage, and with C the methodology, based on the JTA during the detection stage. From Table 2 we see that method A achieves the highest accuracy value of 91% for the process xlock, while the lowest accuracy value of 72% is obtained for the process synthetic ftp. As one can see in Tables 3-6 method B achieves its highest accuracy value of 91,1% for the process xlock, since its lowest value of 87,8% is achieved for the process synthetic ftp. At last method C achieves its highest accuracy value of 94% for the process synthetic ftp, and reaches its lowest accuracy value of 78% for the process synthetic sendmail. Comparing all methods when accuracy alone is concerned, we can conclude the method B outperforms other methods, since it produces stable and reliable accuracy results for all examined processes.
Comparing the proposed methods when *MCC* alone is concerned, we see that method C yields the best overall correlation results, followed by methods A and B respectively. This means the overall correlation for all processes between the predicted and observed behavior is greater, when the methodology applies JTA, than the case when BCJR or Max-log MAP is applied.
The results indicate the proposed methodology with HMM, that describes the normal system activity, could lead to development of IDS with qualitative performance and high level of classification accuracy. The major drawbacks of the approach are the relatively high amount of resources necessary for the normal activity description and the relatively high false positives rate. But we have to outline the normal behavior creation is performed only once during system initialization.

5. Conclusion

The present work introduces an intrusion detection methodology that uses HMM for normal activity description and some decoding algorithms for detecting attacks targeted at essential server processes. The methodology relies on probabilistic methods for both algorithm stages: the normal activity description and the intrusion detection itself. The learning-based approach was applied in order to increase the system ability to detect novel attacks, which is among the most important features of the anomaly IDS. The feasibility of the proposed approach was justified by simulation experiments and evaluation of the obtained results.

6. References

Bahl L., J.Cocke, F.Jelinek, and J.Raviv, (1974). Optimal Decoding of Linear Codes for minimizing symbol error rate, *IEEE Transactions on Information Theory*, vol. IT-20(2), pp. 284-287.

Bahrololum M., M. Khaleghi (2008). Anomaly Intrusion Detection System Using Gaussian Mixture Model, *Third International Conference on Convergence Information Technology*, pp. 1162-1167, Busan, Nov. 2008, vol. 1, no. 1.

Benedetto S., D. Divsalar, G. Montorsi, F. Pollara, "A soft-input soft-output APP module for iterative decoding of concatenated codes," IEEE Comm. Letters, Vol. 1, No. 1, pp. 22-24, Jan. 1997.

Dagorn N. (2008). WebIDS: A Cooperative Bayesian Anomaly-Based Intrusion Detection System for Web Applications, *Recent Advances in Intrusion Detection*, LNCS, Vol. 5230/2008, Springer Berlin / Heidelberg, pp. 392-393.

Ferri C., N. Lachinche, S. A. Macskassy, A. Rakotomamonjy, eds., (2005). Second Workshop on ROC Analysis in ML, Bonn, Germany, August 2005.

Forrest S., S.A. Hofmeyr, A. Somayaji, (1998). Intrusion detection using sequences of system calls, *Journal of Computer Security*, Vol. 6, pp. 151-180.

Forrest S., S.A. Hofmeyr, A. Somayaji, T.A. Longtaff, (1996). A Sense of Self for Unix Processes, *Proceedings of the 1996 IEEE Symposium on Security and Privacy*, pp.120-128, IEEE Computer Society Press, Los Alamitors, CA.

Ghosh K.A. et.al (1999). Study in Using Neural Networks for Anomaly and Misuse Detection, *Proceedings of the 8th SENIX Security Symposium*, pp 131-142, August 1999, Washington D.C.

Hanley JA, McNeil BJ (1982). The meaning and use of the area under the Receiver Operating Characteristic (ROC) curve. *Radiology*, Vol 143, pp. 29-36.

Hoang X.D., J. Hu, P. Bertok, (2003). A Multi-layer Model for Anomaly Intrusion Detection Using Program Sequences of System Calls, *11th IEEE International Conference on Networks (ICON 2003)*, Sydney, Australia.

Jecheva V., E. Nikolova, (2007). An Application of Learning Problem in Anomaly-based Intrusion Detection Systems, *Second International Conference of Availability, Reliability and Security ARES 2007*, pp. 853-860, Vienna, April 2007.

Joshi S.S., V.V. Phoha (2005), Investigating hidden Markov models capabilities in anomaly detection, *Proceedings of the 43rd ACM annual Southeast regional conference*, pp. 98 - 103, Vol. 1, Kennesaw, Georgia, USA.

Lauritzen S.L., (1996). *Graphical Models*, Oxford Science Publications.

Lauritzen, Steffen L.; Spiegelhalter, David J. (1988). Local Computations with Probabilities on Graphical Structures and their Application to Expert Systems, *Journal of the Royal Statistical Society*, Series B (Blackwell Publishing) 50, pp.157–224.

Matthews B.W., (1975). Comparison of the predicted and observed secondary structure of T4 phage lysozyme. *Biochim*. Biophys. Acta, 405, pp.442-451.

Nikolova E., V. Jecheva, (2007). Anomaly Based Intrusion Detection Based on the Junction Tree Algorithm, *Journal of Information Assurance and Security*, Dynamic Publishers Inc., Vol. 2, Issue 3, pp. 184-188.

Nikolova E., V. Jecheva, (2008). Some Evaluations of the Effectiveness of Anomaly Based Intrusion Detection Systems Based on the Junction Tree Algorithm, *Proceedings of the 5th CITSA 2008*, Orlando, Florida, June 29th - July 2nd, 2008, vol. 1, pp.115-120.

Qiao, Y., Xin, X.W., Bin, Y. & Ge, S.(2002) Anomaly intrusion detection method based on HMM, *IEEE Electronic Letters,* Online No: 20020467.

Rabiner L. R., B. H. Juang, (1986). An introduction to Hidden Markov Models, *IEEE ASSP Magazine*, pp.4-16.

Robertson P., E. Villebrun, P. Höher, (1995). A comparison of optimal and sub-optimal MAP decoding algorithms operating in the log domain, *IEEE Int. Conf. On Communications*, pp. 1009-1013, Seattle, WA, Jun. 1995.

Tan X., H. Xi (2008), Hidden semi-Markov model for anomaly detection, *Applied Mathematics and Computation*, Vol. 205, Issue 2, November 2008, Special Issue on Advanced Intelligent Computing Theory and Methodology in Applied Mathematics and Computation, pp. 562-567.

Taylor J. R., (1999). *An Introduction to Error Analysis: The Study of Uncertainties in Physical Measurements*, University Science Books, pp.128-129.

University of New Mexico, Computer Immune Systems Project, http://www.cs.unm.edu/~immsec/systemcalls.htm

Vigna G., E. Jonsson, C. Kruegel, (2003). Recent Advances in Intrusion Detection, *Proceedings of 6th International Symposium, RAID 2003*, Pittsburgh, PA, USA, September 2003, Springer.

Zweig M.H., G. Campbell, (1993). Receiver-operating characteristic (ROC) plots: a fundamental evaluation tool in clinical medicine, *Clinical Chemistry*, Vol. 39, Num. 4, pp. 561-577.

20

Transition Parameters For Successful Reuse Business

Jasmine K.S.
Dept. of MCA, R.V. College of Engineering
Bangalore-59, Karnataka
India

1. Introduction

For any industrial organizations, improving the business performance often means the improvement in their software development performance. The growing popularity of developing the software using reusable components could dramatically reduce development effort, cost and accelerate delivery. Software professionals generally need most help in controlling requirements, coordinating changes, managing (and making) plans, managing interdependencies, and coping with various systems' issues. Since the energy spent on these and similar problems generally consumes a large part of every software professional's time, these are where management can provide the most immediate help.

The primary function of ongoing business management is to monitor the progress of the rollout plans towards achieving these business goals, and to adjust expectations and schedule to meet business and organizational realities. Detailed measurement is crucial to ensure that overall reuse business goals are met. Management should clearly define what is meant by reuse to different parts of the organization, and how to match reuse measurements to business goals of the organization. Reuse measurements must take into account political and organizational realities. When setting up a measurement program, it is must decide what kind of metrics, or what changes in current metrics, are needed to successfully manage a reuse business at the hands-on level. Most of the metrics that software managers use today are aimed at a standalone project group, which does its own estimating, requirements capture, architecting, analysis, design, implementation, and testing.
The need of adjustment in goals and metrics and changes in process and development and implementation methods are mandatory to become success in the transition to reuse business process.

The chapter mainly focuses on the results obtained from my own study and also the lessons learned from the literature survey. In writing this chapter, I have incorporated ideas; suggestions and experience of leading software reuse experts working in various software companies. I am convinced that the lessons and insight provided in this chapter will be of crucial value to any company dependent on software reuse.

2. Transition management –An essential step towards New Business Opportunities

The interest in system innovations is motivated by environmental and economic reasons. The alternative systems should be attractive not only from an environmental point of view but also from an economic point of view (in terms of generating ROI and services to end-users). It is accepted that any system innovations will have disadvantages, which may or may not be overcome. The solution to this problem is the simultaneous exploration of multiple options and adaptive policies, based on iterative and interactive decision making. New systems should not be implemented but "grown" in a gradual manner, relying on feedback and decentralized decision-making (Larry, 2002).

> – *"Radical innovation is the process of introducing something that is new to the organization and that requires the development of completely new routines, usually with modifications in the normative beliefs and value systems of organization members."* -- Nord and Tucker, *Routine and Radical Innovations*, 1987

Transitions here refer to important changes in functional systems. They involve multi-level changes through which an organization fundamentally changes. The transitions are required in the areas such as

- Economy
- Culture
- Management
- Technology

For a transition to occur different development have to come together causing a path of development based on new practices, knowledge, social organization and different guiding principles.

2.1 What exactly is transition management?

Transition management is a new steering concept that relies on 'darwinististic' processes of variation and selection. It makes use of "bottom-up" developments and long-term goals both at the organizational and process level (Garcia, 2003). Learning and institutional change are key elements which means that transition management not so much concerned with specific outcomes but rather with mechanisms for change. The basic philosophy is that or goal-oriented modulation: the utilization of ongoing developments for business and organizational goals. An important question therefore is: what do people really want, both as users and developers?

Collective choices are made "along the way" on the basis of learning experiences at different levels. Different trajectories are explored and flexibility is maintained, which is exactly what a manager would do when faced with great uncertainty and complexity: instead of defining end states for development he sets out in a certain direction and is careful to avoid premature choices.

2.2 Elements of transition management

Transition management consists of following elements:

1. Development of long-term visions
2. Organizing a transition arena for a transition theme
3. Monitoring and evaluation of experiments and transition processes
4. Implementation and Monitoring of transition mechanisms
5. Learning and adjusting to support for future transitions

Key elements of the transition management cycle are: anticipation, learning and adaptation. The starting point is the structuring of problems - to achieve a common outlook. This is followed by the development of long-term visions and goals. Goals are being set via the process and deliberations in transitions arenas. The management acts as a process manager, dealing with issues of collective orientation and adaptation of policy. It also has a responsibility for the undertaking of strategic experiments and programmes for system innovation. Control policies are part of transition management. Transition management aims for generating "momentum" for sustainability transitions. Not all companies will contribute to a transition, but once a new development takes shape, others will follow suit, including companies invested in the old system. When this happens the change process becomes a force of its own. This is a critical phase in a transition in which also unwanted path dependencies occur. Management has to develop assessment tools to measure the effectiveness of this transition process. Transition management requires continuous anticipation and adaptation (Graves, 1989).

2.3 Policy integration

The integration of various policy areas is part of transition management. Areas for integration are: Technological policy, infrastructural policy, adoption & decision making policy and innovation& implementation policy (across organization). This is an important but difficult task. The use of transition agendas and transition arenas should help to achieve this. Policy integration is probably aided by a more open approach of policy making in which learning is institutionalized. Policy renewal is officially part of transition policy. Interactive approach is a better coordination of different policies.

Some findings about adoption policy (Rotmans, 2001):

- Learning and professional development are important to organizations both before and after the adoption
- The adoption decision should be communicated to every developer at all levels
- Adoption should be treated as a continuous process

2.4 What makes transition management different?

Transition management does not rely on blueprints but relies on iterative decision making in which also goals may change. Decisions are made on the basis of experiences and new insights. Policy choices would be more based on long-term desirability instead of on short-term solutions. Long-term possibilities are given support but still need to prove themselves to customer needs. This way, customer may discover what is best.

Through transition management space is being created for change. The space should not be too narrow, lest organization will get locked into suboptimal solutions. To prevent this from happening, transition management opts for a portfolio approach and 'evolutionary' steering.

2.5 Preparing for Transition management

Transition management is well-accepted in software industry. The management is ready to support it. The transition management builds upon interests and "movements" (change processes) in development methodology. Transition management helps to establish a partnership with business and to stimulate new business based on sustainable innovation.

Transforming a business and its core processes to compete effectively is not just a technology issue however. A successful approach will require careful collaboration between (Griss et al., 1993):

- People e.g. stakeholders, accountability, internal politics)
- Technology e.g. service enablement / integration, governance, business process management/ workflow analytics)
- Processes e.g. improved business / IT alignment, delivery methodology, consolidation/rationalization continuous process improvement initiatives).

Only through careful alignment and management of these three distinct disciplines will an organization embark on a successful business transformation journey.

The recent history of successful market transformations consistently demonstrate that embracing relevant technology principles, standards and industry best practice are all differentiating actors between mere market participation and market leadership. Latest advances in architectural principles such as loosely coupled distributed systems, separation of logic from implementation and common information models all indicate the importance of service orientated techniques in the design and development of flexible and hence sustainable solutions. These new architectural approaches coupled with complementary project delivery methodologies help provide the agility required to liberate existing assets and better align IT with ever changing business needs in timely and repeatable fashion.

2.6 Effects of successful transition

The software industry has just started with transition management. In the short term, few results in terms of reduced development cost, Quality improvement, time-to-market and realization of new business opportunities are to be expected. Expectations are rather high, whereas transitions research shows that transitions defy control and effective steering. Policy can do little more than increase the chance for a transition to occur and shape the features of it. This is also what transition management tries to do by way of evolutionary steering, oriented at processes of variation and selection. Processes of adaptation, learning and anticipation are institutionalized through transition management. Conditions for success and application are: 'sense of urgency', leadership, commitment, willingness to change political culture (based on short-term goals), active management, guidance, trust, and willingness to invest the right resources at right time (Graves, 1989).

It is hoped that the commitment to sustainability transitions helps to make such choices, but whether this will happen is far from certain. Transition management is not an instrument but a framework for policy-making and governance. It is believed that transition management offers an interesting model for policy & governance, combining the advantages of incrementalism (do-able steps which are not immediately disruptive) with those of planning (articulation of desirable futures and use of goals).

2.7 Transition to a Reuse Business

There are a number of approaches to deal with large-scale organization and process change that can be used by a software organization to introduce or improve its reuse practice. Among the approaches mentioned above, by focusing on process and organizational models and dealt with people issues, one can have a successful transition to reuse business.

The proper implementation of following steps will guarantee a successful reuse transition process:

Step1.Assess reuse feasibility by assessing business opportunities and needs, organizational readiness and observing the kind and variety of application systems produced, sort of process, tools and technology used.

Step2. Prepare a transition plan to meat the long term goals (e.g. with emphasis on product line approach)

Step3.Address people issues such as awareness about reuse, convincing reasons for reuse, fear for reuse etc.

Step4.Allow the reuse program to grow naturally and mature through a distinct well defined stages.

Step5. Customize and adapt the traditional software engineering approach to Component system engineering and Application family engineering.

Step 6.Testing, appropriate tool development and deployment of the steps1-5.

3. Assess Reuse Risks and Costs

"*The use of commercial products can have profound and lasting impact on the spiraling cost and effort of building Defense systems, particularly information systems. It is important, however, to remember that simply 'using COTS' is not the end in itself, but only the means.*"--David Carney

Component based software development is becoming more generalized, representing a considerable market for the software industry. The perspective of reduced development costs, shorter life cycles, lower cost of sustainment, and better quality acts as motivation factors for this expansion. However, several technical issues remain unsolved before software component's industry reaches the maturity exhibited by other component industries. Problems such as the component selection by their integrators, the component

catalogs formalization and the uncertain quality of third-party developed components, bring new challenges to the software engineering community. Even the reuse actually slowing it down and making the overall design of the system unwieldy, and unstable. It can actually increase the long-term cost of the system. Requirements, algorithms, functions, business rules, architecture, source code, test cases, input data, and scripts can all be reused. Architecture reuse is the primary means for achieving the cost savings potential of code reuse.
To exploit reuse, the development team must recognize the realities of reused products (Jacobson et.al, 1997).

- The product being reused must closely match the need that it is trying to solve. Otherwise, the components with which it interfaces will become more complex.
- The reused product should be well documented with a well-understood interface in the perspective of future maintenance.
- The reuse product should have been designed for a scenario similar to that for which it is going to be used. If not, extensive testing should be conducted to verify the correctness of the product. Changes in the operational environment may require further overhead in testing
- The reuse product should be stable. Any change to the product must be incorporated into the current development.
- The key to successful reuse is determining the components and functions that are needed before forcing a decision to reuse products.
- The quality of the components and their usage has impact on the software process itself. Introducing software components of unknown quality may have catastrophic results
- The requirements should be made flexible in order to support the usage of components
- The third party certification can be made compulsory to ensure that the components confirm to well-defined standards and are adequate to fulfill the given requirements.

Reuse is a powerful technique, because it allows functionality to be provided rapidly to the user. A decision to reuse a software product is also a constraint on the development team. Rather than being allowed to structure the system in the most effective way possible, a decision to reuse software limits the options available.
Also the reuse of commercially available software has some unique disadvantages. Commercial entities are motivated to limit a user's ability to change products. This is often accomplished by including and then recommending the use of proprietary features. In addition, the update cycle for a commercial package can be a significant drain on maintenance resources. The costs of keeping personnel current in and then integrating new product releases should be assessed as a part of overall life cycle costs.

3.1 Risk Analysis

"Reuse is like a savings account. Before you collect any interest, you have to make a deposit, and the more you put in, the greater the dividend attributed to" -Ted Biggerstaff, 1983 ITT Reuse workshop.

There were two types of approaches I could observe from the survey, for establishing a reuse program: centralized and distributed.

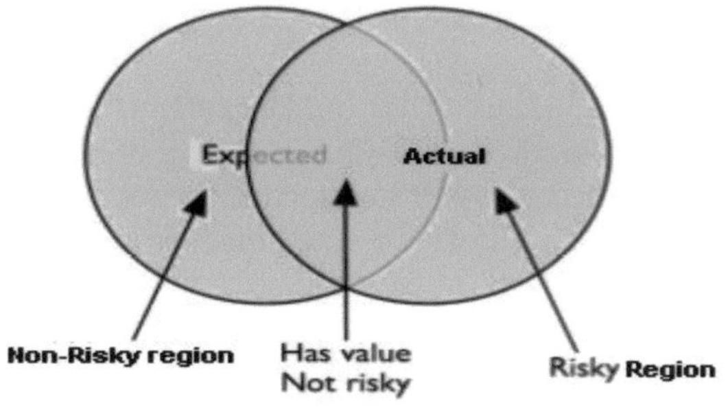

Fig. 1. Prediction region for acceptable values

Fig 1 tells about the prediction region for acceptable values- tend to give good information about value in reuse context. Each region will coincidentally give some information about the other regions, but neither is sufficient by itself. Concentrating on the basis of expectation will not tell as much as information needs to know about risk. The figure gives an insight of savings expected in terms of percentage of reuse used.

	Centralized	Distributed
Risk Factors		
	1) Cost of maintaining a dedicated team (60%)	1) Difficult to coordinate asset development responsibilities (40%)
	2) Cost of training employees (40%)	2) Reluctant to make their own investment for others (60%)
	3) Need for strong management commitment (55%)	3) Need of convincing cost-benefit model (45%)

Table 1. Risk factors identified from the survey

New professional competences in the development teams are required to deal with the introduction of the changes for reuse in the software process. The majority of the estimation models produced during the last decades are found not suitable for reuse products. A discussion on the research difficulties in the software measurement area (which is, of course, crucial to estimation) can be found in (Poulin, 1994). The shift to a new approach to software development requires new estimation models to better capture the essence of CBD. Due to the novelty of CBD and related estimation models, there is still a lack of past experience in which one can support his estimation efforts. An example of a face lifted model that aims supporting cost estimation in CBSE is the COCOTS (Abts et al.2000), an evolution from COCOMO II(Boehm et al.1995,2000).

"Reuse is something that is far easier to say than to do. Doing it requires both good design and very good documentation. Even when we see good design, which is still infrequently, we won't see the components reused without good documentation". - D. L. Parnas, Software Aging, 16th International Conference Software Engineering, 1994

There are many informal arguments that make software reuse an appealing and economically. In the following section I will discuss some models and theories that have been developed to assess economics of software products and the developed reuse models based on my study. The majority of work on economics of reuse is on the reuse of source code.

3.2 Cost Estimation

3.2.1 Traditional COCOMO

COCOMO was first published in 1981 as a model for estimating effort, cost, and schedule for software projects (Boehm, 1981). References to this model typically call it COCOMO 81. In 1997 COCOMO II was developed and finally published in 2001 in the book Software Cost Estimation with COCOMO II. COCOMO II is the successor of COCOMO 81 and is better suited for estimating modern software development projects. It provides more support for modern software development processes and an updated project database. The need for the new model came as software development technology moved from mainframe and overnight batch processing to desktop development, code reusability and the use of off-the-shelf software components.

COCOMO consists of a hierarchy of three increasingly detailed and accurate forms. The first level, Basic COCOMO is good for quick, early, rough order of magnitude estimates of software costs, but its accuracy is limited due to its lack of factors to account for difference in project attributes (Cost Drivers). Intermediate COCOMO takes these Cost Drivers into account and Detailed COCOMO additionally accounts for the influence of individual project phases.

Basic COCOMO is a static, single-valued model that computes software development effort (and cost) as a function of program size expressed in estimated lines of code. COCOMO applies to three classes of software projects (Boehm et.al, 2000; Sunita Chulani, 2000):

- Organic projects - are relatively small, simple software projects in which small teams with good application experience work to a set of less than rigid requirements.
- Semi-detached projects - are intermediate (in size and complexity) software projects in which teams with mixed experience levels must meet a mix of rigid and less than rigid requirements.
- Embedded projects - are software projects that must be developed within a set of tight hardware, software, and operational constraints.

The basic COCOMO equations take the form

$$E=a_b(KLOC)^{b_b}$$

$$D=c_b(E)^{d_b}$$

$$P=E/D$$

Where E is the effort applied in person-months, D is the development time in chronological months, KLOC is the estimated number of delivered lines of code for the project (expressed in thousands), and P is the number of people required. The coefficients a_b, b_b, c_b and d_b are given in the following table.

Software project	a_b	b_b	c_b	d_b
Organic	2.4	1.05	2.5	0.38
Semi-detached	3.0	1.12	2.5	0.35
Embedded	3.6	1.20	2.5	0.32

Basic COCOMO is good for quick, early, rough order of magnitude estimates of software costs, but it does not account for differences in hardware constraints, personnel quality and experience, use of modern tools and techniques, and other project attributes known to have a significant influence on software costs, which limits its accuracy (Boehm et al.2000; Sunita Chulani, 2000).

3.2.2 Intermediate COCOMO

Intermediate COCOMO computes software development effort as function of program size and a set of "cost drivers" that include subjective assessment of product, hardware, personnel and project attributes. This extension considers a set of four "cost drivers", each with a number of subsidiary attributes:

- Product attributes
  - Required software reliability
  - Size of application database
  - Complexity of the product
- Hardware attributes
  - Run-time performance constraints
  - Memory constraints
  - Volatility of the virtual machine environment
  - Required turnabout time
- Personnel attributes
  - Analyst capability
  - Software engineering capability
  - Applications experience
  - Virtual machine experience
  - Programming language experience
- Project attributes
  - Use of software tools
  - Application of software engineering methods
  - Required development schedule

Each of the 15 attributes receives a rating on a six-point scale that ranges from "very low" to "extra high" (in importance or value). An effort multiplier from the table below applies to the rating. The product of all effort multipliers results in an *effort adjustment factor (EAF)*. Typical values for EAF range from 0.9 to 1.4.

	Ratings					
Cost Drivers	Very Low	Low	Nominal	High	Very High	Extra High
Product attributes						
Required software reliability	0.75	0.88	1.00	1.15	1.40	
Size of application database		0.94	1.00	1.08	1.16	
Complexity of the product	0.70	0.85	1.00	1.15	1.30	1.65
Hardware attributes						
Run-time performance constraints			1.00	1.11	1.30	1.66
Memory constraints			1.00	1.06	1.21	1.56
Volatility of the virtual machine environment		0.87	1.00	1.15	1.30	
Required turnabout time		0.87	1.00	1.07	1.15	
Personnel attributes						
Analyst capability	1.46	1.19	1.00	0.86	0.71	
Applications experience	1.29	1.13	1.00	0.91	0.82	
Software engineer capability	1.42	1.17	1.00	0.86	0.70	
Virtual machine experience	1.21	1.10	1.00	0.90		
Programming language experience	1.14	1.07	1.00	0.95		
Project attributes						
Use of software tools	1.24	1.10	1.00	0.91	0.82	
Application of software engineering methods	1.24	1.10	1.00	0.91	0.83	
Required development schedule	1.23	1.08	1.00	1.04	1.10	

The Intermediate COCOMO formula now takes the form:

$$\mathbf{E}=a_i(\mathbf{KLOC})^{(b_i)}.\mathbf{EAF}$$

where E is the effort applied in person-months, **KLOC** is the estimated number of thousands of delivered lines of code for the project, and **EAF** is the factor calculated above. The coefficient $\mathbf{a_i}$ and the exponent $\mathbf{b_i}$ are given in the next table.

Software project	a_i	b_i
Organic	3.2	1.05
Semi-detached	3.0	1.12
Embedded	2.8	1.20

The Development time **D** calculation uses **E** in the same way as in the Basic COCOMO

3.2.3 Detailed COCOMO

Detailed COCOMO - incorporates all characteristics of the intermediate version with an assessment of the cost driver's impact on each step (analysis, design, etc.) of the software engineering process

3.2.4 COnstructive COst MOdel version II (COCOMO II)

COCOMO II can be used for the following major decision situations (Boehm et al. 2000)

- Making investment or other financial decisions involving a software development effort
- Setting project budgets and schedules as a basis for planning and control
- Deciding on or negotiating tradeoffs among software cost, schedule, functionality, performance or quality factors
- Making software cost and schedule risk management decisions
- Deciding which parts of a software system to develop, reuse, lease, or purchase
- Making legacy software inventory decisions: what parts to modify, phase out, outsource, etc
- Setting mixed investment strategies to improve organization's software capability, via reuse, tools, process maturity, outsourcing, etc
- Deciding how to implement a process improvement strategy, such as that provided in the SEI CMM

The full COCOMO II model includes three stages.
Stage 1 supports estimation of prototyping or applications composition efforts.
Stage 2 supports estimation in the Early Design stage of a project, when less is known about the project's cost drivers. Stage 3 supports estimation in the Post-Architecture stage of a project.
This version of USC COCOMO II implements stage 3 formulas to estimate the effort, schedule, and cost required to develop a software product. It also provides the breakdown of effort and schedule into software life-cycle phases and activities from both the Waterfall model and the Mbase Model. The Mbase model is fully described in Software Cost Estimation with COCOMO II.

3.2.5 COCOTS

COCOTS is the acronym for the COnstructive COTS integration cost model, where COTS in turn is short for commercial-off-the-shelf, and refers to those pre-built, commercially available software components that are becoming ever more important in the creation of new software systems.

The rationale for building COTS-containing systems is that they will involve less development time by taking advantage of existing, market proven, vendor supported products, thereby reducing overall system development costs (Abs et al., 2000). But there are

two defining characteristics of COTS software, and they drive the whole COTS usage process:
1) The COTS product source code is not available to the application developer, and
2) The future evolution of the COTS product is not under the control of the application developer.
Because of these characteristics, there is a trade-off in using the COTS approach in that new software development time can indeed be reduced, but generally at the cost of an increase in software component integration work. The long term cost implications of adopting the COTS approach are even more profound, because considering COTS components for a new system means adopting a new way of doing business till the retirement of that system. This is because COTS software is not static; it continually evolves in response to the market, and the system developer must adopt methodologies that cost-effectively manage the use of those evolving components.

3.2.5.1 Relation to COCOMO II

COCOMO II creates effort and schedule estimates for software systems built using a variety of techniques or approaches. The first and primary approach modeled by COCOMO is the use of system components that are built from scratch, that is, new code. But COCOMO II also allows to model the case in which system components are built out of pre-existing source code that is modified or adapted to current purpose, i.e., reuse code.
What COCOMO II currently does not model is that case in which there is no access to a pre-existing component's source code. We have to take the component as is, working only with its executable file, and at most are able to build a software shell around the component to adapt its functionality to our needs.
This is where COCOTS comes in. COCOTS are being designed specifically to model the unique conditions and practices highlighted in the preceding section that obtain when we have to incorporate COTS components into the design of our larger system.

3.2.5.2 COCOTS Model Overview

COCOTS at the moment are composed of four related sub models, each addressing individually what we have identified as the four primary sources of COTS software integration costs (Grady, 1997).
Initial integration costs are due to the effort needed to perform (1) candidate COTS component assessment, (2) COTS component tailoring, (3) the development and testing of any integration or "glue" code (sometimes called "glue ware" or "binding" code) needed to plug a COTS component into a larger system, and (4) increased system level programming and testing due to volatility in incorporated COTS components.
The following figure illustrates how the modeling of these effort sources in COCOTS is related to effort modeled by COCOMO II.

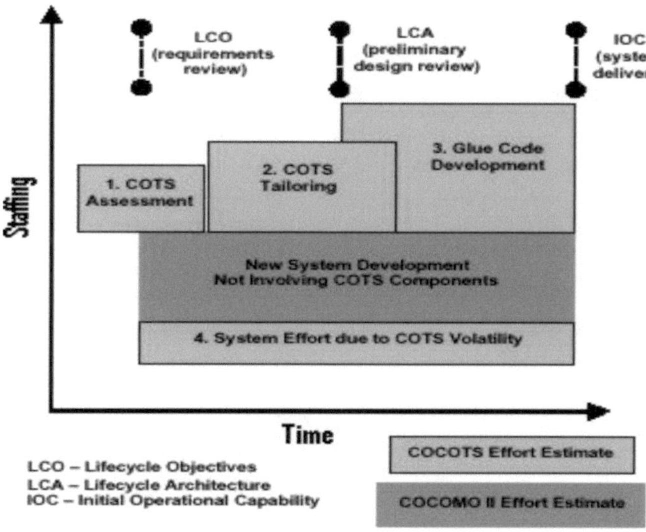

Fig. 2. Sources of Effort (Abts.et.al, 2000b)

The figure represents the total effort to build a software system out of a mix of new code and COTS components as estimated by a combination of COCOMO II and COCOTS. The central block in the diagram indicates the COCOMO II estimate, that is, the effort associated with any newly developed software in the system. The smaller, exterior blocks indicate COCOTS estimates, that effort associated with the COTS components in the system. The relative sizes of the various blocks in this figure is a function of the number of COTS components relative to the amount of new code in the system, and of the nature of the COTS component integration efforts themselves. The more complex the tailoring and/or glue code-writing efforts, the larger these blocks will be relative to the assessment block.

4. Software Metrics

Software development is a complex undertaking. Successful management requires good management skills and good management information. Software metrics are an integral part of the state-of the-practice in software engineering. A sound software metrics program can contribute significantly to providing great management information. Successful metrics programs must provide sound management information to better understand, track, control and predict software projects, processes and products while ensuring low- cost, simplicity, accuracy, and appropriateness.

According to Goodman, software metrics as, "The continuous application of measurement-based techniques to the software development process and its products to supply meaningful and timely management information, together with the use of those techniques to improve that process and its products" (Goodman,1993).

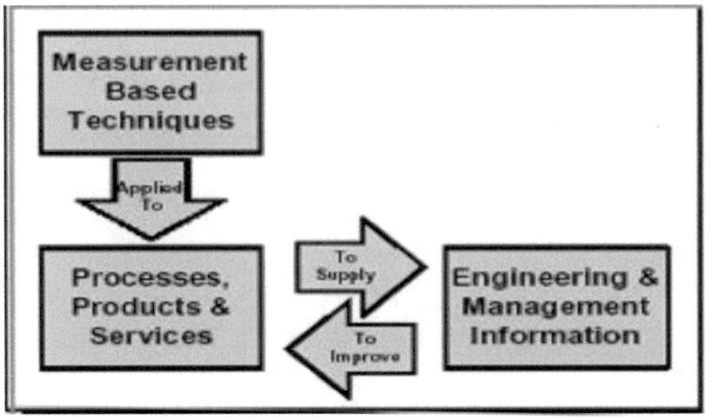

Fig. 3. What are Software Metrics?

Fig. 3 illustrates that metrics can provide the information needed by engineers for technical decisions as well as information required by management.
A software metrics program has many purposes such as cost and schedule estimation, identifying and controlling of risks, evaluation of bids, resource allocation, requirements management, predicting schedules, reducing defects, assessing progress, and improving processes.

4.1 The Keys to Setting Up a Successful Software Metrics Program

The keys to setting up a successful software metrics program are (Chidamber &Kemerer, 1994):

1. Keep the metrics simple keeping in mind that the goal of a metrics program is management not measurement.
2. Understand the different types of metrics indicators.

   E.g: a. Metrics designed to provide an accurate assessment of complicated development path.

   b. Metrics designed to provide an early identification of processes that have broken down.

   c. Metrics designed to provide an advanced warning of trouble ahead. All types are important, but they require different management attention.

   d. Metrics designed to provide an accurate picture of where the project is with regard to cost and schedule.
3. Keep the metrics measurement cycle short.
4. Use a balanced set of metrics. Unbalanced metrics programs can fail because they drive an organization into undesirable behavior.
5. Keep the metrics collection cost down. Normally, software metrics collection program costs should not exceed 5 percent of the development cost. Automated tools can be implemented to collect many metrics.
6. Focus on a small set of important metrics. Some metrics programs suffer from a tendency to collect more and more information over time. Additional metrics do not always provide sufficient additional information to justify their expense.

Keep in mind that metrics will not replace management, and are most effectively used to provide data about potential problem areas to focus management attention (Poulin & Caruso, 1993).

4.2 Deciding and Managing the Metrics

There are literally thousands of possible software metrics to collect and possible things to measure about software development. There are many books and training programs available about software metrics. Later in this document, I am trying to provide a "minimum set" of top-level metrics suitable for reuse program,
For each metric, one must consider *(*Henderson-Sellers, 1996*)*:

1. What are you trying to manage with this metric? Each metric must relate to a specific management area of interest in a direct way
2. What does this metric measure? Exactly what does this metric count?
3. If your organization optimized this metric alone, what other important aspects of your software development phases would be affected?
4. How hard/expensive is it to collect this information? This is where you actually get to identify whether collection of this metric is worth the effort.
5. Does the collection of this metric interact with (or interfere with) other business processes?
6. How accurate will the information be after you collect it?
7. Can this management interest area be measured by other metrics? What alternatives to this metric exist?

Metrics are not useful if they can not be easily reviewed, analyzed for trends, compared to each other, and displayed in a variety of manners. Periodic review of existing metrics against the points mentioned above is recommended.
Be sure to take advantage of free metrics tools available where they are appropriate (example sources of tools include: Software Technology Support Center (STSC), the Software Engineering Institute (SEI), the Software Productivity Consortium (SPC), and the Software Program Managers Network (SPMN)).With this guidance in mind, let's turn to selecting the proper metrics to measure reuse cost and effort.

4.3 Measuring Software Reuse Cost

Economic considerations are at the center of any discussion of software reuse. Economic models and software metrics are needed that quantify the costs and benefits of reuse Models for software reuse economics try to help us answer the question, “when is it worthwhile to incorporate reusable components into a development and when is custom development without reuse preferable?” *(*Heinemann &Councill, 2001*)*.Further, different technical approaches to reuse have different investment and return on investment profiles (Poulin & Caruso, 1993; Frakes & Terry, 1994).Generally metrics can be categorized into two namely product metrics, which determine the characteristics of components and process metrics, which measure time, cost etc.Only recently the researchers started to tackle this problem (Frakes & Terry, 1996; Barnes & Bollinger, 1991; Mili et.al, 1995). But even such studies couldn't help to convince the management to understand the advantage of reuse. Most

existing software engineering economic models need to be customized to each specific reuse business. Several authors have modified the cost models that are today used to estimate time and effort and for the development both of components and of applications using components (Malan & Wentzel, 1993; Poulin, 1994; Boehm & Papaccio, 1988).Because high levels of reuse can reduce the overall cost and time to deliver applications, the extra funding and time can be directed to several alternative projects.
In the following section, the implications of various approaches for software reuse in the organizations are discussed and proposed few economic models for cost analysis.

4.4 Software Reuse Cost Estimation Models

We can categorize the type of reuse in the context of cost estimation as follows (Barnes & Bollinger,1991):

i) Component Reuse without Modification

ii) Component Reuse with modification

In the case of component reuse without modification, the average cost of developing using reusable components can be formulated as follows:

$$\text{Cost}_{\text{search}} + (1-p)*\text{Development}_{\text{no-reuse}} \tag{1}$$

where $\text{Cost}_{\text{search}}$ is the cost of performing a search operation, $\text{Development}_{\text{no-reuse}}$ is the cost of developing without reuse (i.e., the cost of developing the component from scratch) and p is the probability that the component is found in the component library. It is observed that the reuse option would be preferable only if:

$$\text{Cost}_{\text{search}} + (1-p)*\text{Development}_{\text{no-reuse}} < \text{Development}_{\text{no-reuse}} \tag{2}$$

In the case of component reuse with modification, the average cost of developing using reusable components can be formulated as follows:

$$\text{Cost}_{\text{search}} + \text{Cost}_{\text{adapt}} + (1-p)*\text{Development}_{\text{no-reuse}} \tag{3}$$

where $\text{Cost}_{\text{search}}$ is the cost of performing a search operation (the cost depends on the whether the search is a manual search or search using a search tool), $\text{Cost}_{\text{adapt}}$ is the cost required to adapt the component, $\text{Development}_{\text{no-reuse}}$ and p means the same as in the case of equation (1). It is observed that the reuse option would be preferable only if:

$$\text{Cost}_{\text{search}} + \text{Cost}_{\text{adapt}} + (1-p)*\text{Development}_{\text{no-reuse}} < \text{Development}_{\text{no-reuse}} \tag{4}$$

In both the cases, the cost saving due to reuse can be formulated using a simple equation:

$$\text{Cost}_{\text{saved}} = \text{Cost}_{\text{no-reuse}} - \text{cost}_{\text{reuse}} \tag{5}$$

In addition to the above costs, we should also consider some overhead costs associated with reuse include (Jasmine & Vasantha, 2008a):

- Domain analysis (Balda & Gustafson,1990;Pressman,2001)
- Increased documentation to facilitate reuse

- Maintenance and enhancement of reuse artifacts (documents and components)
- Royalties and licenses for externally acquired components
- Creation (or acquisition) and operation of a reuse repository (If the decision is to build a reusable component, then the cost of initial development and also the expected usage frequency of the component also should be considered (Mili.et.al,1995)
- Training of personnel in design for reuses and designs with reuse.

To maximize reuse profits, by analyzing process, organizational and technical aspects with reduced asset development cost and management cost, we have to consider the following points

i) When and Where Capital investment is to be made

Two approaches were observed namely, proactive and reactive. 80% of identified population supported proactive approach and 20% supported reactive approach. If the domain is stable, where the product features can be predicted, organizations can go for upfront investment to develop reusable assets (proactive approach). If the domain is unstable, reusable assets can be developed as when required (reactive approach). This approach may result in reengineering and retrofitting existing products with reusable assets, if there is no common architectural basis.

ii) Whether to go for a dedicated team for development/distribute/maintain assets or not and associated costs involved.

Again the Cost no-reuse and cost reuse depends on the % size of parts (components) reused and % of parts (components) not reused.

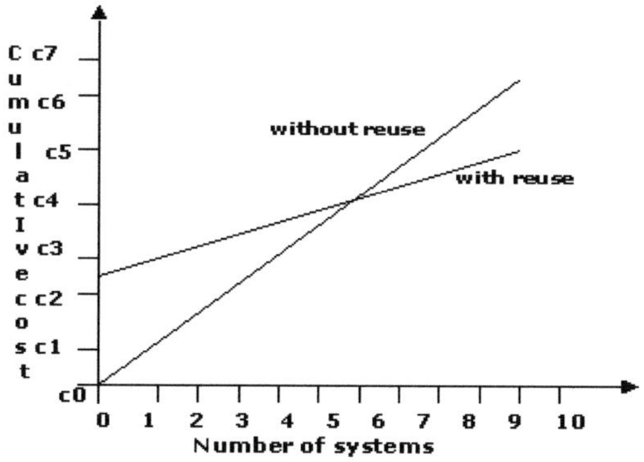

Fig. 4. Cumulative costs of software systems without reuse vs. with reuse

Fig 4 illustrates that for a reuse oriented software development; there will be an initial cost increase. Then gradually cost will decrease due to reusing the same component again and again across similar products.

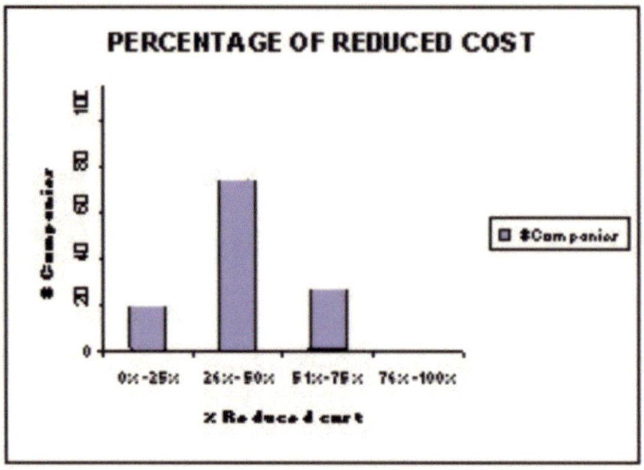

Fig. 5. Percentage of reduced cost of software products due to reuse

Fig 5 illustrates the percentage of reduced cost in the surveyed software companies. The % of cost reduction due to reuse is observed as three ranges such as between 0% and 25%, 26% and 50% & 51% and 75%. Also none of the companies are completely saved their development cost due to reuse.

4.5 Measuring software reuse effort

4.5.1 Suggested estimation Model

A common approach to estimate effort is to make it a function of project size and equation of effort is considered as follows:

$$\text{Effort}=a*\text{size}^{b} \qquad (6)$$

where a and b are constants (Pressman, 2001).A similar study on smaller projects showed that the data fits a straight line quite well, and the equation is of the form:

$$\text{Effort}=a*\text{size}+b \qquad (7)$$

where a and b are constants that are obtained by analysis of data of past projects. Where a is termed the effort adjustment factor and b the scale factor.
Taking into consideration of reusable components these two equations can be modified as follows (Jasmine & Vasantha, 2008b):

$$\text{Effort} = a1*(\text{size of Part}_{reuse})^{b1} + a2*(\text{size of Part}_{no\text{-}reuse})^{b2} \qquad (8)$$

$$\text{Effort} = (a1*(\text{size of Part}_{reuse}) + b1) + (a2*(\text{size of Part}_{no\text{-}reuse}) + b2) \qquad (9)$$

where a1, b1 a2, b2 are constants, part $_{reuse}$ is part developed from reusable components and part$_{no\text{-}reuse}$ is part developed without reusable components.

4.5.2 Incremental development and effort estimation

The effort estimation model used here relates the development effort (in project per-son-months, PM) to software size (in thousands of delivered source lines of code or in number of function points) as by replacing effort by y and size by x the equation (5) becomes

$$y = ax^b \tag{10}$$

In incremental development the target system S is delivered in n stages (Mili.et.al, 1995). The development is seen as a sequence of component integration C1, C2... Cn where each component is a functionally independent system delivered to a customer and the functionality increases with each delivery with one or more component integrations. C1 is considered to be the start of a new system .At the end of the development Cn is equivalent to the target system, S.

The size of the target system S is represented by x. In a one-off (non-incremental) development this effort is estimated with equation (10).

A nominal size of increment i (i.e. the additional functionality, or code, needed to move from Ci-1 to Ci) is represented by n_i and the totality of the increments make up the target system so that

$$x = \sum_i n_i \tag{11}$$

The effective size, x_i, of each increment for effort estimation purposes is expressed as

$$x_i = n_i + o_i n_{i-1} \tag{12}$$

where the parameter O reflects the overhead associated with the previous increment. For example if O has a value of 0.25, it corresponds to 25% overhead.

The development effort in enhancing system from stage Ci-1 to Ci involves developing an increment of effective size x_i and the effort is thus estimated by using expression (10):

$$y_i = a_i x_i^{b_i} \tag{13}$$

giving

$$\sum_i a_i x_i^{b_i} \tag{14}$$

Replacing x_i by $n_i+o_in_{i-1}$,
The final equation for y_i is as follows

$$\sum_i a_i(n_i + o_i n_{i-1})^{b_i}$$ (Jasmine & Vasantha, 2008b) (15)

In a similar manner equation (6) also can be modified.
In incremental development (except for agile development) significant one-time tasks need to be undertaken up front: product design for incremental systems must be well thought out and open-ended so that each additional increment can be incorporated into the architecture defined initially for the whole product. The architecture of the solution needs to allow for breakdown into increments thereby enabling staged development. This requires an upfront effort (encompassing core capability and overall architecture included in the first release), which is over and above the effort needed to develop each increment (Laraman&Basili, 2003).The initial effort can be of considerable magnitude, especially if domain architecting and reuse considerations are taken into account.

Models for software reuse economics helps the organizations to decide When is it worthwhile to incorporate reusable components into a development and when is to perform custom development without reuse. It is observed from the study that existing software engineering economic models need to be adjusted to include reuse and customized to each specific reuse business. An extensive work relating more elaborate software structure reuse metrics and economical factors, with a wide variety of representative set of industrial organizations is still necessary to standardize the reuse cost metrics field. Future research can be performed in these directions.

5. Systematic reuse and economic feasibility

Generally, the knowledge about the problem domain is realized through a set of components that are reusable within a formerly defined framework. A practical problem in defining the problem domain is that the domain knowledge usually isn't immediately available. An essential difficulty herewith is the impossibility to predict all possible variations and evolutions of the software (and the problem domain) beforehand.

Systematic reuse should not only recognize the need for a reusable asset to evolve both during its initial design and when it is being reused, it should actually advocate the development of a methodology for managing change in the process of engineering reusable software. The development of reusable assets is inherently an evolutionary process. A reuser can only gain insights in the qualities of reusable assets by actually reusing them. A provider can only improve the qualities of assets if the experience of reuse is fed back to him. Successful assets can have a long life span and thus need to evolve and adapt to new reusers and their requirements. The inability to do so turns a reusable asset into legacy. Such iterative development is also important because it allows the construction of reusable assets in a bottom-up fashion. This is crucial for reuse to become economically feasible: it allows finding a delicate balance between the longer term investments needed for constructing reusable assets and the need to meet shorter term (customer) deadlines. To be able to leverage on the investment made in building an asset, reusers must be able to benefit from future improvements of the assets they reuse: proper evolution of reused assets should not invalidate previous reuse. In a similar vein, reuse should go beyond the act of copying out code fragments and adapting them to current requirements without regard for the evolution of the reused fragments. This implies the management of some kind of consistency in the evolution of reusable software, to prohibit different versions of a reusable asset from propagating through different applications. While systematic reuse should present an opportunity to reduce maintenance effort, a proliferation of versions actually increases it, as older versions of an asset behave differently than newer versions. The absence of change management mechanisms is recognized as an important inhibitor to successful reuse.

To reconcile the bottom-up approach of iterative development with reuse with the top-down approach of systematic reuse (development for reuse), a methodology that combines the best of both worlds by introducing systematic reuse in the object-oriented software engineering process can be adopted. My conjecture is that incrementally building reusable assets requires a strong co-operation between providers of reusable assets and asset reusers.

5.1 Product-Line Architectures and Reusable Assets

Product family/line engineering is all about reusing components and structures as much as possible. This method creates an underlying architecture of an organizations product platform, one that is based on commonality and similarity. The various product variants can be derived from the basic product family, which creates the opportunity to reuse and differentiate on products in the family. It focuses on the process of engineering new products in such a way that it is possible to reuse product components and apply variability with decreased costs and time.
A product line involves core asset development and product development using the core assets, both under the aegis of technical and organizational management. Core asset development and product development from the core assets can occur in either order: new products are built from core assets, or core assets are extracted from existing products. Often, products and core assets are built in concert with each other. The following figure illustrates these activities.

The Three Essential Activities for Software Product Lines are (Bosch, 1998b)
1. Core Asset Development
2. Product development
3. Management

All three are linked together and they are all essential, inextricably linked, and highly iterative, and can occur in any order .Core assets are used to develop products, but that revisions of existing core assets or even new core assets might, and most often do, evolve out of product development.

5.1.2 What are core assets?

In some contexts, already existing products are mined for generic assets-perhaps a requirements specification, an architecture, or software components-which are then

migrated into the product line's core asset base. In other cases, the core assets may be developed or procured for later use in the production of products.
There is a strong feedback loop between the core assets and the products. Core assets are refreshed as new products are developed. The use of core assets is tracked, and the results are fed back to the core asset development activity. In addition, the value of the core assets is realized through the products that are developed from them. As a result, the core assets are made more generic by considering potential new products on the horizon. There is a constant need for strong, visionary management to invest resources in the development and sustainment of the core assets. Management must also precipitate the cultural change to view new products in the context of the available core assets. Either new products must align with the existing core assets, or the core assets must be updated to reflect the new products that are being marketed. Iteration is inherent in product line activities–that is, in turning out core assets and products and in coordinating the two.

5.1.3 Problems related to Reusable assets

Based on the interviews and other documentation collected from the various organizations as part of the study, I have identified a number of problems related to reusable assets that I believe to have relevance in a wider context than just these organizations. The problems are categorized into three categories, related to multiple versions of assets, dependencies between assets and the use of assets in new contexts.

5.1.3.1 Multiple versions of assets

Product-line architectures have associated reusable assets that implement the functionality of architectural component. These assets can be very large and contain up to a hundred KLOC or more. Consequently, these assets represent considerable investments, multiple man-years in certain cases. Therefore, it was surprising to identify that in some cases, the interviewed companies maintained multiple versions (implementations) of assets in parallel. One can identify at least four situations where multiple versions are introduced (Dikel et.al, 1997; Bass et.al, 1997) which are mentioned below.

- **Conflicting quality requirements**: The reusable assets that are part of the product line are generally optimized for particular quality attributes, e.g., performance or code size. Different products in the product-line, even though they require the same functionality, may have conflicting quality requirements. These requirements may have so high priority that no single component can fulfill both. The reusability of the affected asset is then restricted to only one or a few of the products while other products require another implementation of the same functionality.
- **Variability implemented through versions**: Certain types of variability are difficult to implement through configuration since the effect of a variation spreads out throughout the reusable asset e.g., operating system, for an asset. Although it might be possible to implement all variability through, often it is decided to maintain two different versions.
- **High-end versus low-end products**: The reusable asset should contain all functionality required by the products in the product-line, including the high-end products. The problem is that low-end products, generally requiring a restricted subset of the functionality, pay for the unused functionality in terms of code size

and complex interfaces. Whenever the hardware cost play an important role in the product price, the software engineers may be forced to create a low-end, scaled-down version of the asset to minimize the overhead for low-end Products.

- **Asset evolution**: When the business units are responsible for asset evolution, assets are sometimes extended with very product-specific code or code only tested for one of the products in the product-line (Jacobson et.al,2000). The problems caused by this create a tendency within the affected business units to create their own copy of the asset and maintain it for their own product only. This minimizes the dependency on the shared product-line architecture and solves the problems in the short term, but in the long term it generally does not pay off. There will be several instances of cases where business units had to rework considerable parts of their code to incorporate a new version of the evolved shared asset that contained functionality that needed to be incorporated in their product also.

5.1.3.2 Dependencies between assets

Since the reusable assets are all part of a product-line architecture, they tend to have dependencies between them. Although dependencies between assets are necessary, assets often have dependencies that could have been avoided by another modularization of the system or a more careful asset design. From the examples from the surveyed companies, I have learned that the initial design of assets generally defines a small set of required and explicitly defined dependencies. It is often during evolution of assets that unwanted dependencies are created. Addition of new functionality may require extension of more than one asset and in the process often dependencies are created between the involved assets to implement the functionality. These new dependencies could often have been avoided by another decomposition of the architecture and have a tendency to be implicit, in that their documentation is often minimal and the software engineer encounters the dependency late in the development process. Dependencies in general, but especially implicit dependencies, reduce the reusability of assets in different contexts, but also complicate the evolution of assets. Based on my research at various software companies, I have identified the following situations where new, often implicit, dependencies are introduced:

- **Component decomposition** With the development of the product-line architecture generally also the size of the reusable assets increases. With the increasing size of asset components, there is a point where a component needs to be split into two components. These two components, initially, have numerous relations to each other, but even after some redesign often several dependencies remain because the initial design did not modularize the behavior captured by the two components.
- **Extensions cover multiple assets**: During implementation of the extension, it is very natural to add dependencies between the affected assets since one is working on functionality that is perceived as one piece, even though it is divided over multiple assets. By separating the authorization access from the two assets and representing as a single asset, we can decrease the dependencies.

5.1.3.3 Assets in new contexts

Since assets represent considerable investments, it is mandatory to use assets in as many products and domains as possible to save money. However, the new context differs in one or more aspects from the old context, causing a need for the asset to be changed in order to fit. Two main issues in the use of assets in new context can be identified (Bass et.al, 1997; Bosch, 1998b):

• **Mixed behavior**: An asset is developed for a particular domain, product category, operating context and set of driving quality requirements. Consequently, it often proves to be hard to apply the asset in different domains, products or operating contexts. The design of assets often hardwires design decisions concerning these aspects unless the type of variability is known and required at design time.

E.g., Assets used for fire-alarm system and intruder-alarm systems due to the similarities in the domains

• **Design for required variability**: A reusable asset often requires new variability dimensions. So assets should be designed so that the introduction of new variability requires minimal effort.

E.g, fire-alarm and intruder alarm system share, to a large extent, the same operating context and quality requirements. Since the fire-alarm framework is designed for its domain and the intruder alarm domain has different requirements and concepts, one is forced to introduce variability for application domain functionality.

5.2. Cause Analysis for the Identified problems

The problems discussed in the previous section present an overview over the issues surrounding the use of reusable assets in product-line architecture.

The following are the identified primary underlying causes for these problems. These causes are discussed in the following section (Bosch, 1998b).

5.2.1 Early intertwining of functionality

The early intertwining of functionality is a primary cause to several of the problems discussed in the previous section. Multiple versions of assets are required because the different categories of functionality cannot be separated in the implementation and implemented through variability. The use of layers in asset design separating operating context dependent from context independent functionality avoids the mixing. Also, some design patterns (Gamma et al., 1994; Buschmann et.al, 1996) support this.

5.2.2 Organization

Having explicit groups for domain and application engineering requires a relatively large software development department consisting of at least fifty to a hundred engineers. Several of the problems discussed earlier can be related to the lack of independent domain engineering. Business units focus on their own quality attributes and design for achieving those during asset extension. Because of that, multiple versions of assets may be created where a domain engineering unit may have found solutions allowing for a single version. In addition, asset extension without sufficient focus on the product-line as a whole may introduce more dependencies than strictly necessary, complicating the use of assets as well as the reuse of assets in new contexts.

Solutions exist to minimize the negative effects of organizational structures. Asset redesigns are performed when a consensus is present that an asset needs to be reorganized. During an asset redesign, the software architects from the business units using the asset gather to redesign the asset in order to improve its structure.

5.2.3 Time To Markert

A third important cause for the problems related to reusable assets at the interviewed companies is the time-to-market (TTM) pressure. The problem most companies are dealing with is that products appearing late on the market will lead to diminished market share or, in the worst case, to no market penetration at all. Sacrificing some time-to-market for one product may lead to considerable improvements for subsequent products, but this is generally not appreciated. To address the problems resulting from TTM pressure, it is important for software development organizations to identify the development of product-line architecture with associated assets is a strategic issue and decisions should be taken at the appropriate level. The consequences for the time-to-market of products under development should be balanced against the future returns.

5.2.4 Economic models

Reusable assets may represent investments up to several man years of implementation effort. For most companies, such an asset represents a considerable amount of capital, but both engineers and management are not always aware of that. For instance, an increasing number of dependencies between assets is a sign of accelerated aging of software and, in effect, decreases the value of the assets. Economic models are necessary to visualize the effects of quick fixes causing increased dependencies, in order to establish the economic losses of these dependencies versus the time-to-market requirements. The lack of suitable economic models for these influences several of the identified problems.

There is a need for economic models in two situations. First, models for calculating the economic value of asset, based on the investment (man hours) but also on the value of the asset for future product development and/or for an external market. In addition, models visualizing the effects of various types of changes and extensions on the asset values are also required.

5.3 Some Issues and considerations for product-line approach

In the context of product line approach, the following issues to be considered (Griss et. al, 1993; Basili et.al, 1994).

- Business
    - Number of new starts subscribing to a software product line may be insufficient to offset the costs of building/maintaining product line
    - Incentive must be provided to the contractor community to engage in product line asset development
    - Contractor liability must be addressed and resolved
- Technical
    - Need for software engineering practices and processes that apply technology to create and evolve product line assets and products

  - Managing the evolution of product line architectures
- Organizational
  - Importance of infrastructure and cross organizational cooperation
  - Need for strong visionary management to invest resources into the development/containment of product line architectures

6. Reuse Capability maturity Model (RCMM)

The RCMM was developed in the early 1990's at the Software Productivity Consortium (SPC) as part of a systematic approach to reuse adoption. It is an effective guide primarily to help organizations identify opportunities for improving a reuse-based process. It also provides criteria by which an organization can target a level of reuse capability that matches its particular needs and capabilities (SPC-CMC, 1993).However, the interaction between these two purposes and with the CMM has not been fully understood. Now, our study with various software organizations established that the critical success factors defined by the RCMM can be entirely partitioned according to these two purposes.

Capability Maturity Model is a reference model of mature practices in a specified discipline, used to assess a group's capability to perform that discipline (Craig& Allgood, 2001)
• CMMs differ by
-Discipline (software, systems, acquisition, etc.)
-Structure (staged versus continuous)
-How Maturity is Defined (process improvement path)
-How Capability is Defined (institutionalization)
As per Carnegle Mellon Software Engineering institute's study, CMMI transition from traditional approach to reuse oriented CMMI is a technology transition. Because CMMI is a process technology (Garcia, 2003).

CMMI will require
- Development of new routines(procedures)
- Modification in the norms and beliefs of the organization members

6.1 Need of Technology Transition Practices (TTP) with CMMI transition

TTP is business unit within the Technology Transition Services Directorate focused on enabling organizations to build their own capability for managed, accelerated and affordable software technology transition.TTP works with all SEI software technologies.TTP's current focus is on working primarily with technology developers and deployers. The role of TTP is to work with CMMI team to monitor /refine transition strategy (CMU/SEI, 1993; Garcia, 2003).

6.2 Key elements in successful technology transition

1. Understanding the goals of different roles involved in the transition process
2. Understanding the characteristics of the technology

3. Understanding what is needed to make the technology work.
4. Identifying and mitigating the identified risks

6.3 Different roles in Technology transition

1. Technology developers :Those who create new technologies

E.g. SEI initiatives, Commercial product motivation teams

2. Technology acquirers Those who determine which technologies will be used to support their own system development efforts

E.g. Individual acquisition program offices and corporate business units

3. Technology deployers Those who determine which technologies will be used to support their own system development efforts

E.g. SEI transition partners, military organizations like STSC

4. Technology adopters: The organization or group that will actually be using a new technology

E.g. War fighter units in military, organizations adopting a new maturity model

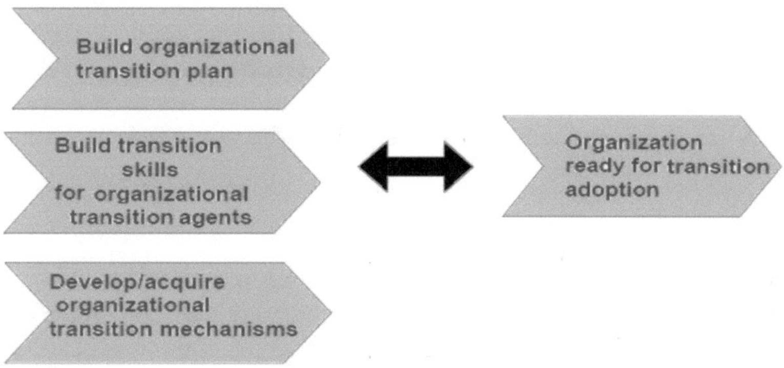

Fig. 6. Adaption and Planning for Transition Adopting Organization

6.4 Motivation for Reuse CMM

Motivation for developing the Reuse Maturity Model comes from observing the enormous impact the Software Engineering Institute's software Capability Maturity Model has had. The SEI has focused attention on process issues in a most remarkable way by examining characteristic engineering practices and providing a means to classify an organization into one of five maturity levels (CMU/SEI, 1993; Garcia, 2003). Moreover, the SEI has established the principle in people's minds that the quality of a software product is dictated by the quality of the processes used to develop that product. Furthermore, the SEI has convinced executive managers that process improvement must come a step at a time, by laying a foundation for process improvement on which other improvement activities can build. Through my Reuse Maturity Model, I hope that achieving reuse requires a comprehensive approach.

From the survey of software companies, a numerous obstacles are identified that must be overcome in order to achieve high levels of reuse, are listed below:

Cultural: Incentives and management backing must be put in place and (``Not Invented Here'') syndrome must be eliminated.

Institutional: A corporate-wide forum is needed to identify product development cycle where reuse concerns can always be raised and resolved.

Financial: The costs and benefits must be understood for a product life cycle based on a "Design for Reuse" philosophy. Reusable work-products must be viewed as capital assets.

Technical: Proper mechanisms are needed to ensure that guidelines, techniques, and standards for making things reusable are developed and followed.

Legal: Negotiations must be undertaken to determine how to retain rights to components developed under customer contract and recover costs in a reuse context. Mechanisms will be needed for payment and collection of royalties for use and reuse in the commercial arena.

Out of the hundred industrial organizations considered, I could see many Level 1 Reuse organizations, only a handful of companies at the intermediate levels, and only hypothesize what a Level 5 Reuse company would look like, I expect some significant revisions are needed to the model. An additional step which augments the reuse maturity questionnaire and by organizing subsets of the questions to address each level of reuse maturity separately is required to objectively measure the Progress toward reuse process improvement.

6.5 How to achieve effective reuse

To provide organizations with detailed guidance on how to achieve effective reuse, the Reuse-driven Software Processes (RSP) methodology was also developed at SPC in the early 1990's. All RSP processes consist of two distinct lifecycle activities of domain engineering and application engineering. The conceptual basis of any RSP process is the formalization of commonalities and variabilities that characterize a set of similar products to represent a product family and an associated process for deriving instance products to meet diverse and changing customer needs.

Other authors have proposed different models to structure the breadth of reuse involvement provided by an organization. Among them one was proposed by (Koltun & Hudson, 1991), that proposed by the Software productivity Consortium and that used in the UE project REBOOT (Reuse Based on Object oriented Techniques)

The model proposed by Koltun and Hudson, five maturity levels are defined for reuse:

1- Initial Chaotic
2- Monitored
3- Co-coordinated
4- Planned
5- Ingrained

The criteria that permit the evaluation of the level of each organization in the model are: Motivation, Planning for reuse, Breadth of reuse involvement, Responsibility for making reuse happen, process by which reuse is leveraged, reuse inventory, classification activity, Technology support, metrics and legal considerations.
The model suggested by Llorens Morillo et. al, is based on the monitoring of three different factors

- Repository structure
- Software development architecture
- Administrative management

Each factor encompasses a certain part of the reuse environment, covering the following areas of control.

Repository structure deals with information representation of the available information in a manner to reuse in the future, classification of existing components and suitable recovery techniques to obtain wherever necessary, and management of authorizing, rejecting and modification of existing components and automated announcement of incorporation or modification of components (Topaloglu et. al, 1996)

Software Development architecture includes developing the architecture according to its orientation towards reuse, type of reuse systematically achieved by the organization and component testing.

Under administrative management, three aspects are covered (Baumert & Mark, 1992) Reuse support towards human resources

- Incentives and planning towards reuse
- Reuse level of previous projects ,applied to the strengthening of the level of improvement

The complete infrastructure graph recommended by (Prieto-diaz et. al, 1993) is shown in following figure.

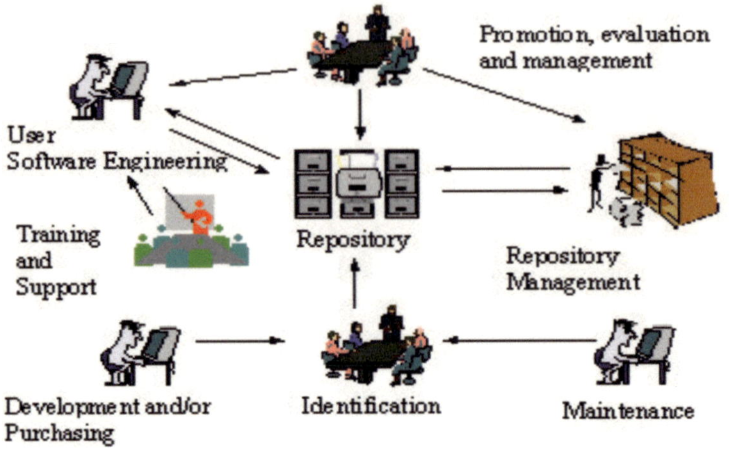

Fig. 7. Reuse Infrastructure

According to (Grady,1997), a reuse-driven process is a framework for performing domain-specific engineering which helps to optimize the software practices to build products of a particular type, resulting in improved productivity and product quality .This focusing and standardization of effort is the key to systematic reuse, leading ultimately to a manufacturing discipline.

As with any process, the CMM and RCM process improvement factors can motivate improvements in a reuse-driven process. In this, some of the corresponding RCM factors ought to be addressed in attaining CMM levels 2 and 3. The 17 process definition factors in the RCM concern differences in the types of reuse based process that an organization may adopt (Grady, 1997). The RCM, in its implementation model, defines four types of reuse-based process: opportunistic, integrated, leveraged, and anticipating. These types, ordered by increasing cost-risk and benefit, provided a categorization for the diversity of approaches already envisioned by the RSP methodology as a family of processes. These process definition factors do not fit into the proper scope of the CMM because they involve a choice among equally valid alternative process conceptions; no one approach is best for everyone.

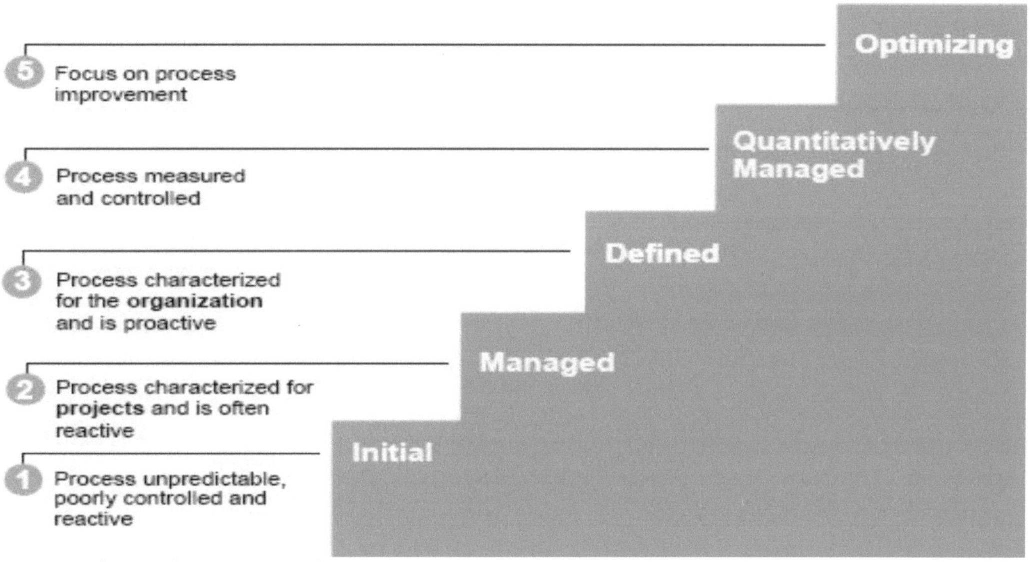

Fig. 8. Traditional CMM Levels

6.6 Proposed CMM levels by the author for reuse

Although process maturity is extremely important in delivering high quality software, there is no standardized maturity model adopted for reuse based software development process. Some organizations which are primarily involved in reuse based software development are following some versions of reuse maturity models. After an extensive literature review (Almeida et al. ,2004; Koltun & Hudson,1991;Frakes and Fox ,1995; Rine, 1997a; Rine & Nada ,2000a) and from my study on reuse projects, I have identified some factors related to software reuse (Brito et al., 2006;Lucr´edio et al. ,2007), that were considered as a basis for this maturity model specification, in order to guide the organizations in the reuse evaluation and/or adoption.

RCMM is a maturity model with focus on reuse and describes which are basic in order to ensure a well planned and controlled reuse oriented software development. In RCMM, there are 5 levels inspired by SEI's Capability Maturity Model. Each level represents a stage in the evolution to a mature reuse process. A set of maturity goals for each level and the activities, task and responsibilities, needed to support are shown in the figure below.

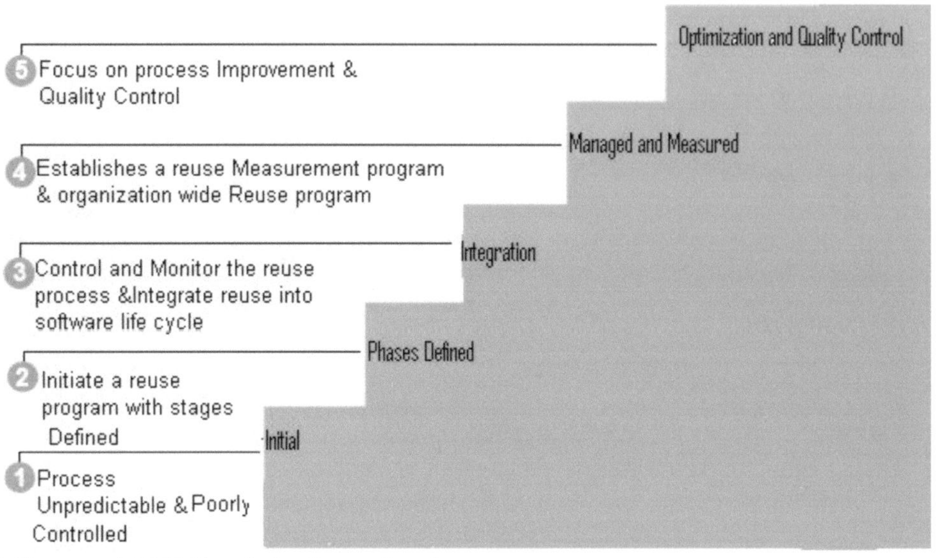

Fig. 9. Proposed CMM levels by the author for reuse

The RCMM model suggested here can be used as s a basis for estimating the level of software reuse practice within an organization. As future work, Maturity Model aims at identifying the strengths of an organization with respect to software reuse and the opportunities for improvements can be adopted. Correct implementation of software reuse and the benefits for an organization adopting reuse in their processes can be evaluated only based on quantitative data. Therefore appropriate Reuse Business and Engineering metrics are recommended to be used within the maturity model to measure the achievement of the respective objectives, the efficiency of the applied practices and the quality of the results obtained. To evaluate the suggested model, it has to be put in the industrial environment and there is a need to get more feedbacks from experts to evaluate the current reuse practice stage and plan the next activities to implement the reuse program.

7. Summary

Good management can make a difference for success in the case of reuse based software development. Proper monitoring and control of the progress towards the business goals and the performance compliance needs an effective management program. However the nature of the reuse business changes the character and extent of the issues. By suitably applying some modifications to the traditional management techniques by keeping in mind the reuse business goals and proper planning will lead to success in reuse business.

By gathering issues associated with people, process and product measurements and by estimating and validating using estimation formulas and economic models ensures that proper usage of resources will follow the right process and right product.

Typically, significant cultural change is needed and will not happen overnight. Just-in-time education and ongoing senior management leadership are needed to make such cultural changes.

8. References

Abts, C., Boehm, B. & Bailey Clark, B., (2000a). COCOTS: a COTS software integration cost model, *Proceedings ESCOM-SCOPE 2000 Conference*, April.

Abts, C.; Boehm, B & Bailey Clark, B. (2000b). Empirical Observations on COTS Software Integration Effort Based on the Initial COCOTS Calibration Database, *ICSE 2000 COTS Workshop* - mip.sdu.dk

Almeida, E. S., Alvaro, A., Lucr´edio, D., Garcia, V. C., & Meira, S. R. L. (2004). Rise project: Towards a robust framework for software reuse. *IEEE International Conference on Information Reuse and Integration (IRI)*, pp. 48–53, Las Vegas, USA.IEEE/CMS.

Balda, D.M. & Gustafson, D.A. (1990). Cost-estimation models for the reuse and prototype software development, *ACM SIGSOFT*, pp. 42-50, July.

Basili, V.R.; Briand, L. C. & Thomas, W. M. (1994). Domain Analysis for the Reuse of Software Development Experiences, *Proceedings of the 19th Annual Software Engineering Workshop*, NASA/Goddard Space Flight Center, November.

Balda, D. and Gustafson, D.(1990). Cost estimation Models for the Reuse and Prototype Software Development Life-cycles.*ACM SIGSOFT Software Engineering Notes* Vol. 15, No. 3, Pages 42-50, July.

Bass, L.; Clements & Cohen. S. et al. (1997). Product Line Practice Workshop Report, *Technical Report CMU/SEI-97-TR-003*, Software Engineering Institute, June.

Baumert, John; Mc Whinney &Mark.(1992).Software Measures and the Capability Maturity Model., Software Engineering Institute,*CMU/SEI-92-TR-25*, Pittsburgh, PA USA, September.

Bosch, J. & Molin, P. (1997). Software Architecture Design: Evaluation and Transformation, *Research Report* 14/97, University of Karlskrona/Ronneby, August.

Bosch, J. (1998a). Object Acquaintance Selection and Binding, *Theory and Practice of Object Systems*, February.

Bosch, J. (1998b). Product-Line Architectures in Industry: A Case Study, *Proceedings of the 21st International Conference on Software Engineering*, November.

Bosch, J. (1999). Evolution and Composition of Reusable Assets in Product-Line Architectures: A Case Study. www:http://www.ide.hk-r.se/~bosch

Boehm, B.M & Papaccio, P.N.(1998).Understanding and controlling software costs, *IEEE transactions on software engineering*, 14(10), 1462-77

Boehm, B., Clark, B.et al.(1995) Cost Models for Future Software Lifecycle Processes: COCOMO 2.0, *Annals of Software Engineering*.

Boehm, B.W (1981). *Software Engineering Economics*, Englewood Cliffs, NJ Prentice Hall.

Boehm, B. & Abts, C.et al. (2000).*Software Cost Estimation with COCOMO II*, Prentice Hall, NJ, June.

Barnes, B.H. & Bollinger, T.B. (1991), Making reuse cost-effective, IEEE software, Vol. 8,No.1, pp. 13-24, January.

Banker, R. D. & Kauffman, R. J. et.al(1993).Evaluation of Software Reuse, *IEEE Transactions on Software Engineering*, Vol. 19, No. 4, pp. 379-389, April.

Brito, K. S., Alvaro, A., Lucr´edio, D., Almeida, E. S., and Meira, S. R. L. (2006). Software reuse: A brief overview of the brazilian industry's case. *5th ACM-IEEE International Symposium on Empirical Software Engineering (ISESE)*, Short Paper, Rio de Janeiro, Brazil. ACM Press.

Buschmann, F; Jäkel,C & Meunier,R.et al.(1996).Pattern-Oriented Software Architecture- A System of Patterns, John Wiley & Sons.

Chidamber, S. R. & Kemerer, C. F.(1994). A Metrics Suite for Object Oriented Design, *IEEE Transactions on Software Engineering*, vol. 20, pp. 476-493.

Dikel, D.; Kane, D. & Ornburn, S. et al (1997). Applying Software Product-Line Architecture,'IEEE Computer, pp. 49-55, August.

Frakes, W. & Terry, C. (1994).Reuse Level Metrics, *Proceedings of the 3rd International Conference on Software Reuse: Advances in Software Reusability, IEEE.*

Davis, T. (1993). The reuse capability model: A basis for improving an organization's reuse capability. *Proceedings of 2nd ACM/IEEE International Workshop on Software Reusability*, pp. 126–133. IEEE Computer Society Press / ACM Press.

Frakes, W. B. and Fox, C. J. (1995). Sixteen questions about software reuse. *Communications of the ACM, 38(6):75–87. ACM Press. New York, NY, USA.*

Frakes, W. & Terry, C. (1996).Software Reuse: Metrics and Models, *ACM Computing Surveys*, Vol. 28, No. 2, June.

Favaro, J. A. (1996).Comparison of Approaches to Reuse Investment Analysis. *Proceedings of the Fourth International Conference on Software Reuse, IEEE Computer Society Press*, pp.136-145, Los Alamitos, CA.

Geels. (2005). *Technological Transitions and System Innovations: A co-evolutionary and socio-technical analysis*, Edward Elgar, Cheltenham.

Guo, J. & Luqui.(2000).A Survey of Software Reuse Repositories, *7th IEEE International Conference and Workshop on the Engineering of Computer Based Systems*, April.

Grady, Campbell.(1997) Tailoring Reuse-Driven Processes In A Process Improvement Context, *ERW-97 Position Paper*, October.

Graves, S. B.(1989).The Time-Cost Tradeoff in Research and Development: A Review, *Engineering Costs and Production Economics,* 16, pp. 1-9, Elsevier Science Publishers.

Griss, M. L., Favaro, *&* P. Walton.(1993). Managerial and Organizational Issues - Starting and Running a Software Reuse Program, *Software,* Shaefer, March.

Harris, K.(1992).Using an Economic Model to Tune Reuse Strategies", *Proceedings of the 5th Annual Workshop on Software Reuse.*

Henry, E. & Faller,B. (1995).Large-Scale Industrial Reuse to Reduce Cost end Cycle Time, *IEEE Software*, Vol. 12, No. 5, September.

Hafedh Mili; Fatma Mili & Ali Mili. (1995).Reusing Software: issues and research Directions, *Proc. IEEE trans. software Engineering*, Vol .21, No.6, June.

Henninger, S.(1997).An Evolutionary Approach to Constructing Effective Software Reuse Repositories, *ACM Transactions on Software Engineering and Methodology*, Vol. 6, No. 2, pp. 111-140, April.

Henderson-Sellers, *B.(1996). Object-Oriented Metrics -Measures of Complexity. Upper Saddle River*, NJ, EUA: Prentice Hall PTR.

Heinemann, *G. T. &* Council, W. T.*(2001).Component-Based Software Engineering - Putting the Pieces Together*. Boston, MA: Addis on-Wesley.

Van Jacobson; Martin Griss & Patrik Jonsson. (2000).Software Reuse- Architecture, Process and Organization for Business Success, *ACM Press.*

Jacobson, I.; Griss, M. & Jönsson, P. (1997). Software Reuse - Architecture, Process and Organization forBusiness Success, Addison-Wesley.

Jasmine, K.S., & Vasantha, R.(2008a). Cost Estimation Model For Reuse Based Software products, Proc. *IAENG International MultiConference of Engineers and Computer Scientists 2008 (IMECS 2008),* Hong Kong, pp.951-954, March.

Jasmine, K.S., & Vasantha, R., (2008b). Effort Estimation in Reuse-Based Software Development Approach, *Proc.National Conference on Wireless network security -Issues & Challenges (WNSIC-08),* Department of CSE, R.V.College of Engineering, Bangalore, pp.63-67, March.

Johnson & Foote (1988).Designing Reusable Classes, *Journal of Object-Oriented Programming,*Vol. 1 (2), pp. 22-25.

Koltun, P. & Hudson, A., (1991). A reuse maturity model. *4th Annual Workshop on Software Reuse,* Hemdon, Virginia: Center for Innovative Technology.

Laraman, C. & Basili, V.R., (2003). Iterative and Incremental Development: A Brief History. *IEEE Computer,* 2003. 36(6): p. 47-56.

Larry McCarthy.(2002). Motorola CMMI Working Group,CMMI^{SM} Transition in a Commercial Environment, *2nd CMMI^{SM} Technology Conference and User Group,* Hyatt Regency Denver Technical Center, November, Denver, Colorado

Lim, W. (1994). Effects of Reuse on Quality, Productivity, and Economics, *IEEE Software,* Vol. 11, No. 5, September.

Llorens Morillo; A.Amescua Seco & Martinez Orga, V.,Carls III University of Madrid, Spain, *http://www.ie.inf.uc3m.es/grupo/Investigacion/LineasInvestigacion/Congresos/RMM97_Docum_Final.doc.*

Loingtier, Irwin, J. (1997).Aspect-Oriented Programming, *Proceedings of ECOOP'97,* pp. 220-242, LNCS 1241.

Lucr´edio, D., Brito, K. S., Alvaro, A., Garcia, V. C., Almeida, E. S., Fortes, R. P. M., and Meira, S. R. L. (2007). Software reuse: The brazilian industry scenario. *Journal of Systems and Software,* Elsevier.

Malan, R. &Wentzel, K. (1993).Economics of software reuse revisited, *Proc. 3rd Irvine Software Symposium,* University of California, Irvine, 30 April, pp.109-21.

Macala, R.R.; Stuckey, L. D. & Gross, D.C. (1996). Managing Domain-Specific Product-Line Development,*IEEE Software,* pp. 57-67.

Mascena, Almeida & Meira.(2005).A Comparative Study on Software Reuse Metrics and Economic Models from a Traceability Perspective, *IEEE.*

Paul Goodman. (1993).*Practical Implementation of Software Metrics,* McGraw Hill, London.

Poulin, J.S., & Caruso, J. (1993). A Reuse Metrics and Return on Investment Model, *Proceedings of the 2nd Workshop on Software Reuse: Advances in Software Reusability, IEEE.*

Poulin, J.S., (1994).Measuring Software Reusability, *Proceedings of the 3rd International Conference on Software Reuse: Advances in Software Reusability, IEEE.*

Poulin, J.S., (2006). The business case for software reuse: Reuse metrics, economic models, organizational issues, and case studies. *Tutorial notes.*

Prieto-D´ıaz, R. (1993). Status report: Software reusability. *IEEE Software,* 10(3):61–66, IEEE Computer Society Press. Los Alamitos, CA, USA.

Prieto-D´ıaz, R. & Frakes W.b.,eds (1993).Advances in software reuse: *Selected papers from the second International Workshop on software reusability*, Los Alamitos, California, March, IEEE Computer Society Press.

Pressman, R. (2001).Software Engineering-A practitioner's Approach, Fifth edition, McGraw-Hill.

Rotmans, Kemp & van Asselt. (2001) More Evolution than Revolution. Transition Management in Public Policy, Foresight 3(1): 15-31

Rine, D. C. (1997a). Success factors for software reuse those are applicable across domains and businesses. *ACM Symposium on Applied Computing*, pages 182–186, San Jose, California, USA. ACM Press.

Rine, D. C. and Nada, N. (2000a). An empirical study of a software reuse reference model. *Information and Software Technology*, 42(1):47–65.

Rine, D. C. and Nada, N. (2000b). Three empirical studies of software reuse reference model. *Software: Practice and Experience*, 30(6):685–722.

Rine, D. C. & Sonnemann, R. M. (1998). Investments in reusable software. a study of software reuse investment success factors. *The Journal of Systems and Software*, 41:17–32.

Rushby Craig& Bruce Allgood (2001).CMMI: A Comprehensive Overview.CMMI User Group, *Computer Resources Support Improvement Program*, Hill AFB, UT, November.

Sunita Chulani (2000).COCOMOII. *Wiley Software Engineering Encyclopedia*, Fall.

Svahnberg, M. & Bosch, J. (1999).Evolution in Software Product Lines: Two Cases., *Journal of Software Maintenance - Research and Practice*, 11(6), pp. 391-422.

Svahnberg, M. &Bosch, J. (1999) .Characterizing Evolution in Product-Line Architectures., *Proceedings of the IASTED 3rd International Conference on Software Engineering and Applications*

Szyperski. C. (1997).*Component Software - Beyond Object-Oriented Programming*, Addison-Wesley.

Suz Garcia. (2003),On the TRIAL to CMMI® : A Framework for Effective Transition Management Practices, *SEI Technology Transition Practices*, Carnegie Mellon University, Pittsburgh, PA 15213-3890.

WWW.sei.cmu.edu/publications/documents/*02.reports*/02tr007.html

SEI/CMU. (2003). INDIA 2003 presentation on TTP website www.sei.cmu.edu/ttp

SPC-CMC. (1993). Software Productivity Consortium, *Reuse-driven Software Processes Guidebook*, SPC-92019-CMC, version 2.0.

SPC-CMC. (1993).Software Productivity Consortium, *Reuse Adoption Guidebook*, SPC-92051-CMC, Version 2.0.

CMU/SEI. (1993). Software Engineering Institute, *Capability Maturity Model for Software*, CMU/SEI-93-TR-024, version 1.1.

Topaloglu,Y.;Dikenelli,O & Sengonca,H. (1996),Afour Dimensional reuse Maturity Model, Symposium on Computer and Information Sciences. ISCIS-XI, Antalya, Turkey. November.

http://en.wikipedia.org/wiki/COCOMO

http://sunset.usc.edu/COCOMO II/Cocomo.html

http://sunset.usc.edu/COCOTS/cocots.html.

21

Interactivity of 3D social Internet as a marketing tool

Urszula Świerczyńska-Kaczor
Jan Kochanowski University, Kielce
Poland

1. Introduction

Until recently the 3D Internet interface has been characterized as an element within the traditional web-site used predominantly by companies selling clothing or cars. However business is waking up to the idea of new marketing possibilities created by the 3Dimensional Internet. Virtual worlds such as Second Life, There, HiPiHi have set a high standard by offering significantly more than 3D changing rooms to view your most recent purchase or imaging the car in your driveway. They have actively transformed the traditional Internet interface from 2D 'flat' web-sites into new worlds with their own societies, economies, competitions and markets of real and purely virtual products. Virtual worlds are defined "as immersive, three-dimensional, multi-media, multi-person simulation environments, where each participant adopts an alter ego and interacts with other participants in real time. World activity persists even if a player is off-line" (Wagner 2008, p. 263). Communications within the virtual world is a background for the creation of new social ties and a new virtual community. Virtual worlds have been subject to different scientific research (e.g. as an educational tool, new market, social phenomenon, environment for teamwork), still very little is known about how 3D virtual environment affects the users' interaction with companies and influences customers' attitude towards brands. Are the rules for interacting the same in virtual worlds as on the traditional web-sites? On the traditional web-site the interactivity is increased by hyperlinks and clickable buttons, graphics, animation, channels for on-line communication, easy navigation, personalization, design and color, speed, search tools, relevance of topic and so on (Sohn et al. 2007). In the 3D Internet 'clickable buttons' are transformed into 'clickable and movable 3D objects' and 'graphics' are turned into 3D virtual objects which can be explored 'inside and outside'. Moreover the users presence on a traditional web-site is limited to a nickname or photo. Inside the 3D virtual world the user experiences virtual space as a 3D avatar and this environment allows the user to be immersed in cyberspace: touching objects, moving them, making changes or even building them. The virtual word is a new marketing platform. Companies trying to embrace virtual worlds in their marketing research and promotion or sales strategy face many new challenges. They have little experience (and often knowledge) as to how to develop communication with potential customers and thus do not fully realize the potential offered by the interactivity in the virtual world. The aim of this chapter is to examine the nature of 3D Internet interactivity and to discuss chosen aspects of virtual worlds' marketing. The material includes both theoretical and empirical issues. The survey presented and consequent discussion focuses on an analysis of one of the biggest virtual worlds for adult users - Second Life and the analysis refers to companies which both operate in the real market and implement Second Life as their marketing tool. The following section presents a proposed model of interaction between company and virtual world's users. The third section describes the methodology used in the survey. This is followed by two sections focusing on analysis of obtained data and their interpretation in the context of the limitations of the survey and future research. The sixth and final summarizes the findings.

2. The nature of 3D marketing Internet interactivity

2.1. The model of building interaction between avatar and company within the virtual world

In order to obtain marketing objectives (see Fig. 1) companies can use both passive and active means of interaction. Passive interaction requires only observation within virtual worlds e.g. avatars hang out in the virtual company's land and they simply watch graphical objects. This situation is similar to brand exposure on television, with the exception that in virtual worlds the potential customer is immersed in the environment. Active forms of interaction demand that the user be 'a co-creator' and becoming a 'prosumer' of interaction (prosumer is involved in the process of production). 'Active-creation' interactions refer to building objects within the virtual world e.g. a company organizes a contest based on the user's building skills. 'Active – without creation' interactions demand a higher level of engagement in interaction from the user to that of 'passive interaction', but it does not demand building skills. For example an avatar can wear a garment (T-shirt, shoes) with the company logo or use an object with company's logo (drive a car of a particular brand etc.). If the user estimates company interactivity as valuable (in fig. 1 the variable 'perceived value of interactivity'), the chances that avatars will continue to build a relationship with the company increase. The value of interaction is a similar construct to the value of a service encounter. According to Heinonen (2008), a service encounter has a value for customers both in process and outcomes elements. In the virtual world the process is linked with the avatar's effort in interacting with the company and the resulting outcomes lay in areas such as entertainment, making social connections or educational value.

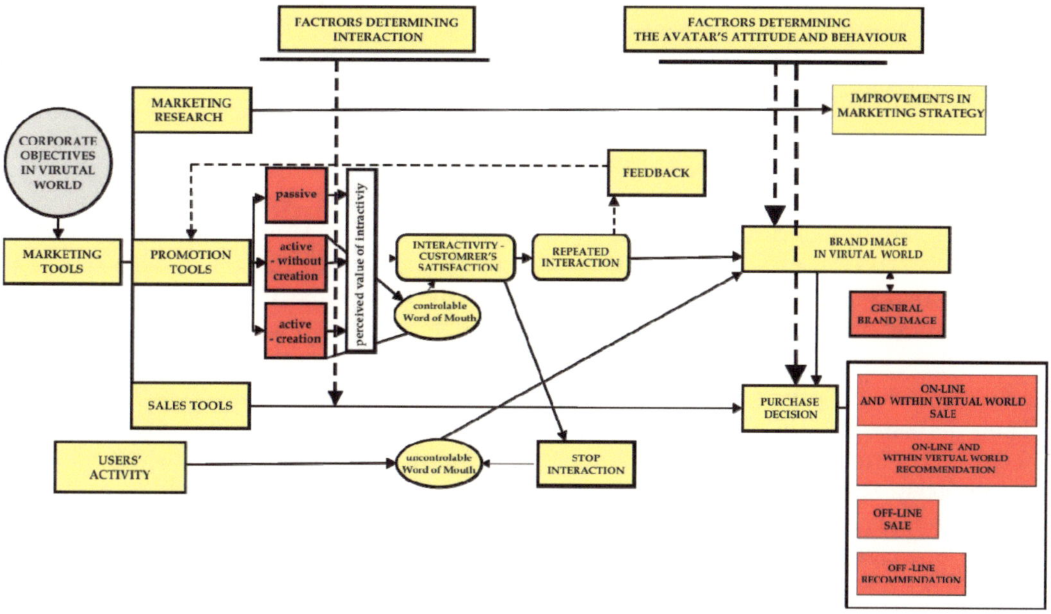

Fig. 1. The model of interaction between company and users within Second Life

Positive contacts lead to a better perception of the company's brand and actively enhance potential purchasing decisions in markets. The term 'markets' is used as opposed to 'a market', is because the presence of a real brand within the virtual world can affect the image of the company in three markets: (1) in the virtual world's market, (2) 'real market' (Castronova (2002) uses the term Earth market) and (3) on-line market offered by traditional web-sites. Active forms of interaction, such as the taking part in discussions by avatars, creates 'Word of Mouth' about a particular brand (WOM) and the reputation of a brand spreads among users. Apart from this controllable WOM (from the company's point of view), many strong and well-known brands (such as Addidas, Sony, Mercedes) are created by an individual user within the virtual world and this way the uncontrollable World Of Mouth for the brand is being formed (unWOM). Both controllable and uncontrollable WOM affect brand image and a consumer's behaviour, that is a user's brand recommendation and purchase. Other factors such as knowledge about the brand from the real market or a customer's budget also play a role in the process of building a brand image (in the fig. 1 – 'factors determining the avatar's attitude and behaviour'). Although the process of building digital WOM within a 2D web-site has been the subject of many studies (e.g. Brown et al. 2007), many aspects about building and spreading WOM within a 3D Internet are still unknown. Within literature also little research exists as to how a company's activity within virtual worlds influences the marketing performance of the brand, specifically selling or brand value (e.g. Arakji & Lang (2008) presented an interesting model of Avatar Business Value, Barnes & Mattsson (2008) analyzed the virtual brand value). The way of describing the nature of the virtual world as presented above (as in the fig.1) refer to a deterministic way of seeing the correlation between indicated factors. This way of presenting interrelations between variables is helpful especially in designing a survey which could show the indicated correlations, but it is necessary to point out that there is also a different approach focused on a nondeterministic way of perceiving the usage of advanced technology (as in Adaptive Structuration Theory – DeSanctis&Poole, 1994 or in the interesting model of Metaverse Research founded by Davis et al. 2009).

2.2. The characteristics of interactivity within virtual world

Referring to the 'media richness' theory, the 'richness' of the Second Life environment, within the virtual world is based on a combination of graphics, sound and communication tools, which can create a different experience in comparison to traditional web-sites. For example, if an avatar is falling down into the water the immersive 3D space allows the user to 'experience' the fear of this accident, more positively an avatar can feel the joy of dancing (maybe this is a reason why Second Life is useful for autistic people – Biever 2007). Some companies activity within the virtual world can be viewed as a form of product placement. There are some variables characterizing product placement in traditional media such as modality, congruity with the plot, type of program or placement prominence (Cowley & Barron 2008). Some of these variables can be used in analysis of interactivity in the 3D Internet. For example, interaction can be assessed as congruent with the type of brand (e.g. offering virtual cars is congruent for a car manufacturer or dealer). Placement prominence can refer to the centrality of the product's presentation in the virtual land (e.g. vending machine with cars is a central point of Nissan virtual land). Finally, duration of the interaction refers to the avatar's exposure to particular stimuli to the extent that organizing a concert is a form of time limited interaction, but offering a virtual car is not. A traditional web-sites interactivity is often limited to the contact user-website, while within the virtual world, the community is the basis for the avatar's virtual existence. Hence, the next aspect of interactivity involves cooperation between the avatars themselves and cooperation between a company and a group of avatars (e.g. a group of brand users).

2.3. The factors influencing avatar's response to company's interaction

Before the avatars decide to interact with a company, they ask themselves: 'Am I able to take part in this interaction?', 'How much effort should I put in in order to take part in this interaction?" and 'Is the outcome of this interaction worth it?' On the other hand companies look to a spectrum of factors affecting the avatar's willingness to respond to a company's invitation. One of these factors is a user's knowledge about Second Life e.g. a user must know how to use an avatar's 'inventory' in order to wear a company's T-shirt or keep the model of its virtual car. Another factor is the user's level of acceptance of marketing activity inside a virtual world. Some users, perceiving the virtual world as fantasy, reject the companies' presence and this means that the consumers can reject interaction with company. Research conducted on traditional web-sites (Sohn et al., 2007), identifies the factor of 'expected interactivity'. This factor can play a significant role in an evaluation of virtual interaction. Avatars visiting the land of a well-known car manufacture expect some interaction connected with driving a virtual car, while visiting the land of an IT company avatars expect free courses about building and scripting in Second Life. Therefore, an avatar's assessment can be higher when a company's interactivity exceeds expectations. These three elements: expected interactivity, avatar's knowledge and users' acceptance of virtual world are only examples of factors which may influence the analyzed process of interaction.

3. The research questions and method

The aim of this empirical study was to examine chosen aspects of a virtual world's interactivity. In this study the following specific questions were formulated: (1) What forms of interactivity are preferred by avatars? (2) Is there any difference in avatars' preferences between active and passive forms of interaction? (3) Can company's interactivity influence brand image within the virtual world in such a dimension as trustworthiness? (4) How do interactions influence the customer's behaviour in three areas: buying a product in the real market, recommendation of a brand to another user and repeated contact with a company in the future? The two first specified questions are connected with the avatar's preference of interactions embedded in the proposed model (fig.1) as variables: 'passive interaction', 'active without creation', 'active – creation' and 'perceived value of interactivity'. The next following two questions refer to the outcomes in the proposed model: brand image in the virtual world and the link indicated between interactivity and the avatar's behaviour within the virtual world, on-line and the real market. The survey was conducted within the virtual world of Second Life. The procedure was based on the following steps: (1) on the basis of observations of companies' activities within the virtual world the possible forms of interactions between company and avatar were identified, (2) respondents - avatars visited the lands of two chosen companies and then avatars were redirected to Jan Kochanowski University's web-site in order to complete a questionnaire, (3) in the first part of the questionnaire avatars evaluated different forms of interactions without referring to any specific company, (4) In the second part of questionnaire avatars assessed the visited companies' interactions and assessed their attitude to companies' brands. Brand attitude can be assessed in many dimensions, but research about e-branding, indicated brand trustworthiness as one of the crucial elements of brand perception within the e-market. For instance Kossecki (2004) analyzed trust among other factors enhancing e-purchase, Kim, Cho, and Rao examined the role of trust and perceived benefit in e-commerce (Joia & de Oliveira 2008). Steward (2003) pointed out that the novelty of a distribution channel may weaken customer's trust. Presumably in the virtual world, customers are less willing to trust a company than at a traditional web-site. Subsequently customer's brand attitude is connected with behaviour such as 'brand recommendation, 'intention to buy product' and 'willingness to repeat contact with a brand'. Reichheld (2004) found that 'on Earth economy' the question about product's recommendation is a very good indicator for customers' loyalty and the company's growth. Similarly in the virtual world two, examined in the survey, variables - 'recommendation of company to other avatars' and 'willingness to repeat contact with company' can be good indicators for the customer's loyalty and brand relevancy to customer. 'Intention to buy a product in real life' can be a strong indicator of the avatar's brand perception and consequently the indicator of company's marketing effectives within virtual world. The survey was conducted in February 2009 and 51 Polish avatars responded to the questionnaire. 94% of respondents (48) have been living in Second Life for at least 6 months (the date of birth of avatar is visible in the avatar's profile), thus presumably most respondents are experienced in virtual interactivity. In this survey avatars visited lands of two companies: (1) well-known car manufacturer Nissan and (2) Polish language school Lingualand. These firms have existed in Second Life for at least a few months, have strong links with the real market and represent different business sectors (auto manufacturer and educational service).

4. Preferred forms of interactivity

In the first part of questionnaire avatars answered two questions: (a) 'If the company proposes interaction 'X', how willingly do you respond?', (b) 'If the company proposes interaction 'X', does this interaction encourage you to repeat contact with company?' All questions were scaled from 1 to 5 points (1 being the lowest mark, 'I do not like'; 5 – highest mark, 'I do like'). This research showed that the avatars' responses significantly vary compared to different interactions. Three active form of interactions: 'taking part in events organized by a company', 'conversation with salesmen within the virtual world' and 'taking part in a contest which does not demand building skills, but money prize is offered' - strongly influence an avatar's willingness to participate in interaction (see Table 1). Three passive form of interactions: 'The visual display of the company's land', 'interest in the company's product presentation' and 'playing nice music' also have a significant positive effect on avatars' participation in interaction. The statistical analysis shows that there is no significant differences between the distribution of interaction which received the highest grades (all six interactions both passive and active). Therefore all six forms of interaction are similar in the avatar's perception ($p>0.05$ Wilcoxon test). On the other hand the avatars do not appreciate the following forms of interactions: (1) within the active interactions: 'offering a free product trail', 'giving feedback to the company e.g. writing notes on a board or filling a questionnaire' and (2) within the passive interactions: 'video or slide presentations and 'receiving a company's landmark' (landmark is a virtual address within Second Life). 'Receiving the landmark' is an interaction evaluated significantly lower ($p<0.05$) in comparing it to both active interactions and the other passive form (video and slides). The active form of 'offering a free product trial' was assessed significantly higher than slides and video presentations and receiving landmarks ($p<0.05$). This study also showed a huge gap between an avatar's willingness to interact with a company for the first time (in the table nr 1 variable 'mean 1') and then repeating the interactions (variable 'mean 2' – the variables tested using Wilcoxon test: p – presented in the table, the distributions of variables are not normal). This result proved a well-known marketing principle – it is much easier to attract customer's (in this case avatar's) attention than to create a long-lasting relationship between customer (avatar) and company.

Form of interaction	Expected response from an avatar	Mean (1)	Mean (2)	p (1/2)
Active interaction				
Organizing events within SL such as concert, meetings, presentation, debates	Taking part in the event organized by company, positive recommendation to other users	4,37	3,94	0,00
Avatar can talk with sales people who are able to answer customer's question.	Avatar's interest in company's products. Giving feedback about company's product	4,25	3,86	0,01
Contest with a money prize (the contest does not require building skills)	Taking part in the contest	4,12	3,94	0,15

The possibility of placing an order for real products within Second Life (in the same way as at a traditional web site)	Ordering real company's products within SL	3,75	3,53	0,13
Offering virtual objects within the virtual world (not necessary connected with real company's product)	Acceptance and usage of an object e.g. driving virtual car or wearing virtual garments with company logo	3,53	3,10	0,00
Organizing contests requiring building skills	Taking part in contest	3,20	3,00	0,16
Giving feedback to company e.g. writing notes on a board or completing questionnaire	Engaging avatar in giving feedback to company	3,20	2,76	0,00
Offering a free product's trail (the virtual product is connected with real company's product)	Virtual consumption of product	3,18	3,12	0,81
Passive interaction				
Interesting presentation of a product on a company's virtual land	Visiting a company's land	4,24	3,69	0,00
Visual display of a company's land	Visiting a company's land	4,10	3,71	0,01
Playing nice music on a particular land	Visiting a company's land	4,10	3,55	0,00
Receiving detailed information about an object	Visiting a company's land. Arousing avatar's interest in a company and its products.	3,90	3,55	0,01
Receiving information about a company within virtual world, but outside its land (eg. billboard on merchants' land, ads within search engine)	Visiting a company's land	3,47	3,12	0,01
Communications between a company and the users who participate in the company's group	Avatar's response depends on the proposed interactions within the message e.g. visiting a new products' exhibition	3,10	2,75	0,00
Video or slide presentations on a company's land	Watching the presentation	2,90	2,59	0,01
Receiving the landmark	Repeated visits to a company's land	2,65	2,49	0,20

Table 1. The assessment of different forms of interactions

5 The case of Nissan and Lingualand

5.1. The assessment of companies' interactivity

Respondents evaluated marketing forms of interactions offered by two companies: Nissan and Lingualand. Nissan set up its virtual business on an virtual island. Its interactivity gives visitors a large spectrum of active and passive interaction: (1) the company offers a free virtual car - avatars can get it when they input a 'secret code' into a special vending machine, (2) the avatars can drive the virtual car on a specially designed racing track , (3) users get more information about Nissan if they click on a hyperlink connected to the virtual island and are redirected to a traditional web-site. Lingualand is a brick-and-mortar Polish school, set up in the Polish city of Krakow and they conduct their business in the real world. The school has also set up its virtual replica within the Polish part of Second Life – Second Poland. Survey respondents evaluated both companies one for active interaction (variable: 'offering free product trail') and for passive interactions (variables: 'visual company's features', 'the features of surrounding area', 'product presentation', 'sufficiency of information about products', 'reliability of information about product' and 'information about company at websites outside SL'). The analysis of interactions showed that there was a statistically significant difference between the assessment of Lingualand and Nissan, except one variable: 'information at the web-site outside SL' (see Table 2, in the analysis - the distribution of variables were not normal, differences tested using Wilcoxon test). The virtual school Lingualand was better evaluated than Nissan , although some interactions do not have the same meanings for both companies: (1) Lingualand does not offer material products, therefore 'product presentation' can not been estimated, (2) Nissan built its presence in a separate virtual land, whereas the Lingualand office is only one element of the whole land – virtual Krakow, hence, the 'perception of the surrounding area' was included in Lingualand's analysis. The meaning of the variable 'offering free product trial' is also different for Nissan and for Lingualnad. For Lingualand the avatars can attend a virtual language lesson (e.g. English and Italian), thus the virtual experience is a real educational service. In the Nissan land virtual consumption does not mean driving real car, but only playing with a virtual one. The results showed that there was no differences in assessment of information about a company at an outside website (avatars can find the link to 'outside' web-site within Second Life).

	The interaction (code for interation)	Nissan (N)	Lingualand (L)	p Wilcoxon
		Mean/Median/SD		
Passive interactions	A company's visual features (F1)	3,41/4/1,22	3,82/4/1,18	0,05
	The features of the surrounding area (F2)	-	4,06/4/0,95	-
	Presentation of the product (F3)	3,94/4/1,03	-	-
	The spectrum of information about products – is the information sufficient? (F4)	3,31/3/0,91	3,92/4/0,84	0,00
	Reliability of information about the products (F5)	3,51/4/0,88	3,98/4/0,99	0,01
	Information about a company at the traditional websites (F7)	3,53/4/0,90	3,69/4/0,99	0,33
	Active interaction - Offering free trial product (F6)	3,73/4/1,11	4,39/5/0,98	0,01

Table 2. Comparison between companies' interaction within Second Life

On the basis of data obtained from the first part of this survey and the assessment of companies, Nissan and Lingualand, interactivity can be evaluated within two dimensions: weak and strong points of a company and the importance of interactivity. Figure 2 graphically represents which virtual companies' activity should be maintained at the highest level because of its importance (the code of variables as in table 2, Lingualand marked 'L' and red, Nissan 'N' and green, the interaction 'information about company outside SL' was not evaluated in aspect of importance, the cross point is the mean of assessment of companies interactions and the mean of importance of all interactions).

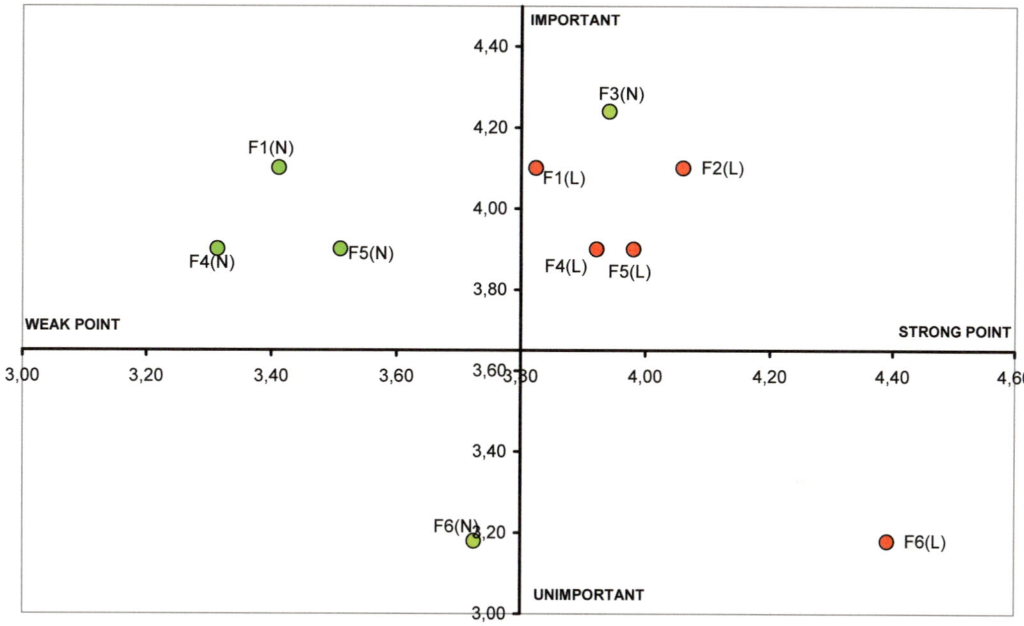

Fig. 2. Comparison between strong and weak companies' points and the importance of interactions

5.2. Analysis of brand trustworthiness and customer's behaviour

The avatars answered the questions about Nissan and Lingualand image and their attitude to the brands. The analysis shows that there are statistically no significant differences between distributions of such variables as: 'trust in the company', 'recommendation of a company to other avatars' and 'willingness to re-visit the virtual company'. For Nissan it would be difficult for respondents to assess how virtual activities would affect their willingness to buy products, therefore users were asked for the assessment of the link between virtual activity and general brand image. In Lingualands school the situation is different. After attending virtual lessons, the users can asses whether the image of the school (if it were real in their neighborhood) is appealing enough to sign up for real classes. Only in this area are respondents' answers significantly different statistically (Table 3, Figure 3). The survey shows that although there are significant differences between perception of interaction between Nissan and Lingualand, the avatars' bonds to the brands in most dimensions are similar.

The interaction	Nissan (N)	Lingualand (L)	p. Wilcoxon N/L
	Mean/Median/SD		
Trust in the company (R1)	3,86/4/0,98	3,82/4/0,97	0,75
Virtual presentations positive effect on Nissan image / Intention to sign up for real language lessons (R2)	3,75/4/0,89	3,27/3/1,27	0,02
Recommendation of company to other avatars (R3)	3,75/4/1,02	3,84/4/0,90	0,57
Willingness to re-visit the virtual company(R4)	3,55/4/1,21	3,80/4/1,00	0,21

Table 3. The differences between the perception of brand image and consumer's attitude towards brands

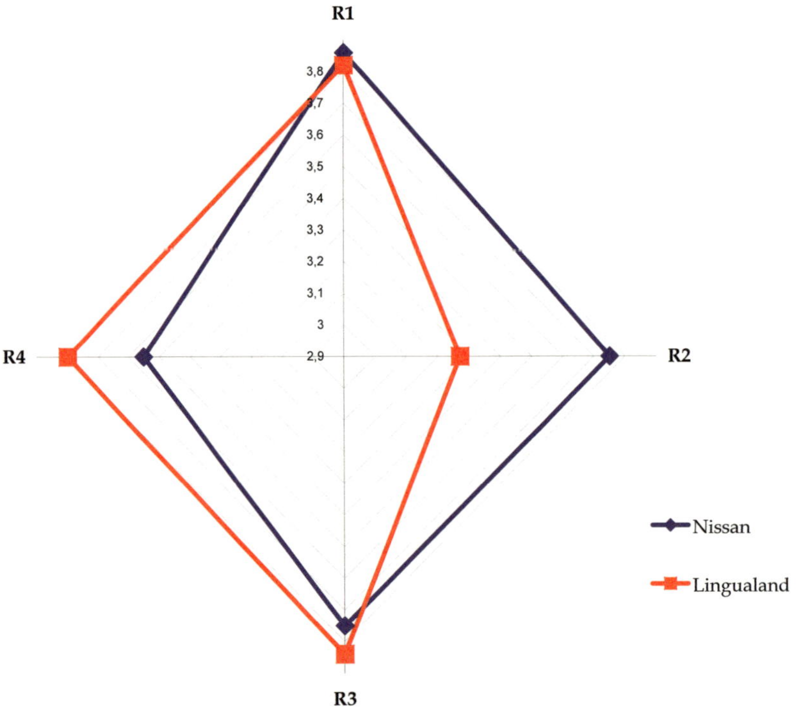

Fig. 3. Four dimensions of consumer's brand attitude and behaviour

Among the tools of the virtual Lingualand marketing, avatars appreciate the possibility of attending free English lessons - this active form of interaction is estimated significantly higher than others (see Table 2). However, the analysis shows that 'the intention to sign up to real lessons' was assessed significantly statistically lower than the three other aspects of brand: 'trust', 'recommendation visiting' and 'willingness to re-visit the company'. Analysis within the interactions offered by Nissan shows that avatars especially appreciate the uncommon form of product presentations – vending machine for distributing the virtual car. In the analysis of Nissan brand outcomes, there are no differences between the four analyzed variables - 'trust', 'virtual presentation has a positive effect on Nissan image', 'recommendation of company to other avatars' and 'willingness to re-visit the company' ($p>0.5$ Wilcoxon test). In the next step of analysis the correlation between interaction and customer's response was assessed (Table 4, Table 5, Figure 4). Results for Nissan show that a strong correlation exists between (a) the visual company's virtual features and creating a positive image in customer's mind and (b) between offering a virtual car and recommendation to other avatars to visit Nissan land and between (c) presentation of cars and recommendation visit. In Lingualand most examined variables are highly correlated and the results are: (1) Six examined factors (reliability and sufficiency of information, the offer of free language classes, the features of the surrounding area, information about the school outside SL) very strongly correlate with the recommendation of school services to other avatars. (2) Four examined factors (reliability and sufficiency of information, offering free language classes and features of surrounding area) strongly correlate with recommending other avatars visit school and also with the intention of re-visiting the school themselves. (3) All indicated interactions strongly correlate with trust.

	F1(N)	F6(N)	(F3(N))	(F4(N))	(F5(N))	(F7(N))
Trust in company	0,22	0,35	0,34	0,06	0,42	0,20
The effect of virtual presentations on Nissan image	0,59	0,21	0,37	0,16	0,38	0,47
Recommendation of visiting Nissan land to other avatars	0,47	0,51	0,51	0,44	0,44	0,44
Willingness to re-visit Nissan land	0,47	0,47	0,44	0,37	0,38	0,23

Table 4. Correlation between Nissan interactivity and avatars' attitudes (Gamma correlation - codes for variables as in table 2)

	(F1(L))	(F2(L))	(F6(L))	(F4(L))	(F5(L))	(F7(L))
Trust in company	0,49	0,60	0,64	0,77	0,80	0,54
Intention to sign up for real courses in real life	0,36	0,47	0,30	0,50	0,50	0,51
Recommendation of visiting school to other avatars	0,56	0,85	0,85	0,90	0,84	0,65
Intention to re-visit the school	0,56	0,79	0,70	0,76	0,81	0,70

Table 5. Correlation between Lingualand interactivity and avatars' attitudes (Gamma correlation – codes for variables as in table 2)

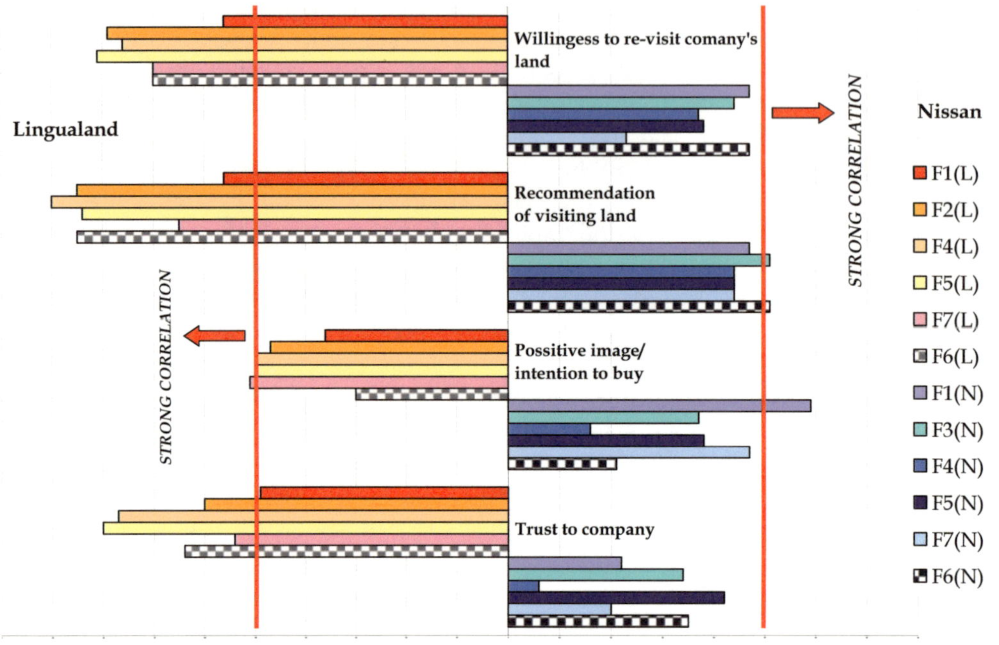

Fig. 5. The correlation between variables

The results show that despite the statically significant differences between assessment of companies' interactions, the avatar's brand attitude is similar to both companies. What are the possible explanations for this? The following section indicates some factors which can play a role in this survey. Factors are presented according to the scheme: (1) the factor influencing the link between interaction and brand attitude, (2) reference to this study results, (3) marketing implications, (4) study limitation and future research in a discussed field.

5.3. Indicating factors which may moderate the avatar's attitude to the brand

5.3.1. Brand familiarity

(1) The factor: The 'brand familiarity' creates the background of perception of interactivity ('brand familiarity is understood as 'as the number of brand-related direct or indirect experiences that have been accrued by the consumer' - Park & Stoel, 2005). This factor refers to the dichotomy of well known brands vs. unknown brand and also global vs. local brand. (2) Reference to the results of this study – Correlation analysis shows that avatars' attitude to well-known manufacturer Nissan is not based on proposed interaction. On the contrary, Lingualand, which is known from virtual world (few avatars have a chance to the know company in the real world), built its image through its marketing interactivity within the virtual environment. For this company, analysis shows very strong correlation between proposed interaction and brand attitude (3) Marketing implications – The meaning of interactivity in the virtual world's is different for well-known brands than for unknown brands. Avatar's recommendations of well-known brand or willingness to repeat contact may depend less on proposed interactions. For lesser known brands, their interactivity

should create user's awareness of brand. (4) Study limitation and future research - Future study should examine the influence of previous brand image on brand attitude within the virtual world. Further study should use a larger sample including different business sectors, and also examine differences between brick-and-mortar companies and purely virtual ones.

5.3.2. Avatar's motive

(1) The factor: Avatars form highly diversified communities, hence the perception of interactivity and its outcome – brand attitude - are different for various segments of avatars. (2) Reference to this study - Looking at the 'average' image of a company and an 'average' consumer's attitude and not distinguishing the data obtained from different segments led to unclear results. In this study the additional question - 'If a company from the real world organizes language courses in Second Life, how willingly will you take part?' can be used as a criteria of segmentation (This question was included in an additional part of the questionnaire, not referring to Lingualand or any other particular company, a scale from 1 to 5 points was used). Implementing this question into analysis it is possible to distinguish two different segments: the group of users who answered 5 (called 'educationally-orientated') and the group of users who answered 1 ('non-educationally-orientated'). The analysis showed that the intention to sign up for real courses offered by Lingualand is significantly higher in the group of 'educationally-orientated' avatars than 'non-educationally orientated' users (U Mann-Whitney test, $p<0.05$). Moreover, the differences between both segments are significant in the assessment of other Lingualand dimensions: brand trustworthiness, making recommendations to other avatars, willingness to re-visit the land (there are no differences between users choosing 4 and 5). (3) Marketing implications - This finding confirms that the 'average' customer does not exist in the market of the virtual world. Proposed interactions should take into account the specific needs of a particular segment of users. (4) Study limitation and future research –The findings of this survey are limited by a small chosen sample. Hence it was not a cross-cultural study and potential cultural differences among segments can be overlooked. Future research should examine different factors which can be used as segmentation criteria such as user's attitude to interaction or a user's self-expression (e.g. Arakji & Lang. (2008) argued that the avatars' needs depend on the image which user wants to create within virtual world - adopting human avatars or non-human).

5.3.3. Facilitating factors

(1) The factor: Facilitating factors. Brand perception is not a simple sum of the proposed interactions and one particular interaction can change overall perception. (2) Reference to this study - No elements on Nissan land were particularly negatively assessed, therefore a positive element, such as with the vending machine, can strongly influence the perception of the brand. (3) Marketing implications – Maybe it is enough to create one engaging form of interactions that is worth seeing. It may turn out that 'overloaded' interactivity is assessed lower than the more simplified and easily noticeable interaction. (4) Study limitation and future research – Future research should be focused on indicating different facilitating factors including those not connected with graphics.

5.3.4. Avatar's interactivity expectation

(1) The factor: Avatar's interactivity expectations, (2) Reference to the study results - Avatars visiting the land of a well-known car manufacture expect interactivity connected with a virtual car. But while avatars visit a school their expectations may not be so clear – they would expect free lessons or slide or video presentations or some other forms of interaction. Hence, the element of 'being surprised' can play a role in the higher assessment of interactivity of Lingualand, but it does not lead to a higher assessment of the brand in outcomes such as trustworthiness or recommendation (3) Marketing implications – 'interactivity expectations' depend on the product category. Maybe the best working interaction should trigger the avatar's curiosity and surprise them. 4) Study limitation and future research –Future research should examine the avatar's interactivity expectation toward a particular brand in order to find a 'reference point' in perception and then from that perspective examine the proposed interactivity.

5.3.5. Cooperation

(1) The factor: Avatar's willingness to cooperate with others. Interactivity can be differently perceived when a group, not a single user, is involved. (2) Reference to this study – Lingualand interactivity which was based on cooperation was highly assessed. Also in the first part of the survey avatars positively evaluated interactions such as organizing concert, debates or contest, which require social contact. (3) Marketing implications – Companies can build their own virtual communities within the virtual world and this way create their own 'fan-clubs'. 4) Study limitation and future research - . Future research should focus on the role of cooperation between avatars in the process of building marketing interactivity.

5.3.6 Emotions

(1) The factor: Emotions play a significant role in building an avatar's attitude toward a brand and perception of interactivity, (2) Reference to the study results - In this survey the avatar's response to interaction was defined in behavioral aspects, omitting many emotional aspects. It is possible that primary interactivity influences the users' emotions and then the users' behaviour. This study did not show this process. (3) Marketing implications – The avatars can be 'moved' from 'liking' the brand to 'buying' or 'recommending brand' thanks to a company's interactivity. (4) Study limitation and future research - Future studies should also examine the aspects of emotions and not only focus on the beliefs and behavior.

5.3.7 Avatar's attitude to 'real world'

(1) The factor: Avatar's attitude to the virtual world can influence the perception of a company's interactivity, (2) Reference to the study results - The presented survey shows that avatars are unwilling to transfer consumption of a product from the virtual world into real world - in this analysis to sign up for real language courses. (3) Marketing implications – The users are so immersed in cyberspace that if it is possible to use the product virtually they do not think about an actual purchase. Offering a product where customers are, (in the virtual world) not where the company is, is a change in the direction of thinking from traditional forms of commerce. Study limitation and future research - Future research should give more a holistic picture of integration 'earth' marketing and marketing within into virtual world.

6. Conclusion

The results of the survey conducted among Polish users of Second Life partly explained the proposed model of interactions presented in section 2.1. The first part of the survey identified the spectrum of possible interaction (indicated in the model in section 2.1. as passive, active without creation and active- creation), and investigated which interactions can be assessed as particularly interesting for avatars (variable 'perceived value of interactivity'). The result emphasizes the importance of 'bringing the brand to life'. Engaging activities such as debates, concerts or contests with a prize are users' preferred forms of interaction. At the same time, the survey showed that avatars also appreciate unusual and creative forms of passive interactions such as interesting graphics for product presentation or embedding sound in the land. Surprisingly when users were asked to assess the a product free trail, they assessed this interaction poorly. The data also highlights that companies could face huge difficulties in keeping avatar's responses during subsequent contacts at the same level as in the first. The study shows that there is no clear evidence that marketing interactivity can directly enhance the probability of buying real products, avatar's recommendations of brand to other users and perceived trustworthiness of the brand. The interpretation and discussion on the findings of the second part of this survey pinpoint many factors which should be taken into consideration when building a company's interactivity within the virtual world. These factors may influence the avatar's response to marketing interactivity determining whether the avatar takes part in the interaction or they may influence the outcome - that is - the avatar's willingness to recommend the brand, trust toward the brand or the avatar's willingness to renew contact with the company (as the proposed model in fig. 1). These factors (table 6) can be used as a list of dimensions for marketing interactions which should be considered and described before the company builds its presence in virtual 3D society.

Factor/Factors	Description
Characteristics of interactivity	Interactivity congruence with the brand, interactivity duration and interactivity prominence. Active forms or passive forms of interactions
Characteristics of ties between avatar and brand	The characteristics of the ties between avatar and brand - their strength and emotional intensity. The avatar's response can depend on the familiarity of the brand.
Relationship between avatars	The perception of a company's interactivity changes when user-user relationship is building. The friend-avatar can influence the user to take part in interaction. The opinions leaders (virtual world influentials) can also play important role.
Avatar's motives	The user's response to interaction varies depending on the motives for existing within the virtual worlds e.g. 'relationship-orientated' avatars could be more willing to take part in social events as compared to 'educational-orientated' or 'building-orientated' avatars

Avatar's profile	Factors influencing an avatar's attitude to interaction and promoted brands connected with the avatar's profile: demographical, economical and behavioral variables (e.g. How many hours does an avatar spend within a virtual world? How do computer skills limit the ability to take part in the interactions?). It can be also important how strongly attached the user is to the virtual world - this means how willingly the user chooses virtual world activities as a substitute for real world activities.
Avatar's engagement in the process of co-creation	The virtual world allows users to create their own objects. If the company encourages users to be co-creators of interaction, this can influence the brand attitude and perception of interactivity

Table 6. Factors which may influence the process of company-avatar interaction

7. References

Arakji, R. Y. & Lang, K. R. (2008), Avatar Business Value Analysis: A Method For The Evaluation Of Business Value Creation In Virtual Commerce, Journal of Electronic Commerce Research. Long Beach: 2008. Vol. 9, Iss. 3, p. 207-218

Barnes, S. & Mattsson, J. (2008), Brand Value In Virtual Worlds: An Axiological Approach, Journal of Electronic Commerce Research, Long Beach: 2008. Vol. 9, Iss. 3, p.195-206

Biever, C. (2007), Let's meet tomorrow in second life, New Scientist 6/30/2007, Vol. 194 Issue 1610, p. 26-27

Brown, J., Broderick, A. J. & Lee, N. (2007), Word of mouth communication within online communities: Conceptualizing the online social network, Journal of Interactive Marketing; Summer2007, Vol. 21 Issue 3, p2-20

Castronova, E. (2002), On Virtual Economies, CESifo Working Paper No. 752, http://ssrn.com/abstract_id=338500

Cowley, E. & Barron, Ch. (2008), When product placement goes wrong: The effects of Program Liking and Placement Prominence, Journal of Advertising, Spring 2008; 37, 1; ABI/INFORM Global, pg. 89

Davis A., Murphy J., Owens D., Khazanchi D. (2009), Zigurs I, Avatars, People, and Virtual Worlds: Foundations for Research in Metaverses, Journal of the Association for Information System, Volume 10, Issue 2, February 2009, pp. 90-117

DeSanctis G., Poole M. S. (1994), Capturing the Complexity in Advanced Technology Use: Adaptive Structuration Theory, Organization Science, Vol. 5, No. 2, May 1994, pp. 121-147

Heinonen K. (2008), The Role of Digital Service Encounters on Customers' Perceptions of Companies', Journal of Electronic Commerce in Organizations, Volume 6, Issue 2, 2008 IGI Global

Joia, L.A.& de Oliveira L. C. B. (2008), Development and Testing of an E-commerce Web Site Evaluation Model, Journal of Electronic Commerce in Organizations, Volume 6, Issue 3, edited by Mehdi Khosrow-Pour, 2008, IGI Global

Kossecki, P., (2004), Building Trust in eCommerce - Quantitative Analysis, Available at SSRN: http://ssrn.com/abstract=633843

Park, J.& Stoel (2005), L., Effect of brand familiarity, experience and information on online apparel purchase, International Journal of Retail & Distribution Management. Bradford:2005. Vol. 33, Iss. 2/3, p. 148- 160

Reichheld, F. (2004), Najważniejszy jest wskaźnik wzrostu, Harvard Business Review Polska, May 2004, p. 43-53

Sohn D., Ci C. & Lee B-K (2007), The Moderating Effects of Expectation on the Patterns of the Interactivity-Attitude Relationship, Journal of Advertising, Fall 2007; 36,3; ABI/INFORM Global, p. 109

Stewart, Katherine (2003), Trust Transfer on the World Wide Web, Organization Science; Jan/Feb2003, Vol. 14 Issue 1, p 5-17,

Wagner, Ch. 2008, Learning Experience with Virtual Worlds, Journal of Information Systems Education 2008, vol. 19, No. 3, p. 263-266

22

Performance evaluation of protocols of multiagent information retrieval systems

Zofia Kruczkiewicz
Wrocław University of Technology, Wybrzeże Wyspiańskiego 27
Poland

1. Introduction

It is aimed at the limitation of the network traffic which is generated during the realization of protocol in distributed environment of multiagent systems. This paper presents the way of the decrease of the number and the way of the diminution of the size of messages sent between agents as the manner of the limitation of the network traffic. Multiagent system can be employed agents in searching information in distributed databases.

In literature, performance evaluation of the following multi-agent systems: *ZEUS* (Camacho et al., 2002), *JADE* (Camacho et al., 2002), *Skeleton Agent* (Camacho et al., 2002), *Aglets IBM* (Dikaiakos et al., 2001), (Yamamoto & Nakamura, 1999), *Concordia* (Dikaiakos et al., 2001), *Voyager* (Dikaiakos et al., 2001) is presented. When new MAS with performance requirements is designed then, according to software performance engineering (Smith, 1990), (Smith & Lloyd, 2002), (Wooldridge & Rao, 1999), (Babczyński et al., 2004), (Babczyński et al., 2005) performance requirements have to be considered at each phase of life cycle.

The paper presents the method of design communication protocols (FIPA00025, 2000), (FIPA00037, 2000), (Specification of JADE) which based on the limitation of the network traffic in multiagent systems as the use of dynamic protocols instead of static protocols embedded in system.

The method consists in assumption that agent communications and semantics based on Agent Communication Language (ACL), Interaction Protocols etc. (Odell et al., 2001), (Specification of FIPA), (Specyfication of JADE), (Pautret, 2005-2006). At a basic level, it is checked syntactic and semantic consistency of received and sent messages (for example, it is not possible to send an *agree* message with a content representing an action instead of a proposition). The behaviour of an agent is based on analyzing incoming messages and on drawing the conclusion from this analyze. Therefore, the agent semantics consists in setting up its initial beliefs, the rules for handling its beliefs, the domain-specific actions it is expected to handle, and in customizing its cooperative abilities. This way of designing agents of multiagent information retrieval systems will simplify adapting their protocols to the actual meaning of the exchanged messages. These protocols are named the dynamic protocols. This semantic adjustment of agent protocols during exchanging messages will improve the performance of retrieval tasks.

Each agent is built of components, which analyze the received or sent messages. If it is the incoming message, the agent chooses the action and communication act with regard to possibility of minimal loss of performance. It means that an agent sends messages to these agents who understand the content of messages and they are able to realize instructions of messages.

The method of the agent components consists in processing six lists of semantic and interpretation expressions:

- the lists of semantic expressions are FIPA-SL (FIPA00008, 2000), (FIPA00070, 2000) expressions that represent the sense of the message according to the FIPA-ACL semantics (FIPA00037, 2000)
- the belief knowledge, uncertainty knowledge and intention knowledge are lists of expressions that store the beliefs, uncertainties and intentions of the agent. A belief, uncertainty or intention can be a simple predicate, or a more complex formula;
- the lists of semantic actions store the description of the model components of communicative act. The reasons for which the act is selected are referred to as the rational effect (RE) and the conditions that have to be satisfied for the act to be planned are related to as the feasibility preconditions (FPs) (FIPA00037, 2000). They are qualifications for the act. Each action is associated to a semantic behaviour that performs the action;
- the lists of interpretation components perform semantic adjustment of the agent protocol.

Alike just the interpretation algorithm in (Pautret, 2005-2006), the presented interpretation algorithm of the content of semantic components is based on messages and on internal events the form of which are SL expressions. It is a loop, which applies all possible interpretation components to all existing semantic expressions and evaluates the performance of select dynamic protocols and stops when one of the following conditions holds:

- the semantic expressions list becomes empty,
- no interpretation components can be further applied to any semantic expression,
- the one of the semantic expressions is a false formula (e.g., in the case of inconsistency).

The chapter also presents the performance experiments enabling the comparison the dynamic protocols.

The paper is organized as follows. In Section 2, the project of multiagent information retrieval system adapting their protocols to the actual meaning of the exchanged messages is presented. In Section 3, performance metrics of protocols are defined and the methods of formation of the dynamic protocols are presented from performance point of view. The results of simulation experiments are described. Then there are conclusions.

2. System design

This section presents the project of retrieval multiagent system taking benefit from the semantic dimension of the FIPA-ACL language (FIPA00037, 2000), that applies in systems for presentation of interaction between agents. Language of agent includes communication acts so called a message and the grammar (FIPA00008, 2000). The project is done in MaSE technology (Deloach et al., 2001).

2.1 Concepts

It takes advantage of MaSE technology for identification of agents. During analysis, in AgentTool environment of MaSE technology (Deloach et al., 2001), model of goals is built (fig.1). Goals diagram expresses the mission fulfilled by the system. Then the use cases model is created, which presents interactions between roles using the sequence diagram (fig.2, fig.3). In next step of modeling multiagent system, the roles diagram is created, expressed the roles of system, executable tasks of each role and protocols of interactions between tasks (fig.4). The plan of each task is modeled by using the statecharts diagram.
The first step of formation of the design model is built the agent template diagram (fig.5). This diagram is created by the arbitrary choice of agents relate with individual roles they become tasks of agents - task role. Next, it is possible to generate the design model on base of the analysis model and the agent diagram, automatically. Diagram of agent architecture is built of components (fig.6) which represent agent tasks as classes on the design level. The conversation sends a message to another agent or receives a message from another agent (fig.7). The statecharts diagram of the task on analysis level is transformed to the statecharts diagram of the relative component on the design level (fig.8-14). The trigger as the communication act of the statecharts diagram of the task is transformed to the action as the conversation of the relative transition of the component statecharts diagram.

The goals diagram of the retrieval multiagent system

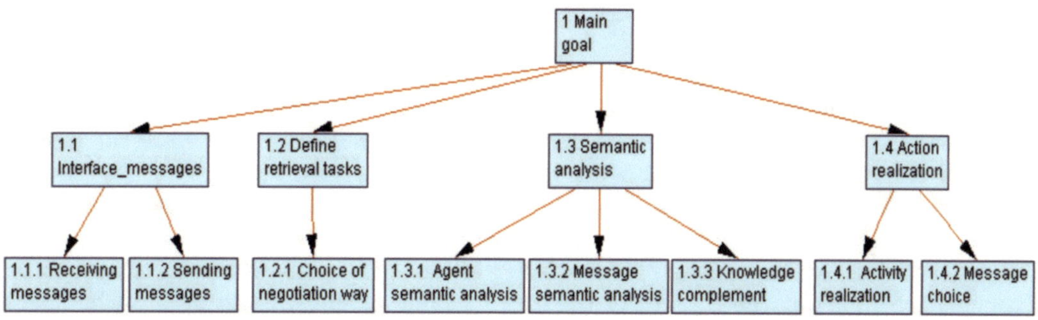

Fig. 1. The goals diagram

The goals diagram belongs to the analysis model. The *Main* goal of the retrieval multiagent system is adapting their protocols to the actual meaning of the exchanged messages because it is the way of the limitation of the network traffic which is generated during the realization of protocol in distributed environment of multiagent systems. The *Main* goal consists of a few goals of the first level. One of them is an *Interface_messages* which consists of a goal of the interface of the *Receiving messages* and a goal of the interface of *Sending messages*. The second goal of the first level is to define the retrieval tasks which include the goal of the choice of the negotiation way. The third goal of the first level is the *Semantic analysis* of communication acts at the point of view of agent properties. It consists of the three following goals. The *Message semantic analysis* goal aims at taking better benefit from semantic dimension of the FIPA-ACL language. The *Agent semantic analysis* goal takes into account the belief knowledge, uncertainty knowledge and intention knowledge in choice of the actions and the communication acts. The third *Knowledge complement* goal refers to gathering the knowledge of an agent properties and facts of actions and communicative acts. The fourth *Action realization* goal executes the communicative acts or internal event. This goal consists of two goals. The first *Activity realization* goal refers to the realization of activity of the task. The second *Message choice* goal deals with the choice of an appropriate message which would be sent to another agent. This is a choice at a point of view of the result of the agent action and the retrieval tasks.

The use cases and sequence diagrams of the retrieval multiagent system

The use cases and its sequence diagrams belong to the analysis model, too. The each use case presents the scenario of the multiagent system. The sequence diagram represents these interactions of system in a more formal way. The agents of the system fulfil the different roles. Each role accomplishes a few tasks.

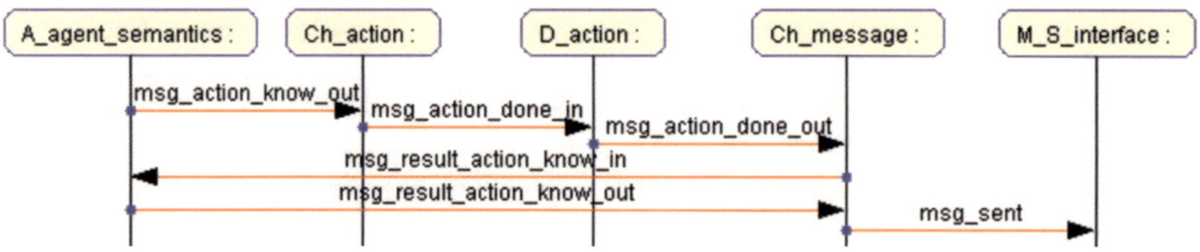

Fig. 2. Sequence diagram of sent process of the *send* use case

The sequence diagram of the *send* use case (fig.2) represents the scenario of fulfilling the process of sending communication acts, which is represented by the interactions between the roles of system over the protocols (fig.4). The *A_agent_semantics* role sends *msg_action_know_out* message by use the *Knowledge_complement* task of this role. There are two reasons of sending this message. The first one is the preparing the response of message received from another agent. The second reason refers to the initiation of the new action of agent.

The received message represents the knowledge of the agent need of activity of system for searching information. The content of the sent message includes these facts of the agent. This message is received by the *Action_choice* task of the *Ch_action* role. The *Action_choice* task choices the proper action which has to be done by the *Action_done* task of the *D_action* role. The *Action_choice* task choices the action by use the belief, uncertainty and intention knowledge of the agent. Each agent has itself knowledge.

Then the *Action_choice* task sends the *msg_action_done_in* message to the *Action_done* task of the *D_action* role. The received message gives information for executing the action or no principles for doing anything. Then the *Action_done* task of the *D_action* role sends the *msg_action_done_out* message to the *Message_choice* task of the *Ch_message* role. This task choices the appropriate message for the result of the *Action_done* task of the *D_action* role. The *Message_choice* task sends the *msg_result_action_know_in* message to the *Knowledge_complement* task of the *A_agent_semantics* role and receives the *msg_result_action_know_out* message with information supporting the choice of the proper message. At last the *Message_choice* task sends the chosen *msg_sent* message to the *Message_sending* task of the *M_S_interface* role.

The process of sending and receiving the *msg_in* result message to another agent is presented by the sequence diagram of the *receive* use case (fig.3) and role diagram (fig.4).

The *Message_sending* task of the *M_S_interface* role of the *ag1* agent sends the *msg_in* message to the *Message_receiving* task of the *M_R_interface* role of the *ag2* agent. The next interactions occur between tasks of roles of the *ag2* agent. The message as the communication act of FIPA ACL language (FIPA00037, 2000) is transformed to FIPA-SL expression (FIPA00008, 2000). The expression represents the semantics of the message.
Then the *msg_sl* message is sent to the *Message_sem_analysis* task of the *A_message_semantics* role. The reasons for which the act is selected are referred to as the rational effect (RE). The conditions that have to be satisfied for the act to be planned are related to as the feasibility preconditions (FPs). They are qualifications for the act (FIPA00037, 2000). Each action is associated to a semantic behaviour that performs the action. The *msg_know_in* message and the *msg_know_out* messages are sent between the *Message_sem_analysis* task of the *A_message_semantics* role and the *Knowledge_complement* task of the *A_agent_semantics* role.

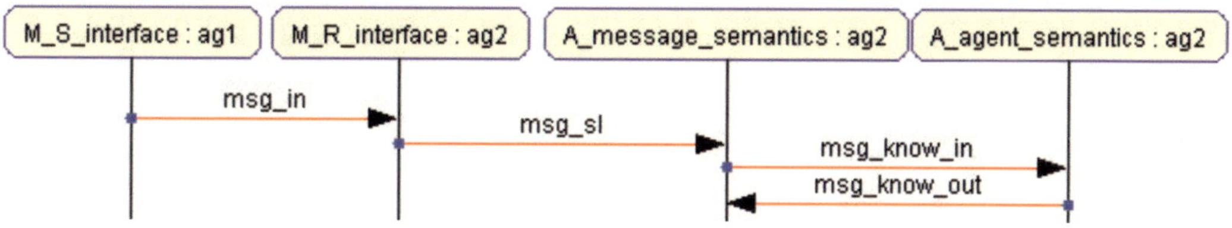

Fig. 3. Sequence diagram of receive process of the *receive* use case

The role diagram of the retrieval multiagent system

The role diagram is the next diagram of the analysis model. The role diagram expresses the roles of the system, executable tasks of each role and protocols of interactions between tasks (fig.4). Each agent of the system fulfils a few roles or the one role at least. These roles are defined at the sequence diagrams. Each role accomplishes different tasks.
The tasks exchange the messages over the protocols. For example, the *Message_sem_analysis* task sends the *msg_know_in* message to the *Knowledge_complement* task and receives the *msg_know_out* message from this task over *message_know* protocol. They are presented at the following diagrams: the sequence diagram of *receive* use case (fig.3), two statecharts diagrams - the *Knowledge_complement* task (fig.11) and the *Message_sem_analysis* task (fig.10), and the role diagram (fig.4).

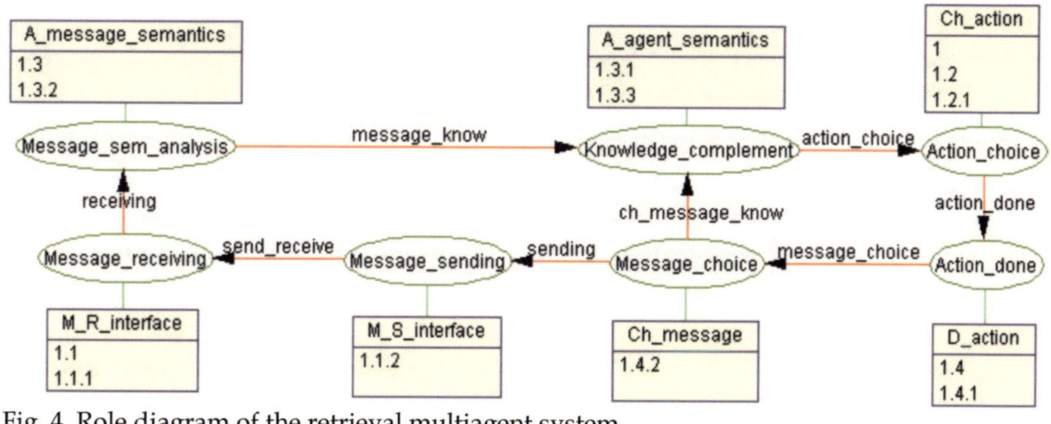

Fig. 4. Role diagram of the retrieval multiagent system

2.2. Design

On the figure 5 there is the *Agent Template Diagram.* It represents the roles fulfilled by each agent. The agent is the universal program, which realizes the same tasks by use itself belief, uncertainty and intention knowledge gathered during the life cycle. Therefore the each agent has the following features: flexibility in adaptation to environment changes, possibility of increasing the number of functions, mobile data and programs, etc. The *send_receive1* and *send_receive2* conversations are used to exchange the messages. The order of these messages realizes the dynamical protocols. The behaviour of the agents will simplify adapting their protocols to the actual meaning of the exchanged messages.

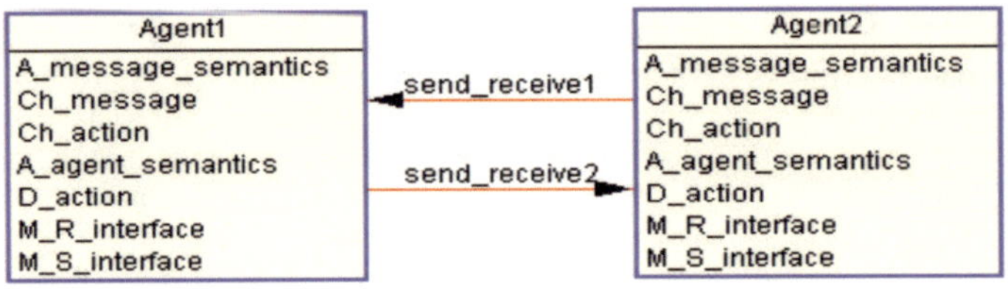

Fig. 5. Agent template diagram

The fig.6 shows the architecture diagram for each agent, which includes components transformed from the task of roles fulfilled by the each agent.

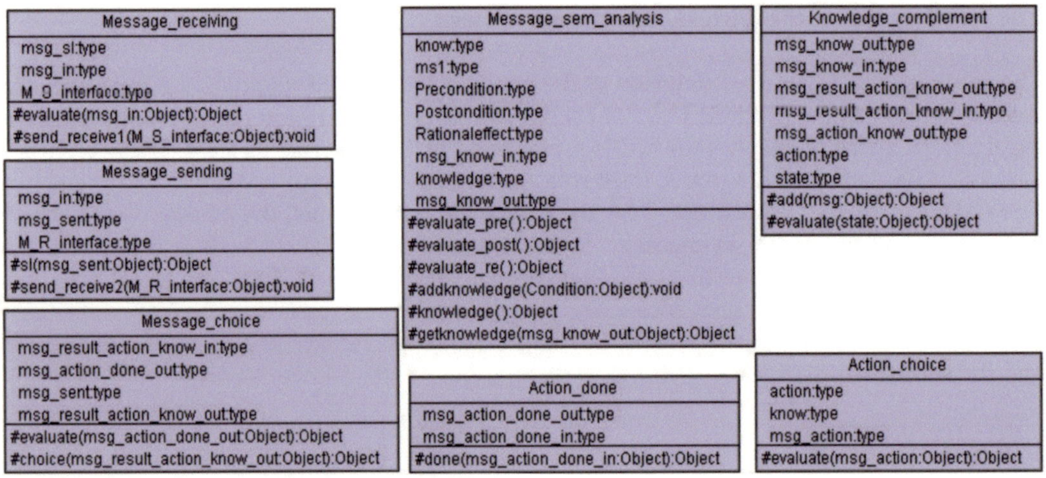

Fig. 6. Architecture diagram for each agent

On the figure 7, it is presented statecharts diagrams of the *send_receive1* and *send_receive2* conversations. Each conversation consists of two statecharts diagrams (Deloach et al., 2001), (Specification of UML): *send_receive1* or *send_receive2 Initiator* (the left statechars diagram of fig.7) and *send_receive1* or *send_receive2 Responder* (the right statechars diagram of fig.7).

Fig. 7. Statecharts diagrams of *send_receive1* or *send_receive2 Initiator* conversation (the left statecharts diagram) and *Responder* conversation (the right statecharts diagram).

The statecharts diagram of the *Message_receiving* component (fig.8) represents the actions executing during the receiving process.

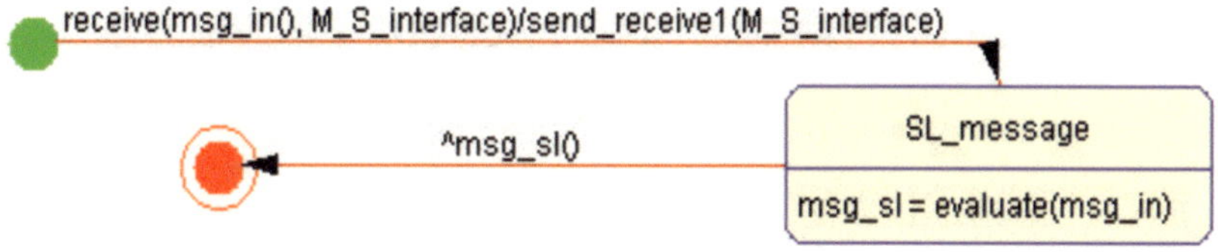

Fig. 8. Statecharts diagram of *Message_receiving* component

The statecharts diagram of the *Message_sending* component represents the actions executing during the sending process. The *send_receive1* and *send_receive2* conversations are used as the action of the transition of the statecharts diagram of the *Message_receiving* (fig.8) and *Message_sending* components (fig.9).
When the agent receives the *msg_in* message (fig.8), the *send_receive1 Responder* conversation is created. When the agent wants to send the message (fig.9), the *send_receive2* conversation *Initiator* is created.

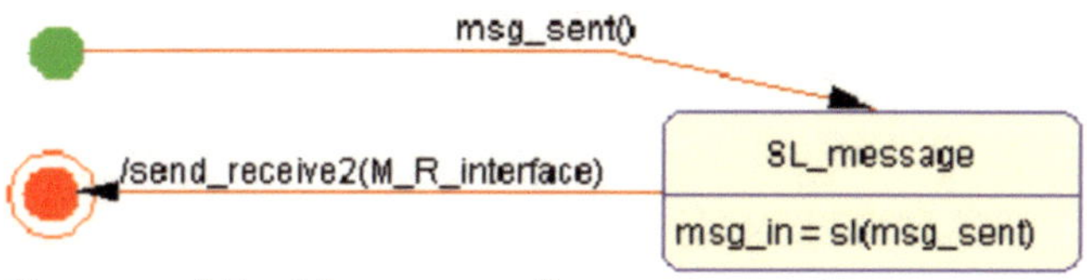

Fig. 9. Statecharts diagram of the *Message_sending* component

The statecharts diagram of the *Message_sem_analysis* component (fig.10) presents the process of interpreting of the received message.

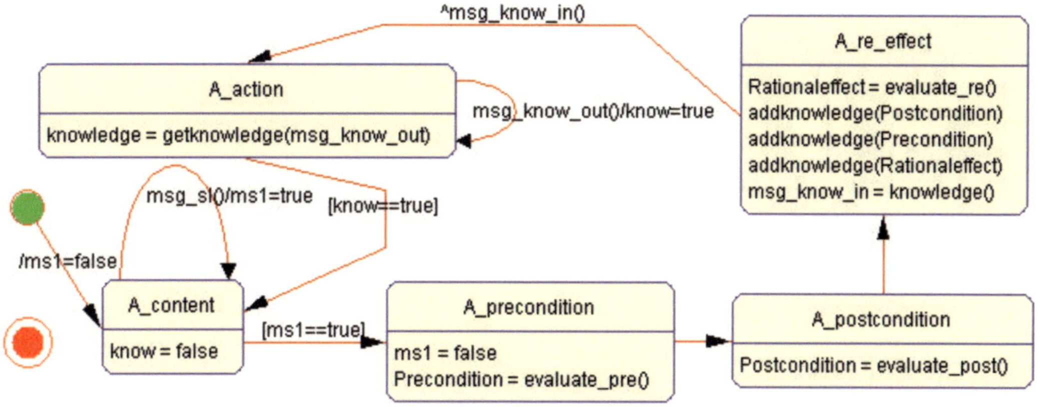

Fig. 10. Statecharts diagram of *Message_sem_analysis* component

The *Message_sem_analysis* component produces the data structure of the semantic representation handled by the mechanisms of gathering knowledge of the *Knowledge_complement* component and interpretation formulas of the following components: *Knowledge_complement, Action choice, Action_done, Message_choice.*

The data structure of the semantic representation defined by the following attributes represented by the SL formulas that represents the sense of the received message:
• a term that represents the agent of the action;
• the feasibility precondition FP, which represents a condition that must hold for an agent to be able to perform the action;
• the rational effect RE, which represents a state intended by the agent performing the action;
• the semantic behaviour, which implements its performance by the agent.

A communication act model of the request act is presented as follows (FIPA00037, 2000):
<i, request (j, a)>
FP: $\varphi1$
RE: $\varphi2$
where *i* is the agent of the act, *j* the recipient, *request* the name of the communication act, *a* stands for the semantic content or propositional content1, and $\varphi1$ and $\varphi2$ are propositions. This notational form is used for brevity, on the formal basis of ACL. The correspondence to the standard transport syntax (FIPA00070, 2000) adopted above is illustrated by a simple translation of the above example:

```
(request
 :sender i
 :receiver j
 :content
   a)
```

FP: FP (a) [i\j] ∧ Bi Agent (j, a) ∧ ¬ Bi Ij Done (a)
RE: Done (a)
where FP(a) [i\j] denotes the part of the FPs of a which are mental attitudes of i.

Example 1 (FIPA00037, 2000): Agent *i* requests *j* to reserve a ticket for *i*.

```
(request
:sender (agent-identifier :name i)
:receiver (set (agent-identifier :name j))
:content
"((action (agent-identifier :name j)
          (reserve-ticket LHR MUC 27-sept-97) ))"
:protocol fipa-request
:language fipa-sl
:reply-with order567)
```

The *Knowledge_complement* component (fig.11) stores facts believed by the agent and uncertain and intentional facts for this agent, according to the specific application domain. These facts are defined as SL semantic formulas. The *Knowledge_complement* component can only store and retrieve facts without actually interpreting their meaning. For instance, if an empty component is informed that (ac12345 100) there are 100 pounds in its ac12345 account, then agent *j* will correctly answer a Request-When message about (Done (reserve-ticket LHR MUC 27-sept-97, ac12345 100)) meaning about "Agent *i* tells agent *j* to notify it as soon as a reserve-ticket occurs and there are 100 pounds in its account just before that.".

However, it will not be able to answer a Request-Whenever message about (Done (reserve-ticket LHR MUC 27-sept-97, (> (price-ticket) 100))) meaning about "Agent *i* tells agent *j* to notify it whenever a reserve-ticket occurs and the price of tickets is lower than 100 before that.", because agent *j* cannot guess the semantic relationships between the ac12345 and the price-ticket predicates. This component includes the different operations towards the belief uncertainty and intention bases, which are needed by the interpretation process of other components.

These knowledge bases would have the following properties:

- storing the facts believed by the agent and uncertain and intentional facts for the agent (the *knowledge_message_out* state);
- providing a mechanism of listening changes in the contents of the knowledge bases by using formulas (the *knowledge_message_in* state);
- initializing the process of the internal action as the response of received message or as the initiation of the new task of the agent (the *knowledge_action* state).

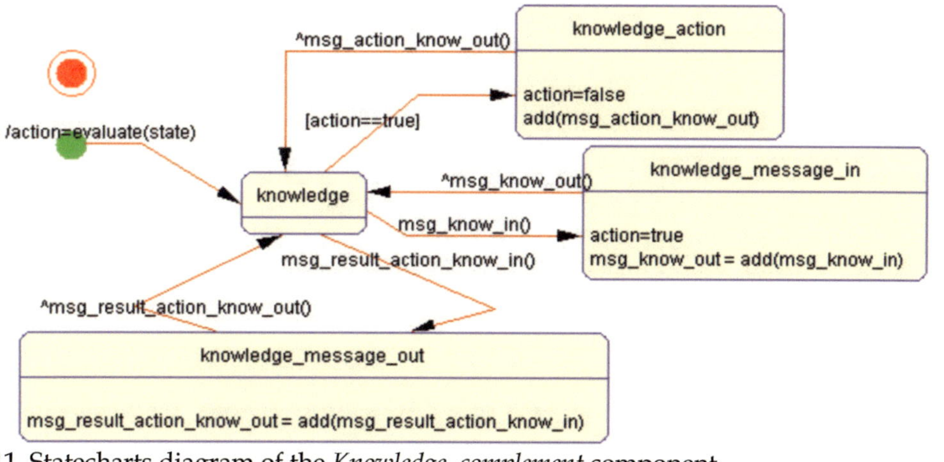

Fig. 11. Statecharts diagram of the *Knowledge_complement* component

The *Action_choice* component (fig.12) supports choices of the internal and the ontological actions.

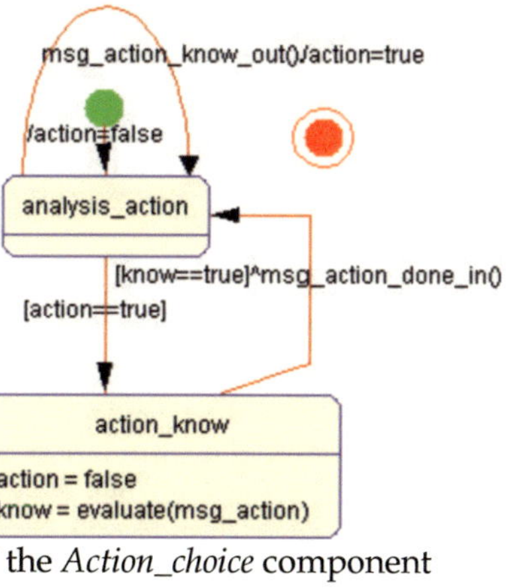

Fig. 12. Statecharts diagram of the *Action_choice* component

The ontological actions gather the actions related to the specific application. The internal actions gather the actions related to the response of the content of the received message or to a specific application. The action choice is based on the interpretation of the belief knowledge, uncertainty knowledge and intention knowledge and on the rules of FIPA- ACL language. The semantic interpretation formulas are related to the behaviours of the agent. They provide the interpretation mechanism of semantic SL formulas. Each semantic interpretation formula is applicable on a specific SL pattern. The use of semantic interpretation formulas is based on querying and updating the knowledged bases as the first result. The second result of the interpretation is based on adding to, or removing behaviours from the agent.

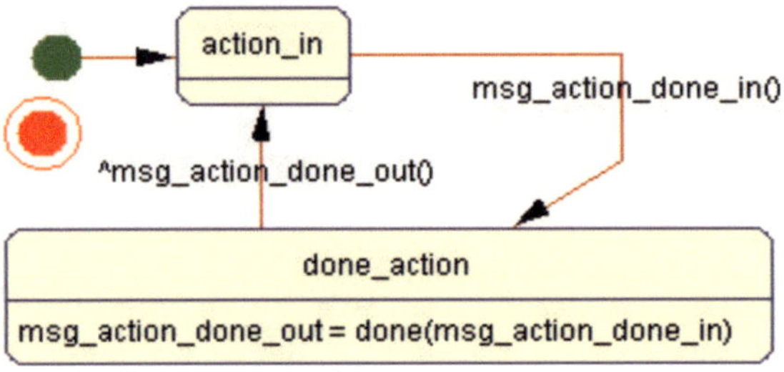

Fig. 13. Statecharts diagram of the *Action_done* component

The *Action_done* component (fig.13) executes the internal action choiced by the *Action_choice* component during the interpretation process. Then it delivers the results of this action to the *Message_choice* component. These results are defined in SL formulas.

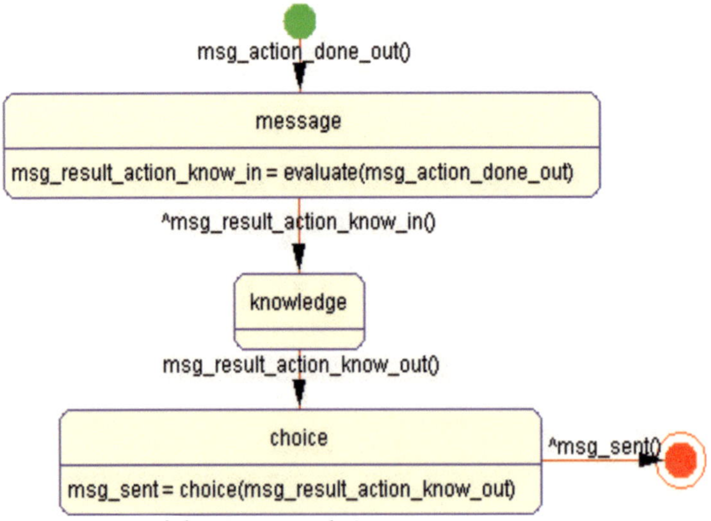

Fig. 14. Statecharts diagram of the *Message_choice* component

The *Message_choice* component (fig.14) choices the communicative act as the response for the received message or as the initialization of the interaction with other agents related to a specific application. The communicative actions gather all the FIPA Communicative Acts. The message choice is based on the semantic interpretation of the belief, uncertainty and intention knowledge databases and on the rules of FIPA- ACL language. The message

choice uses the semantic interpretation formulas that are based on querying and updating the knowledge bases as the first result. The second result of the interpretation is based on adding to, or removing behaviours from the agent.
The example 2 resumes the example 1: if the agent is able to do the action included in the content of the received message as the *request* communicative acts, it sends the *agree* message to the sender agent:

<i, agree (j, <i, request>, φ))> ≡ <i, inform (j, Ii Done (<i, act>, φ))>

FP: Bi α ∧ ¬ Bi (Bifj α ∨ Uifj α)

RE: Bj α

where: α = Ii Done(<i, act>, φ)

The example 3 continues the example 1: the agent *j* answers that it agrees to reserve a ticket for *i*, since there are sufficient funds in its account.

```
(agree
:sender (agent-identifier :name j)
:receiver (set (agent-identifier :name i))
:content
  "( (action (agent-identifier :name j)
    (reserve-ticket LHR MUC 27-sept-97))
    (sufficient- funds ac12345))"
:in-reply-to order567
:protocol fipa-request
:language fipa-sl)
```

The example 4 continues the example 2: if the agent is able to do the action defined in the content of the received message as the *request* communicative acts, it sends the *refuse* message to the sender agent: Agent *i* informs *j* that action act is not feasible, and further that, because of proposition *φ*, act has not been done and *i* has no intention to do act.

<i, refuse (j, <i, act>, φ)> ≡ <i, disconfirm (j, Feasible(<i, act>))>;

<i, inform (j, φ ∧ ¬ Done (<i, act>) ∧ ¬ Ii Done (<i, act>))>

FP: Bi ¬ Feasible (<i, act>) ∧ Bi (Bj Feasible (<i, act>) ∨
          Uj Feasible (<i, act>)) ∧ Bi α ∧ ¬ Bi (Bifj α ∨ Uifj α)

RE: Bj ¬ Feasible (<i, act>) ∧ Bj α

where: α = φ ∧ ¬ Done (<i, act>) ∧ ¬ Ii Done (<i, act>)

Example 5 continues the example 3: Agent *j* answers that it refuses to reserve a ticket for *i*, since there are insufficient funds in its account.

```
(refuse
:sender (agent-identifier :name j)
:receiver (set (agent-identifier :name i))
:content
"((action (agent-identifier :name j)
  (reserve-ticket LHR MUC 27-sept-97))
  (insufficient- funds ac12345))"
:in-reply-to order567
:protocol fipa-request
:language fipa-sl)
```

The process of semantic interpretation enables to simplify adapting their protocols to the actual meaning of the exchanged messages.

3. Communication protocols

It is possible to create protocol for exchanging most appropriate messages between agents. These messages represent the role of the agent in community of agents taking part in conversations. The table 1 presents the properties of communicative acts.

Communitive act	Information passing	Requesting information	Negotiation	Action performing	Error handling
accept-proposal			+		
agree, cancel				+	
cfp			+		
confirm, disconfirm	+				
failure, not-understood					+
inform, inform-if (macro act), inform-ref (macro act)	+				
propose			+		
query-if ,query-ref		+			
refuse				+	
reject-proposal			+		
request, request-when, request-whenever				+	
subscribe		+			

Table 1. Communicative acts (Specification of FIPA, 2000)

3.1. Dependency between messages

This section presents the list of communicative acts with a concise description (tab.2). The *cancel, request, request-when, request-whenever* messages can be sent by the agent fulfilling superior role. This agent demands the execution action of the subordinate agent.

If there is the client-server relationship between agents, *subscribe, cfp, accept-proposal, query-if, query-ref* messages are sent by client agent concerned with making of cooperation with recipient agent. The recipient agent executes the task for sender agent. The client agent sends the *reject-proposal* message if it is not interested in services of the recipient agent. This is the response of the received *propose* message, that is sent by the recipient agent.

The *inform, inform-if(macro act), inform-ref (macro act)* messages are sent by agent that remains in neutral relationship with other agents. If sender assums, that recipient agent cannot believe to received information, then this receiver sends the *confirm* message to confirm acceptance of received information. If however, the sender assums that the recipient agent believes to received information, the receiver agent sends the *disconfirm* message, if it rejects this information. Subordinate or servicer agent can send the *agree* message as the answer to the *request* or the *subscribe* message from the superior or client agent. The *refuse* message can be sent by the subordinate or the client as the answer of the *request, subscribe* or *cfp* message from the superior or the client agent, if it declines execution of the action. The *failure* message is sent by the subordinate agent, which cannot execute the action. In opposite case, if executable task will end progress, the subordinate agent sends the *inform* message as the result to the superior agent. Independently on the role, the each agent can send the *not-understood* message if it not understand the message that other agent has just sent to it.

Communicative acts	Description
accept proposal	The action of accepting a previously submitted proposal to perform an action.
agree	The action of agreeing to perform some action, possibly in the future.
cancel	The action of one agent informing another agent that the first agent no longer has the intention that the second agent performs some action.
cfp - call for proposal	The action of calling for proposals to perform a given action.
confirm	The sender informs the receiver that a given proposition is true, where the receiver is known to be uncertain about the proposition.
disconfirm	The sender informs the receiver that a given proposition is false, where the receiver is known to believe, or believe it likely that, the proposition is true.
failure	The action of telling the another agent that an action was attempted but the attempt failed.
inform	The sender informs the receiver that a given proposition is true.
inform if (macro act)	A macro action for the agent of the action to inform the recipient whether or not a proposition is true.
inform ref (macro act)	A macro action for sender to inform the receiver the object which corresponds to a descriptor, for example, a name.
not understood	The sender of the act (for example, i) informs the receiver (for example, j) that it perceived that j performed some action, but that i did not understand what j just did. A particular common case is that i tells j that i did not understand the message that j has just sent to i.
propose	The action of submitting a proposal to perform a certain action, given certain preconditions.
query if	The action of asking another agent whether or not a given proposition is true.
query ref	The action of asking another agent for the object referred to by a referential expression.
refuse	The action of refusing to perform a given action, and explaining the reason for the refusal.
reject proposal	The action of rejecting a proposal to perform some action during a negotiation.
request	The sender requests the receiver to perform some action. One important class of uses of the request act is to request the receiver to perform another communicative act.
request when	The sender wants the receiver to perform some action when some given proposition becomes true.
request whenever	The sender wants the receiver to perform some action as soon as some proposition becomes true and thereafter each time the proposition becomes true again.
subscribe	The act of requesting a persistent intention to notify the sender of the value of a reference, and to notify again whenever the object identified by the reference changes.

Table 2. Characteristics of messages of ACL language (FIPA00037, 2000)

Such dependencies between messages allow designing effective protocols of communications, without redundancy in sent message. It is the first way of improve performance of multiagent systems. The limitation number of messages is the second way to correct performance of protocols.

3.2. Performance evaluation of interaction protocols

Applications working in distributed environment use the distributed data and the distributed clients. Clients send a lot of messages during realizing operations by using e-mail, web services, communicators programs etc. Therefore these applications generate the large network traffic lowering performance of the internet applications.

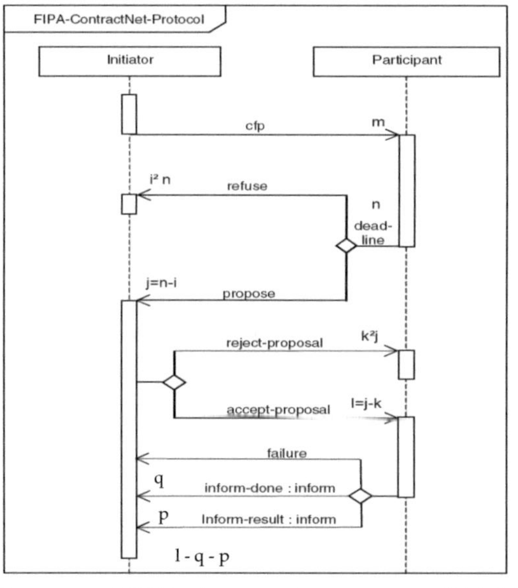

Fig. 15. The interaction diagram of *FIPA-Contract-Net* protocol (FIPA00029, 2002)

In section 2, it is introduced agents, which adapt their communicative acts (FIPA00037, 2000) to actual state of knowledge databases, main goal of application and character of interactions between agents. These interactions have the dynamic character of protocols based on negotiations, subscriptions, auctions. This sending proper sequence of messages is related to the state of realized task. As a proof that the dynamic protocols can limit the network traffic, it is presented two protocols as the products of adapting the communicative acts. These protocols are *FIPA-Contract-Net* (fig.15) (FIPA00029, 2002) and user defined protocol as the *Order-Request-NET* (fig.16) based on *FIPA-Request-Net* protocol (FIPA00026, 2002). The protocols are defined by use interaction diagram (FIPA00025, 2000), (Odell et al., 2001). If the choices of the sequences of messages as the protocol are proper, an agent can reduce the network traffic by sending messages only to these agents who are be able to collaborate over executing the task.

The *FIPA-Contract-Net* protocol (FIPA00029, 2002) is a small modification of the original protocol by added the reject and accepts communicative acts. The *initiator* agent fulfils the role of manager in this protocol. The *initiator* sends a *call for proposals* act (*cfp*) to m agents.

These messages are received by *n participants* of the protocol. They send the *proposal* message which specifies the task, as well as any conditions the *initiator* is placing upon the execution of the task or *refuse* message if they decline the proposal for the *initiator*. The *initiator* receives *i* the *refuse* messages and *j=n-i* the *proposal* acts. The *participant* finishes protocol if it sends the *refuse* message. Therefore *2i* messages generate the needlessly network traffic.
The manager evaluates *j* proposals according to certain function and accepts *j-k* (*n-i-k*) proposals. This estimate of proposal messages is expressed behind assistance of price, time etc. The *initiator* sends *j-k accept-propose* messages to accepted *participant* and *k reject-proposal* messages to remaining *participants*. Therefore *3k* messages generate the needlessly network traffic.
At last the accepted *participants* send the result of the task by sending together *n-i-k-q inform-result* and *inform-done* messages. If *participant* cannot finish the task, it sends a *failure* message to the manager (*initiator*) - the *initiator* receives *q* failure messages. Therefore *4q* messages generate the needlessly network traffic. At last, it can be *2i+3k+4q* messages generating the needlessly network traffic.

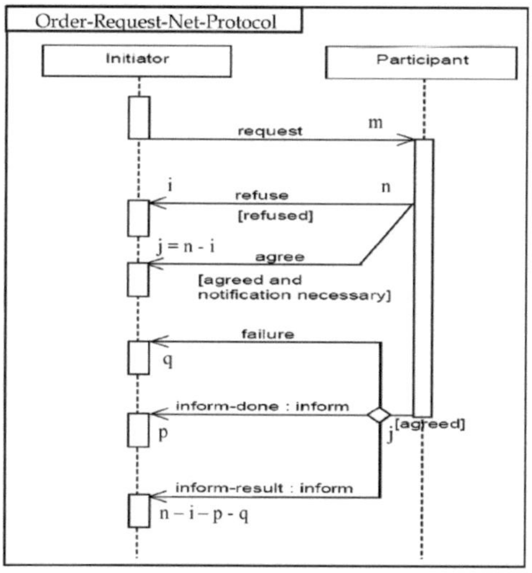

Fig. 16. The interaction diagram of user defined *Order-Request-Net* protocol (FIPA00026, 2002)

The *Order-Request-NET* protocol is based on the *FIPA-Request-Net* protocol (fig.16). It includes the informatiom about the multiplicity of participants. The *initiator* agent fulfils the role of the superior in this protocol. It sends *m request* messages with information about necessity of performing some action. These messages are received by *n participants* as subordinates. They send *agree* messages if they can perform the request action or *refuse* messages if they decline the request for the *initiator*. The *initiator* receives *i refuse* messages and *n-i agree* messages. Therefore *2i* messages generate the needlessly network traffic.
At last *participants* send the result of the task by sending together *n-i-q inform-result* and *inform-done* messages. If the *participant* cannot finish the task, it sends a *failure* message to the manager (*initiator*) - the *initiator* receives *q* failure messages. Therefore *3q* messages generate the needlessly network traffic. At last, it can be *2i+3q* messages generating the needlessly network traffic.

Meaning of messages and their possibility of occurrence during interactions allow to value number of messages in extreme and average cases (Smith, 1990), (Smith & Lloyd, 2002). It assumes that each message has the same size or the same transmission *t* time by network. Average duration transmission of all messages is evaluated by using the probability *p* of occurance messages in both protocols.
The *cfp* messages of the *FIPA-Contract-Net* protocol (tab.3) reach participants with the probability *p1*. The *refuse* message is sent with the probability *p2* and the *propose* message with *1-p2* probability. The *acept-proposal* message is sent with propability *p3* and the *reject-proposal* message with the probability *1-p3*. At last the *failure* message is sent with the probability *p4*, the *inform-done* message with the probability *p5* and the *inform-result* message with probability *1-p4-p5*. The average duration *t1* of *FIPA-Contract-Net* protocol is equal

$$t1=tm(1 + p1(3-2p2-p3+p2p3)) \quad (1)$$

however, maximum time is *4tm* and it is minimal equal with *tm*.
The *Loss1* avarage of duration of messages of *FIPA-Contract-Net* protocol which are the types of *failure, refuse* and *reject-proposal* messages etc. is equal

$$Loss1=tm\ p1(2p2+3(1-p2)p4) \quad (2)$$

estimation of number of messages	The number of messages								
	cfp	refuse	propose	reject-proposal	accept-proposal	failure	inform-done	inform-result	total
All messages	m	i	n - i	k	n – i - k	q	p	n–i–k– q-p	m + 3n – 2i - k
Average t1 t=1	m	m p1 p2	m p1 (1-p2)	m p1 (1-p2) p3	m p1 (1-p2) (1-p3)	m p1 (1-p2) (1-p3) p4	m p1 (1-p2) (1-p3) p5	m p1 (1-p2) (1-p3) (1–p4-p5)	m (1 + p1 (3-2p2-p3 +p2p3))
Maximum p1=1 (m=n) p2=0 (i=0) p3=0 (k=0) p4=0 (q=0)	m	0	m	0	m	0	mp5	m(1-p5)	4m
Minimum p1=0 (n=0)	m	0	0	0	0	0	0	0	m
Loss1, t=1		2m p1 p2		3m p1 (1-p2) p3		4m p1 (1-p2) (1-p3) p4			m p1 (2p2+(1-p2) (3p3+ 4p4(1-p3)))

Table 3. Performance parameters of *FIPA-Contract-Net* protocol

The *request* message of the *Order-Request-Net* protocol (tab.4) reaches participants with the probability *p1*. The *refuse* message is sent with the probability *p2* and the *agree* message with the probability *1-p2*. At last the *failure* message is sent with the probability *p4*, the *inform-done* message with the probability *p5* and the *inform-result* message with probability *1-p4-p5* however. Average duration of protocol is equal

$$t2=tm(1 + p1(2-p2)) \quad (3)$$

however, maximum time is *3tm* and it is minimal equal with *tm*.
The avarage of duration of messages *Loss1* of the *Order-Request-Net* protocol which are the types of *failure* and *refuse* messages etc. is equal

$$Loss2= m\, p1(2p2+3(1-p2)p4) \quad (4)$$

The metric of lost messages *Lost1*, which excludes some agents from executing the task realizing over the *FIPA-Contract-Net* protocol is equal

$$Lost1=Loss1/t1 \quad (5)$$

The metric of lost messages *Lost2*, which excludes some agents from executing the task realizing over the *Order-Request-Net* protocol is equal

$$Lost2=Loss2/t2 \quad (6)$$

Measure of messages	The number of messages						
	request	refuse	agree	failure	inform-done	inform-result	total
All messages	m	i	n - i	q	p	n – i - q - p	m + 2n – i
Average t2 t=1	m	m p1 p2	m p1 (1-p2)	m p1 (1-p2) p4	m p1 (1-p2) p5	m p1 (1-p2) (1-p4-p5)	m (1 + p1(2- p2))
Maximum p1=1 (m=n) p2=0 (i=0) p4=0 (q=0)	m	0	m	0	mp5	m(1-p5)	3m
Minimum p1=0 (n=0)	m	0	0	0	0	0	m
Loss2, t=1		2m p1 p2		3m p1 (1-p2) p4			m p1 (2p2+3(1-p2)p4)

Table 4. Performance parameters of *Order-Request-Net* protocol

The table 5 presents the results of simulation experiments for estimation of the duration of both protocols.

Protocol	Evalution of transmission time	Duration			
		m=10	m=100	m=1000	m=10000
FIPA-Contract-Net	value of expression (1) (t=1)	t1=18.76	t1=187.67	t1=1876.60	t1=18761.15
	Minimum: m	10	100	1000	10000
	Maximum: 4m	40	400	4000	40000
	Loss1, value of expression (3)	12.26	112.59	1127.43	11264.69
	Lost1, value of expression (5)	0.6536	0.5999	0.6008	0.6004
Order-Request-Net	value of expression (2) (t=1)	t2=17.50	t2=175.14	t2=1751.38	t2=17510.79
	Minimum: m	10	100	1000	10000
	Maksimum: 3m	30	300	3000	30000
	Loss2, value of expression (4)	9.53	87.45	877.54	8756.15□
	Lost2= value of expression (6)	0.5444	0.4993	0.5011	0.5000

Table 5. Results of performance experiments of *FIPA-Contract-Net* protocol and user defined protocol as the *Order-Request-NET* protocol

The number of messages sending over the protocols is calculated by using the generator of uniform distribution values. The experiment relied on 100000 repetition of measurements for number of 10, 100, 1000, 10000 agents. The time of transmission (*t*) of the one message is equal with the 1 time unit. The table 5 includes values of measurements of average values and values of maximum and minimum. Results of performance experiments in the table 5 and on the figure 17 are presented the influence of number of agents and their behaviour on performance of the multiagent system. For example, if the interpreting mechanism detects the relationship superior-subordinate, the *Order-Request-Net* protocol is better than *FIPA-Contract-Net* because of smaller generated network traffic. If the interpreting mechanism enables the selection of proper agents which are capable of executing actions of the task, the network traffic will be smaller because the number of the *refuse, failure and reject* messages can be reduced.

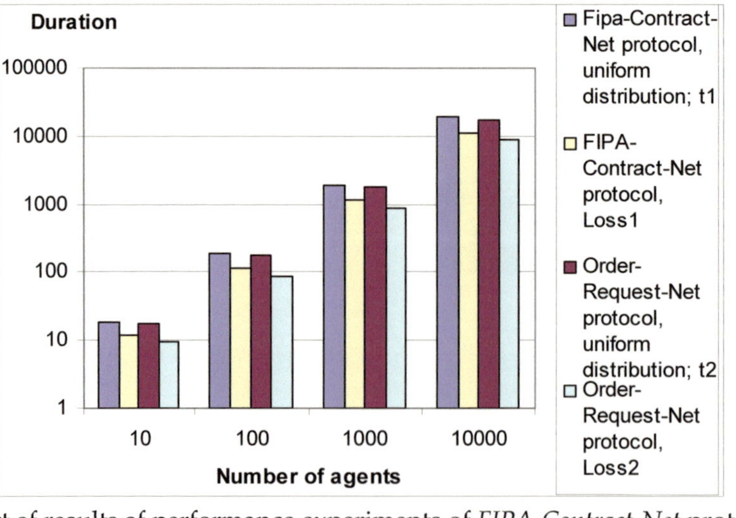

Fig. 17. The chart of results of performance experiments of *FIPA-Contract-Net* protocol and user defined protocol as the *Order-Request-NET* protocol

4. Conclusion

In the paper it is presented the design of multiagent system, which includes agents with special abilities. They are able to interpret the communicative acts and they can adapt to actual state of executing task. This is the way to choice the proper sequence of messages for example the *Order-Reqest-Net* protocol instead of the *FIPA-Contract-Net protocol*.
The other ability of an agent is reduction of the *refuse, failure, and reject* etc. messages by interpreting belief, uncertainty and intention knowledge databases. In the paper agent reduces the messages with propabilites generated from uniform distribution. In the future, it can complete the mechanism of interpreting messages with learning process of behaviours of agents collaborating over the tasks. These are reasons of reduction the network traffic and improving the performance of multiagent systems.
Results of performance experiments authenticate the influence of number of exchanging messages between agents and agent's abilities on performance of the multiagent system. Therefore, if the interpreting mechanism can detect properly the relationship between agent and their abilities, the generated network traffic can become smaller. The first reason is the possibility of choice of the protocol with smaller duration, for example the *Order-Reqest-Net* protocol instead of the *FIPA-Contract-Net protocol*. The second reason is the possibility of reduction the *refuse, failure, and reject* etc. messages by the selection of proper agents which are capable of executing action of the task.

5. References

Babczyński, T.; Kruczkiewicz, Z.; Magott, J. (2004). Performance Analysis of Multiagent Industrial System, *Proceedings of 8th International Workshop, CIA 2004, Cooperative Information Agents VIII*, LNAI 3191, pp. 242-256, ISBN-13 978-3-540-29046-9, Erfurth, Germany, September, 2005, Lecture Notes in Computer Science/Lecture Notes in Artificial Intelligence, Springer-Verlag, Berlin Heidelberg New York

Babczyński, T.; Kruczkiewicz, Z.; Magott, J. (2005). Performance Comparison of Multi-agent Systems, *Proceedings of 4th Central and Eastern European Conference on Multi-Agent Systems, CEEMAS 2005, Multi-Agent Systems and Applications IV*, LNAI 3690, pp. 612-615, ISBN 3-540-23170-6, Budapest, Hungary, September, 2005, Lecture Notes in Computer Science/Lecture Notes in Artificial Intelligence, Springer-Verlag, Berlin Heidelberg New York

Bennett, A. J.; Field, A. J.; Woodside, C. M. (2004). Experimental evaluation of the UML Profile for Schedulability, Performance, and Time, In: *The Unified Modelling Language*, Baar, T. et al., eds, Lecture Notes in Computer Science, pp. 143-157, Vol. 3273, Springer, ISBN 978-3-540-23307-7, Berlin Heidelberg

Camacho, D.; Aler, R.; Castro, C.; Molina, J. M. (2002). Performance evaluation of ZEUS, JADE, and SkeletonAgent frameworks, *Proceedings of the 2002 IEEE Systems, Man, and Cybernetics Conference*, on page(s): 6 pp., ISBN: 0-7803-7437-1, October 2002

Deloach, S.A.; Wood, M.F.; Sparkman, C.H. (2001), Multiagents systems engineering, *International Journal of Software Engineering and Knownledge Engineering*, Vol 11, No.3 June 2001, pp. 231-258, World Scientific Publishing Company

Dikaiakos, M.; Kyriakou, M.; Samaras, G. (2001). Performance evaluation of mobile-agent middleware: A hierachical approach, *Proceedings of the 5th IEEE International Conference on Mobile Agents*, Picco, J.P. (ed.), Lecture Notes in Computer Science series, pp. 244-259, ISBN 978-3-540-42952-4, Springer, December 2001, Berlin Heidelberg

FIPA00008 (2000), FIPA SL Content Language Specification. Foundation for Intelligent Physical Agents, http://www.fipa.org/specs/fipa00008/

FIPA00025 (2000), FIPA Interaction Protocol Library Specification. Foundation for Intelligent Physical Agents, http://www.fipa.org/specs/fipa00025/

FIPA00026 (2002), FIPA Request Interaction Protocol Specification. Foundation for Intelligent Physical Agents

FIPA00029 (2002), FIPA Contract Net Interaction Protocol Specification. Foundation for Intelligent Physical Agents

FIPA00037 (2000), FIPA Communicative Act Library Specification. Foundation for Intelligent Physical Agents, http://www.fipa.org/specs/fipa00037/

FIPA00070 (2000), FIPA ACL Message Representation in String. Foundation for Intelligent Physical Agents, http://www.fipa.org/specs/fipa00070/

http://jade.cselt.it/doc/tutorials/SemanticsProgrammerGuide.pdf

Odell, J.; Parunak, V.D.H.; Bauer, B. (2001). Representing Agent Interaction Protocols in UML, In: *Agent-Oriented Software Engineering*, Ciancarini, P. and Wooldridge, M., Eds., pp. 121-140, Springer - Verlag, ISBN 3-540-41594-7, New York

Pautret V. (2005-2006). Jade Semantics Add-on Programmer's guide, *Research & Development*, Version: 1.0, France Telecom,

Smith, C.U. (1990). *Performance Engineering of Software Systems*, Addison – Wesley, ISBN 0-201-53769-9, United States of America

Smith, C.U.; Lloyd G.W. (2002). *Performance Solutions, A Practical Guide to Creating Responsive, Scalable Software*, Addison - Wesley, ISBN 0-201-72229-1, Canada

Specification of FIPA, http://www.fipa.org/specs/

Specification of JADE, http://sharon.cselt.it/projects/jade/doc/

Specification of UML, http://www.uml.org/

Wooldridge, M.; Rao, A. (Eds.) (1999). *Foundations of Rational Agency*, Kluwer Academic Publishers, ISBN 0-7923-5601-2, The Netherlands

Yamamoto, G.; Nakamura, Y. (1999). Architecture and performance evaluation of a massive multi-agent system, *Proceedings of the third annual conference on Autonomous Agents*, pp. 319-325, ISBN 1-58113-066-X, Seattle, 1999, ACM, New York, NY, USA

Measurement of Production Efficiency in Semiconductor Assembly House: Approach of Data Envelopment Analysis

[1]Chien-wen Shen, [2]Ming-Jen Cheng and [3]Ming-Chia Chi
[1]*Department of Business Administration, National Central University, 300 Jhongda Road, Jhongli City, Taoyuan County 32001, Taiwan*
[2]*Graduate Institute of Management, National Kaohsiung First University of Science & Technology, 1 University Road Yenchao, Kaohsiung County 824, Taiwan*
[3]*Advanced Semiconductor Engineering Inc., Nantze Export Processing Zone Kaohsiung City, Taiwan*

Abstract

Because semiconductor assembly plants generally apply individual indicators to monitor manufacturing processes, this research proposes the approach of data envelopment analysis (DEA) to evaluate production performance from the perspective of overall efficiency. Our DEA models are composed of 3 input variables (average employee number, average labor hours, and cost of goods sold) and 4 output items (production output, average overall equipment effectiveness, production cycle time, and production ratio). To test the practicability of proposed models, one semiconductor assembly company was selected to investigate the relative efficiency of its 10 manufacturing plants. DEA-based Malmquist productivity index was also applied to describe the productivity change over time. Findings show that the main cause of technology inefficiency for the sample company is its inappropriate resource allocation in the aspect of operation efficiency. From the viewpoint of efficiency variation, the productivity of six relatively efficient plants was increasing during 2 years of observations while the productivity of the other four plants was decreasing at the same period. Through the analysis of slack variable and sensitivity analysis, number of employees in the relatively inefficient manufacturing plants may cause additional hidden costs and wastes. Our analysis results not only demonstrate the applicability of DEA approach for the measurement of production efficiency in semiconductor assembly industry but also provide this industry with methodology to indentify where to improve operational performance.

Keywords: *Efficiency Assessment, Data Envelopment Analysis, Malmquist Analysis*

1. Introduction

As the semiconductor assembly industry is capital-intensive, operations management becomes one of the important issues for its business effectiveness. Especially under the pressure of limited profit margin and customer requirements, plants have to enhance their operating efficiency so as to improve the competitive advantage. Currently, the manufacturing process of semiconductor assembly plant faces bottlenecks of die bond, wire bond and potting sites. For instance, the outputs of most die bonding machines are contricted by their actuation modes of absorption and desorption. Moreover, wire bonding machine is constricted by the number and arc of wire bond, while potting machine is restrained by the time of potting. In terms of cost, although employees account for 15%-20% of total expenditure, machines of die bond, wire bond and potting sites are still the largest investments for the semiconductor assembly house. Accordingly, management tends to focus on enhancing man-machine ratio and simplifing SOP to reduce human cost and improve productivity. In addition, various performance indexes are also applied routinely to monitor operational efficiency and quality for further improvement. However, the performance indexes adopted by the semiconductor manufacturing factories usually consider single angle like machine breakdown or yield rate. Although this kind of method is easy to calculate and understand, index approach has limitations because it's unable to identify the causes of inefficiency and to reflect the actual relative efficiency among plants. Therefore, evaluation methods that can consider both the inputs and outputs of manufacturing plants could provide more reliable findings for management to adjust their production operations.

In order to bridge the gap between practical and theoretical issues in the semiconductor manufacturing industry, this paper considered Data Envelopment Analysis (DEA) method for performance assessment. This approach not only takes into account input-output variables but also proves to be useful for efficiency analysis. Without specifying the production functions in advance, we are also able to trace the sources of inefficiency for every evaluated plant. Together with DEA-based Malmquist productivity measurement, productivity rate of growth for each plant can be further analyzed to understand their progress or regression during a specific period. Hence, the main purposes of this study include the analysis of operational performance and changes for the semiconductor assembly house, and the improvement solutions for inefficient plants assessed. In the following discussion, we start with the brief review of past research regarding the efficiency assessment in the electronics industry. Then section 3 describes the DEA methodology used in this study. To validate the applicability of our proposed approach, one semiconductor assembly company was selected to investigate the relative efficiency of its 10 manufacturing plants. Findings of this case study are discussed in section 4. Finally, we conclude our research in the final section.

2. Efficiency Assessment of Electronics Industry

In the electronic manufacturing industry, common methods of efficiency assessment include machine utilization rate, regression analysis, and DEA. Leachman and Hodges (1996) used regression analysis to study 16 wafer factories, and obtained the production cycle and yield rate for each product line. Thore et al. (1996) applied DEA method to evaluate the cycle time efficiency of computer manufacturing industry in the U.S., so as to find out how to improve machine's production rate and to maintain efficiency. Shang and Sueyoshi (1995) analyzed the efficiency of flexible production systems, and found that DEA method could be applied to evaluate different manufacturing systems. Their study also compares the efficiency of different production lines and gives managers the suggestions for improvements. Beeg (2004) used crash time and average repair time to establish the capability indicators of machine and personnel. Besides, Beeg took into considerations the variables of production amount, overall equipment efficiency (OEE), and production ratio as the items of outputs for DEA models. Ertray and Ruan (2004) employed DEA method to evaluate workers' efficiency in mobile manufacturing plants. Work hours and staff allocation are listed as the efficiency assessment of inputs. Hosseinzadeh and Ghasemi (2007) investigated the efficiency and productivity in telecommunication companies through DEA models and Malmquist productivity index. Pan et al. (2008) explored the managerial and productive technical efficiencies of Taiwan's IC design industry. They also adopted DEA models and DEA-based Malmquist method to examine the performance of 72 companies from 2003 to 2005.

In the semiconductor industry, OEE is often employed to measure productivity (SEMI, 1999). Other common indicators include: availability efficiency, efficiency ratio, operating efficiency, and quality efficiency (Nakajima, 1988; Leachman, 1995; Konopka, 1996). Availability efficiency is defined by the difference between total production time and downtime over total production time. Meanwhile, efficiency ratio is the ratio of ideal cycle time to actual cycle time. Operating efficiency is the ratio of total production time to facility operating time. Accordingly, we can rank performance by the cross product of efficiency ratio and operating ratio. Additionally, quality efficiency is defined by the difference between total production volume and total returns over total production volume. Hence, each machine can use one of the above indicators to evaluate their respective performance. Integrated performance index can be also computed by the average performance of all machines. Furthermore, Thomas (2000) applied DEA approach to measure efficiency of semiconductor manufacturing operations. Input variables in DEA models include mean time between failures, scrap/1000 wafer moves, cycle time, and downtime. Meanwhile, wafer moves, OEE, activity ratio (actual moves/planned moves) are output variables. Liu and Wang (2007) also employed DEA models to assess the Malmquist productivity of semiconductor packaging and testing firms in Taiwan. Their Malmquist productivity considers 3 major measurements, which are technical change, frontier forward shift, and frontier backward shift of a company over two consecutive periods. From the above review of past studies, DEA has been proved to be a successful evaluation approach for efficiency performance in the semiconductor industry. Hence, this study would like to further investigate how to apply the DEA method to measure the production efficiency and efficiency change in the semiconductor assembly industry.

3. Methodology

3.1 Decision Making Unit (DMU)

Decision making unit is any entity that is to be assessed by its abilities to convert inputs into outputs (Charnes et al., 1978). According to Golany and Roll's (1989) definition, DMUs must be a group of homogeneous units, but there should be some differences between them.

Thus, this study took 10 independent factories (denote Pi, $i = 1,...,10$) of a certain semiconductor assembly company in Taiwan as the target of assessment. Monthly data of activities were retrieved from the manufacturing execution system during the period of 2005/01-2006/12. These 10 factories generally had common manufacturing machines. For example, the same type of wire bonder machines can produce lead frame and BGA products. Factories could support each other and do cross feeding. P1, P2, P3, P4, P5 and P6 factories mainly manufactured consumptive IC products, the general logic and IC control lead-frame products, such as PDIP, PLCC, QFP, and TQFP; while P7, P8, P9 and P10 factories mainly manufactured graphics chip, CPU, LCD driver chip and other mid and high-end BGA products, such as BGA, TFBGA, QFN, and FBGA.

3.2 Inputs and Outputs

To select the input variables and output variables for the DEA models used in this study, factors that affect overall production processes, costs, operating time, product quality, and machine efficiency were under our considerations. Based on the results of past research and on-site investigation of engineers, three input variables were chosen and are summarized as follows:

(1) Average employee number: the average number of employees per month;
(2) Average labor hour: the average work hours per month;
(3) Average cost of goods sold: the average cost of goods sold divided by the net sales per month.

All of the input data were collected from the personnel database of target manufacturer for each plant.

Besides, the output variables of DEA models are defined as follows:

(1) Production output: the actual production of each factory per month;
(2) Average OEE: OEE = Availability Ratio x Performance Ratio x Quality Ratio, where availability ratio is the share of the actual production time and the planned production time, performance ratio is the loss of production due to under-utilization of the machinery, quality ratio is the amount of the production that has to be discharged or scrapped;
(3) Production cycle time: time it takes for production personnel to make the product available for shipment to the customer;
(4) Production ratio: the actual delivery of each factory per month divided by the planed delivery.

All of the output observations were collected from the manufacturing execution system of each plant.

3.3 Research Models

The basic DEA model of efficiency analysis is composed of the inputs and outputs of DMUs. This approach tends to reduce the multiple-output/multiple-input situation to a single 'virtual' output and 'virtual' input. The ratio of single output to single input for a particular DMU, which is a function of the multipliers, forms the objective function for optimization. Because DEA approach is empirically-oriented and has no a priori assumptions like other approaches, it has been applied to a number of studies involving efficient frontier estimation. To encounter different problem issues, there is a variety of alternate DEA models to evaluating performance. The CCR model with constant returns to scale (Charnes et al., 1978) and the BCC model with variable returns to scale (Banker et al., 1984) were applied in this study to evaluate efficiency performance among manufacturing plants of semiconductor assembly house. Suppose we have *m* different inputs and *s* outputs for *n* DMUs. The CCR model can be described by

$$\begin{aligned} & Min\ h_k = \theta - \varepsilon\left(\sum_{i=1}^{m} s_i^- + \sum_{r=1}^{s} s_r^+\right) \\ & s.t. \\ & \sum_{j=1}^{n} \lambda_j X_{ij} - \theta X_{ik} + s_i^- = 0 \\ & \sum_{j=1}^{n} \lambda_j Y_{rj} - s_r^+ = Y_{rk} \\ & X_{ik} = \theta X_{ik} - s_i^- \\ & Y_{rk} = Y_{rk} + s_r^+ \\ & \forall \lambda_j, s_i^-, s_r^+ \geq 0; j = 1,\ldots,n; i = 1,\ldots,m; r = 1,\ldots,s; \theta \in R \end{aligned} \tag{1}$$

The mathematical meaning of Eq. (1) is to get the minimum value of h_k in restriction conditions, where Y_{rj} is *r*-th output for plant *j*, X_{ij} is *i*-th input for plant *j*, s_i^- is slack variable, and s_r^+ is surplus variable. The optimal solution of θ must be positive and yield an efficiency score for a specific DMU. The necessary and sufficient condition of every DMU with relative efficiency is $\theta = 1$ and $s_i^- = s_r^+ = 0$. However, CCR model is assumed to be the linear programming model with constant returns to scale, which is not necessarily in line with the actual situation of industry. Therefore, Banker et al. (1984) replaced with variable returns to scale, that is, $\Sigma\lambda=1$ was added into the above formula and get the BCC model in Eq. (2):

$$\begin{aligned} & Min\ h_k = \theta - \varepsilon\left(\sum_{i=1}^{m} s_i^- + \sum_{r=1}^{s} s_r^+\right) \\ & s.t. \\ & \sum_{j=1}^{n} \lambda_j X_{ij} - \theta X_{ik} + s_i^- = 0 \\ & \sum_{j=1}^{n} \lambda_j Y_{rj} - s_r^+ = Y_{rk} \\ & \sum_{j=1}^{n} \lambda_j = 1 \\ & X_{ik} = \theta X_{ik} - s_i^- \\ & Y_{rk} = Y_{rk} + s_r^+ \\ & \forall \lambda_j, s_i^-, s_r^+ \geq 0; j = 1,\ldots,n; i = 1,\ldots,m; r = 1,\ldots,s; \theta \in R \end{aligned} \tag{2}$$

After solving the technical efficiency values based on CCR and BCC models specified in Eq. (1) and (2), scale efficiency (SE) is obtained, which is the ratio of two values. SE = 1 represents scale efficiency and SE < 1 represents scale inefficiency, where SE can be divided into increasing returns to scale (IRS) and decreasing returns to scale (DRS). $\Sigma\lambda = 1$ implies constant returns to scale, $\Sigma\lambda > 1$ indicates IRS, and $\Sigma\lambda < 1$ describes DRS.

In order to find out the real value of comparative efficiency in different periods, and solve the shortcomings of assessed unit, this study used Malmquist productivity analysis as the basis for measurement and comparison. This approach can show the changes in technical efficiency and technical change process with the definition of Malmquist index specified in Eq. (3):

$$M_0 = \left[\frac{\theta_0^t(x^{t+1}, y^{t+1})}{\theta_0^t(x^t, y^t)} \frac{\theta_0^{t+1}(x^{t+1}, y^{t+1})}{\theta_0^{t+1}(x^t, y^t)} \right]^{1/2} \quad (3)$$

where $\theta_0^t(x^{t+1}, y^{t+1})$ denotes the relative efficiency of a particular DMU in period $t + 1$ against the performance of those DMUs in period t. Productivity $M_0 > 1$ implies that the productivity is improved over time whereas the productivity is declined when $M_0 < 1$. This approach not only reveals patterns of productivity change but also identifies the strategy shifts of individual plant.

4. Results

4.1 Efficiency analysis

Table 1 and 2 summarize the efficiency scores evaluated by the CCR and BCC models respectively for each plant in year 2005 and 2006. The CCR model assumes constant returns to scale while the BCC model allows for variable returns to scale.

DMU	Efficiency	Jan	Feb	Mar	Apr	May	Jun	Jul	Aug	Sep	Oct	Nov	Dec
	CCR	0.815	1	0.692	0.682	0.682	0.701	0.701	0.701	0.701	0.701	0.700	0.700
P1	BCC	1	1	1	1	1	1	1	1	1	1	1	1
	SE	0.815	1	0.692	0.682	0.682	0.701	0.701	0.701	0.701	0.701	0.700	0.700
	CCR	1	1	1	1	1	1	1	1	1	1	1	1
P2	BCC	1	1	1	1	1	1	1	1	1	1	1	1
	SE	1	1	1	1	1	1	1	1	1	1	1	1
	CCR	1	1	1	1	1	1	1	1	1	1	1	1
P3	BCC	1	1	1	1	1	1	1	1	1	1	1	1
	SE	1	1	1	1	1	1	1	1	1	1	1	1
	CCR	1	1	1	1	1	1	1	1	1	1	1	1
P4	BCC	1	1	1	1	1	1	1	1	1	1	1	1
	SE	1	1	1	1	1	1	1	1	1	1	1	1
	CCR	1	1	1	1	1	1	1	1	1	1	1	1
P5	BCC	1	1	1	1	1	1	1	1	1	1	1	1
	SE	1	1	1	1	1	1	1	1	1	1	1	1
	CCR	0.819	0.790	0.802	0.802	0.802	0.846	0.846	0.917	0.917	0.917	0.914	0.914
P6	BCC	1	1	1	1	1	1	1	1	1	1	1	1
	SE	0.819	0.790	0.802	0.802	0.802	0.846	0.846	0.917	0.917	0.917	0.914	0.914
	CCR	1	1	1	1	1	1	1	1	1	1	1	1
P7	BCC	1	1	1	1	1	1	1	1	1	1	1	1
	SE	1	1	1	1	1	1	1	1	1	1	1	1
	CCR	0.745	0.629	0.612	0.612	0.612	0.612	0.610	0.612	0.648	0.648	0.691	0.741
P8	BCC	1	1	0.98	0.932	0.933	0.933	1	1	1	1	1	1
	SE	0.745	0.629	0.624	0.656	0.656	0.656	0.610	0.612	0.648	0.648	0.691	0.741
	CCR	0.860	0.831	0.829	0.818	0.818	0.812	0.806	0.806	0.829	0.829	0.824	0.827
P9	BCC	1	1	1	1	1	1	1	1	1	1	1	1
	SE	0.860	0.831	0.829	0.818	0.818	0.812	0.806	0.806	0.829	0.829	0.824	0.827
	CCR	0.809	0.832	0.847	0.813	0.813	0.916	0.916	0.916	0.916	0.916	0.916	0.919
P10	BCC	1	0.907	1	1	1	1	1	1	1	1	1	1
	SE	0.809	0.916	0.847	0.813	0.813	0.916	0.916	0.916	0.916	0.916	0.916	0.919

Table 1. The efficiency scores of DMUs in 2005

DMU	Efficiency	Jan	Feb	Mar	Apr	May	Jun	Jul	Aug	Sep	Oct	Nov	Dec
	CCR	0.701	0.679	0.734	0.811	0.785	0.785	0.801	0.867	0.857	0.815	0.835	0.810
P1	BCC	1	1	1	1	1	1	1	1	1	1	1	1
	SE	0.701	0.679	0.734	0.811	0.785	0.785	0.801	0.867	0.857	0.815	0.835	0.810
	CCR	1	1	1	1	1	1	1	1	1	1	1	1
P2	BCC	1	1	1	1	1	1	1	1	1	1	1	1
	SE	1	1	1	1	1	1	1	1	1	1	1	1
	CCR	1	1	1	1	1	1	1	1	1	1	1	1
P3	BCC	1	1	1	1	1	1	1	1	1	1	1	1
	SE	1	1	1	1	1	1	1	1	1	1	1	1
	CCR	1	1	1	0.986	1	1	1	1	1	1	1	1
P4	BCC	1	1	1	0.996	1	1	1	1	1	1	1	1
	SE	1	1	1	0.989	1	1	1	1	1	1	1	1
	CCR	1	1	1	1	1	1	1	1	1	1	1	1
P5	BCC	1	1	1	1	1	1	1	1	1	1	1	1
	SE	1	1	1	1	1	1	1	1	1	1	1	1
	CCR	0.916	0.828	0.828	0.828	0.828	0.828	0.862	0.863	0.843	0.863	0.833	0.859
P6	BCC	1	1	1	1	1	1	1	1	1	1	1	1
	SE	0.916	0.828	0.828	0.828	0.828	0.828	0.862	0.863	0.843	0.863	0.833	0.859
	CCR	1	1	1	1	1	1	1	1	1	1	1	1
P7	BCC	1	1	1	1	1	1	1	1	1	1	1	1
	SE	1	1	1	1	1	1	1	1	1	1	1	1
	CCR	0.714	0.628	0.627	0.605	0.605	0.599	0.637	0.612	0.640	0.640	0.657	0.647
P8	BCC	1	1	1	1	1	1	1	1	1	1	1	1
	SE	0.714	0.628	0.627	0.605	0.605	0.599	0.637	0.612	0.640	0.640	0.657	0.647
	CCR	0.808	0.766	0.752	0.752	0.752	0.753	0.752	0.762	0.766	0.681	0.681	0.708
P9	BCC	1	1	1	1	1	1	1	1	1	1	1	1
	SE	0.808	0.766	0.752	0.752	0.752	0.753	0.752	0.762	0.766	0.681	0.681	0.708
	CCR	0.916	0.922	0.921	0.921	0.888	0.889	0.874	0.864	0.874	0.826	0.846	0.840
P10	BCC	1	1	1	1	1	1	1	1	1	1	1	1
	SE	0.916	0.922	0.921	0.921	0.888	0.889	0.874	0.864	0.874	0.826	0.846	0.840

Table 2. The efficiency scores of DMUs in 2006

If taking the time interval of month for analysis, plants P2, P3, P4, P5 and P7 are efficient in CCR Model during the observation period. On the other hand, plants P1, P6, P8, P9, and P10 are inefficient for all 24 months. In terms of factory analysis, plant P_1 has only one month achieving technical efficiency, and the rest are scale inefficiency. Besides, plants P2, P3, P4, P5 and P7 all have scale efficiency. But plants P6, P8, P9 and P10 are scale inefficiency.

From the SE analysis, the study found that plants P2, P3, P5 and P7 maintained efficient during the observation period, whereas plants P6, P8, P9 and P10 had no scale efficiency for 24 months. But the SE inefficiency factories all had efficiency value of 1 in the BCC model. This phenomenon implies that their inefficiency is possibly from the influence of scale inefficiency. Additionally, the efficiency scale of plant P1 is 1 in only one month while its performance remains inefficient for the remaining 23 months. This finding also indicates the possibility of scale inefficiency. Therefore, reducing the scale of production can improve scale inefficiency.

Moreover, although plant P4 had technical and scale inefficiency only in April 2006, it had the overall relative efficiency of 1 for the rest of observations. The main reason is the input imbalance between average employee number and average labor hours. After adjusting the related imbalanced variables, the overall relative efficiency was recovered to 1. Meanwhile, plant P8 has similar situation like plant P4. It had technical and scale inefficiency from March to July in 2005 and the rest had the overall relative efficiency of 1. After adjusting related variables, the overall relative efficiency can be recovered to 1. Similar implication can be inferred for plant P10. Therefore, although each factory couldn't use input resource effectively to achieve the output with scale efficiency in a short time, it can still achieve efficiency if related variables were adjusted. This information provides an important managerial impact on resource control of manufacturing plants.

4.2 Analysis of Slacks and Returns to Scale

We further performed the analysis of slack variables to understand the improvements of inefficient DMUs on inputs. Meanwhile, returns to scale analysis was applied to identify whether a proportional change in inputs result in the same proportional change in outputs. IRS indicates that proportional changes in inputs result in a more than proportional changes in outputs. On the other hand, DRS implies the opposite changes in outputs. Therefore, after analysis of slacks and returns to scale, this study summarizes the influential elements of the efficiency in each inefficient factory as follows:

(1) P1 is DRS, which should be improved through reducing its input of resources, especially the control of employee number and labor hours.

(2) P6 is DRS, which should be improved through reducing its input of resources, especially the control of employee number.

(3) P8 is DRS, which should be improved through reducing its input of resources, especially the control of employee number and labor hour.

(4) P9 is DRS, which should be improved through reducing its input of resources, especially the control of labor hour.

(5) P10 is DRS, which should be improved through reducing its input of resources, especially the control of employee number and average cost of goods sold.

4.3 Sensitivity Analysis

The sensitivity analysis is mainly to get CCR overall efficiency of each assessed factory through respectively removing inputs and outputs. The resulted value is compared with the original input-output efficiency. Sensibility analysis can be used to understand the impact of each variable on efficiency and to find out the sources of efficiency and inefficiency for each unit assessed. After sensitive analysis, the findings of this study are as follows:

(1) When deleting "average employee number": P8's efficiency is significantly reduced by about 10%, so average employee number is the advantage to enhance the overall efficiency. P4's efficiency decreases significantly only in 6 months. Its efficiency scores are among 0.98-0.99, which results in decreased overall efficiency.

(2) When deleting "average labor hour": The efficiency scores of P6, P8, and P10 are reduced by 1%, 1% and 5% respectively. Because plant P4's efficiency decreases significantly only in 3 months, it can explore whether the labor hour is excessive in the period.

(3) When deleting "average cost of goods sold": P2's efficiency values are reduced by about 15%. Meanwhile, P4's efficiency decreases to 0.98 significantly only in one

month, and the rest months are not affected. Similarly, P5's efficiency decreases significantly only in 6 months. Thus, the average cost of goods sold has a significant impact on efficiency score.

(4) When deleting "production output": P2's efficiency values are reduced by about 50%, P6 was about 30%, P7 was about 77%, P8 was about 10%, P9 was about 30 %, and P10 was about 40%. Moreover, P3's efficiency decreases significantly only in 9 months, which are among 0.93-0.97. Hence, the production output also has a significant impact on efficiency score.

(5) When deleting "average OEE": P4's efficiency decreases significantly in 2 months, which are among 0.98-0.99. Its efficiency scores are not affected for the rest of months. So the average OEE is the advantage to enhance the overall efficiency.

(6) When deleting "production cycle time": P4's efficiency decreases to 0.98 significantly in one month, and the rest are not affected. So the production cycle time is the advantage to enhance the overall efficiency.

(7) When deleting "production ratio": P4's efficiency decreases to 0.99 significantly in 2 months, and the rest are not affected. So the production ratio is the advantage to enhance the overall efficiency.

Therefore when deleting average employee number, labor hour and production output, more than half of factories are affected (P2, P6, P7, P8, P9 and P10) and their efficiency scores decrease. Accordingly, these three variables are advantages enhancing the overall efficiency.

4.4 Malmquist Analysis

Finally, Malmquist productivity measure was used by this study to compare the efficiency value of each factory at different times. Table 3 shows the result of total factor productivity change (TFPC), technical efficiency change (TEC), and technical change (TC) in assembly factories.

Factory	TFPC, TEC, TC
P1	TFPC ↑, TEC ↑, TC ↑
P2	TFPC ↑, TEC ↑, TC ↑
P3	TFPC ↑, TEC ↑, TC ↑
P4	TFPC ↑, TEC ↑, TC ↑
P5	TFPC ↑, TEC ↑, TC ↑
P6	TFPC ↓, TEC ↓, TC ↓
P7	TFPC ↑, TEC ↑, TC ↑
P8	TFPC ↓, TEC ↑, TC ↓
P9	TFPC ↓, TEC ↓, TC ↓
P10	TFPC ↓, TEC ↓, TC ↑

Table 3. The Malmquist Productivity Measure results of each assembly factory
Note: ↑ represents progress; ↓ represents backward

According to the results of Table 3, plants P1, P2, P3, P4, P5, and P7 have TFPC sustained progress, showing an improvement in productivity. On the other hand, plants P6, P8, P9 and P10 show a backward trend, which means the recession in productivity. Moreover, plants P1, P2, P3, P4, P5, P7 and P8 have enhancing changes in technical efficiency, showing an improvement in technical efficiency. But plants P6, P9 and P10 have recession in technical efficiency with no improvement in TEC. Besides, plants P1, P2, P3, P4, P5, P7 and P10 have enhancing technical changes, showing an improvement in production technology. However, plants P6, P8, P9 and P10 have recession in production technology with no improvement in TC.

4.5 Summary

This study conducted efficiency analysis, returns to scale analysis, analysis of slacks variable, sensitivity analysis and Malmquist productivity index analysis to assess the efficiency of 10 semiconductor assembly factories. The results are summarized as follows:

(1) Efficiency analysis: Plants P2, P3, P4, P5, and P7 have efficiency in 24 months. But plants P1, P6, P8, P9, and P10 have scale inefficiency in 24 months. Besides, plants P8 and P10 have a total of five months with technical and scale inefficiency.

(2) Analysis of slacks variable and returns to scale: plants P2, P3, P4, P5 and P7 have achieved returns to scale while plants P1, P6, P8, P9 and P10 are DRS.

(3) Sensitivity analysis: when deleting "production output", plants P2, P6, P7, P8, P9 and P10 have significantly decreased efficiency scores.

(4) Malmquist productivity index analysis: plants P1, P2, P3, P4, P5, and P7 have continued progress in TFPC, showing an improvement in productivity. But plants P6, P8, P9 and P10 have backward trend, which means the productivity has recession.

5. Conclusions

According to our empirical test in a semiconductor assembly house, this study found that the applications of DEA method could improve the shortcomings of single performance measurements with the considerations of influential inputs and outputs during the manufacturing processes. DEA approach also proves to provide constructive suggestions to enhance resource allocation. For example in our case company, the managers can reduce the corresponding resource if the employee number or labor hour is found over-allocated from DEA results. Together with the Malmquist productivity measure, engineers are able to assess the patterns of productivity change after strategy shifts. This also helps management to evaluate whether or not such shifts are making progress. As for future studies, the same research methods and input elements could be used to assess the efficiency among different semiconductor assembly plants for the other company. Robustness of DEA approach for semiconductor assembly house can be verified then. More important factors may be included in DEA models to enhance its practicability for semiconductor assembly house. Models other than CCR and BCC can be explored to extend the explanation power of DEA approach.

6. References

Banker, R. D.; Charnes, A. & Cooper, W. W. (1984). Some models for estimating technical and scale inefficiencies in data envelopment analysis. *Management Science*, Vol. 30, No. 9, pp. 1078-1092.

Beeg, T. (2004). Wafer fab cycle forecast under changing loading situations, *IEEE/SEMI Advanced Semiconductor Manufacturing Conference and workshop*, pp. 339-343, May 2004.

Charnes, A.; Cooper, W. W. & Rhodes, E. (1978). Measuring the efficiency of decision making units. *European Journal of Operational Research*, Vol. 2, No. 6, pp. 29-444.

Ertray, T. & Ruan, D. (2005). Data envelopment analysis based decision model for optimal operator allocation in CMS. *European Journal of Operational Research*, Vol. 164, pp. 800-810.

Golany, B. & Roll, Y. (1989). An application procedure for DEA. *OMEGA: International Journal of Management Science*, Vol. 17, No, 3, pp. 237-250.

Hosseinzadeh, F. & Ghasemi, M. V. (2007). Malmquist productivity index on interval data in telecommunication firms, application of data envelopment analysis. *Applied Mathematical Sciences*, Vol. 1, No. 15, pp. 711-722.

Konopka, J. (1996). Improving output in semiconductor manufacturing environments. Ph. D. Dissertation, Arisona Graduate College.

Leachman, R. C. (1995), Benchmarking manufacturing performance in the semiconductor industry. *Production and Operations Management*, Vol. 4, No. 3, pp. 201-216.

Leachman, R. C. & Hodges, D. A. (1996). Benchmarking semiconductor manufacturing, *IEEE Transaction on Semiconductor Manufacturing*, Vol. 7, pp. 158-169.

Liu, F. H. & Wang, P. H. (2007). DEA Malmquist productivity measure: Taiwanese semiconductor companies. *International Journal of Production Economics*, Vol. 112, 367-379.

Nakajima, S. (1988). *Introduction to total Productive Maintenance*, Productivity Press, Cambridge, MA.

Pan, W., Feng, Y., Huang, Y., and Chen, Y. (2008). Performance review of Taiwanese IC design industry: DEA-based Malmquist productivity measure. *WSEAS Transactions on Computers*, Vol. 7, No. 8, pp. 1291-1299.

SEMI, (1999). Standard for definition and measurement of equipment reliability, availability, and maintainability.

Shang, J. & Sueyoshi, T. (1995). Theory and methodology: A unified framework for the selection of a flexible manufacturing system. *European Journal of Operational Research*, Vol. 85, pp. 297-315.

Thomas, H. R. (2000). Schedule acceleration, work flow, and labour productivity. *Journal of Construction Engineering and Management*, Vol. 123 No. 2, pp. 181-8.

Thore, S. P. F.; Ruefli, T. W. & Yue, P. (1996). DEA and the management of the product cycle: The U.S. computer industry, *Computer Ops Res.*, Vol. 23, No. 4, pp. 341-356.

Portable ID Management Framework for Security Enhancement of Virtual Machine Monitors

Manabu Hirano[1], Takeshi Okuda[2], Eiji Kawai[9], Takahiro Shinagawa[3], Hideki Eiraku[3], Kouichi Tanimoto[3], Shoichi Hasegawa[3], Takashi Horie[3], Seiji Mune[3], Kazumasa Omote[4], Kenichi Kourai[5], Yoshihiro Oyama[6], Kenji Kono[7], Shigeru Chiba[8], Yasushi Shinjo[3], Kazuhiko Kato[3], and Suguru Yamaguchi[2]

[1] Toyota National College of Technology,
[2] Nara Institute of Science and Technology (NAIST),
[3] University of Tsukuba, [4] Japan Institute of Science and Technology (JAIST),
[5] Kyusyu Institute of Technology, [6] The University of Electro-communications,
[7] Keio University, [8] Tokyo Institute of Technology,
[9] National Institute of Information and Communications Technology
Japan

1. Introduction

Most governmental and commercial organizations are processing a massive amount of data everyday. In such organizations, end-users' computers are physically distributed and they can be moved outside of organizations. Therefore, it is difficult to monitor, and enforce security policies to these distributed end-users' computers. Although a security administrator in organizations can install monitoring software, an end-user can remove and bypass this kind of software on conventional operating systems. Most existing commercial operating systems cannot enforce a mandatory security policy to end-users. This chapter shows a security policy enforcement mechanism based on a virtual machine monitor (VMM).

A VMM is a technology to encapsulate an operating system, which was originally developed for mainframe computers like IBM VM/370 (Seawright & MacKinnon, 1979). Original VMM mechanism was intended to support legacy software of mainframe computers in new hardware. An ideal VMM technology provides complete isolation of virtual machines (VMs) (Madnick & Donovan, 1973). This feature enables us to separate domains with different security levels in a same physical machine. A layer of a VMM can, without modifying a guest operating system, provide useful and strong security functions transparently for client and server computers. We call this kind of VMM system ``a secure VMM''. A concept of a secure VMM is useful to insert a security layer without modifying existing operating systems. In this chapter, we use terms, both *VMM* and *hypervisor*, to express this mediation software. In particular, a *hypervisor* means a bare-metal VMM which does not need a host operating system.

In recent research, some VMM systems designed for security-purposes have been proposed as follows.

sHype. sHype (Secure Hypervisor) (Sailer et al., 2005) is developed by IBM Research. The purpose of the sHype project is to construct a secure foundation for server platforms. sHype provides an access control and an isolation mechanism of virtual resources in hypervisor software. sHype is intended to provide a mandatory access control (MAC) for inter-VM communication of server VM coalitions. sHype is implemented on Xen hypervisor and rHype (Research Hypervisor). sHype implementation supports some major security policy mechanisms such as Chinese wall policy and the simple Type Enforcement (TE) policy. Main components of sHype are an access control module for virtual resources and inter-VM communication, hypervisor mediation hooks, callback functions and a policy management VM.

NetTop. NetTop is designed by NSA (Meushaw & Simard, 2000). NetTop is constructed with commercial off-the-shelf technology, VMware products and SELinux as a host operating system. NetTop provides security mechanisms using isolation of VMs, and it is based on reliability of a host operating system and VMM software. NetTop project also states the importance of trusted BIOS because all host platform security is dependent on an initial boot-up process. NetTop can provide a transparent VPN VM and a Filtering VM to protect and filter communication channels of end-users' OS like Microsoft Windows. NetTop is intended to be deployed in a governmental environment. NetTop also provides a secure data transfer mechanism, called the "Regrade" server protocol, between two VMs with different security levels. The regrade server achieves data transfer based on a token-based user identity and a regrade policy. It can also check and sanitize malicious content, and record audit logs. NetTop also provides a transparent storage encryption service.

Terra. Terra architecture provides a trusted virtual machine monitor (TVMM) that isolates and protects each virtual machine (Garfinkel et al., 2003). Terra architecture is designed to construct a trusted computing platform based on a VMM technology. Terra architecture supports a remote attestation mechanism to establish a trusted path. The trusted path is achieved by attestation certificate chains for BIOS, a boot loader and a VM image. Terra also supports an encrypted disk and an integrity-checked disk in the VMM layer. A prototype implementation of Terra architecture employs the VMware ESX server product and python scripts.

BitVisor. We are developing novel secure VMM software called BitVisor (Shinagawa et al., 2009). The first version of BitVisor has been released to the public in March 2008. BitVisor has been developed by 6 universities and college, companies with the help of NISC (National Information Security Center), Japan. BitVisor can be downloaded as complete source codes. Developers can download and extend source codes of this novel security software. BitVisor provides transparent security functions like a built-in IPsec-VPN module with IKEv1 (RFC4301 and RFC2409) and a storage encryption module based on XTS-AES algorithm (IEEE1619 standard) in the VMM layer. The IPsec-VPN module enables users to establish VPN without modifying guest operating systems. The IPsec-VPN module provides encrypted communication and mutual authentication functions between distributed end-point computers and a VPN gateway. The transparent storage encryption function can force the use of encrypted storages (ex. ATA hard disk drives and USB thumb drives) in end-point computers to prevent information leak cases.

As described above, there are many secure VMM systems. This chapter presents a portable ID management framework for secure VMM systems. The proposed ID management framework provides useful services to VMM software. For instance, the proposed portable ID management framework provides a user authentication function using PKI-based ID cards and a user ID based authorization function for transparent security services in a VMM layer.

In the following sections, we first describe a basic concept of a secure VMM. Then, we show a design and a prototype implementation of the proposed portable ID management framework for secure VMM systems. Then, we present our novel secure VMM software called BitVisor and its integration with the proposed portable ID management framework.

2. Overview of Secure VMM Systems

Security frameworks using a VMM technology are based on an isolation mechanism of that technology. Each VM works on same VMM cannot influence the other VMs. For this mechanism, we can separate the purpose of each isolated VM. For example, one VM can connect to the Internet, but another VM can restrict network connections except for intranet accesses. NetTop takes this approach to reduce the number of physical machines for different purposes and different security levels in a governmental environment. We can construct isolated domains with different security levels as different VMs using the VMM technology.

NetTop and Terra support a transparent storage encryption mechanism. The advantage of this mechanism is that it does not require modifying the guest operating system. The secure VMM layer can provide storage encryption and decryption automatically. Even a guest operating system is attacked; an encryption key is not leaked - on the assumption that a secure VMM layer is strongly protected from untrusted guest operating systems and other malicious actions. NetTop also provides a transparent VPN function for guest operating systems using a VPN gateway VM. It has the same effect as two physical separated machines, an end-user machine and an administrator-controlled VPN gateway server machine.

Figure 1 illustrates a basic concept of a secure VMM architecture. Secure VMM systems have the following features: (1) thin, light-weight, and minimum overhead for security processing with high performance and high testability; (2) a trusted bootstrap architecture and an attestation mechanism for each component (e.g. BIOS codes, a boot-loader, VMM software and VM images). We need a measured launch mechanism using Intel's TXT (Trusted Execution Technology) hardware, formerly known as LaGrande, and TPM (Trusted Platform Module) chip to check software integrity at the boot time; (3) a strong isolation mechanism for each VM; (4) a mandatory access control (MAC) function based on an access control list (ACL) or a security policy (e.g. the Chinese wall policy and the Type

Enforcement policy). The MAC function basically consists of a policy decision point (PDP), a policy enforcement point (PEP; i.e. hook points for virtual/physical resources), and a policy management function to update distributed policy files; (5) transparent security functions like automatic storage encryption and encrypted communication channel using a VPN function; and (6) a protection mechanism against run-time attacks to VMM software.

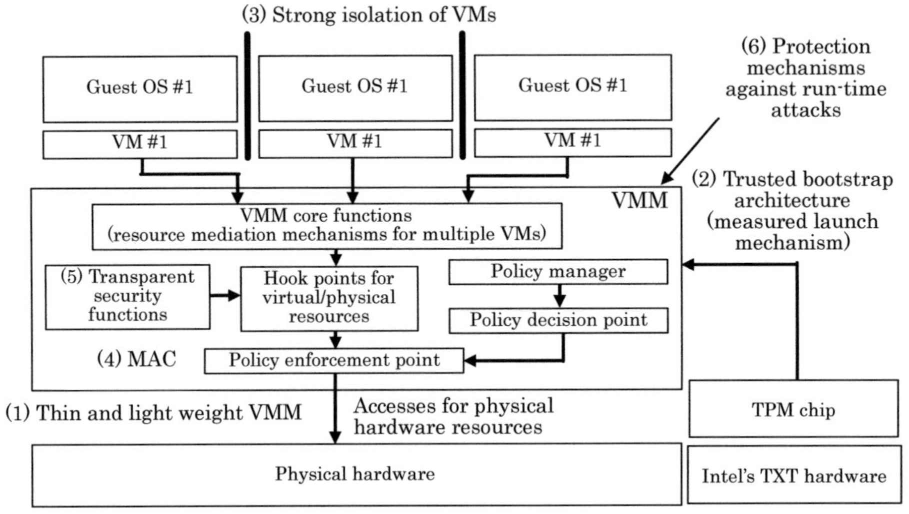

Fig. 1. Basic concept of a secure VMM architecture

A key component of secure VMM systems is MAC functions. The secure VMM software can control virtual/physical resources of each VM. In this chapter, the word *resource* refers to devices like a NIC which handles network packets and a USB thumb drive which holds a user's data. As shown in Figure 1, secure VMM systems hooks I/O data of these devices and they enforce security policies in the PEP. The policy manager updates and validates a security policy which is distributed by a central policy distribution server in an organization. The PDP processes an authorization decision for VM operations and sends the result to the PEP. Finally, the PEP enforces security policies based on retrieved authorization result.

The foundation of a MAC function is dependent on there being only one administrator that can access a management function of a secure VMM system. We have to prevent that an end-user cannot bypass the administrator-controlled secure VMM layer. Secure VMM systems provides a policy enforcement mechanism for end-users' computers based on above methods.

3. ID Management Problems in a VMM Layer

In existing secure VMM systems, a VM entity is identified by VMM software, and a secure VMM enforces a security policy based on the each VM identity (VM ID). However, to deploy a secure VMM system as a policy enforcement mechanism, we need to manage a user-identity in a secure VMM system. Figure 2 shows access control models of a secure VMM system. The figure (A) shows an access control model based on a VM ID only. The figure (B) shows an access control model based on both a VM ID and a user identity (User

ID). In the latter case, secure VMM software first authenticates a user and identified her or his user ID. Then, secure VMM software enforces a security policy using the user ID.

In the conventional system like the figure (A), a user authentication mechanism is still dependent on a guest operating system (e.g. Windows Logon and UNIX-like OS's password mechanism). Conventional secure VMM systems cannot handle the mapping between a VM ID and a user ID of a guest OS. From the usability and the security, ID management mechanisms on multiple guest operating systems on multiple VMs are not efficient, because the administrator have to maintain multiple user IDs on multiple guest operating systems on each VM.

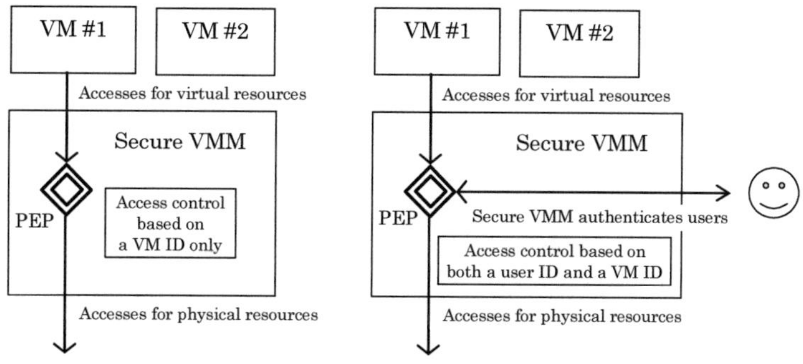

(a) Access control based on a VM ID

(b) Access control based on a user ID and a VM ID

Fig. 2. Access control models of a secure VMM system

Secure VMM layer can provide many security functions transparently to upper guest operating systems. Employing user identification and authentication in a VMM layer has many advantages. First, a secure VMM will be able to control many VMM functions based on a user ID, like a VM boot operation and disk encryption. Furthermore, access control of virtual/physical devices will be effective using an authenticated user ID because a security administrator in most organizations prefers a user ID-based authorization, instead of a VM ID-based authorization only. The user ID-based authorization also enables a secure VMM to record audit logs based on the user ID. An audit log is an essential component of security systems. Audit logs also achieve non-repudiation of users' actions on an administrator-controlled secure VMM system. In the following sections, we describe a method to integrate a proposed portable ID management framework based on a PKI-based smart card (ID card) into secure VMM systems.

4. Portable ID Management Framework for Secure VMM Systems

Figure 3 shows a design of the proposed portable ID management framework for secure VMM systems. We assume that each employees of an organization has their PKI-based ID cards. We mainly employ PKI technology to manage an employee's identity of an organization. For instance, governments in Belgium, France and many countries are considering a national ID card system based on PKI to authenticate citizens' identities. ID management based on a PKI technology is growing in the public sector world wide. We show a method to integrate PKI-based authentication and authorization mechanisms into secure VMM systems to enforce security policies for distributed end-users' computers.

Our proposed smart card stores the secure VMM application we developed. Middleware layers in a secure VMM system support PKCS#11 APIs, PC/SC (Personal Computer/Smart Card) APIs, and the minimum cryptographic APIs. The proposed portable ID management framework libraries also include a USB CCID (Chip/smart Card Interface Devices) device driver for generic smart card readers. The secure VMM ID management library provides user authentication functions based on PKI-based ID card and authorization functions based on a security policy. The proposed ID management framework libraries also provide a standard ID/password authentication API. These functions can be used to authorize VM operations based on an authenticated user ID.

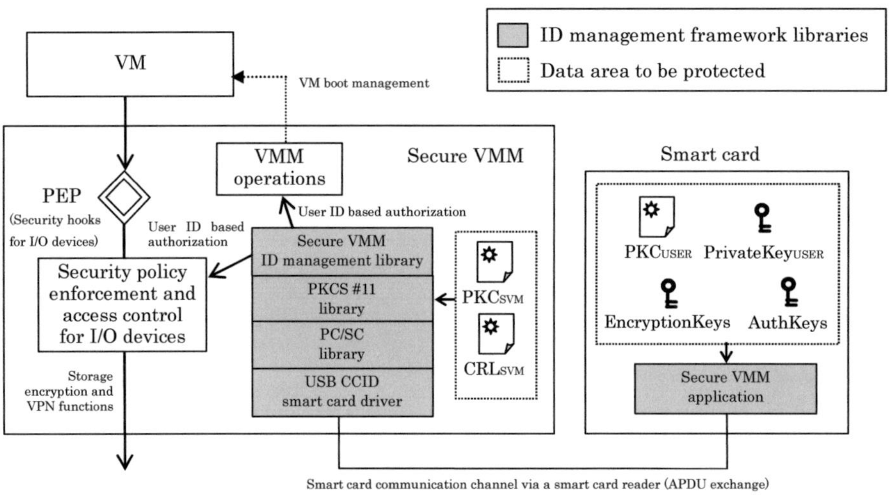

Fig. 3. Design of the portable ID management framework for secure VMM systems

In addition, the secure VMM software can enforce storage encryption/decryption services to guest operating systems transparently. An encryption key ($\text{EncryptionKey}_{\text{USER}}$) is stored in the user's smart card. Secure VMM software encrypts and decrypts storages using the encryption keys. Each encryption key is associated with the user's identity. Therefore, an attacker without a valid smart card cannot decrypt a user's storage. Secure VMM software also provides a VPN service in hook points of a physical NIC device. PKI-based authentication functions can be used for the initial user authentication between a user's machine and a VPN gateway machine.

Figure 4 shows the details of user authentication of the proposed ID management framework. The user authentication function employs a simple challenge and response mechanism. First, a user inputs a PIN number of her or his smart card, and the smart card authenticates the user. Then, authentication data are exchanged between the smart card and the ID management framework libraries in secure VMM software. Secure VMM software sends a challenge as R, and the smart card then returns the user's Public Key Certificate (PKC_{USER}) and the signature of R ($\{R\}_{\text{USER}}$) generated by the user's private key ($\text{PrivateKey}_{\text{USER}}$). The ID management framework libraries validate retrieved PKC_{USER} using a trust anchor certificate for a secure VMM (PKC_{SVM}). The ID management framework libraries check certificate revocation status by a Certificate Revocation List (CRL_{SVM}). If the authentication is successful, then a secure VMM will be able to enforce security policy based on a user ID in the secure VMM layer. As a result, administrator-controlled secure VMM software with the ID management framework libraries provides the fundamental part of an end-point policy enforcement mechanism in an organization.

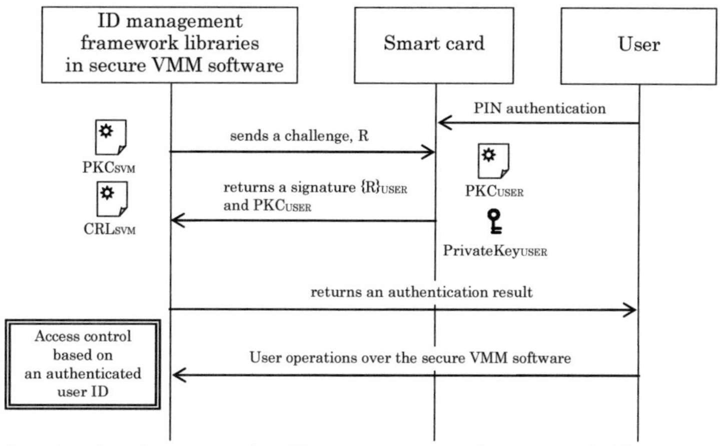

Fig. 4. User authentication between the ID management framework libraries and a user

5. Implementation of the Portable ID Management Framework Libraries

We have implemented the portable ID management framework libraries shown in Figure 3. Table 1 shows the hardware and software environment for the implementation. Because the portable ID management framework libraries have middleware software and device drivers completely, the libraries can run on the hardware directly without the help of operating systems and specific external libraries. As a result, we can integrate our portable ID management framework libraries into any VMM and hypervisor software. We employ eLWISE smart card manufactured by NTT Communications. The eLWISE smart cards are employed as Japanese national ID cards (i.e. the Basic Resident Register system in Japan). We have implemented secure VMM libraries compatible with PKCS#11 interfaces. We have merged our portable ID management framework libraries with BitVisor.

6. BitVisor

In section 1, we have described BitVisor briefly. BitVisor is a bare metal hypervisor. In the following sections, we use not *VMM* but *hypervisor* because BitVisor does not need host operating system. For the same reason, we also use not *secure VMM* but *secure hypervisor* in the following sections. BitVisor employs CPUs and chipsets supporting Intel Virtualization Technology (Intel VT) or AMD-V. We have presented a detailed design and implementation of BitVisor in the previous paper (Shinagawa et al., 2009). BitVisor supports both 32 bit and 64 bit mode. Current version of BitVisor can run Windows XP/Vista, Linux, and FreeBSD as a guest OS. BitVisor can run only one guest OS at the same time. However, BitVisor achieves very small code sizes and light weight performance. These characteristics are suitable for a foundation of security policy enforcement. This section shows highlights of BitVisor architecture.

Smart card	NTT Communications eLWISE (ISO/IEC 14443 and 7816)
Smart card reader	Axalto Reflex USB v3 (ISO/IEC 7816)
PC	Intel VT or AMD-V support
Hypervisor	BitVisor
Compiler	gcc

Table 1. Software and hardware used in the implementation

First, why do we need to develop a novel hypervisor for security purpose? The purpose of BitVisor is to provide a foundation of security policy enforcement for end-point client computers. There are several implementations of general-purpose hypervisors like Xen and VMware. Although these hypervisors provide general purpose and stable VM execution environments, they are not specialized for security purpose. BitVisor is originally designed for security purpose. If a hypervisor has vulnerabilities, attackers compromise the hypervisor and gain the control of the secure hypervisor software. Therefore, we have to prevent attacks to hypervisors. In general, the large code size of hypervisor causes poor testability and much vulnerability. For instance, VMKernel of VMware ESX server has 200 KLOC (Kilo-lines of codes) (VMware, 2005) and Xen hypervisor has 100 KLOC (Murray et al., 2008). BitVisor (version 0.8) has only 30 KLOC. BitVisor employs a two-step execution mechanism to reduce the code size of core hypervisor (Hirano et al., 2009). Thin hypervisors like BitVisor provide the low risk of vulnerabilities and high testability.

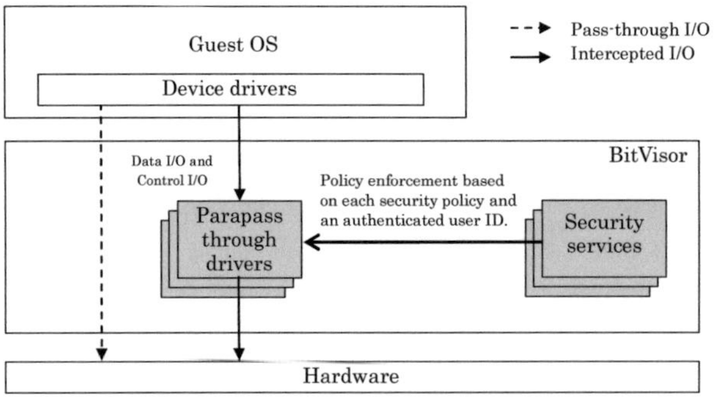

Fig. 5. Parapass-through architecture of BitVisor

Figure 5 shows basic architecture of BitVisor. BitVisor employs parapass-through architecture to process I/O devices. In this architecture, most accesses from a guest OS are passed through BitVisor simply. Therefore, it can provide high performance like native hardware. Some I/O data from specific devices are intercepted by parapass-through drivers. BitVisor can hook I/O data and apply security policies in conjunction with the parapass-through drivers. BitVisor can enforce security services like a storage encryption function and a VPN function based on each security policy. Intercepted I/O are divided into data I/O and control I/O. BitVisor can intercept control I/O and record it to audit logs in the hypervisor layer. BitVisor can intercept data I/O to inspect and encrypt them.

A parapass-through driver of BitVisor has essential codes only to enforce security services. A device driver on the guest OS executes most tasks other than security processing. Therefore, a parapass-through driver can keep the small code size. To employ a new device to monitor and encrypt, BitVisor needs this small parapass-through driver and its security service library only. Other general purpose hypervisors need much larger code sizes of the new device because of its architecture.

BitVisor also intercepts memory accesses using shadow paging to isolate memory area o f each device. BitVisor employs a novel scheme called shadow DMA (Direct Memory Access) descriptors. Shadow DMA descriptors enable us to intercept data transferred by a DMA mechanism. By employing shadow DMA descriptors, we can prevent attacks using a DMA mechanism from guest OSs.

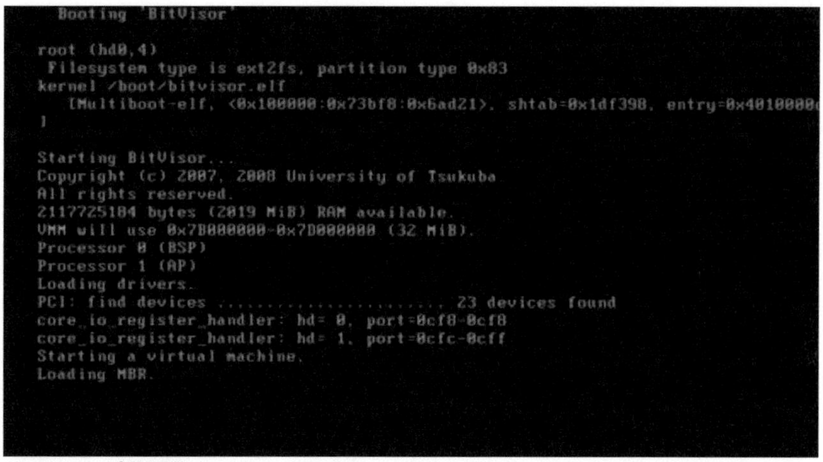

Fig. 6. Start screen of BitVisor

Figure 6 shows a start screen of BitVisor. BitVisor has been developed by 6 universities and college, and many companies with the help of NISC (National Information Security Center), Japan. BitVisor can be downloaded from http://sourceforge.net/projects/bitvisor/.

7. Integration of Portable ID Management Framework and BitVisor

We have integrated the proposed portable ID management framework libraries to BitVisor. The portable ID management framework libraries are not dependent on other external libraries and system calls of host operating systems. Therefore, we can integrate the ID management framework libraries into BitVisor directly. The libraries can run with bare metal hypervisors on the hardware directly without the help of host operating systems.

Figure 7 shows the relation between the proposed portable ID management framework libraries and security services of BitVisor. The proposed ID management framework provides the following functions to BitVisor: (1) a PKI-based user authentication function using smart card to start a BitVisor system (a simple ID/password authentication function is also provided), (2) a storage function of encryption keys in smart cards (BitVisor provides an XTS-AES storage encryption service), (3) a PKI-based user authentication function using smart cards for IPsec-VPN/IKEv1 service, and (4) a periodical checking mechanism to verify user's presence. The final feature can be used to detect illegal physical access to the end-point computers. If a user removes her or his smart card from the smart card reader, BitVisor detects it and immediately shuts down the BitVisor system.

The portable ID management framework libraries support both contact and contact-less smart cards (ISO/IEC 7816 and 14443) for BitVisor. As shown in Figure 3, the portable ID management framework libraries are constructed as layered libraries. If other service provider needs to handle other smart card and reader products, the provider has to develop a new CCID driver. If a provider needs to customize partitions of smart cards, the provider also has to develop customized PKCS#11 libraries.

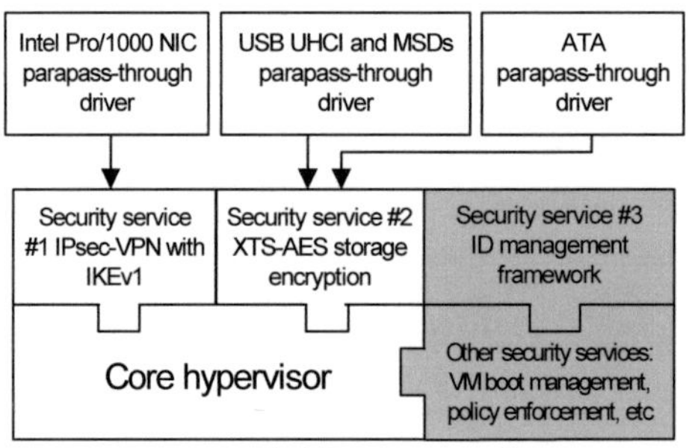

Fig. 7. Portable ID management framework libraries and security services of BitVisor

8. Two-step Execution Mechanism for Thin Secure Hypervisors

This section shows a method to minimize the core portion of BitVisor software. A trusted computing base (TCB) is a component to enhance the security of existing operating systems. We employ hypervisors to construct a TCB. In general, the complexity of hypervisors is not preferable to construct a TCB. Some researchers have proposed tiny hypervisors specialized for security-purpose. Murray et al. propose a mechanism to reduce the complexity of Xen hypervisor to construct a TCB (Murray et al., 2008). SecVisor is developed as a tiny hypervisor that ensures code integrity for commodity OS kernels (Seshadri et al., 2007). SecVisor has small code size, only 1,112 LOC (Lines of code), for the run-time portion using CPU-supported virtualization. Xia et al. shows a small hypervisor called Palacious VMM (Xia et al., 2008). Palacious VMM hooks I/O operations between device drivers on a guest OS and physical hardware. The core of Palacious VMM has 20 KLOC and the additional part to hook I/O operations has 10 KLOC. As described above, the code size of a TCB is one of the important aspects to evaluate whether reliable security mechanisms or not.

We have proposed the two-step execution mechanism in the previous paper (Hirano et al., 2009). Figure 8 shows the flow of the proposed two-step execution mechanism. Our proposal is intended to reduce the code sizes of the run-time portion of BitVisor as possible. Basic idea is simple, we separate a conventional hypervisor-based TCB into the following two parts: (1) a thin hypervisor with minimum security services and (2) a special guest OS for security preprocessing. Thus, we introduce an additional TCB domain for security preprocessing as the special guest OS runs on a hypervisor.

We can move the many tasks from BitVisor to the special guest OS. For example, the special guest OS can execute the following tasks before booting a target guest OS to be protected: (a) a PKI-based user authentication function using a PKI-based smart card for VM boot operations, and (b) an acquisition function of encryption keys for future encryption services from a smart card, and (c) an acquisition function of user certificates for VPN services from a smart card. We have also designed a data passing part between the special guest OS and BitVisor using *kexec* system call of Linux OS. By employing the proposed two-step execution mechanism, we have reduced approximately 8.5 % of LOC in run-time portion of BitVisor in total. Especially, we have reduced 24.5 % of LOC of ID management framework libraries.

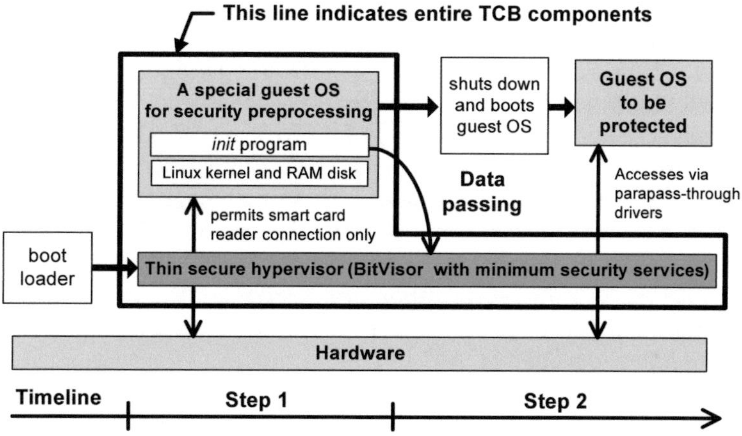

Fig. 8. Flow of the proposed two-step execution mechanism for thin secure hypervisors

To guarantee the authenticity of the special guest OS (the special guest OS consists of the minimum Linux kernel, initial RAM disk and init program only), we can introduce a measured launch mechanism based on a TCG extended boot loader (Sailer et al., 2004) like TrustedGrub. We can also guarantee the authenticity of BIOS codes and the first part of TCG extended boot loader using Intel TXT (Trusted Execution Technology) hardware and TPM chip.

9. Future Direction

We have described a basic concept of BitVisor and its portable ID management framework. From the perspective of IT resource management, these basic TCB components can be used as a policy enforcement mechanism for distributed end-point computers in organizations. Current version of BitVisor provides an XTS-AES storage encryption function and an IPsec-VPN function to prevent information leak cases. We must consider further security services to prevent information leak cases via other I/O devices. Policy management problem and certificate management problem are also important to deploy the proposal to real governmental and commercial organizations. Moreover, we need further on-site verifications of the prototype implementation. We have to improve the source codes continuously to prevent attacks to their potential vulnerabilities and increase the usability.

10. Conclusion

This chapter has shown the portable ID management framework for secure hypervisors. We have introduced an architectural overview of the novel secure hypervisor software called BitVisor. We have shown the design and the prototype implementation of the portable ID management framework libraries and BitVisor. The source codes of BitVisor including the portable ID management framework libraries can be downloaded from the following web sites, http://sourceforge.net/projects/bitvisor/.

11. References

Garfinkel, T.; Pfaff, B.; Chow, J.; Rosenblum, M. & Boneh, D. (2003). Terra: a virtual machine-based platform for trusted computing, *Proceedings of the ACM Symposium on Operating Systems Principles*, pp. 193–206

Hirano, M.; Okuda, T.; Kawai, E. & Yamaguchi, S. (2007). Design and Implementation of a Portable ID Management Framework for a Secure Virtual Machine Monitor, *Journal of Information Assurance and Security*, Vol.2, No.3, pp.211-216

Hirano, M.; Shinagawa, T.; Eiraku, H.; Hasegawa, S.; Omote, K.; Tanimoto, K.; Horie, T.; Mune, S.; Kato, K.; Okuda, T.; Kawai, E. and Yamaguchi, S. (2009). A Two-step Execution Mechanism for Thin Secure Hypervisors, In *Proceedings of the 3rd International Conference on Emerging Security Information, Systems and Technologies*

Madnick, S. & Donovan, J. (1973). Application and analysis of the virtual machine approach to information system security and isolation, *Proceedings of the workshop on virtual computer systems*, pp.210-224, ACM Press

Meushaw, R. & Simard, D. (2000). NetTop: Commercial Technology in High Assurance Applications, *National Security Agency Tech Trend Notes*, pp. 3-9

Murray, D. G.; Milos, G. and Hand, S. (2008). Improving Xen security through disaggregation. *In Proceedings of the Fourth ACM SIGPLAN/SIGOPS international Conference on Virtual Execution Environments*, pp.151-160

Sailer, R.; Zhang, X.; Jaeger, T. and Doorn, L. V. (2004). Design and Implementation of a TCG-based Integrity Measurement Architecture, *In Proceedings of thirteenth USENIX Security Symposium*, pp.223-238

Sailer, R.; Jaeger, T.; Valdez, E.; Caceres, R.; Perez, R.; Berger, S.; Griffin, J. & Doorn, L. (2005). Building a MAC-Based Security Architecture for the Xen Open-Source Hypervisor, Proceedings of *ACSAC 2005*, IEEE CS, pp. 276-285

Seawright, L. & MacKinnon, R. (1979). VM/370 - a study of multiplicity and usefulness, *IBM Systems journal*, pp.4-17

Seshadri, A.; Luk, M.; Qu, N. and Perrig, A. (2007). SecVisor: a tiny hypervisor to provide lifetime kernel code integrity for commodity OSes. *In Proceedings of Twenty-First ACM SIGOPS Symposium on Operating Systems Principles*, pp.335-350

Shinagawa, T.; Eiraku, H.; Tanimoto, K.; Omote, K.; Hasegawa, S.; Horie, T.; Hirano, M.; Kourai, K.; Oyama, Y.; Kawai, E.; Kono, K.; Chiba, S.; Shinjo, Y. & Kato, K. (2009). BitVisor: A Thin Hypervisor for Enforcing I/O Device Security, *Proceedings of the 2009 ACM SIGPLAN/SIGOPS International Conference on Virtual Execution sEnvironments*, pp.121-130

Xia, L.; Lange J. and Dinda, P. A. (2008). Towards Virtual Passthrough I/O on Commodity Devices., USENIX Workshop on I/O Virtualization

Task Jitter Measurement in Multi-purpose Real-time Systems

Pavel Moryc and Jindrich Cernohorsky
Technical University of Ostrava
Czech Republic

1. Introduction. Scope and problem definition

1.1 Real-time task and its physical realization.

A real-time task is a task, which meets its prescribed deadline. (More precisely, it is a task, which benefit depends on its execution time.)
A control system is a computing system used to control a production technology (fig. 1). Usually, a production technology includes many interacting sub-processes, which all need to be controlled. A real-time task runs in parallel with other real-time tasks and interacts with them. This type of parallelism can be called predictable.

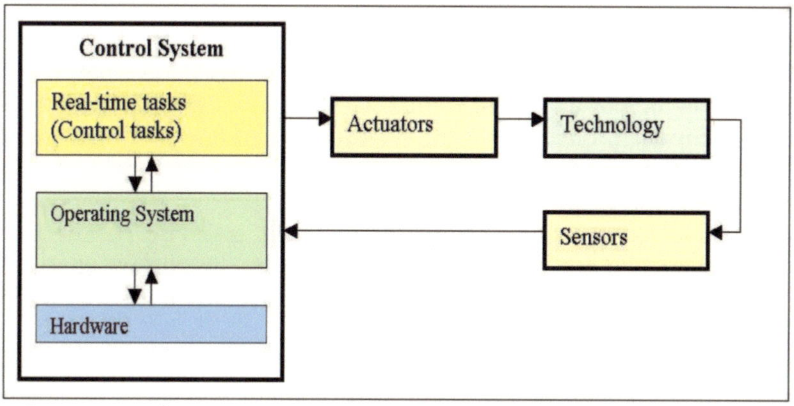

Fig. 1. Technology control

However, another type of parallelism can be seen in the controlled technology as well. The nature of the controlled technology is not fully known, and can only be described with statistical methods. Hence, it is not possible to fully plan, how the technology will be controlled, but from time to time it is necessary to interrupt the currently running control task, and to react on an unplanned urgent condition.
A production system works for years, and during that time, it enters its various conditions repeatedly. Thus, planned system operation means periodicity, while required reactions on unplanned conditions (errors, hazards, etc.) present aperiodicity. The aperiodicity naturally

stems from noise, disturbances, delays, and all other unpredictable phenomena in the real world.
A very simple control system can be realized as a monolithic block having no vertical layers, but usually, a layered structure involving both hardware and software layers is applied. Typically, three domains of control can be recognized in the layered control system structure:

- real-time task. It is a realization of a control algorithm, which controls the technology. Its precise execution is a goal of the control system. But, the control task itself is a pure design abstraction, which has to use services provided by underlying system layers.
- operating system. The real-time operating system provides resources that support control algorithm realization, and make possible that the control algorithm meets its deadline. The operating system is a design abstraction as well.
- hardware. The hardware physically realizes the control task algorithm and the operating system algorithm.

The real-time task directly uses not the basic resources provided by the hardware, but the virtual resources provided by the operating system. Hence, the operating system can significantly mitigate or amplify adverse effects of the hardware used. The quality of the control system is assessed as its ability to support specified accuracy of control, which first of all implies the ability to keep specified deadlines.
A real-time operating system is an operating system, which supplies resources that support the execution of a given real-time task on the specified hardware this way, the real-time task meets deadlines required by the controlled technology.
A real-time operating system should not enforce strict rules that nature cannot meet, but rather provide resources that help to smooth the conflicts. As these resources are supplied by the operating system, they are called virtual. Their quality depends not only on quality of the operating system itself, but also on the quality of the underlying hardware resources. The periodic task is designed to handle deterministic events. Hence, its basic characteristics are its starting time and its deadline.
The aperiodic task is designed to interrupt the periodic task and handle an unplanned, urgent, or even emergency event. Thus, its basic and most important characteristic is the delay between the time when action is required and the time when it is started. This delay is called latency.
Jitter is a variable deviation from ideal timing event. Scheduling jitter is the delay between the time when a periodic task is scheduled to be started, and the time when the task is started. Interrupt latency is the delay between the time when the interrupt is triggered and the time when the interrupt service routine is started. The interrupt latency varies, and therefore, it shows jitter. Kernel latency is defined as the delay between a nominal time when a periodic task shall be switched to the running state, and the actual time when the periodic task is switched to the running state (see Ripoll, 2001).
Both the virtual and hardware resources that support real-time task realization are standardized in the POSIX 1003.13 specification, which defines four resource profiles that can be used to design control systems. A higher profile extends the lower one (see tab. 1).

Profile No.	Profile Name
PSE 51	Minimal
PSE 52	Controller
PSE 53	Dedicated
PSE 54	Multi-purpose

Table 1. POSIX 1003.13 profiles

1.2 Multi-purpose real-time system

A multi-purpose real-time system can be defined as a resource set specified by the POSIX 1003.13 PSE 54 profile. It can be realized as an embedded PC computer, running multi-purpose operating system. The multi-purpose operating system can be based on a general-purpose operating system (e.g. Linux or Windows).
It has been measured (Ripoll, 2001), that the Linux kernel latency can reach up to several hundreds of milliseconds. It is evident, that such latency makes the system unusable in most technology control applications. This problem is well known, and basically, there solutions were proposed:

- low-latency kernel,
- preemptible kernel,
- hardware abstraction layer.

Low-latency kernel cannot be preempted by task. It is designed as a non-preemptible (monolithic) block, but with the intention to minimize latencies and jitters of API services typically used by real-time tasks.
Preemptible kernel can be preempted by task. Preemptivity by task means, that while a task is being serviced by the kernel, another task can successfully call a kernel API service and preempt the current flow of the kernel operation. This type of preemptivity is called reentrancy. However, at least some parts of the kernel cannot be made reentrant. Moreover, the idea of preemptivity itself does not imply, that the kernel is deterministically preemptible, i.e. the kernel latency and its jitter are kept acceptably low.
Hardware abstraction layer (HAL, fig. 2) is a software layer installed between the hardware and the operating system kernel. It is built as a module that is plugged into the operating system kernel. It receives timer interrupts and sends virtual (software) interrupts to the general-purpose operating system kernel, thus providing a virtual (slower) clock for the general-purpose operating system. This can be seen as a cycle stealing. Because the HAL microkernel can postpone the general-purpose kernel operation, it can make spare time to run real-time tasks. Obviously, latencies and jitters of the HAL layer must be kept low enough by design. In this publication, we will focus on the HAL based solutions only.

1.3 Multi-purpose real-time system based on Hardware Abstraction Layer

The HAL-based multi-purpose real-time system architecture is obtained from the general-purpose operating system by installing the HAL layer into the general-purpose operating system kernel space (see figure 2). In the Linux environment, the HAL layer is called RTLinux microkernel.

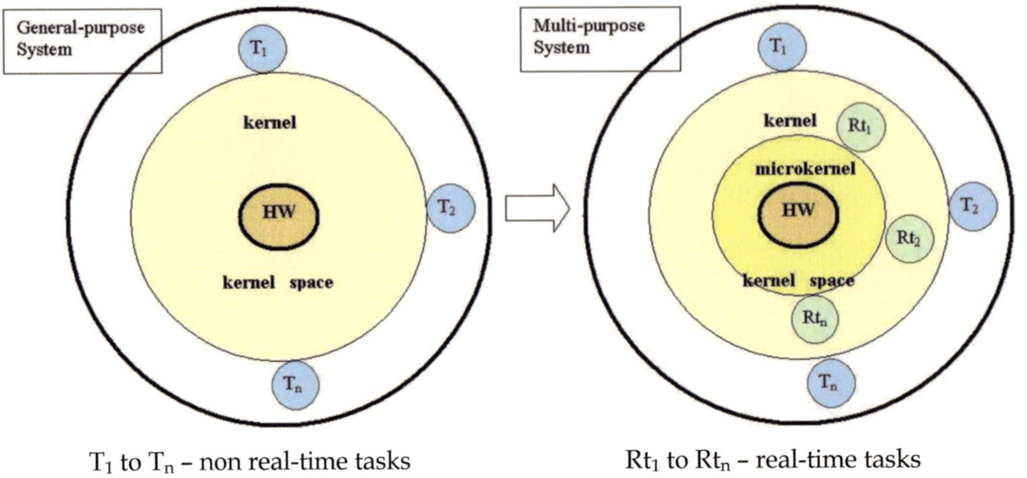

Fig. 2. POSIX PSE-54 multi-purpose system constructed as real-time extension of general-purpose system by adding hardware abstraction layer.

As the RTLinux Free source code is available, it can be analyzed. Basically, it catches interrupts from hardware, and sends them to the Linux kernel as software interrupts. The software interrupts are special signals with low latencies, i.e. with very short times of delivery. However, other software interrupts can preempt and postpone their delivery. If the microkernel is heavily loaded, many internal and external signals can wait in queues for delivery, and their delivery times could significantly vary.

The microkernel runs in the kernel space, as a kernel module. It shares the kernel space with the rest of the kernel and with the real-time tasks. The safety barriers between the kernel, the microkernel, and the real-time tasks are thin. It can be supposed, that a more safe solution would adversely affect both the microkernel and the kernel real-time characteristics, their overhead, latency and jitter.

It can be concluded, that the system must be forethoughtfully tested. However, a number of possible iterations in an industrial technology design process is rather limited, and each such iteration can be quite expensive. Hence, a model architecture that makes possible to simulate and verify system behavior in various design stages is needed.

2. Existing measurement methods

First, existing measurement methods were studied. (Ripoll, 2001) is only partially focused on tasks jitter measurement under RTLinux, but it can provide at least a starting point. More details on yet existing approaches were found in (Proctor, 2001), and (Dougan, 2004). Taking these approaches and experience into consideration, a model architecture design has been approached.

3. Designed measurement methods

As it has been yet mentioned before, the real-time task and the operating system resources are mere abstractions, and the overall architecture including hardware must be taken into consideration. Hence, the effort has been focused not on the formal approach only, but on its applicability as well. A measurement architecture (a control system model) has been designed and realized. The design has been intended tightly connected with an application study. Therefore, it can be assumed, that obtained results will be useful for engineering practice.

3.1 Generalized data acquisition program

The multi-purpose real-time system is typically used in applications, where both real-time and non-real-time tasks co-exist in one computing system. Many of these applications are interfaces between dedicated real-time and non-real-time IT levels. As a representative case, a data acquisition system has been chosen. Based on that case, a model architecture has been created. The data acquisition system has been reasonably simplified, generalized, and extended with additional diagnostic timestamp outputs.

The obtained model architecture (fig. 3) contains and integrates resources, which make possible to apply a defined workload to the system, as well as to measure, how the workload task is executed on the system. Its core part is a model of a real-time task, named RT-golem.

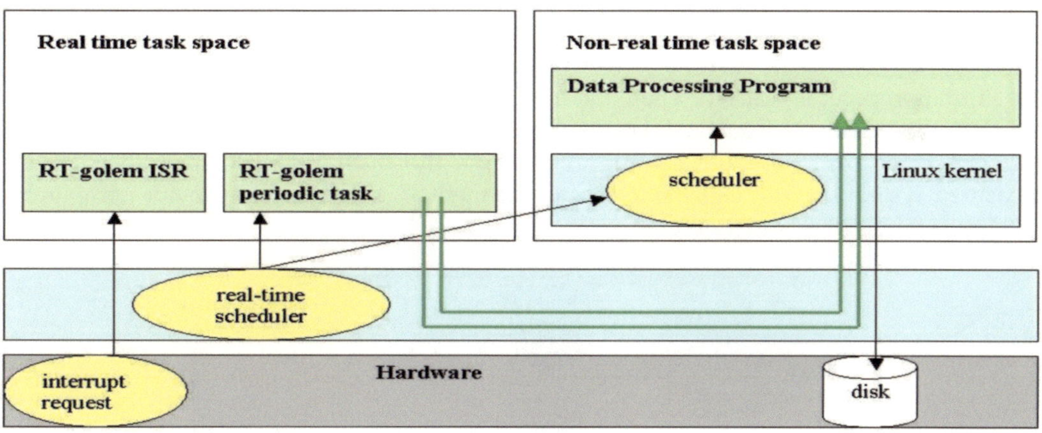

Fig. 3. RT-golem architecture

The RTLinux microkernel creates two separate software areas. First, it is a real-time space (compare fig. 2), in which real-time tasks run. Second, it is a non-real time task space, which contains the non-real-time Linux kernel space, and the Linux application space. (As it has been yet noted (see section 1), the real-time task space is realized inside the kernel space, and barriers between the two task spaces are realized by software means only). The RT-golem contains a periodic task, and an interrupt service routine. The periodic task represents the generalized data acquisition task, which in each instance measures its starting time and its finishing time, and sends the time stamps to a mass storage device (a hard disk).

In general, it would be possible to process the values either online, at the time in which they were being produced, or offline, after the simulation has been finished. The RT-golem operation creates a basic load in the system. Both theory and experience require testing under load, however, on certain PC hardware architectures, more jitter has been observed under less workload (Proctor, 2001). Hence, it has been decided to minimize the inevitable basic load caused by the measurement device as possible, and the offline data processing has been used. RTLinux itself does not provide a resource, which makes possible to access hard disk directly. Therefore, data has to be transferred from the real-time space to the non-real-time space first, and it can be stored to the hard disk using standard Linux API kernel calls then.
The interrupt service routine (ISR) is designed to support the ISR latency measurement. For the ISR latency measurement, a new method has been designed (Moryc, 2007). It is called the saturation method.

3.2 Interrupt latency measurement

Interrupt latency is one of the most important real-time system characteristics, as it describes the system ability to react to (and upon) unplanned conditions. A saturation method has been designed for measuring interrupt latency (see fig. 4). A rectangle-wave signal from a precise X-tal driven signal generator enters the system hardware input and triggers an interrupt request. The request is further processed by the system, and at the end, the control is given to the interrupt service routine. As the input signal is periodic and its period is stable, the interrupt service routine is run periodically, and it is possible to observe a time interval between two successive ISR routine starts, and its jitter. When the incoming interrupt rate is boosted, the time between two successive ISR routine starts decreases, until the saturation point is reached. Then, the minimum time between two successive ISR starts equals to the interrupt latency. It consists of latency times caused both by hardware and software resources. Since the saturation presents the maximum IRQ rate load on the measured system that it is capable to accept, the method is expected to provide comparable results across various hardware platforms.

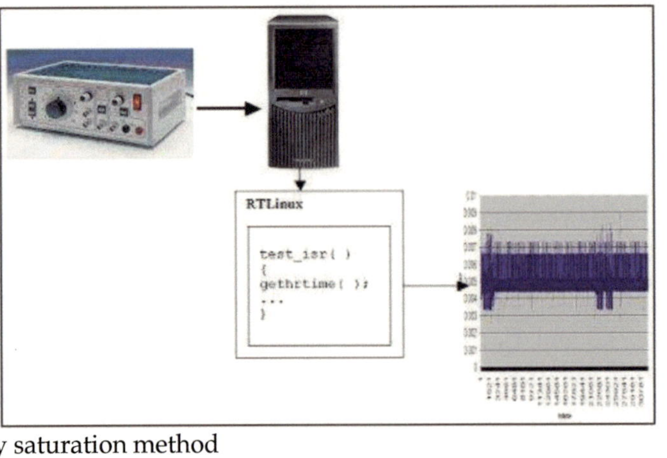

Fig. 4. ISR latency saturation method

3.3 RT-golem development and evaluation

The model architecture design and development process had been iterative, and the model had been verified after each step had been finished. Analyzing the verification results, it has been recognized, that a measurement tool, which encompasses the whole range of typical RTLinux resources and provides a deeper insight, is needed. Based on the RTLinux analysis, the following important RTLinux characteristics have been identified:

- scheduler precision (measured as task starting time jitter),
- interrupt latency time,
- execution time of typically used API services,
- pipe write and read operations,
- shared memory write and read operations,
- thread switching time, and
- I/O port read and write access time.

(The I/O access is included here, as it presents the basic (and sometimes the only) method of communication with many I/O cards. Nonetheless, it shall be avoided as possible, as it bypasses the operating system, which causes a potential for significant problems.) During the iterative design and development process, the RT-golem has been evolved from a mere data acquisition task to an advanced measurement tool. The advanced version of RT-golem consists of a periodic task, and an interrupt service routine. The periodic task includes two threads. It is possible to set priority and period of both threads, as well as to disable one or more parts of the task. This way, it is possible to balance the workload that the RT-golem causes inside of the model architecture.

4. Experimental setup

A set of measurements has been designed and performed. The periodic task starting time and finishing time jitters have been measured, under different system workload conditions:

- basic load (operating system kernel, standard daemons, RT-golem test task),
- basic load and additional non-real-time load (routine that copies short files),
- basic load and additional real-time load (additional 15 RT-golem tasks).

on two test systems (see tab. 2) :

- PC Dell GX 280,
- PC no name.

The source code of the RTLinux scheduler contains a comment suggesting that this scheduler should not be used for scheduling more than 10 tasks. For the verification of the scheduler behavior, an experiment was designed, where the system is heavily loaded with additional 15 RT-golem workload tasks, and the RT-golem test task jitter is measured. The additional 15 RT-golem tasks have been configured that way, they have created maximum acceptable load for the system, that is, the highest load at which the Linux kernel yet does not report lost timer interrupts.

Experimental results are given and discussed in details later (see section 6, Experimental results discussion, and section 9, Conclusion and future work). Briefly, they have shown, that:

- The implemented simple RTLinux scheduler manages to handle more tasks than it was suggested by its authors.

- The Linux kernel operation increases the amount of internal RTLinux microkernel signals, which in turn increases the RTLinux microkernel latency. This influence is measurable and significant.
- The influence of the hardware on the real-time characteristics of the operating system virtual resources is measurable and significant.
- The jitter values can be sorted by their amplitude into classes (Proctor, 2001).

Operating system

Linux kernel	v. 2.2.19
RTLinux microkernel	RTLinux Free v. 3.1

Hardware

PC DELL GX 280

CPU	Intel P4 at 3.0 GHz, 1 MB of L2 cache
RAM	1024 MB (only 64 MB used by Linux)
HDD	SAMSUNG SV0842D, 75 GB, SATA
	WDC WD800JD-75JNC0, 8 GB, ATA-66

PC no name

CPU	Intel P4 at 2.4 GHz, 32 K of L1 cache
mainboard	MSI 865 PE Neo2-P
RAM	256 MB (only 64 MB used by Linux)
HDD	Seagate Barracuda ST380011A, 80 GB, ATA-100
	Maxtor WDC WD100EB-00BHF0, 10 GB, ATA-66

Table 2. Test systems details

5. Win-golem, a RT-golem port to MS-Windows

After the RT-golem method has been evaluated by experiments, it has been required to port it to another target environment, based on Microsoft Windows and RTX for Microsoft Windows Real-time Extension, and to perform comparison of both real-time environments (RTLinux and RTX for Microsoft Windows).

First, the new intended target platform had been analyzed. The RTX microkernel is similar to the RTLinux microkernel in functionality, but different in realization. RTX is a proprietary solution, hence we have to rely on its description supplied by the vendor (Cherepov, 2002). The RTX microkernel supports real-time tasks, which are called RTSS (real-time subsystem) threads. It is interconnected with the Windows kernel via two access paths. The first access path is created in the Windows HAL, and the second one is the interface for connecting device drivers. Basically, it is necessary to modify the Windows HAL, because:

- interrupt isolation between the Windows kernel and the RTSS threads has to be added,
- high-speed clocks and timers need to be supported,
- shutdown handlers need to be provided.

The two interconnection points between Windows kernel and RTX microkernel mentioned above make possible to realize connection between the RTX microkernel and the Windows kernel, providing the same functionality as the interface between the RTLinux microkernel and the Linux kernel (compare fig. 4, fig. 5). The communication interface between Windows and the RTX kernel implements a low-latency client-server mechanism, which includes both buffers and Service Request Interrupts (SRI). Due to the communication interface, a subset of Windows application programming interfaces (API) services is callable from within a RTSS thread. It includes APIs for storing data to file, thus real-time pipes are neither needed nor available in the API services set. However, we can reasonably suppose, that similar IPC mechanisms are necessary to provide similar functionality, no matter whether they are hidden for the programmer. Some of the Windows APIs available from the RTSS threads are listed as non-deterministic, i.e. they can cause significant jitter when called from a RTSS thread. High-speed (and high resolution) clocks are needed for realization of precise real-time timers. Within a RTSS thread, time is recognized with 100 ns step and resolution. Shutdown handler is a mechanism delivering more robustness to the real-time RTSS subsystem when the Windows subsystem is crashed or regularly shut down.

It can be summarized, that following significant differences from RTLinux exist:

- no real-time pipes or their equivalents are available in the API service set,
- it is possible to call a subset of Windows API services directly from a RTX (RTSS) real-time task,
- time is recognized with 100 ns resolution,
- Windows-controlled interrupts are masked while the RTX (RTSS) real-time task runs,
- a real-time interrupt routine has two mandatory parts, which can be seen as the upper and bottom ISR part,
- it is possible to implement a shutdown handler as the last resort resource.

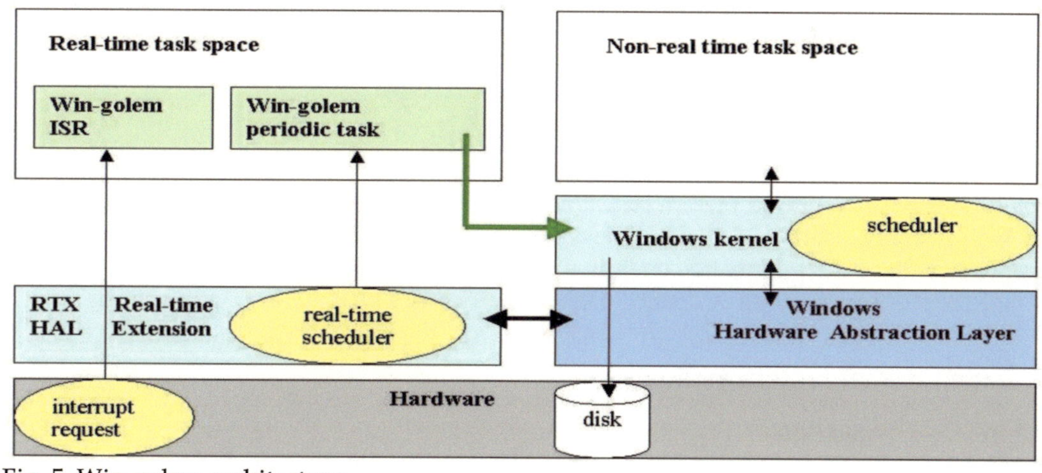

Fig. 5. Win-golem architecture

As the RTLinux and RTX operating environments are functionally similar and their key resources are almost the same, it can be supposed, that the RT-golem architecture design can be adapted for the jitter measurement in the RTX operating environment as well. After the target environment analysis had been performed, the realization issues have been approached. The RT-golem is written in C language, thus it should be easily portable. Nonetheless, both the environments contain many non-portable extensions, and as a result, the design had to be partially re-written. The RT-golem task re-written for the RTX environment is called Win-golem. For the RTX environment properties evaluation, it has been used the same experimental setup as described in section 4 (Experimental setup).

6. Experimental results

Experimental results are given below. For the evaluation, hundreds of data sets and graphs have been used, but here only a handful of them, which contains typical or interesting cases, is meaningful to be presented. The graphs are often arranged in pairs for easy comparison. (In the pair, the left graph is referred to as fig. x a, while the right graph is referred to as fig. x b.) There are presented relative starting time (RST) graphs, relative finishing time (RFT) graphs, and statistical evaluation graphs. Relative starting time is the time when the given instance of a periodic task starts, measured from the previous instance starting time. Because of the relative starting time definition given above, the relative starting time jitter graph consists of spikes oscillating up and down around the nominal value (fig.6, fig. 7).

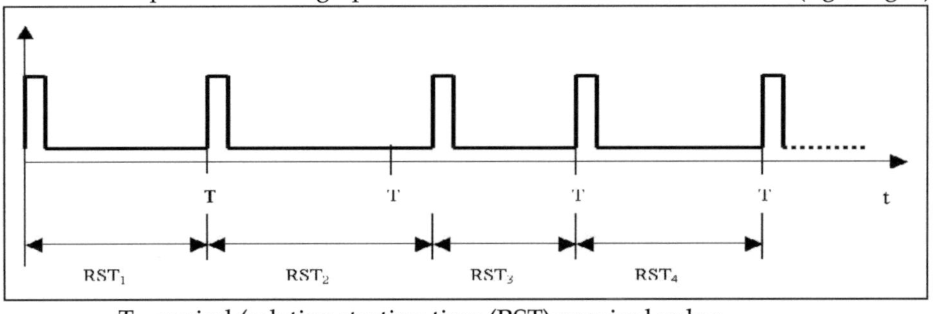

T - period (relative starting time (RST) nominal value
RST1,..RSTn - relative starting time of the 1-st,..n-th instance

Fig. 6. Relative starting time measurement

The instance's relative finishing time is measured from this instance's relative starting time. The statistical evaluation graphs present statistical measures comparison bar graphs, showing mean vs. median comparisons, and standard deviation vs. interquartile range (IQR) comparisons. The graphs provide useful information on typical values as well as outlying values importance in the sample, but further statistical evaluation could be needed (see section 7.2).

7. Experimental results evaluation

7.1 Intuitive evaluation

It can be concluded from the presented experimental results, that the benchmark periodic task relative starting time jitter (kernel latency jitter) is significantly lesser on the RTX-based measurement architectures, than on the RTLinux Free-based architectures (fig. 7, 9, 13). The median of the task finishing time is approximately the same within the applied range of test architectures and workloads. Under RTLinux Free, the port write time median value is ca. 15% less than the port read time median value, but under RTX both medians are the same (fig. 11). Similarly to the task starting time, task finishing time shows lesser jitter on the RTX-based architectures (fig. 8, 10, 14). Evaluating the RTLinux Free-based measurement architecture, it has been observed on the graphs presented above, that most of the jitter instances are near the best-case values, but sometimes significantly higher spikes occur.

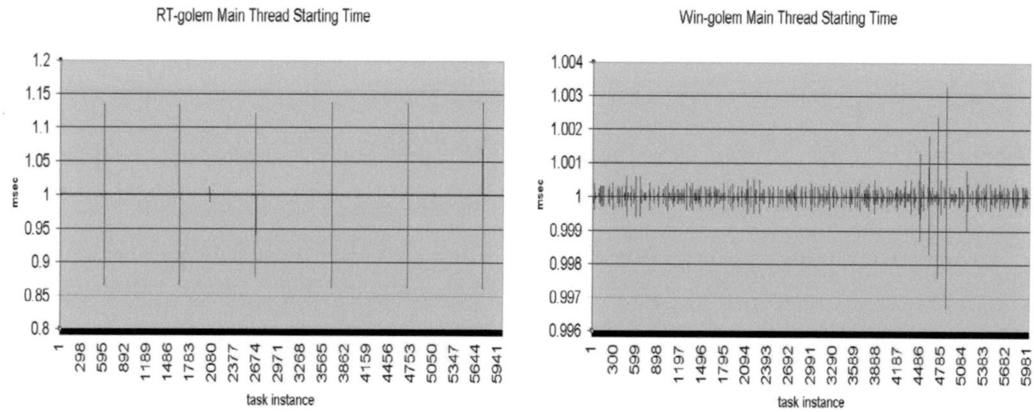

Fig. 7. RT-golem and Win-golem results comparison: periodic task starting time, PC Dell, basic workload only

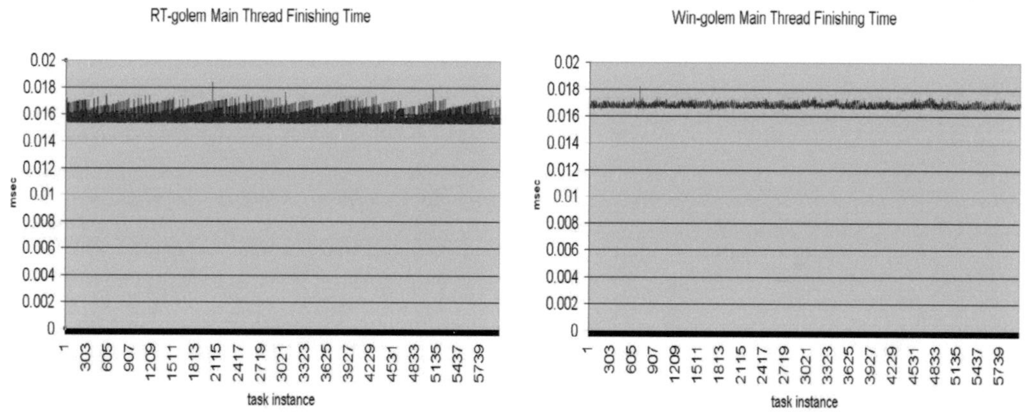

Fig. 8. RT-golem and Win-golem results comparison: periodic task finishing time, PC Dell, basic workload only

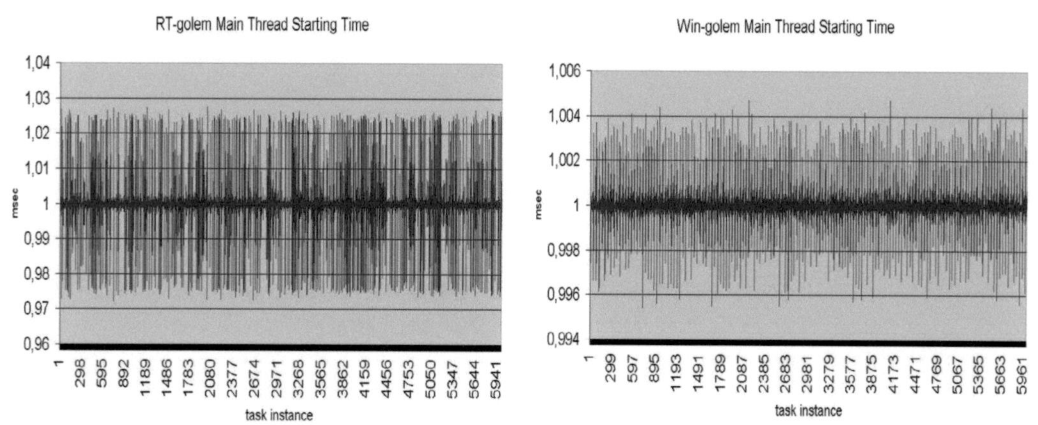

Fig. 9. RT-golem and Win-golem results comparison: periodic task starting time, PC Dell, basic and additional workload (copying files)

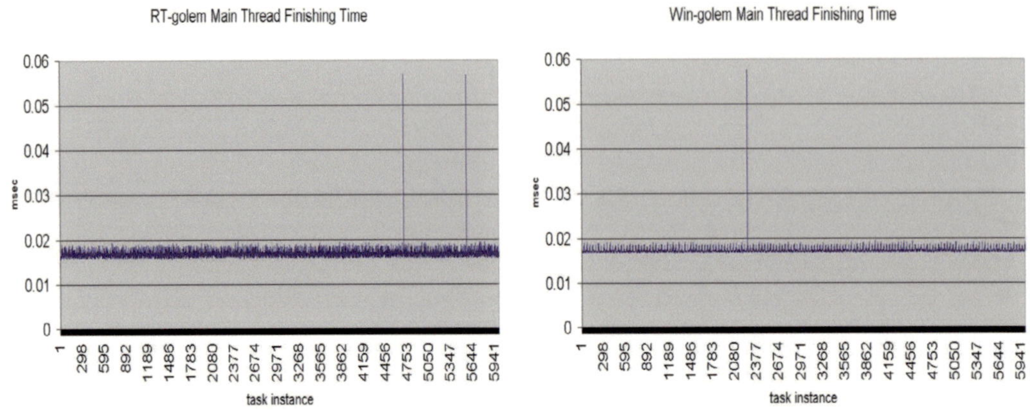

Fig. 10. RT-golem and Win-golem results comparison: periodic task finishing time, PC Dell, basic and additional workload (copying files)

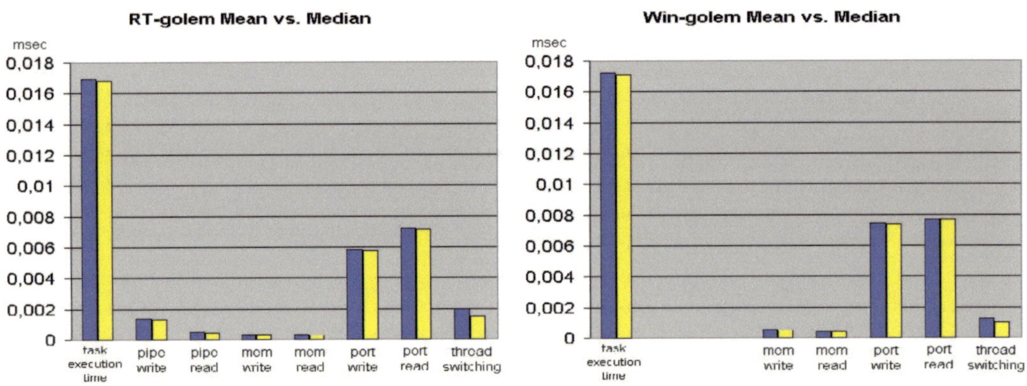

Fig. 11. RT-golem and Win-golem results comparison: execution time means vs. medians, PC Dell, basic and additional workload (copying files)

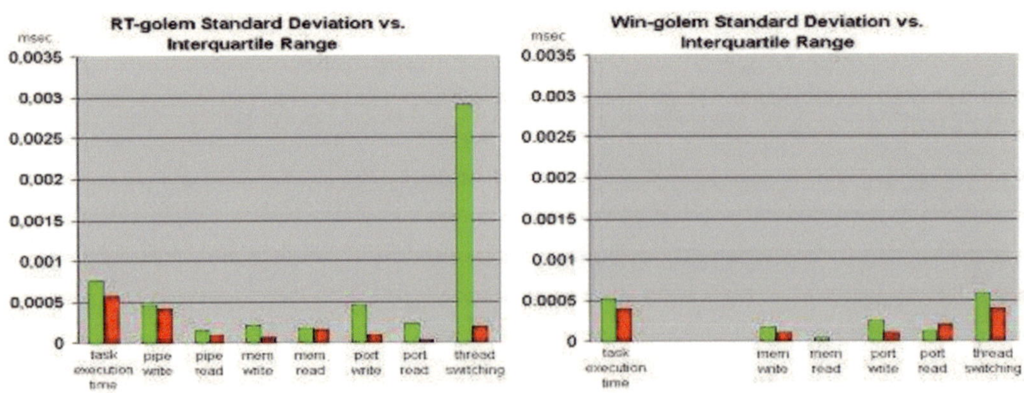

Fig. 12. RT-golem and Win-golem results comparison: execution time standard deviations vs. interquartile ranges, PC Dell, basic and additional workload (copying files)

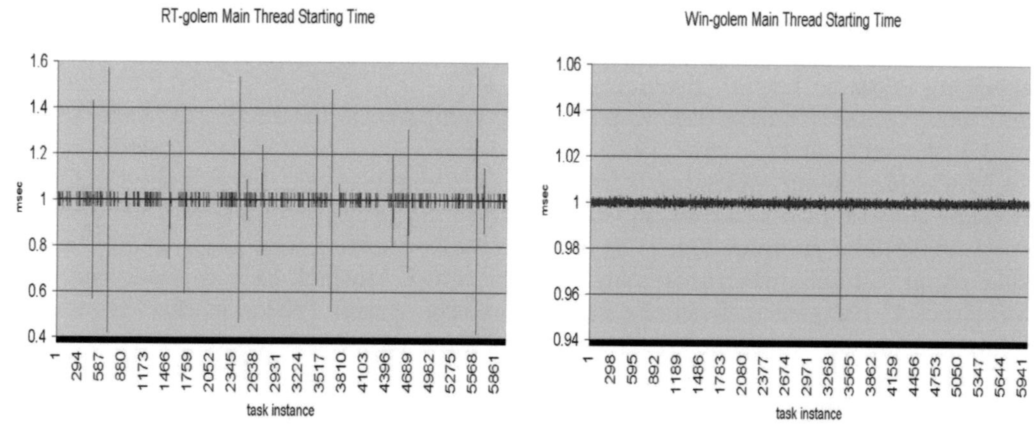

Fig. 13. RT-golem and Win-golem results comparison: periodic task starting time, PC no name, basic and additional workload (copying files)

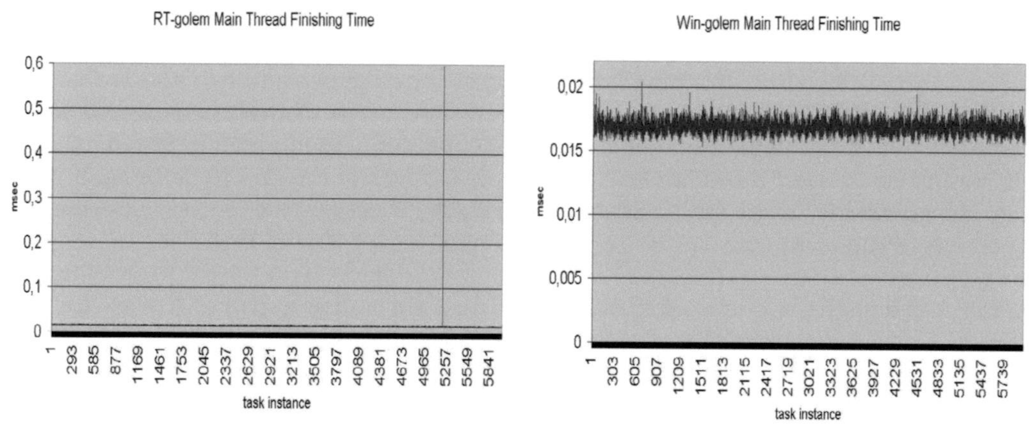

Fig. 14. RT-golem and Win-golem results comparison: periodic task finishing time, PC no name, basic and additional workload (copying files)

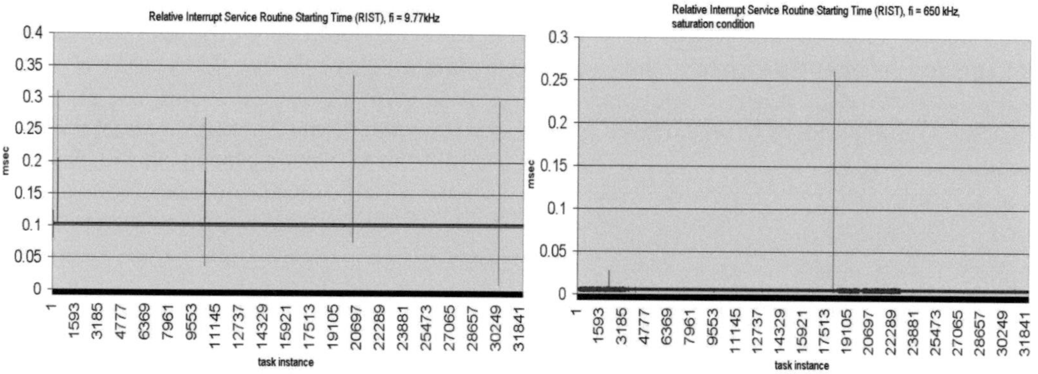

Fig. 15. Interrupt service routine starting time, RT-golem, PC Dell

These spikes can form typical patterns (relative starting time measurement, fig. 7a, 13a), or can be observed randomly (fig. 10a, fig 14a), but in any case their amplitude is typical for the underlying system layers. Evaluating the RTX and Windows-based architecture, significantly less spikes have been found (fig. 7b compared to fig. 7a, fig. 13b compared to fig. 13a), or none at all.
Last but not least, interrupt latency measurements have been evaluated (see fig. 15). On the left frame (fig. 15 a) can be seen the ISR starting time jitter at input signal frequency of 10kHz, while the right frame (fig. 15 b) provides the ISR starting time graph at input signal frequency of 650 kHz, when the saturation condition is reached. In both cases, the same hardware (PC Dell) as well as the same operating system (RTLinux) has been used. Apparently, the load conditions are very different, but the observed spikes have the same amplitude of ca. 25 msecs. It can be concluded, the spikes are independent on the workload, and they characterize the measurement architecture.

7.2 Statistical evaluation

Background

All task jitter instances that occurred or will occur in given measurement architecture under given load are considered a population, and measured task jitter instances represent a known sample drawn from this population. It can be formulated a null hypothesis about the population, that the population can be described with given distribution, as well as the alternative hypothesis to the aforementioned null hypothesis. Then, it can be tested, whether it is reasonable to reject the alternative hypothesis in favor of the null hypothesis. If it has been not possible to reject the alternative hypothesis, it could be expected, that the null hypothesis is valid and true, but it is not possible to be ever sure of that, because of type I and type II errors existence. The type I error (α, significance level) means the probability that the true null hypothesis is rejected in favor of the false alternative hypothesis, while the type II error (β) means the probability that the false null hypothesis is not rejected in favor of the true alternative hypothesis. Unfortunately, it is not possible to minimize both the type I and type II errors simultaneously. In engineering applications, usually it is chosen α=0.05. When the resulting β value is not sufficiently low, it can be lowered by changing the test statistic used, or by drawing larger sample from the population.

Application

The instances of a real-time task shall be started in intervals specified by the task period, and not affected by previous system state or by previous system activity. Thus, they shall be independent to each other. If they can be described with Poisson distribution, they are sufficiently independent to each other. It has been formulated the hypothesis, that the task instance starting times follow Poisson distribution, and the hypothesis has been tested using χ^2 test. Results are given in table 3.

workload applied	χ^2 test result
basic load and additional RT load	H_A rejected in favor to H_o
basic load and additional non-RT load	H_A not rejected

H_o : The task instance starting times follow Poisson distribution.
H_A : The task instance starting times do not follow Poisson distribution.
Significance level: $\alpha=0.05$.
Measurement architecture: PC Dell GX 280 (see tab 2.), RT Linux

Table 3. χ^2 test results

8. Feasibility Study

Based on the outcomes, it has been designed and realized a data acquisition system for physical model of a steel flow in an interladle.

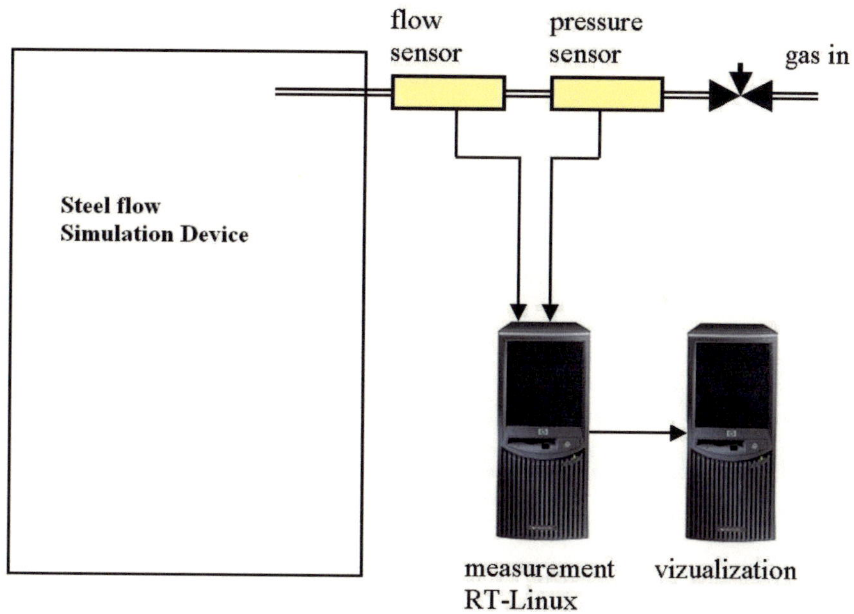

Fig. 16. Steel flow model

In the model, the steel flow is simulated by a gas flow in a liquid environment. The data acquisition system consists of

- pressure and flow rate sensors,
- measurement subsystem,
- control and visualization subsystem.

It is required by the end-user, that both the gas flow and the gas pressure are acquired once per two microseconds, with maximum tolerance of +/- 100 μsecs. The control and visualization subsystem shall provide:

- control of the measurement subsystem via rcmd utility,
- graphical presentation of currently measured values,
- graphical presentation of previously acquired values stored in database.

At the beginning of the design process, it has been intended, that the measurement subsystem will be built using industrial PC (Pentium P2 Celeron 333 MHz), and ICP-DAS 823 A/D card, which were available.

Most of the design and verification effort has been concentrated on the measurement subsystem, as the subsystem contains the core of the design, and has to meet relatively strict deadlines. At early design stages, it has been concentrated on the question, whether the intended hardware will fit the deadline specifications. Series of simulations have been performed using the RT-golem architecture ported on the target hardware. The task has been configured as close to the intended target design as possible, and various workload conditions have been used to get the possibly most adverse results (see fig. 17, the blue, red and yellow curves). It is commonly supposed, that the worst jitter is produced when the system is heavily loaded, but due to cache loading and flushing effects, the system behavior under lower workloads needs to be examined too (Proctor, 2001).

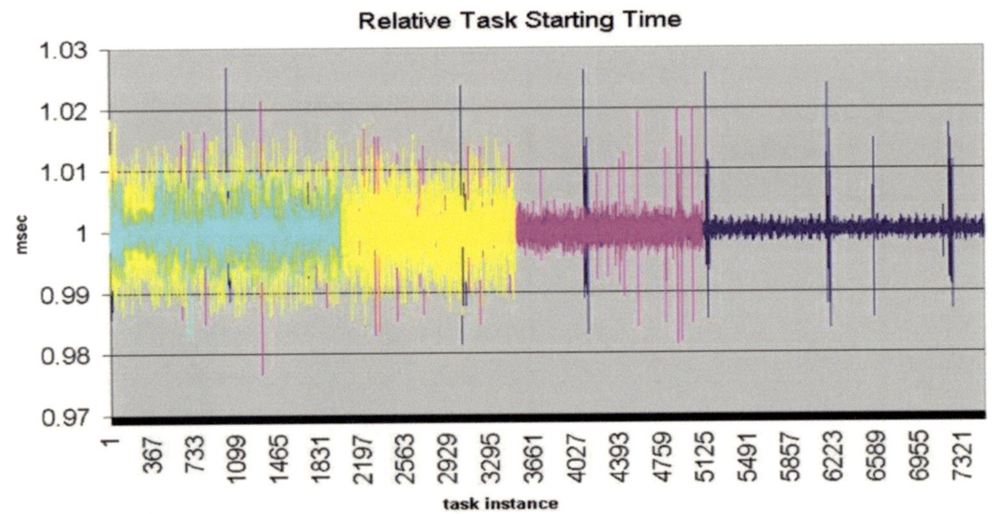

blue - RT-golem, basic workload only
red - RT-golem, basic and real-time workload
yellow - RT-golem, basic and non-real-time workload
cyan - Steel flow model realization, real workload

Fig. 17. Steel flow model: measurement task relative starting time jitter, simulation vs. realization

The control of the measurement system is realized using the rcmd protocol, as both the computers are connected with a cross-wired Ethernet cable in secure environment. The measured data messages delivery is realized using the Microsoft Server Message Block (SMB) protocol.

The control and visualization subsystem ensures experiment control and supplies results visualization. It's typical latency has been stipulated to meet a common human reaction time (which is not less than 200 msecs). The visualization subsystem displays flow vs. time and

pressure vs. time online graphs. Its design consists of two periodic threads, the first one timed at sample rate, and the second one timed at display rate. It is necessary to adjust both the sample and display rates on the given hardware to achieve optimum performance. On the used Dell notebook (Pentium 4 Celeron at 2.4 GHz), the sample rate has been set to 10 msecs, while the display rate has been set to 100 msecs.
During the commissioning process, ca. 100 measurements were made under various possible working conditions specified, and the measurement and visualization system has been found meeting the requirements (see fig. 17, the cyan curve).

9. Conclusion. Future work

9.1 Results discussion

It can be supposed, that the significant worst-case jitter spikes observed in the experiments with RTLinux Free are caused by cache writing and flushing effects. (Proctor, 2001) suggested the same conclusion, what can be seen as another argument supporting this opinion. But, as the measurements are performed on the top of the hardware and software stack, and the virtual resources presented to the measurement task by the operating system API services are quite distant to the resources presented to the operating system by the hardware (more precisely, by the part of the operating system realized in hardware), it is not possible to validate such hypothesis by methods described here. The mere absence of this phenomenon on both test architectures using the RTX operating system can imply, that the RTX microkernel prevents the hardware from flushing the cache arbitrarily. Moreover, some further tracks can be given. (Cherepov, 2004) notes that video drivers are the most cache demanding part of the Windows operating system, and in the RTX platform evaluation kit, video is used as a workload. Video is a real-time task as well as a RTX microkernel (RTSS) task. Thus, the conflict between a video and a real-time RTSS task can be seen as the conflict between two real-time cache-demanding tasks, which can lead to swapping the RTSS task code out of the cache. Unfortunately, the RTX microkernel source code is not freely available, and therefore it is not possible to verify the tracks given above with the code analysis. However, the aforementioned discussion can suggest, that the mechanism of locking the real-time code in the hardware cache is worthy to be studied and implemented.

9.2 Applicability in engineering practice

In most today applications, it is used a PLC for technology control or data acquisition, and a PC with the Microsoft Windows for data visualization. However, a fully PC-based technology control and visualization system can be considered as well. In the present time, RTLinux and RTX-based control system solutions are yet recognized by business vendors (e.g. Siemens WinAC platform). The published method of jitter measurement in multipurpose real-time systems has been successfully applied, and it is ready to be used in similar designs.

9.3 Vision. Future work

The outcomes of the published work are going to be used in Experimental real-time database testing system (see Acknowledgement below). The proposed benchmark methods yet have been used to evaluate possible platforms for the real-time database realization, and two more applications are intended:

- RT-golem port on QNX,
- design and realization of a communication architecture, which makes possible to measure time needed for various TCP/IP communication steps and phases.

It can be suggested, that real-time databases will present an interesting field of study. Applications in flight supporting devices, mobile communication devices, speech recognition systems, and many other areas can be foreseen.

10. Acknowledgement

This research has been performed at the Technical University of Ostrava, Faculty of Electrical Engineering and Computer Science, Department of Measurement and Control, Centre for Applied Cybernetics, and supported by the Ministry of Education, Youth and Sports of the Czech Republic under Project 1M0567.

11. References

Cherepov, M. et. al. (2002). Hard Real-Time with Ardence RTX on Microsoft Windows XP and Windows XP Embedded, source: www. ardence.com

Dougan, C. & Mwaikambo, Z. (2004). Lies, Misdirection and Real-time Measurements, source: www.rtl.com

Krol V., Pokorny J., & Cernohorsky, J. (2006). Architecture of experimental real-time databases for embedded systems, *Proceedings of IFAC Workshop on Programmable Devices and Embedded Systems PDeS 2006,* pp. 384-388, ISBN 80-214-3130-X, Brno, Czech Republic, Feb. 2006

Krol V., Pokorny J. (2006). *Design of V4DB - Experimental Real-Time Database System, The 32-nd Anunual Conference of the IEEE Industrial Electronics Socienty,* Paris, France, Nov. 2006

Moryc, P. & Cernohorsky, J. (2007). Task jitter measurement under RTLinux operating system, *Proceedings of the International Multiconference on Computer Science and Information Technology,* pp. 849-852, ISSN 1896-7094, Wisla, Poland, 15.-17. Oct. 2007

Moryc, P. & Cernohorsky, J. (2008). Task jitter measurement under RTLinux and RTX operating systems, comparison of RTLinux and RTX operating environments, *Proceedings of the International Multiconference on Computer Science and Information Technology,* pp. 703-709, ISBN 978-60810-14-9, ISSN 1896-7094, Wisla, Poland, Oct. 2008

Moryc, P. & Cernohorsky, J. (2009). Task jitter measurement under RTLinux operating system, *Journal of Automation, Mobile Robotics and Intelligent Systems,* Vol. 4, 01/2009, pp. 62-65, ISSN 1897-8649

Pokorny J., Franek Z. (2008). *Databases in Real-Time: Experimental Research.* IT&T 8-th International Conference on Information Technology and Telecommunications, ISSN 1649-1246, Galway, Ireland, 2008.

Proctor, F.M. (2001). Measuring Performance in Real-Time Linux, *Proceedings of the Third Real-Time Linux Workshop,* Milan, Italy, Oct. 2001

Ripoll I. et al. (2001). WP1: RTOS State of the Art Analysis: Deliverable D1.1: RTOS Analysis, OCERA, source: www.ocera.org